Quilting Makes the Quilt

Lee Cleland

ACKNOWLEDGMENTS

My thanks go to:

My husband, Bob, and our family, Kim, Clive, and Derek, who have lived with this book for the past two years.

Sandra Edwards of Windsor, who first suggested this book and convinced me that I could write it. My friends Nonie Fisher, Pam Heagney, and Chris Wood, owners of the Quilting Bee in Gordon, for their encouragement and support.

Christine Barnes, my book editor, who helped me to put my thoughts into words.

My father, Noel Selman, who organized me, typed the manuscript, and got me finished on time.

MISSION STATEMENT

WE ARE DEDICATED TO PROVIDING QUALITY PRODUCTS THAT ENCOURAGE CREATIVITY AND PROMOTE SELF-ESTEEM IN OUR CUSTOMERS AND OUR EMPLOYEES.

WE STRIVE TO MAKE A DIFFERENCE IN THE LIVES WE TOUCH.

That Patchwork Place is an employee-owned, financially secure company.

That Patchwork Place, Inc.
PO Box 118,
Bothell, WA 98041-0118 USA

Printed in Hong Kong
03 02 01 00 99 12 11

Library of Congress Cataloging-in-Publication Data

Cleland, Lee,
Quilting makes the quilt/Lee Cleland.
p. cm.
ISBN 1-56477-075-3:
1. Machine quilting—Patterns.
2. Patchwork—Patterns.
I. Title.
TT835.C595 1994
746.46—dc20 94-29983
CIP

CREDITS

EDITOR-IN-CHIEF	BARBARA WEILAND
TECHNICAL EDITOR	CHRISTINE BARNES
MANAGING EDITOR	GREG SHARP
COPY EDITOR	TINA COOK
PROOFREADER	LESLIE PHILLIPS
DESIGN DIRECTOR	JUDY PETRY
TEXT AND COVER DESIGNER	AMY SHAYNE
PHOTOGRAPHER	BRENT KANE
ILLUSTRATOR	JOHN PARAMORE
	LAUREL STRAND

Table of Contents

About This Book

After color concerns, the question I hear most often from quilters is, "How should I quilt my quilt?" In reply, I offer a collection of ideas for quilting, from simple filler grids to complex border designs inspired by Greek friezes and Celtic art. Some of these designs will be familiar to you and others will be unknown, perhaps even startling. All show how quilting designs can change the look of a quilt.

I owe the idea for this book to Sandra Edwards, an avid quilter from Windsor, Australia, a town at the foot of the Blue Mountains near Sydney. Several years ago she suggested I write a book on machine quilting. At first I said no: "Haven't enough machine quilting books been done?" But soon I began thinking about ways to illustrate the impact of quilting designs. Being a prolific machine quilter, I came up with an ambitious plan: I would quilt identical pieced tops in different designs. I chose twelve traditional quilt patterns and made each five times, using the same fabric and batting. Then I quilted the quilts in a variety of designs, a process that took two years, dogged persistence, and many miles of thread. The result? Instead of wondering how various designs might look on a quilt, you'll be able to see in an instant what a difference the quilting makes.

The quilts and their quilting designs are the heart of the book. Turn to the photos on pages 25–96 to get a feel for how different designs look on the same quilt pattern. With each pair of photos, you'll find a detailed caption describing the quilting designs and explaining the design principles at work. Many of these designs reflect Australia's British heritage; several are decidedly Australian. Eleven quilting designs are included in the pullout patterns at the back of the book.

"Making Designs Fit" (pages 6–24) guides you in choosing and drawing quilting designs, with particular attention to calculating and drawing designs to fit borders. To make any of the twelve quilts, turn to the step-by-step instructions in "Quilt Patterns" (pages 97–121). In "Quiltmaking Techniques" (pages 122–33), you'll find basic methods, as well as my own special hints and methods. I encountered a number of practical and creative problems while working on so many quilts. My solutions are included throughout the book.

My hope is that the quilts in this book will start you thinking about quilting designs now, long before you've finished piecing your quilt top. As you'll see, just about anything goes when it comes to quilting. Be willing to imagine, experiment, and create. Above all, enjoy your quilting—it makes the quilt!

Lee Cleland
St. Ives, New South Wales
Australia

Before You Begin

Something special, even magical, happens when you begin to quilt. Smooth fabrics take on intriguing texture, motifs stand out in crisp relief, and graceful patterns swirl across blocks with no regard for piecing boundaries. Quilting is a process, a stitch-by-stitch transformation of fabric and batting into something difficult to describe and pleasing to behold.

As even a beginning quilter knows, the interplay of piecing and quilting lines creates a powerful visual image. You contribute a vital personal ingredient to that image when you select quilting designs. Choose a classic design, and your quilt will possess a timeless beauty. For a contemporary or wild-and-way-out quilt, take your inspiration from unexpected, nontraditional sources. The options are endless.

The choices can also be overwhelming, for there are as many quilting designs as there are quilters. Which designs will most enhance your quilt top? How much stitching is enough? Should you follow the piecing lines or impose a larger-than-life design? How should you quilt the borders?

Many quilters find it difficult to select quilting patterns because they can't visualize how various designs might look on their pieced tops. That's why quilts have been quilted the same way for centuries. Every quilter wants to be happy with her finished quilt—and no quilter wants to undo her stitching! The more you look, really look, at quilting designs, the more confident you'll become. An awareness of your many design choices will free you to think, and quilt, more creatively.

In the Know

You'll enjoy the many hours spent quilting if you know your quilt will look as good as you imagined it. A few quilting facts will help you make wise decisions:

- Quilting shows up better on solid fabrics than on prints, which is why I chose many solid fabrics for this book. Sharp color contrast affects quilting, too, causing quilting lines to appear broken. Interestingly, the reverse happens: curved quilting lines can visually bend straight piecing lines and merge colors.
- Outlining a shape emphasizes it.
- Dense background quilting, such as echo quilting, close grids, and stippling, compresses the quilt layers and makes unquilted areas look like trapunto (stuff work). Stippling has other intriguing effects: When stitched in dark thread on a light fabric, stippling creates a tone, a darker variation of the original color. Stippling also obscures piecing lines and blends colors.
- Stitching in-the-ditch holds the layers together and functions as the framework for additional quilting. A pieced top usually deserves more quilting than stitching in-the-ditch.
- Battings are often overlooked in the quilt "recipe." A variety of battings are available; each kind produces a different look and feel. In general, the thicker the batting, the more difficult it is to quilt.

Making Designs Fit

Once you understand the process, it's not difficult to draw designs to fit a quilt top. Using the instructions that follow, you'll be able to adapt motifs from other sources or create original designs.

Borders give quiltmakers the most headaches, so this chapter concentrates on ways to make quilting designs fit borders and neatly turn corners. These methods will save you the trouble of finding a design that fits your pieced top or trying to piece your top to fit an existing design.

Drawing Tools and Supplies

As a quiltmaker, you appreciate the need for accuracy in cutting and piecing. You must be just as accurate when drawing quilting designs. Tools and supplies I frequently use include:

- Rotary rulers and squares. Make sure you have an 18" ruler with ⅛" divisions. Check your rulers for consistency and accuracy; measurements may vary.
- Mechanical pencil with soft leads
- Eraser
- Calculator
- Waterproof permanent marker
- Bar compass
- Large pad (19" x 24") or roll (various widths and lengths) of artist-quality tracing paper. Technical/drafting paper is another option; it's transparent and durable.

In place of tracing or technical paper, you can use large sheets of plain paper or a roll of shelf paper. However, many papers tear more readily than tracing or technical paper, which creates a problem with large designs. Tracing and technical papers have several other advantages: Once you've drawn your design, you can easily alter it by placing a fresh sheet over your original and redrawing. Lines on tracing and technical papers are also crisp, making them easy to follow if you use a light box to mark your quilt top.

There are many quilting designs to choose from. Following are descriptions of the four main types of quilting designs and instructions for drawing them.

Filler Designs

Filler designs usually form a backdrop for other quilted elements, such as motif designs. Occasionally, a filler is the main, allover quilting design. Most fillers are geometric, with echo quilting and stipple quilting the notable exceptions.

On borders, be sure to quilt filler designs all the way to the seam lines and outer edges.

----- STRAIGHT GRIDS -----

Grids, in a variety of patterns, are the most common filler designs. Two traditional straight grids are the 1" diagonal grid and the straight-grain grid.

A diagonal grid (left) is a classic filler design.

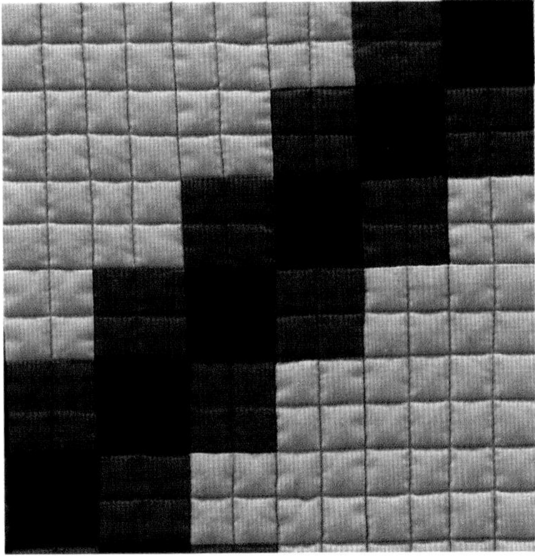

A straight-grain grid (right) lends visual stability to a quilt.

Some grids are a continuation of the piecing lines. The various grid designs in Scrap Star, Quilt 1 on page 68 are based in part on the piecing lines.

If following the piecing lines to form a grid is not an option, the easiest way to draw a straight-line grid is to mark the quilt top with dots along the top, bottom, and side edges. Join the dots, using a 10' length of molding or aluminum window trim, or an extendible straightedge (available at building supply stores). Joining dots is more accurate than working from the previous line, which invariably leads to compounding errors. Even a pencil-width difference from one end of a line to the other distorts the grid pattern.

CLAMSHELL AND WINEGLASS

These designs introduce pleasing curves to pieced quilt tops.

Clamshell (left) is a traditional English filler design.

Wineglass (right) consists of a series of overlapping circles.

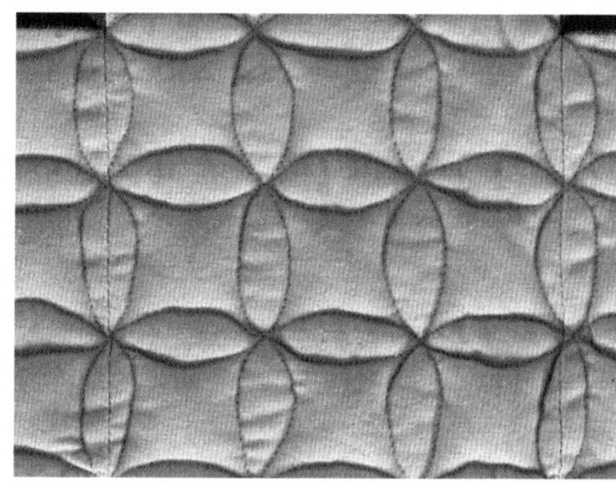

To draw these interlocking filler designs, divide the area to be filled, whether it's a block or the entire quilt, into squares equaling the desired size of each motif. Draw the individual motif in the square so that it touches all edges; make a pattern with a number of repeats. For a neat look, start the design at the bottom of the block or quilt and work up, offsetting rows as you go. In many antique quilts, the designs begin at the edges and repeat toward the center, with extra lines filling the center gap.

ECHO AND STIPPLE QUILTING

These designs add dimension and visual interest to a quilt. Echo quilting outlines a motif or appliqué with close, evenly spaced lines of stitching. Hawaiian quilting is perhaps the finest example of echo quilting around appliqué. Stipple quilting is a continuous, meandering line of stitching that never crosses itself. Both echo and stipple quilting are stitched without marking the quilt top.

A feather swag (left) stands out in relief against echo quilting.

Dense stipple quilting (right) makes circles appear sculptured.

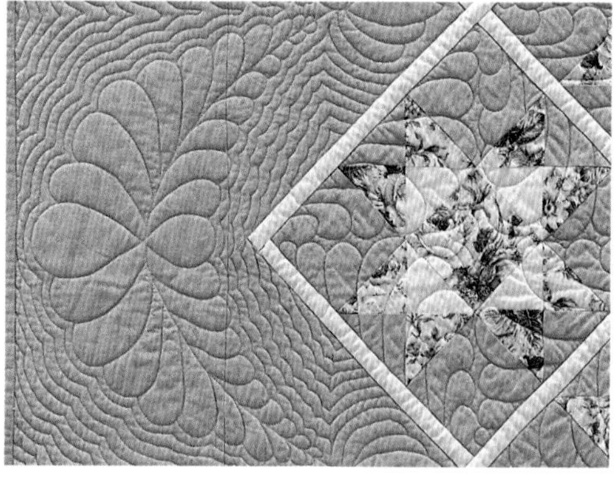

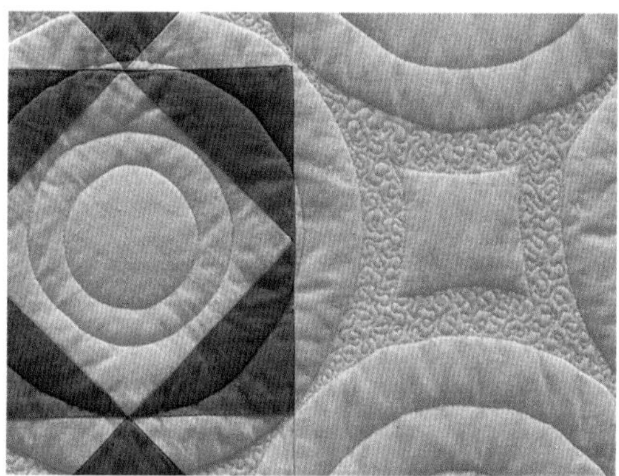

Motif/Block Designs

These decorative designs fit within a well-defined area, often a block or border. The motifs may be geometric, representational, or abstract. Popular motif/block designs include stylized leaves, feathers, wreaths, and flowers.

A wreath motif (left) is a traditional favorite.

A mirror-image flower motif (right) adds curves to a Double Four Patch block.

Motif/block designs should fill the intended area without crowding. They can also cross major piecing lines to create new areas. See Scrap Star, Quilt 5 on page 72 for an example of large motif designs that redefine areas.

To draw a motif design:

1. Measure the area to be quilted. (Don't assume that your quilt measurements are exactly what they should be.) Draw this area on tracing paper.
2. Measure and draw a line ¼" inside each edge. The reduced area allows you a little leeway if some of the areas to be filled vary slightly. This reduced area also gives the motif "breathing room" and, if you want the motif to fill a block, keeps the quilting safely out of the seam allowances—especially important for hand quilters.
3. Draw your design in the reduced area, enlarging or reducing it if necessary with a grid (below) or a photocopy machine (page 11). If you add a filler outside of the motif, be sure to quilt the filler all the way to the seam lines.

Enlarging or Reducing a Design with a Grid

This simple technique allows you to adapt a motif design to fit your quilt top.

1. Tape a piece of tracing paper over the design you wish to enlarge or reduce. Use graph tracing paper or draw a uniform grid. The more detailed the design, the more detailed the grid should be.
2. On tracing paper, measure and draw the area you plan to fill; draw a line ¼" inside each edge. Using the inner line as your perimeter, draw the same number of squares as are on your original design. These squares will be larger than those on the original if you're enlarging a design and smaller if you're reducing it.
3. Using the grids as a guide, copy every line in the original design onto the enlargement or reduction, square by square.

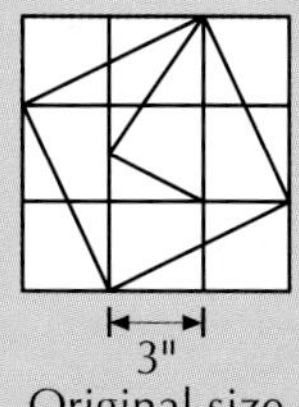

Original size

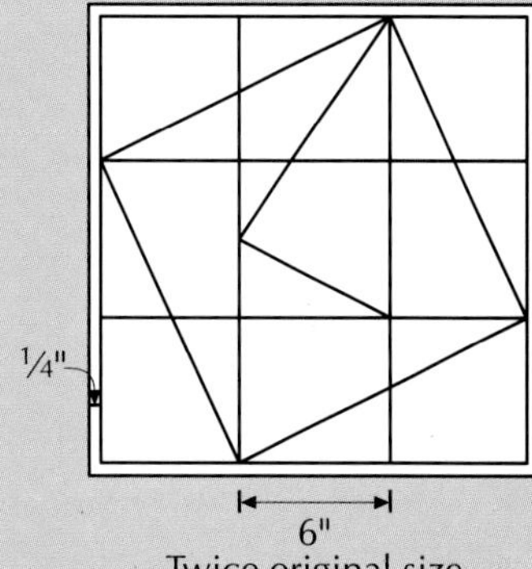

Twice original size

Allover Designs

These large-scale designs cover the whole quilt, disregarding piecing lines and borders. Reminiscent of still-life compositions, allover designs are often inspired by scenes from nature.

An allover design crosses piecing lines.

Allover designs can also be abstract patterns or combinations of grids or lines arranged as a complete design. Single Wedding Ring, Quilt 4 on page 89 is a contemporary allover design composed of swirling lines. In Ohio Star, Quilt 1 on page 44, the in-the-ditch stitching extends into the border to form an allover design.

Use large sheets of tracing paper to draw allover designs. If the design repeats around the center of the quilt, you may need to draw only one-fourth of the design.

To draw an allover design:

1. Tape together as many sheets of paper as necessary to make one large piece the size of your quilt top or, if the design repeats, the size of the repeat.
2. Using a colored pencil, lightly draw the piecing design so that you don't confuse it with the quilting design. Draw a line ½" inside the outer edges to allow for the binding seam allowance and breathing room for the design.
3. Draw your design, enlarging it if necessary with a grid (page 9) or a photocopy machine (facing page). Once you've enlarged the design, you may find that some areas require more quilting to hold the layers together. One approach is to add detail to the design to fill in blank spots. Another option is a filler design. To maintain the impact of the primary design, choose a small filler that won't blend with the allover design. Traditionally, ¼" diagonal or straight-grain grids are used as fillers with allover designs.

Photocopy Machines and Computers

A photocopy machine can save you time and frustration, so don't hesitate to use it. In addition to copying designs, photocopy machines can enlarge and reduce designs, combine designs, rotate designs, and create mirror-image designs—all in a matter of seconds. Copy shops and some libraries have photocopy machines with these capabilities.

To enlarge or reduce designs with a photocopy machine, you must work with percentages. The original size of a design is 100%. To enlarge a design to one-and-a-half times its original size, copy it at the 150% enlargement setting. To reduce a design by half, use a 50% reduction setting. Maximum percentages vary from machine to machine. Many photocopy machines must enlarge designs in steps; that is, you may need to copy the design at the maximum enlargement setting, then further enlarge the copy to reach the size you need.

Computers are another useful tool. A drawing program with the ability to repeat, rotate, merge, and combine designs provides unlimited design possibilities.

Border Designs

Most border designs form a pattern that flows around the quilt, framing the central area and drawing the eye in. Popular border designs include continuous feathers, cables, and scrolls. Occasionally, a border design consists of a single motif that repeats.

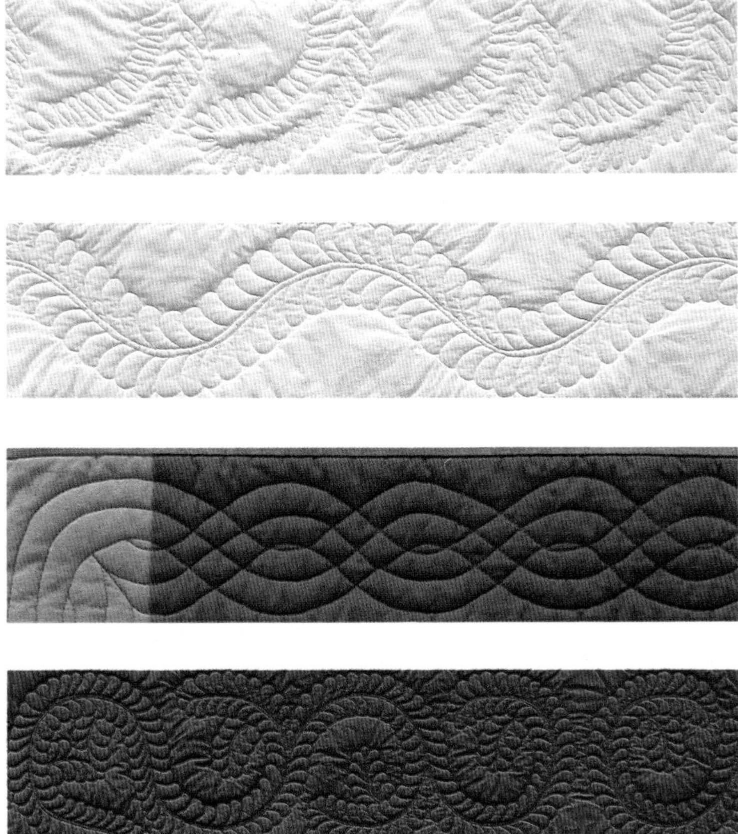

Single Feather Motif

Continuous Feather

Continuous Cable

Continuous Scroll

Border designs relate to the designs in the central area of the quilt in several ways:

- A border design may repeat a motif or part of the design from the central area of the quilt. The border design in Single Wedding Ring, Quilt 1 on page 86 repeats the feather from the central Princess Feather.
- A border design may consist of continuous designs that relate to, but do not repeat, the central quilting design. See Square in a Square, Quilt 5 on page 36 and Log Cabin, Quilt 1 on page 92 for examples of related designs.
- A border design may be modified from the central quilting design. The border designs in Ohio Star, Quilt 3 on page 46 and Log Cabin, Quilt 5 on page 96 are variations of the central designs.
- The quilting design from the central area of the quilt may spill into the border; for an example of this type of design see Fans, Quilt 5 on page 66.

For a pleasing visual effect, quilting designs should fit the borders as precisely as possible. Border designs that turn the corners require careful calculations; even designs that run off the edges of the quilt, disregarding the corners, must be well planned.

One important point: with the exception of the straight-line design shown on page 23, it's best to calculate and draw border designs after you attach the borders. It doesn't matter whether your corners are straight or mitered; the quilting will hide the seams.

BORDER CORNERS

Quilt borders consist of corners and sides. When choosing and planning a border design, consider the border corners first. To find the corner areas, imagine extending the seam lines joining the borders and the central area of the quilt. (It's helpful to disregard the actual seam that occurs at the corner.) The corner areas will be square if the borders are the same width.

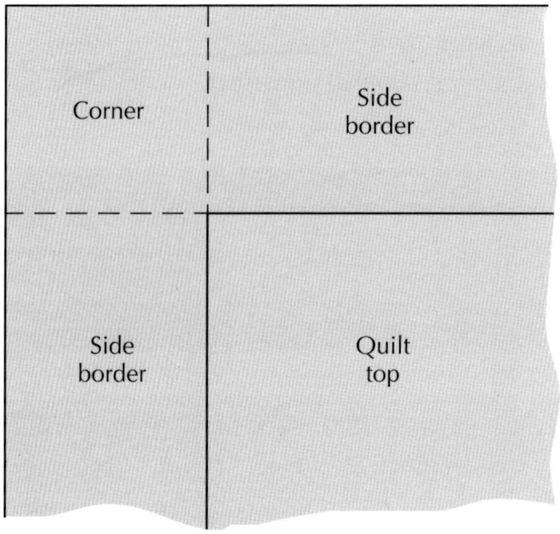

Corner

Side border

Side border

Quilt top

Decide how to treat the corner areas. You may treat corners as:

- Separate design areas, with border designs that stop at the corners.
- A continuation of a flowing design, with border designs that turn the corners.
- A continuation of the side borders, with border designs that run off the edges of the quilt.

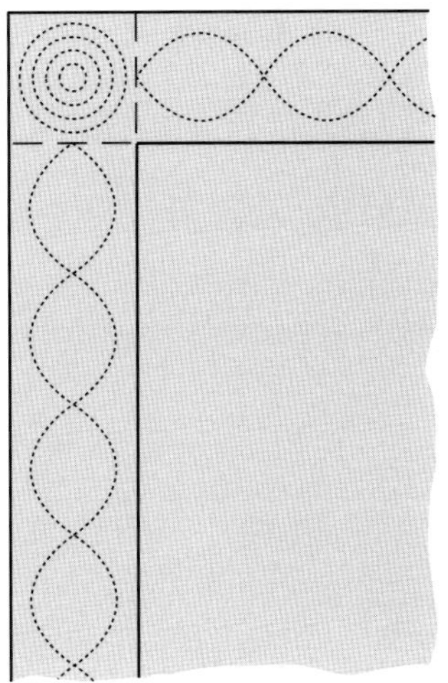
Separate design

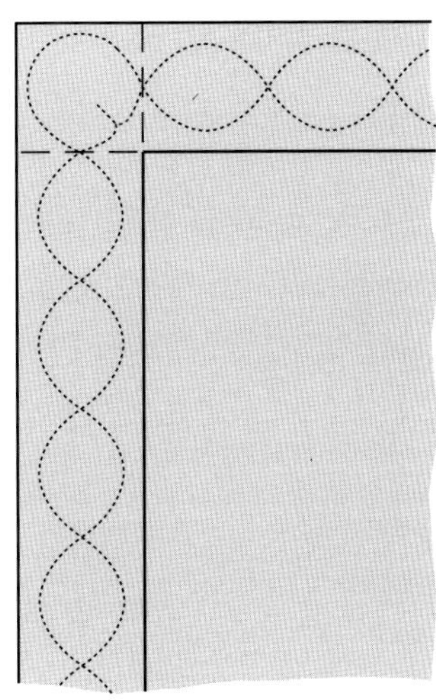
Flowing design

Off-the-edge design

Corners as Separate Design Areas

See Log Cabin, Quilt 3 on page 94 for an example of distinct corner motifs.

1. On tracing paper, draw a square the same size as the corner area on your quilt. Draw lines ½" inside the two outer edges to allow for the binding seam allowance and to create breathing room for the design. Also draw lines ¼" inside the two inner edges where the corner area joins the border sides to give the design breathing room.

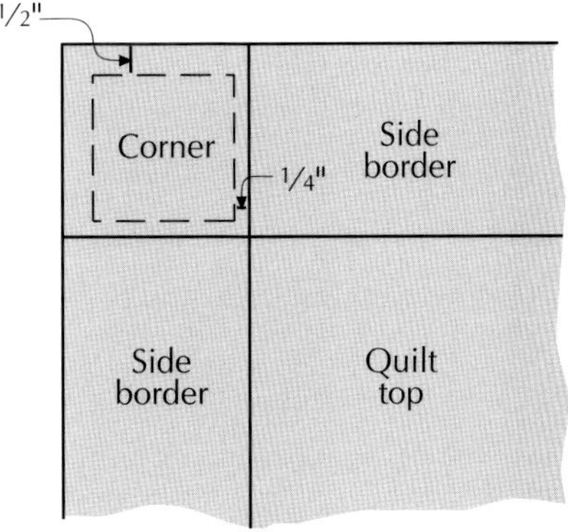

2. Draw your design in the reduced area, enlarging or reducing it if necessary with a grid (page 9) or a photocopy machine (page 11). If you add a filler behind the motif, be sure to quilt the filler all the way to the seam lines.

Borders That Turn Corners

See Single Wedding Ring, Quilt 3 on page 88 for an example of a border design that turns corners.

1. On tracing paper, draw a square the same size as the corner area on your quilt. Draw lines ½" inside the two outer edges to allow for the binding seam allowance and to create breathing room for the design.

2. Draw a small ¼" square at the inner corner of the square to allow breathing room for the design. If the corner design is symmetrical, also draw a diagonal line as shown.

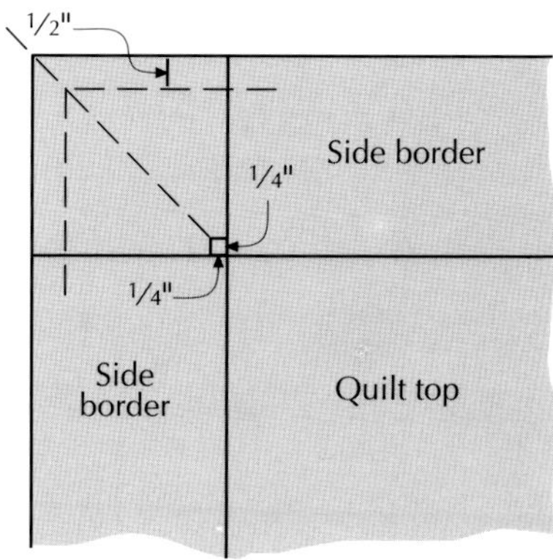

3. Mark the point where the border design will enter the corner area. Straight designs enter the corner at the midpoint (see A and B below). Curved designs might enter closer to the outer edge of the border (C and D) or closer to the inner edge of the border (E and F). The design should enter and leave the corner at the same point on each side.

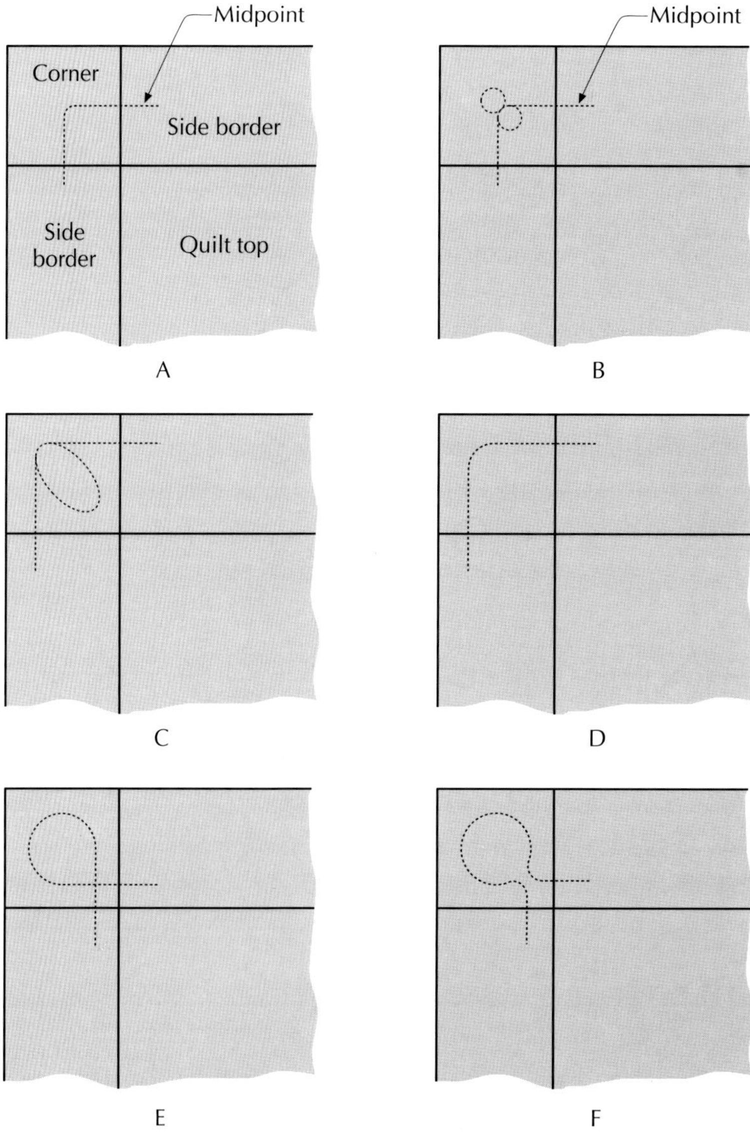

4. Draw half of the corner design, using the diagonal line as a guide. Fold the paper on the diagonal line and trace the other half for a symmetrical motif.

Borders That Run Off the Edges

In antique quilts, border designs on opposite sides often included the corners and ran off the edges of the quilt; the remaining border designs met the first two borders at right angles. Usually, the pairs of borders were different lengths.

Borders that run off the edges

In a variation of this type of border, the design on each border includes only one corner. At the other end of the border, the design meets the adjoining border at a right angle. The effect is similar to the pattern created by the last round of logs in a Log Cabin block.

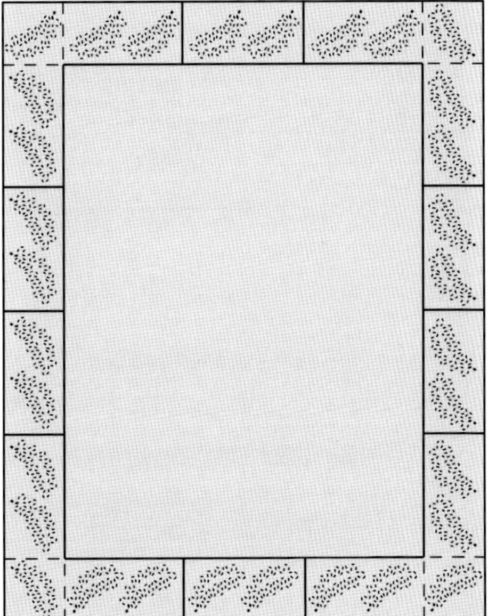

Borders that include one corner

These designs are relatively easy to draw, yet they still require planning. If you draw the designs without regard to where the motifs begin and end, the borders may look cut off or unfinished. It's better to draw designs that fit the length of the border strips exactly; see the instructions that follow.

----- BORDER SIDES -----

Once you've decided how to handle the corners, turn your attention to the sides of the border. The following instructions explain how to draw single-motif repeat designs; instructions for continuous-motif repeat designs, such as cables and feathers, begin on the facing page.

Remember, in calculating and drawing border designs, you're working with the width and length of the border once it's attached to the quilt top.

Single-Motif Repeat Designs

Stencils and designs from books are good sources of single-motif repeat designs. To draw a single-motif border design, you must consider both the length and number of repeats. The term "repeat length" refers to the size of a design element, including any space on either side of the element. If, for example, your motif is a flower that measures 7" across, with ½" of space on either side, the repeat length of each motif is 8". (Keep in mind that the adjoining flower also has ½" of space on either side, so the total distance between flowers is 1".)

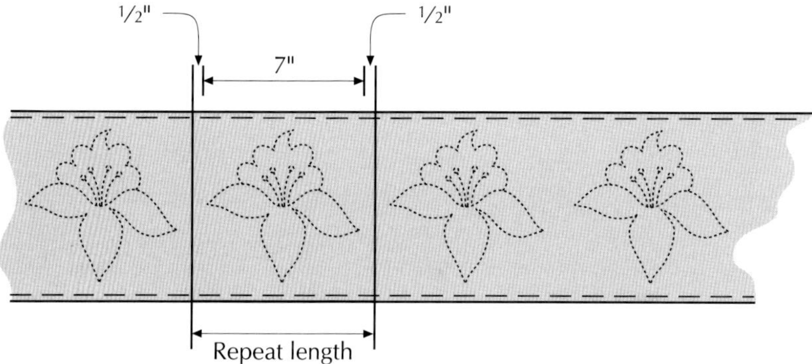

To determine the repeat length and draw your design:

1. Measure the repeat length of the motif you've chosen to use in your border.
2. Measure the length and width of the borders. Exclude the corners if the design will stop at or turn the corners. Include one corner if the design will run off one edge. Include both corners if the design will run off both edges. For each corner that runs off the edge of the quilt, subtract ½" from the border length to allow for the binding seam allowance and to create breathing room for the design.

   If the borders are different lengths, as on a rectangular quilt, you may draw different-sized repeat designs for both borders. The corners remain constant. The motifs in Single Wedding Ring, Quilt 1 on page 86 vary slightly, but the eye doesn't detect the difference.

3. Divide the length of the border by the repeat length; the result is the number of design elements needed for the border. For example, if the border length is 80" and the repeat length is 8", you'll need 10 design elements (80" ÷ 8" = 10"). You can then draw the border design using the design element at its original size.

   What if the result isn't a whole number of elements? If, for example, the border is 86" and the repeat length is 8", you'll arrive at 10.75 design elements (86 ÷ 8 = 10.75). In this case, round up to 11 and divide the length of the border by this number (86 ÷ 11 = 7.8). The result is the repeat length required by one design element. If this repeat length is a long number, use the whole number and the first number after the decimal point (7.8 rather than 7.835); don't round the number up or down.

4. Draw an area equal to the repeat length and the width of the border; subtract 1/4" on the edge next to the quilt and 1/2" on the outer edge to allow for the binding seam allowance and breathing room for the design. Don't subtract anything from either end.

5. Draw the design in the area, enlarging or reducing it if necessary with a grid (page 9) or a photocopy machine (page 11). Make several copies to use for marking the quilt. On your quilt top, lightly mark the repeat length on the border and use these marks to position the pattern.

Continuous Repeat Designs

Although continuous repeat designs, such as cables and feathers, require special handling, their elegance makes them well worth the effort. Most of these designs are based on a curve that remains constant for the length of the border. These designs usually turn corners, so you'll begin by drawing border sides, excluding corners.

To draw a continuous repeat border design, you must consider both the length and number of repeats. With this type of design, the term "repeat length" refers to the length of one design element from the beginning of one element to the beginning of the next identical element. With continuous repeat designs, the repeat length is generally estimated to be twice the border width.

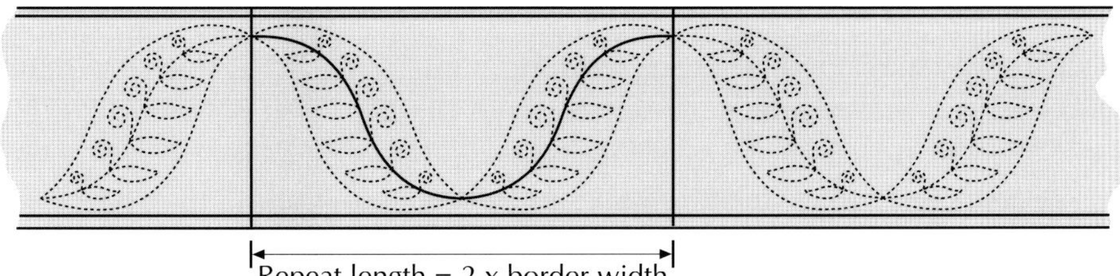

Borders may have an odd or even number of repeats on the sides, and rectangular quilts may have both. An example of a quilt with an odd number of repeats on the top and bottom borders and an even number of repeats on the side borders is shown at right. See also Single Wedding Ring, Quilt 3 on page 88.

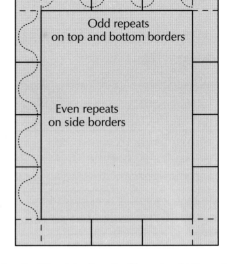

Odd repeats on top and bottom borders

Even repeats on side borders

To determine the repeat length:

1. Measure the length and width of the border excluding the corners, less ¼" on the edge next to the quilt and ½" on the outer edge to allow for the binding seam allowance and breathing room for the design.

2. To determine the approximate repeat length for a continuous design, multiply the width of the border by two. For example, if the border is 9" wide (excluding the ¼" and ½" on the edges), the approximate repeat length is 18".

3. Divide the border length by the approximate repeat length to arrive at the number of repeats (87" ÷ 18" = 4.83 repeats). Round up to 5 repeats.

4. Divide the border length by the whole number of repeats to arrive at the exact repeat length (87" ÷ 5 = 17.4"). You'll have 5 repeats, each 17½" long. Draw one repeat.

   If this formula produces repeat lengths that are too short (causing tight curves), round the number down to 4 repeats. In the example, the exact repeat length would then be 21¾" (87" ÷ 4 = 21.75").

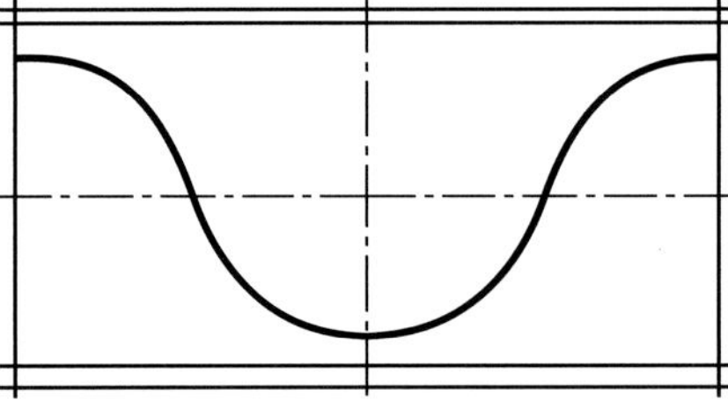

Five repeats make the curve tight.

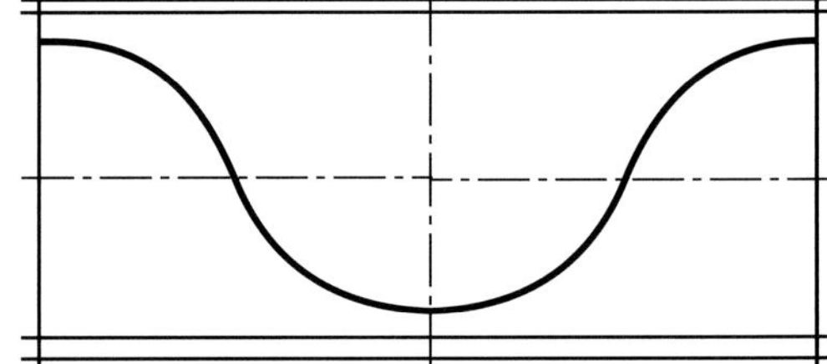

Four repeats create a more open curve.

Another way to determine the repeat length is to cut (or tape together) a piece of paper the length and width of your border. Fold the strip into equal spaces that are pleasing to the eye, usually 3, 4, or 5. This method does away with the calculator, but until you fold the paper, you won't know how many elements will look best or if you need an even or odd number of repeats.

If the quilt is rectangular, you may need two different-sized repeats—one for the sides and one for the top and bottom borders. Normally, repeat length differences of 2" or less are not noticeable.

Even if you measured correctly, a design may not fit exactly. In this case, you'll need to make slight adjustments in the design size. Never adjust designs at the corners, where changes are most obvious. Instead, adjust the center three repeats evenly. A little adjustment to the center repeats is better than a large adjustment to one repeat and is unlikely to be noticed.

Sometimes the error is too large or the design too complex, or you're just tired of trying to get it right. One solution is to add a small element at the midpoint of the border if a gap exists; see Square in a Square, Quilt 5 on page 36. If you plan to use a standard stencil and the border can't accommodate a whole number of repeats, put a single related motif at the midpoint of the border.

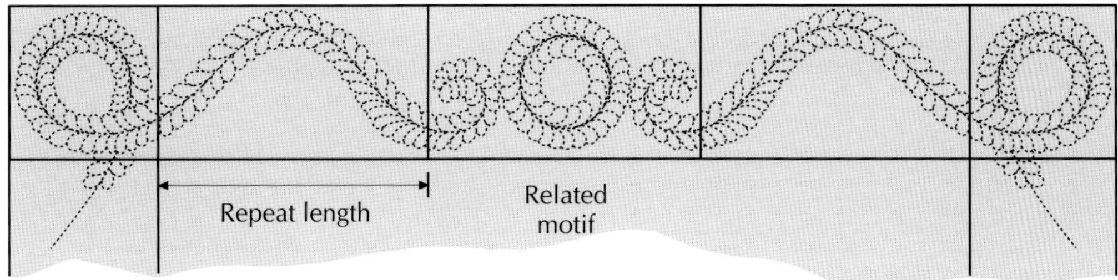

To draw curved designs:

Curved designs, such as vines, florals, scrolls, feathers, and cables, have a full curve at the bottom and two half-curves at the top of each repeat.

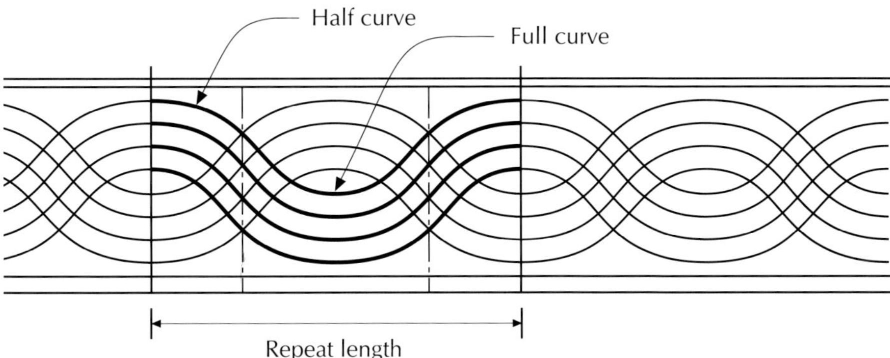

1. Draw the design for one repeat length (not the entire border) equal to the width of the border, less 1/4" on the edge next to the quilt and 1/2" on the outer edge to allow for the binding seam allowance and to create breathing room for the design. Don't subtract anything from either end because one element will flow into the next.

2. Draw a horizontal line midway between the top and bottom lines. Draw three vertical lines, dividing the area into fourths. Going over the vertical and horizontal lines with a colored pen or pencil will keep them separate from the quilting lines.

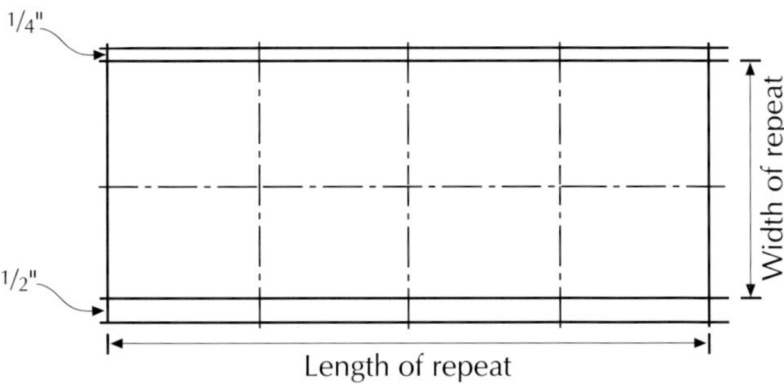

3. For *vines, florals,* and *scrolls,* start the curve ¼" from the top of the design area. Start *feathers* and *cables* halfway between the top of the design area and the horizontal dividing line to allow the feathers or cables to extend above and below the curve.

   Draw the curve from the starting point to the intersection of the horizontal line and the first vertical line.

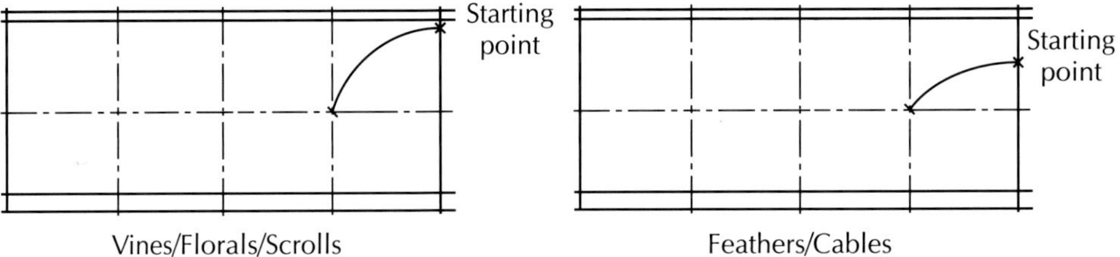

Vines/Florals/Scrolls　　Feathers/Cables

4. Draw the remaining curves in the design area. To make smooth, even curves, take a piece of tracing paper a little larger than the area of the first curve and, with a dark pencil or pen, trace the curve and the surrounding lines. Position this piece of paper (rotated 180° or turned over, or both) under your main drawing and trace uniform curves in the three remaining areas. These are your basic curves for the repeat.

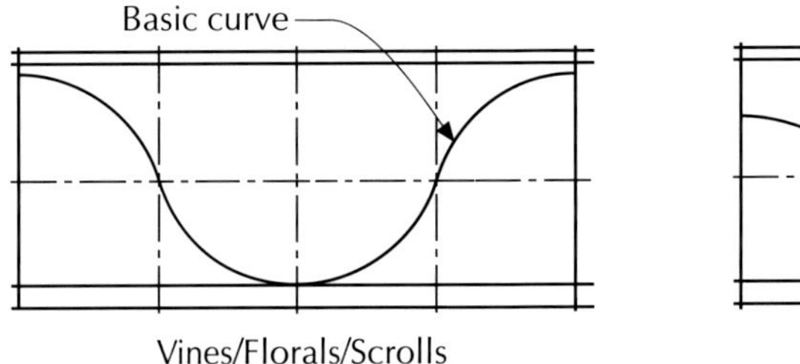

Vines/Florals/Scrolls

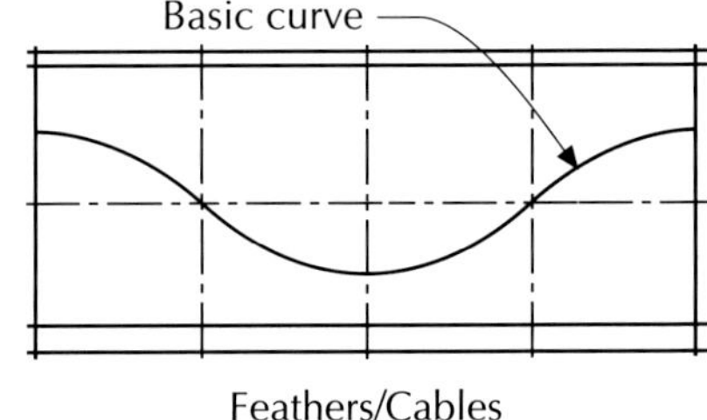

Feathers/Cables

5. Complete the design. For *vines, florals,* and *scrolls,* add the secondary curves and motifs to the basic curve. You can also use this method to design repeat appliqué borders.

   With *feathers,* the basic curve becomes the spine of the feather; parallel lines drawn on either side of the basic curve keep the height of the feathers constant. These lines may extend to the edge of the design area. Measure equal distances on either side of the basic curve, mark with dots, and join the dots smoothly to make parallel curved lines. Draw the feathers all the way from the spine to these parallel lines.

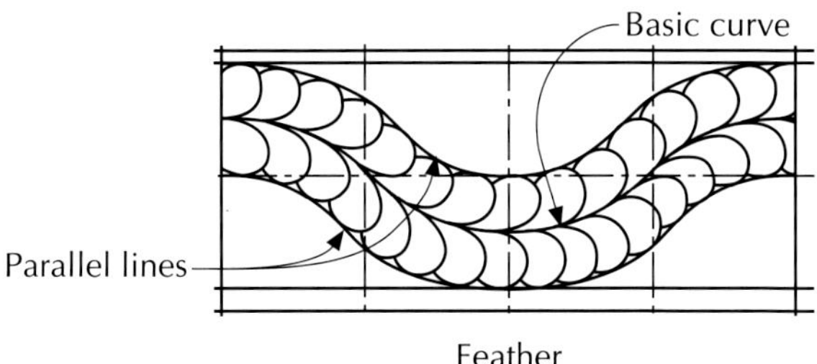

Feather

Fine Feathers, a book by Marianne Fons, contains detailed instructions for drawing feather designs.

Cable designs may have as many parallel cables as you like. Once you've drawn the basic curve, which is the same as for feathers, decide if you want an odd or even number of cables in your design.

With an odd number of cables, the basic curve is the center of the middle cable. To draw the middle cable, measure half the desired cable width on either side of the basic curve and mark with dots. For the other cables, measure and mark the cable width on either side of the middle cable. Join the dots to make parallel curved lines. Erase the basic curve.

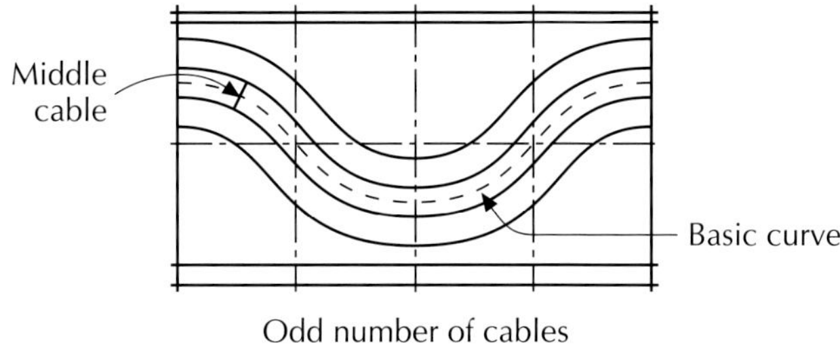

Odd number of cables

For an even number of cables, draw the outer lines first, spacing them the desired total width of the design and measuring from the basic curve. Divide the total width by the number of cables desired—four in the illustration below—to arrive at the width of each cable. Measure, mark with dots, and join the dots to make parallel curved lines.

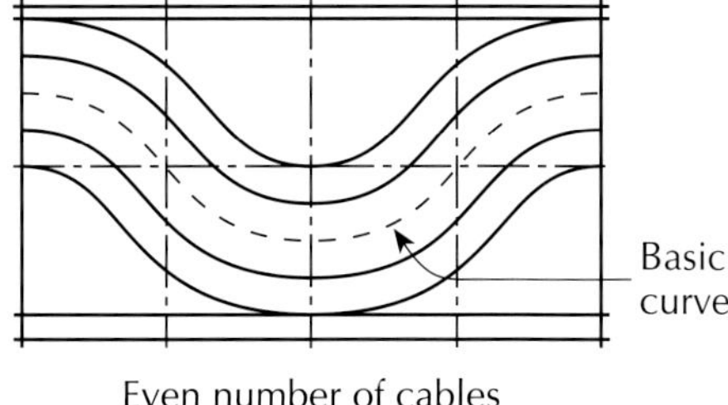

Even number of cables

To complete either design, fold your tracing paper in half along the horizontal center line and trace the cables on both sides. Erase the lines where the cables cross.

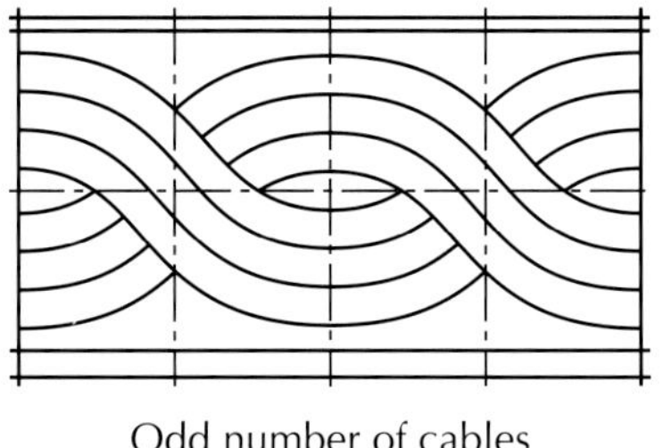

Odd number of cables

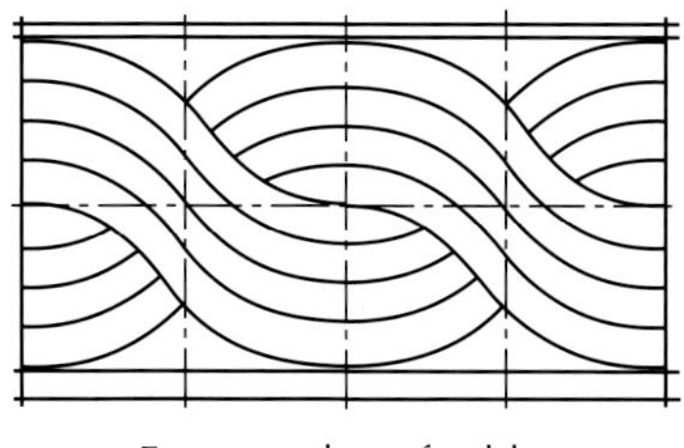

Even number of cables

PUTTING IT ALL TOGETHER

Once you've drawn the corner design and the border side repeat, position the designs as they will occur on the quilt. If you're using a separate corner motif, make sure there is breathing room around the corner design.

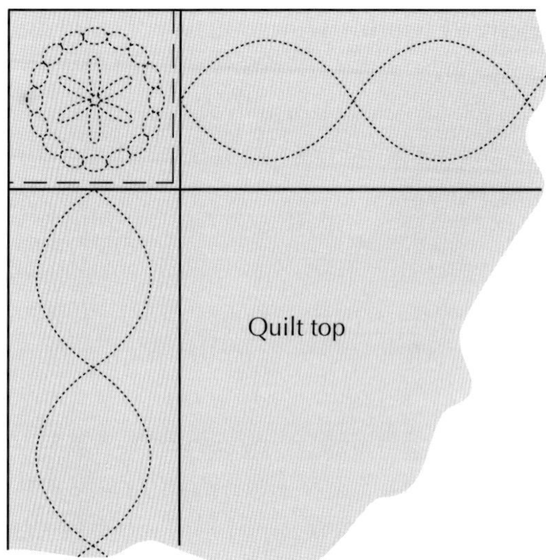

If your side border design is a continuous repeat, make sure the design meets the corner design and flows smoothly around the corners. You may need to redraw a few connecting lines or feathers to make a smooth transition from the side border into the corner.

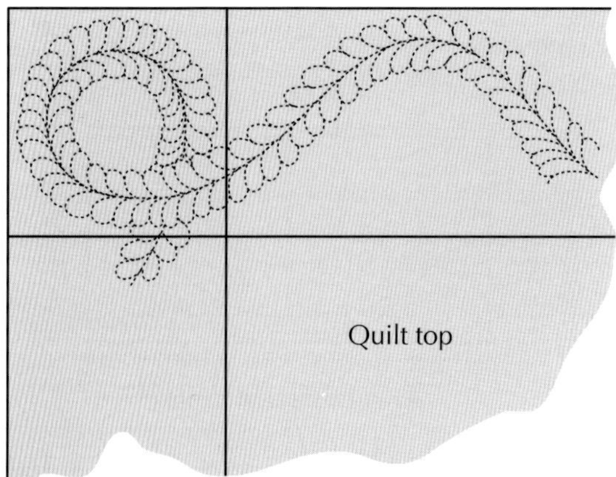

STRAIGHT-LINE DESIGNS

See Single Wedding Ring, Quilt 2 on page 87 for an example of a straight-line design. In the past, quiltmakers had trouble with this geometric border design, and many simply ran the repeat off the borders. For a more pleasing effect, work out the repeat before you cut and attach your borders.

The design consists of right-angle triangles quilted in straight lines. The length of the repeat is the longest side of the triangle and is placed against the edge of the quilt top.

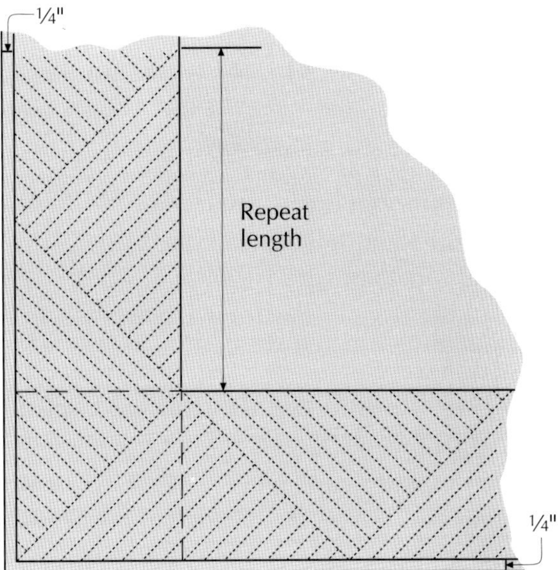

This border design is very simple to use on a quilt composed of blocks in a side-by-side setting. In this case, the repeat length is equal to the finished block size, and the finished border width is one-half the block size. If, for example, the finished block is 12", the repeat is 12" and the finished border is 6".

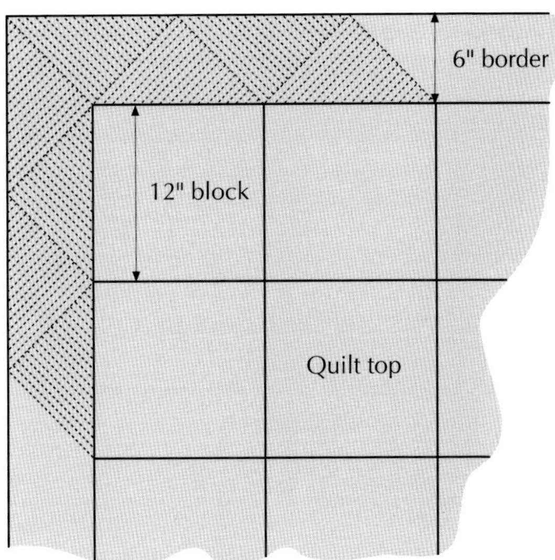

For other quilts, you must choose a border width and calculate the repeat length as follows:

1. Measure your quilt before the borders have been attached. Subtract ¼" from all edges for seam allowances. In this example, the quilt top, less the seam allowances, measures 64" x 96".

2. Choose a border width and multiply by two. In the following example, assume a desired border width of 8" (8" x 2 = 16").

3. Divide the quilt length and width by the number in step 2 to arrive at the number of repeats. In the example, there are 4 repeats on the short borders (64" ÷ 16 = 4) and 6 repeats on the long borders (96" ÷ 16" = 6), each 16" long. The cut borders will measure 96½" x 8½" and 80½" x 8½".

If however, the number of repeats is not a whole number (the usual case), choose a border width that, when multiplied by 2, divides evenly into the short side of the quilt top. This calculation takes some experimentation.

In this example, the quilt top, less seam allowances, measures 60" x 89".

1. Choose a border width that, when multiplied by 2, divides evenly into the short side of the quilt top. A border width of 6, when multiplied by 2, divides evenly into 60 (60 ÷ 12 = 5). You will have 5 repeats on the short side, each 12" long.

2. Divide the long side by the same border width multiplied by 2 (89 ÷ 12 = 7.4 repeats, rounded to 7 repeats). Divide the long side by this whole number of repeats for the exact repeat length (89 ÷ 7 = 12.71, or 12¾"). You will have 7 repeats on the long side, each 12¾". The cut borders will measure 89½" x 6½" and 72½" x 6½".

The ¾" difference in repeat length on the short and long sides won't be noticed. The angles on the long sides won't be true right angles, but you'll still be able to draw 45° angles in the corners.

When you measure and cut your borders for this design, add a ¼" seam allowance to each edge. No breathing room is allowed for the quilting design because the quilting goes all the way to the seams and outer edges.

TRIANGLES

48" x 72½"

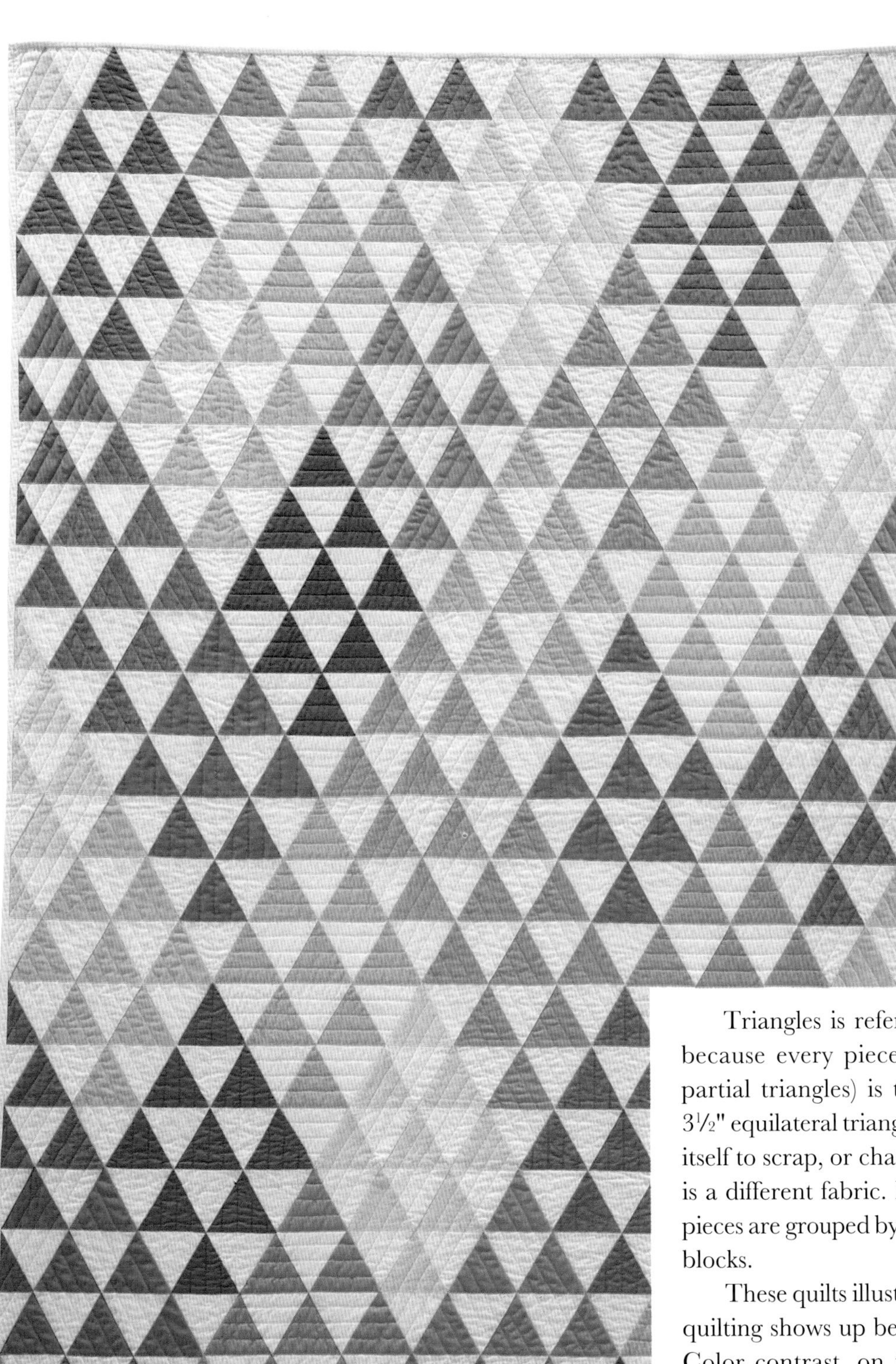

Triangles is referred to as a One Patch quilt because every piece (with the exception of the partial triangles) is the same size and shape—a 3½" equilateral triangle. A One Patch pattern lends itself to scrap, or charm, quilts, where every patch is a different fabric. In the quilts shown here, the pieces are grouped by color to create large diamond blocks.

These quilts illustrate a basic quilting principle: quilting shows up best on fabrics of similar value. Color contrast, on the other hand, can disrupt quilting designs. Where white triangles touch dark triangles, the quilting lines are broken. To showcase your quilting and maintain the continuity of the design, choose similar-value colors.

1 This design of parallel lines is perhaps the simplest form of quilting. The vertical white stitching bisects the pairs of triangles, creating half-diamonds. A minimal design like this one is a good choice for a true scrap quilt, where elaborate stitching might get lost.

To make the quilt more stable and durable, stitch in-the-ditch horizontally, following the seams that form the bases of the triangles.

Stitching in-the-ditch, although not seen, plays an important role in holding the layers of fabric and batting together.

Diagonal rows of quilting outline the individual diamonds. An off-center zigzag pattern, stitched with machine-embroidery thread, echoes the piecing design and emphasizes the length of the quilt.

You can use many different decorative machine stitches on this quilt. A larger stitch would draw attention to the zigzag pattern and diminish the visual impact of the piecing. Variegated machine-embroidery thread could be used to good effect, too.

Narrow bands of straight lines and wide bands of stippling zigzag across this quilt in an abstract allover design.

The straight-line design echoes the One Patch triangle. A second row of stitching, ³⁄₈" from the piecing lines, defines each band.

The wider bands of stippling imitate rippling water, a fitting design for a quilt made of blue-green fabrics. This curvilinear pattern can also be used to indicate wood grain and plant textures in nature quilts.

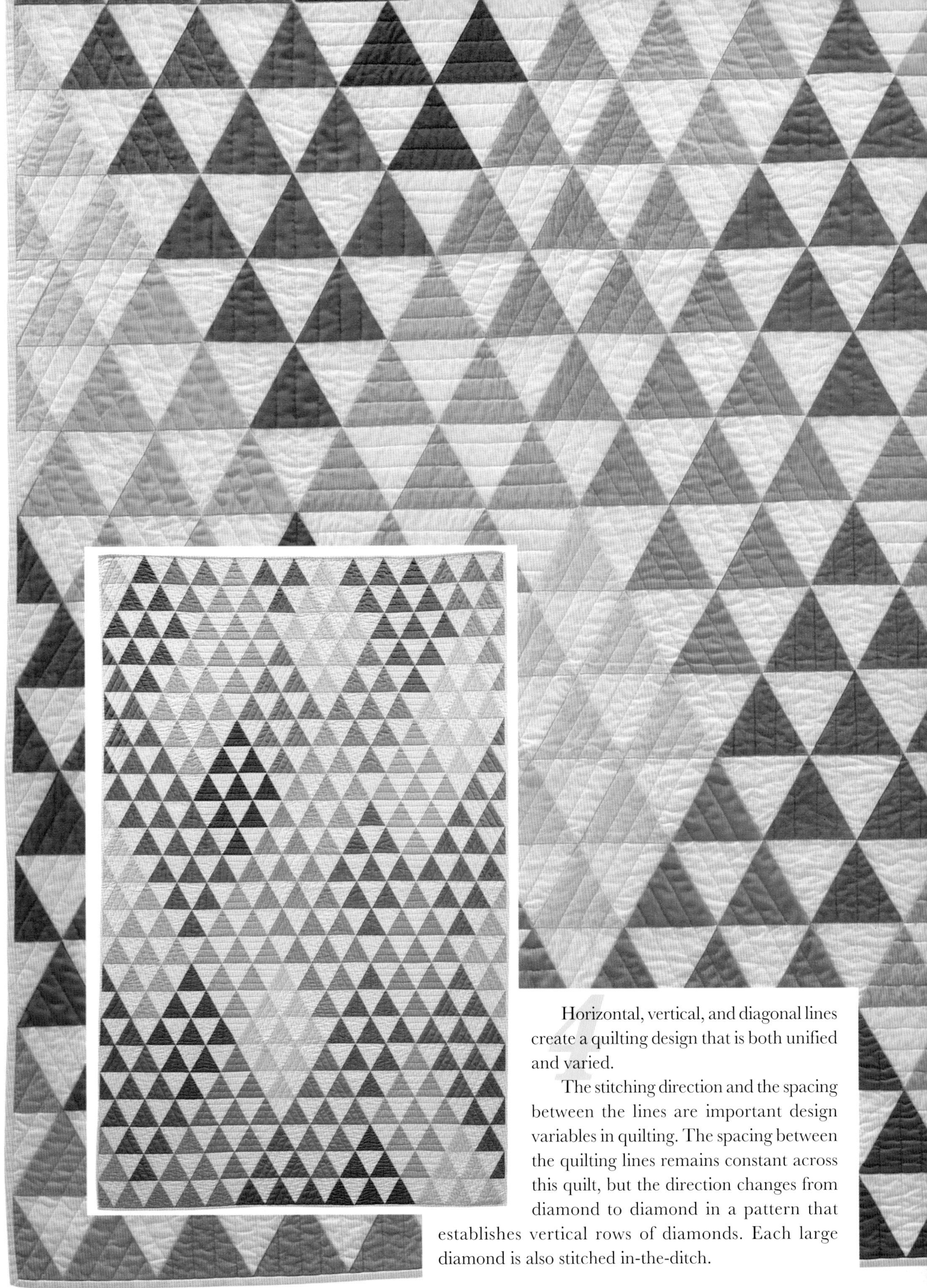

Horizontal, vertical, and diagonal lines create a quilting design that is both unified and varied.

The stitching direction and the spacing between the lines are important design variables in quilting. The spacing between the quilting lines remains constant across this quilt, but the direction changes from diamond to diamond in a pattern that establishes vertical rows of diamonds. Each large diamond is also stitched in-the-ditch.

5

An allover Art Nouveau floral design lends unexpected curves to a geometric quilt. A variety of machine-embroidery threads outlines the leaf shapes, and heavy pearl cotton defines the flowers.

To achieve this effect, first quilt the top with dressmaking thread. Then wind pearl cotton onto the bobbin and quilt the flowers from the back, following your previous stitching. You must work from the back because heavy threads cannot be threaded through the machine needle.

I enlarged this design from Gregory Mirow's *A Treasury of Design for Artists and Craftsmen*, using the grid technique described on page 9.

This quilt features the two most basic shapes in quiltmaking—the square and the half-square triangle. Alternating the colors in each block makes this simple design appear more complex.

The quilts in this series illustrate the power of quilting to affect the look of a simple pieced quilt. The gentle curves in Quilt 1 subdue the angles of the blocks, while concentric circles in Quilt 3 blur the piecing and create intriguing negative space. Curved motifs centered in the squares in Quilts 4 and 5 maintain the piecing design.

Square in a Square

65½" x 78½"

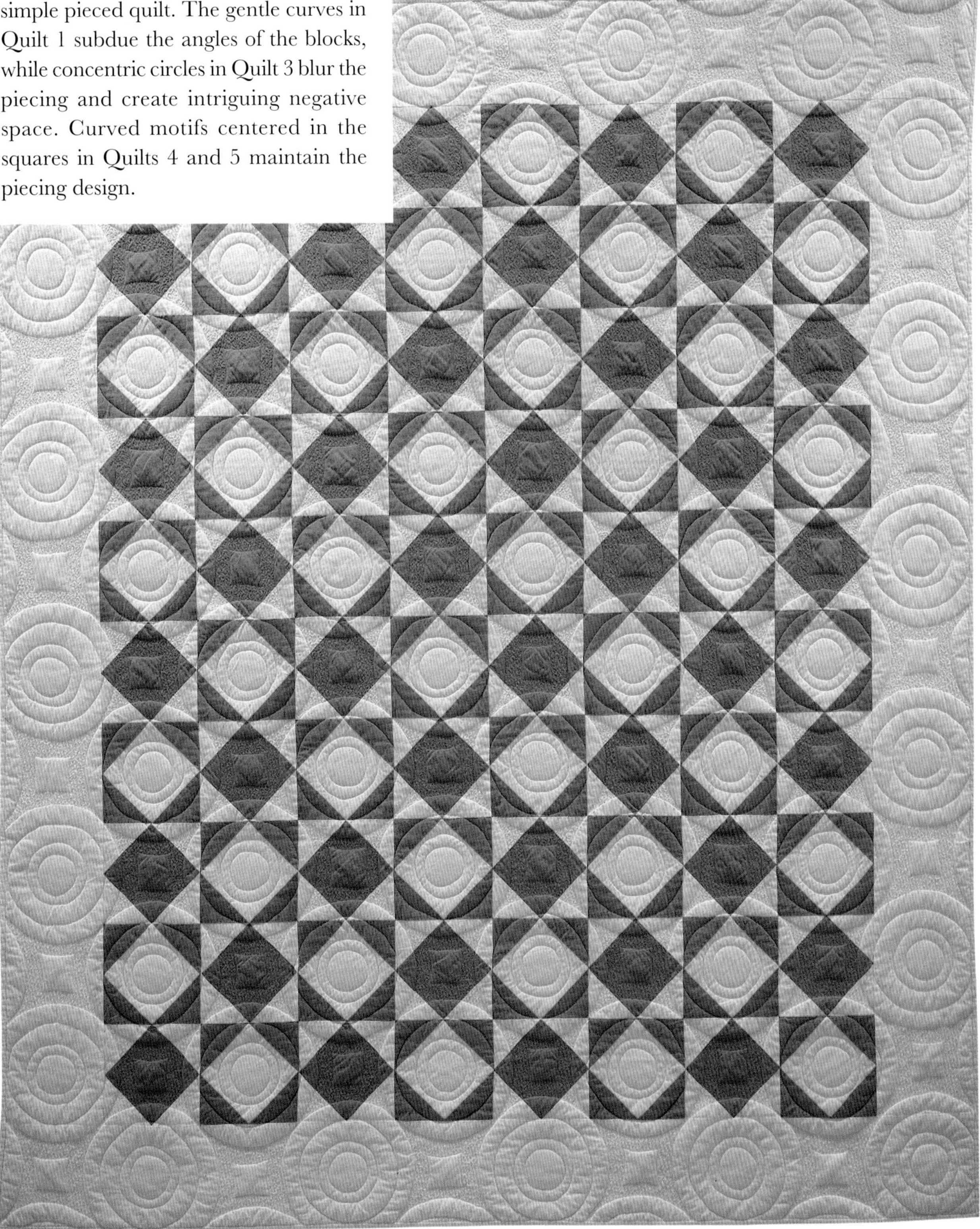

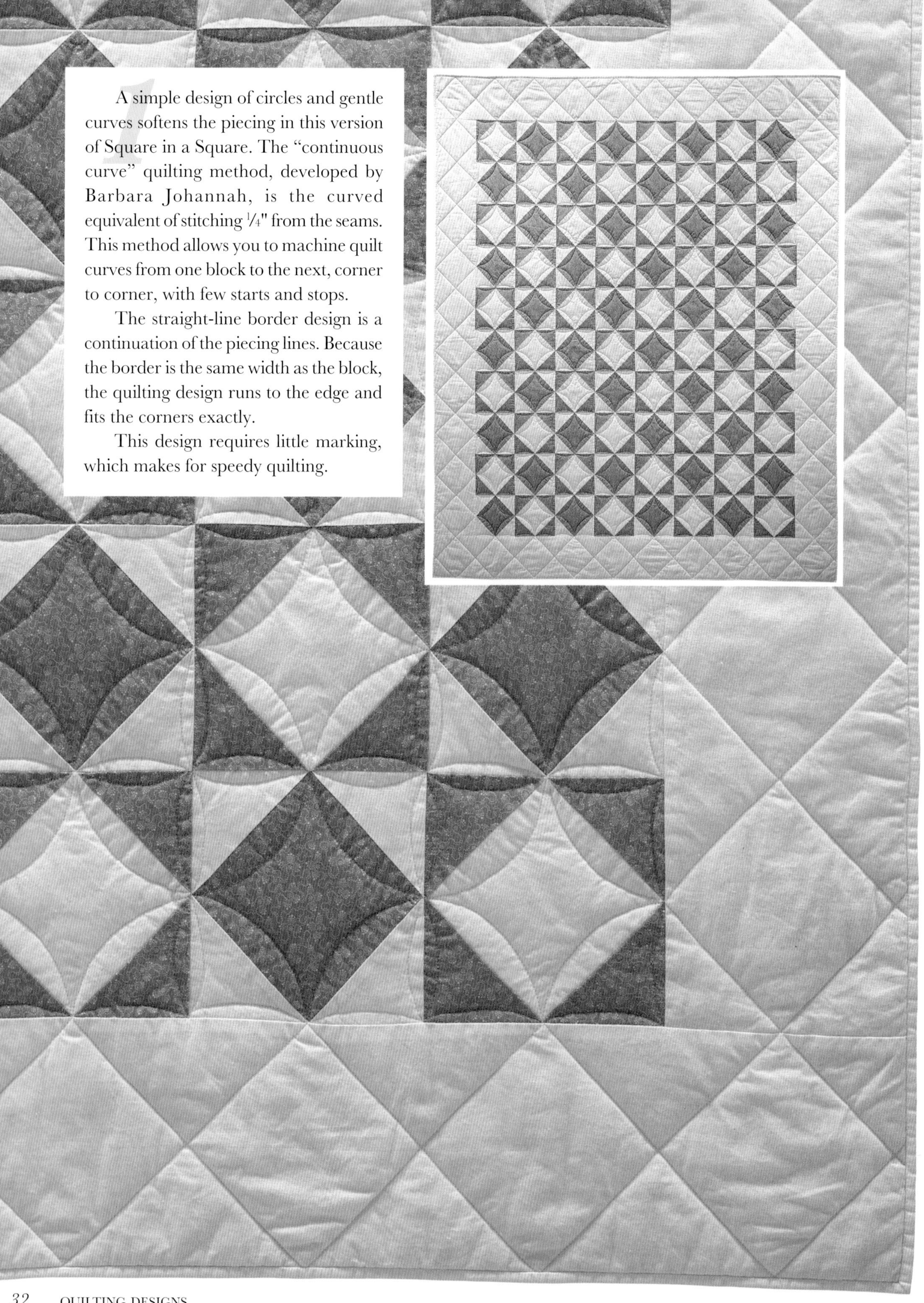

A simple design of circles and gentle curves softens the piecing in this version of Square in a Square. The "continuous curve" quilting method, developed by Barbara Johannah, is the curved equivalent of stitching 1/4" from the seams. This method allows you to machine quilt curves from one block to the next, corner to corner, with few starts and stops.

The straight-line border design is a continuation of the piecing lines. Because the border is the same width as the block, the quilting design runs to the edge and fits the corners exactly.

This design requires little marking, which makes for speedy quilting.

This contemporary design, a combination of satin and zigzag stitching, is strictly for machine quilters. Vary the distance between rows and use a variety of threads and stitches to achieve the distinctive dimensional effect.

Because the diagonal lines go in the same direction, the finished quilt is slightly out of square. On a small quilt you can compensate for this distortion by quilting alternate rows in opposite directions. But this strategy is impractical on a large quilt, and you must be willing to live with the less-than-square results.

The border design echoes the internal line work with an elongated zigzag pattern. To ensure a precise fit at the corners, you must carefully plan this border design; see "Border Designs" on pages 11–24.

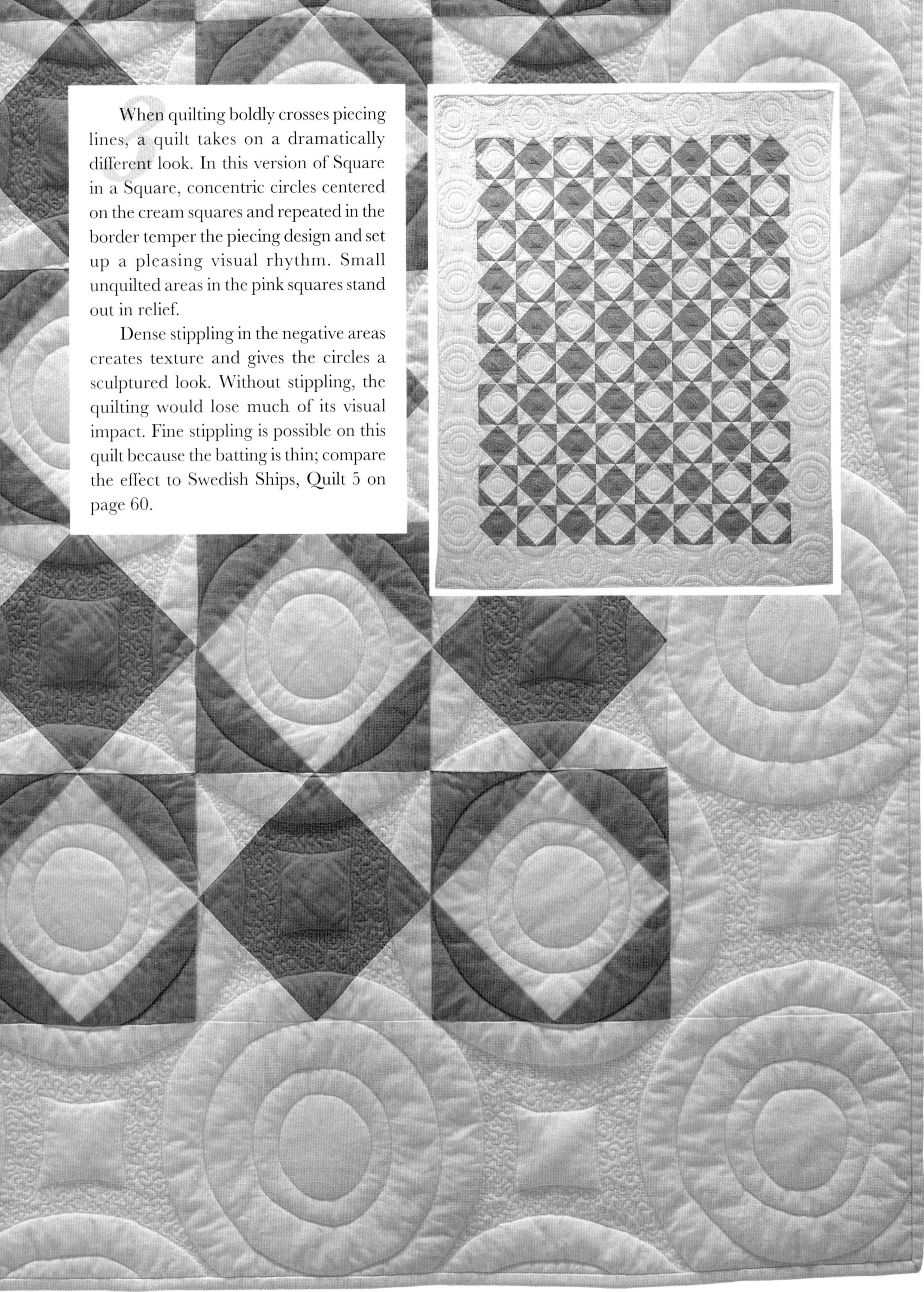

When quilting boldly crosses piecing lines, a quilt takes on a dramatically different look. In this version of Square in a Square, concentric circles centered on the cream squares and repeated in the border temper the piecing design and set up a pleasing visual rhythm. Small unquilted areas in the pink squares stand out in relief.

Dense stippling in the negative areas creates texture and gives the circles a sculptured look. Without stippling, the quilting would lose much of its visual impact. Fine stippling is possible on this quilt because the batting is thin; compare the effect to Swedish Ships, Quilt 5 on page 60.

Parallel lines quilted in the pink triangles frame letters and numerals in the cream squares. An inward-spiraling maze in the pink squares keeps the eye moving; for visual relief, the cream triangles are left plain. All piecing lines are stitched in-the-ditch.

An interlocking Celtic key design, modified from *Celtic Art* by George Bain, decorates the border. Without the zigzag stitching, the design would be a distracting jumble of lines. Turning the corner with this border design is tricky. The repeat must be calculated the same way as a border of straight lines; see the instructions on pages 22–24.

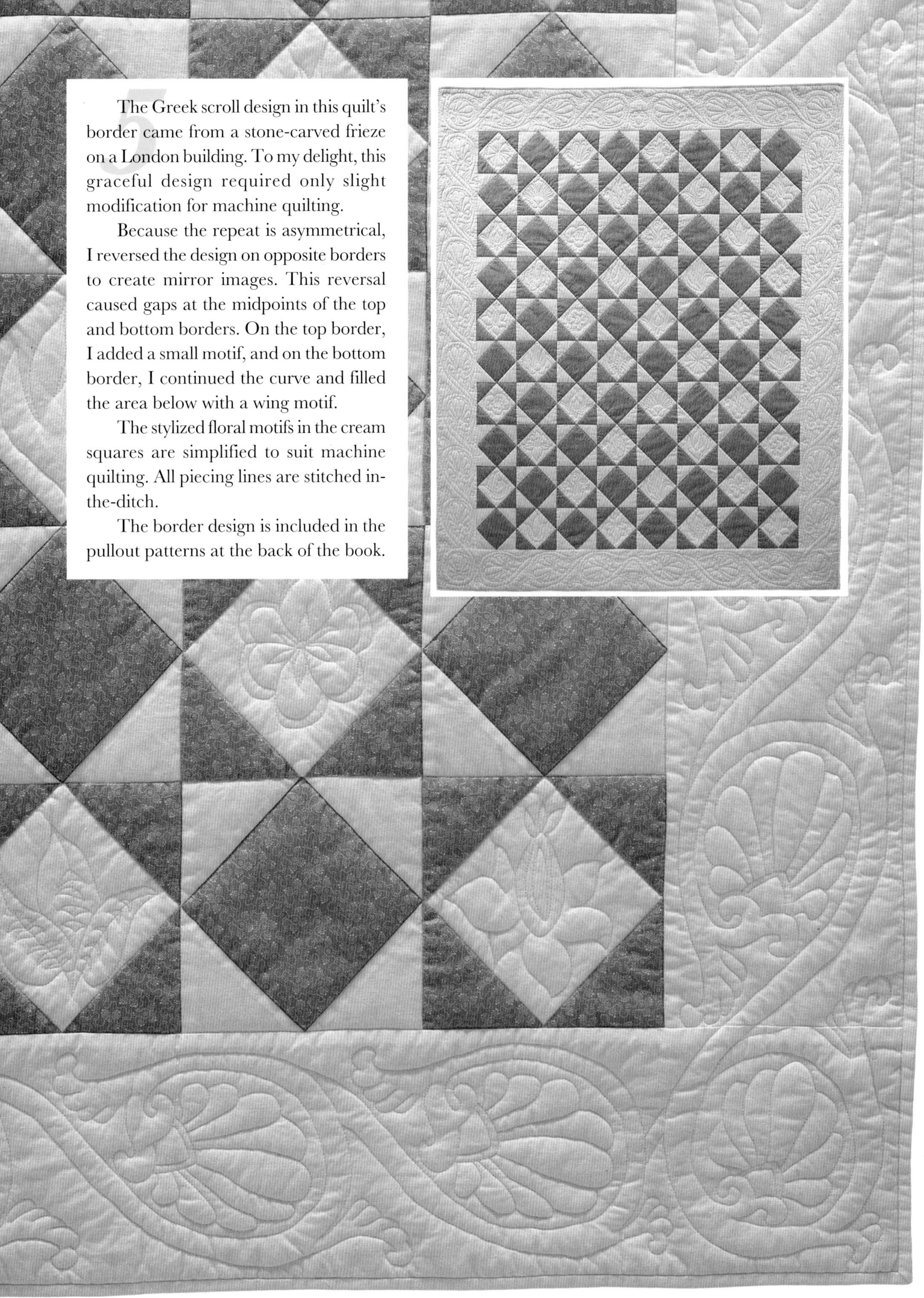

The Greek scroll design in this quilt's border came from a stone-carved frieze on a London building. To my delight, this graceful design required only slight modification for machine quilting.

Because the repeat is asymmetrical, I reversed the design on opposite borders to create mirror images. This reversal caused gaps at the midpoints of the top and bottom borders. On the top border, I added a small motif, and on the bottom border, I continued the curve and filled the area below with a wing motif.

The stylized floral motifs in the cream squares are simplified to suit machine quilting. All piecing lines are stitched in-the-ditch.

The border design is included in the pullout patterns at the back of the book.

Double Irish Chain

53″ x 68″

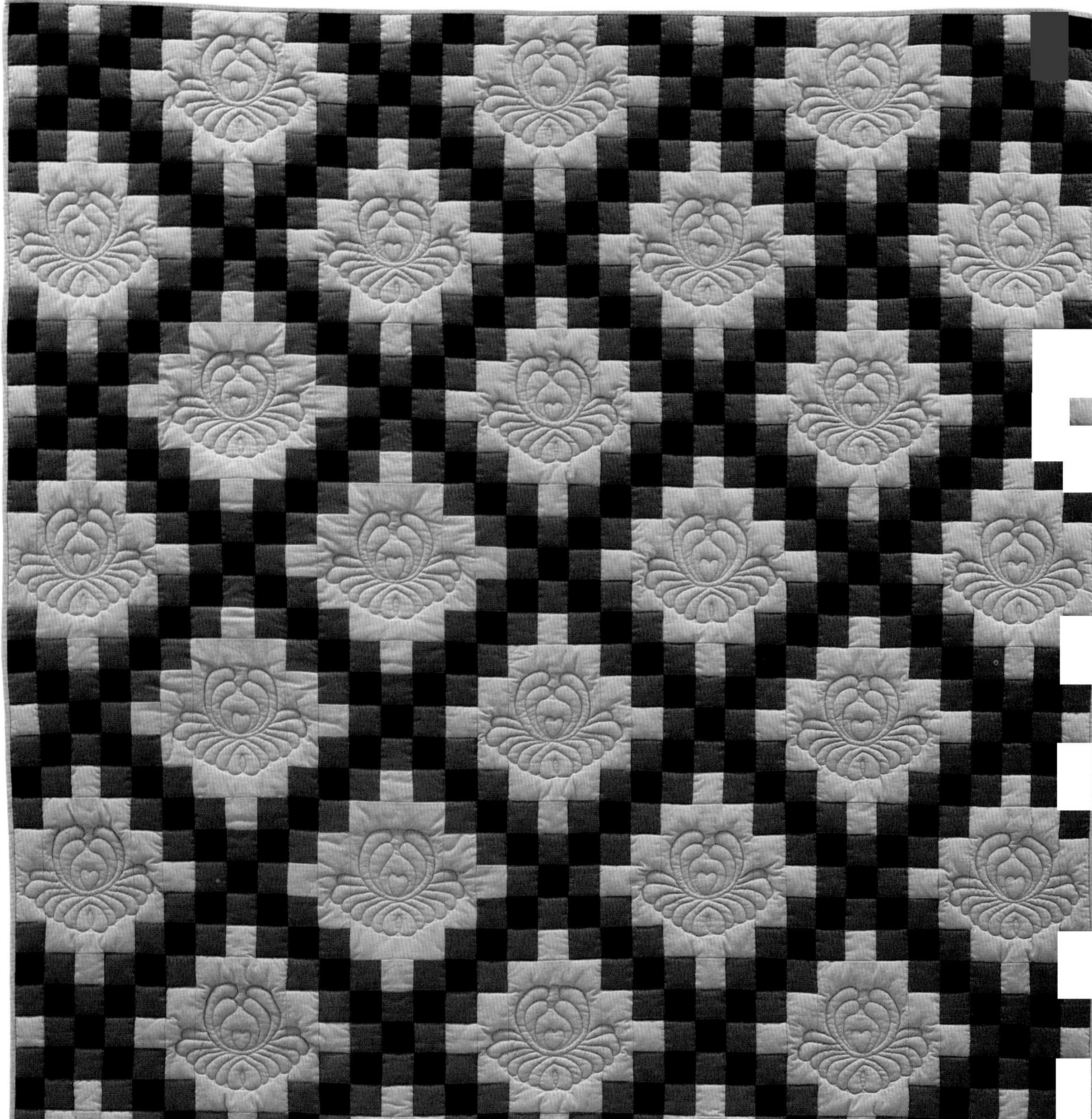

A traditional favorite among quiltmakers, the Double Irish Chain forms strong diagonal bands, or "chains," that appear to float on the background. This pattern is typically quilted in a diagonal grid, or the chains are stitched in-the-ditch, with a repeating motif quilted in alternate blocks. In the quilts that follow, a subdued palette of rust, black, and khaki displays a variety of quilting designs.

A Double Irish Chain quilt takes on an entirely different look when floral fabrics are used. And when fabric colors blend, the lines between chains and alternate blocks blur, creating an orderly but Impressionistic pattern.

1 Geometric quilts are always pleasing when quilted in diagonal grids. In a Double Irish Chain quilt, a diagonal grid balances the horizontal and vertical piecing lines of the chains. Be sure to keep the grid uniform, with true parallel lines; see "Straight Grids" on page 7 for tips on drawing a diagonal grid.

Log Cabin quilts are good candidates for this basic grid because the diagonal stitching breaks up the perpendicular piecing lines while maintaining a sense of order. A diagonal grid also works on an appliqué quilt. To make the appliqué motifs appear to float on the background, stop and start the grid at the edges of the appliqué.

2

While a diagonal grid emphasizes the chains, a straight-grain grid repeats the square shapes for a visually restful design. Who's to say which design is correct? It's a matter of personal preference.

This basic grid consists of horizontal and vertical lines stitched in-the-ditch of the chain squares. Each resulting square is further divided horizontally and vertically to create a smaller grid-within-a-grid. Although both diagonal and straight-grain grids divide each chain square into fourths, a straight-grain grid requires more sewing.

When quilters think of the Double Irish Chain, they often imagine a quilt like this one, with the diagonal chains stitched in-the-ditch and traditional motifs quilted in the alternate blocks.

The stylized feather motif shown here came from *Tried and True—Favorite Old-time Quilting Designs* by Shirley Thompson. This motif illustrates the power of quilting to subtly alter color: the stitching creates highlights and shadows, which the eye reads as a slight variation in tone.

Other popular motifs include flowers and feather wreaths. Almost any design that fills the area evenly is a good choice.

A traditional wineglass design relates well to the scale of the chains in this quilt. The stylized flowers stitched in bronze metallic thread are linked for ease of stitching. If you quilt with metallic threads, make sure they can be seen, or the effect will be lost and the effort wasted. To keep the thread from shredding, use a specialized needle with a larger eye and elongated scarf (the groove on the back of the needle) and reduce the top tension. Some metallic threads can be sewn successfully on unpieced areas but break when going over seams. As with any unfamiliar materials, test threads to find one that works with your fabrics and batting.

5

Heavy satin stitching in khaki and black thread accentuates the diagonal chains and adds an unusual decorative element to this quilt. If you try this technique, use a thin batting and do not stretch the quilt on the bias as you stitch.

Other quilting options include stitching a continuous flower motif in the center chain, with the three chains stitched in-the-ditch or the outer chains satin-stitched.

Quilting on-point squares in the alternate blocks is a dramatic departure from tradition. Smaller squares stand out against a backdrop of heavy black stippling. Seen from afar, the stippling creates a variation in tone and a pattern reminiscent of Ocean Waves.

Ohio Star

56½" x 70"

The Ohio Star block has been a favorite with quiltmakers since the early nineteenth century, when it first appeared in pieced tops. It is a versatile pattern, adapting well to plain or patterned fabrics and side-by-side or on-point settings, with or without sashing.

In the quilts shown here, narrow cream sashing forms a latticelike frame that lends structure to the design. Wide borders and setting triangles that are larger than the blocks create the illusion of blocks floating on the background.

These quilts illustrate what happens when quilting lines cross from plain to patterned fabrics: designs that show clearly on solid fabrics may get lost in prints. If you want the quilting design to have the same impact in all areas of the quilt, consider using only plain fabrics.

1 Duplicating the star piecing pattern in the quilting design produces a tailored effect. For simplicity, the blocks and sashing are stitched in-the-ditch. These lines extend into the setting triangles and the border, where they echo the piecing design.

For an entirely different look, quilt continuous curves in the blocks but repeat the piecing design in the setting triangles and the borders; see Square in a Square, Quilt 1 on page 32 for a similar design.

What a difference a quilting design makes! A double clamshell pattern obscures the piecing lines of the stars, blending the solid and print fabrics. Curved quilting over straight-line piecing often adds texture and character to a quilt, especially when the quilt is viewed from afar.

Clamshell is an English piecing pattern that's been used for hundreds of years as a quilting design. In the Japanese quilting tradition of Sashiko, this design is referred to as a wave pattern.

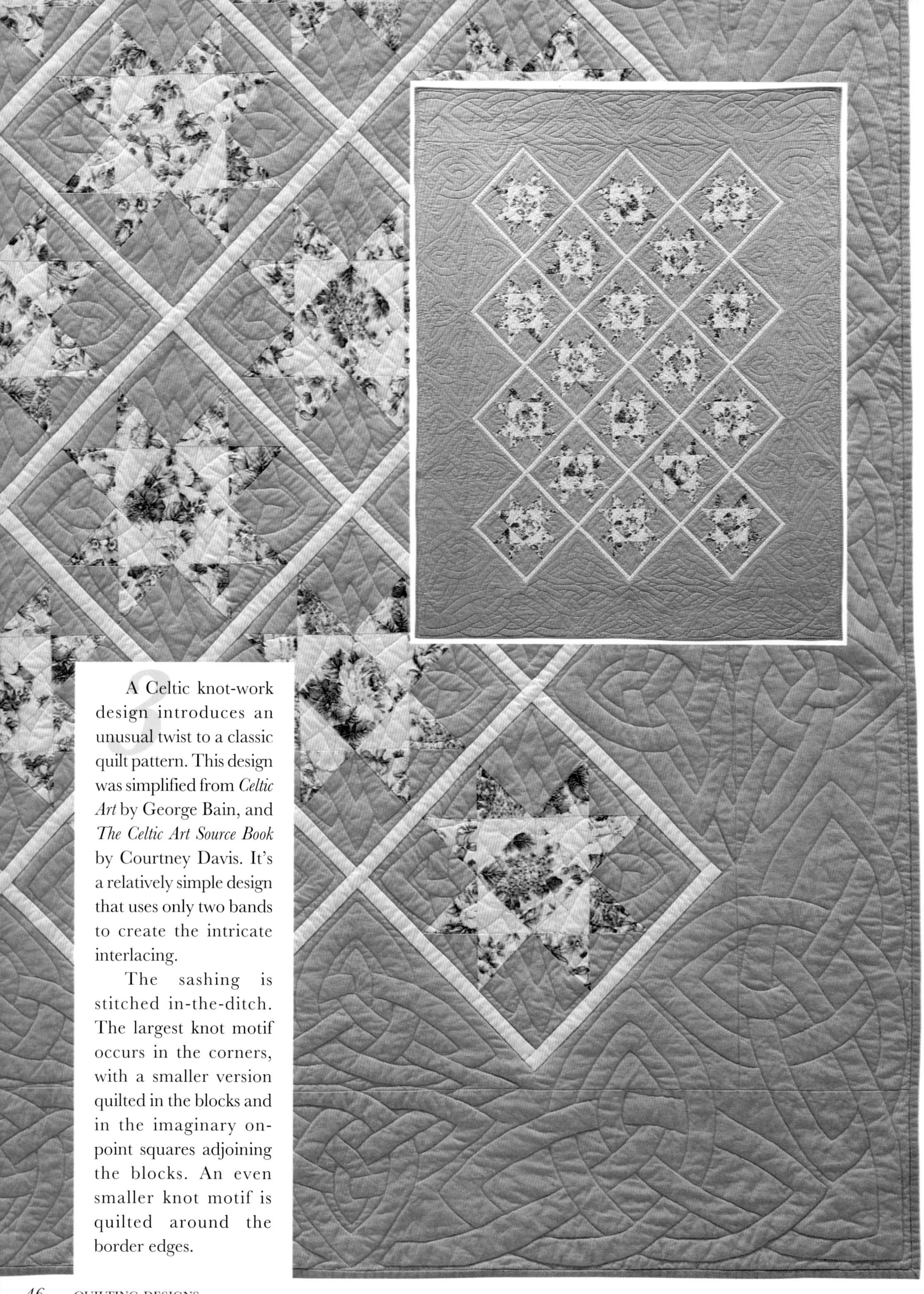

A Celtic knot-work design introduces an unusual twist to a classic quilt pattern. This design was simplified from *Celtic Art* by George Bain, and *The Celtic Art Source Book* by Courtney Davis. It's a relatively simple design that uses only two bands to create the intricate interlacing.

The sashing is stitched in-the-ditch. The largest knot motif occurs in the corners, with a smaller version quilted in the blocks and in the imaginary on-point squares adjoining the blocks. An even smaller knot motif is quilted around the border edges.

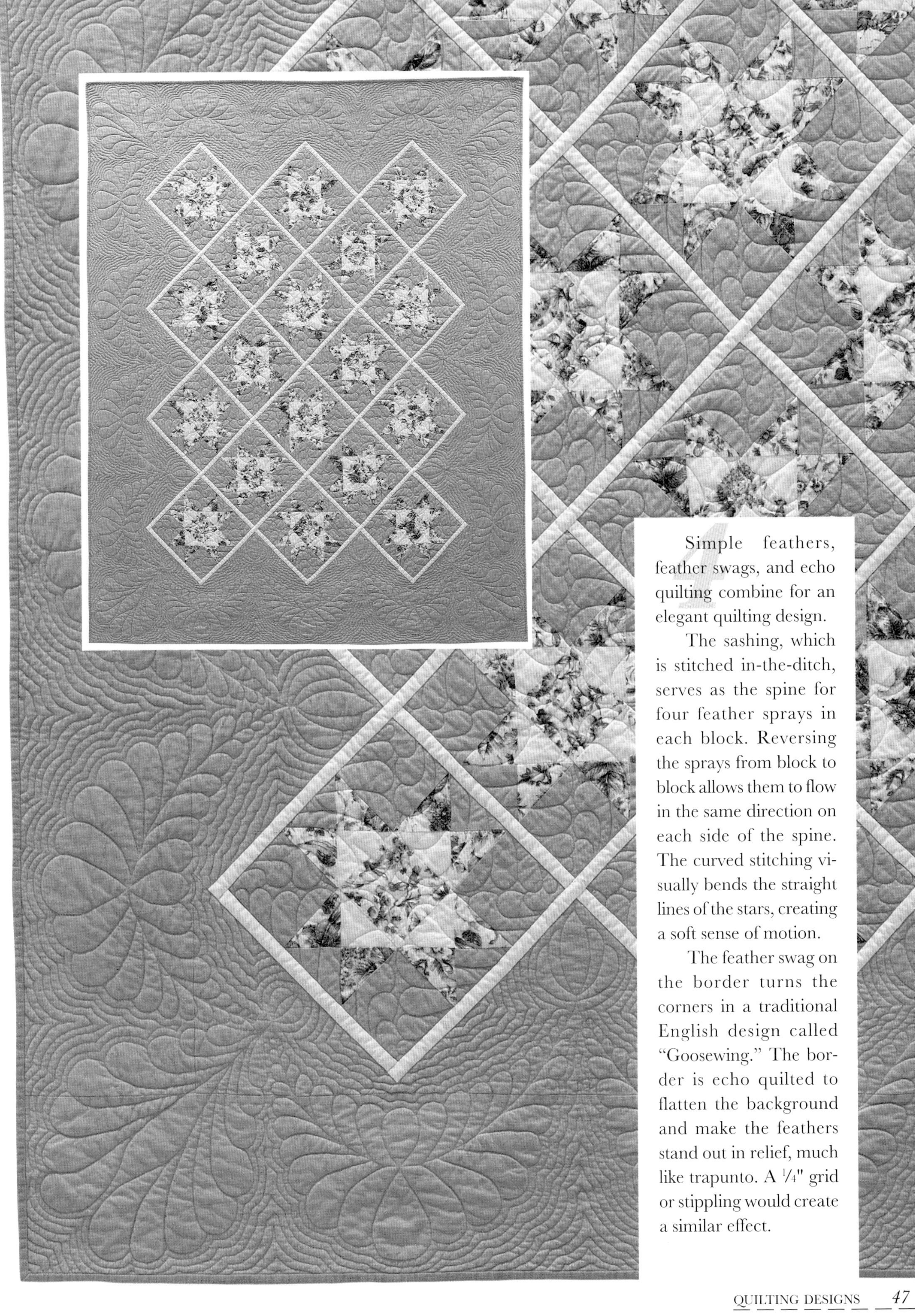

4 Simple feathers, feather swags, and echo quilting combine for an elegant quilting design.

The sashing, which is stitched in-the-ditch, serves as the spine for four feather sprays in each block. Reversing the sprays from block to block allows them to flow in the same direction on each side of the spine. The curved stitching visually bends the straight lines of the stars, creating a soft sense of motion.

The feather swag on the border turns the corners in a traditional English design called "Goosewing." The border is echo quilted to flatten the background and make the feathers stand out in relief, much like trapunto. A ¼" grid or stippling would create a similar effect.

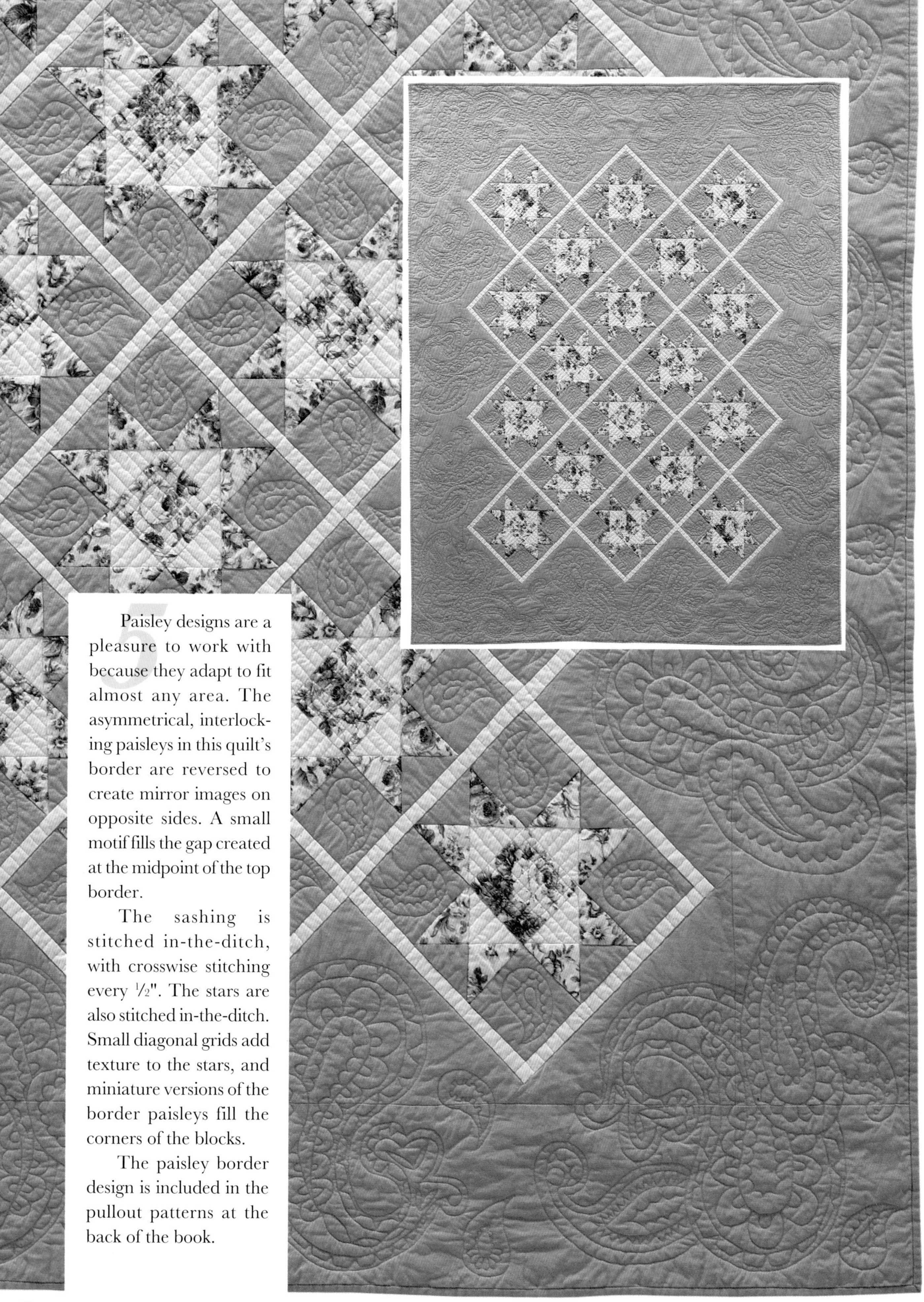

5 Paisley designs are a pleasure to work with because they adapt to fit almost any area. The asymmetrical, interlocking paisleys in this quilt's border are reversed to create mirror images on opposite sides. A small motif fills the gap created at the midpoint of the top border.

The sashing is stitched in-the-ditch, with crosswise stitching every ½". The stars are also stitched in-the-ditch. Small diagonal grids add texture to the stars, and miniature versions of the border paisleys fill the corners of the blocks.

The paisley border design is included in the pullout patterns at the back of the book.

Le Moyne Star

59" x 78½"

This traditional design takes on a decidedly contemporary look with the addition of six-strip sashing. Orange Peel sashing squares, with their gentle curves and alternating colors, provide a counterpoint to classic Le Moyne Stars. Three yellow sashing strips brighten the color scheme.

Choose simple quilting designs to maintain distinct sashing strips; intricate designs may get lost in the multicolored strips. If you wish to soften the seam lines joining the strips, stitch complex designs that blur the piecing and allow the colors to merge.

When working with eight-pointed stars, it's best to quilt every other diamond to the center and stop the quilting on the remaining diamonds ¼" to ½" short of the center.

Minimal quilting designs can have maximum impact, as this quilt demonstrates. The outline of each star is stitched in-the-ditch; concentric stars accentuate the star shape and add texture and depth.

The sashing strips are also stitched in-the-ditch, with the quilting lines continuing across the Orange Peel blocks to form 1¼" grids.

To set the stars apart from the sashing, consider stipple quilting the background of each star, or quilt a very fine ¼" grid.

Concentric squares set on point break up the star blocks in an unexpected way. Although the squares are centered on the sashing strips, a secondary focal point forms at the center of each star. This simple line work sets up a pleasing visual rhythm, and the overall effect is one of order and balance, much like that created by a grid. The design also works on a quilt without sashing: simply center the squares on the seams joining the blocks.

Another option is to center the concentric squares straight on the blocks, rather than on point. This design would be different but perhaps less interesting—a good example of how a slight variation in a design can dramatically affect the look of the quilt.

This spirited quilting design is a variation on the star theme. What looks like randomly scattered stars is actually two linked star patterns, each with fifteen or sixteen stars, that repeat across the quilt in an allover design. Varying the size of the stars and the spacing between stars sets an informal mood, yet the design remains balanced.

To some extent, the piecing lines and the quilting design compete in the quilt. (In fact, the design shows more clearly on the back of the quilt.) But this pattern-on-pattern effect lends vitality and excitement to a quilt.

In a departure from the usual background grid, this filler design is superimposed on the star blocks. The grid must be placed in exactly the same position on each block, or the effect is distracting.

The Orange Peel motifs quilted in the sashing strips are reduced slightly to fit two motifs in each strip, but the proportions are still pleasing.

The sashing is stitched in-the-ditch on the outer edges only. The pieced Orange Peel blocks are stitched-in-the-ditch on the outer edges and along the curves.

Continuous curve quilting gives each star in this quilt a softer, more open look. Compare this version of Le Moyne Star, with its generous use of curves, to Quilts 1 and 2, which feature only straight-line quilting.

The sashing and Orange Peel blocks are treated as they are in Quilt 4, with one important difference: in this quilt the background is stipple quilted. This dense stitching flattens the areas and allows the Orange Peel motifs to stand out in relief. The stippling also blends the colors in the sashing strips, a good example of how texture modulates color.

This playful quilt was adapted from a design in *The It's Okay If You Sit on My Quilt Book* by Mary Ellen Hopkins. I redrew one of her on-point sailboat designs and rearranged the blocks into a simple side-by-side setting. Reversing the colors on six of the ships defines the central area and creates a frame.

The primary-colored fabrics in this quilt almost defy quilting. In fact, it takes a great deal of stitching to effect any change in the surface of such a boldly colored quilt.

You may notice that one ship is pieced differently from the rest. This variation was a simple mistake in my first quilt, but because the block still looked like a ship, I repeated it in the other quilts.

Swedish Ships

28½" x 35½"

1

Stitching the horizontal and vertical piecing lines in-the-ditch and leaving the angled lines unquilted set up a strong horizontal pattern in this quilt; the rhythm varies slightly because the top and bottom strips in each block are different widths.

To break up the straight piecing lines and create an entirely different look, quilt a design of concentric circles; see Square in a Square, Quilt 3 on page 34.

You can quilt this jaunty design without marking the quilt top. Begin by stitching the ship outlines in-the-ditch to accentuate the shapes and establish quilting guidelines.

Quilt the waves freehand from the back, varying their height and filling the background. Use a heavy, silver hand-embroidery thread in the bobbin (adjust the tension screw until the thread flows smoothly) and dressmaking thread on top.

When you embroider by machine, pull the top thread to the back of the quilt. Make a knot in each tail, close to the surface of the quilt, then thread each tail onto a needle and weave it back into the quilt, popping the knot into the quilt layers. Other starting and stopping methods, such as backtacking, detract from a quilt.

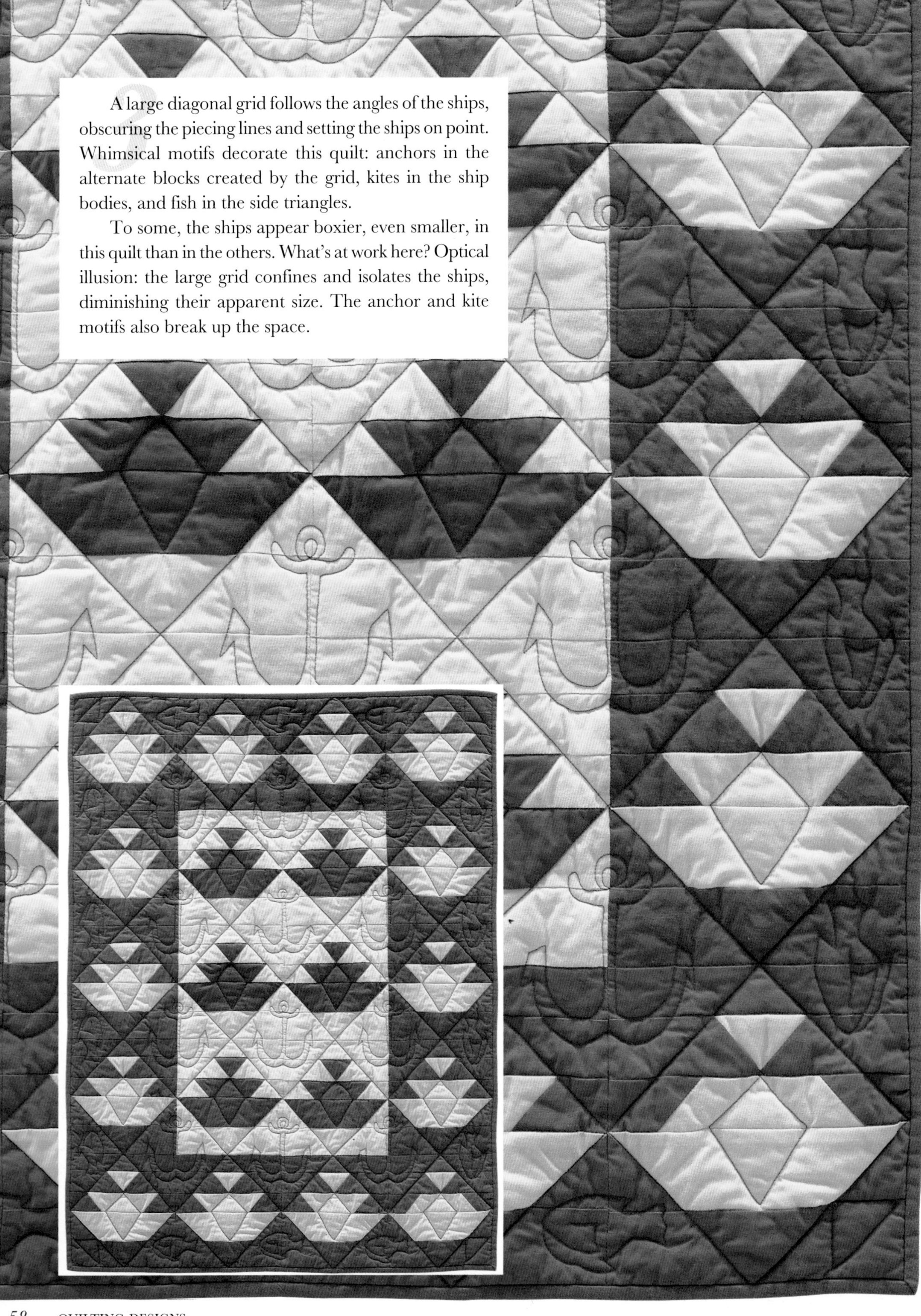

A large diagonal grid follows the angles of the ships, obscuring the piecing lines and setting the ships on point. Whimsical motifs decorate this quilt: anchors in the alternate blocks created by the grid, kites in the ship bodies, and fish in the side triangles.

To some, the ships appear boxier, even smaller, in this quilt than in the others. What's at work here? Optical illusion: the large grid confines and isolates the ships, diminishing their apparent size. The anchor and kite motifs also break up the space.

4

A multitude of lines spaced ¼" apart gives this quilt a highly textured, almost woven, look. Be prepared for curious fingers, for work like this is very tactile and will always be touched. Horizontal quilting lines in the blue background impart a tranquil mood. Changing the direction of the lines in the yellow areas accentuates the strong color contrast.

The ships are stitched in-the-ditch. Because the batting has a high loft, the six unquilted blue ships stand out in relief.

The inspiration for this allover design came from seaweed, an appropriate motif for a ships-at-sea quilt.

Covering a quilt with such a large-scale design effectively merges the pieced areas. Heavy stippling in navy thread accentuates the seaweed shapes and makes them advance visually. Stippling also adds background texture and subdues strong colors. The batting in this quilt is a wool/polyester blend with a relatively high loft. A thinner batting would make it possible to stipple quilt the background even more.

*F*ANS

58½" x 58½"

This is a traditional pattern, quilted in a variety of traditional designs. There are two popular, and very different, approaches to quilting a Fans quilt: you can isolate the blocks with outline quilting or, by quilting a filler design, create a continuous background on which the blocks appear to float. A nontraditional method, shown in Quilt 4 on page 65, is to quilt an allover design that adds texture but little depth.

In these quilts, the fans are set on point with side and corner setting triangles. Another traditional arrangement is a side-by-side setting, with or without sashing. Familiar curvilinear patterns include Dresden Plate, consisting of four blocks joined in a circular design; and patterns in which pairs of diagonal blocks join to create abstract butterflies.

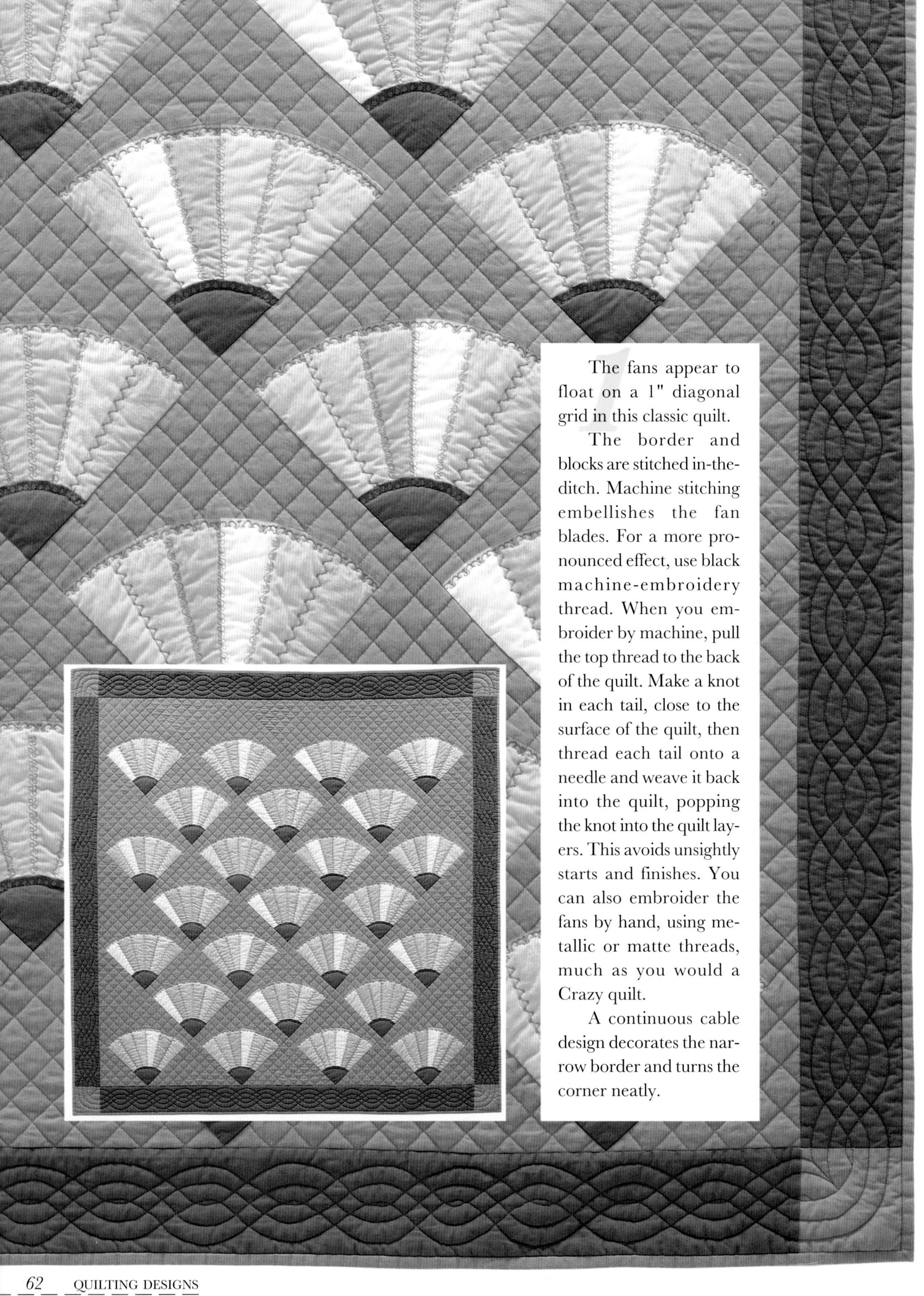

1

The fans appear to float on a 1" diagonal grid in this classic quilt.

The border and blocks are stitched in-the-ditch. Machine stitching embellishes the fan blades. For a more pronounced effect, use black machine-embroidery thread. When you embroider by machine, pull the top thread to the back of the quilt. Make a knot in each tail, close to the surface of the quilt, then thread each tail onto a needle and weave it back into the quilt, popping the knot into the quilt layers. This avoids unsightly starts and finishes. You can also embroider the fans by hand, using metallic or matte threads, much as you would a Crazy quilt.

A continuous cable design decorates the narrow border and turns the corner neatly.

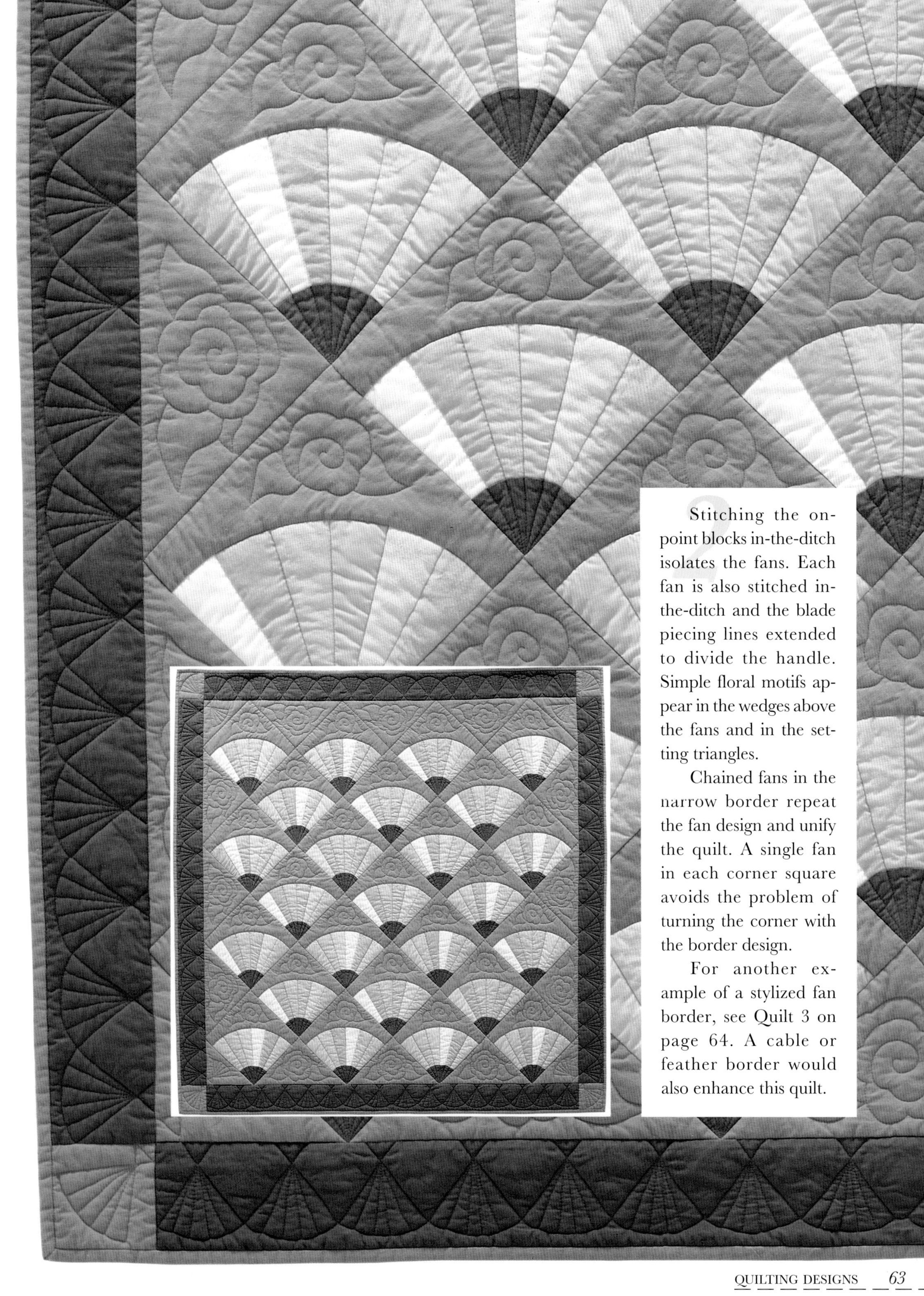

2

Stitching the on-point blocks in-the-ditch isolates the fans. Each fan is also stitched in-the-ditch and the blade piecing lines extended to divide the handle. Simple floral motifs appear in the wedges above the fans and in the setting triangles.

Chained fans in the narrow border repeat the fan design and unify the quilt. A single fan in each corner square avoids the problem of turning the corner with the border design.

For another example of a stylized fan border, see Quilt 3 on page 64. A cable or feather border would also enhance this quilt.

Rays of quilting are well suited to fan blocks, the blades of which radiate in a similar pattern. This ray design is also appropriate for the blocks in Strippy on Point, Quilt 4 on page 83.

The border and blocks are stitched in-the-ditch. The rays begin at the base of each handle, follow the blade piecing lines, and extend to fill the background. A second line of stitching divides each blade and completes the pattern. The design repeats in the setting triangles, unifying the quilt.

Alternating wedge fans quilted in the border add texture and echo the piecing design.

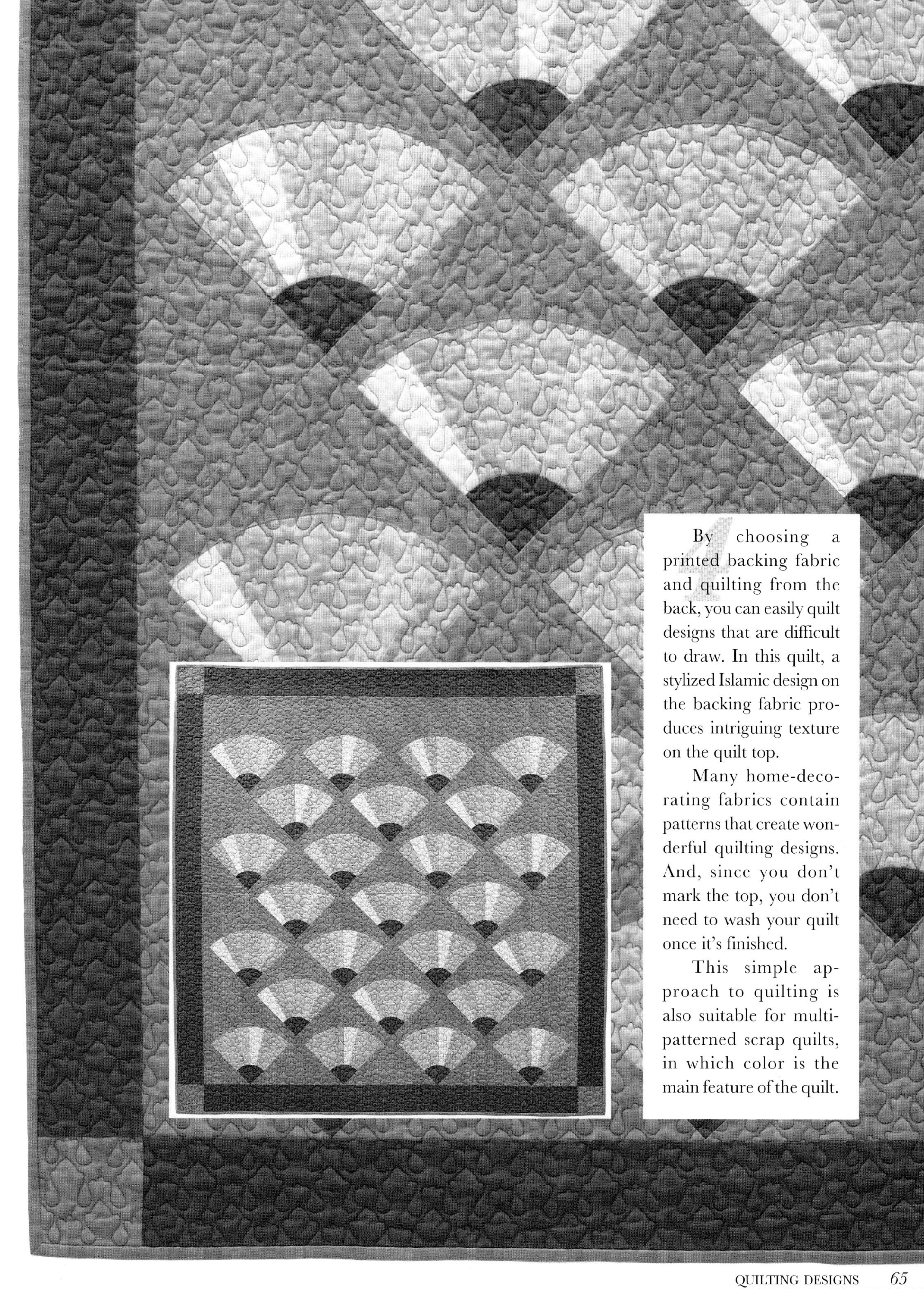

By choosing a printed backing fabric and quilting from the back, you can easily quilt designs that are difficult to draw. In this quilt, a stylized Islamic design on the backing fabric produces intriguing texture on the quilt top.

Many home-decorating fabrics contain patterns that create wonderful quilting designs. And, since you don't mark the top, you don't need to wash your quilt once it's finished.

This simple approach to quilting is also suitable for multi-patterned scrap quilts, in which color is the main feature of the quilt.

An unusual three-to-one plaid design forms the backdrop for the fans in this quilting variation. Any harmonious combination of lines will contribute surface interest to a quilt. Just make sure the grid is smaller than the design it touches, or the lines will merge and the effect will be lost.

The fan shapes are stitched in-the-ditch and embellished with symmetrical feather motifs.

Classic feathered hearts fill the setting triangles and, in a break with tradition, cross the border. Because the border fabric is dark, the hearts recede and remain background elements.

SCRAP STAR

57½" x 57½"

This quilt offers a wonderful opportunity to use up small scraps of fabric and experiment with new quilting designs. The plain areas behind the stars give scope for lots of quilting and allow a wide selection of colors in the triangles.

Quilting designs from other quilts may be interchanged with Scrap Star designs. In place of the grids shown in Quilt 1, consider concentric squares like those in Le Moyne Star, Quilt 2 on page 51. Specialized feather designs are featured in Scrap Star, Quilt 5 on page 72, but other feather designs are suitable, such as a running feather in the border and sashing, or feather wreaths in the blocks. Because a 2½"–3" sashing is traditional, you can use the three sashing designs shown here in other quilts.

This "grid sampler" quilt features four different background designs. Any combination of grids will work, as long as the designs are similar in scale. Another option is to quilt the grids shown here with closer lines for more texture.

The outer edges of the blocks are stitched in-the-ditch. The sashing and border display a simplified version of the traditional pumpkin seed design seen in Amish quilts. The lines enclosing the pumpkin seeds have a common turning point. This makes the design easy to machine quilt.

In this version of Scrap Star, the four large blocks and all triangles are stitched in-the-ditch.

The stylized flowers in the sashing were simplified from a small English quilt I saw at the Victoria and Albert Museum in London. These daisylike flowers adapt easily to any area; just alter the length of the petals. In the background squares and triangles, they're modified and quilted in groups of three, similar to designs from the sixties.

The sashing strips surrounding the upper right and lower left blocks feature a continuous stem motif; in the remaining sashing strips, the stem stops at the sashing squares.

Five different-sized triangles, satin stitched with machine embroidery and metallic threads, overlap for a very contemporary quilting design. This use of bold shapes and heavy decorative stitching fragments the piecing lines. To some, the effect is messy, while others find the random placement of shapes a refreshing change.

This type of quilting design breaks from tradition, and it's up to you to decide if it has a place in your quilt. If you find the design too strong, don't dismiss it entirely but try using it in a different way. Stitching small random triangles in the sashing, with more traditional quilting in the blocks, will give your quilt texture without affecting the piecing design.

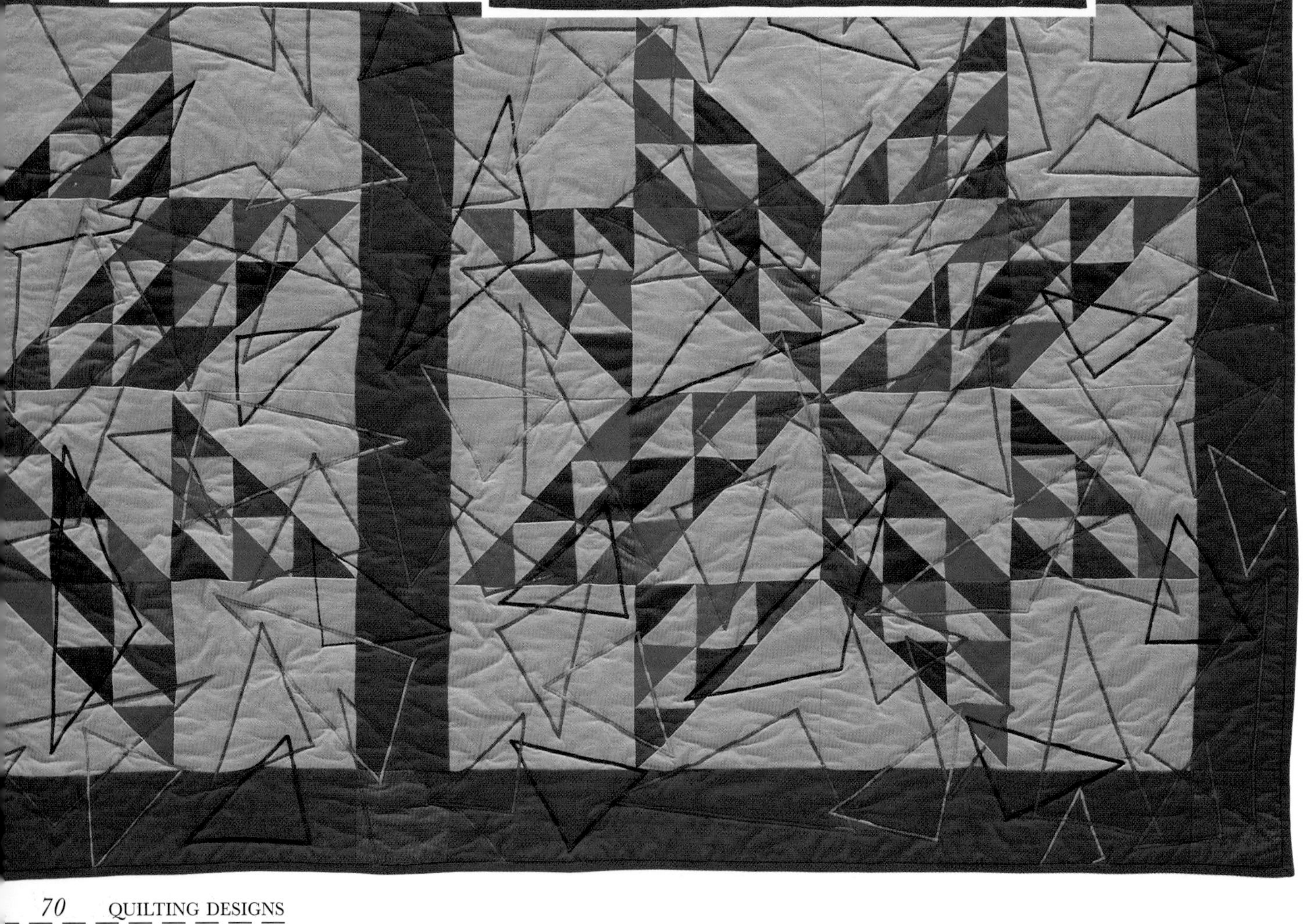

This vibrant quilting design introduces shapes unrelated to the piecing pattern.

The outside edge of each block is stitched in-the-ditch. The heart design centered on each star appears to have many separate lines and circles, but the lines and circles touch, making it possible to stitch continuously from shape to shape using a previously stitched line.

The linked hearts in the sashing strips were originally intended to be circles. Extending a line from one circle to the next and modifying the shapes formed a chain of stylized hearts.

The heart design is included in the pullout patterns at the back of the book.

Only the points of each star are stitched in-the-ditch, leaving large areas to showcase feather designs.

Rather than use circular feather wreaths, I drew feathers to fit squares. One feather fills the large square created by the four central cream squares; another feather fills each of the four on-point squares surrounding the central square. (To see these squares, ignore the sashing that divides them.) To maintain a consistent scale, I drew different designs for the two squares, rather than enlarging the smaller feather to fill the larger area.

Two feather designs are included in the pullout patterns at the back of the book.

Strippy Bars

56½" x 65½"

As a pieced design, Strippy Bars is as basic as you can get, but watch it come alive with quilting. This old quilt style, found throughout Great Britain, offers unlimited quilting possibilities. Designs ranging from small grids to large-scale florals enhance its simple lines.

If you choose colors of similar intensity and value, as in the quilts shown here, you can treat Strippy Bars as a whole-cloth quilt and disregard the piecing lines. If, however, the colors contrast sharply, it's best to quilt in the traditional manner and confine the designs to the strips.

The fabrics used in these quilts are the only ones in the book that weren't prewashed. The cotton batting was not presoaked. Quilt shrinkage, after washing, was minimal.

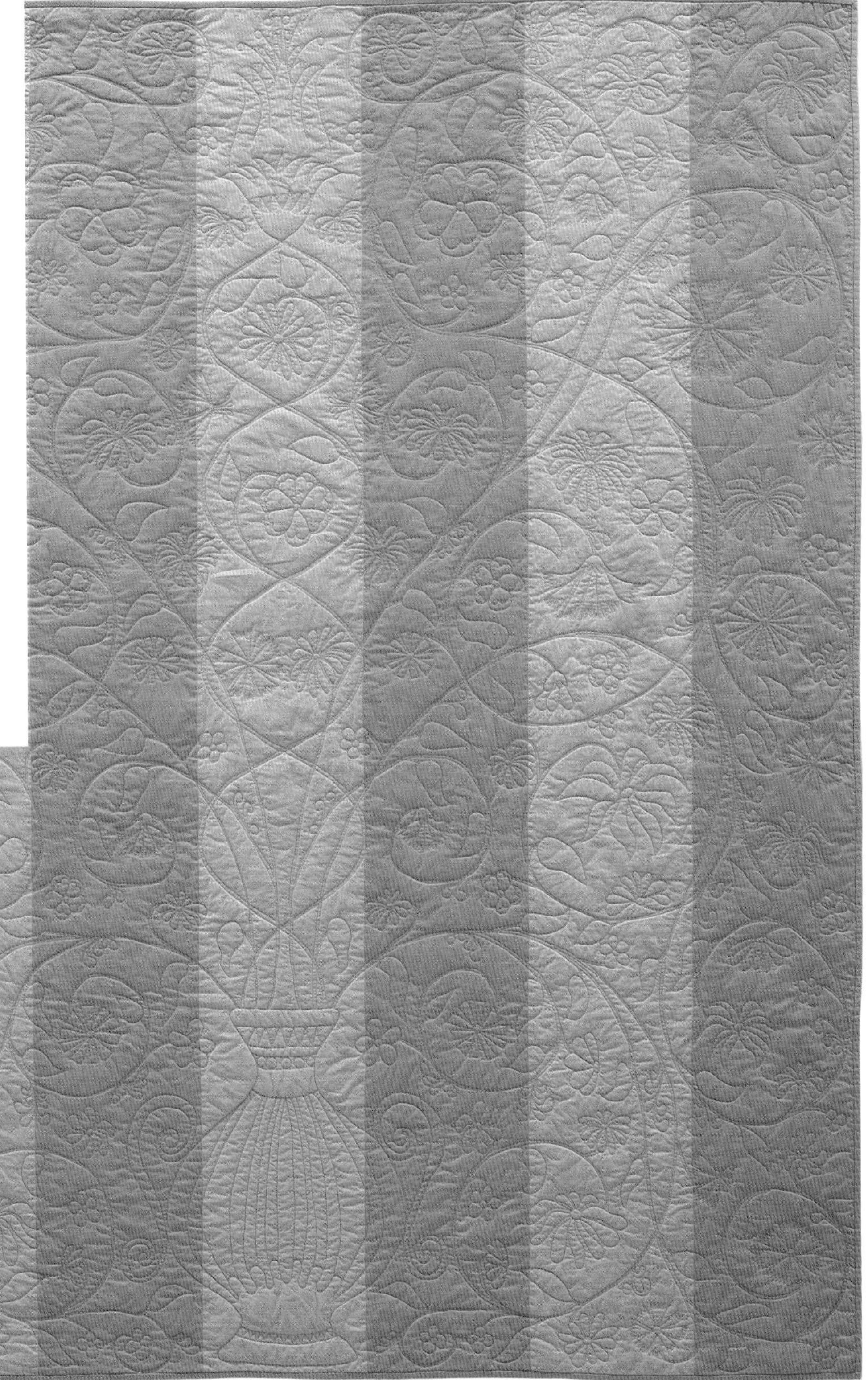

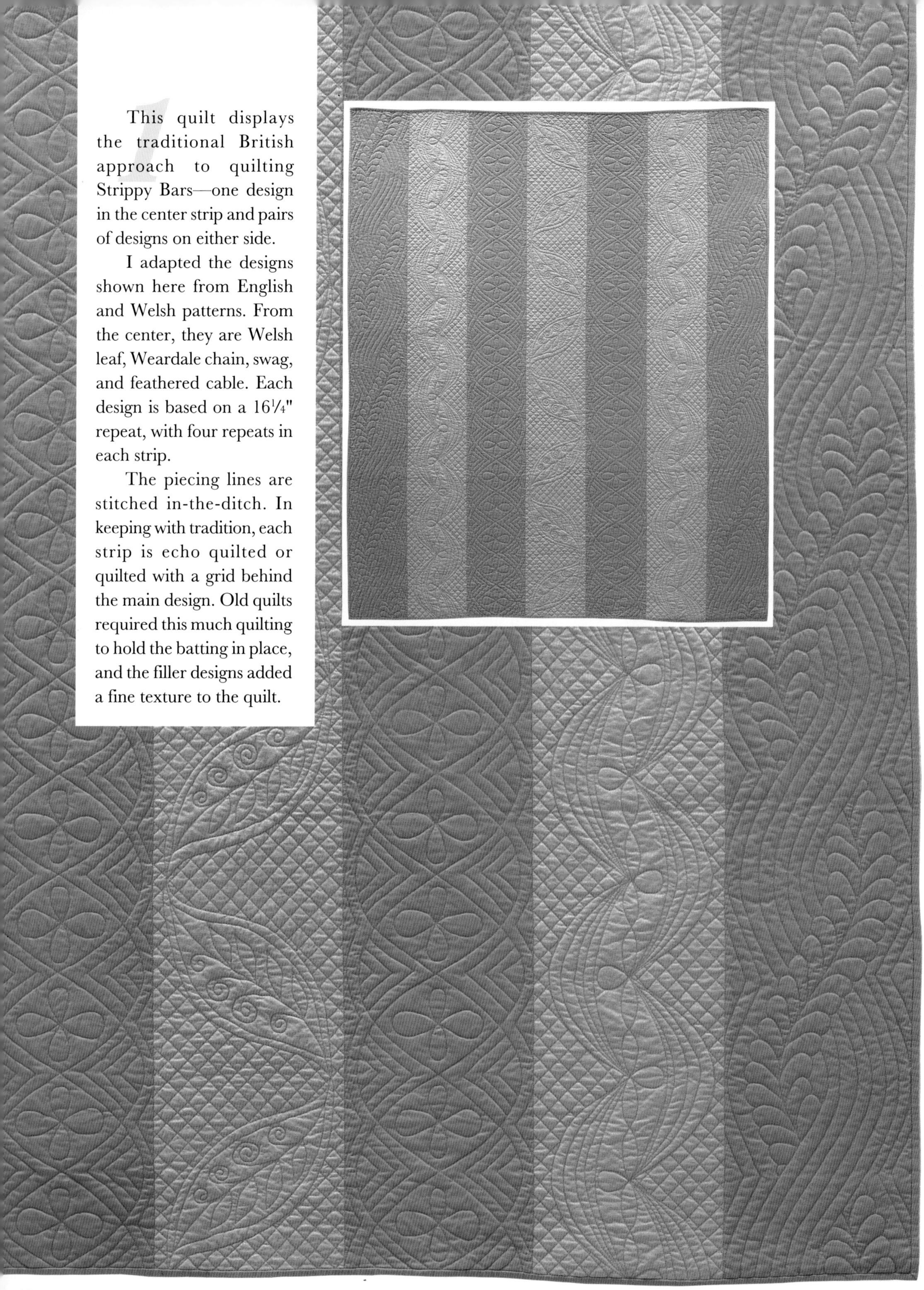

This quilt displays the traditional British approach to quilting Strippy Bars—one design in the center strip and pairs of designs on either side.

I adapted the designs shown here from English and Welsh patterns. From the center, they are Welsh leaf, Weardale chain, swag, and feathered cable. Each design is based on a 16¼" repeat, with four repeats in each strip.

The piecing lines are stitched in-the-ditch. In keeping with tradition, each strip is echo quilted or quilted with a grid behind the main design. Old quilts required this much quilting to hold the batting in place, and the filler designs added a fine texture to the quilt.

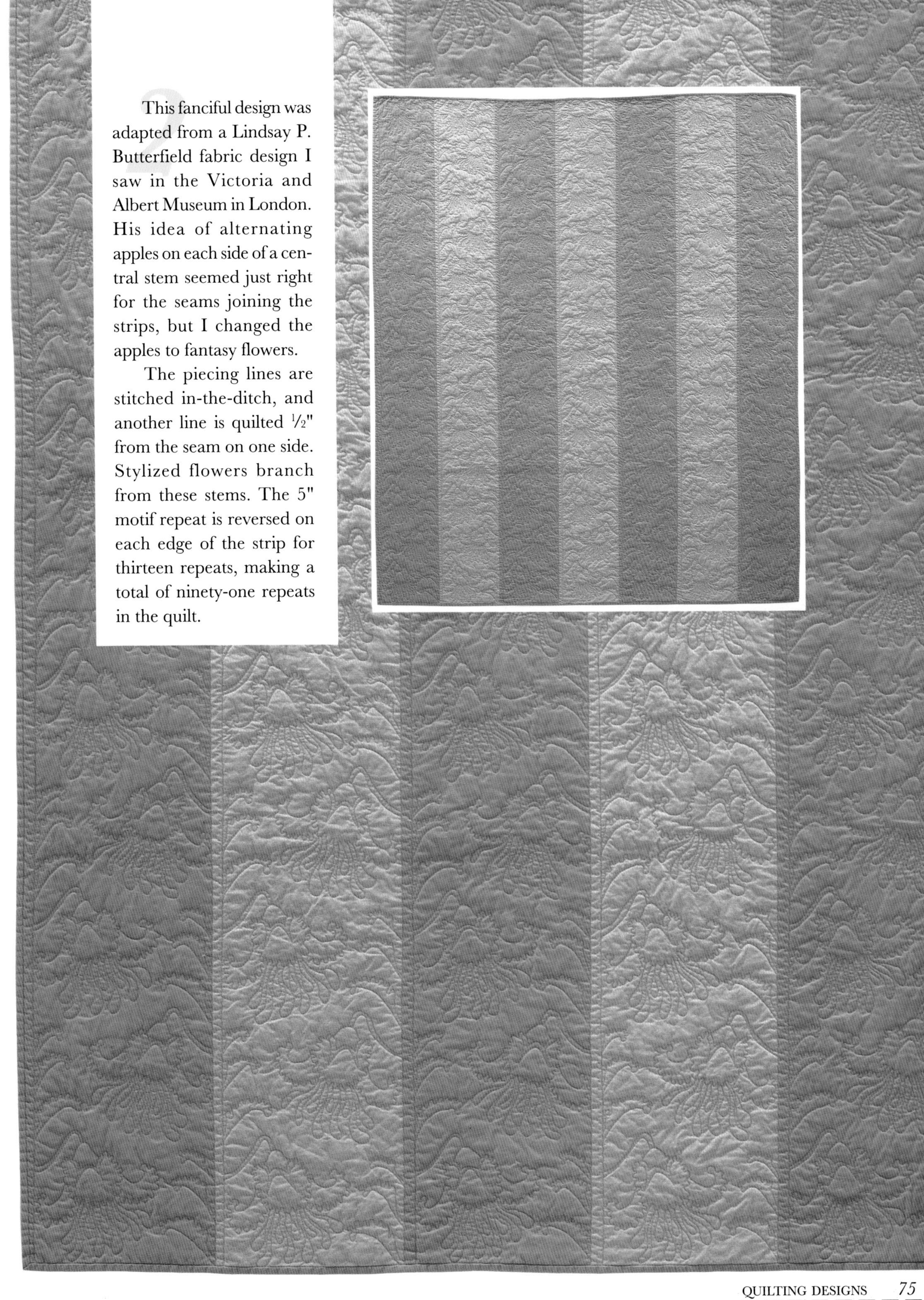

This fanciful design was adapted from a Lindsay P. Butterfield fabric design I saw in the Victoria and Albert Museum in London. His idea of alternating apples on each side of a central stem seemed just right for the seams joining the strips, but I changed the apples to fantasy flowers.

The piecing lines are stitched in-the-ditch, and another line is quilted ½" from the seam on one side. Stylized flowers branch from these stems. The 5" motif repeat is reversed on each edge of the strip for thirteen repeats, making a total of ninety-one repeats in the quilt.

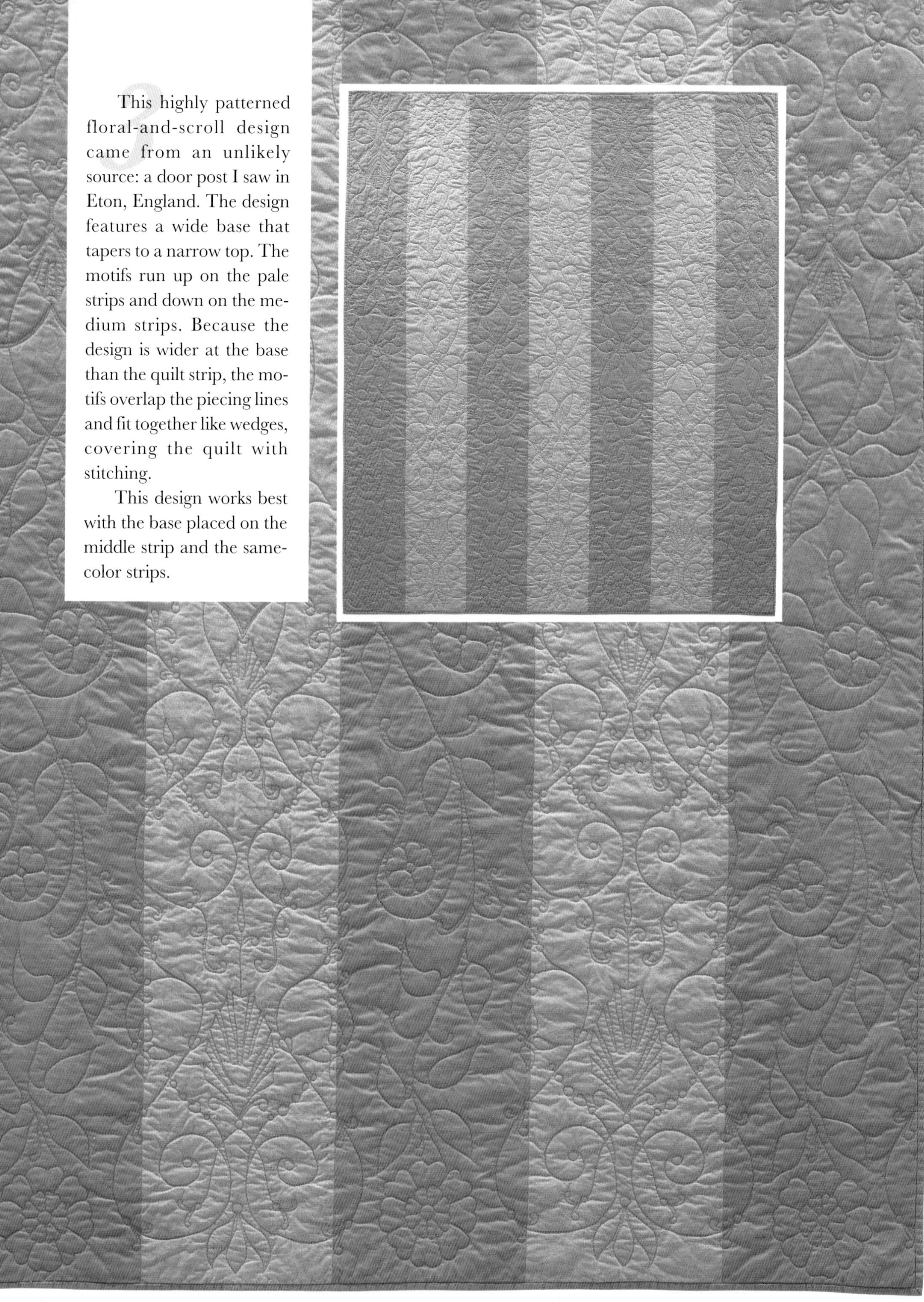

This highly patterned floral-and-scroll design came from an unlikely source: a door post I saw in Eton, England. The design features a wide base that tapers to a narrow top. The motifs run up on the pale strips and down on the medium strips. Because the design is wider at the base than the quilt strip, the motifs overlap the piecing lines and fit together like wedges, covering the quilt with stitching.

This design works best with the base placed on the middle strip and the same-color strips.

4 An assortment of quilting designs, many based on traditional English patterns, lends a look of sophistication to this version of Strippy Bars.

Large-scale ogee motifs, zigzag quilted with a wide stitch, overlap the piecing lines. The stylized daisies, seen in Scrap Star, Quilt 2 on page 69, demonstrate their versatility here as circular designs. The oversized tulip design at the top of the center strip is from a Welsh quilt a friend found at a garage sale. Other designs are combinations of traditional English designs.

This mélange of patterns softens the piecing lines yet maintains a sense of order. Combining designs also provides the opportunity to experiment with different designs on the same quilt.

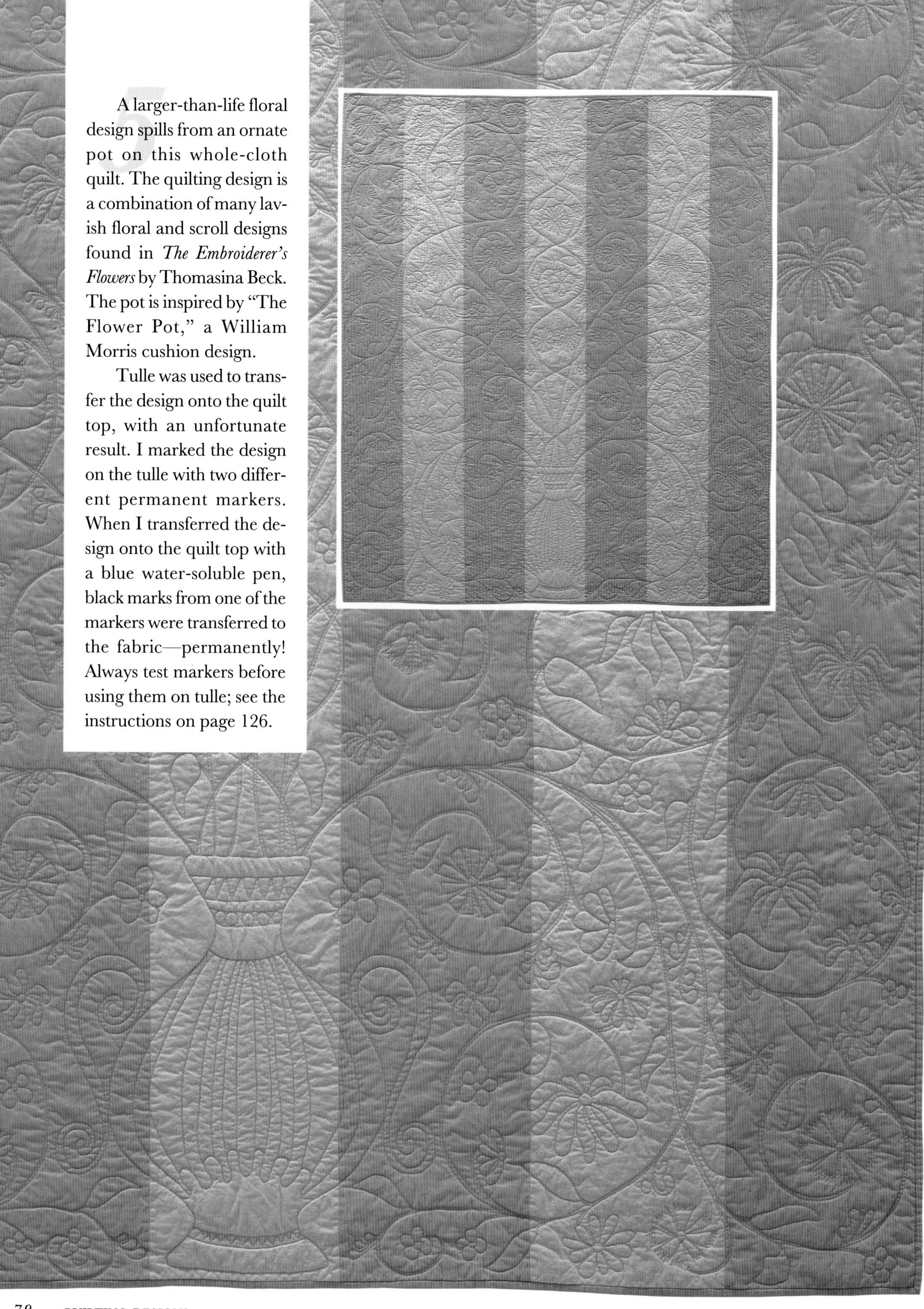

A larger-than-life floral design spills from an ornate pot on this whole-cloth quilt. The quilting design is a combination of many lavish floral and scroll designs found in *The Embroiderer's Flowers* by Thomasina Beck. The pot is inspired by "The Flower Pot," a William Morris cushion design.

Tulle was used to transfer the design onto the quilt top, with an unfortunate result. I marked the design on the tulle with two different permanent markers. When I transferred the design onto the quilt top with a blue water-soluble pen, black marks from one of the markers were transferred to the fabric—permanently! Always test markers before using them on tulle; see the instructions on page 126.

*S*TRIPPY ON *P*OINT

$53^{1}/_{2}$" x 64"

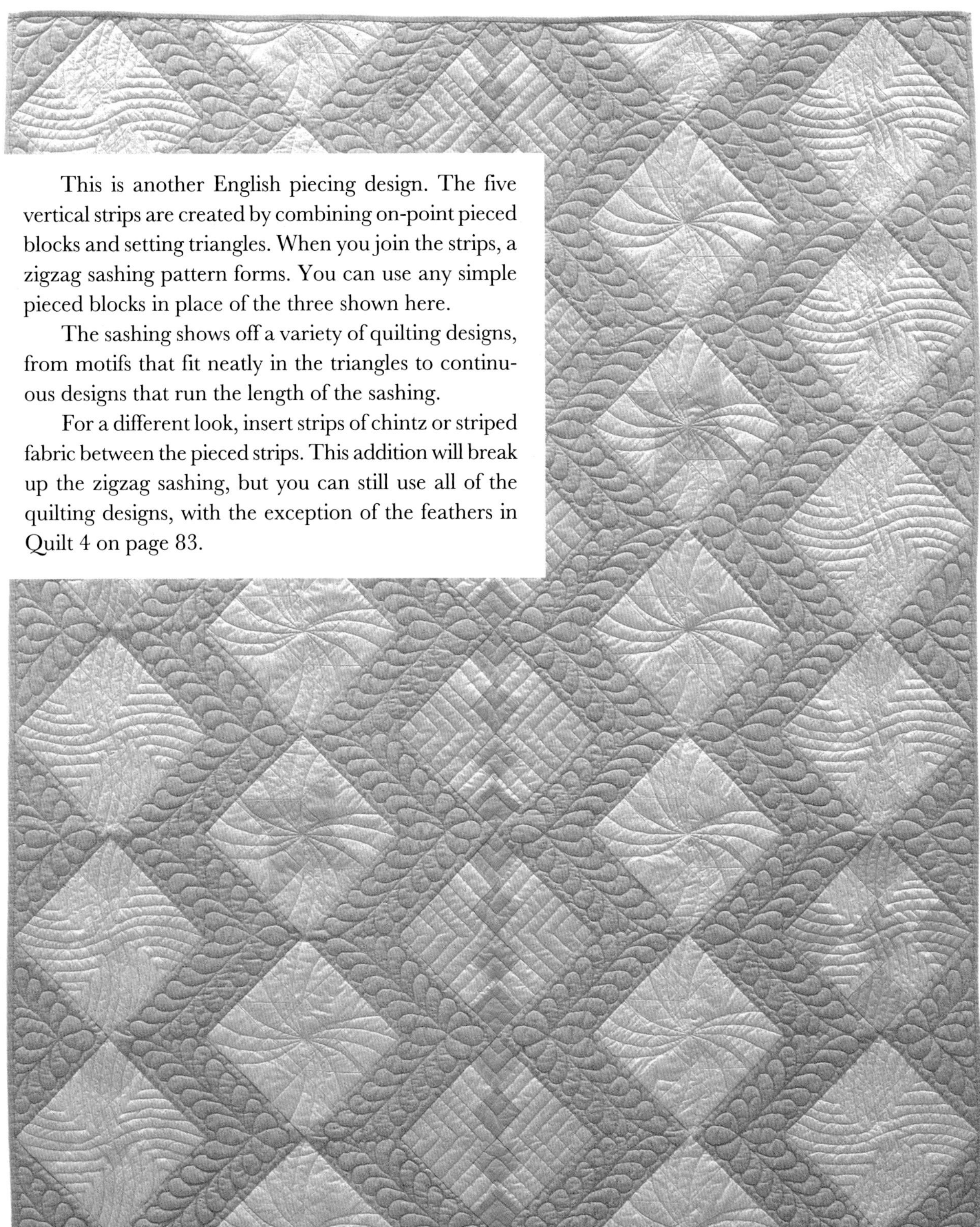

This is another English piecing design. The five vertical strips are created by combining on-point pieced blocks and setting triangles. When you join the strips, a zigzag sashing pattern forms. You can use any simple pieced blocks in place of the three shown here.

The sashing shows off a variety of quilting designs, from motifs that fit neatly in the triangles to continuous designs that run the length of the sashing.

For a different look, insert strips of chintz or striped fabric between the pieced strips. This addition will break up the zigzag sashing, but you can still use all of the quilting designs, with the exception of the feathers in Quilt 4 on page 83.

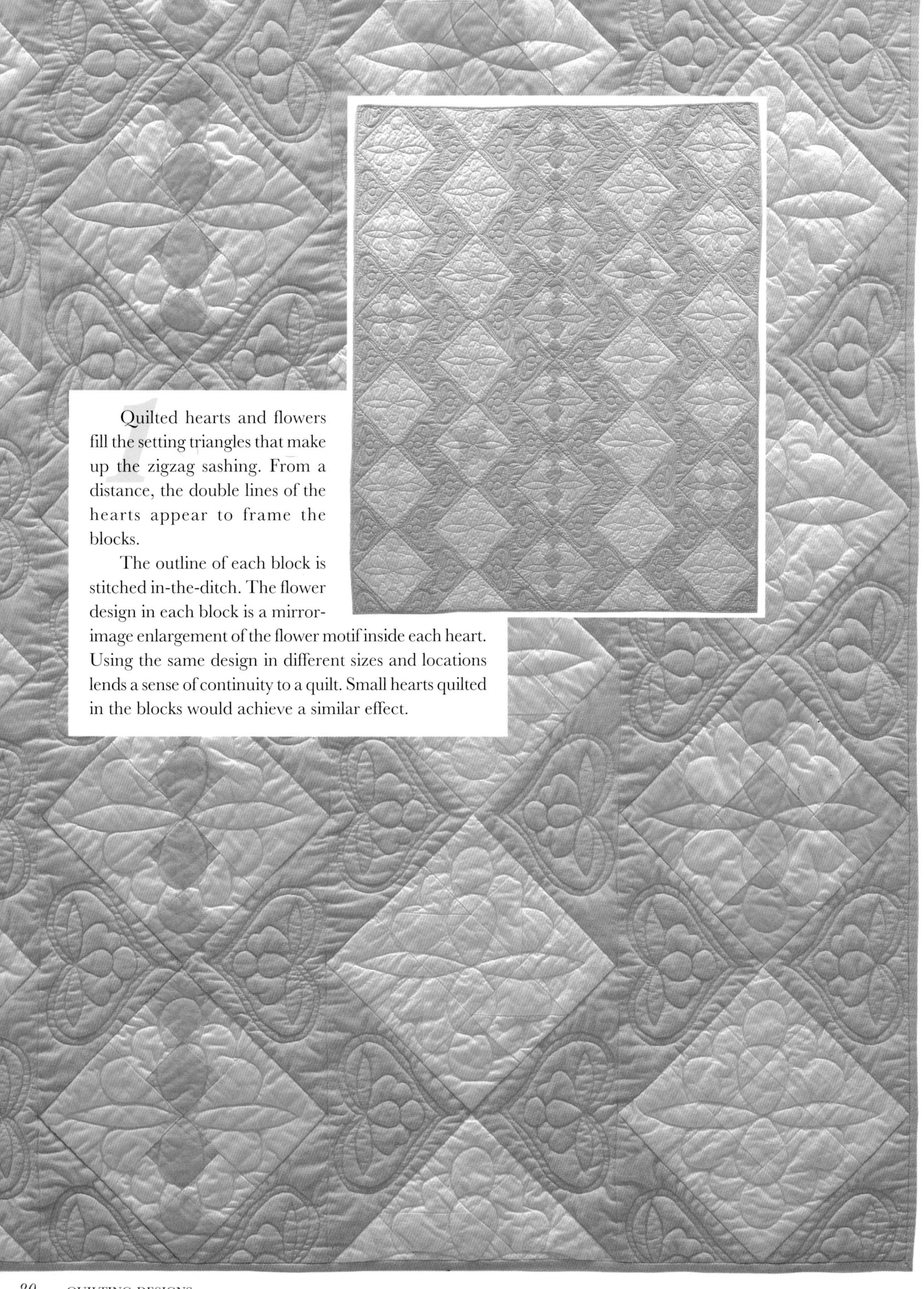

1

Quilted hearts and flowers fill the setting triangles that make up the zigzag sashing. From a distance, the double lines of the hearts appear to frame the blocks.

The outline of each block is stitched in-the-ditch. The flower design in each block is a mirror-image enlargement of the flower motif inside each heart. Using the same design in different sizes and locations lends a sense of continuity to a quilt. Small hearts quilted in the blocks would achieve a similar effect.

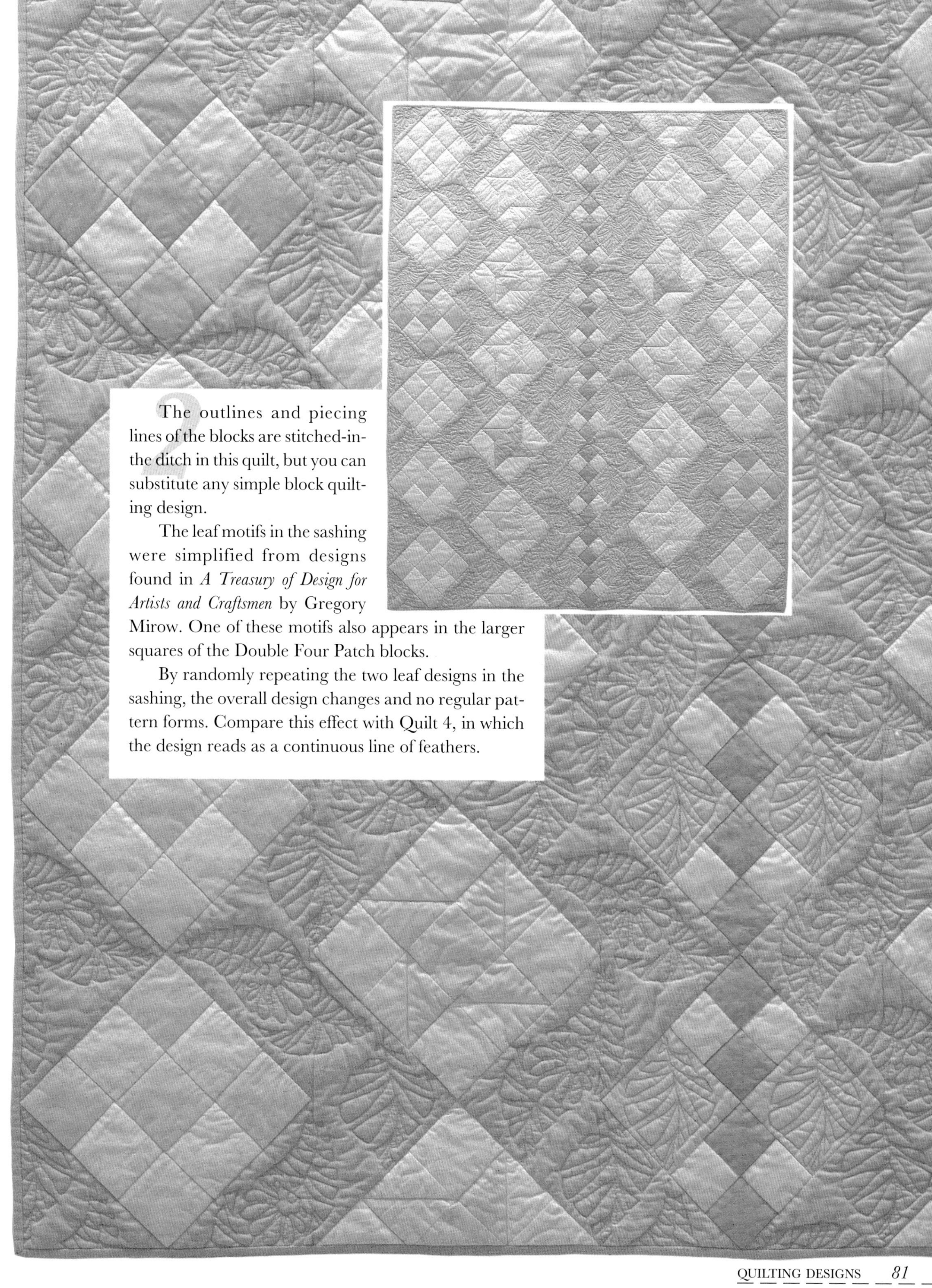

The outlines and piecing lines of the blocks are stitched-in-the ditch in this quilt, but you can substitute any simple block quilting design.

The leaf motifs in the sashing were simplified from designs found in *A Treasury of Design for Artists and Craftsmen* by Gregory Mirow. One of these motifs also appears in the larger squares of the Double Four Patch blocks.

By randomly repeating the two leaf designs in the sashing, the overall design changes and no regular pattern forms. Compare this effect with Quilt 4, in which the design reads as a continuous line of feathers.

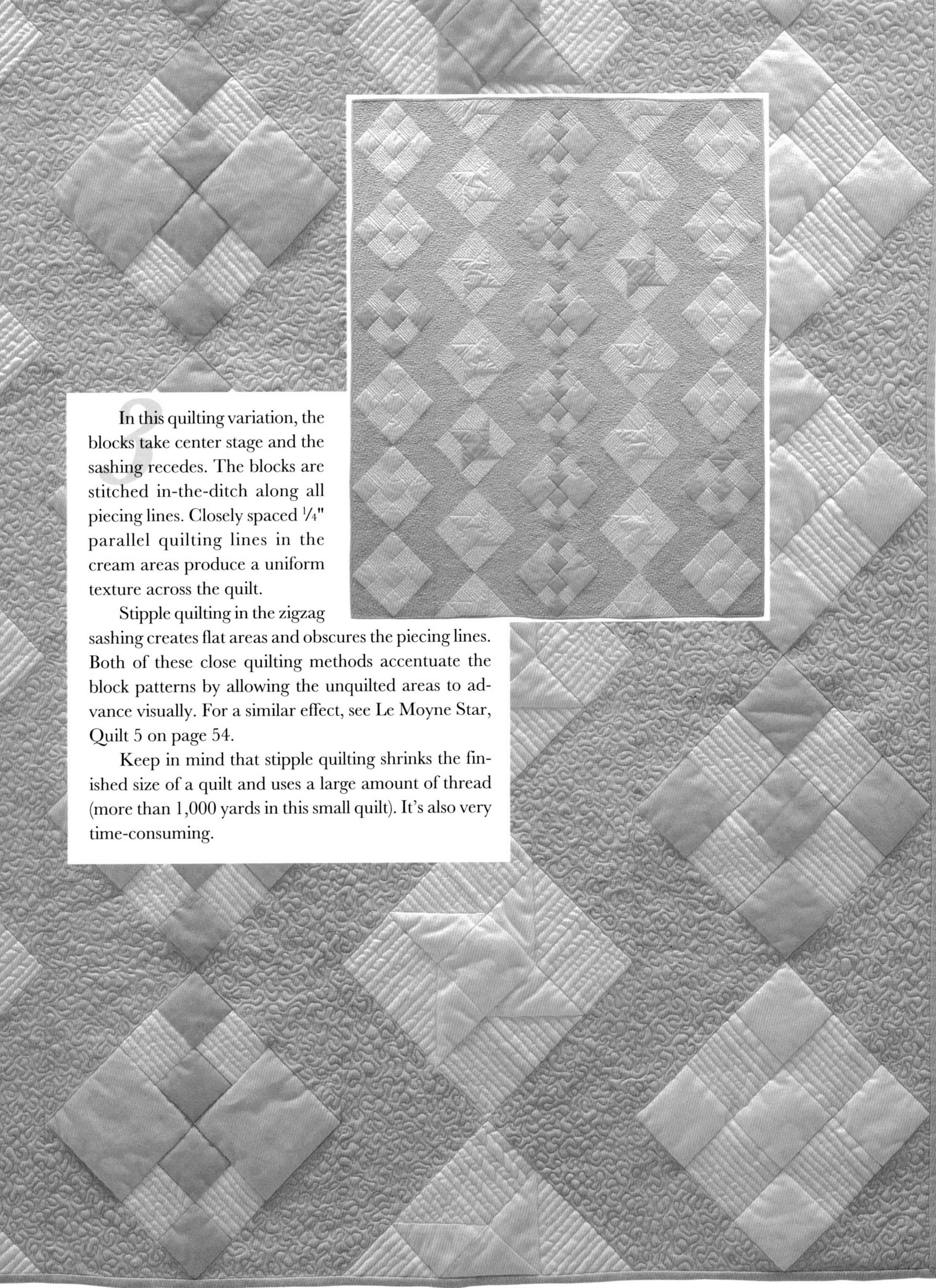

In this quilting variation, the blocks take center stage and the sashing recedes. The blocks are stitched in-the-ditch along all piecing lines. Closely spaced ¼" parallel quilting lines in the cream areas produce a uniform texture across the quilt.

Stipple quilting in the zigzag sashing creates flat areas and obscures the piecing lines. Both of these close quilting methods accentuate the block patterns by allowing the unquilted areas to advance visually. For a similar effect, see Le Moyne Star, Quilt 5 on page 54.

Keep in mind that stipple quilting shrinks the finished size of a quilt and uses a large amount of thread (more than 1,000 yards in this small quilt). It's also very time-consuming.

4

Although the feathers in the sashing strips are not continuous, they look as though they are. Each feather flows in two directions from a figure-eight base motif. (You'll find these motifs in the sashing corners that point inward.) The space between the feather designs is so small that the eye reads the motifs as one flowing design. This approach is much easier than attempting to quilt a continuous feather design that turns the corner.

The outline of each block is stitched in-the-ditch. Simple, but vigorous, quilting designs disregard the piecing lines of the blocks and complement the sashing.

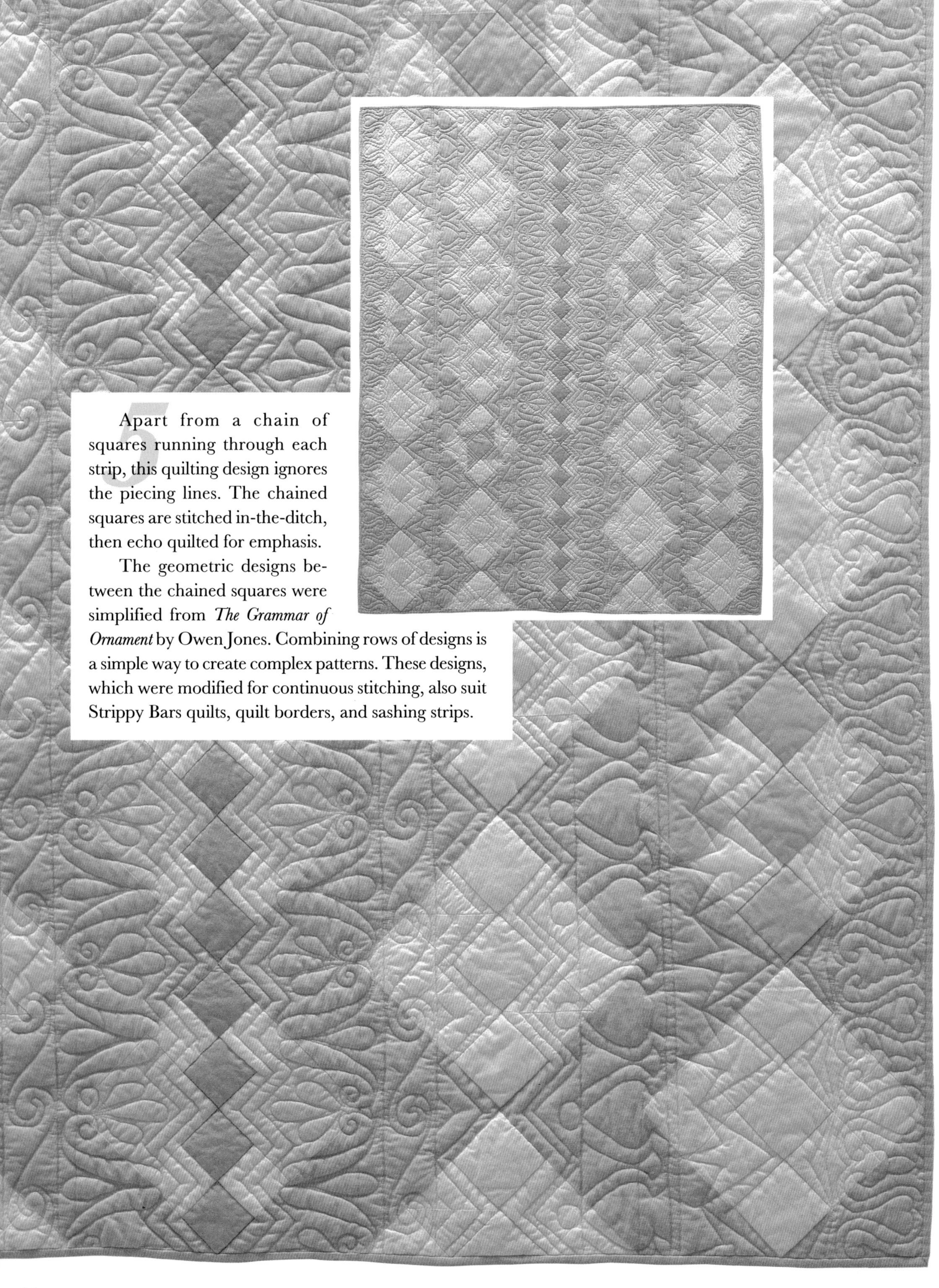

5

Apart from a chain of squares running through each strip, this quilting design ignores the piecing lines. The chained squares are stitched in-the-ditch, then echo quilted for emphasis.

The geometric designs between the chained squares were simplified from *The Grammar of Ornament* by Owen Jones. Combining rows of designs is a simple way to create complex patterns. These designs, which were modified for continuous stitching, also suit Strippy Bars quilts, quilt borders, and sashing strips.

Single Wedding Ring

76" x 90"

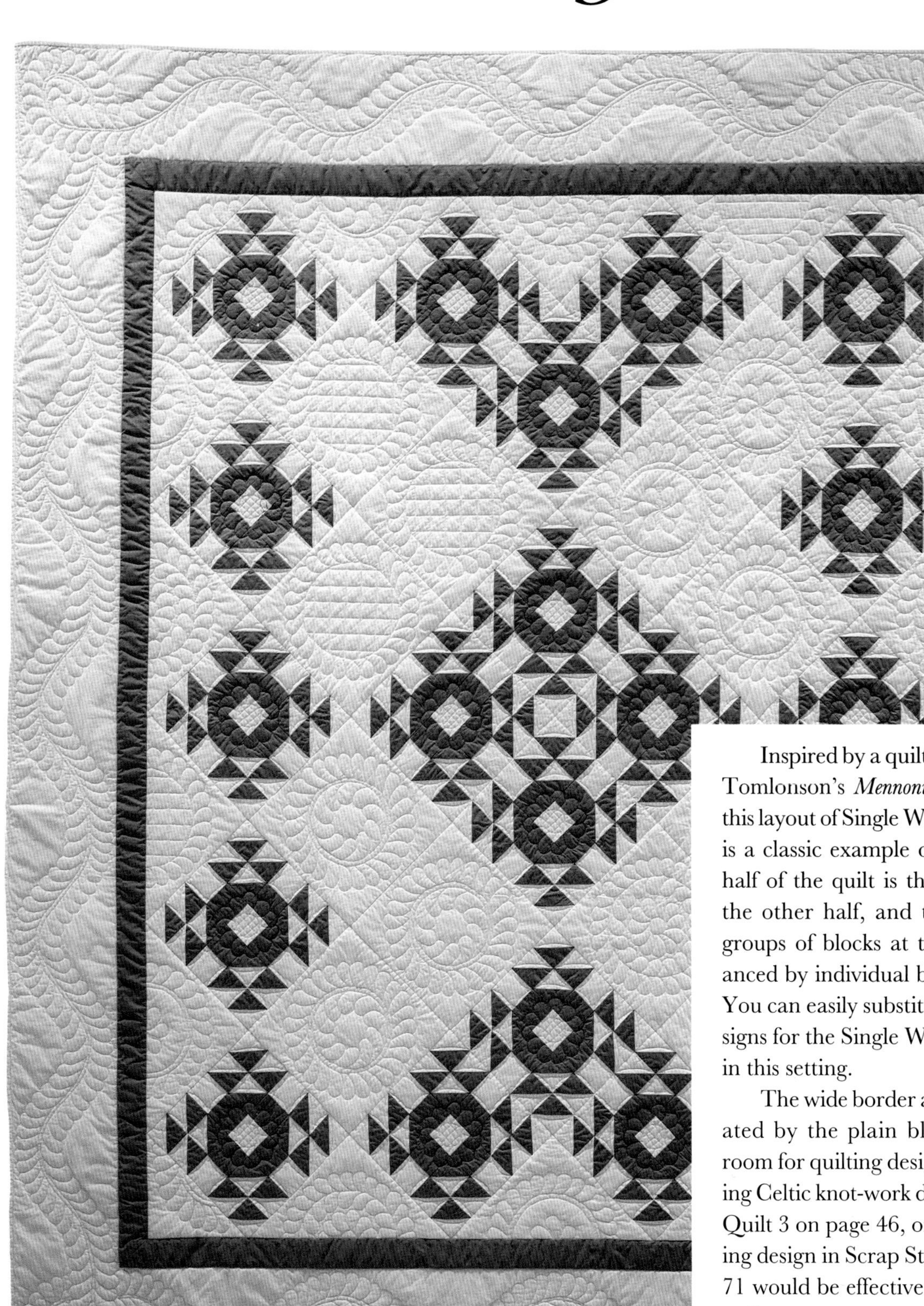

Inspired by a quilt in Judy Schroeder Tomlonson's *Mennonite Quilts and Pieces,* this layout of Single Wedding Ring blocks is a classic example of symmetry. Each half of the quilt is the mirror image of the other half, and the visually heavy groups of blocks at the center are balanced by individual blocks at the edges. You can easily substitute other block designs for the Single Wedding Ring block in this setting.

The wide border and open areas created by the plain blocks allow ample room for quilting designs. The interlocking Celtic knot-work design in Ohio Star, Quilt 3 on page 46, or parts of the quilting design in Scrap Star, Quilt 4 on page 71 would be effective if drawn to fit this quilt.

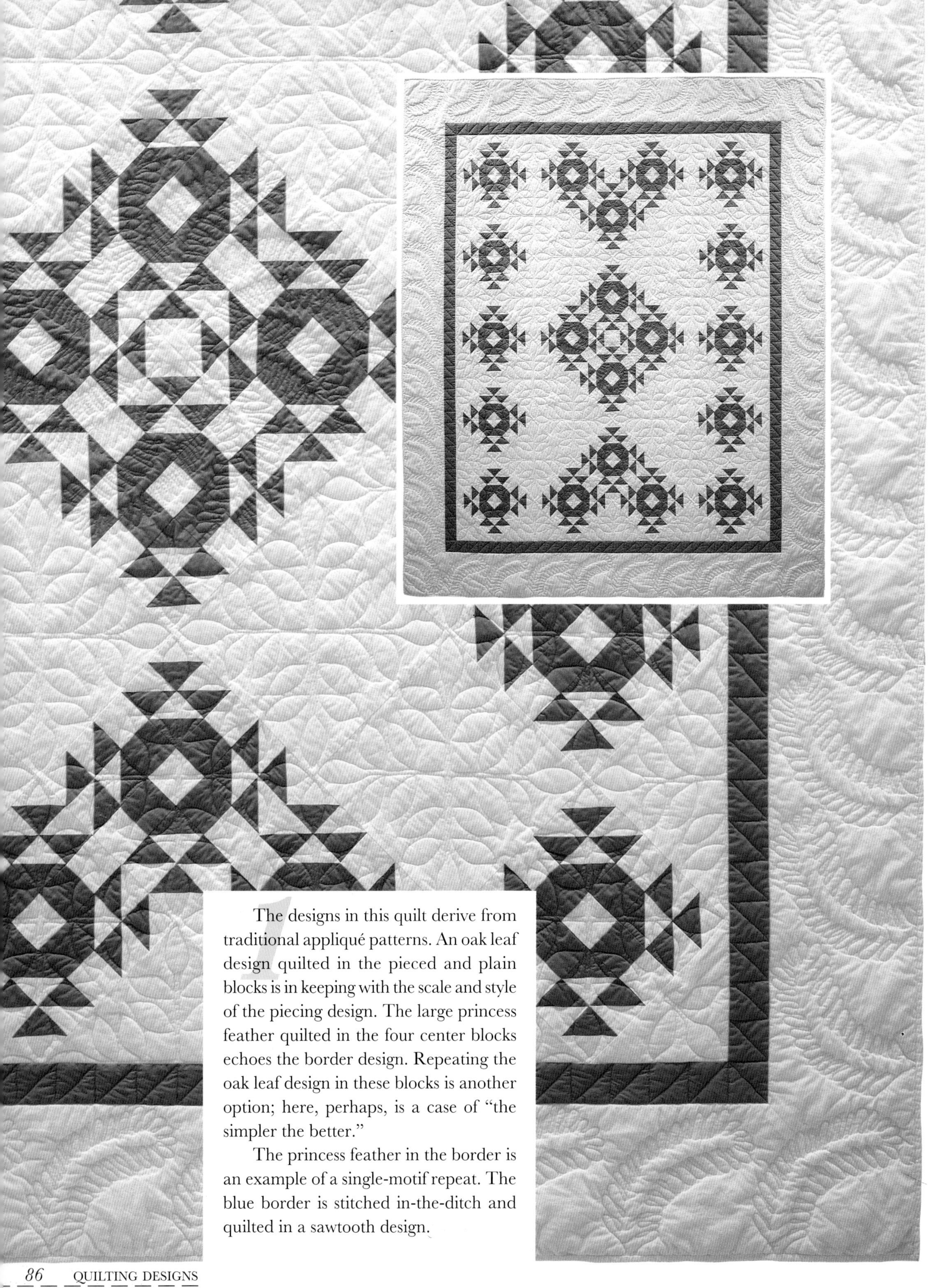

The designs in this quilt derive from traditional appliqué patterns. An oak leaf design quilted in the pieced and plain blocks is in keeping with the scale and style of the piecing design. The large princess feather quilted in the four center blocks echoes the border design. Repeating the oak leaf design in these blocks is another option; here, perhaps, is a case of "the simpler the better."

The princess feather in the border is an example of a single-motif repeat. The blue border is stitched in-the-ditch and quilted in a sawtooth design.

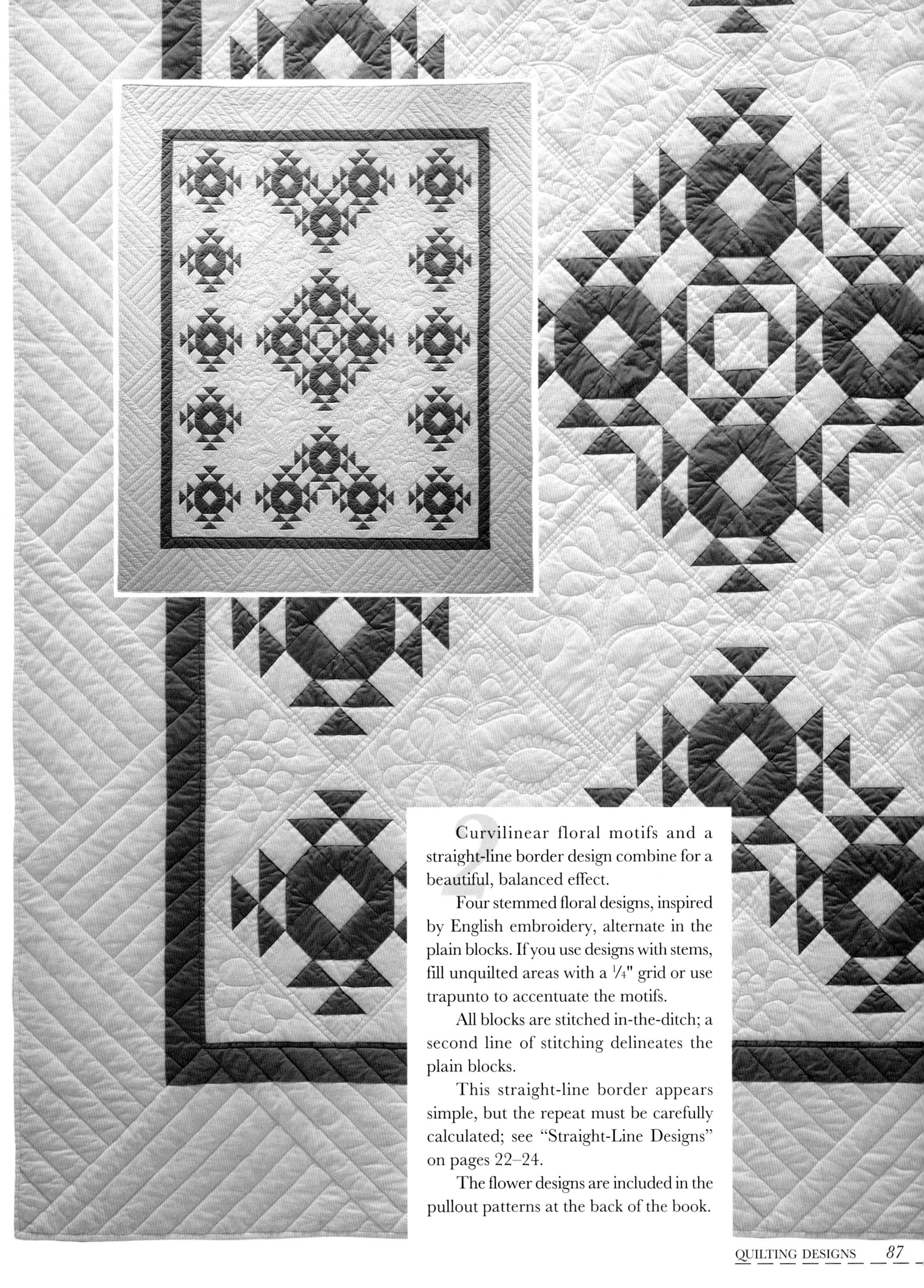

Curvilinear floral motifs and a straight-line border design combine for a beautiful, balanced effect.

Four stemmed floral designs, inspired by English embroidery, alternate in the plain blocks. If you use designs with stems, fill unquilted areas with a ¼" grid or use trapunto to accentuate the motifs.

All blocks are stitched in-the-ditch; a second line of stitching delineates the plain blocks.

This straight-line border appears simple, but the repeat must be carefully calculated; see "Straight-Line Designs" on pages 22–24.

The flower designs are included in the pullout patterns at the back of the book.

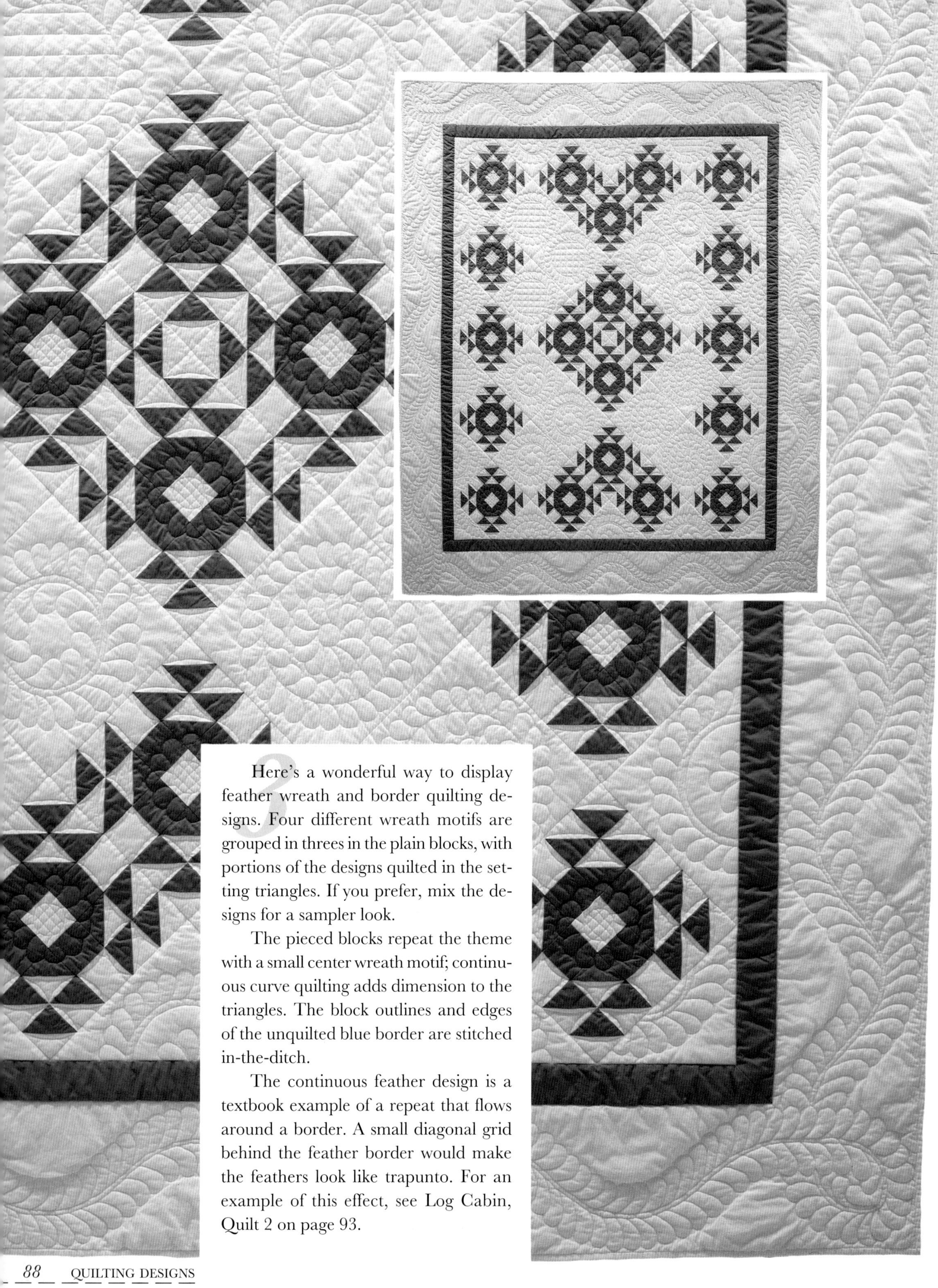

Here's a wonderful way to display feather wreath and border quilting designs. Four different wreath motifs are grouped in threes in the plain blocks, with portions of the designs quilted in the setting triangles. If you prefer, mix the designs for a sampler look.

The pieced blocks repeat the theme with a small center wreath motif; continuous curve quilting adds dimension to the triangles. The block outlines and edges of the unquilted blue border are stitched in-the-ditch.

The continuous feather design is a textbook example of a repeat that flows around a border. A small diagonal grid behind the feather border would make the feathers look like trapunto. For an example of this effect, see Log Cabin, Quilt 2 on page 93.

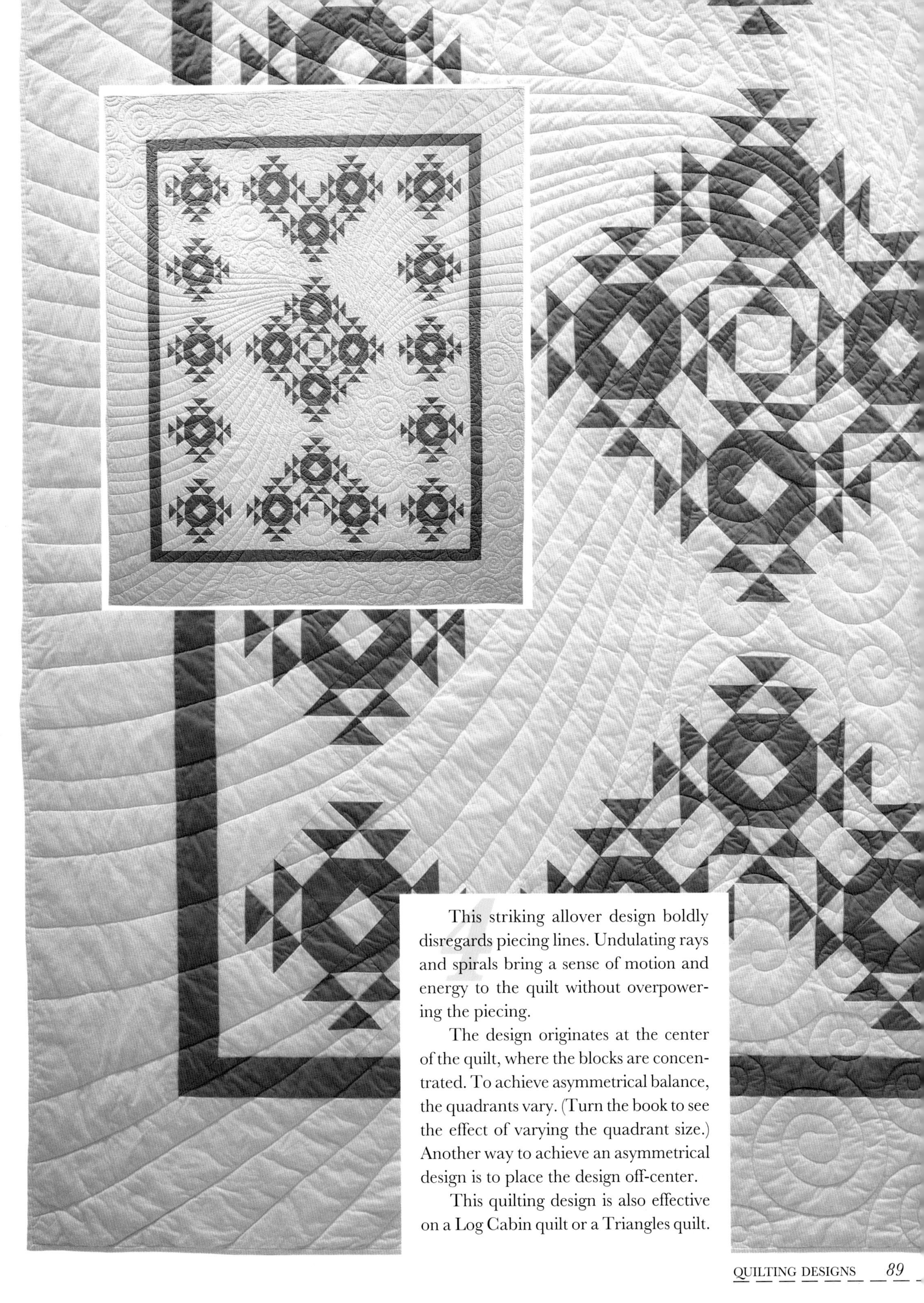

This striking allover design boldly disregards piecing lines. Undulating rays and spirals bring a sense of motion and energy to the quilt without overpowering the piecing.

The design originates at the center of the quilt, where the blocks are concentrated. To achieve asymmetrical balance, the quadrants vary. (Turn the book to see the effect of varying the quadrant size.) Another way to achieve an asymmetrical design is to place the design off-center.

This quilting design is also effective on a Log Cabin quilt or a Triangles quilt.

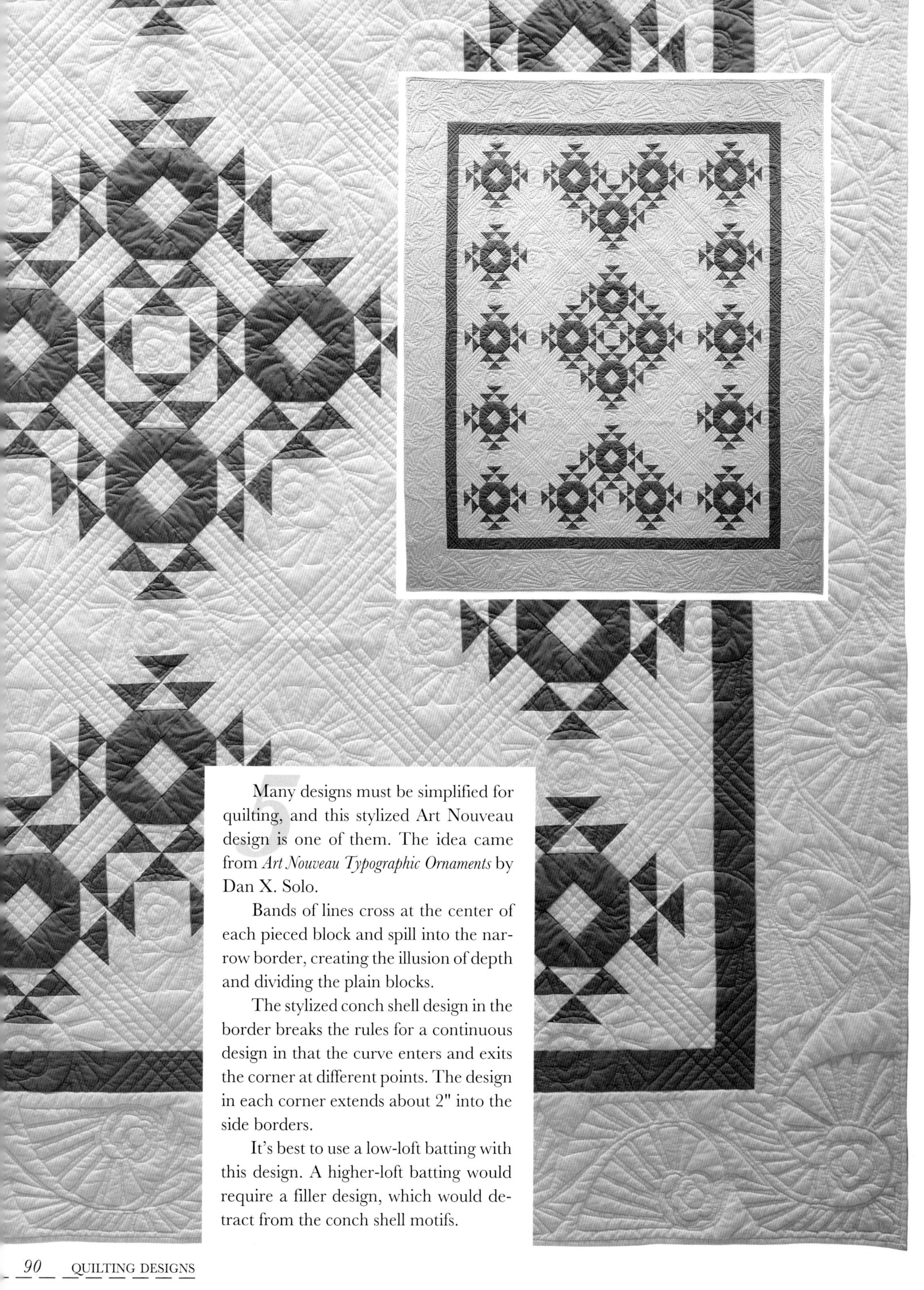

Many designs must be simplified for quilting, and this stylized Art Nouveau design is one of them. The idea came from *Art Nouveau Typographic Ornaments* by Dan X. Solo.

Bands of lines cross at the center of each pieced block and spill into the narrow border, creating the illusion of depth and dividing the plain blocks.

The stylized conch shell design in the border breaks the rules for a continuous design in that the curve enters and exits the corner at different points. The design in each corner extends about 2" into the side borders.

It's best to use a low-loft batting with this design. A higher-loft batting would require a filler design, which would detract from the conch shell motifs.

79½" x 79½"

One of the best known and loved of all quilt patterns, Log Cabin offers a seemingly endless array of settings. In the quilts shown here, the blocks are arranged in the classic Barn Raising setting. A 12½"-wide border gives ample room for impressive border designs.

The Log Cabin block is often stitched-in-the ditch of each round of logs, or ¼" away from the ditch of each round of logs. The quilts that follow ignore that tradition and feature a variety of innovative quilting designs. Background designs, such as fan, clamshell, and wineglass, or straight-grain or diagonal grids, are but a few of your other options.

1

A reverberating design of cables and feathers accentuates the traditional Barn Raising setting. A feather wreath in the center four blocks creates a focal point.

The large feather scroll design in the border consists of four separate scrolls. Each scroll begins in a corner and flows in each direction to the border midpoint, where it meets another scroll. The design is worked out like a continuous repeat.

You may prefer to fill the plain circular areas in the scroll with quilting; for two ideas, see Quilt 2 on the facing page.

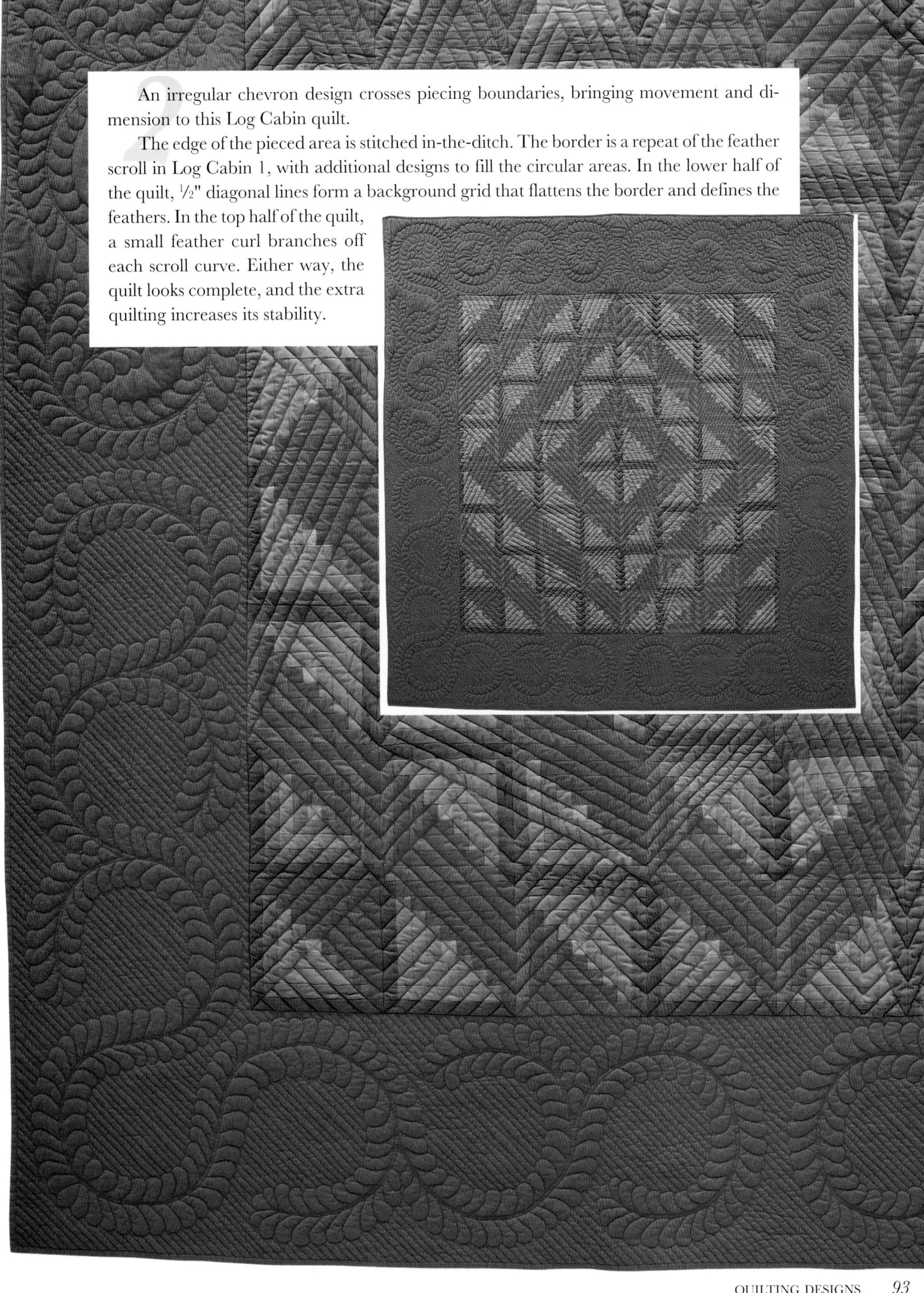

An irregular chevron design crosses piecing boundaries, bringing movement and dimension to this Log Cabin quilt.

The edge of the pieced area is stitched in-the-ditch. The border is a repeat of the feather scroll in Log Cabin 1, with additional designs to fill the circular areas. In the lower half of the quilt, ½" diagonal lines form a background grid that flattens the border and defines the feathers. In the top half of the quilt, a small feather curl branches off each scroll curve. Either way, the quilt looks complete, and the extra quilting increases its stability.

Shallow curves break up the blocks in an unusual pattern and establish a pleasing visual rhythm. The edges of the pieced area are stitched in-the-ditch.

The blues and rusts are evocative of the Australian outback, so it seemed fitting to quilt one of our best-known poems, "My Country," by Dorothea McKellar, in the border. Each corner features an Australian animal inside a circular motif. Clockwise from the top left, the animals are the frilled lizard, koala, kangaroo, and emu.

When you use poetry, or any wording, in a quilt, you may be left with unquilted areas. Solve this design problem by adding small motifs in the unquilted areas, such as the gum-nut and leaf designs shown here.

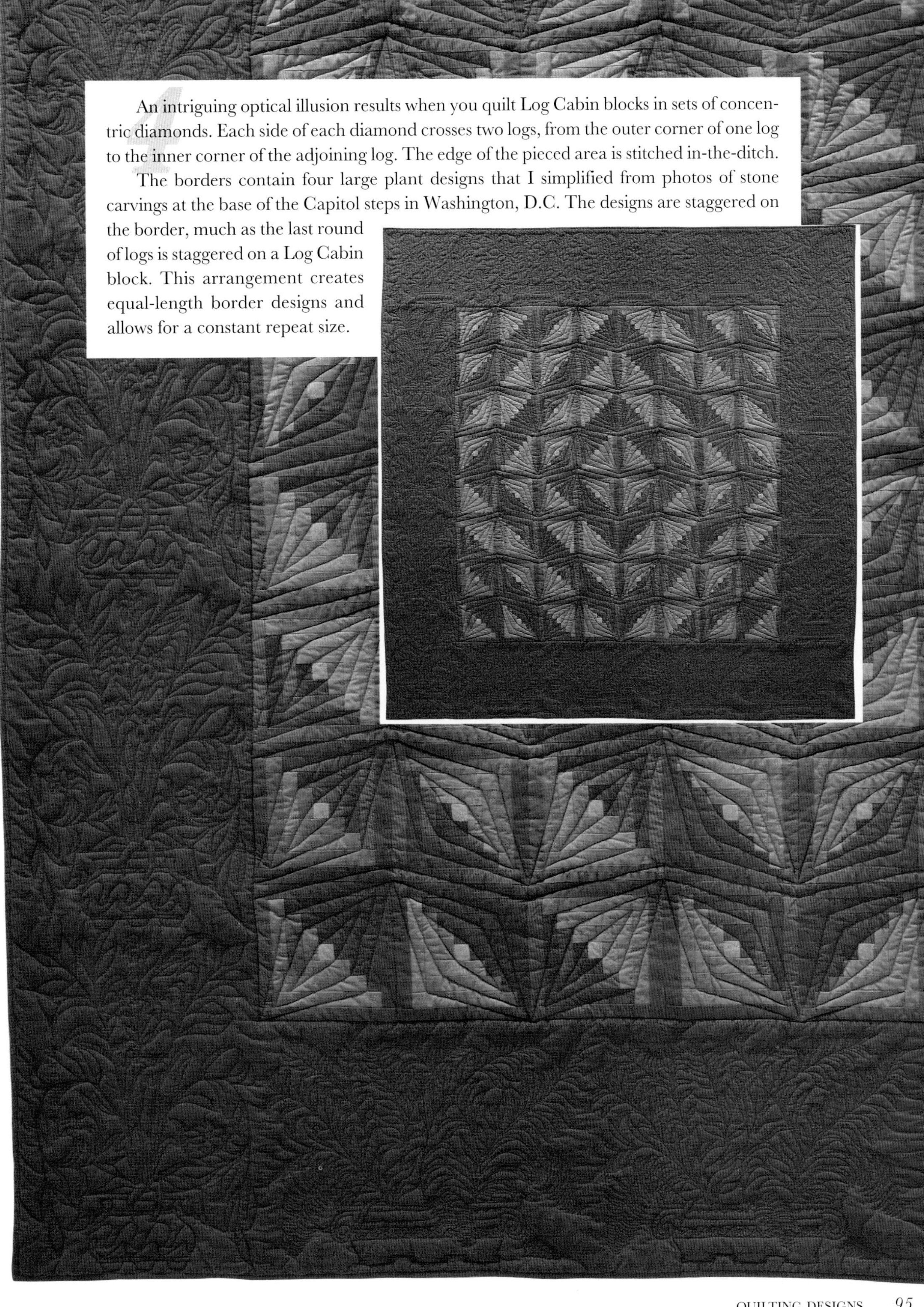

An intriguing optical illusion results when you quilt Log Cabin blocks in sets of concentric diamonds. Each side of each diamond crosses two logs, from the outer corner of one log to the inner corner of the adjoining log. The edge of the pieced area is stitched in-the-ditch.

The borders contain four large plant designs that I simplified from photos of stone carvings at the base of the Capitol steps in Washington, D.C. The designs are staggered on the border, much as the last round of logs is staggered on a Log Cabin block. This arrangement creates equal-length border designs and allows for a constant repeat size.

A stylized arch border design, simplified from *The Grammar of Ornament* by Owen Jones, is framed by bands of straight lines and waves. These bands don't turn the corners but stop and start with a single corner motif.

The large-scale design in the pieced area is a variation on the border theme. Modifying and repeating design elements in a quilt creates a sense of harmony and completeness. Varying the scale of the two major designs ensures that the areas remain distinct.

The border design is included in the pullout patterns at the back of the book.

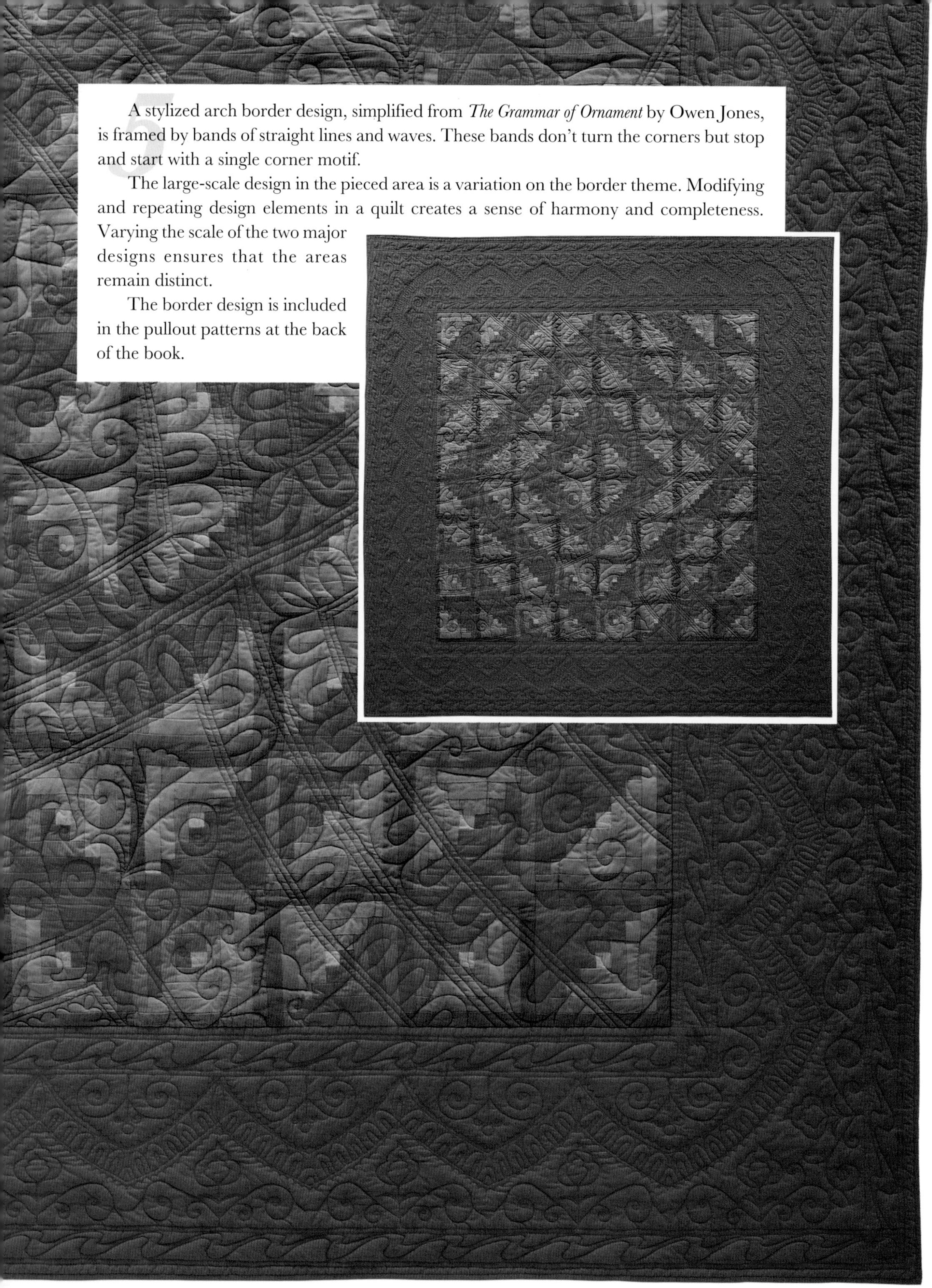

This section contains instructions for making each of the twelve quilts. Eight quilts require rotary cutting, and four quilts require templates. Read the complete cutting and piecing instructions for the quilt you plan to make before you begin. A template letter with a small "r" following it, such as Br, means "reverse." Flip the template over and cut a mirror image of it.

The "Materials" section of each project includes fabric and color suggestions. Fabric requirements are based on 44"-wide fabric that has 42 usable inches. If you prewash your fabric and it has less than 42 usable inches, you may need to purchase more fabric.

QUILT PATTERNS

Many projects call for strips that are 42" long when cut across the fabric width. If your fabric is wider than 42", it's not necessary to trim the excess. If it's narrower than 42", you may need an additional strip of fabric to cut the required number of pieces.

The backing yardage for each quilt includes an 8"-wide rod sleeve.

All measurements include 1/4"-wide seam allowances. *Do not add seam allowances to the dimensions given in the cutting section or on the templates.*

TRIANGLES

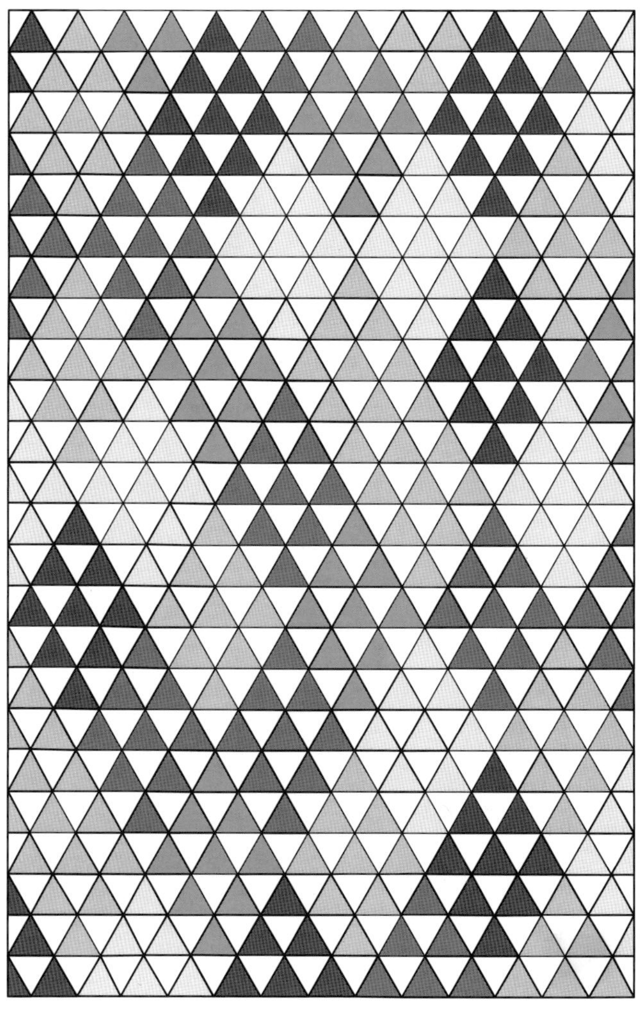

Triangles
10 1/2" block

DIMENSIONS: 48" x 72 1/2"
PHOTOS ON PAGES 25–30.

28 large diamond blocks, 10 1/2" on each side; 7 vertical half-diamonds; 8 horizontal half-diamonds; and 2 quarter-diamonds, set diagonally; finished without a border.

MATERIALS

44"-WIDE FABRIC

2 1/2 yds. white for blocks and binding
1/2 yd. each of 7 different blue-green solids for blocks
3 yds. fabric for backing (seamed crosswise) and rod sleeve
Batting (100% cotton, packaged)

CUTTING

All measurements include ¼"-wide seams.

From the white:

Cut 19 strips, 3¾" x 42". Cut these strips into 312 equilateral triangles using Template A.

Cut 24 side triangles, 12 using Template B and 12 using Br.

Cut 7 strips, 2" x 42", for binding.

From the blue-green solids:

Cut 3 strips each of 7 different blue-green solids, 3 ¾" x 42". Cut these strips into 312 equilateral triangles, using Template A.

Cut 24 side triangles, 12 using Template B and 12 using Br.

DIRECTIONS

1. Join 1 colored piece A and 1 white piece A to make 1 diamond as shown. Make a total of 252 diamonds.

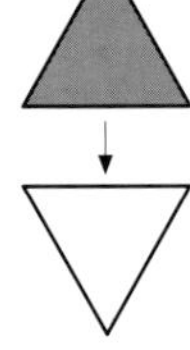

2. Join 9 diamonds of the same color to make 1 large diamond block as shown. Make a total of 28 assorted large diamond blocks.

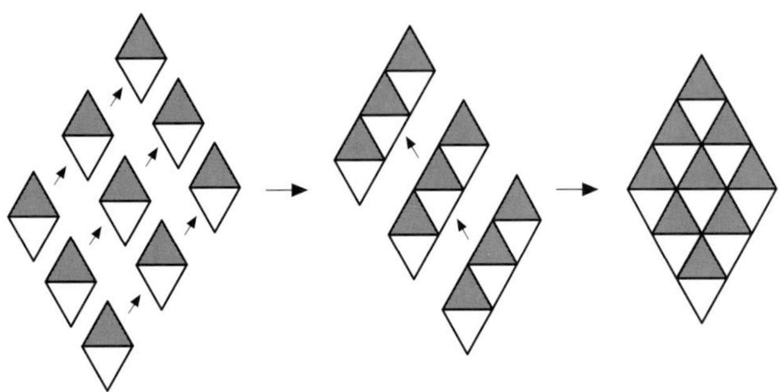

3. Make 7 vertical half-diamonds, using pieces A, B, and Br.

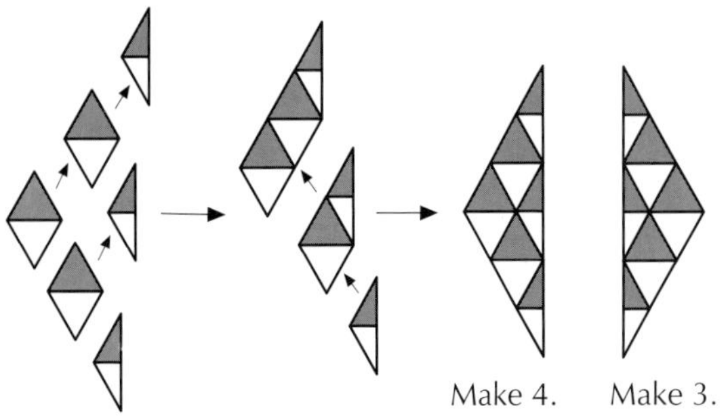

4. Make 8 horizontal half-diamonds, using piece A.

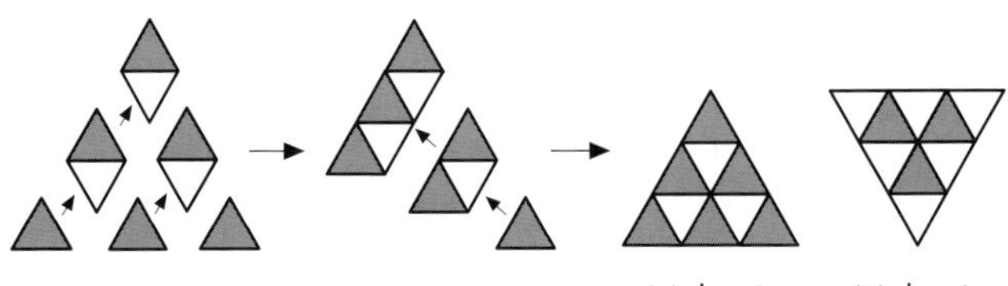

5. Make 2 quarter-diamonds, using pieces A, B, and Br.

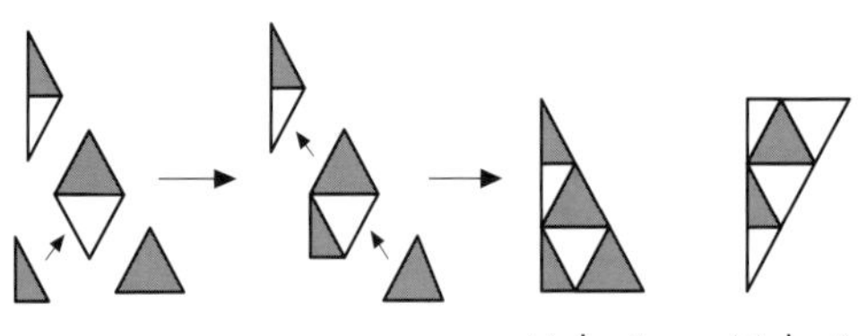

6. Join the large diamond blocks into diagonal rows, using the half- and quarter-diamonds as shown. Join the rows.

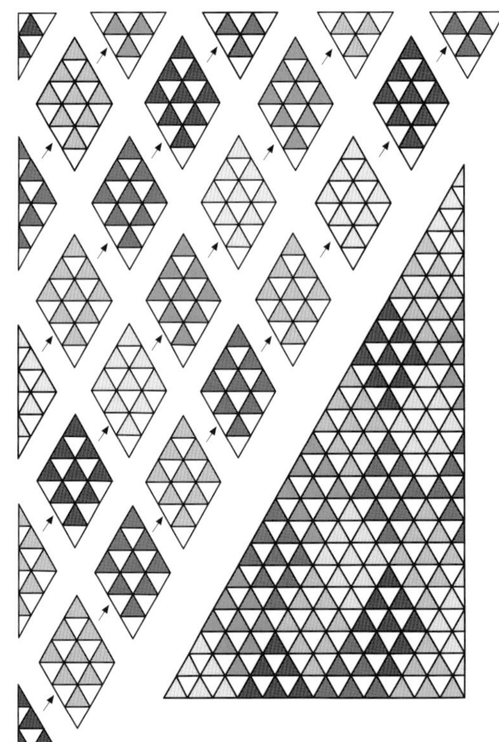

7. Layer the quilt top with batting and backing. See "Quiltmaking Techniques" on pages 122–33. Quilt; refer to the photos on pages 25–30 for ideas.

8. Bind with the 2" x 42" white strips.

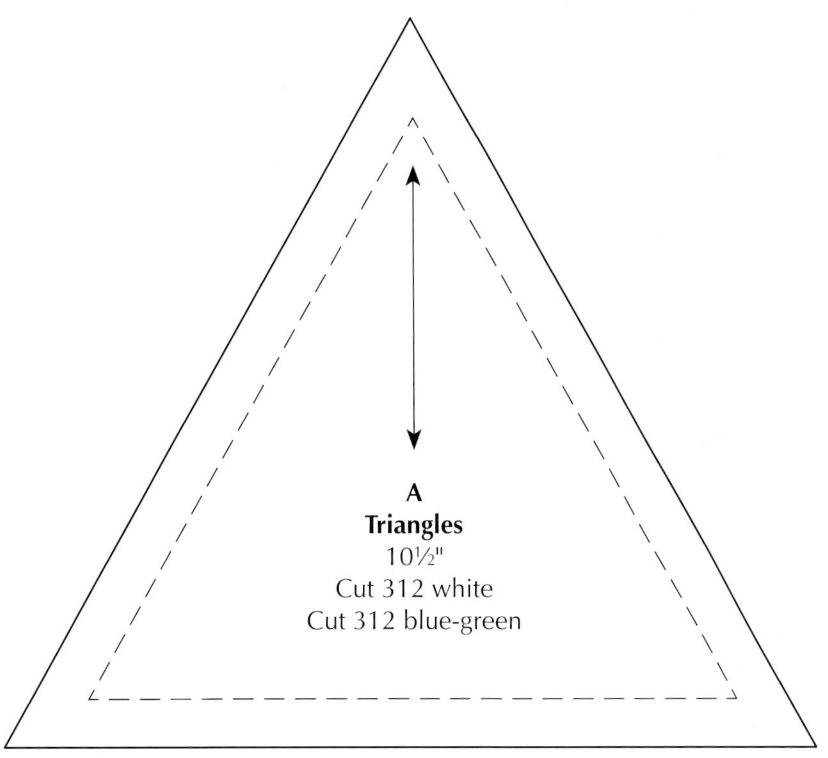
A
Triangles
10½"
Cut 312 white
Cut 312 blue-green

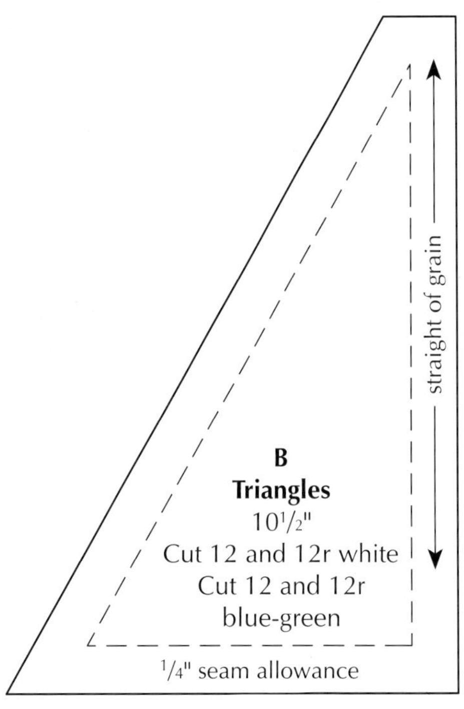
straight of grain
B
Triangles
10½"
Cut 12 and 12r white
Cut 12 and 12r
blue-green
¼" seam allowance

SQUARE IN A SQUARE

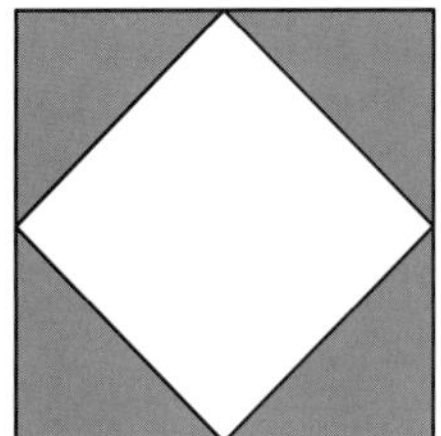

Square in a Square
6½" block

DIMENSIONS: 65½" x 78½"
PHOTOS ON PAGES 31–36.

80 blocks, 6½", set 8 across and 10 down; 6½"-wide border.

MATERIALS

44"-WIDE FABRIC

1¾ yds. pink print for blocks
3¾ yds. cream solid for blocks, border, and binding
4½ yds. fabric for backing (seamed crosswise) and rod sleeve
Batting (100% polyester, packaged)

CUTTING

ALL MEASUREMENTS INCLUDE ¼"-WIDE SEAMS.

From the pink print:
Cut 5 strips, 5" x 42". Cut these strips into a total of 40 squares, 5" x 5", for the center squares.
Cut 8 strips, 4⅛" x 42". Cut these strips into a total of 80 squares, 4⅛" x 4⅛". Cut once diagonally into 160 half-square triangles.

From the cream solid:
Cut 5 strips, 5" x 42". Cut these strips into a total of 40 squares, 5" x 5", for the center squares.
Cut 8 strips, 4⅛" x 42". Cut these strips into a total of 80 squares, 4⅛" x 4⅛". Cut once diagonally into 160 half-square triangles.
Cut 4 lengthwise strips, 7" x 68", for borders.
Cut 5 lengthwise strips, 2" x 72", for binding.

DIRECTIONS

1. Join 1 pink center square and 4 cream triangles to make a block. Make a total of 40 blocks.

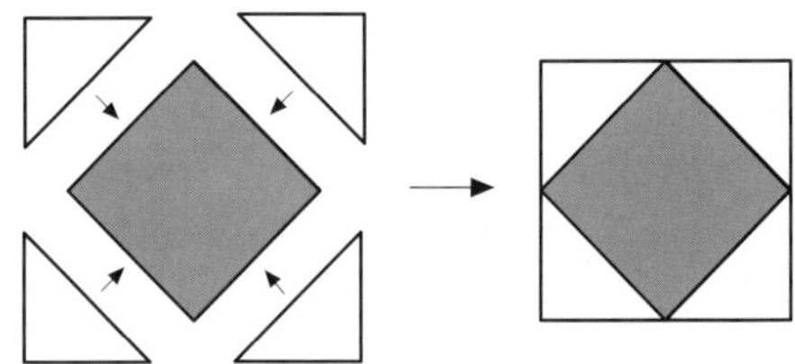

2. Join 1 cream center square and 4 pink triangles to make a block. Make a total of 40 blocks.

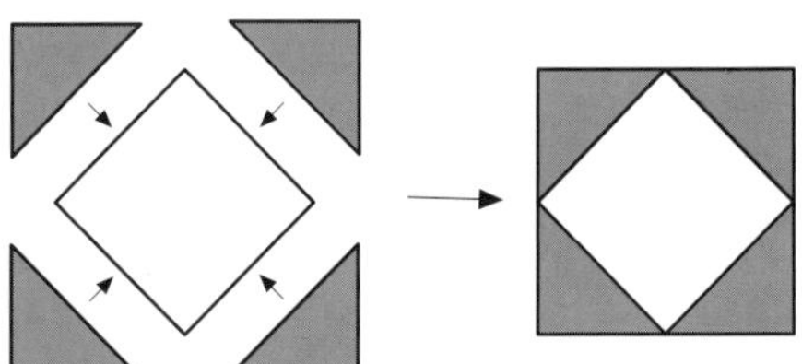

3. Join the blocks in rows of 8, alternating pink and cream centers as shown in the quilt plan. Join the rows.
4. Add cream borders. See "Straight-Cut Borders" on page 123.
5. Layer the quilt top with batting and backing. See "Quiltmaking Techniques" on pages 122–33. Quilt; refer to the photos on pages 31–36 for ideas.
6. Bind with the 2" x 72" cream strips.

DOUBLE IRISH CHAIN

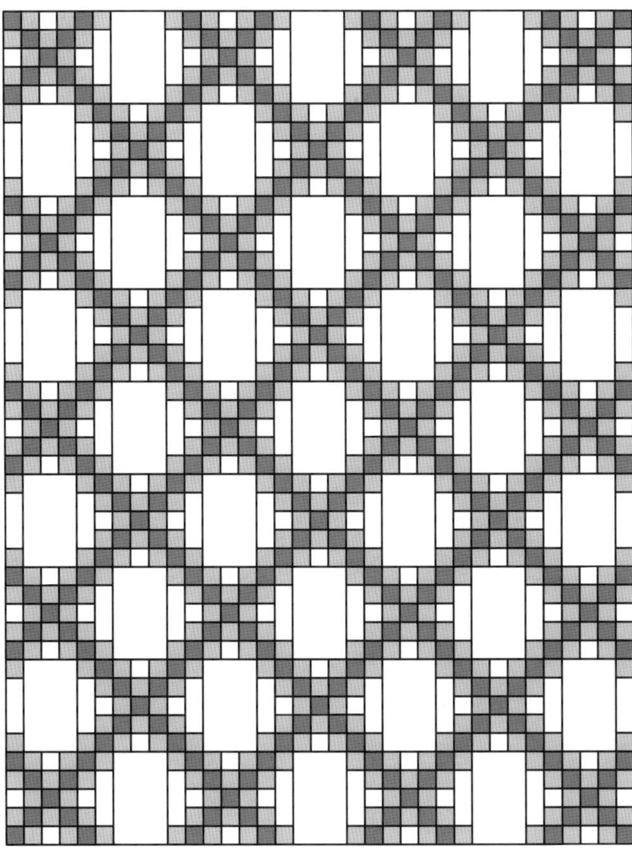

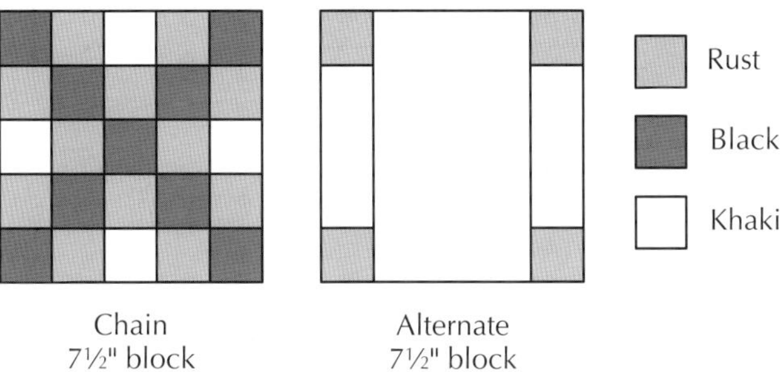

Chain
7½" block

Alternate
7½" block

DIMENSIONS: 53" x 68"
PHOTOS ON PAGES 37–42.

63 blocks (32 Chain and 31 alternate), 7½", set 7 across and 9 down; finished without a border.

MATERIALS

44"-WIDE FABRIC

2 yds. rust solid for Chain and alternate blocks
1⅛ yds. black solid for Chain blocks
2½ yds. khaki solid for Chain and alternate blocks and binding
3¼ yds. fabric for backing (seamed crosswise) and rod sleeve
Batting (100% polyester, 3 oz. off the roll)

CUTTING

ALL MEASUREMENTS INCLUDE ¼"-WIDE SEAMS.

From the rust solid:
Cut 30 strips, 2" x 42", for Chain and alternate blocks.

From the black solid:
Cut 18 strips, 2" x 42", for Chain blocks.

From the khaki solid:
Cut 8 strips, 2" x 42", for Chain blocks.
Cut 4 strips, 8" x 42". Cut these strips into a total of 31 rectangles, 5" x 8", for alternate blocks.
Cut 3 strips, 5" x 42", for alternate blocks.
Cut 6 strips, 2" x 42", for binding.

DIRECTIONS

Chain Blocks

1. Join 2" x 42" rust, black, and khaki strips into units as shown. Make 4 each of Units A and B and 2 each of Unit C. The units should measure 8" wide when sewn. Cut Units A and B into 64 segments and Unit C into 32 segments, each 2" wide.

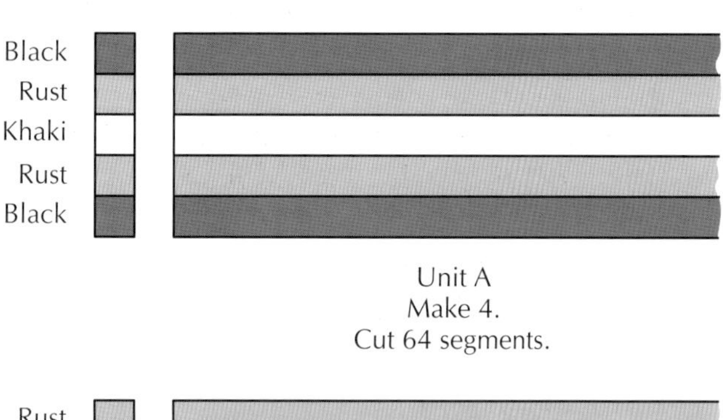

Unit A
Make 4.
Cut 64 segments.

Unit B
Make 4.
Cut 64 segments.

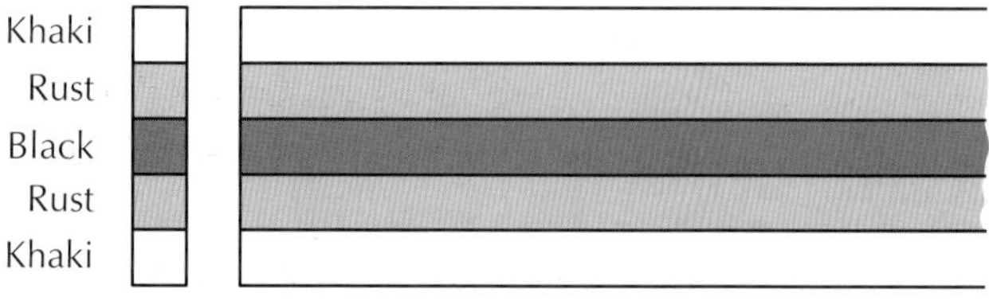

Unit C
Make 2.
Cut 32 segments.

2. Join the segments as shown to make 32 Chain blocks.

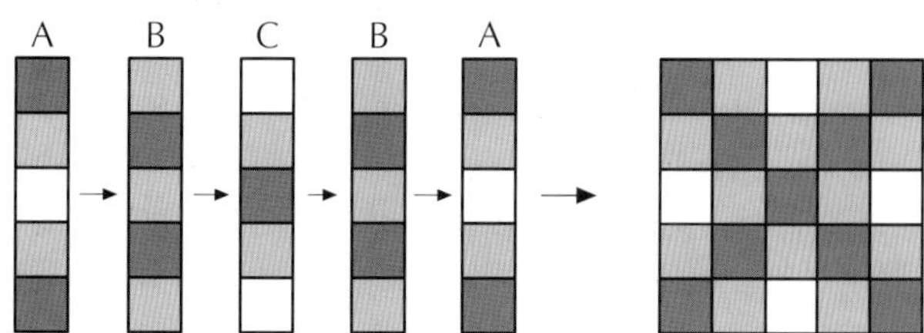

Alternate Blocks

1. Join two 2" x 42" rust strips and one 5" x 42" khaki strip into a unit. Make 3 units. The units should measure 8" wide when sewn. Cut the units into a total of 62 segments, each 2" wide.

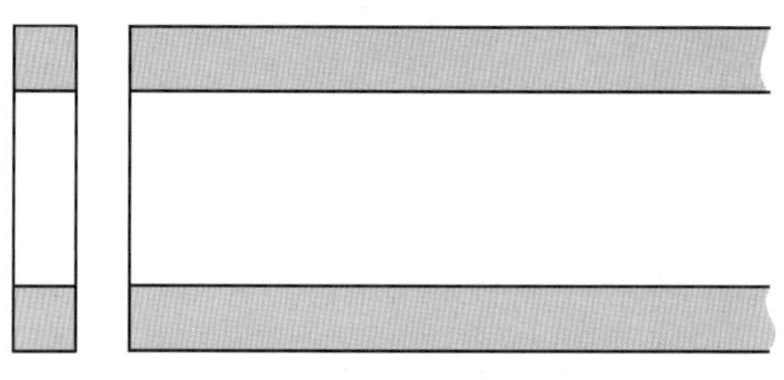

Make 3.
Cut 62 segments.

2. Join the rust/khaki segments and the 5" x 8" khaki rectangles to make 31 alternate blocks.

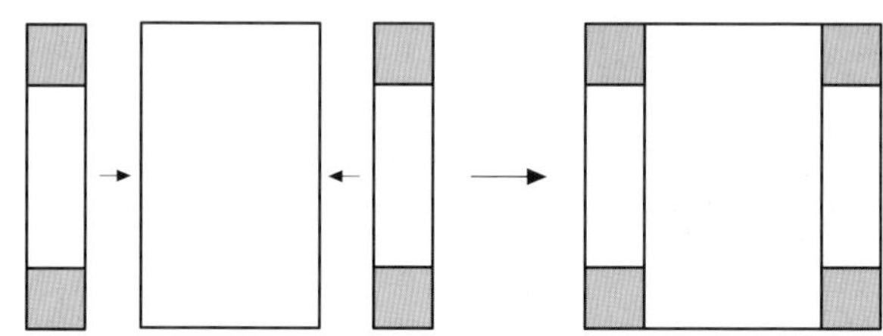

3. Join the blocks in rows of 7, alternating Chain and alternate blocks as shown in the quilt plan. Join the rows.
4. Layer the quilt top with batting and backing. See "Quiltmaking Techniques" on pages 122–33. Quilt; refer to the photos on pages 37–42 for ideas.
5. Bind with the 2" x 42" khaki strips.

Ohio Star

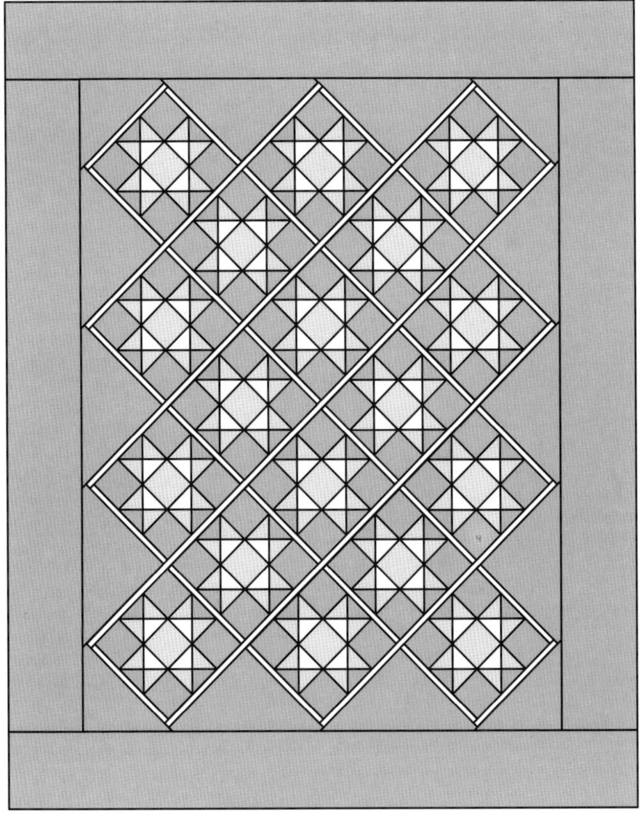

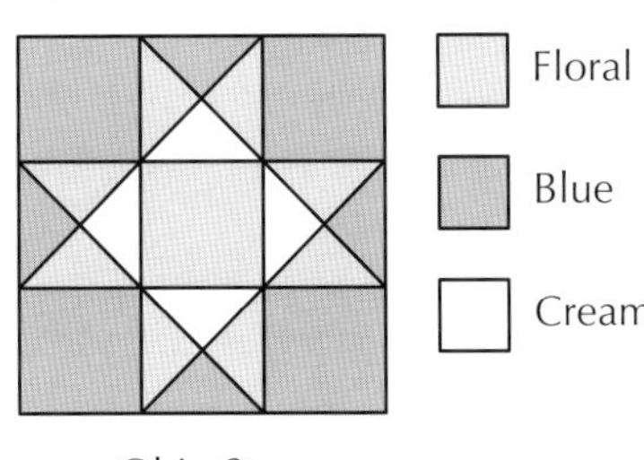

Ohio Star
9" block

Dimensions: 56½" x 70"
Photos on pages 43–48.

18 blocks, 9", set on point 3 across and 4 down with ½"-wide sashing, with large setting triangles; 6½"-wide border.

MATERIALS

44"-wide fabric

¾ yd. floral print for stars

¾ yd. cream solid for sashing and stars

3⅔ yds. blue solid for blocks, setting triangles, border, and binding

3½ yds. fabric for backing (seamed crosswise) and rod sleeve

Batting (100% cotton, packaged)

CUTTING

All measurements include ¼"-wide seams.

From the floral print:

Cut 4 strips, 4¼" x 42", for star points. Cut these strips into a total of 36 squares, 4¼" x 4¼". Cut twice diagonally into 144 quarter-square triangles.

Cut 2 strips, 3½" x 42", for star centers. Cut these strips into a total of 18 squares, 3½" x 3½".

From the cream solid:

Cut 2 strips, 4¼" x 42", for star points. Cut these strips into a total of 18 squares, 4¼" x 4¼". Cut twice diagonally into 72 quarter-square triangles.

For sashing cut:

24 strips, 1" x 9½"
2 strips, 1" x 10½"
2 strips, 1" x 29½"
3 strips, 1" x 40"; from these, piece 2 strips, each 1" x 48½"
2 strips, 1" x 40"; from these, piece 1 strip, 1" x 58"

From the blue solid:

Cut 2 strips, 4¼" x 42", for star background. Cut these strips into a total of 18 squares, 4¼" x 4 ¼". Cut twice diagonally into 72 quarter-square triangles.

Cut 6 strips, 3½" x 42", for star background. Cut these strips into a total of 72 squares, 3½" x 3½".

Cut 3 squares, 16" x 16". Cut these squares twice diagonally into 12 setting triangles; you will use only 10.

Cut 2 squares, 11" x 11". Cut these squares once diagonally into 4 corner triangles.

Cut 4 lengthwise strips, 7" x 60", for borders.

Cut 5 lengthwise strips, 2" x 60", for binding.

DIRECTIONS

1. Join 1 floral quarter-square triangle and 1 cream quarter-square triangle to make 1 half-square triangle. Make a total of 72 half-square triangles.

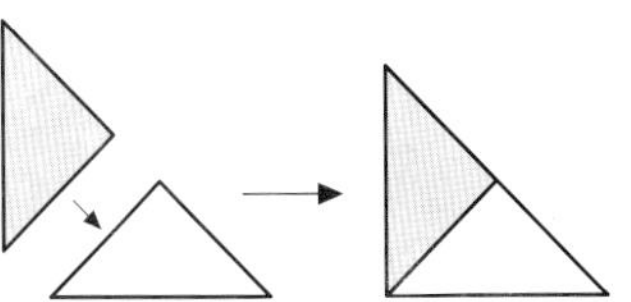

2. Join 1 floral quarter-square triangle and 1 blue quarter-square triangle to make 1 half-square triangle. Make a total of 72 half-square triangles.

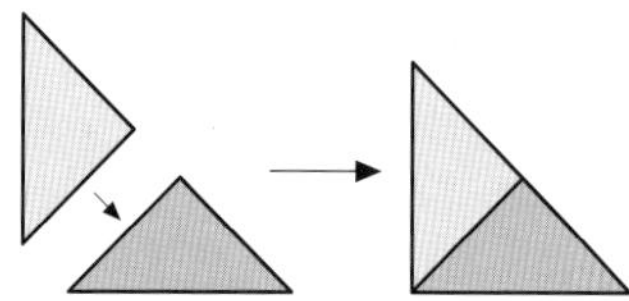

3. Join 1 floral/cream half-square triangle and 1 floral/blue half-square triangle to make 1 square. Make a total of 72 squares.

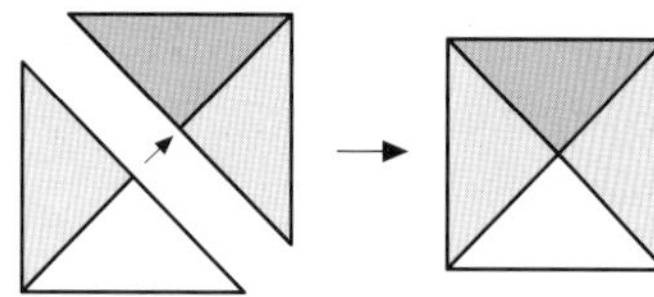

4. Join 4 pieced squares, 4 blue squares, and 1 floral square to make 1 block. Make a total of 18 blocks.

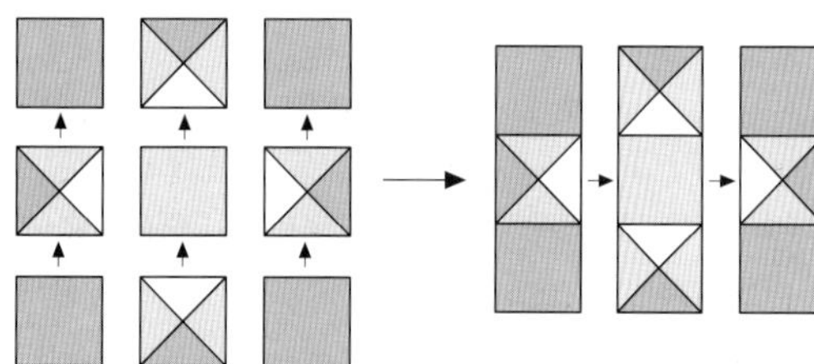

5. Join the star blocks into diagonal rows, adding the shortest sashing strips between blocks and at either end of each row. At the upper end of row 4, add a setting triangle.

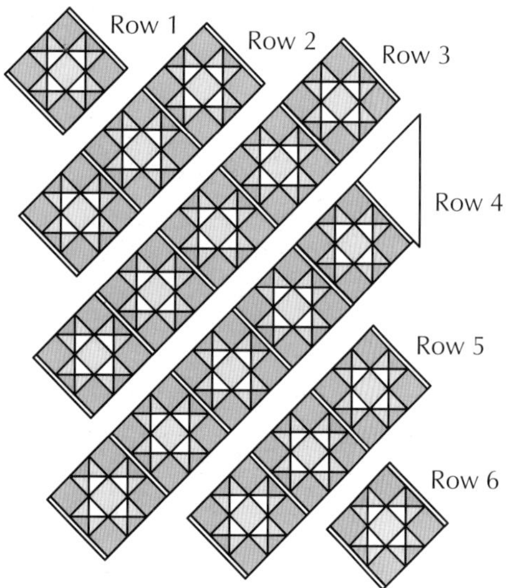

6. Join the remaining sashing strips to one long edge of each row.

7. Join the side and corner setting triangles to the rows as shown. These triangles are larger than the blocks.

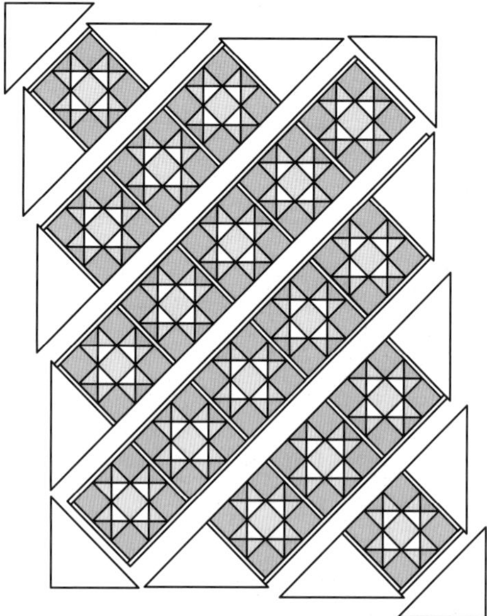

8. Join the rows. Trim the edges of the quilt top just enough to straighten, leaving at least ¾" beyond block points so blocks will "float."

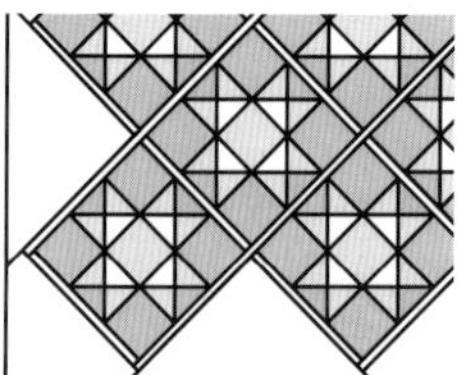

9. Add the blue border. See "Straight-Cut Borders" on page 123.

10. Layer the quilt top with batting and backing. See "Quiltmaking Techniques" on pages 122–33. Quilt; refer to the photos on pages 43–48 for ideas.

11. Bind with the 2" x 60" blue strips.

Le Moyne Star

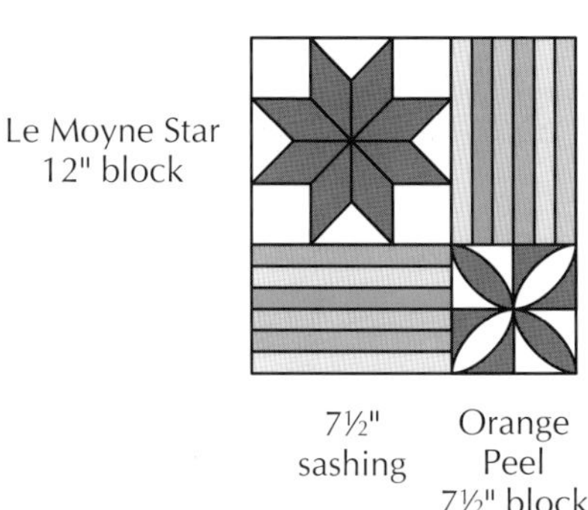

Dimensions: 59" x 78½"
Photos on pages 49–54.

12 Le Moyne Star blocks, 12", set 3 across and 4 down with 7½"-wide sashing and 7½" Orange Peel blocks as sashing squares; finished without a border.

MATERIALS

44"-wide fabric

2½ yds. total of assorted pastel solids for sashing
2⅓ yds. blue solid for Le Moyne Star blocks, Orange Peel blocks, and binding
2 yds. cream solid for Le Moyne Star blocks and Orange Peel blocks
4 yds. fabric for backing (seamed crosswise) and rod sleeve
Batting (100% polyester, packaged)

CUTTING

All measurements include ¼"-wide seams.

From the assorted pastel solids:
Cut 144 strips, 1¾" x 12½", for sashing.
From the blue solid:
Cut 7 strips, 2" x 42", for binding.
From the blue and cream solids:
Stars

From each color:
Cut 48, using Template A.
Cut 3 strips, 4" x 42". Cut the strips into a total of 24 squares, 4" x 4".
Cut 1 strip, 6¼" x 42". Cut the strip into a total of 6 squares, 6¼" x 6¼". Cut twice diagonally into 24 quarter-square triangles.

Orange Peel blocks

From each color:
Cut 24, using Template B.
Cut 48, using Template C.

DIRECTIONS

1. Arranging colors as desired, join the pastel strips to make 17 sets of 6 strips and 14 sets of 3 strips.

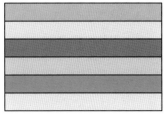

Make 17.

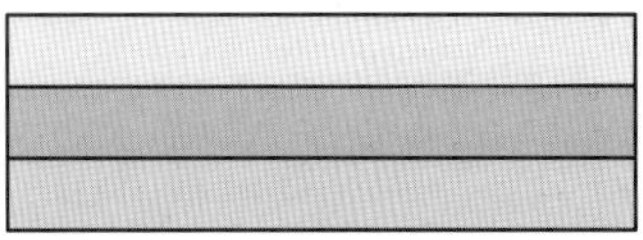

Make 14.

2. Piece 24 blue-centered Orange Peel squares and 24 white-centered Orange Peel squares, using pieces B and C.

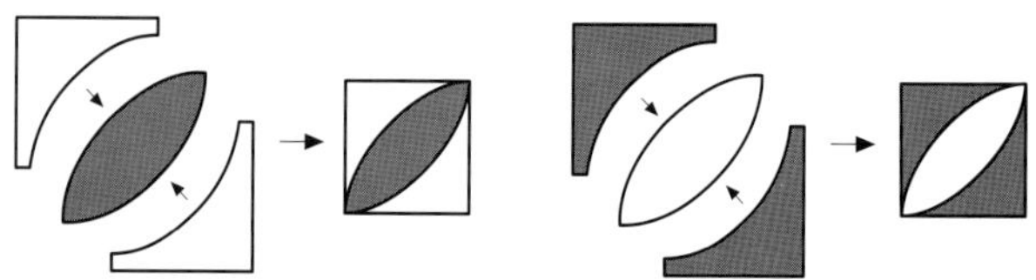

3. Alternating the center colors, join 4 Orange Peel squares to make 1 block. Make a total of 6 blocks.

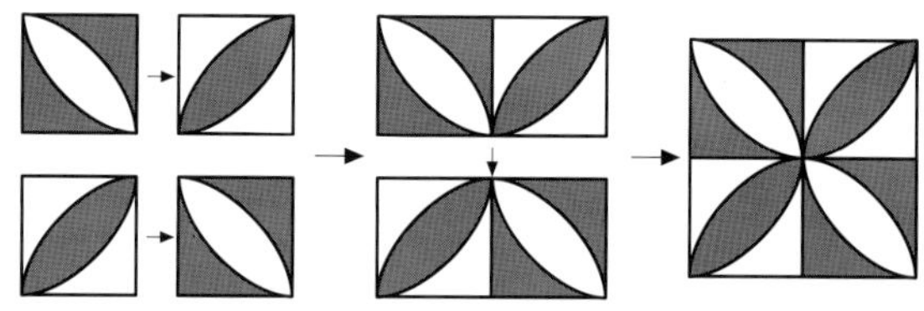

4. Alternating the center colors, join 2 Orange Peel squares to make a half-block. Make a total of 10 half-blocks.

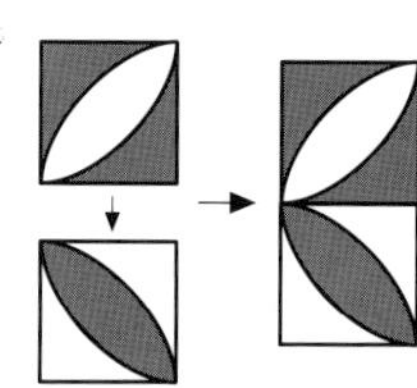

5. Piece 1 cream Le Moyne Star block with blue background, using 8 cream pieces A, 4 blue squares, and 4 blue quarter-square triangles. Piece a total of 6 blocks.

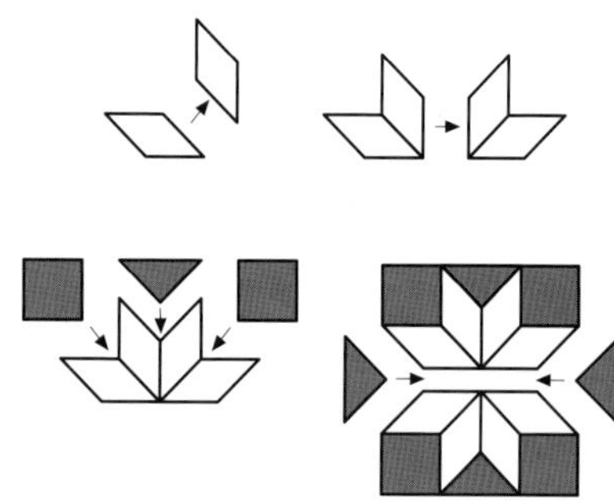

6. Piece 6 blue Le Moyne Star blocks with cream background.

7. Join 3 Le Moyne Star blocks, two 6-strip sashing units, and two 3-strip sashing units to make a row, alternating the colors of the stars. Make a total of 4 rows.

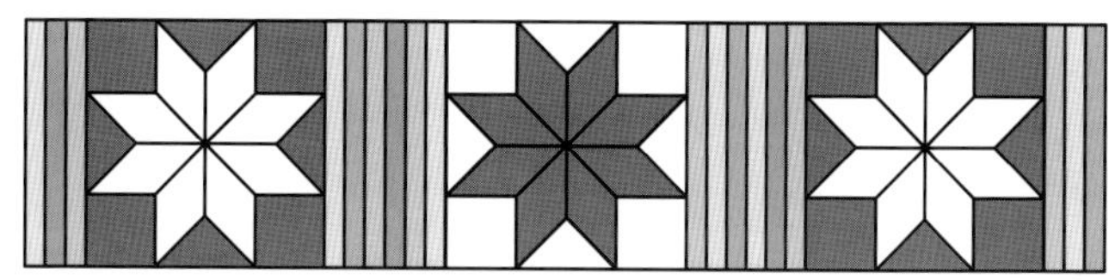

8. Join three 3-strip sashing units, 2 Orange Peel squares, and 2 Orange Peel half-blocks to make the top and bottom rows.

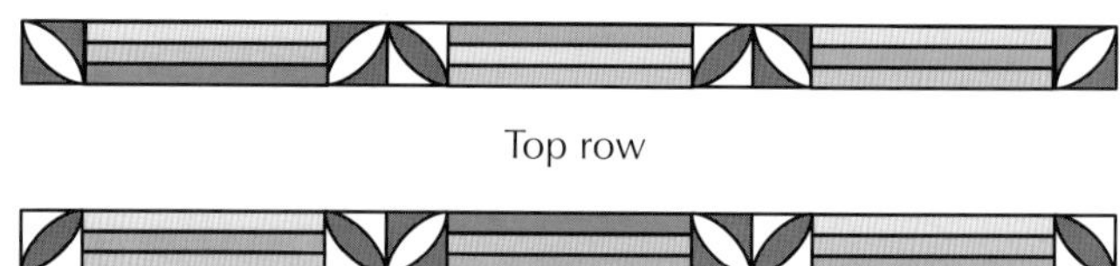

Top row

Bottom row

9. Join the remaining 6-strip sashing units, Orange Peel blocks, and Orange Peel half-blocks into the middle 3 sashing rows.

Make 2.

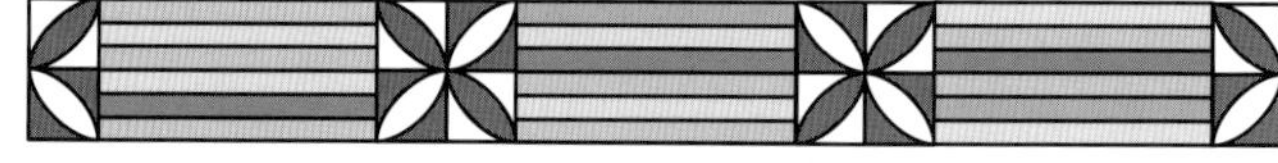

Make 1.

10. Join the rows as shown in the quilt plan.

11. Layer the quilt top with batting and backing. See "Quiltmaking Techniques" on pages 122–33. Quilt; refer to the photos on pages 49–54 for ideas.

12. Bind with the 2" x 42" blue strips.

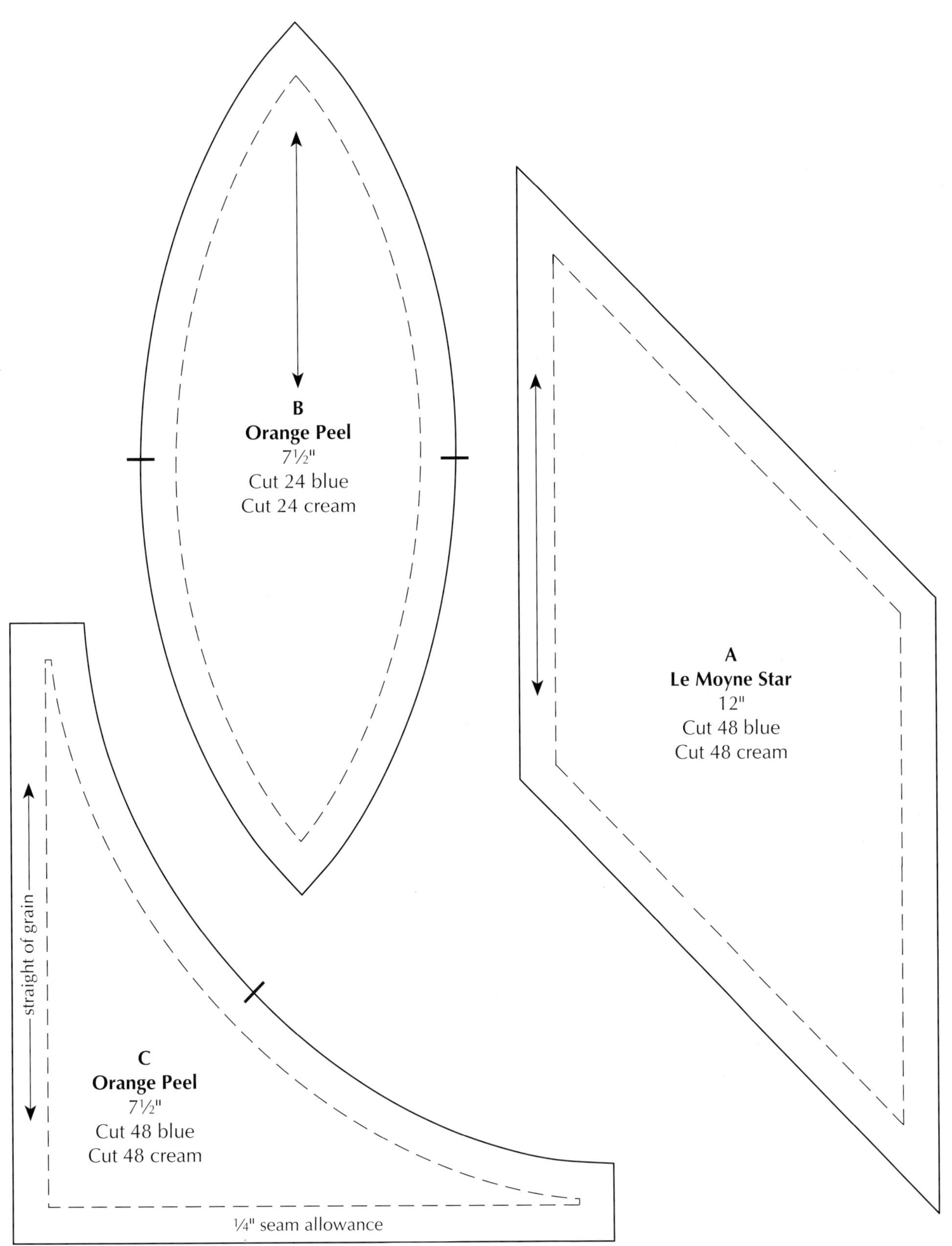
B
Orange Peel
7½"
Cut 24 blue
Cut 24 cream
A
Le Moyne Star
12"
Cut 48 blue
Cut 48 cream
straight of grain
C
Orange Peel
7½"
Cut 48 blue
Cut 48 cream
¼" seam allowance

SWEDISH SHIPS

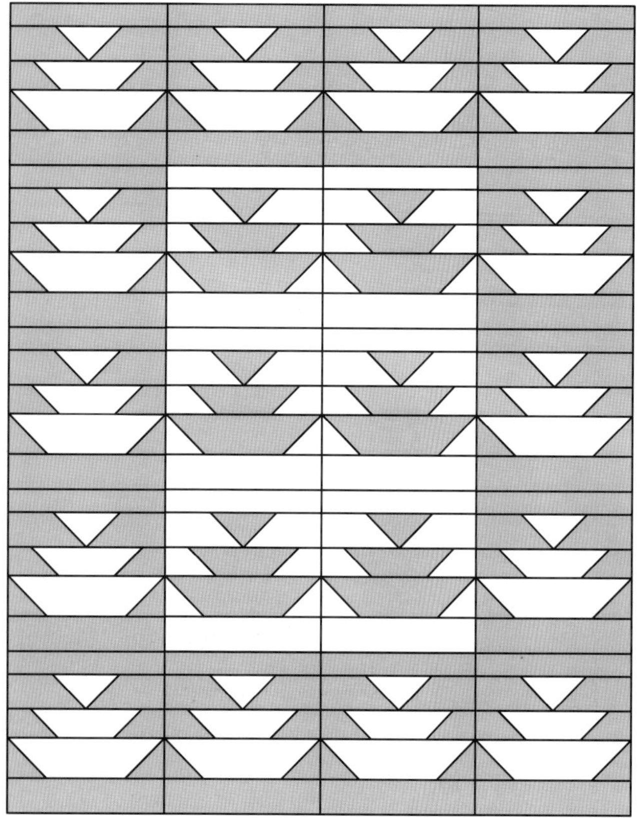

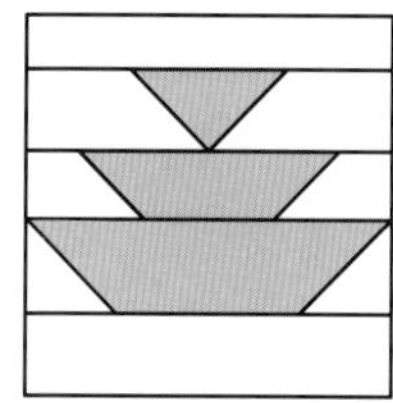

Swedish Ship
7" block

DIMENSIONS: 28½" x 35½"
PHOTOS ON PAGES 55–60.

20 blocks (14 yellow ships and 6 blue ships), 7", set 4 across and 5 down; finished without a border.

MATERIALS

44"-WIDE FABRIC

1⅓ yds. blue solid for blocks and binding
1 yd. yellow solid for blocks
1⅛ yds. fabric for backing and rod sleeve
Batting (60/40 wool/polyester, off the roll)

CUTTING

ALL MEASUREMENTS INCLUDE ¼"-WIDE SEAMS.

From the blue solid:
Cut 14 rectangles, 1⅝" x 7½".
Cut 14 rectangles, 2¼" x 7½".
Cut 6 ship bases, using Template A.
Cut 6 ship midsections, using Template B.
Cut 6 ship tops, using Template C.
Cut 14 each, using Template D and Dr, Template E and Er, and Template F and Fr.
Cut 4 strips, 2" x 42", for binding.

From the yellow solid:
Cut 6 rectangles, 1⅝" x 7½".
Cut 6 rectangles, 2¼" x 7½".
Cut 14 ship bases, using Template A.
Cut 14 ship midsections, using Template B.
Cut 14 ship tops, using Template C.
Cut 6 each, using Template D and Dr, Template E and Er, and Template F and Fr.

DIRECTIONS

1. Join blue piece C to yellow pieces F and Fr. Join blue piece B to yellow pieces E and Er. Join blue piece A to yellow pieces D and Dr.

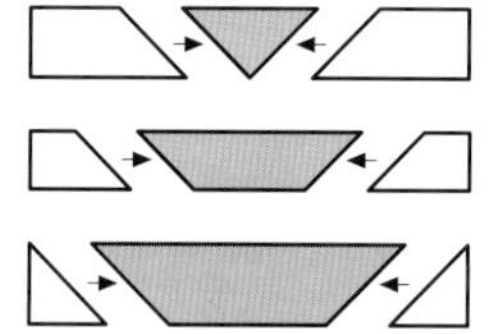

2. Join the 3 rows.

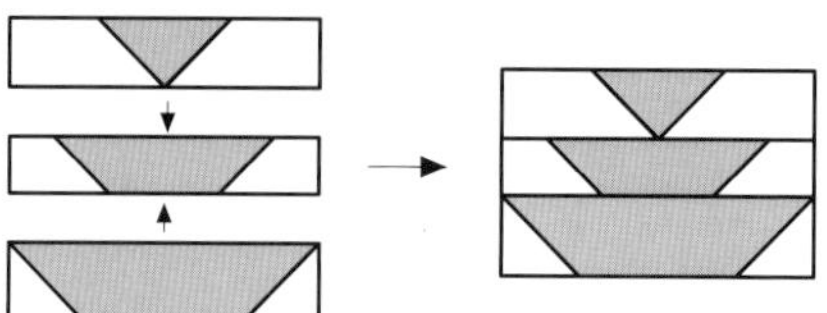

3. Join the 1⅝" x 7½" rectangle to the top of the ship and the 2 ¼" x 7½" rectangle to the bottom of the ship to make 1 block. Make a total of 6 blocks.

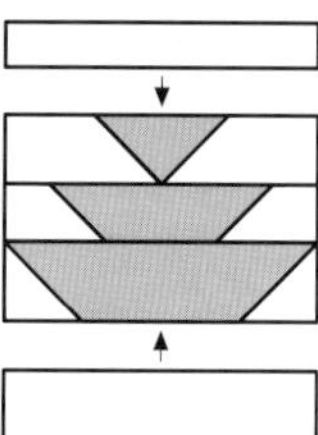

4. Piece 14 ship blocks in the reverse colors.

5. Join the blocks into rows of 4 as shown in the quilt plan. Join the rows.
6. Layer the quilt top with batting and backing. See "Quiltmaking Techniques" on pages 122–33. Quilt; refer to the photos on pages 55–60 for ideas.
7. Bind with the 2" x 42" blue strips.

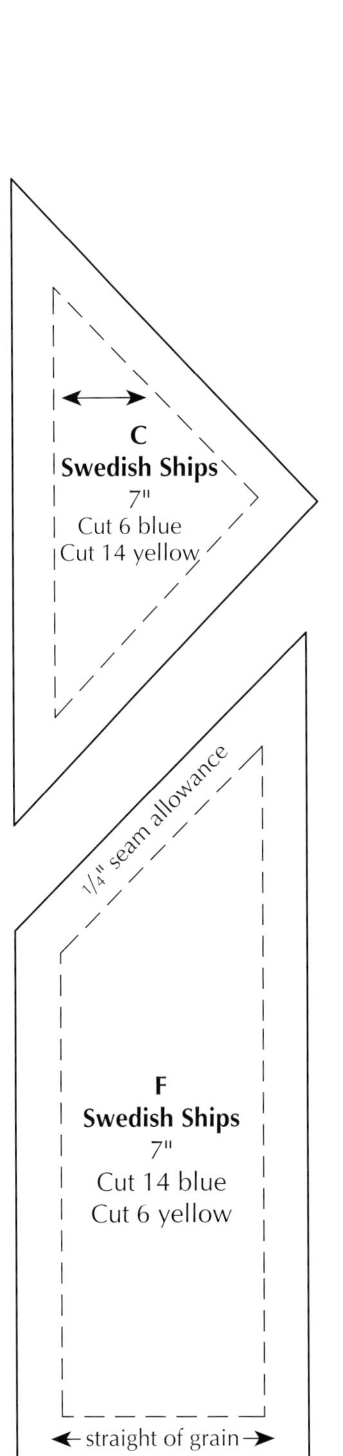

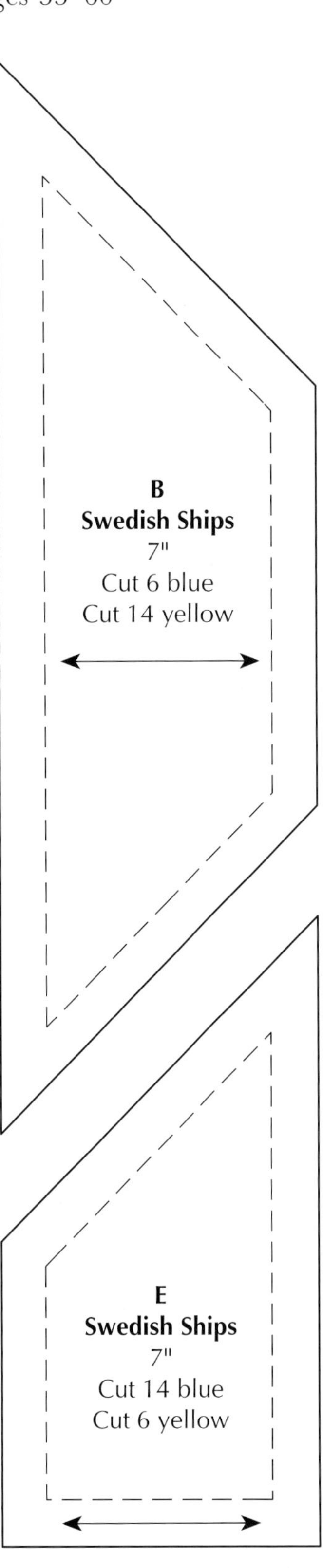

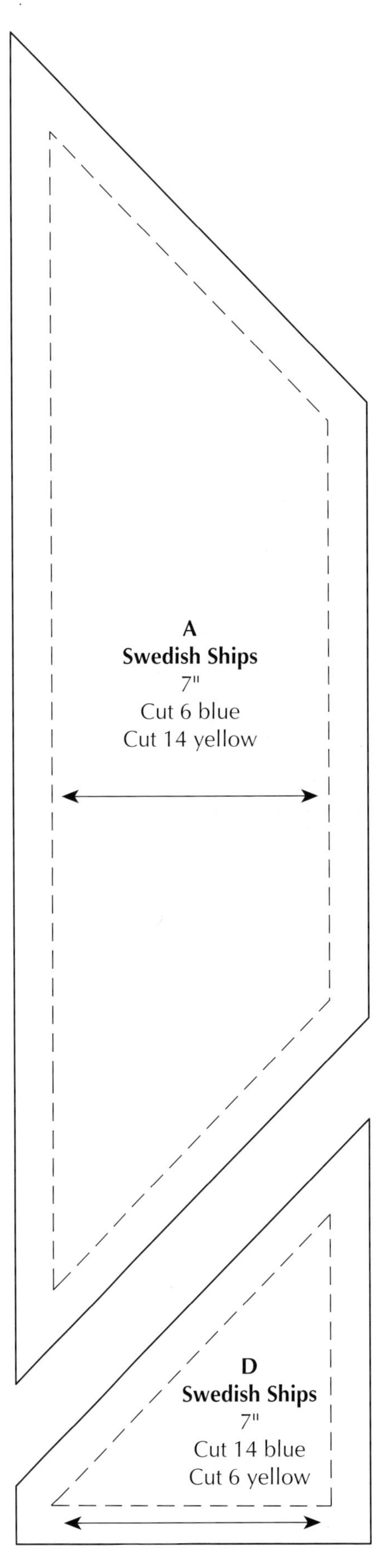

*F*ANS

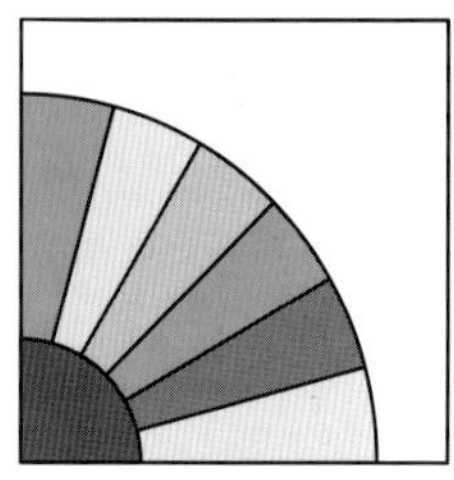

Fan
9" block

DIMENSIONS: 58½" x 58½"
PHOTOS ON PAGES 61–66.

25 blocks, 9", set on point with side and corner setting triangles; 3½"-wide border with corner squares.

MATERIALS

44"-WIDE FABRIC

½ yd. each of 6 different solids for fan blades
1 yd. deep purple solid for border and fan handles
3 yds. purple solid for background, corner squares, and binding
3½ yds. fabric for backing and rod sleeve
Batting (100% polyester, packaged)

CUTTING

ALL MEASUREMENTS INCLUDE ¼"-WIDE SEAMS.

From each of 6 different solids:
Cut 25 fan blades, using Template A.
From deep purple solid:
Cut 6 strips, 4" x 42", for border.
Cut 25 fan handles, using Template B.
From purple solid:
Cut 25 squares, 9½" x 9½", for background. Trim the squares using Template C.
Cut 3 squares, 14" x 14". Cut twice diagonally into 12 setting triangles.
Cut 2 squares, 7¼" x 7¼". Cut once diagonally into 4 corner setting triangles.
Cut 4 squares, 4" x 4", for border corners.
Cut 7 strips, 2" x 42", for binding.

DIRECTIONS

1. Join 6 different fan blades (piece A) to make 1 colored fan blade set. Make a total of 25 fan blade sets, varying color placement as desired.

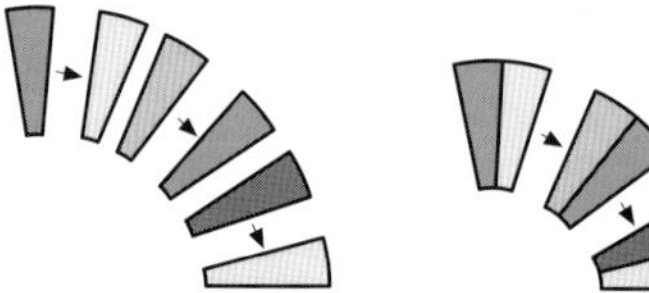

2. Join a fan handle (piece B) to each fan blade set.

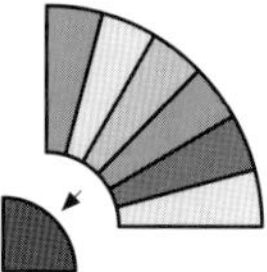

3. Join a piece C to each fan. Make 25 blocks.

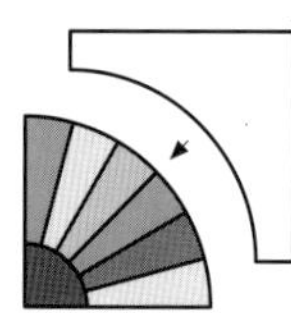

4. Join Fan blocks into diagonal rows with side and corner setting triangles. Join the rows.

5. Add the deep purple border. See "Borders with Corner Squares" on page 125.

6. Layer the quilt top with batting and backing. See "Quiltmaking Techniques" on pages 122–33. Quilt; refer to the photos on pages 61–66 for ideas.

7. Bind with the 2" x 42" purple strips.

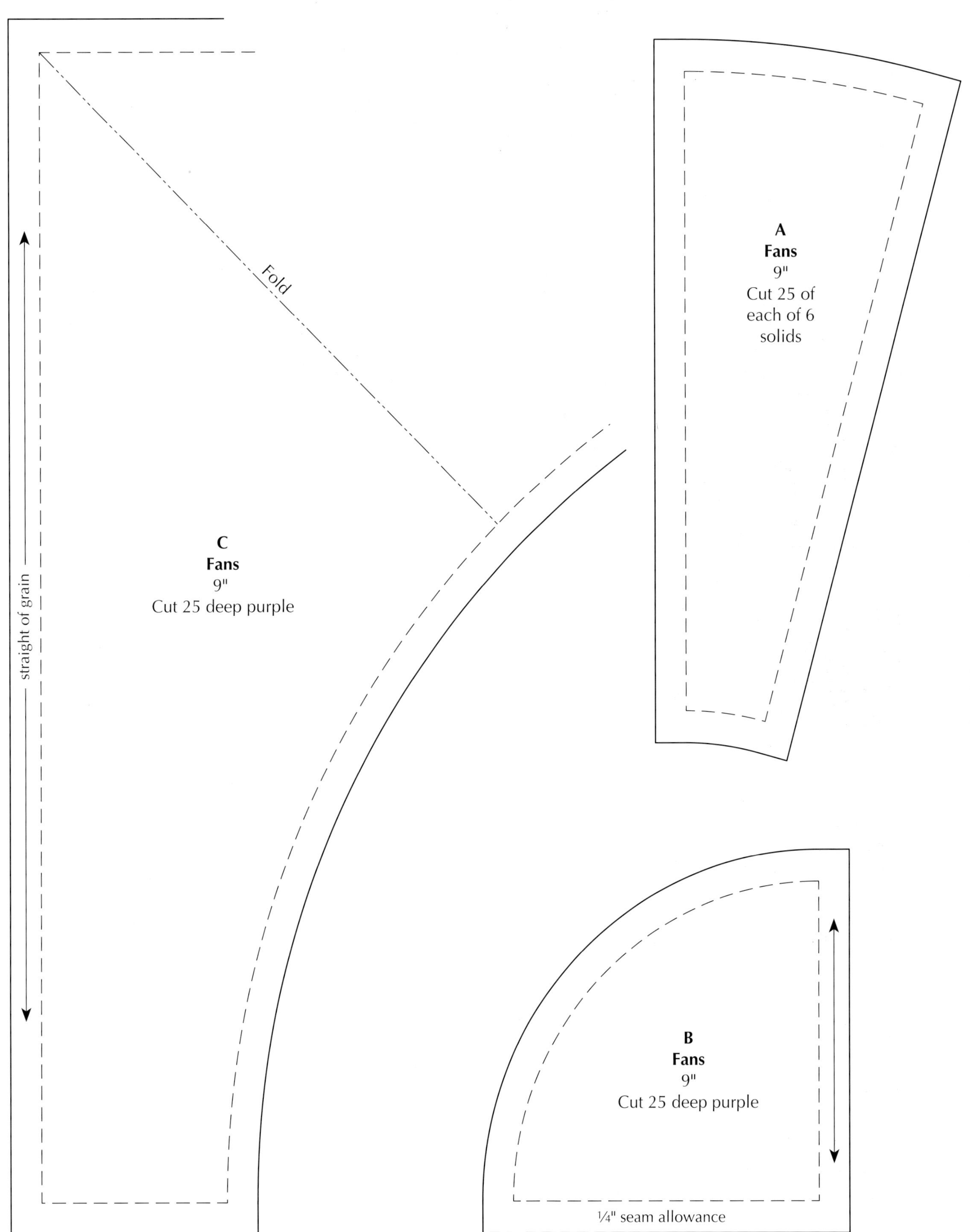
Fold
C
Fans
9"
Cut 25 deep purple
straight of grain
A
Fans
9"
Cut 25 of
each of 6
solids
B
Fans
9"
Cut 25 deep purple
¼" seam allowance

Scrap Star

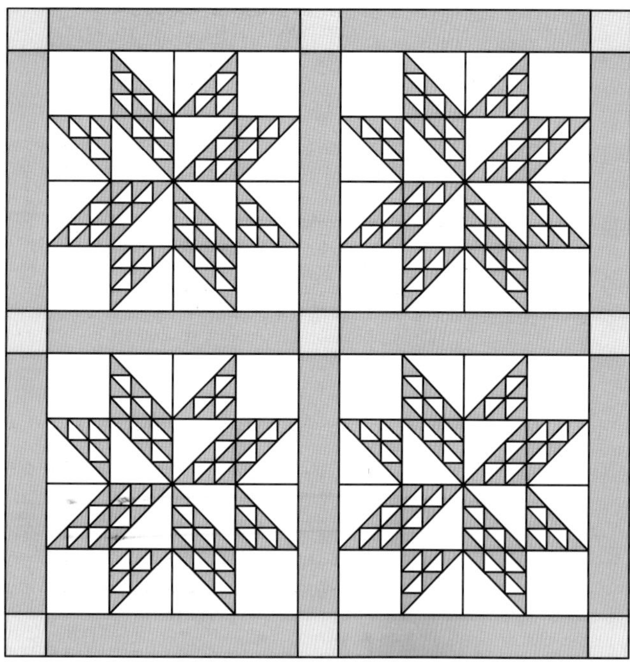

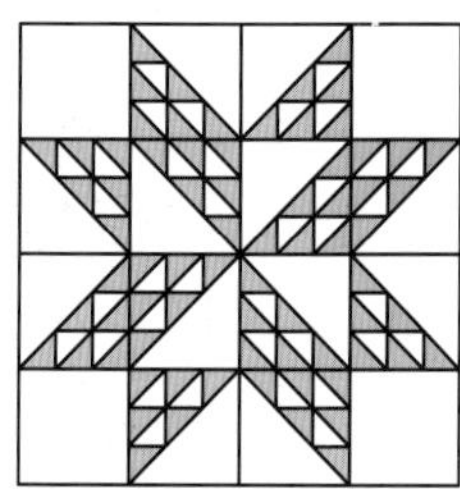

Scrap Star
24" block

Dimensions: 57½" x 57½"
Photos on pages 67–72.

4 blocks, 24", set 2 across and 2 down with 3"-wide sashing and sashing squares; finished without a border.

MATERIALS

44"-wide fabric

¼ yd. each of 9 different red solids for stars
1¼ yds. red solid for sashing and binding
¼ yd. magenta solid for sashing squares
2 yds. caramel solid for stars
3½ yds. fabric for backing and rod sleeve
Batting (100% cotton, packaged, presoaked*)
*Check the manufacturer's directions for presoaking.

CUTTING

All measurements include ¼"-wide seams.

From each of 9 different red solids:
Cut 16 squares, 2⅞" x 2⅞". Cut these squares once diagonally into 32 half-square triangles for a total of 288 triangles.

From the red solid:
Cut 7 lengthwise strips, 2" x 42", for binding.
Cut 12 strips, 3½" x 24½", for sashing.

From the magenta solid:
Cut 9 squares, 3½" x 3½", for sashing squares.

From the caramel solid:
Cut 16 squares, 6½" x 6½", for star background.
Cut 24 squares, 6⅞" x 6⅞". Cut these squares once diagonally into 48 half-square triangles.
Cut 6 strips, 2⅞" x 42". Cut these strips into a total of 72 squares, 2⅞" x 2⅞". Cut once diagonally into 144 half-square triangles.

DIRECTIONS

1. Join 3 different red half-square triangles and 3 caramel half-square triangles to make 3 squares.

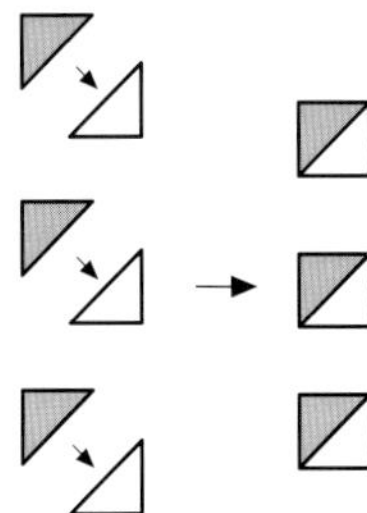

2. Join the 3 squares and 3 red half-square triangles to make 1 large pieced triangle. Make a total of 48 large pieced triangles.

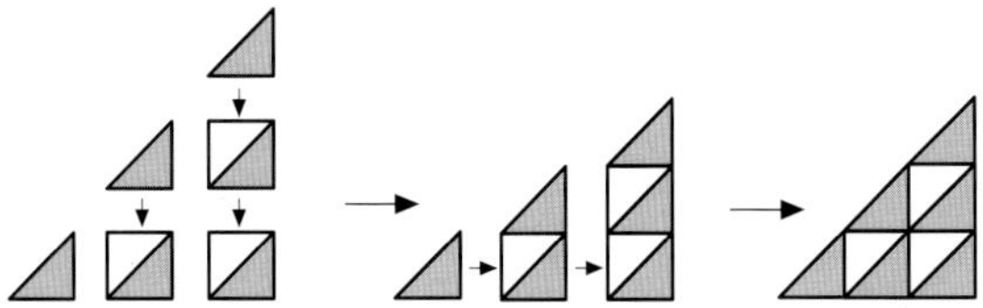

3. Join 1 large pieced triangle and 1 large caramel triangle to make 1 pieced square. Make a total of 48 pieced squares.

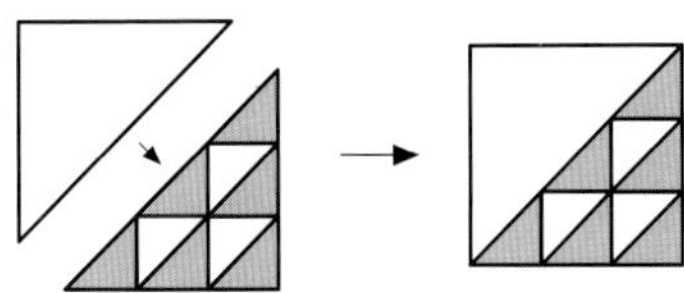

4. Join the pieced squares and plain caramel squares to make rows A and B. Make 8 rows of each.

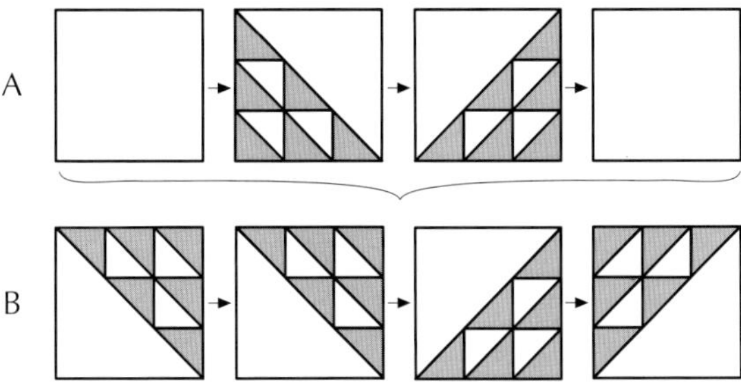

5. Join the rows to make 1 Star block. Make a total of 4 blocks.

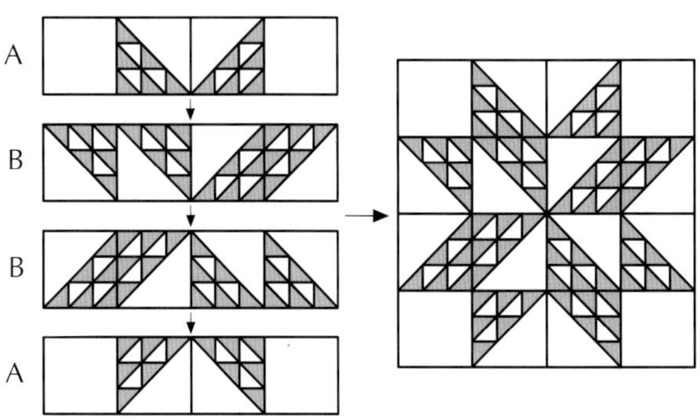

6. Join 3 magenta squares and 2 red sashing strips to make 1 sashing row. Make a total of 3 rows.

7. Join 2 Star blocks and 3 sashing strips to make 1 star row. Make 2 rows.

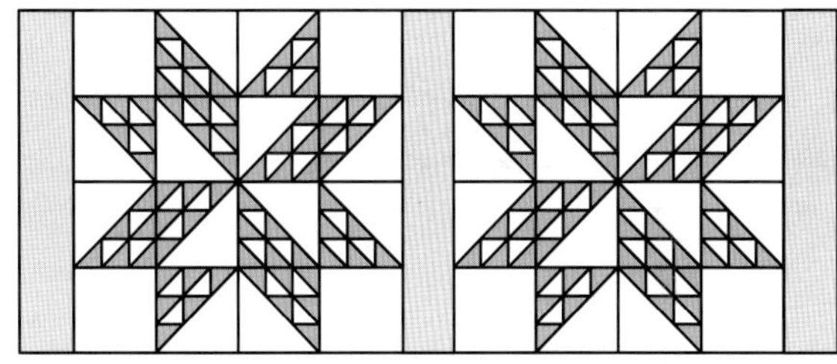

8. Join the sashing rows and the star rows as shown in the quilt plan.
9. Layer the quilt top with batting and backing. See "Quiltmaking Techniques" on pages 122–33. Quilt; refer to the photos on pages 67–72 for ideas.
10. Bind with the 2" x 42" red strips.

STRIPPY BARS

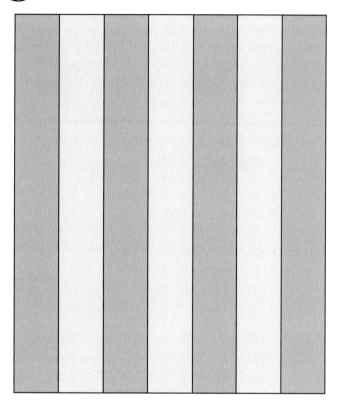

DIMENSIONS: 56½" x 65½"
PHOTOS ON PAGES 73–78.

7 bars (4 dark apricot and 3 pale apricot), 8" wide; finished without a border.

MATERIALS

44"-WIDE FABRIC

2 yds. dark apricot solid for bars and binding
2 yds. pale apricot solid for bars
3½ yds. fabric for backing (seamed crosswise) and rod sleeve
Batting (100% cotton, packaged)

CUTTING

ALL MEASUREMENTS INCLUDE ¼"-WIDE SEAMS.

From the dark apricot solid:
Cut 4 lengthwise strips, 2" x 72", for binding.
Cut 4 lengthwise strips, 8½" x 72", for bars.

From the pale apricot solid:
Cut 3 lengthwise strips, 8½" x 72", for bars.

DIRECTIONS

1. Join the dark apricot and pale apricot strips, alternating the colors as shown in the quilt plan. Trim to 65½" long.
2. Layer the quilt top with batting and backing. See "Quiltmaking Techniques" on pages 122–33. Quilt; refer to the photos on pages 73–78 for ideas.
3. Bind with the 2" x 72" dark apricot strips.

Strippy on Point

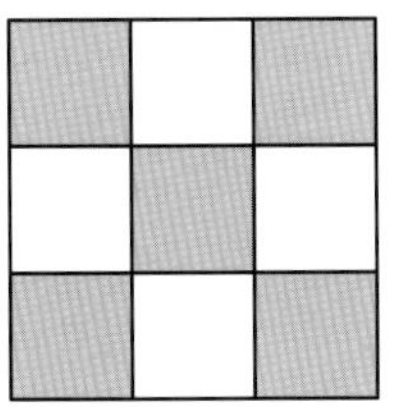

Ninepatch
7½" block

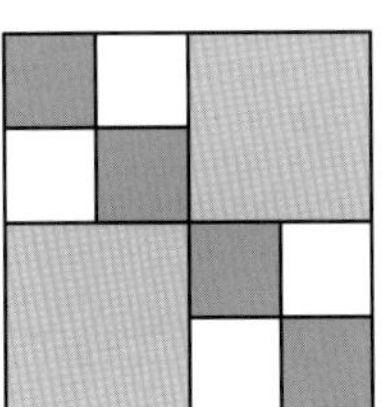

Double Four Patch
7½" block

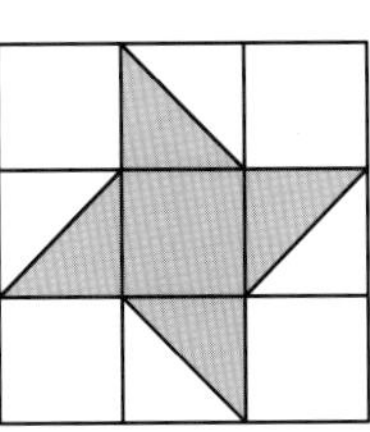

Friendship Star
7½" block

Dimensions: 53½" x 64"
Photos on pages 79–84.

28 blocks (12 Ninepatch, 6 Double Four Patch, and 10 Friendship Star) and 4 half-blocks (Friendship Star), 7½", set on point in 5 vertical rows of 6 blocks each; finished without a border.

Materials

44"-wide fabric

1⅛ yds. cream solid for blocks
1¼ yds. total assorted yellow solids for blocks
2¼ yds. mint green solid for setting triangles and binding
3¼ yds. fabric for backing (seamed crosswise) and rod sleeve
Batting (100% polyester, packaged)

Cutting

All measurements include ¼"-wide seams.

Ninepatch

From the cream solid:
Cut 4 strips, 3" x 42".
From the assorted yellow solids:
Cut 5 strips, 3" x 42".

Double Four Patch

From the cream solid:
Cut 2 strips, 2⅜" x 42".
From the assorted yellow solids:
Cut 2 strips, 2⅜" x 42".
Cut 2 strips, 4¼" x 42". Cut these strips into a total of 12 squares, 4¼" x 4¼".

Friendship Star

From the cream solid:
Cut 4 strips, 3" x 42". Cut these strips into a total of 56 squares, 3" x 3".
Cut 3 strips, 3⅜" x 42". Cut these strips into a total of 28 squares, 3⅜" x 3⅜". Cut once diagonally into 56 half-square triangles.
From the assorted yellow solids:
Cut 1 strip, 3" x 42". Cut this strip into a total of 14 squares, 3" x 3".
Cut 3 strips, 3⅜" x 42". Cut these strips into a total of 28 squares, 3⅜" x 3⅜". Cut once diagonally into 56 half-square triangles.
From the mint green solid:
Cut 14 squares, 11⅞" x 11⅞". Cut these squares twice diagonally into 56 setting triangles; you will use 54.
Cut 6 squares, 6⅛" x 6⅛". Cut these squares once diagonally into 12 half-square setting triangles for the upper and lower edges of the quilt.
Cut 6 strips, 2" x 42", for binding.

DIRECTIONS

Ninepatch

1. Join 4 yellow 3" x 42" strips and 2 cream 3" x 42" strips to make 2 units as shown. The units should measure 8" wide when sewn. Cut the units into 24 segments, each 3" wide.

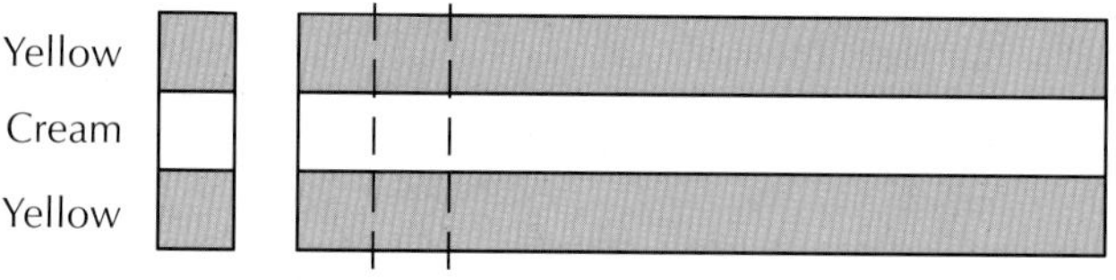

Make 2.

2. Join 1 yellow 3" x 42" strip and 2 cream 3" x 42" strips to make 1 unit as shown. The unit should measure 8" wide when sewn. Cut the unit into 12 segments, each 3" wide.

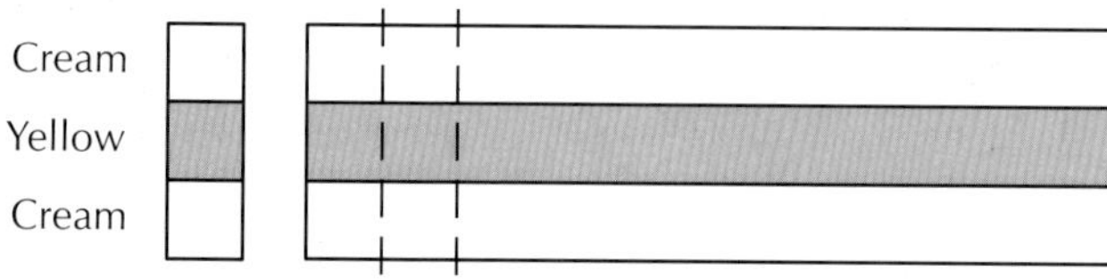

Make 1.

3. Join the segments as shown to make 1 Ninepatch block. Make a total of 12 blocks.

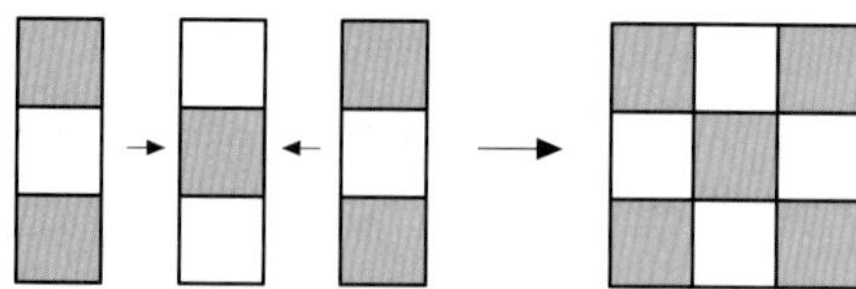

Double Four Patch

1. Join 2 yellow 2⅜" x 42" strips and 2 cream 2⅜" x 42" strips to make 2 units as shown. The units should measure 4¼" wide when sewn. Cut the units into 24 segments, each 2⅜" wide.

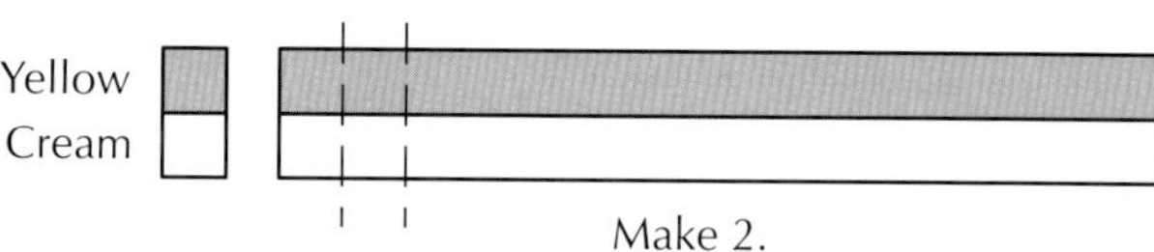

Make 2.

2. Join the segments, alternating colors, to make 1 Four Patch square. Make a total of 12 squares.

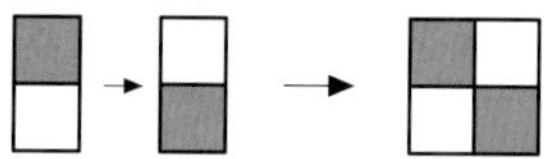

3. Join 1 Four Patch square and 1 yellow square to make a rectangle. Make a total of 12 rectangles.

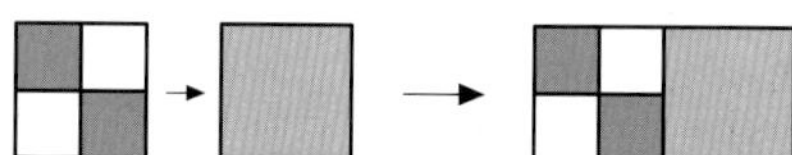

4. Join 2 rectangles from step 5, reversing the pieces, to make a Double Four Patch block. Make a total of 6 blocks.

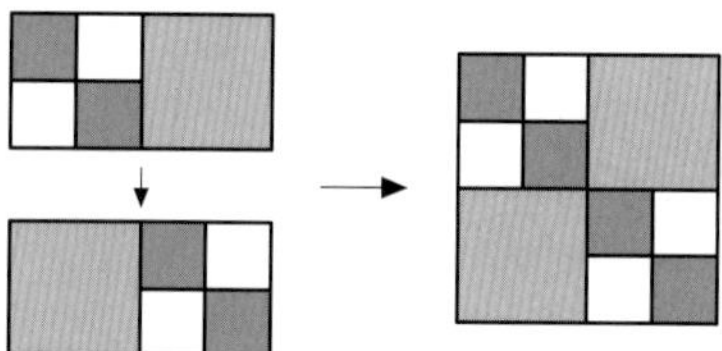

Friendship Star

1. Join a yellow half-square triangle and a cream half-square triangle to make a square. Make a total of 56 squares.

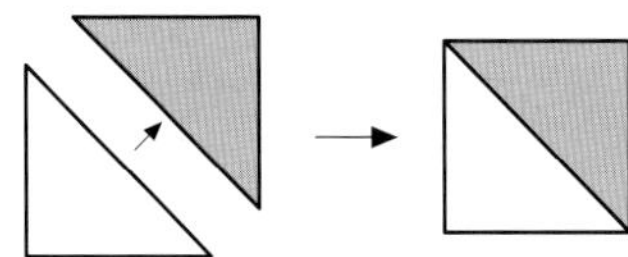

2. Join 4 cream squares, 1 yellow square, and 4 pieced squares to make 3 rows. Join rows to make 1 block. Make a total of 14 blocks.

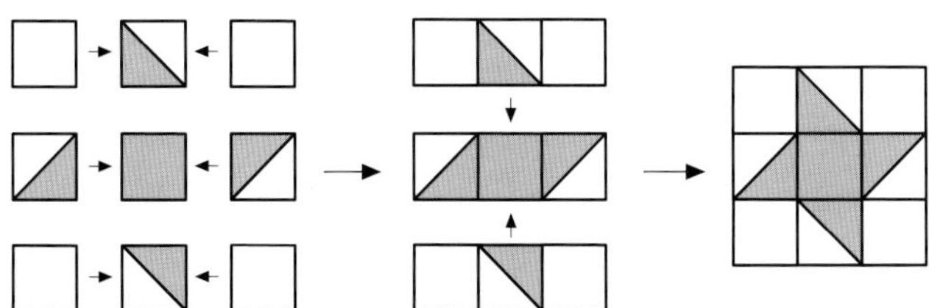

3. Cut 4 Friendship Star blocks in half from corner to corner, adding a ¼"-wide seam allowance to the edge, to make 4 half-blocks for the top and bottom of each row. Discard the smaller half-blocks.

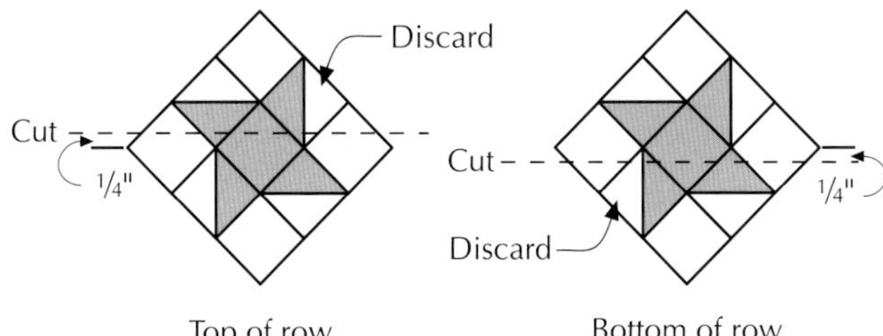

Assembling the Quilt Top

1. Join the blocks and mint green setting triangles into vertical strips as shown. Make 2 strips of Ninepatch blocks, 2 strips of Friendship Star blocks, and 1 strip of Double Four Patch blocks.

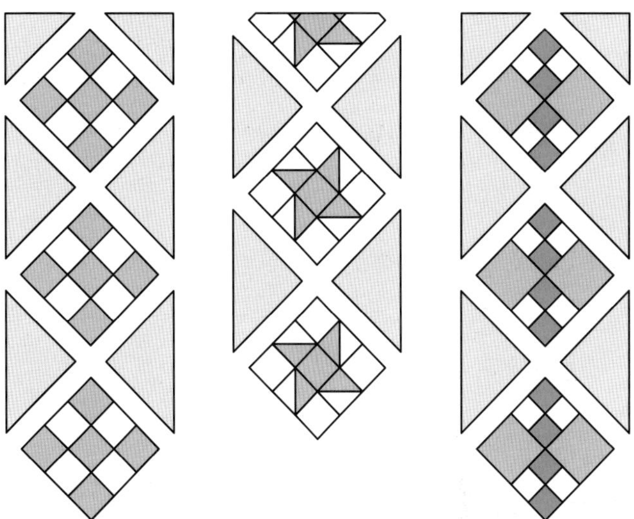

2. Join the strips as shown in the quilt plan.
3. Layer the quilt top with batting and backing. See "Quiltmaking Techniques" on pages 122–33. Quilt; refer to the photos on pages 79–84 for ideas.
4. Bind with the 2" x 42" mint green strips.

Single Wedding Ring

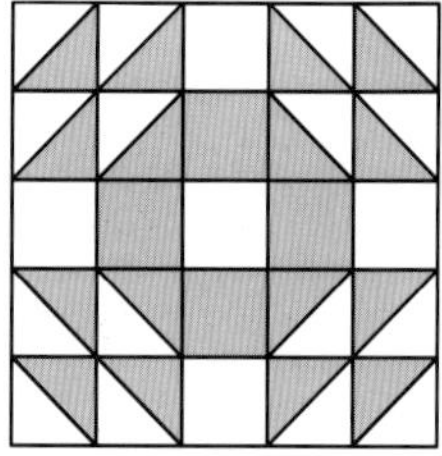

Single Wedding Ring
10" block

Dimensions: 76" x 90"
Photos on pages 85–90.

32 blocks (20 pieced and 12 plain), 10", set on point 4 across and 5 down; 2"-wide inner border and 7½"-wide outer border, mitered.

MATERIALS

44"-wide fabric

6¼ yds. white for blocks, outer border, and binding
2¾ yds. blue solid for blocks and inner border
5⅔ yds. fabric for backing (seamed lengthwise) and rod sleeve
Batting (100% polyester, packaged)

CUTTING

All measurements include ¼"-wide seams.

From the white:

Cut 12 squares, 10½" x 10½".
Cut 2 squares, 8" x 8". Cut once diagonally into 4 corner setting triangles.
Cut 4 squares, 15⅜" x 15⅜". Cut twice diagonally to make 16 side setting triangles; you will use 14.
Cut 7 strips, 2½" x 42". Cut these strips into a total of 100 squares, 2½" x 2½".
Cut 12 strips, 2⅞" x 42". Cut these strips into a total of 160 squares, 2⅞" x 2⅞". Cut once diagonally to make 320 half-square triangles.
Cut 2 lengthwise strips, 8" x 93", and 2 lengthwise strips, 8" x 79", for outer border.
Cut 4 lengthwise strips, 2" x 93", for binding.

From the blue solid:

Cut 2 lengthwise strips, 2½" x 93", and 2 lengthwise strips, 2½" x 79", for inner border.
Cut 3 lengthwise strips, 2½" wide. Cut these strips into a total of 80 squares, 2½" x 2½".
Cut 6 lengthwise strips, 2⅞" x 93". Cut these strips into a total of 160 squares, 2⅞" x 2⅞". Cut once diagonally to make 320 half-square triangles.

DIRECTIONS

1. Join 1 blue half-square triangle and 1 white half-square triangle to make 1 square. Make a total of 320 squares.

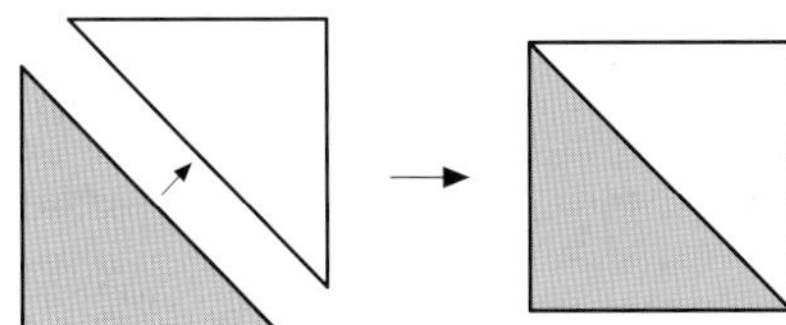

2. Join 16 pieced squares, 4 blue squares, and 5 white 2½" squares to make 1 block. Make a total of 20 blocks.

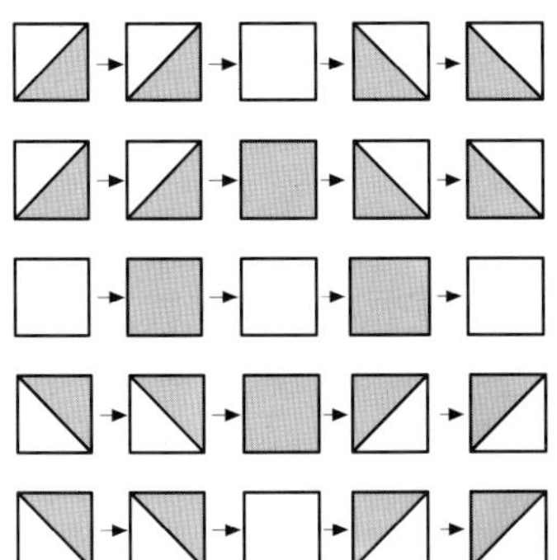

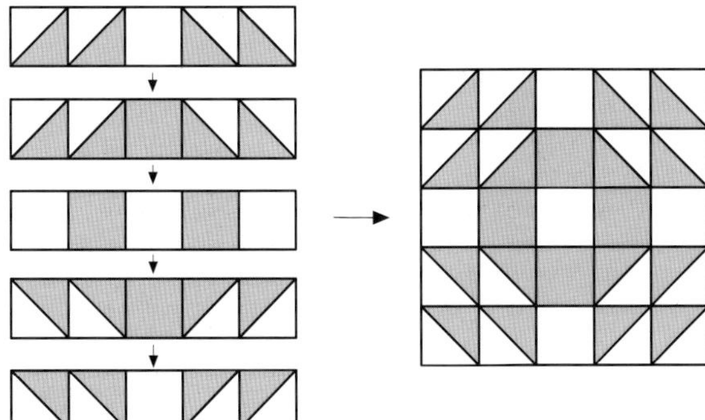

3. Join the pieced blocks and the white 10½" squares into diagonal rows with side and corner setting triangles. Join the rows.

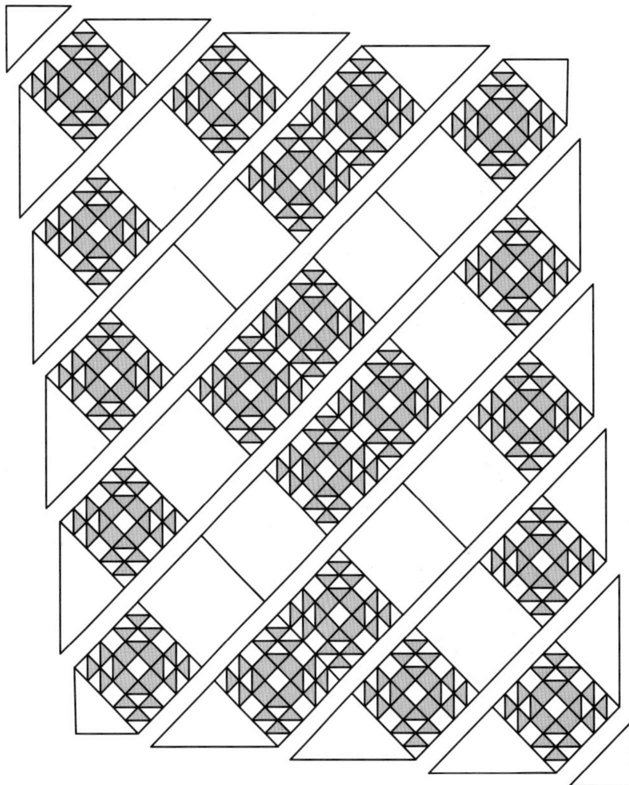

4. Add the border. See "Borders with Mitered Corners" on pages 124–25.

5. Layer the quilt top with batting and backing. See "Quiltmaking Techniques" on pages 122–33. Quilt; refer to the photos on pages 85–90 for ideas.

6. Bind with the 2" x 93" white strips.

Log Cabin

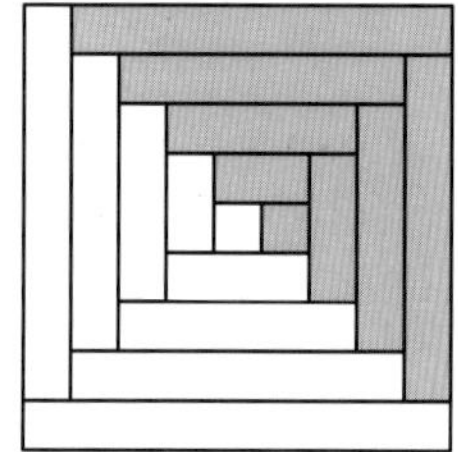

Log Cabin
$6^{3}/_{4}$" block

Dimensions: $79^{1}/_{2}$" x $79^{1}/_{2}$"
Photos on pages 91–96.

64 blocks, $6^{3}/_{4}$", set 8 across and 8 down; $12^{1}/_{2}$"-wide border.

MATERIALS

44"-wide fabric

$^{1}/_{4}$ yd. caramel solid for center squares
$3^{3}/_{4}$ yds. rust solid for borders and binding

Assorted rust solids for blocks in the following amounts:
$^{1}/_{4}$ yd. for round 1
$^{1}/_{2}$ yd. for round 2
$^{5}/_{8}$ yd. for round 3
$^{3}/_{4}$ yd. for round 4

Assorted blue solids for blocks in the following amounts:
$^{3}/_{8}$ yd. for round 1
$^{1}/_{2}$ yd. for round 2
$^{2}/_{3}$ yd. for round 3
$^{7}/_{8}$ yd. for round 4
$5^{1}/_{8}$ yds. fabric for backing and rod sleeve
Batting (60/40 wool/polyester, off the roll)

CUTTING

All measurements include $^{1}/_{4}$"-wide seams.

From the caramel solid:
Cut 2 strips $1^{1}/_{4}$" x 42". Cut these strips into 64 squares, $1^{1}/_{4}$" x $1^{1}/_{4}$".

From the rust solid for border and binding:
Cut 2 strips, 13" x $57^{1}/_{2}$", for border.
Cut 2 strips, 13" x 80", for border.
Cut 8 strips, 2" x 42", for binding.

From the assorted rust solids:
Cut strips $1^{1}/_{4}$" x 42". Cut 64 of each of the following:

- $1^{1}/_{4}$" squares and $1^{1}/_{4}$" x 2" rectangles for round 1.
- $1^{1}/_{4}$" x $2^{3}/_{4}$" and $1^{1}/_{4}$" x $3^{1}/_{2}$" rectangles for round 2.
- $1^{1}/_{4}$" x $4^{1}/_{4}$" and $1^{1}/_{4}$" x 5" rectangles for round 3.
- $1^{1}/_{4}$" x $5^{3}/_{4}$" and $1^{1}/_{4}$" x $6^{1}/_{2}$" rectangles for round 4.

From the assorted blue solids:
Cut strips $1^{1}/_{4}$" x 42". Cut 64 of each of the following:

- $1^{1}/_{4}$" x 2" and $1^{1}/_{4}$" x $2^{3}/_{4}$" rectangles for round 1.
- $1^{1}/_{4}$" x $3^{1}/_{2}$" and $1^{1}/_{4}$" x $4^{1}/_{4}$" rectangles for round 2.
- $1^{1}/_{4}$" x 5" and $1^{1}/_{4}$" x $5^{3}/_{4}$" rectangles for round 3.
- $1^{1}/_{4}$" x $6^{1}/_{2}$" and $1^{1}/_{4}$" x $7^{1}/_{4}$" rectangles for round 4.

DIRECTIONS

1. Join a 1¼" rust square to the right edge of a 1¼" caramel center square.

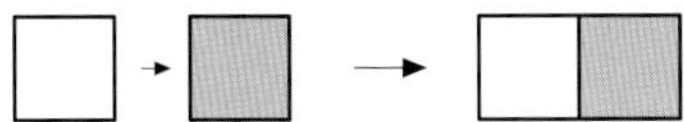

2. Join a 2" rust rectangle to the unit.

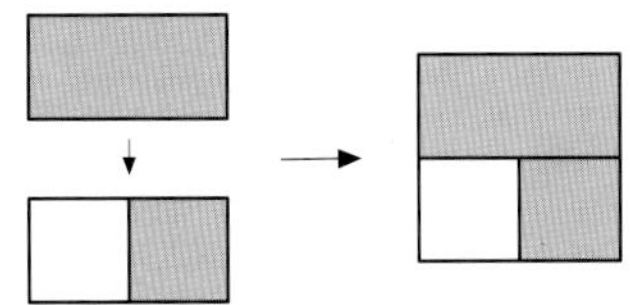

3. Join a 2" blue rectangle to the unit.

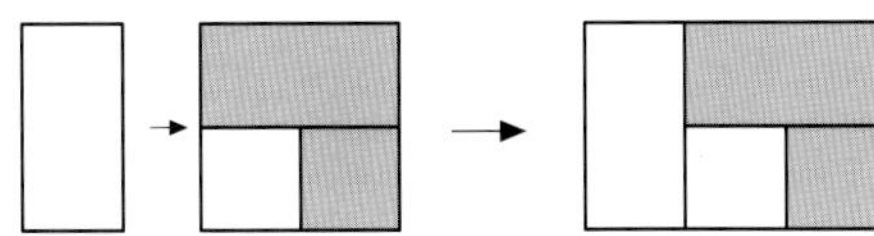

4. Join a 2¾" blue rectangle to the unit.

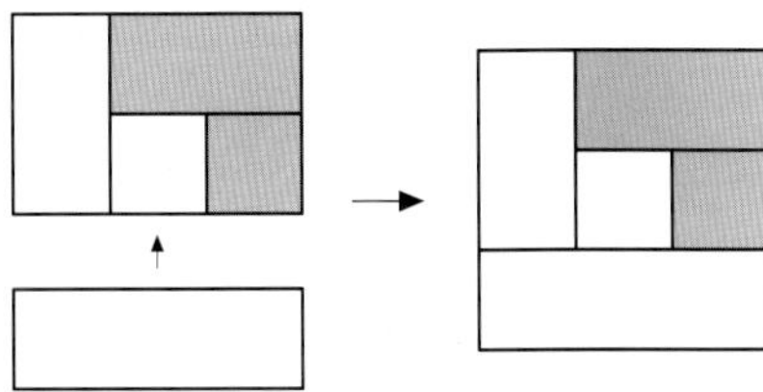

5. Working in a counterclockwise direction, continue to join rust and blue rectangles to fit the unit. Make a total of 64 blocks.

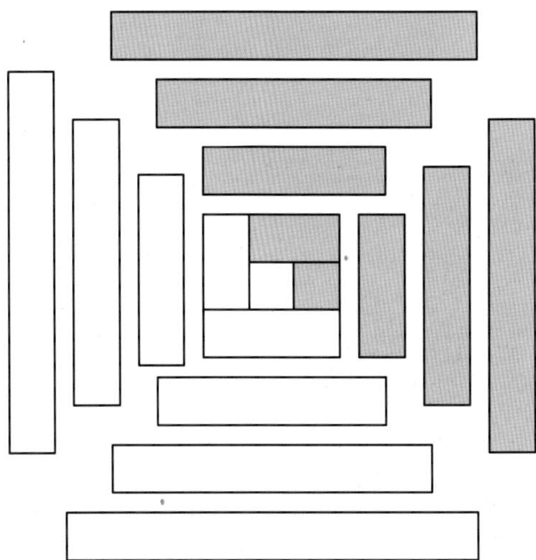

6. Join blocks in rows of 8 as shown in the quilt plan. Join the rows.
7. Add rust borders. See "Straight-Cut Borders" on page 123.
8. Layer the quilt top with batting and backing. See "Quiltmaking Techniques" on pages 122–33. Quilt; refer to the photos on pages 91–96 for ideas.
9. Bind with the 2" x 42" rust strips.

Quiltmaking Techniques

The following pages include basic techniques for cutting, assembling, marking, and finishing your quilt. You'll also find information on batting and tips for machine quilting.

Rotary Cutting

The proper rotary equipment will speed the measuring and cutting of your fabric.

Rotary cutters. These round-bladed cutters enable you to quickly cut strips and pieces without templates. Rotary cutters are available in large and small sizes.

Rotary mats. A self-healing rotary cutting mat holds the fabric in place and protects both the blade and the work surface. An 18" x 24" or 24" x 36" mat allows you to cut most pieces; a smaller mat is ideal for scrap fabrics.

Rotary rulers. These clear acrylic guides are ⅛" thick and come in a variety of sizes. The 6" x 12" and 12" x 24" rulers are appropriate for most cutting; a 15" x 15" square is useful for cutting large squares.

To cut strips:

1. Fold the fabric in half lengthwise, with selvages matching. Lay the fabric on the cutting mat.
2. Align a square ruler with the fold of the fabric and place a cutting ruler to the left.

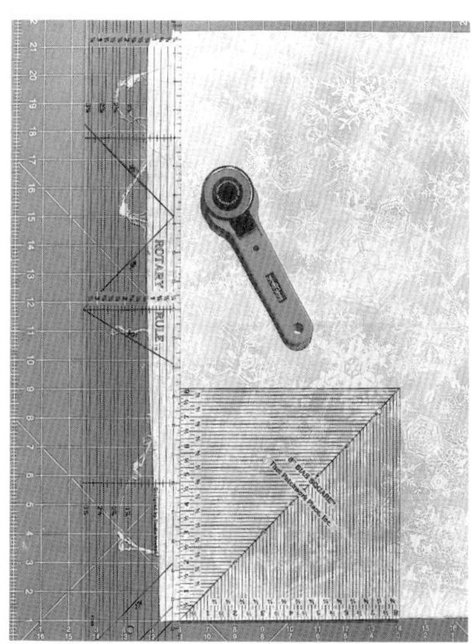

3. Remove the square and cut along the edge of the ruler, rolling the cutter away from you.

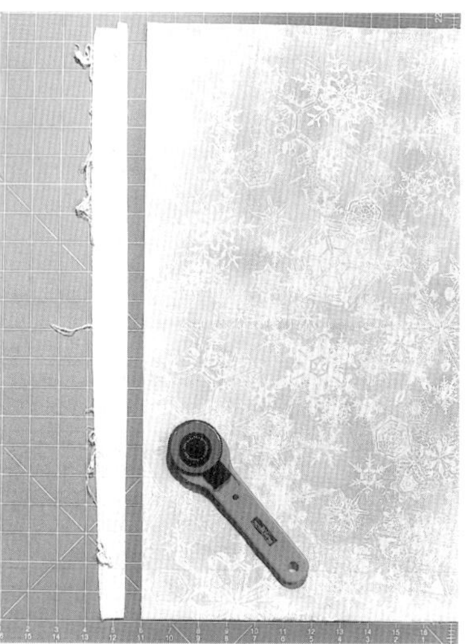

4. Move the ruler to the right, aligning the ruler markings at the desired width with the cut edge of the fabric. Cut fabric into strips.

To cut squares:

Cut strips into squares the width of the strip. You may cut through several layers of strips at once.

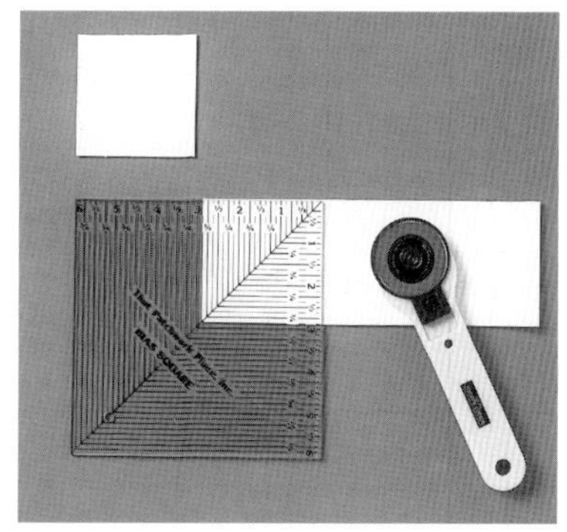

To cut half-square triangles:

1. Cut strips into squares the width of the strip.
2. Place the ruler on each square diagonally from corner to corner. Cut into 2 triangles.

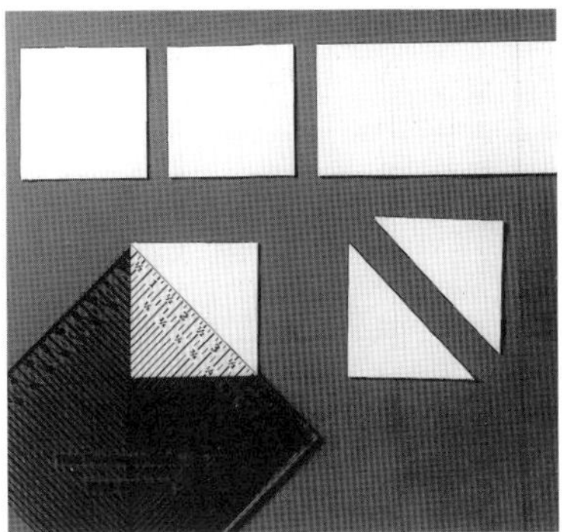

To cut quarter-square triangles:

1. Cut strips into squares the width of the strip.
2. Cut the squares twice diagonally into 4 triangles.

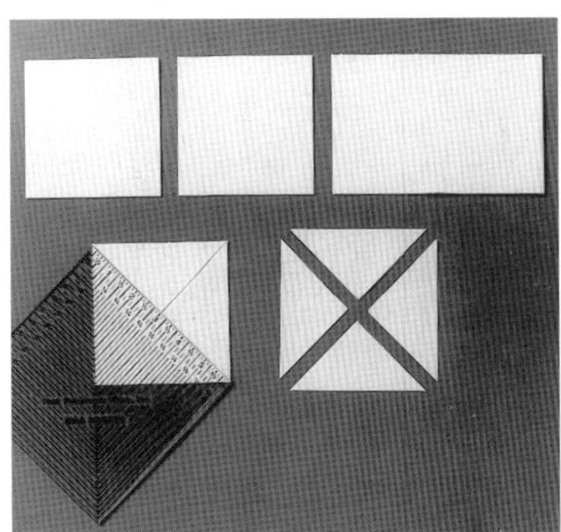

Adding Borders

The assembly instructions for each quilt will tell you whether to cut border strips crosswise or lengthwise. If you cut lengthwise borders, extra inches are allowed in the cutting instructions. If you cut crosswise borders, you'll need to seam the strips for the necessary length and press the seams open. With lengthwise and crosswise strips, you'll trim the strips to the correct length once you've measured the quilt top.

Square in a Square, Ohio Star, and Log Cabin have straight-cut borders. Single Wedding Ring has a double mitered border, and Fans has a border with corner squares. Directions for these three borders follow.

-- STRAIGHT-CUT BORDERS --

1. Measure the length of the quilt at the center, from the top edge to the bottom edge.

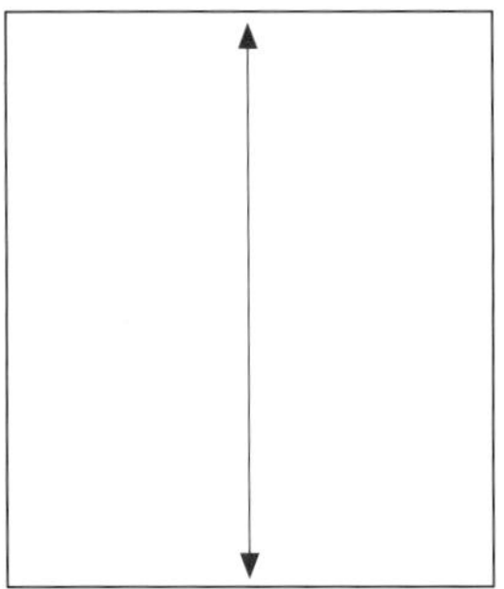

2. Cut two strips equal to the quilt length measured in step 1. Fold each strip in half and place a pin at the center. Find the center point of each half and mark with a pin to divide the strip into quarters. Repeat this pinning procedure along the raw edge of the quilt top.

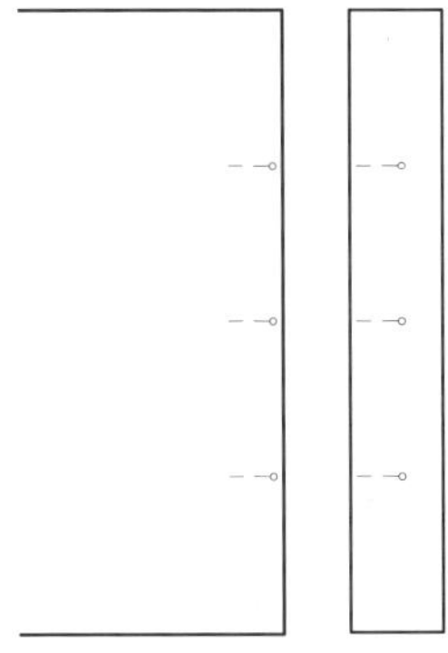

3. Pin the border strips to the sides of the quilt, matching the pins and easing to fit as necessary. Stitch, using a ¼"-wide seam allowance. Press seams toward borders.
4. For the top and bottom borders, measure the width of the quilt top at the center, including the side borders. Cut two border strips to this length and attach to the quilt top as described for the side borders in steps 2 and 3.

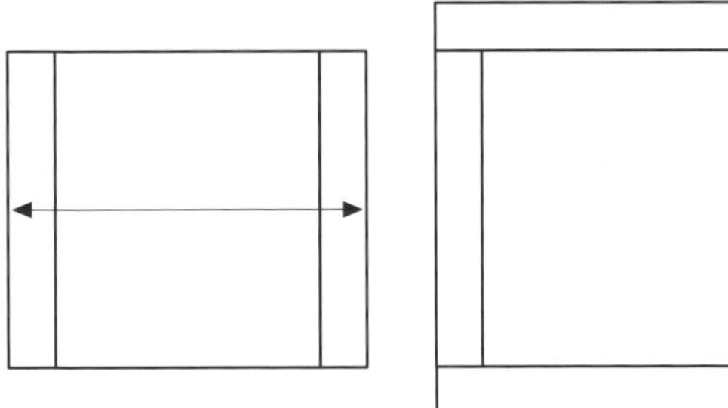

––––– BORDERS –––––
WITH MITERED CORNERS

1. For crosswise-cut borders, estimate the outside dimensions (length and width) of the completed quilt with the borders and add 3" to each measurement. Piece the strips as necessary and cut them to these lengths.

2. If your quilt has more than one border, as in Single Wedding Ring on page 85, seam the border strips using a ¼"-wide seam allowance.

3. Measure the quilt top at the center to determine the finished size. Record the length and width, minus ½" each for seam allowances.

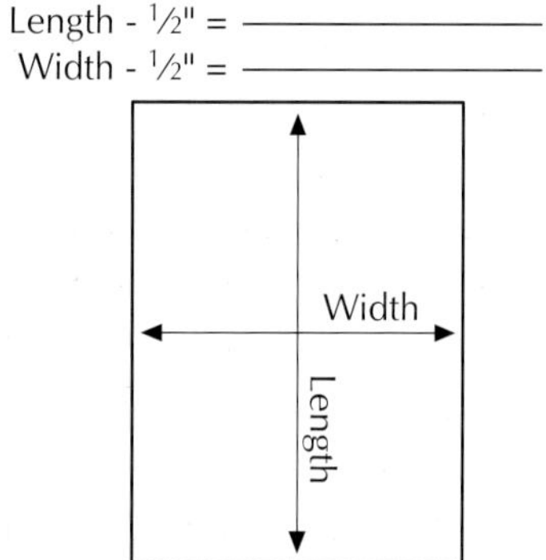

4. Find the center of each border strip and mark with a pin. Measure from this point, in both directions, a distance equal to half the length measurement from step 3 for the lengthwise borders and half the width measurement from step 3 for the crosswise borders. Place pins at these points. Establish the center of each half of the strip and mark with a pin to divide the border strip into quarters.

5. Find the center of each side of the pieced quilt top and mark with a pin. Measure ¼" from the outer edge of each corner and mark with a pin. When attaching the borders, this is the point where the stitching starts or ends. Establish and pin the quarter marks on the quilt top as you did on the border strips.

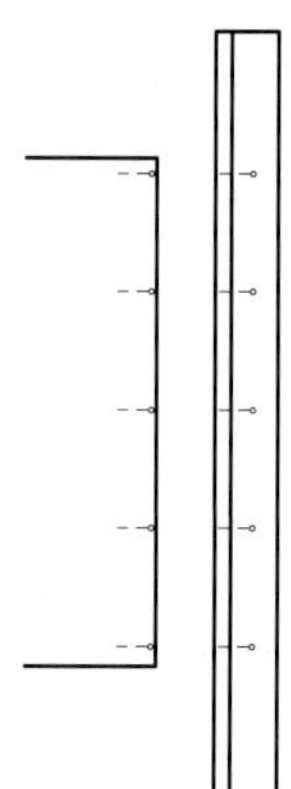

6. Pin the borders to the quilt top, matching pins and easing to fit as necessary. Stitch, using a ¼"-wide seam allowance. Begin and end stitching ¼" from each corner of the quilt top. Backstitch to anchor.

7. Miter one corner at a time. Spread a corner of the quilt smooth and straight on the pressing area with the strip on Side A overlapping the strip on Side B. Make sure the borders form a 90° angle.

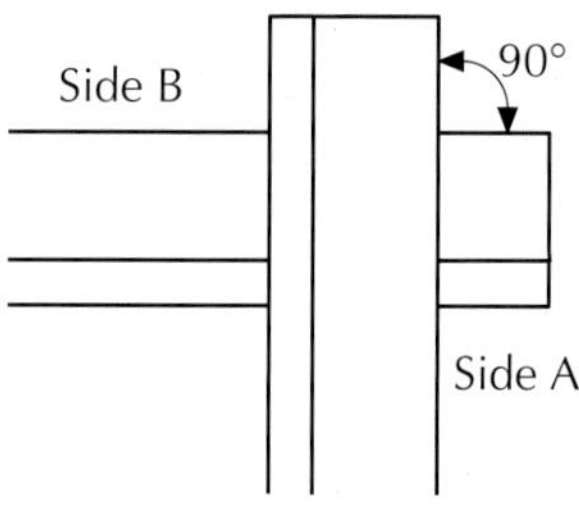

8. Fold under the excess border fabric on Side A at a 45° angle. Make sure the top and bottom edges of the strips line up exactly. Press the fold flat; pin to secure. This fold is the sewing line.

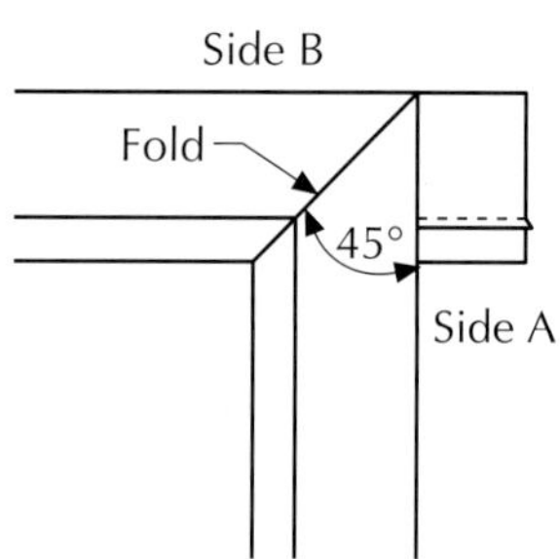

9. Flip the Side A border to match the raw edge of the Side B border, folding the quilt on the diagonal with the wrong side showing. Pin across the fold to secure. Stitch on the fold from the outside edge of the border toward the pieced center. Stop stitching ¼" from the inner edge of the border and backstitch. Trim the excess border strips ¼" from the stitching. Press the seam open. Repeat on the remaining corners.

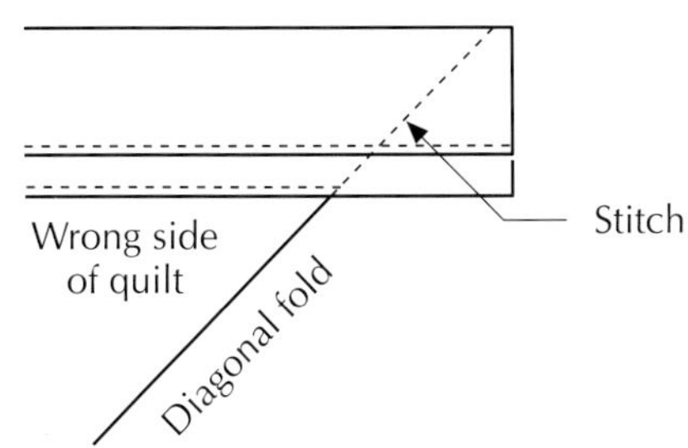

----- BORDERS ----- WITH CORNER SQUARES

1. Measure the length and width of the quilt through the center from edge to edge.

2. Follow steps 2 and 3 for "Straight-Cut Borders" on page 123 to cut the strips, mark with pins, and seam to the side edges of the quilt top.

3. Cut two border strips to the original width measurement. Seam the corner squares to the ends of these strips.

4. Pin and stitch the strips with corner squares to the top and bottom edges of the quilt as you did the side strips, matching seams at the corners.

Marking the Quilt Top

Clear, accurate marking of your quilt top is the prelude to successful machine quilting. The marking tools and techniques discussed below will make easy work of this important step.

----- MARKERS -----

Fabric Markers. You'll find a vast array of fabric markers at quilt shops and fabric stores. You can't be too careful when choosing a marker. The marks must be easily seen during quilting, yet they must wash out completely when the quilt is finished.

Read about fabric markers in recently published magazines and books and ask other quilters which markers they use and why. Then test different markers on your fabrics to decide which one is best for your project.

To test a marker, cut an extra 3" x 3" square of each fabric you're using on the quilt top. Mark these pieces with the markers you're considering using and indicate which marker made each mark. Set aside. Once you've finished piecing the top, wash the marked squares the way you plan to wash the finished quilt. It takes about as long to machine piece a quilt top as it does to machine quilt it, so if the marks come out of your samples, they will come out of your finished quilt.

Pencils. A variety of colored pencils are available: white, yellow, blue, and silver are common choices. Select a brand that doesn't contain a large percentage of wax, which is difficult to remove, and sharpen the pencil to a fine point when using.

Some hand quilters use soft- or hard-lead pencils, but they tend to be difficult to see when machine quilting. Hard-lead pencils may distort fabric.

Soap slivers. Fine soap slivers work well on small quilts made of very dark fabrics.

Chalk wheels. Use chalk only if you're quilting by hand and marking as you go. Chalk isn't suitable for machine quilting because it brushes off quickly.

Masking tape. Tape isn't recommended for machine quilting. If you accidentally sew over the tape, you'll find it difficult to remove the sticky pieces.

Water-Soluble Marking Pens. If you use one of the water-soluble marking pens or fading pens (they resemble felt-tip pens), be aware that heat permanently sets the chemicals, which means you can't iron your quilt top once it's been marked. Even if the marks seem to have disappeared, the chemicals remain in the quilt and may reappear over time.

The marks from fading pens generally disappear within twenty-four hours, sooner in areas of high humidity.

MARKING METHODS

There are many ways of transferring a quilting design to your quilt top. My favorites are the light box or glass-topped table for light to medium fabrics, tulle for large designs or whole-cloth quilts, and stencils for dark fabrics.

Light box. A light shining through a light box or glass-topped table enables you to trace your design onto the quilt top. Before you begin, photocopy your design so that you have the original to refer to. Tape your design to the light box or table, position the quilt top, and trace the design. Make light but distinct lines that you can follow when machine quilting.

Tulle. This method is suitable only if you plan to use a quilter's water-soluble marking pen to mark your quilt top; pencils distort the tulle. You'll also need a waterproof permanent marker. Be sure the pen says "waterproof" and "permanent." A pen that is not can lead to disaster.

Before you make your tulle pattern, test both pens, because the chemicals in the water-soluble pen may transfer ink from the permanent marker onto your quilt top—where it *will* be permanent!

To make a tulle pattern:

1. Photocopy your design and, using the permanent marker, trace a portion of it onto a small piece of tulle. Wash the tulle to remove the excess ink.
2. Lay the tulle test pattern over a scrap of fabric and mark the design onto the fabric using the water-soluble pen. If no ink from the permanent marker is transferred to the fabric, it's safe to make your full-size tulle pattern and mark your quilt top.

Stencils. Many precut stencils are available in quilt shops and fabric stores. However, if you draw your own quilting designs and your fabrics are too dark to mark using a light table, you'll need to make your own stencils.

Use heavy cardboard or template plastic for your stencils. Cardboard must be stiff enough to stand up to the marking yet easy to cut.

To make a stencil:

1. Photocopy your design, then glue the copy onto the cardboard or trace it onto template plastic with a permanent marker.
2. Using a double-bladed craft knife and a rotary mat, carefully cut the narrow spaces for the quilting lines. Be sure to leave bridges every 1"–2" so the stencil doesn't fall apart.

– – REMOVING THE MARKINGS – –

Whatever you use to mark your quilt, you must remove the markings completely once the quilt is finished. Some quilters attempt to remove marks from water-soluble pens as they go, but spraying or dabbing with a wet cloth only moves the chemicals into the batting. The marks may reappear at any time.

The only truly satisfactory way to remove markings is to wash your quilt. Don't be reluctant to wash your quilt; if it's made well enough to withstand day-to-day use, it can certainly be washed.

To wash your quilt, fill the machine with cold water. Immerse the quilt (without soap, detergents, or water softener), agitate it for 3 to 4 minutes, and spin it dry. Remove the quilt and fill the machine again with cold water. This time, use a quilt washing compound such as Orvus Paste® or Mountain Mist Ensure®, or use a nonmedicated horse or dog shampoo. Run the quilt through a short wash and a complete rinse and spin cycle.

Don't put your quilts in the clothes dryer. It's too hard on the fabric. You can hang your quilts on the line to dry. To avoid clothespin marks on the quilt, hang it by the rod sleeve before it is stitched down. Or, cut a separate length of fabric about 4" wide and equal in length to the width of the quilt. Using large stitches, sew the strip to the quilt close to the binding or in-the-ditch of the binding; hang the quilt from the strip.

If you have two closely spaced clotheslines, you can attach strips of fabric to the top and bottom edges and hang the quilt in a U-shape. Hang the quilt, backing side up, or cover it with a sheet.

You can dry your quilts flat, outside or inside. Put a sheet over and under the quilt to protect it. A trampoline makes a great drying rack because it allows air to circulate. The faster a quilt dries, the better, because dye transfer is less likely to happen when quilts dry quickly.

Dye Transfer

Prewashing removes excess dye, but color may still be transferred from one fabric to another in a quilt when the fabrics are wet. This dye transfer may be permanent. The problem doesn't happen often, but if you've ever had a quilt discolored in this way, you know the heartbreak it causes.

To prevent dye transfer, test your fabrics after prewashing but before cutting them. Cut two pieces of your lightest-colored fabric, each large enough to accommodate 1" squares of all your other fabrics. Thoroughly wet all fabrics and make a fabric sandwich by placing the 1" squares between the two large squares. Press the fabrics together and, keeping the sandwich flat, leave overnight or until dry. If color from a small square appears on the light fabric, replace the problem fabric and test again. Sometimes the lightest fabric is the offender, and by changing it you may be able to use all the colors you wish.

Choosing Batting

Even for the experienced quilter, selecting a batting is no simple task. Battings possess different properties that greatly affect the look of a finished quilt. Battings also respond differently to machine and hand quilting.

Experiment with different brands and kinds of batting until you find one that suits your needs. This search can take years and many quilts! To short-cut the process, tap into the knowledge of your local quilt-shop owner and quilt-guild members. Some quilt shops and quilt-supply catalogs offer batting swatch samples you can experiment with.

Batting comes prepackaged or "off the roll" in a variety of weights and fibers. Most battings are made of one or a combination of three fibers: cotton, wool, and polyester. The fiber content governs, to a degree, the amount of quilting necessary to hold the quilt together. Always take note of the manufacturer's recommendations on how far apart to space the quilting lines. If there are no instructions on the package or with the roll, follow these spacing guidelines:

- 100% cotton or wool: ½"–1"
- Cotton/polyester or wool/polyester blends: 1"– 2"
- 100% polyester: up to 4"

As you consider your choices, keep in mind that all quilts shrink as they're being quilted, whether by hand or machine. The more quilting you do and the thicker the batting, the more a quilt will shrink.

COTTON AND COTTON/POLYESTER

Most cotton and cotton/polyester battings are relatively dense and hold the fabric layers in place, preventing them from shifting. Quilts made with cotton or cotton/polyester batting retain their loft, or spring, over the years. Some quilters find 100% cotton batting difficult to hand quilt because it resists the needle, but you won't have this problem with machine quilting.

Cotton batting may shrink slightly when washed, giving a quilt an antique look. Because it breathes, cotton is considered more comfortable than polyester. And cotton is durable—just think how long cotton quilts have been around.

WOOL AND WOOL/POLYESTER

Battings made of wool or a blend of wool and polyester have a higher loft than cotton batting. Wool batting clings to the fabrics like cotton batting, but because it's softer, wool tends to shift slightly. Good quilting techniques are especially important with wool batting. Wool is wonderfully warm, soft, and durable and well worth a little extra effort.

POLYESTER

This batting comes in a variety of weights and lofts and is usually bonded or glazed to prevent fiber migration. The thicker the batting, the more difficult it is to quilt. The maximum batting thickness recommended for hand or machine quilting is 3 ounces off the roll, which is approximately ⅜" thick; anything thicker is best left for tied quilts. Heavily bonded polyester batting does not drape well and is stiff and harsh to the touch. Thin batting is relatively easy to quilt, but the finished quilt may appear limp. Close quilting can add texture and body to quilts made with this batting.

One advantage of polyester batting is cost. It is less expensive than cotton, wool, or blends. A disadvantage is that it tends to compress and become thin over the years. In the past, bearding was also a common occurrence with 100% polyester or wool batting. Today, you can usually avoid this problem by choosing a good-quality batting and using natural-fiber fabrics with a high thread count. To be on the safe side, choose a black or gray batting for quilt tops made of dark fabrics.

Another important concern with polyester batting is safety: the resins and bonding agents will melt or burn when exposed to direct heat, so carefully consider a quilt's use when choosing a batting.

With thicker, softer batting, such as 100% polyester off the roll and wool/polyester, the quilt edges might not lie flat once you've finished quilting. We've all seen them at shows—the quilts with the wavy edges. To prevent this problem, make a separate row of stitching ¼" from each edge through all thicknesses, using the longest machine stitch. Gather each edge, pulling the bobbin thread carefully so it doesn't break; the quilt will curl up like a shallow bowl. Ease out the gathering until the quilt lies flat, then bind the edges.

Battings generally stretch more one way than the other, just like fabric. If a batting is used with the most stretch running lengthwise, a wall hanging with minimal quilting may sag over time. To prevent this problem, use the batting with the most stretch running crosswise. You can successfully join batting with the stretch going different directions as long as the quilt is well quilted. Lay the batting with the edges touching but not overlapping; hand stitch together using a herringbone stitch or whipstitch.

When using a soft, high-loft batting such as wool/polyester, choose a backing fabric the same weight as the fabrics on the quilt top, or slightly heavier. If the backing fabric is very different from the top fabrics, the layers may shift, creating pleats and puckers. Most cotton and cotton/polyester battings are denser and don't cause this problem.

Layering and Basting for Machine Quilting

Pin basting is best if you plan to quilt by machine. Basting threads get caught in the presser foot while you're quilting, and the layers tend to shift and roll.

Take time to do a good job of pin basting. Layers that are well pinned are much easier to quilt. Careful pin basting also helps prevent distortion and stretching during stitching and eliminates unwanted tucks and puckers.

Do not work on a good table! When pin basting, you'll be sliding each pin along the tabletop, possibly scratching the surface.

To layer for machine quilting:

1. Cut the backing and batting approximately 2" larger than the quilt top on all sides.
2. Fold the quilt top in half lengthwise and mark the center of the top and bottom edges with a pin. Mark the backing fabric and batting in the same manner. Measure the quilt top along the fold, from edge to edge, for the lengthwise measurement.

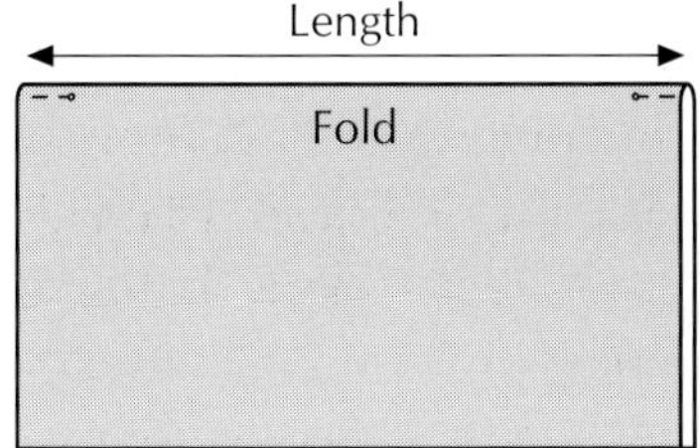

If the quilt is large, you'll also need to fold and mark the quilt top, batting, and backing across the width.

3. Working on a flat surface or table at least 3' x 5', mark the center of the tabletop on one of the short sides. If the quilt is large, also mark the center on the long sides. Use a toothpick secured by masking tape to make a bump you can feel when centering the layers of fabric and batting. Measure the length of the surface from the marked center point until you reach the lengthwise measurement of the quilt top plus 3". Place another toothpick secured by masking tape on the table to mark this point. If the measurement is longer than the table, mark the center of its edge.

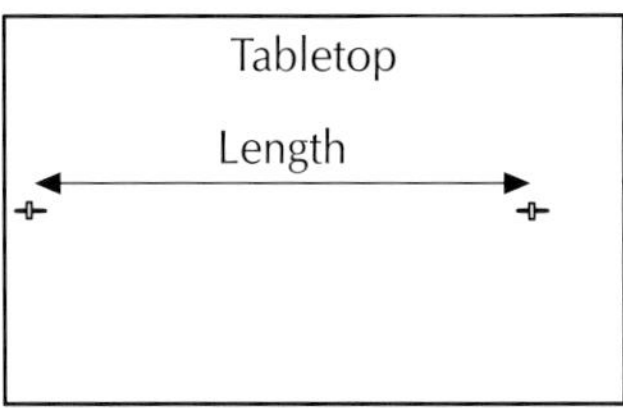

4. Fold the backing fabric in half lengthwise, wrong sides together. Place on the table, matching the center marks on the backing with the toothpicks.

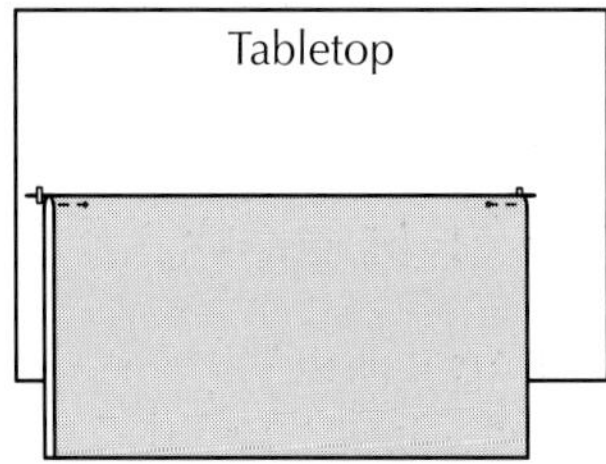

5. Unfold the backing with the wrong side up, allowing the excess to hang over the edges of the table if necessary. Check to make sure the centers are still aligned by feeling the toothpick bumps. Carefully smooth the fabric open. Use binder clamps to gently stretch and securely hold the backing to one side of the table. Also attach clamps to the opposite side of the table. If your backing is long enough to reach the ends of the table, use clamps on the remaining two sides. If not, apply several pieces of masking tape to the unclamped backing edges to secure them to the table. The backing fabric should now be taut but not stretched or distorted.

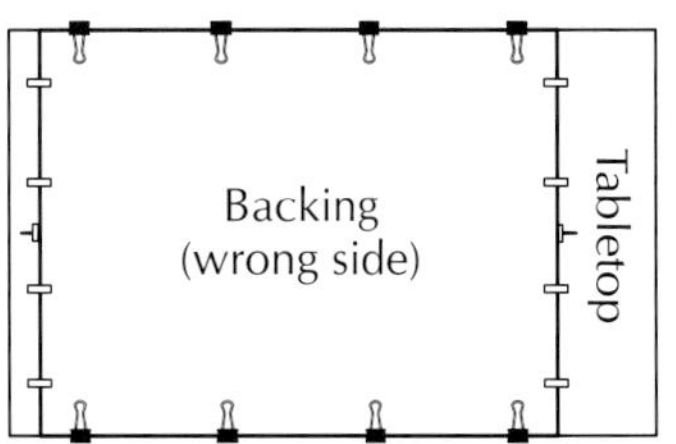

6. Fold the batting in half lengthwise and gently place it on top of the backing, making sure the center of the batting matches the toothpick bumps. Unfold the batting and carefully smooth it so there are no bumps or wrinkles. Do not clamp to the table.

7. Fold the quilt top in half lengthwise, right sides together, and place it on top of the batting and backing. Match the center of the quilt top to the toothpick bumps. Unfold the quilt top and carefully smooth it out. The quilt sandwich is ready for pin basting.

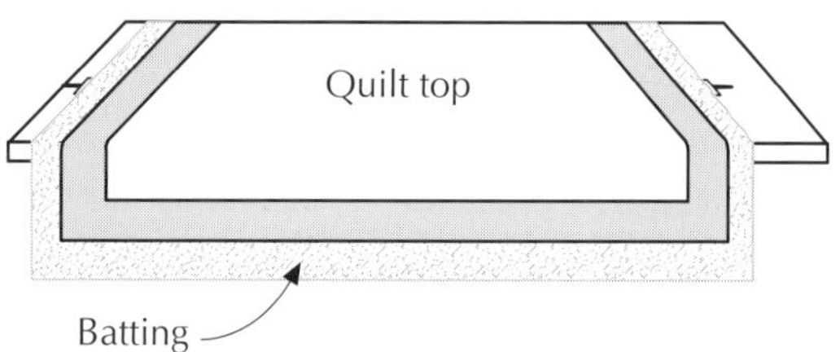

8. Use #2 nickel-plated safety pins to pin-baste. These pins are 1½" long (½" longer than the pins normally used for basting), which makes them easy to close. Starting around the edges of the table, begin pinning the layers together. Pin into the fabric and slide the point along the table to make sure you've gone through all the layers. Pin every 3"–4" and fill the pins ⅔–¾ full of fabric. When all the edges are pinned, start pinning toward the center.

9. If your quilt is larger than the table, remove the clamps and slide the quilt until an unpinned section is on the tabletop, with one row of pins from the previously pinned area along one edge. Reclamp the backing to the table on the unpinned side or sides only. Smooth the batting and the quilt top again and pin as before, pinning edges before working toward the center.

   If you must work on the floor, use masking tape to secure the backing to the floor, wrong side up. Lay the batting and the quilt top on the backing and smooth, being careful not to disturb the backing fabric. Pin all the edges first, then work toward the center, kneeling on the quilt only in areas that have been pinned.

Machine Quilting Hints

Invisible monofilament nylon thread (size .004) comes in clear for light fabrics and smoky for dark fabrics. Don't use ordinary nylon thread; it's too thick and strong for quilts and can damage the fabrics. Also avoid hand quilting thread, because it is usually coated and may clog the tension disks.

There are a number of brands of invisible thread suitable for machine quilting. Be sure to test thread on your fabric because some threads shine when quilted on dark fabrics. If you can't find an invisible thread that doesn't shine on your fabric, use a dark dressmaking thread (cotton or cotton-wrapped polyester) or machine-embroidery thread instead.

Be aware that some brands of invisible thread melt when ironed. If you're doing invisible machine appliqué, test your thread to make sure it won't melt; change brands if necessary.

Use invisible thread or dressmaking thread on the top of the machine. Always use dressmaking thread, not invisible thread, in the bobbin. Invisible thread tends to stretch and snap if caught, and if used in the bobbin, it's very difficult to find and remove the thread.

You'll probably need to loosen the top tension slightly when using invisible thread; the same is true for metallic and machine-embroidery threads. Consult your manual and experiment with your thread.

The machine quilting stitch may look harsher than the hand quilting stitch, but you can, with patience and practice, achieve a hand-quilted look. If you're going to machine quilt, take the time to do it well. Nothing looks as bad as poorly done machine quilting. And nothing can compare to a beautifully machine-quilted quilt.

All of the quilts in this book are machine quilted, and most contain stitching in-the-ditch. It's best to stitch in-the-ditch first to stabilize large areas before doing more detailed quilting.

Study your quilt to find the best place to start machine quilting. Begin where you'll have the least number of starts and stops. Sometimes, starting where a few lines cross allows you to quilt in a continuous line with one start and one finish. If this strategy isn't possible, you can minimize the number of starts and stops by stitching once over already-stitched lines for short distances.

For best results, keep the bobbin and feed dog areas clean and change the needle after every 10–12 hours of sewing time. Be consistent in the amount of quilting across your quilt. If the quilting density varies too much from one area to another, the quilt will not lie flat or hang straight.

To ensure straight lines, always quilt with a walking foot. However, where there are many short (less than 3"), closely spaced straight lines, you can avoid turning the quilt by using the darning foot with the feed dog dropped or covered. It's not necessary to mark short straight lines. Use the width of the darning foot as a guide. Some lines may waver slightly, but the eye won't pick up these subtle differences.

When machine quilting on dark and light fabrics, choose your backing fabric carefully. If you use a light-colored backing and a similar-colored thread in the bobbin, the bobbin thread may show on the quilt top's dark fabrics. The reverse may also happen: dark bobbin thread may show on the quilt top's light fabrics. This problem is usually the result of incorrect tension. If the tension is adjusted correctly and the bobbin thread still shows on the top, the thread may be showing through the holes your needle makes. Try a smaller needle or change the bobbin thread to dark for dark quilt-top fabrics and light for light quilt-top fabrics and ignore the backing fabric.

Attaching Binding

Double-fold bindings are cut lengthwise or crosswise as specified in the quilt project instructions. Do not trim the backing and batting until after you attach the binding.

1. Sew the cut strips together at a 45° angle and press the seams open.

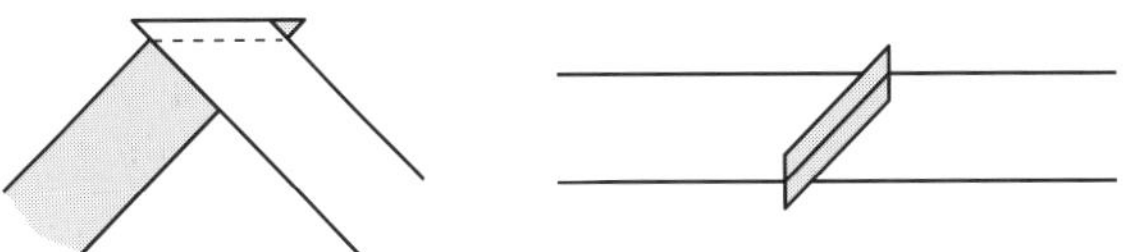

2. Fold the strip in half lengthwise, wrong sides together, and press.
3. Starting approximately 10" from a top corner, pin the binding to the quilt front, leaving a 6" tail. Align the raw edges of the binding with the raw edge of the quilt top.

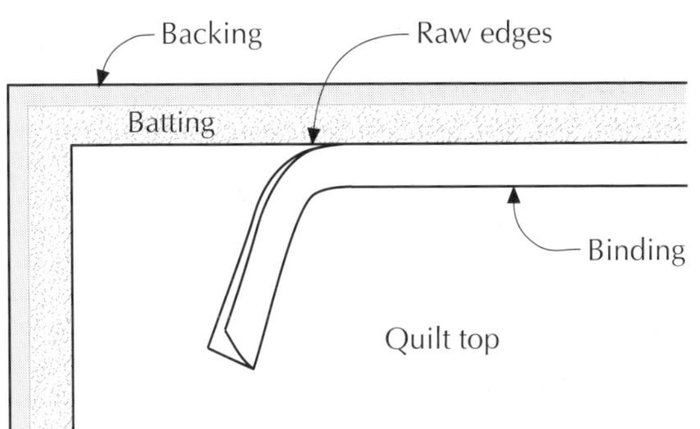

4. Using an even-feed foot, if available, stitch the binding to the quilt using a ¼"-wide seam allowance. Backstitch at the beginning to secure. Be careful not to stretch the binding as you go. At the corner, stop the stitching ¼" from the edge; backstitch and clip the threads.

5. Turn the quilt. Fold the binding straight up and away from the quilt to form a 45° angle. Place a straight pin in the binding in line with the raw edges of the first side.

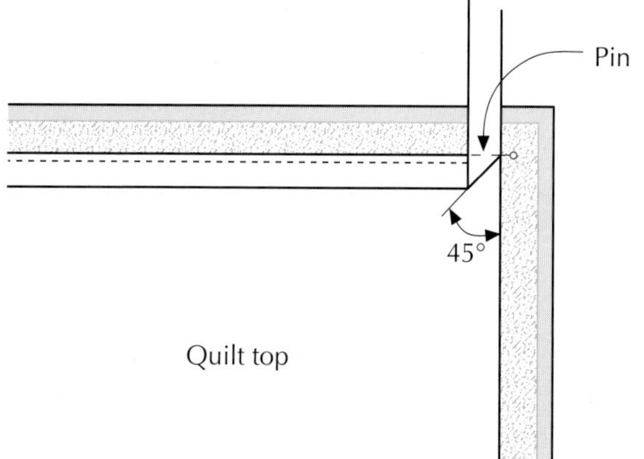

6. Bring the binding straight down, over the pin, and hold firmly. Align the fold in the binding with the raw edge of the first side. Make sure the raw edges of the binding align with the raw edge of the second side. Stitch from the top of the fold down the second side, finishing ¼" from the edge.

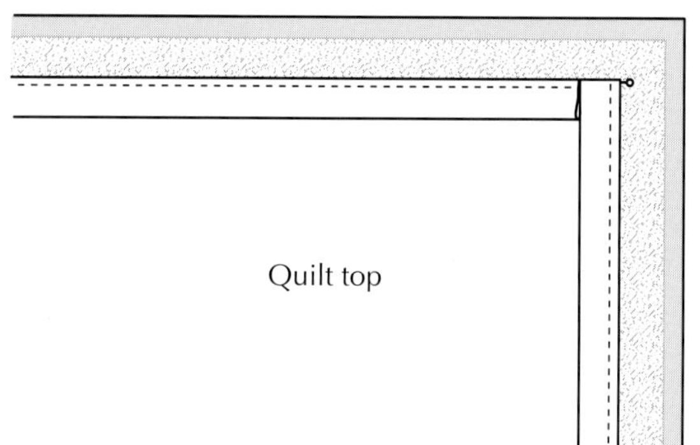

7. Continue sewing and mitering corners on the remaining edges. Finish stitching approximately 6"–8" from the starting point; backstitch and clip the threads.

8. Open the binding and lay one end on top of the other. Trim both ends at a 45° angle, allowing a ½" overlap for the seam allowance. With right sides together, pin and stitch the ends using a ¼"-wide seam allowance. Finger-press the seam open.

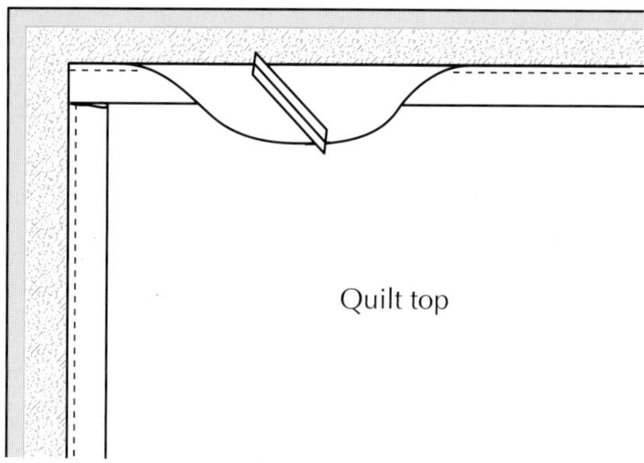

9. Refold the binding lengthwise and finish stitching to the quilt.

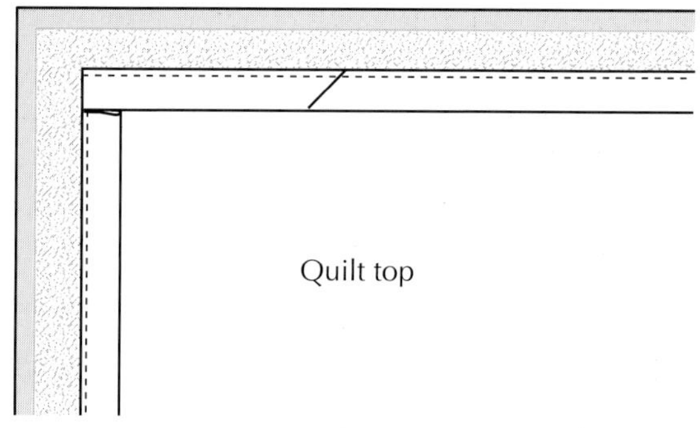

Trim the batting and backing even with the raw edges of the binding. If you're planning to add a rod sleeve, do so now, before sewing the binding to the back. See "Adding a Rod Sleeve" on the facing page.

10. Fold the binding to the back of the quilt and cover the machine stitching with the fold. Blindstitch, making sure the stitches don't show on the front or back of the quilt.

11. A perfect miter will form on the front of the quilt at each corner. Fold the back miter in the opposite direction from the front miter to distribute the bulk evenly. Stitch the miters closed on both sides of the quilt.

Adding a Rod Sleeve

A sleeve at the top of the backing makes hanging your quilt easy. Cut the sleeve from the leftover backing fabric after you layer the quilt top, batting, and backing.

1. Cut a strip of fabric 8" wide and as long as the top edge of the quilt. Turn under 1/2" on each short end and press. Turn under an additional 1/2", press, and stitch close to the fold.

2. Fold the strip in half lengthwise, right side out. Shift one long edge 1/4" below the other, making one side of the sleeve narrower. Press the fold.

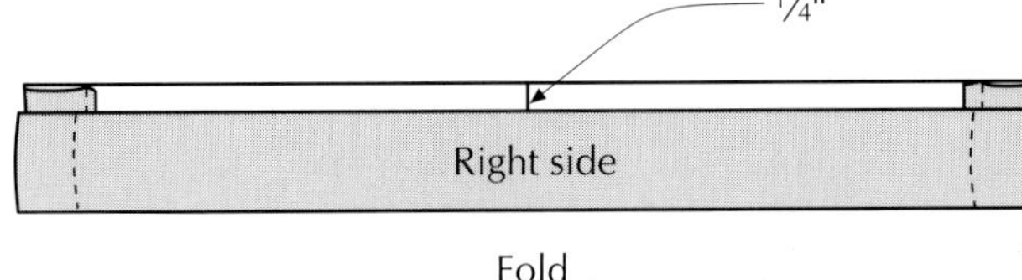

3. Mark the center of the rod sleeve and the quilt. With the narrower side against the quilt, pin the rod sleeve to the top of the quilt, matching the centers and aligning all raw edges. The sleeve will be poufed because there is an extra 1/4" in the side facing up.

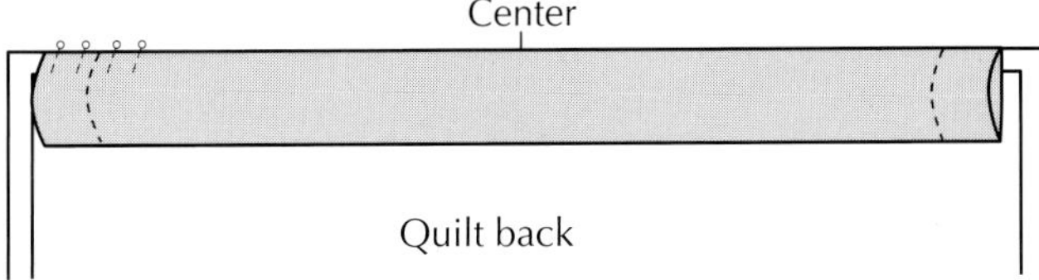

4. Machine stitch the rod sleeve to the top of the quilt through all thicknesses using a 1/4"-wide seam allowance.

5. Keeping the tube open, hand stitch each end of the sleeve to the backing; secure well at the pressed-fold corner. Hand stitch the pressed fold to the quilt, making sure the stitches don't show on the front of the quilt. The extra 1/4" of fabric in the side facing up will prevent the rod from distorting the quilt when you hang it.

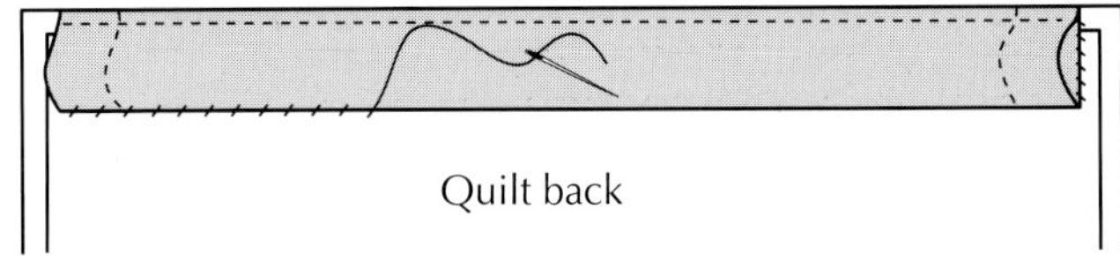

6. See steps 10 and 11 of "Attaching Binding" on page 132 to sew the binding to the back of the quilt.

Bibliography

BAIN, GEORGE. *Celtic Art—The Methods of Construction.* London: Constable, 1992. An excellent source of Celtic designs.

BECK, THOMASINA. *The Embroiderer's Flowers.* Devon, England: David and Charles, 1992.

———. *The Embroiderer's Garden.* Devon, England: David and Charles, 1989. Thomasina Beck's books have hundreds of ideas that can be adapted by quilters.

DAVIS, COURTNEY. *The Celtic Art Source Book.* London: Blanford Press, 1989. Another excellent source of Celtic designs.

FONS, MARIANNE. *Fine Feathers: A Quilter's Guide to Customizing Traditional Feather Quilting Designs.* Lafayette, Calif.: C & T Publishing, 1988. A comprehensive guide to drawing feather designs.

HOPKINS, MARY ELLEN. *The It's Okay If You Sit on My Quilt Book.* Santa Monica, Calif.: ME Publications, 1989. A book of piecing designs.

JONES, OWEN. *The Grammar of Ornament.* New York: Dover Publications, Inc., Dover Pictorial Archives Series, 1987. Books in the Dover Pictorial Archives Series have a wealth of designs, most from historical sources.

MIROW, GEORGE. *A Treasury of Design for Artists and Craftsmen.* New York: Dover Publications, Inc., Dover Pictorial Archives Series, 1969.

SOLO, DAN X. *Art Nouveau Typographic Ornaments.* New York: Dover Publications, Dover Pictorial Archives Series, 1982.

THOMPSON, SHIRLEY. *Tried and True—Favorite Old-time Quilting Designs.* Edmonds, Wash.: Powell Publications, 1987. A collection of wonderful quilting designs.

TOMLONSON, JUDY SCHROEDER. *Mennonite Quilts and Pieces.* Intercourse, Penn.: Good Books, 1985. Noteworthy for the use of color and design in traditional quilts.

Meet the Author

Lee Cleland lives in St. Ives, a suburb of Sydney, Australia, with her husband and adult children. She made her first quilt in 1968 for the birth of her first child, using a pattern in an American needlework magazine and fabrics from her dresses. Never having seen a quilt before, she quilted it by machine. That quilt, "dreadful as it was," began her machine-quilting career.

After years of making contemporary quilts and machine quilting bedspreads for interior designers, Lee turned to traditionally pieced patchwork quilts. She has taught machine quilting for ten years, mostly on the more populous east coast of Australia. She prefers full-size quilts—"I don't like little fiddly things"—and is a firm believer that every quilt should be "quilted to death."

In addition to quilting books, Lee collects architecture and embroidery books, which she uses for design inspiration. Her other loves are cross-stitch, sailboarding, walking, and skiing.

Books from Martingale & Company

Appliqué

Appliqué in Bloom
Baltimore Bouquets
Basic Quiltmaking Techniques for Hand Appliqué
Basic Quiltmaking Techniques for Machine Appliqué
Coxcomb Quilt
The Easy Art of Appliqué
Folk Art Animals
From a Quilter's Garden
Fun with Sunbonnet Sue
Garden Appliqué
Interlacing Borders
Once Upon a Quilt
Stars in the Garden
Sunbonnet Sue All Through the Year
Welcome to the North Pole

Basic Quiltmaking Techniques

Basic Quiltmaking Techniques for Borders & Bindings
Basic Quiltmaking Techniques for Curved Piecing
Basic Quiltmaking Techniques for Divided Circles
Basic Quiltmaking Techniques for Eight-Pointed Stars
Basic Quiltmaking Techniques for Hand Appliqué
Basic Quiltmaking Techniques for Machine Appliqué
Basic Quiltmaking Techniques for Strip Piecing
Your First Quilt Book (or it should be!)

Crafts

15 Beads
The Art of Handmade Paper and Collage
Christmas Ribbonry
Fabric Mosaics
Folded Fabric Fun
Hand-Stitched Samplers from I Done My Best
The Home Decorator's Stamping Book
Making Memories
A Passion for Ribbonry
Stamp with Style

Design Reference

Color: The Quilter's Guide
Design Essentials: The Quilter's Guide
Design Your Own Quilts
The Nature of Design
QuiltSkills
Surprising Designs from Traditional Quilt Blocks

Foundation/Paper Piecing

Classic Quilts with Precise Foundation Piecing
Crazy but Pieceable
Easy Machine Paper Piecing
Easy Mix & Match Machine Paper Piecing
Easy Paper-Pieced Keepsake Quilts
Easy Paper-Pieced Miniatures
Easy Reversible Vests
Go Wild with Quilts
Go Wild with Quilts—Again!
It's Raining Cats & Dogs
Mariner's Medallion
Paper Piecing the Seasons
A Quilter's Ark
Sewing on the Line
Show Me How to Paper Piece

Home Decorating

Decorate with Quilts & Collections
The Home Decorator's Stamping Book
Living with Little Quilts
Make Room for Quilts
Special-Occasion Table Runners
Stitch & Stencil
Welcome Home: Debbie Mumm
Welcome Home: Kaffe Fassett

Joy of Quilting Series

Borders by Design
The Easy Art of Appliqué
A Fine Finish
Hand-Dyed Fabric Made Easy
Happy Endings
Loving Stitches
Machine Quilting Made Easy
A Perfect Match
Press for Success
Sensational Settings
Shortcuts
The Ultimate Book of Quilt Labels

Knitting

Simply Beautiful Sweaters
Two Sticks and a String
Welcome Home: Kaffe Fassett

Machine Quilting/Sewing

Machine Needlelace
Machine Quilting Made Easy
Machine Quilting with Decorative Threads
Quilting Makes the Quilt
Thread Magic
Threadplay

Miniature/Small Quilts

Celebrate! with Little Quilts
Crazy but Pieceable
Easy Paper-Pieced Miniatures
Fun with Miniature Log Cabin Blocks
Little Quilts All Through the House
Living with Little Quilts
Miniature Baltimore Album Quilts
Small Quilts Made Easy
Small Wonders

Quilting/Finishing Techniques

Borders by Design
The Border Workbook
A Fine Finish
Happy Endings
Interlacing Borders
Loving Stitches
Quilt It!
Quilting Design Sourcebook
Quilting Makes the Quilt
Traditional Quilts with Painless Borders
The Ultimate Book of Quilt Labels

Rotary Cutting/Speed Piecing

101 Fabulous Rotary-Cut Quilts
All-Star Sampler
Around the Block with Judy Hopkins
Bargello Quilts
Basic Quiltmaking Techniques for Strip Piecing
Block by Block
Easy Seasonal Wall Quilts
Easy Star Sampler
Fat Quarter Quilts
The Heirloom Quilt
The Joy of Quilting
More Quilts for Baby
More Strip-Pieced Watercolor Magic
A New Slant on Bargello Quilts
A New Twist on Triangles
Patchwork Pantry
Quilters on the Go
Quilting Up a Storm
Quilts for Baby
Quilts from Aunt Amy
ScrapMania
Simply Scrappy Quilts
Square Dance
Strip-Pieced Watercolor Magic
Stripples Strikes Again!
Strips That Sizzle
Two-Color Quilts

Seasonal Projects

Christmas Ribbonry
Easy Seasonal Wall Quilts
Folded Fabric Fun
Holiday Happenings
Quilted for Christmas
Quilted for Christmas, Book III
Quilted for Christmas, Book IV
A Silk-Ribbon Album
Welcome to the North Pole

Stitchery/Needle Arts

Christmas Ribbonry
Crazy Rags
Hand-Stitched Samplers from I Done My Best
Machine Needlelace
Miniature Baltimore Album Quilts
A Passion for Ribbonry
A Silk-Ribbon Album
Victorian Elegance

Surface Design/Fabric Manipulation

15 Beads
The Art of Handmade Paper and Collage
Complex Cloth
Creative Marbling on Fabric
Dyes & Paints
Hand-Dyed Fabric Made Easy
Jazz It Up

Theme Quilts

The Cat's Meow
Everyday Angels in Extraordinary Quilts
Fabric Collage Quilts
Fabric Mosaics
Folded Fabric Fun
Folk Art Quilts
Honoring the Seasons
It's Raining Cats & Dogs
Life in the Country with Country Threads
Making Memories
More Quilts for Baby
The Nursery Rhyme Quilt
Once Upon a Quilt
Patchwork Pantry
Quilted Landscapes
Quilting Your Memories
Quilts for Baby
Quilts from Nature
Through the Window and Beyond
Two-Color Quilts

Watercolor Quilts

More Strip-Pieced Watercolor Magic
Strip-Pieced Watercolor Magic
Watercolor Impressions
Watercolor Quilts

Wearables

Crazy Rags
Dress Daze
Easy Reversible Vests
Jacket Jazz Encore
Just Like Mommy
Variations in Chenille

Many of these books are available through your local quilt, fabric, craft-supply, or art-supply store. For more information, call, write, fax, or e-mail for our free full-color catalog.

Martingale & Company
PO Box 118
Bothell, WA 98041-0118 USA
1-800-426-3126
International: 1-425-483-3313
24-Hour Fax: 1-425-486-7596
Web site: www.patchwork.com
E-mail: info@martingale-pub.com

3/99

LESSON 4

OBJECTIVES

- Students will recognize the sounds made by short vowels
- Students will identify words containing short vowels
- Students will sort words containing short vowels

WORD BANK OF SHORT-VOWEL WORDS

at	Ed	it	on	up
am	hen	in	cot	us
an	beg	if	log	tub
tap	get	sip	mop	bug

MATERIALS

Worktext, page 8
Teacher's Manual, page 5

SHORT VOWELS

- Say the following word slowly: **at**. Ask students to say it slowly. Then have them say it again, but ask them to stop before they get to the last part of the word. By cutting the word in half, they have accessed and emphasized the short-vowel sound. Repeat this routine with other short-vowel words, such as *Ed, it, on,* and *up.*
- For students who speak English as a second language, you may want to use the word *off* instead of *on.*

Teacher Tip

You may want to present the short-vowel sounds in a sequence such as /*a*/, /*e*/, /*i*/, /*o*/, and /*u*/, placing contrasting vowel sounds next to each other so that students are able to discriminate sounds more easily.

Sorting Short-Vowel Words

- Write the following categories on the board: **short a**, **short e**, **short i**, **short o**, and **short u**. Have students brainstorm 25 short-vowel words (five of each short vowel) and write them underneath the correct categories.
- Using index cards, write each of the words. Afterward, have students take turns reading each word and saying the short-vowel sound. Shuffle the cards again, and have them sort each word according to its vowel sound. Invite them to think of other words for this flash-card and sorting routine.

PRACTICE

A. Sort the Words

Ask students to turn to page 8 in their Worktexts. Have them sort the words found in the Word Bank according to their short-vowel sounds.

B. Fill in the Blanks

Invite students to "Fill in the Blanks" by making short-vowel words. Have them check to see if they've made real words by using the dictionary.

LESSON 4

A. Sort the Words

Look at each word found in the Word Bank. Look at the short vowel in each word and say it. Then sort each word according to its short-vowel sound. When you are finished, take turns reading the words with a partner.

WORD BANK				
it	Ed	on	up	at
us	cot	hen	in	am
tub	an	if	beg	log
mop	bug	get	tap	sip

short a	short e	short i	short o	short u
______	______	______	______	______
______	______	______	______	______
______	______	______	______	______
______	______	______	______	______

B. Fill in the Blanks

Look at the words. There is a blank in the middle of the word. Fill in the blank with a vowel that will make a real word. Use a dictionary to check to see if you are making real words. Some of these words can use more than one vowel, such as: **c _ p cap cop cup.**

1. p _ n ________
2. t _ g ________
3. m _ t ________
4. b _ t ________
5. f _ n ________
6. n _ d ________
7. r _ n ________
8. s _ p ________
9. v _ n ________
10. t _ b ________

8 • Chapter 1

Worktext page 8

Getting Ready

LESSON 5

OBJECTIVES

- Students will recognize that diphthongs are comprised of two letters that make up one sound, such as the sound of /*ou*/ and /*ow*/ in *cloud* and *bow*, or the sound of /*oi*/ and /*oy*/ in *coin* and *toy*
- Students will identify words containing diphthongs
- Students will recognize that vowel digraphs /*au*/ and /*aw*/ usually have the same sound, as in *haul* and *paw*
- Students will identify words containing vowel digraphs

WORD BANK FOR WORDS WITH DIPHTHONGS AND VOWEL DIGRAPHS

cloud	bow	coin	toy	haul
paw	house	crown	oil	boy
Paul	crawl	mouth	flower	noise
joy	pause	yawn		

MATERIALS

Worktext, page 9
Teacher's Manual, page 6

DIPHTHONGS AND VOWEL DIGRAPHS

- Write the following categories on the board: **ou–ow**, **oi–oy**, and **au–aw**. Tell students that sometimes two letters can make one special sound that isn't a short-vowel or long-vowel sound. Say each of the above sounds and have students echo you. Then write a word from the Word Bank that matches each category, such as *house, crown, oil, toy, pause,* and *paw*. Invite students to say each word after you.
- Ask students to think of a rhyming word for each of the above words and include them under the correct categories.

PRACTICE

A. Sort the Words

Have students open their Worktexts to page 9. Using the Word Bank, ask them to sort words according to their sound and spelling pattern.

B. Fill in the Blanks

Invite students to "Fill in the Blanks" to make words, using the Word Bank to check their spellings.

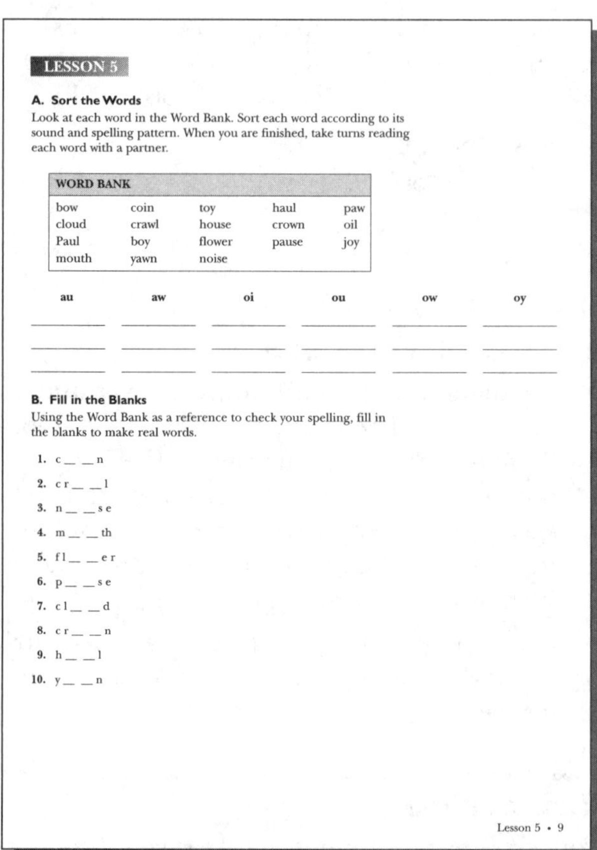

LESSON 5

A. Sort the Words

Look at each word in the Word Bank. Sort each word according to its sound and spelling pattern. When you are finished, take turns reading each word with a partner.

WORD BANK				
bow	coin	toy	haul	paw
cloud	crawl	house	crown	oil
Paul	boy	flower	pause	joy
mouth	yawn	noise		

au	aw	oi	ou	ow	oy
______	______	______	______	______	______
______	______	______	______	______	______
______	______	______	______	______	______

B. Fill in the Blanks

Using the Word Bank as a reference to check your spelling, fill in the blanks to make real words.

1. c __ __ n
2. c r __ __ l
3. n __ __ s e
4. m __ __ th
5. f l __ __ e r
6. p __ __ s e
7. c l __ __ d
8. c r __ __ n
9. h __ __ l
10. y __ __ n

Lesson 5 • 9

Worktext page 9

CHAPTER 2
Three-Sound, Short-Vowel Words

TOKEN LESSON A

OBJECTIVES

- Students will develop phonemic awareness by segmenting short-vowel nonsense words using tokens to represent sounds
- Students will discriminate sounds in the initial, final, and medial positions

WORD BANK OF NONSENSE WORDS

fam	dod	lesh	tib	bev
gis	wak	bim	kem	vel
mosh	chev	thut	whit	gen
cuj	gim	min	naz	thap
luf	daz	leth	shib	whan
rop	juv	zath	fep	roch

WORD BANK OF REAL WORDS

cap	cup	nap	not	shop
sit	fin	cut	lip	tap
sun	thin	mop	zip	
fun	map	rod	ship	

MATERIALS

Teacher's Manual, pages 7–8
Additional list of nonsense words, page 337
Token cards

PHONEMIC AWARENESS

Segmenting Sounds

Place three different tokens such as a circle, triangle, and star in a row on the table in front of a small group of students.

- Say it slowly: ***fam.* What is the first sound you hear in *fam*?** As you say *fam*, stretch each phoneme, elongating each sound. When the first student has identified the /*f*/, have the student point to the first token and say /*f*/.

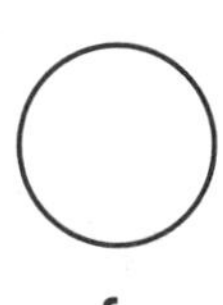

f a m

- Say it slowly: ***fam.* What is the middle sound after /*f*/?** Have the student say the word slowly and listen to the sound made right after saying /*f*/. After saying /*a*/, have the student point to the next token.
- Say it slowly: ***fam.* What is the final sound you hear in *fam*?** When the student says /*m*/, have him or her touch the last token. Ask the student to say the word slowly, stretching out each sound. As the student does this, point to each token. Afterward, ask the student to say it slowly and point to each token while saying each sound.
- Introduce a new nonsense word and have the next student work with another set of tokens to sound out and segment each phoneme. Repeat this routine, providing multiple opportunities for each student to work with the words found in the Word Bank.

Teacher Tip

If . . . students aren't able to identify a particular sound,
Then . . . say the word very slowly, stretching out each sound. Be sure to say the word whole, coaching students to segment each sound by themselves.

SUBSTITUTION ROUTINES

Initial Consonants

Place three new tokens in front of students, such as a circle, square, and rectangle. Demonstrate the following substitution routine.

- Say: **If this says *dod*, I'm going to make the nonsense word *fod*.** Replace the circle with a star.
- Say: **If this now says *fod*, I'm going to make *zod*.** Replace the star with a diamond.
- Say: **If this now says *zod*, I'm going to make *thod*.** Replace the diamond with a triangle.

- After modeling the previous routine, have students take turns substituting the initial sound. Work with three new tokens and say: **If this says *lesh*, make *pesh*. If this says *pesh*, make *nesh*.**

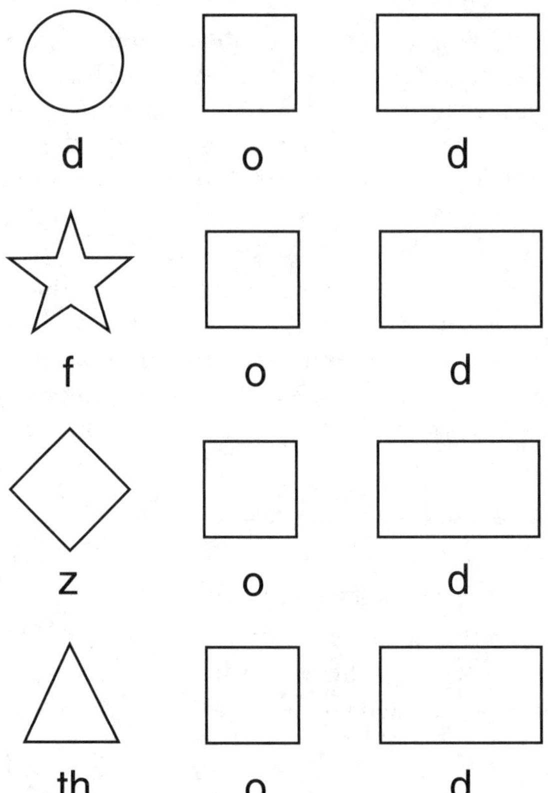

Final Consonants

Place a star, diamond, and rectangle in front of students.

- Say: **If this says *tib*, make *tiz*.** Have a student replace the rectangle with another token. Guide the student in substituting the final consonant sound to make *tid* and *tiv*.

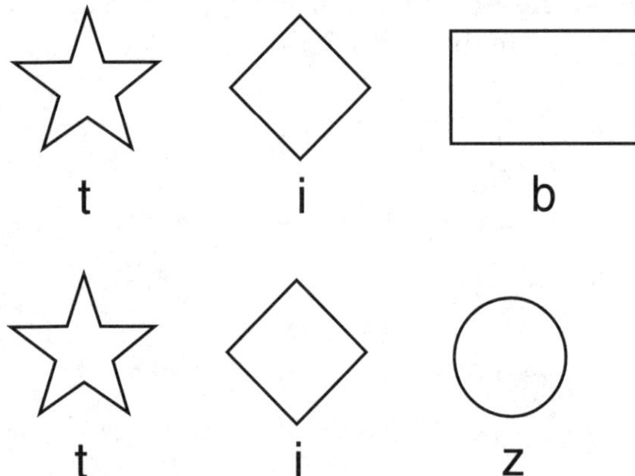

Medial Vowel Sounds

Place a square, triangle, and circle on the table.

- Say: **If this says *bev*, make *biv*.** Have a student replace the triangle with another token. Coach the student in substituting the medial vowel sound to make other nonsense words, such as *bov* and *bav*.
- As you have students continue to work with manipulating and substituting sounds in the initial, final, and medial positions, you may want to use additional short-vowel nonsense words found on page 337.
- After students have worked with short-vowel nonsense words, you can use the Word Bank of Real Words with them.

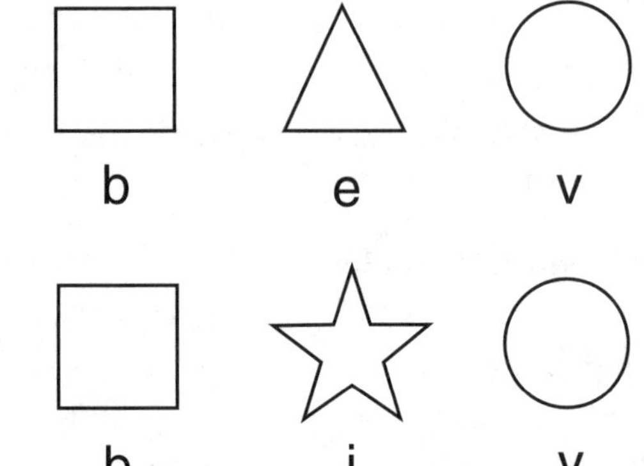

TOKEN LESSON B

OBJECTIVES

- Students will segment three-sound, short-vowel nonsense words by connecting sounds to letters
- Students will make new nonsense words by substituting beginning, final, and medial sounds and letters

WORD BANK OF NONSENSE WORDS

List 1	List 2	List 3	List 4
meb	rop	bam	pid
feb	sop	gam	fid
cheb	fop	nam	nid
chez	foz	nad	nith
ched	foth	naf	nish
chem	fosh	naj	nib
cham	fash	nij	neb
chom	fush	noj	nub
chim	fesh	nej	nab

MATERIALS

Teacher's Manual, pages 9–10
Assessment Checklist, page 62 of the *Assessment Manual*
Token cards
Letter cards, including all vowels, consonants, and consonant digraphs *ch*, *sh*, *th*, and *wh*

PHONICS

Connecting Sounds to Letters

Spread out the letter cards on the table, making them accessible to a small group of students. Place three different tokens in a row on the table.

- Say it slowly: ***meb.*** Point to the first token and say: **What sound does this make?** When the student says /*m*/, ask: **Can you find the letter that makes that sound?** Have the student place the letter *m* below the first token.
- Say it slowly: ***meb.*** Point to the middle token and say: **What sound does this make?** When the student says /*e*/, ask: **Can you find the letter that makes that sound?** Have the student place the letter *e* below the second token.

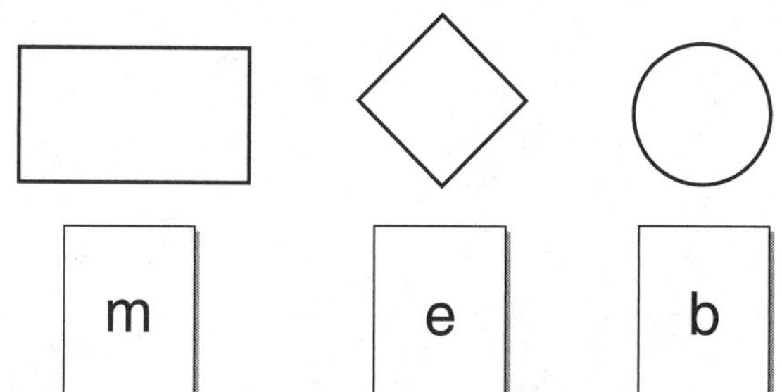

- Say it slowly: ***meb.*** Point to the last token and say: **What sound does this make?** When the student says /*b*/, ask: **Can you find the letter that makes that sound?** Have the student place the letter *b* below the last token.

SUBSTITUTION ROUTINES

Initial Consonants

Remove the three tokens, working with the letter cards only. Say: **If this says *meb*, watch as I find the letter that will make the nonsense word *feb*.** Replace the *m* with the *f*. **Now it's your turn. Can you make *cheb*?** As the student replaces the *f* with the card that says *ch*, you may want to review consonant digraphs. Explain that although *ch*, *sh*, *th*, and *wh* have two letters, each pair of letters represents one sound.

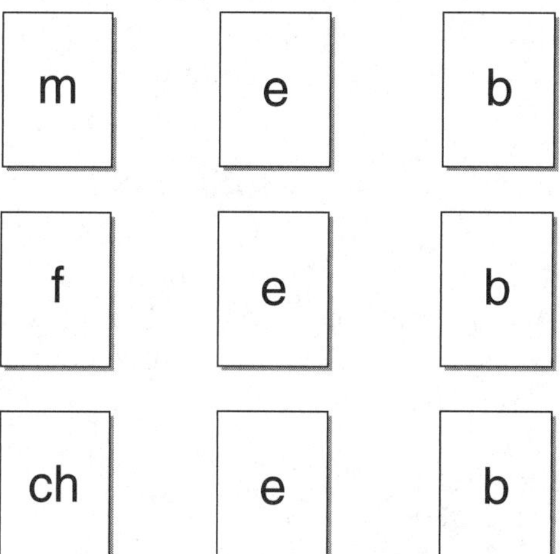

Final Consonants

Invite the next student to find letter cards to make the nonsense word *chez*, then substitute the final letters to make *ched* and *chem*.

Medial Vowels

- Have another student work with changing the medial letter in *chem*, by substituting the short vowel, as in *cham*, *chom*, and *chim*.
- As you continue having students manipulate letter cards in the initial, medial, and final positions, you may wish to refer to page 337 for additional three-sound nonsense words.

READING ROUTINES

Blending Sounds

- Place the nonsense word *rop* in front of students. Ask the first student: **Can you read the word?** If the student can read the word, ask the next student to read another word.
- If students are having difficulty reading any of the nonsense words, point to each letter and ask them to say the sound. If they are able to segment each sound but are having difficulty blending the sounds together to form the word, take apart the word. Cover up the *r* in *rop*. Ask students to blend *op*, conducting them as they say the sounds.
- Remind them not to stop in between each sound, keeping the two sounds continuous. When they can say the two sounds together quickly, uncover the *r* and ask them to read the nonsense word, blending the sounds together slowly, then more quickly, and finally as one word.

INFORMAL ASSESSMENT

To assess whether students are able to decode three-sound, short-vowel nonsense words, you may want to use the Assessment Checklist found on page 62 in the *Assessment Manual*. Use the sample checklist on this page as a guideline.

Teacher Tip

If . . . students aren't able to get eight out of 10 nonsense words correct,
Then . . . determine whether they are having difficulty hearing sounds in the initial, final, or medial position. You may want to review particular consonant or vowel sounds in Chapter 1, or do more sound-stretching activities that focus on a particular position.

ASSESSMENT CHECKLIST

Place letter cards on the table. Say each word slowly. Have students take turns saying and spelling each word. Record student performance here for your records.

	Student name	Nonsense or real word	Score	Notes
1.	Maria	fam	+	
2.	Todd	gis	-	gos
3.	Sam	mosh	+	
4.	Maria	cuj	+	
5.	Todd	luf	+	
6.	Sam	rop	+	
7.	Maria	wak	+	
8.	Todd	chev	+	
9.	Sam	gim	+	
10.	Maria	daz	-	das
11.	Todd	juz	+	
12.	Sam	lesh	+	
13.	Maria	bim	+	
14.	Todd	thut	+	
15.	Sam	min	+	
16.	Maria	leth	+	
17.	Todd	zath	+	
18.	Sam	tib	+	
19.	Maria	kem	-	cem
20.	Todd	whit	-	whid
21.	Sam	naz	+	
22.	Maria	shib	+	
23.	Todd	feb	+	
24.	Sam	vel	+	
25.	Maria	thap	+	
26.	Todd	wham	+	
27.	Sam	roch	-	rosh
28.	Maria	meb	+	
29.	Todd	bam	-	pam
30.	Sam	pid	+	

Score:
Maria 8 out of 10
Todd 7 out of 10
Sam 9 out of 10

Sample Assessment Checklist

Teacher Tip

If . . . you've placed a word in front of a student who cannot read it aloud,
Then . . . have the student sound out each letter, then blend. If the attempt is not accurate, the student goes to the vowel as the nucleus of the syllable and identifies it. Then the student adds one consonant before or after the vowel (whichever is easier to say) and blends them. The student says that piece whole, adds one more consonant, then blends together. The student adds additional consonants one by one until the entire word is constructed.

LESSON 1

OBJECTIVES

- Students will recognize that double consonants such as *ff*, *ll*, and *ss* stand for only one sound
- Students will recognize that words with *ck* stand for only one sound
- Students will identify short-vowel words containing double consonants and words with *ck*

WORD BANK OF REAL WORDS

ff	ll	ss	ck
puff	will	pass	back
cuff	full	boss	pick
tiff	hill	less	kick
stuff	fell	miss	duck
buff	well	mess	pack

MATERIALS

Teacher's Manual, page 11
Worktext, page 10

SPELLING

Double Consonants and Words With *ck*

- Write the following categories on chart paper or the board: **ff**, **ll**, **ss**, and **ck**. Explain to students that when they see words spelled with two consonants next to each other, it signals that the vowel before it is short. Write the following words under each category: **puff**, **will**, **pass**, and **back**. Say each word slowly, emphasizing the final consonant sound.
- Point out that even though *ck* is spelled with two letters, it stands for only one sound, /*k*/.
- Mention that many double consonants stand for only one sound. Have them brainstorm other words that end with these double consonants and write them under the correct categories.
- Have students turn to page 10 in their Worktexts. You may wish to have students work in pairs to complete the spelling activities.

CHAPTER 2

LESSON 1

SPELLING RULE
When you see a word spelled with two consonants next to each other after a vowel, that vowel will be short, as in *miss*. The two consonants stand for only one sound, as in *fill* or *kick*.

A. Say the Words
Say each word in the Word Bank. Remember that the two consonants stand for only one sound.

WORD BANK				
hill	boss	pick	kick	puff
fell	buff	miss	duck	mess
back	full	stuff	will	less
pass	pack	cliff	well	cuff

B. Sort the Words
Look at the spelling of each word in the Word Bank. Sort and write each word under the correct category. Circle the two consonants.

ll	ss	ff	ck
______	______	______	______
______	______	______	______
______	______	______	______
______	______	______	______
______	______	______	______

C. Fill in the Blanks
Add two consonants at the end of the following letters to make real words. Some of these words may not be found in the Word Bank.

1. bo _ _ 3. bla _ _ 5. le _ _ 7. sha _ _ 9. cu _ _
2. chi _ _ 4. mo _ _ 6. fe _ _ 8. pa _ _ 10. hi _ _

D. Find the Words
Use a dictionary to find four other words that end with a double consonant or *ck*. Write them below.

______ ______ ______ ______

10 • Chapter 2

Worktext page 10

Teacher Tip

If . . . students cannot tell what sounds are in a word to encode it,

Then . . .

1. teach them to say the word slowly with you a couple of times, then mouth the word and direct them in saying it. Next, they say it alone. They can hear sounds in words if the word is said more slowly, but not if it is said at the normal rate of speech.
2. if they still can't hear individual sounds when a word is said slowly, warn them and then point to their mouth when they are saying it slowly. This helps them focus attention on what their mouth is doing at the moment they are saying a particular sound.
3. if they still can't hear the sound, have them say the word slowly. When you point, they "freeze" their mouth and stop their voice box. When you point again, they start their voice box again with their mouth "frozen" in place. Then stop again, start again. The effect is that they have segmented the sound.

LESSON 2

OBJECTIVES

- Students will decode and read three-phoneme, short-vowel words
- Students will build and spell short-vowel words using letter cards
- Students will practice reading short-vowel words by unscrambling sounds, finding them on a Word Search board, and playing a vowel substitution game

WORD BANK OF REAL WORDS

chat	man	pet	tan	pat
gem	will	pot	much	back
sit	bag	duck	sad	cuff
tug	fog	chin	met	pick
nap	shop	lip	job	tub

MATERIALS

Worktext, pages 11–13
Teacher's Manual, pages 12–14
Assessment Checklist, page 62 of the *Assessment Manual*
Award Certificate, page 336
Letter cards for each pair of students

SUBSTITUTION ROUTINES

Initial, Final, and Medial Letters

- On chart paper or the board, write the word **chat**. Ask students to read the word, then write it down on paper. Below *chat*, ask them to write the word *bat*. Ask them to think of other words that rhyme with *chat* and *bat* and write them underneath. Remind them that the phonogram *at* will remain the same, while they will substitute the initial consonant. Afterward, ask students to share their words.
- On the board write **man**, and have students read and write it on their papers. Now ask them to substitute the final consonant to build new words, such as *mat* and *map*.
- Have students read and write **pat**, then substitute the short vowel with other vowels to build *pet, pit, pot,* and *put*.

SHIFTING ROUTINES

Place the letter cards in front of students. Say: **If this says *tap*, how would you spell *pat*?** Invite a volunteer to manipulate the two consonants to spell the new word. Explain that you shifted the initial and final letter cards to make another word. Repeat this routine, asking students to write down their responses, with words such as *ten* (*net*), *not* (*ton*), *pit* (*tip*), *gum* (*mug*), *nap* (*pan*), and so on.

WORD-BUILDING ROUTINES

- Words with short *a*: Provide each pair of students with a set of letter cards. Ask them to pull the following letters from the pile: *a, t, n, p, c, f, m, r*. Have them build and write down as many short *a* words as they can in five minutes. Remind students that the initial sound in their word will be a consonant; the second a vowel; and the final a consonant, such as in the word *p-a-t*.
- Award a point to the pair with the most words written and read correctly. Continue the game, having students build other short-vowel words using the letter cards listed below.
- Words with short *e*: *e, b, p, m, l, g, d, n, t*
- Words with short *i*: *i, n, t, g, b, f, p, w*
- Words with short *o*: *o, t, n, p, h, s, d, c*
- Words with short *u*: *u, g, n, p, t, b, c, r*

As students continue the word-building game, award points to each student or pair of students who write and read their new words correctly. Award a certificate found on page 336 to the winning team.

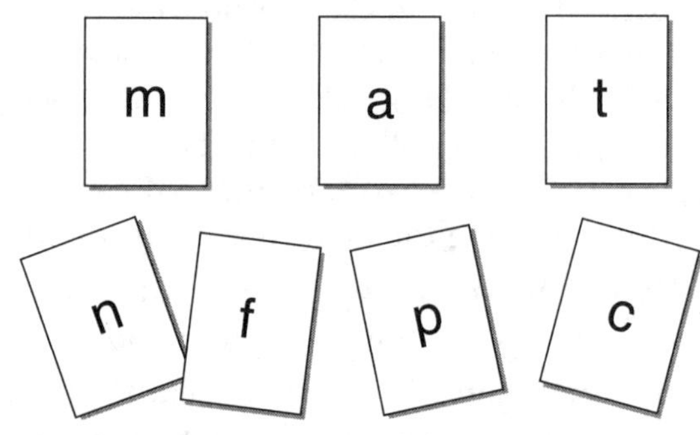

Teacher Tip

As your students work through each chapter and become more proficient in their reading and spelling skills, you may want to post their award certificates on a bulletin board. At the completion of *Getting Ready*, honor the award winners with a special ceremony, reflecting on everyone's efforts as they achieve their personal best. For students who continue to struggle but persevere to make the effort, award them with the certificate found on page 336 to commend their efforts.

PRACTICE

A. Unscramble the Words

Have students work on page 11 in the Worktext to unscramble three-sound, short-vowel words. Review the concept that each word requires a vowel sound in the medial or middle position.

B. Word Search

On Worktext page 12, have students take turns reading the words found in the Word Bank. Then have them work independently to find all 24 words that are hidden.

C. Word Race

Have students work in pairs to play the game found on Worktext page 13. Before playing, read the directions aloud to the class and provide examples of how to change the vowel sound in a word, such as *tip* to *top* to *tap*.

INFORMAL ASSESSMENT

To assess whether students are able to decode three-sound, short-vowel words, you can use the Assessment Checklist found on page 62 in the *Assessment Manual*, or write the Word Bank words on flash cards to test students.

LESSON 2

A. Unscramble the Words

Below are a series of words to unscramble. The first one is done for you. Remember that your words begin with a consonant sound, then have a vowel sound, then a consonant sound. When you unscramble the word, write it. Then read the word and place a check mark (✓) next to the word, indicating that you read it.

				Write the word.	Read the word.
	m	e	g	gem	☑
1.	t	a	ch	________	☐
2.	ff	c	u	________	☐
3.	u	b	t	________	☐
4.	t	i	s	________	☐
5.	t	m	e	________	☐
6.	i	n	ch	________	☐
7.	g	b	a	________	☐
8.	p	o	sh	________	☐
9.	b	ck	a	________	☐
10.	b	j	o	________	☐
11.	i	ck	p	________	☐
12.	p	i	l	________	☐
13.	a	n	p	________	☐
14.	g	f	o	________	☐
15.	ch	u	m	________	☐
16.	ll	w	i	________	☐
17.	t	e	p	________	☐
18.	i	ll	h	________	☐
19.	a	s	d	________	☐
20.	u	d	ck	________	☐

Lesson 2 • 11

Worktext page 11

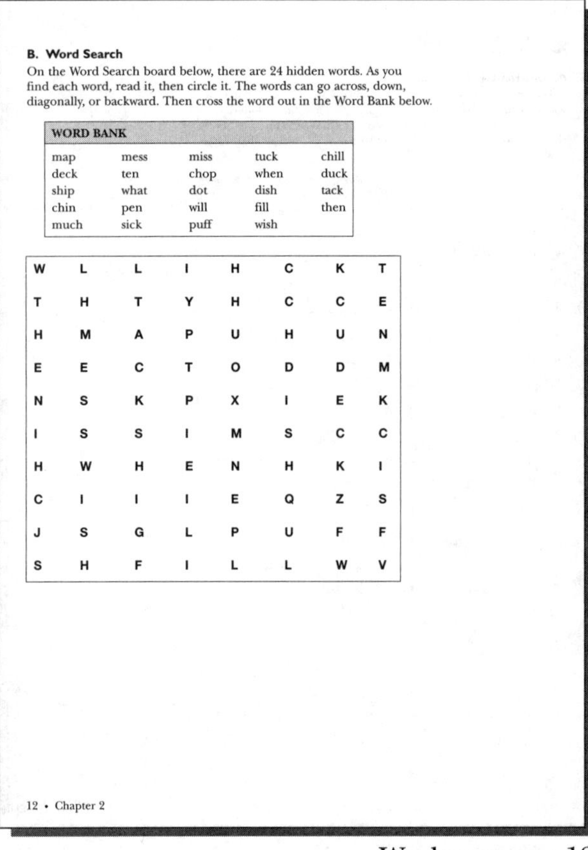

B. Word Search

On the Word Search board below, there are 24 hidden words. As you find each word, read it, then circle it. The words can go across, down, diagonally, or backward. Then cross the word out in the Word Bank below.

WORD BANK				
map	mess	miss	tuck	chill
deck	ten	chop	when	duck
ship	what	dot	dish	tack
chin	pen	will	fill	then
much	sick	puff	wish	

W	L	L	I	H	C	K	T
T	H	T	Y	H	C	C	E
H	M	A	P	U	H	U	N
E	E	C	T	O	D	D	M
N	S	K	P	X	I	E	K
I	S	S	I	M	S	C	C
H	W	H	E	N	H	K	I
C	I	I	I	E	Q	Z	S
J	S	G	L	P	U	F	F
S	H	F	I	L	L	W	V

12 • Chapter 2

Worktext page 12

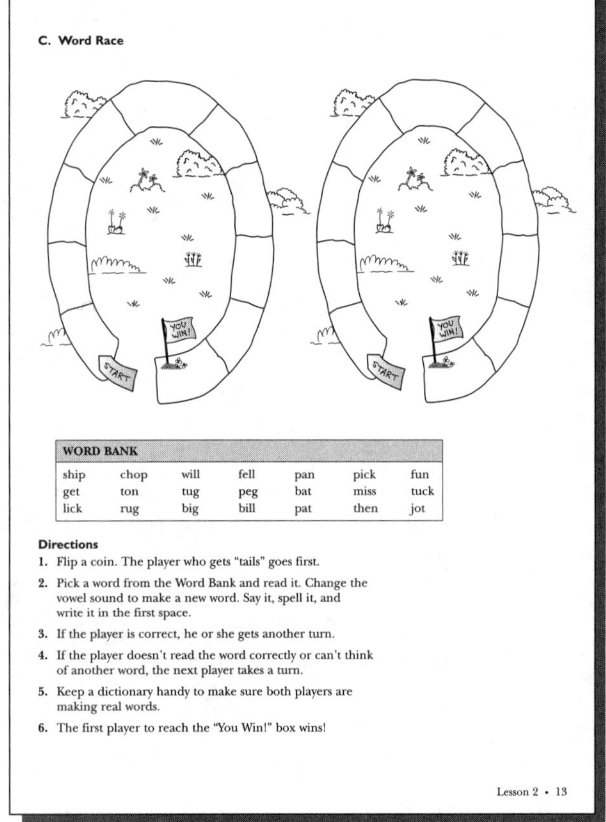

C. Word Race

WORD BANK						
ship	chop	will	fell	pan	pick	fun
get	ton	tug	peg	bat	miss	tuck
lick	rug	big	bill	pat	then	jot

Directions

1. Flip a coin. The player who gets "tails" goes first.
2. Pick a word from the Word Bank and read it. Change the vowel sound to make a new word. Say it, spell it, and write it in the first space.
3. If the player is correct, he or she gets another turn.
4. If the player doesn't read the word correctly or can't think of another word, the next player takes a turn.
5. Keep a dictionary handy to make sure both players are making real words.
6. The first player to reach the "You Win!" box wins!

Lesson 2 • 13

Worktext page 13

LESSON 3

OBJECTIVES

- Students will apply their decoding skills by reading tongue-twister sentences that contain three-sound, short-vowel words
- Students will sort words according to their vowel sounds
- Students will decode and read a poem
- Students will write sentences that sequence the order of events in the poem

MATERIALS

Worktext, pages 14–17
Teacher's Manual, pages 15–16
Award Certificate, page 336

DECODING AND READING

A. Wacky Tongue Twisters

- Read aloud the directions found on Worktext page 14. Guide students in reading each of the tongue twisters. Almost all of the words have a three-sound, short-vowel pattern. Point out any words that don't follow this pattern, such as *pickles*. When students come to this word, have them cover up *les* and decode the word *pick*. Guide them in blending both syllables together.
- When students have practiced the tongue twisters and can read them smoothly, have them use a stop watch or the second hand on the classroom clock to see how many times they can read each tongue twister in a minute.

Award a certificate to the student who not only read it the most times, but read it correctly.

B. Sort the Words

Have students read "Pal and the Pickle Pot" again. Help them begin the sorting activity by asking students to find the first short-vowel word in the tongue twister. Ask them to write it beneath the correct category. Then have students complete the activity independently.

C. Make Up Your Own Tongue Twister

Have students make up their own tongue twisters to share with classmates.

D. My Dog, Red

Have students read the poem silently. Afterward, ask them to circle any words they had difficulty sounding out. Invite students to take turns reading the poem aloud. Coach them in decoding words that are giving them difficulty.

E. What Happens First, Next, and Last?

Have students reread the poem. Taking turns, have them describe the sequence of events in their own words. On Worktext page 17, ask them to write four sentences for each stanza, ordering the events in the proper sequence.

ASSESSMENT

Dictation Routine

Have students write down each sentence as you dictate it. Say the sentence a few times before having them write it. When you're ready for them to write, say each word slowly. If students are having a problem with a particular word, have them write as much of the word as they can.

1. Pat and Peg put the pet pig in a pig pen.
2. Todd will tap on the top of a tin can.
3. Sam and Sal sell shells in a shop.
4. Meg and Mack mop up the mud.
5. Biff has a bug box on his big bed.
6. We go to the vet when my pet is sick.
7. I will put the mop in my van.
8. Red will sit in my lap, and I will pet him.

LESSON 3

A. Wacky Tongue Twisters

On this page, you will read five tongue twisters. Practice reading them with a partner, sounding out any words that you don't know. When you are able to read them smoothly, see how many times you can read one tongue twister in a minute. Remember, you have to read each word correctly. If you don't, please start over. Good luck!

Pal and the Pickle Pot

Pat, Pam, and Peg put Pal, the pet pig, and the pot of pickles in a pig pen. Pal and his pig friends, Pit, Pug, and Pod, pigged out on the pickle pot!

Tuck and the Thin, Tan, Tin Can

Tom and Tim tell Todd to tug with Tuck, the pup. Then Todd and Tuck go tap, tap, tap on the top of that thin, tan, tin can.

Sam and His Sis Sal

Sam and his sis Sal sit in the sun and eat a sub as they sell a sack of six shells by a shop. "Such fun," said Sam to his sis Sal.

My Mutt Mack

Matt, Meg, and Mom mop up the mud mess that my mutt, Mack, made. How much mud did Meg, Mom, and Matt mop up?

Biff's Big Bed

Ben, Bob, and Biff put a bell, bag, bat, and bug box on top of Biff's big bed.

14 • Chapter 2

Worktext page 14

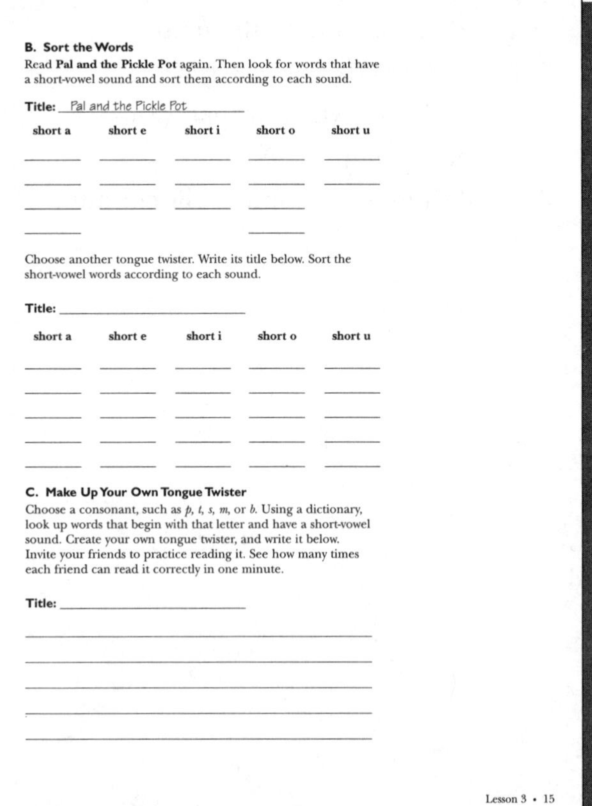

B. Sort the Words

Read **Pal and the Pickle Pot** again. Then look for words that have a short-vowel sound and sort them according to each sound.

Title: Pal and the Pickle Pot

short a	short e	short i	short o	short u
______	______	______	______	______
______	______	______	______	______
______	______	______	______	
______			______	

Choose another tongue twister. Write its title below. Sort the short-vowel words according to each sound.

Title: ____________________

short a	short e	short i	short o	short u
______	______	______	______	______
______	______	______	______	______
______	______	______	______	______
______	______	______	______	______
______	______	______	______	______

C. Make Up Your Own Tongue Twister

Choose a consonant, such as *p, t, s, m,* or *b.* Using a dictionary, look up words that begin with that letter and have a short-vowel sound. Create your own tongue twister, and write it below. Invite your friends to practice reading it. See how many times each friend can read it correctly in one minute.

Title: ____________________

Lesson 3 • 15

Worktext page 15

D. My Dog, Red

Read this poem to yourself. Then practice reading it aloud with a partner, sounding out any words that you don't know.

My Dog, Red

I will wash my dog, Red.
And when he is fed
I will pet him and then
We will sit on my bed.

And when Red is sick
We will go to the vet.
Red will lick the man's chin
And get him all wet!

Then Red and I
Will go to the shop
To get a big pot,
A pan, and a mop.

I will put the big pot,
The mop, and the pan
And my pet dog, Red,
In my big, long van.

And when we get home
Red will sit in my lap.
I will pet him and then
We will take a big nap!

16 • Chapter 2

Worktext page 16

E. What Happens First, Next, and Last?

Read the poem "My Dog, Red" again. Notice that in each stanza, the teenager did something with her dog, Red. First, tell a classmate all the things they did together. For each of the five stanzas, write four sentences about what they did. Be sure to put the sentences in the correct sequence.

1. ____________________

2. ____________________

3. ____________________

4. ____________________

5. ____________________

Lesson 3 • 17

Worktext page 17

CHAPTER 3
Other Three-Sound Words

TOKEN LESSON A

OBJECTIVES

- Students will develop phonemic awareness by segmenting nonsense words comprised of three sounds, using tokens to represent these sounds
- Students will discriminate sounds in the initial, final, and medial positions
- Students will discriminate sounds through the deletions of initial and final consonants

WORD BANK OF NONSENSE WORDS

seev	moez	dawm	naish	soob
loik	gaish	deeg	towp	mooth
laip	laish	muesh	shoob	seef
rawg	vaud	vead	zaid	noat

WORD BANK OF REAL WORDS

pail	boat	nail	reef	fail
seem	need	dawn	coin	goat
weed	sail	coat	rail	leaf
fawn	lawn	shoot	yawn	beet

MATERIALS

Teacher's Manual, pages 17–18
Token cards
Additional list of nonsense words, page 337

Teacher Tip

Before beginning this chapter, you may want to review long-vowel sounds, diphthongs, and vowel pairs, found in Chapter 1, pages 5–9.

PHONEMIC AWARENESS

Segmenting Sounds

Place three different tokens in a row, such as a diamond, square, and circle.

- Say it slowly: ***seev.* What is the first sound you hear in *seev*?** As you say the word, stretch and elongate each sound, without segmenting it. As the first student says /*s*/, have him or her point to the diamond, which represents the initial consonant sound.
- Say it slowly: ***seev.* What is the next sound you hear in *seev*?** Have the student begin saying the nonsense word, and cut him or her off after saying /*ee*/. When the student identifies /*ee*/, have him or her point to the square or token representing the medial vowel sound.
- Say it slowly: ***seev.* What is the final sound you hear in *seev*?** After the student says /*v*/, have him or her touch the circle representing the final consonant sound.
- Invite another student to segment a new word, using nonsense words found in the Word Bank.

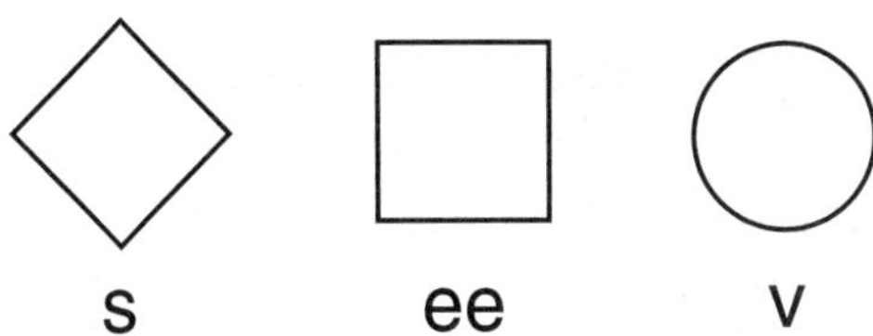

SUBSTITUTION ROUTINES

Initial Consonants

Place three new tokens in front of students, such as a star, rectangle, and triangle.

- Say: **This says *loik.* Now I'm going to make *boik.*** Replace the star with a circle.
- Say: **If this now says *boik*, I'm going to make *noik*.** Replace the circle with a square.
- Say: **If this now says *noik*, I'm going to make *zoik*.** Replace the square with a diamond.
- After modeling this routine, pick another word from the Word Bank of Nonsense Words and rotate students, having each substitute the initial consonant sounds, such as *laip, maip, vaip, daip.*

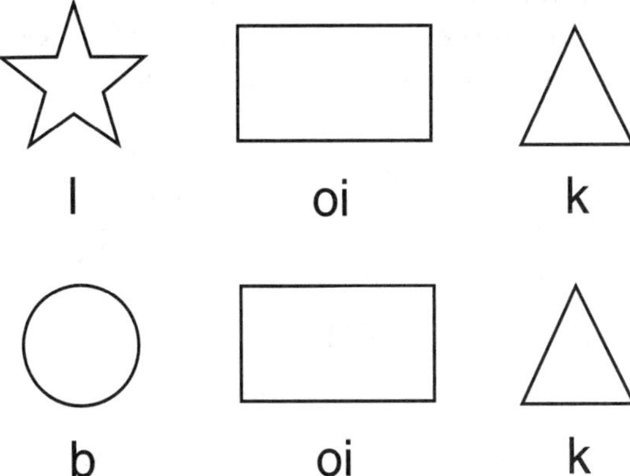

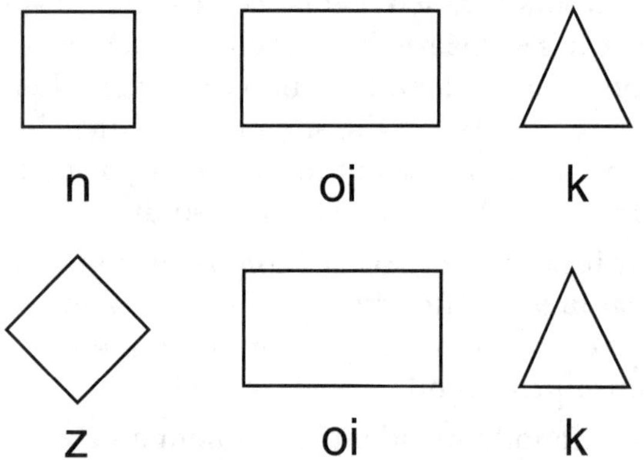

Final Consonants

Place three new tokens in front of students, such as a square, circle, and diamond.

- Say: **If this says *shoob*, make *shoov*.** Have the student replace the diamond with another token, such as a star. Guide students in substituting the final consonant sounds, replacing the last token with a new one.

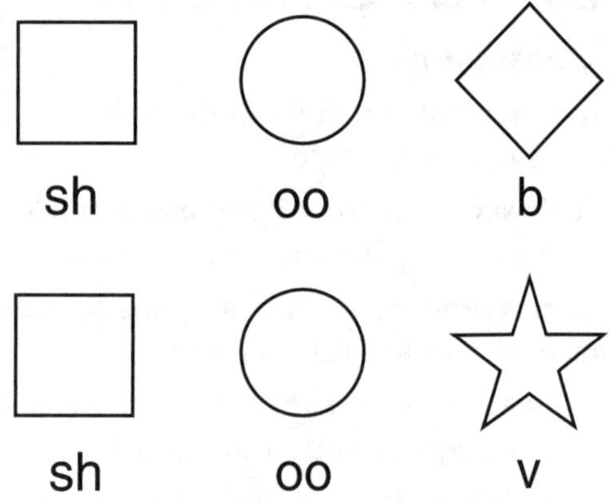

Medial Vowel Sounds

Place a triangle, circle, and star on the table.

- Say: **If this says *vaud*, make *vood*.** Coach students in substituting the medial vowel sound to make other nonsense words, such as *veed*, *vued*, and *voad*.

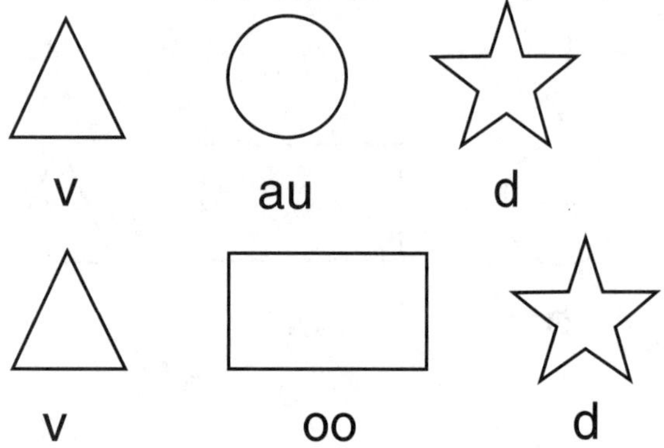

DELETION ROUTINES

Initial and Final Consonants

Place a circle, rectangle, and square on the table.

- Say: **If this says *dawm*, make *awm*.** Coach students in taking away the circle token, which represents the initial consonant sound. Once students become proficient at this, replace the circle and have them delete the final consonant sound to make *daw*, taking away the square.
- Repeat this deletion routine with other nonsense words.

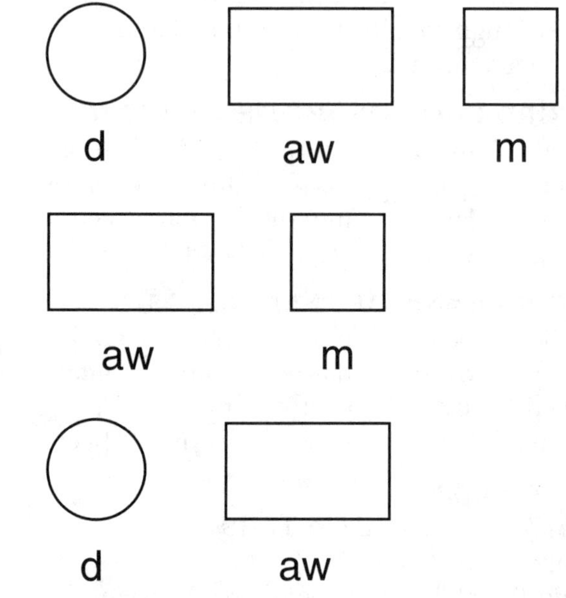

- For additional three-sound, long-vowel nonsense words, turn to page 337.
- After students have worked with three-sound, long-vowel nonsense words, you can use the Word Bank of Real Words with them.

TOKEN LESSON B

OBJECTIVES

- Students will segment three-sound nonsense words comprised of long vowels and vowel pairs by connecting sounds to letters
- Students will make and read new nonsense words by substituting beginning, final, and medial sounds and letters

WORD BANK OF NONSENSE WORDS

List 1	List 2	List 3	List 4
voon	seeg	moish	foat
choon	sheeg	thoish	zoat
thoon	heeg	roish	loat
thooz	heem	roich	loash
thood	heech	roith	loaz
thoom	heef	roid	loag
thaum	hoaf	raed	leeg
thiem	hauf	ruud	laug
theem	hoif	rowd	loog

MATERIALS

Teacher's Manual, pages 19–20
Assessment Checklist, page 62 of the *Assessment Manual*
Token cards
Letter cards, including all vowels, vowel pairs, consonants, and consonant digraphs

PHONICS

Connecting Sounds to Letters

Make a set of letter cards accessible to a small group of students. Place three different-shaped tokens in front of them.

- Say it slowly: ***voon.*** Point to the first token and say: **What sound does this make?** When the student says /*v*/, ask: **Can you find the letter that makes that sound?** Have the student place the letter *v* below the first token.
- Say it slowly: ***voon.*** Point to the middle token and say: **What sound does this make?** When the student says /*oo*/, ask: **Can you find the vowel pair that makes that sound?** Have the student place the letters *oo* below the second token.
- Say it slowly: ***voon.*** Point to the last token and say: **What sound does this make?** When the student says /*n*/, ask: **Can you find the letter that makes that sound?** Ask the student to place the letter *n* below the third token.
- Repeat this routine with other students in the group, using nonsense words from the Word Bank.

SUBSTITUTION ROUTINES

Initial Consonants

Once students are able to identify and connect the sounds to letters, remove the tokens, working with letter cards only.

- Say: **If this says *seeg*, watch as I find the letter card that will make the nonsense word *sheeg.*** Replace the *s* with the consonant digraph *sh.*
- Say: **Now it's your turn. Can you make *heeg*?** Coach the student in locating the letter card *h.*
- Repeat this routine until students are proficient at substituting letter cards in the initial position.

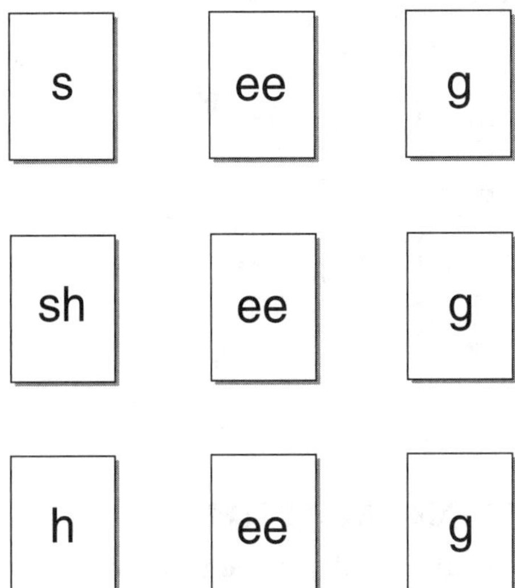

Final Consonants

Invite another student to find letter cards to make new nonsense words, substituting final consonants, such as *heem, heech,* and *heef.*

Medial Vowels

- Have the next student manipulate the letter cards in the medial position by substituting vowel sounds, such as *hoaf, hauf,* and *hoif.*
- For additional nonsense words, refer to page 337.

DELETION ROUTINES

Initial and Final Consonants

Place the following letter cards in front of students: *f-oa-t.*

- Say: **This says *foat*. Make *oat*.** Ask a student to remove the first letter card.
- Say: **This says *foat*. Make *foa*.** Have the student remove the last letter card.

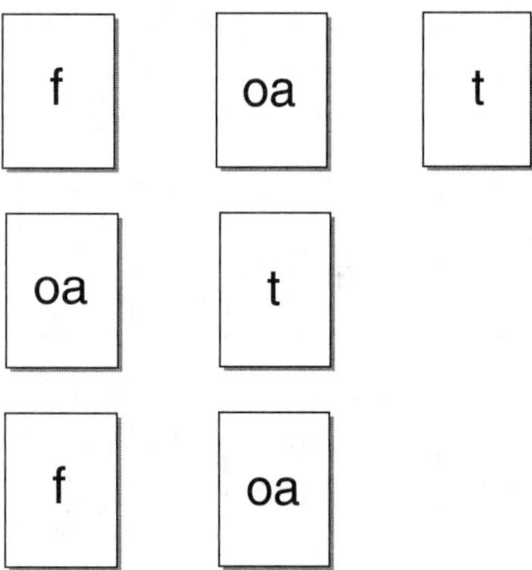

SHIFTING ROUTINES

Place these letter cards on the table: *m-ee-th.*

- Say: **This says *meeth*. Make *theem*.**
Coach students in shifting the initial and final letter cards.
- Say: **This says *theem*. Make *eemth*.**
If students are having trouble with shifting letter card positions, stretch out each sound, saying the word very slowly. Also let them know that no letter cards, other than the three in front of them are needed.

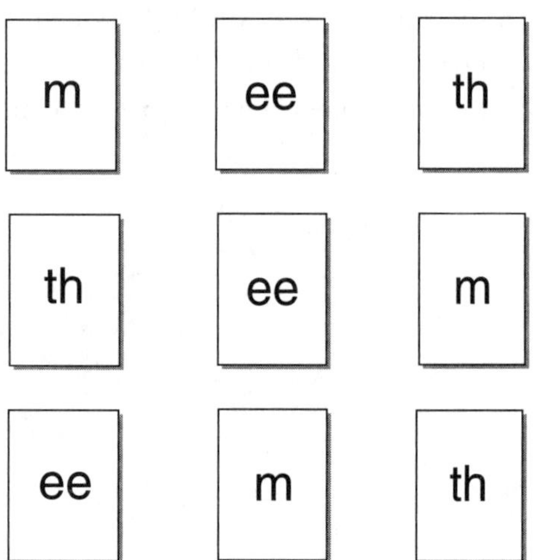

READING ROUTINES

Blending Sounds

- Place the word *loag*—as a whole word—in front of students. Ask one student to read the word. If the student reads it correctly, move on to the next student and have him or her decode another nonsense word.
- When students have difficulty reading a particular word, point to each letter and ask them to say the sound. If they are able to segment each sound, but if they are having difficulty blending the sounds together to form the word, you may want to take apart the word. Cover up the *l* in *loag*. Coach students in sounding out *oag*, conducting them to say the sound in a continuous fashion. Then ask students to blend the *oa-g* more quickly. Now uncover the *l*, getting them to read the nonsense word, blending the sounds together slowly, then more quickly, and finally as one word.

INFORMAL ASSESSMENT

Use the Assessment Checklist on page 62 of the *Assessment Manual* to determine whether students are able to decode three-sound, long-vowel, and vowel-pair patterns.

Teacher Tip

If . . . students aren't able to get eight out of 10 nonsense words correct,

Then . . . assess whether they are having difficulty hearing sounds in the initial, final, or medial positions. You may want to review particular consonants, long vowels, or vowel pairs in Chapter 1.

LESSON 1 (Part 1)

OBJECTIVES

- Students will recognize that when a word with one syllable has two vowels, the first vowel usually has a long sound, while the second vowel is silent
- Students will identify vowel-consonant-*e* spelling patterns
- Students will look at word pairs to distinguish short- and long-vowel patterns, such as *slid/slide*

WORD BANK OF REAL WORDS

mad/made	hid/hide	rob/robe
cub/cube	can/cane	rid/ride
hop/hope	tub/tube	pan/pane
kit/kite	cur/cure	dud/dude
tap/tape	dim/dime	mop/mope
cut/cute	fat/fate	bit/bite
not/note	cop/cope	

MATERIALS

Worktext, page 18
Teacher's Manual, page 21

CHAPTER 3

LESSON 1 (Part 1)

SPELLING RULE
Long-vowel words can be spelled vowel-consonant-e, as in *make, time, hope,* and *cute.* When a word with one syllable has two vowels, the first vowel will say its name, while the e is silent.

A. Say the Words
Say each word in the Word Bank. Remember that the first vowel will say its name, while the *e* will be silent.

WORD BANK				
note	fate	pane	bite	tape
cube	dime	mope	robe	dude
hide	cane	ride	cope	cute
kite	cure	tube	hope	made

B. Sort the Words
Look at the spelling of each word in the Word Bank. Sort and write each word under the correct long-vowel category. Circle the vowel that says its name.

a-consonant-e	i-consonant-e	o-consonant-e	u-consonant-e
________	________	________	________
________	________	________	________
________	________	________	________
________	________	________	________
________	________	________	________

C. Fill in the Blanks
Add a vowel and then a silent *e* to make real words. These are words that are found in the Word Bank.

1. c _ t _ 3. t _ p _ 5. b _ t _ 7. d _ m _ 9. f _ t _
2. m _ p _ 4. n _ t _ 6. d _ d _ 8. k _ t _ 10. r _ d _

D. Make It Short
Each word in the Word Bank can be turned into a short-vowel word by dropping the *e*, as in *made* to *mad.* Read each word, then think of the short-vowel word. Write four word pairs, such as *made/mad* below.

________ ________ ________ ________

18 • Chapter 3

Worktext page 18

SPELLING

Vowel-consonant-e patterns

- Write the following categories on the board: *a*-consonant-*e*, *i*-consonant-*e*, *o*-consonant-*e*, and *u*-consonant-*e*. Explain to students that some long-vowel words can be spelled vowel-consonant-*e*, as in *make, time, hope,* and *cute.* As you say each word, write it under the correct categories. Mention that when a word with one syllable has two vowels, the first vowel will say its name, while the *e* is silent. To help them remember the rule, you can say: **When two vowels go a-walking, the first one does the talking!**
- Have students turn to page 18 in their Worktexts and complete the activities. Coach students who are having difficulty in reading or sorting their words.
- After students complete the "Make It Short" activity, ask them to read their short-vowel and long-vowel word pairs to make sure they are pronouncing the vowel sounds correctly.

LESSON 1 (Part 2)

OBJECTIVES

- Students will recognize that when two vowels are next to each other in a one-syllable word, the first one says its name, while the second one is silent
- Students will identify long-vowel words with *ee, ea, ai, ay,* and *oa*
- Students will recognize that homophones are words that sound alike but have different spelling patterns

WORD BANK OF REAL WORDS

beet	beat	paid	pay	coat
meet	meat	maid	may	boat
cheep	cheap	nail	say	foam
feet	feat	gain	day	goal
peek	peak	fail	hay	soap

MATERIALS

Worktext, page 19
Teacher's Manual, page 22

LESSON 1 (Part 2)

SPELLING RULE
When two vowels are together in a word, the first one usually says its name, while the second one is silent, such as in *meat* or *coat*. *Y* can stand for vowels such as after an *a*, as in the words *day* and *way*.

A. Say the Words
Say each word in the Word Bank. Remember that the first vowel will say its name, while the second vowel is silent.

WORD BANK					
soap	way	nail	coat	hay	boat
peak	gain	day	feet	paid	beat
beet	meat	maid	cheep	meet	goal
cheap	may	peek	foam	feat	pay

B. Sort the Words
Look at the spelling of each word in the Word Bank. Sort and write each word under the correct long-vowel category. Circle the vowel that says its name.

ee	ea	ai	ay	oa
______	______	______	______	______
______	______	______	______	______
______	______	______	______	______
______	______	______	______	______
______	______		______	______

C. Fill in the Blanks
Add two vowels to make each word. All of the words are found in the Word Bank. There is more than one possible answer for some of these words.

1. m _ _ t 3. f _ _ t 5. d _ y 7. b _ _ t
2. f _ _ m 4. p _ _ k 6. c _ _ t 8. n _ _ l

D. Homophones
Homophones are words that sound alike but are spelled differently and have different meanings, such as *beat* and *beet*. Write four other word pairs that are homophones below.

1. ______ and ______ 3. ______ and ______
2. ______ and ______ 4. ______ and ______

Lesson 1 • 19

Worktext page 19

SPELLING

Long Vowels

- Write the following categories on the board: **ee, ea, ai, ay, oa.** Explain to students that when a word with one syllable has two vowels, the first vowel usually has a long sound, while the second vowel is silent. Write words from the Word Bank as you explain each long-vowel sound.
- Ask students to complete Worktext page 19. Help students decode each word, then help them to sort them according to their sounds and spellings. Point out that each word in the "Fill in the Blanks" activity can be found in their Word Bank.
- Explain to students that homophones are words that sound alike but are spelled differently and don't have the same meaning, such as *beat* and *beet.* Say the following sentences to point out the differences: **We're a team that can't be beat. I'll slice a beet and put it in my salad.** Have them look in their Word Bank to find four other homophone word pairs.

LESSON 2

OBJECTIVES

- Students will decode and read three-phoneme words that contain long-vowel spelling patterns and diphthongs
- Students will build and spell words using letter cards
- Students will practice reading by unscrambling sounds to make words, playing Bingo, and sorting words according to spelling patterns

WORD BANK OF REAL WORDS

read	paid	coin	day	oath
name	moan	say	peak	join
hope	sheep	team	raid	pay
soil	wheel	seem	dime	cheek
tube	boil	heal	may	coal

MATERIALS

Worktext, pages 20–22
Teacher's Manual, pages 23–24
Assessment Checklist, page 62 of the *Assessment Manual*
Award Certificate, page 336
Letter cards for each pair of students
Tokens for Bingo game

SUBSTITUTION ROUTINES

Initial Sounds

- Write the word **name** on the board. Ask a student to read the word, then have the group members write it down on their papers. Below *name*, ask volunteers to think of words that rhyme with it, such as *game* and *tame*, and have them suggest the spelling for each word and write it underneath *name*. Remind them that the initial consonant needs to be replaced with a new sound each time.
- Repeat this routine with other words in the Word Bank, such as *peak, heal,* and *may*. As you do this activity as a whole group, students may encounter rhyming words that are spelled differently, such as *peek, beak, week, seek,* and *leak*. Remind them that although these are all long-vowel words, they are spelled differently.

SORTING ROUTINES

Write each word from the Word Bank on index cards. Have students take turns sorting each word according to the vowel pattern. As students sort, have them read each word aloud.

WORD-BUILDING ROUTINES

- Provide each student or pair of students with a set of letter cards. Determine what vowel pattern you'd like students to practice. For example, if they need more practice with long *a*, specifically *a*-consonant-*e*, ask them to pull the *a* and *e* letter cards along with consonants that will make a lot of words, such as *m, k, l, f, w, t, b, c,* and *r*. As one student makes a word, the other can write it down. Then they can switch roles.
- Time individuals or pairs of students. Award a certificate to the person or pair who makes the most words in a five- or 10-minute period. The certificate can be found on page 336.

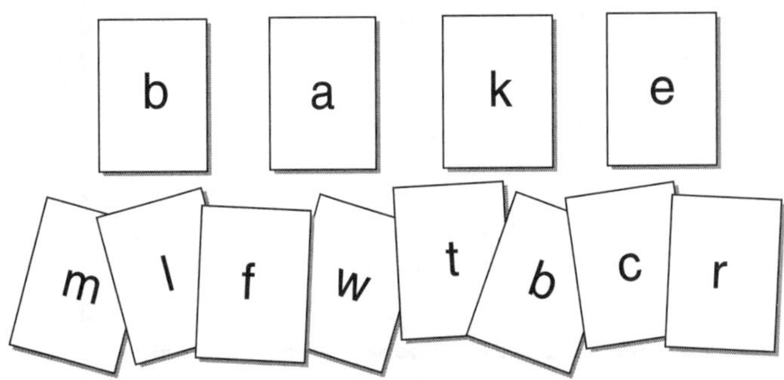

PRACTICE

A. Bingo

Have two or three students play Bingo, using the Bingo cards found on Worktext pages 20–21. Invite one student to be the caller, reading the Word Bank words. Students can use the tokens as chips for each Bingo card.

B. Word Pattern

- Ask students to turn to page 22 in the Worktext. Tell them that they will be using words from their Word Bank to make a pattern of words in the grid.
- As they write a word in the grid, have them read the word, then cross it out. Award a certificate to the student who was able to use the most words and decode each correctly.

INFORMAL ASSESSMENT

Use the Assessment Checklist found on page 62 of the *Assessment Manual* to assess whether students can decode and read three- sound words.

LESSON 2

A. Bingo

Directions

1. Each player should use a different Bingo card.
2. Each player takes some tokens.
3. Pick a caller.
4. The caller reads a word from the Word Bank in any order.
5. The players put a token on the square that contains the word.
6. The first player to get four tokens in a row says, "Bingo!"

WORD BANK				
read	pick	coin	day	oath
name	moan	say	peak	join
hope	sheep	team	raid	pay
soil	wheel	seem	dime	cheek
tube	boil	heal	may	come

Bingo Card 1

dime	heal	soil	seem
read	hope	name	sheep
day	wheel	coin	pay
join	raid	peak	may

20 • Chapter 3

Worktext page 20

Bingo Card 2

come	day	read	hope
team	soil	cheek	tube
boil	may	seem	join
moan	oath	say	wheel

Bingo Card 3

pick	name	join	wheel
say	soil	dime	tube
oath	team	raid	boil
heal	may	seem	day

Lesson 2 • 21

Worktext page 21

B. Word Pattern

Use words in the Word Bank below to create your own word pattern in the grid. Begin by making another word, using one of the letters in the word *take*. As you use words in the Word Bank, cross them out. Be careful that all the connecting words form words both across and down. The student with the most words in his or her word pattern wins!

WORD BANK			
~~take~~	seed	ray	mole
cube	coil	meal	seal
rope	deep	mean	shake
white	lead	loan	coin
day	foil	teeth	leak

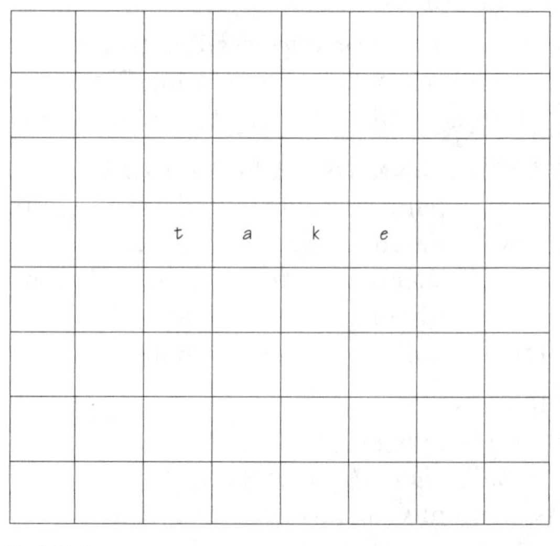

22 • Chapter 3

Worktext page 22

LESSON 3

OBJECTIVES

- Students will apply their decoding skills by reading passages containing words with long vowels
- Students will sort words according to their spelling patterns
- Students will read a passage and fill in missing words that contain long-vowel spelling patterns
- Students will write a sports cheer that includes words containing both short and long vowels

MATERIALS

Worktext, pages 23–25
Teacher's Manual, pages 25–26
Award Certificate, page 336

DECODING AND READING

A. Drop Me a Note!

- Coach students as they read letters written by Mike and Kate. As they read, they will be reviewing many short-vowel words. In addition, they will be focusing on reading words containing the long-vowel patterns learned in this chapter.
- Have students practice reading for fluency, then award certificates, found on page 336, to students who are becoming more proficient.

Teacher Tip

Before students read each letter, write any words that may give them difficulty on the board, such as the two-syllable words **over** and **party**. Help them decode these words. Then write **laps** and **miles** on the board. Cover up the *s* in *laps,* have a volunteer read the word, then add /*s*/ to make it plural. Point out the "P.S.," or postscript, in Kate's letter and write the word **join** on the board. Review the sound a diphthong makes in a word. You can refer to page 6 in Chapter 1 of the *Teacher's Manual* for additional suggestions.

B. Sort the Words

As a group, reread the letter written by Mike. Then ask students to circle the words with the following long-vowel patterns: *a_e, i_e, o_e, ea, ee,* and *oa.* Have them sort the circled words according to their long-vowel spelling pattern.

C. Fill in the Blanks

In this activity, have students read the letter by Kate and fill in the missing long-vowel words using the Word Bank as a guide.

D. A Team Cheer

Before students read the cheer, help them decode the words **three** and **Saturday**, by writing each word on the board.

- Cover up the letters *ree* in *three* and have students say /*th*/. Then cover up the letters *th* and have them sound out /*r*/ and /*ee*/. Ask them to blend the two sounds together. Finally, guide them in blending the three sounds together to make the word.
- Have students look at the word *Saturday* in chunks. Cover up all the letters except *sat* and decode this word first. Then cover up everything except *day* and have them decode that chunk. Next, have them sound out /*ur*/. Finally, blend the whole word together, syllable by syllable.

E. Make Up Your Own Cheer

Take a poll to see which sport the class likes best and have them write a group cheer together.

ASSESSMENT

Dictation Routine

Have students write down each sentence as you dictate it. Say the sentence a few times before having them write. When they're ready, say each sentence slowly and clearly. If students have difficulty figuring out how to spell a particular word, have them leave a blank or write as much of the word as they can.

1. Mike made the team.
2. I need to get in shape.
3. I like to ride my bike and race it.
4. Come to the game this week.
5. Kate will sit with Hope at the game.
6. I will go to the beach with my dog.
7. I need to feed my dog.
8. I may join a team.

LESSON 3

A. Drop Me a Note!
Read the two letters below.

Dear Kate,

I made the team! I need to get in shape by the time of the race. I will hike up the hill. I will ride my bike and race with Gabe. We will take my boat to the lake. Gabe and I will dive in the lake. Gabe will time me while I swim a half mile.

Can you go on a date to the game with me this week? Gabe and Hope will save us seats. Then I will take you to a party at Nate's house. Gabe will take Hope to the party.

I need to get some sleep. I have to wake up at 6:00 A.M. and ride nine miles on my bike. Drop me a note!

Mike

Dear Mike,

Way to go! I will go this week to the game with you. I will cheer for the team. I will look for Gabe and Hope to sit with them. Nate's party will be fun, too.

I need to take my dog, Big Ray, for a run at the beach. Then I need to feed him. I can't wait to see you this week. Good luck!

Kate

P.S. I may join a team, too!

Lesson 3 • 23

Worktext page 23

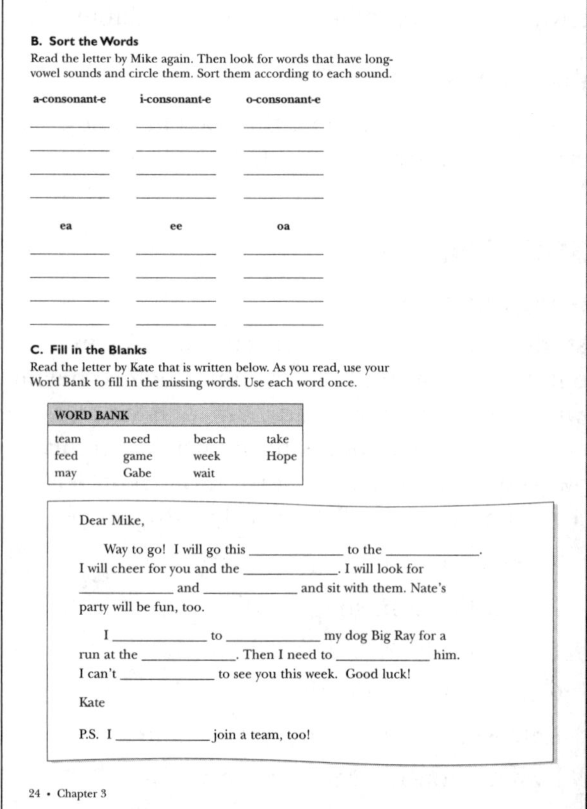

B. Sort the Words
Read the letter by Mike again. Then look for words that have long-vowel sounds and circle them. Sort them according to each sound.

a-consonant-e	i-consonant-e	o-consonant-e
______	______	______
______	______	______
______	______	______
______	______	______

ea	ee	oa
______	______	______
______	______	______
______	______	______
______	______	______

C. Fill in the Blanks
Read the letter by Kate that is written below. As you read, use your Word Bank to fill in the missing words. Use each word once.

WORD BANK			
team	need	beach	take
feed	game	week	Hope
may	Gabe	wait	

Dear Mike,

Way to go! I will go this ____________ to the ____________. I will cheer for you and the ____________. I will look for ____________ and ____________ and sit with them. Nate's party will be fun, too.

I ____________ to ____________ my dog Big Ray for a run at the ____________. Then I need to ____________ him. I can't ____________ to see you this week. Good luck!

Kate

P.S. I ____________ join a team, too!

24 • Chapter 3

Worktext page 24

D. A Team Cheer
Read the poem below.

One, three, five, nine.
See my team. We are so fine!

So join the team. It will be fun.
We kick the ball. We pass and run.

Each of us is lean and mean.
We will beat the other team.

We will play this game to win.
See the goal post and kick it in.

We play ball each Saturday.
"Win, win, win" is what we say!

We will win. We can't be beat.
See us play, so take a seat!

E. Make Up Your Own Cheer
Read the cheer again. Think of a sport that you like best. Then make up your own cheer. Use some long-vowel words, such as *team, beat,* and *game.* Review some of your short-vowel words, such as *win, kick,* and *run.*

Title: ____________________

____
____
____
____
____
____
____
____

Lesson 3 • 25

Worktext page 25

CHAPTER 4
Three-Sound, More Complex Words

TOKEN LESSON A

OBJECTIVES

- Students will develop phonemic awareness by segmenting nonsense words comprised of initial and final consonant blends, using tokens to represent each sound
- Students will discriminate sounds through substitution and deletion routines as well as by shifting the position of sounds

WORD BANK OF NONSENSE WORDS

skai	ploe	tre	fli	smue
gree	dwie	spo	bree	dri
fru	swee	klo	aps	ilf
esk	omp	oest	eebz	inth
ust	ips	ept	aizd	eps

WORD BANK OF REAL WORDS

mask	west	tree	true
must	elf	east	dump
free	greet	ninth	flee
bee	treat	cups	jump

MATERIALS

Teacher's Manual, pages 27–28
Token cards
Additional list of nonsense words, page 337

PHONEMIC AWARENESS

Segmenting Sounds

Place a circle, rectangle, and triangle in front of a small group of students.

- Say it slowly: ***skai.* What is the first sound you hear in *skai*?** As you say the word, stretch each sound without segmenting it. Have a student point to the circle and say /s/.
- Say it slowly: ***skai.* What is the next sound you hear in *skai*?** Have the student stretch out the first two sounds, cutting him or her off after /k/. Ask the student to point to the token representing the second consonant. (*rectangle*)
- Say it slowly: ***skai.* What is the last sound you hear in *skai*?** Have the student say /ai/, pointing to the triangle at the same time.
- Introduce other nonsense words, rotating them among students in the small group.

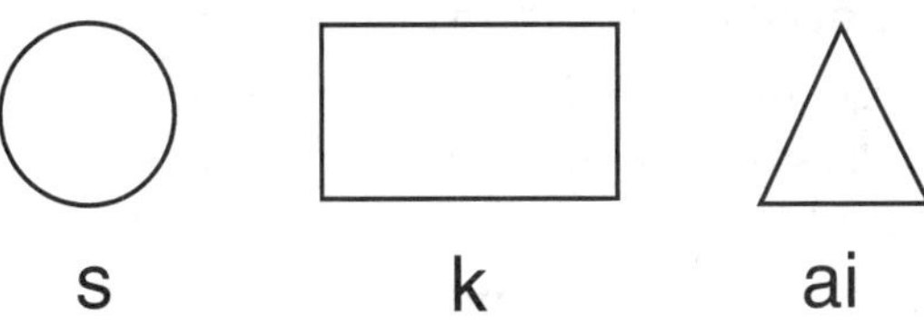

Teacher Tip

Consonant blends can be very difficult for students to hear because they need to distinguish very fine sound differentiations. It is important to model saying each nonsense word very slowly, elongating each sound. As students segment the word, have them listen to and stretch each sound. You can also introduce word pairs, such as *sai/skai, poe/ploe, sue/smue, di/dri.* By working with word pairs, students can compare and hear how a consonant blend sounds different from a single consonant sound.

WORD-PAIR ROUTINES

Making Consonant Blends

Place a star and a diamond next to each other.

- Say: **This says *ko.* Now I'm going to make *klo.*** Add a square between the star and diamond. Ask students to say the new sound that was added. (/*l*/)
- Put a rectangle and circle on the table. Say: **If this says *fu,* make *fru.*** As a student places a new token between the rectangle and circle, have him or her say /*r*/, representing the new consonant.
- Once you've had students work with several initial consonants and consonant blends, use words from the Word Bank of Nonsense Words that have final consonant blends. Say: **If this says *ek,* make *esk.*** Students should add a token in the middle of the two sounds and say /*s*/. Do this routine with other nonsense words, such as *us/ust, eez/eebz,* and *op/omp.*

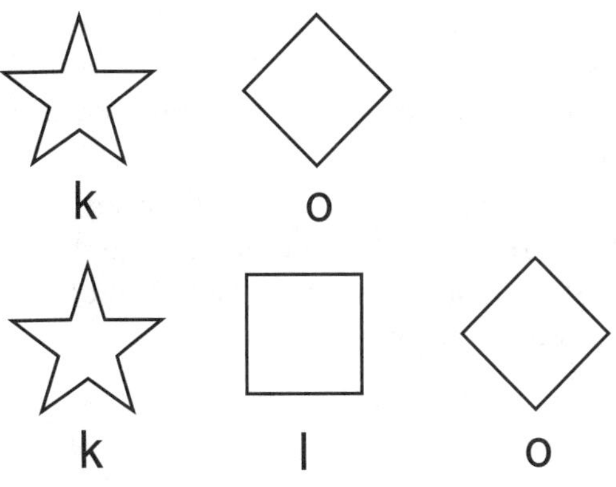

SUBSTITUTION ROUTINES

Initial Consonant Blends

Place a rectangle, circle, and triangle on the table. Substitute consonants to make new consonant blends.

- Say: **If this says *smue*, make *spue*.** Ask a volunteer to point to the token that needs to be replaced (*the circle*), while saying the new sound /*p*/.
- Say: **If this says *spue*, make *skue*.** Coach the student in replacing the second token once again to form a new consonant blend.

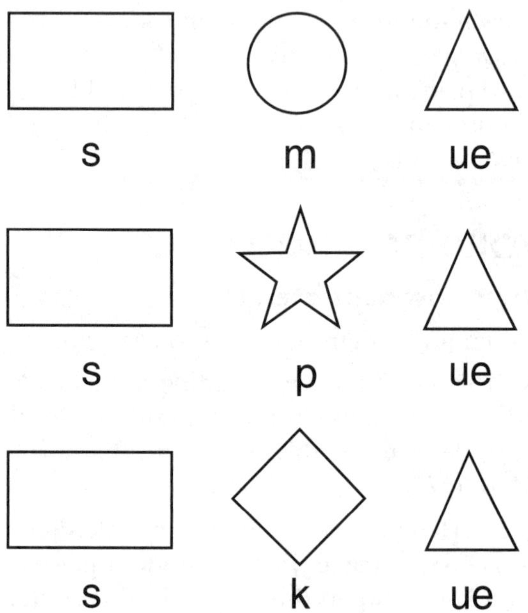

Final Consonant Blends

Use new tokens to have students work with substituting consonants to make final blends, such as *ilf/ ilm/ ilz; omp/ omz/ omd; esk/ esp/ esd.*

SHIFTING ROUTINES

When students are proficient in adding and substituting sounds to make consonant blends, guide them in listening carefully as you shift the position of sounds. This routine can be much more difficult for students to hear, so be sure to stretch each sound as you say it.

- Place a square, triangle, and star on the table. Say: **If this says *osp*, make *pos*.** As the student places the star before the square, have him or her segment each sound, /*p*/ /*o*/ /*s*/.
- Say: **If this says *pos*, make *spo*.** After the student has placed the triangle, star, and square in a row, have the student point to each token while saying /*s*/ /*p*/ /*o*/.
- Invite students to shift positions of sounds in other nonsense words.

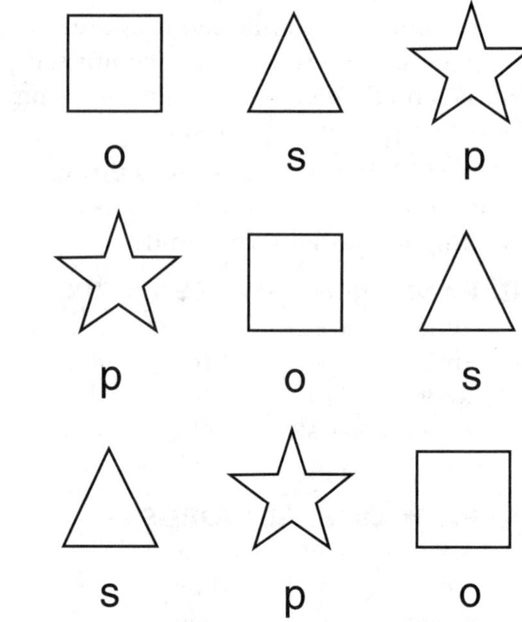

- For additional complex, three-sound nonsense words containing consonant blends, turn to page 337.
- After students have worked with complex, three-sound nonsense words with consonant blends, you can use the Word Bank of Real Words with them.

TOKEN LESSON B

OBJECTIVES

- Students will segment three-sound, more complex words comprised of initial or final consonant blends by connecting sounds to letters
- Students will make and then read new nonsense words by adding, substituting, deleting, or shifting the position of letters

WORD BANK OF NONSENSE WORDS

stoe	bloy	tes	frai	skou
broo	slee	prau	asht	drail
isp	eft	aks	oops	alp
ilk	ort	anth	oemz	uusht

MATERIALS

Teacher's Manual, pages 29–30
Assessment Checklist, page 62 of the *Assessment Manual*
Token cards
Letter cards, including all vowels, vowel pairs, consonants, and consonant digraphs

PHONICS

Connecting Sounds to Letters

Have a set of letter cards handy. Place three different-shaped tokens in front of students.

- Say it slowly: ***stoe.*** Point to the first token and say: **What sound does this make?** When the student responds /*s*/, say: **Find the letter that makes that sound.** Ask the student to place the letter *s* under the first token.
- Say it slowly: ***stoe.*** Point to the middle token and say: **What sound does this make?** Have the student place the letter *t* below the second token and say /*t*/.
- Say it slowly: ***stoe.*** Point to the last token and say: **What sound does this make?** When the student says /*oe*/, ask: **Can you find the letter(s) that make this sound?** The student may place the letter(s) *o* or *oe* beneath the last token.
- Repeat this routine using other nonsense words from the Word Bank. Be sure to practice both initial and final consonant blends.

SUBSTITUTION ROUTINES

Initial Consonant Blends

Once students are proficient in identifying and connecting the sounds to letters, remove the tokens and use letter cards only.

- Say: **This says *bloy.* Make *broy.*** As you say the word slowly, emphasize the second consonant. Guide students in finding the letter *r* and substituting it for the *l.*
- Say: **This says *broy.* Make *skoy.*** Ask students how many sounds have been changed, coaching them to substitute *br* with *sk.*
- Say: **This says *skoy.* Make *sloy.*** Invite a volunteer to substitute /*k*/ with /*l*/.
- Repeat this routine with other nonsense words until all students have had multiple opportunities to manipulate initial consonant sounds.

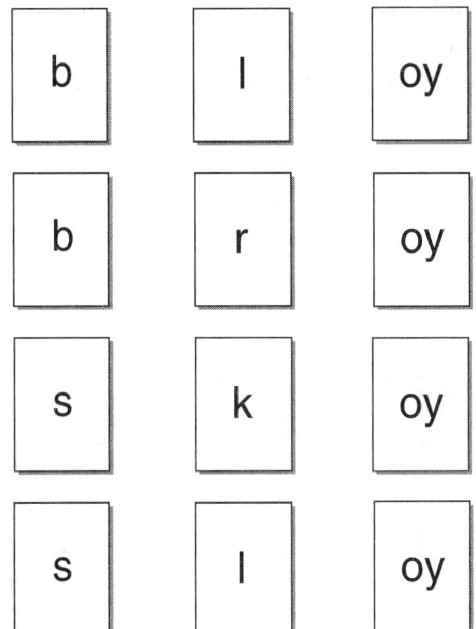

Final Consonant Blends

Mention to students that in this routine, you will be substituting consonants at the end of each nonsense word and that they should listen carefully for those sounds.

- Say: **This says *anth.* Make *anz.*** Help students substitute the *th* letter card with the *z.*
- Say: **This says *anz.* Make *anch.*** Students should substitute the letter *z* with the consonant digraph *ch.*
- Say: **This says *anch.* Make *anf.*** Invite a student to substitute *ch* with the letter *f.*
- Continue this routine with other nonsense words containing final consonant blends.

DELETION ROUTINES

Tell students that you will be deleting a consonant somewhere in each nonsense word and ask them to listen carefully as you stretch out each sound.

- Say: **This says *frai.* Make *rai.*** As students remove the *f*, ask them to say the new word *rai.*
- Repeat this routine with other nonsense words, such as *slee/ see, alp/ ap, uusht/ uush.*

SHIFTING ROUTINES

Mention to students that you are going to challenge them with another routine. Explain that you will be shifting the position of letters within the word, which may be more difficult for them to hear.

- Say: **This says *slee.* Make *seel.*** Repeat each word slowly, stretching out each sound. Once students have shifted the *l* to the end of the word, continue the routine using the same letter cards to make *lees* and *eels.* You may want to demonstrate this routine by providing students with a few examples before they attempt it themselves.

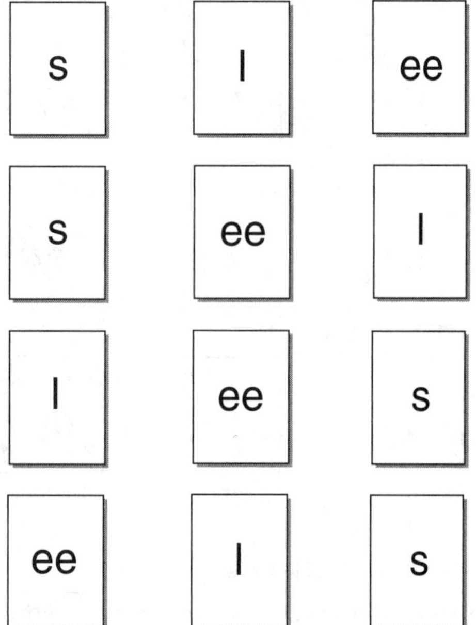

READING ROUTINES

Blending Sounds

After having students practice spelling nonsense words, assess their ability to read the nonsense words that they are making.

- Place the word *prau* in front of students and invite a volunteer to read it. If the student reads it correctly, move on to the next volunteer and place another nonsense word on the table for that student to read.
- If students have difficulty decoding the nonsense words, coach them in stretching out each sound that makes the consonant blend, so that they don't skip over one of these sounds. You can also point out the differences in what a word sounds like with and without the consonant blend, such as in *skou/ sou, oops/ oop,* and *eft/ et.*

INFORMAL ASSESSMENT

Use the Assessment Checklist on page 62 of the *Assessment Manual* to determine whether students are able to decode and read three- sound nonsense words that contain initial and final consonant blends.

Teacher Tip

If . . . a student says a consonant blend together (e.g., */pl/*) and assigns one token for the blend,

Then . . . ask: **How many sounds do you hear in */pl/*? What is the first sound?** When the student identifies it, ask: **What is the second sound?** Then help the student assign two tokens to the blend.

LESSON 1 (Part 1)

OBJECTIVES

- Students will recognize that consonant *c* can sound like /*k*/ or /*s*/
- Students will identify words containing both sounds
- Students will sort words according to their sounds and read sentences to fill in words with hard *c* and soft *c*

WORD BANK OF REAL WORDS

candy	celery	actor	cattle	recess
coal	city	coin	dice	coat
cat	race	cut	rice	cap
cake	mice	cone	face	ice

MATERIALS

Worktext, page 26
Teacher's Manual, page 31

SPELLING

Hard and Soft c

- Write the following categories on the board or on chart paper: /*s*/ and /*k*/. Mention to students that consonant *c* can have two sounds. Sometimes it sounds like /*s*/, as in *celery* and *recess.* Other times it can sound like /*k*/, as in *candy, actor,* and *cattle.* Write each of the words under the correct category. Have students brainstorm other words and add them to each list.
- Have students complete Worktext page 26. Rotating around the small group, ask students to decode and read each of the words found in the Word Bank. Then have them sort the words according to their hard and soft sounds.
- As students complete "Fill in the Blanks," remind them that all of the words can be found in the Word Bank.

CHAPTER 4

LESSON 1 (Part 1)

SPELLING RULE
Words with consonant c can have two sounds. Sometimes it sounds like /k/, in words such as *camel* or *carpet.* When c is followed by an *i, e,* or *y*, it sounds like /s/, as in the words *center* and *civil.*

A. Say the Words
Say each word in the Word Bank. Remember that consonant *c* sounds like /*s*/ when it is followed by an *i, e,* or *y*.

WORD BANK				
coal	city	coin	dice	coat
cat	race	cut	rice	ice
cake	mice	cone	face	

B. Sort the Words
Read the words again in the Word Bank. Sort and write each word under the correct category. Circle the *c* in each word.

/*s*/		/*k*/	
______	______	______	______
______	______	______	______
______	______	______	______
______		______	

C. Fill in the Blanks
Read the sentences and fill in the correct words. The words can be found in the Word Bank. Some sentences may have more than one possible answer.

1. My ________ likes to chase ________.
2. I will ________ down the hill on my bike.
3. The boy has dirt on his ________.
4. The road is a sheet of ________.
5. My ________ is red and white.
6. The ________ cream ________ will taste good.

26 • Chapter 4

Worktext page 26

Getting Ready

LESSON 1 (Part 2)

OBJECTIVES

- Students will recognize that consonant *g* can sound hard, like /g/, or soft, like /j/
- Students will identify words that contain both sounds
- Students will sort words according to their sounds and read sentences to fill in words that have hard *g* and soft *g*

WORD BANK OF REAL WORDS

sugar	gutter	pigeon	arrange	game
gym	page	ago	sage	egg
grid	large	goat	gum	siege
get	huge	rage	gift	age

MATERIALS

Worktext, page 27
Teacher's Manual, page 32

SPELLING

Hard and Soft g

- Make two categories on chart paper that say **/g/** and **/j/**. Explain to students that *g* can sound hard, as in *gutter* or *flag*. Write the two words under /g/. Mention that *g* can also sound soft, as in *giraffe* or *orange*. Ask students where they would place *garage*. Tell them that the word contains both sounds, and write it under each category. Have students think of other words that have these sounds. Students can also look up some words in the dictionary to add to the class list.
- Have students turn to page 27 in their Worktexts and complete the spelling page on hard and soft *g*. Help students decode any words they may not be able to read fluently. Coach students as they sort the words according to their sounds.
- Have students complete "Fill in the Blanks."

LESSON 1 (Part 2)

SPELLING RULE
Words with consonant *g* can have two sounds. Sometimes it sounds hard, as in *gutter* or *flag*. When *g* is followed by an *i*, *e*, or *y*, it usually sounds soft, as in *giraffe* or *orange*. There are some exceptions to the rule. For example, if a word has *ge* at the end of it, consonant *g* sounds like /j/, as in *gauge*. Or, *g* may have a hard sound at times, as in the word *give*.

A. Say the Words
Say each word in the Word Bank. Remember that consonant *g* usually sounds like /j/ when it is followed by an *i*, *e*, or *y*.

WORD BANK				
game	goat	gym	page	siege
sage	huge	egg	gum	gift

B. Sort the Words
Read the words again in the Word Bank. Sort and write each word under the correct category. Circle the *g* in each word.

/g/	/j/
________	________
________	________
________	________
________	________
________	________

C. Fill in the Blanks
Read the sentences and fill in the correct words. The words can be found in the Word Bank.

1. I like to eat an ________ and toast.
2. The boy likes to play a ________.
3. I like to chew ________.
4. I will give my dad a ________.
5. This ________ of work is easy.
6. I like to play ball in the ________.

Lesson 1 • 27

Worktext page 27

LESSON 1 (Part 3)

OBJECTIVES

- Students will recognize that consonant *y* can also stand for vowels, such as long *e* and long *i*
- Students will identify words containing *y* that have the long *e* and long *i* sounds
- Students will sort words according to their sounds as well as read sentences, identifying the targeted sounds

WORD BANK OF REAL WORDS

fly	sty	family	twenty	baby
try	shy	funny	cry	puppy
dry	my	why	very	
sky	many	by	pretty	

MATERIALS

Worktext, page 28
Teacher's Manual, page 33

SPELLING

Y as a Vowel

Write the following two categories on chart paper or the board: **long *e*, long *i*.** Explain to students that *y* can sometimes sound like long *e*, in words such as *family* and *twenty*. Mention that it can also sound like long *i*, in words such as *fly* and *sty*. Have students brainstorm other words that contain these sounds and add them to each category.

- Ask students to turn to page 28 in their Worktexts. Students may need help in decoding some of the words on their list that contain two syllables, such as *baby*, *funny*, *puppy*, *many*, and *pretty*. Rotate around the room, coaching students as they sort their words.
- As students complete "What's the Vowel Sound?" mention that some sentences contain more than one word that contains the targeted sounds. Have them circle words where *y* sounds like long *i*, and underline words where consonant *y* sounds like long *e*.

LESSON 1 (Part 3)

SPELLING RULE
Consonant *y* can stand for vowels, such as long e and long *i*, as in the words *family* and *fly*.

A. Say the Words
Say each word in the Word Bank. Remember that *y* can stand for vowels such as long *e* and long *i*.

WORD BANK			
baby	very	sky	try
funny	many	cry	puppy
fly	my	by	pretty

B. Sort the Words
Read the words again in the Word Bank. Sort and write each word under the correct category. Circle the *y* in each word.

/i/	/e/
________	________
________	________
________	________
________	________
________	________
________	________

C. What's the Vowel Sound?
Read each sentence. Circle words where consonant *y* sounds like long *i*. Underline words where consonant *y* sounds like long *e*.

1. My puppy is shy.
2. The baby will cry when she wakes up.
3. The sky is blue.
4. Tom is so funny.
5. Many of my friends are very funny.
6. I like to fly on a plane.

28 • Chapter 4

Worktext page 28

Getting Ready

LESSON 2

OBJECTIVES

- Students will decode and read three-phoneme words that contain initial and final consonant blends
- Students will build and spell words using letter cards
- Students will practice reading by playing a game, completing a crossword puzzle, and unscrambling words containing consonant blends

WORD BANK OF REAL WORDS

free	play	glue	ears	sky
plea	slow	sway	oink	flee
east	ask	elf	act	oats
arch	aunt	alp	elk	arm

MATERIALS

Worktext, pages 29–31
Teacher's Manual, pages 34–35
Assessment Checklist, page 62 of the *Assessment Manual*
Award Certificate, page 336
Letter cards for each pair of students

SUBSTITUTION ROUTINES

Initial and Final Consonant Blends

- Write the word **play** on the board. Ask a volunteer to read the word, then have the class write the word down on paper. Explain to students that you will say another word that rhymes with *play*, but you will be substituting the initial consonant blend with two other sounds and letters. Say the word **stay** and ask them to write the word below *play*. Do the same routine with *tray*, *clay*, and *gray*.
- Repeat this routine with other words in the Word Bank.
- When students are proficient at substituting initial consonant blends to make rhyming words, have them spell other words, such as *arch*, *elk*, *ears*, and *oink*. As you say each word, elongate each sound without segmenting it.

SORTING ROUTINES

Initial and Final Consonant Blends

Write each word from the Word Bank on index cards. Have students take turns sorting each word according to the vowel pattern. As students sort, have them read each word aloud.

WORD-BUILDING ROUTINES

- Provide each student or pair of students with a set of letter cards. Determine what words you'd like students to practice making. For example, ask them to pull the following letter cards from their sets: *y, c, d, f, r, l, s, k, t.* Ask them to make as many words as they can, using *y* as a long *i* sound, as in the word *sky*. One student can make a word, then the other can write it down, switching roles after every two words they make.
- You may wish to have students time themselves, then award a certificate to the person or pair who makes the most words in a five-minute time period. The certificate can be found on page 336 of this manual.

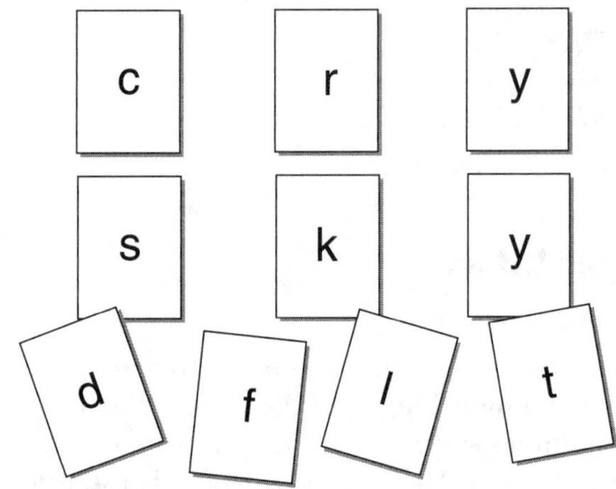

PRACTICE

A. Word Race

Have two students play this game, found on Worktext page 29. Remind them that when they think of a rhyming word, the word needs to have the same spelling pattern as the one found in the Word Bank, such as *crew* and *few* for *flew* and *blue* and *cue* for *true.*

B. Crossword Puzzle

Invite students to complete Worktext page 30. As students work on the crossword puzzle, have them cross out words they've used in the Word Bank.

C. Unscramble the Words

Before students unscramble the words found on Worktext page 31, remind them that each word will contain an initial or final consonant blend, such as in the words *fly* and *end.*

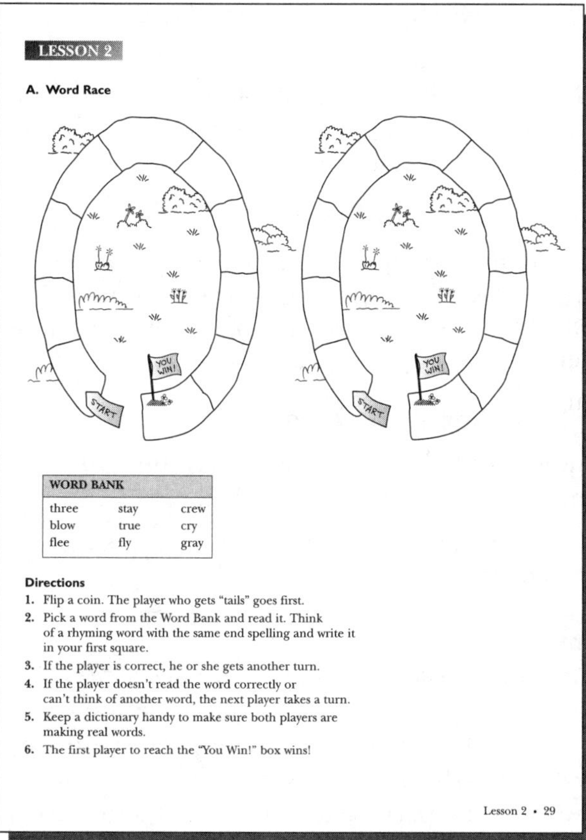
LESSON 2

A. Word Race

WORD BANK		
three	stay	crew
blow	true	cry
flee	fly	gray

Directions

1. Flip a coin. The player who gets "tails" goes first.
2. Pick a word from the Word Bank and read it. Think of a rhyming word with the same end spelling and write it in your first square.
3. If the player is correct, he or she gets another turn.
4. If the player doesn't read the word correctly or can't think of another word, the next player takes a turn.
5. Keep a dictionary handy to make sure both players are making real words.
6. The first player to reach the "You Win!" box wins!

Lesson 2 • 29

Worktext page 29

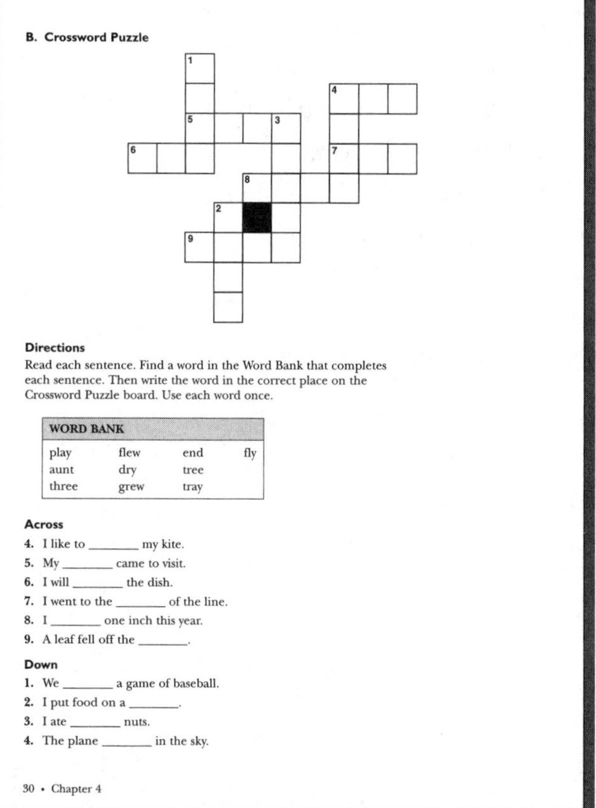
B. Crossword Puzzle

Directions

Read each sentence. Find a word in the Word Bank that completes each sentence. Then write the word in the correct place on the Crossword Puzzle board. Use each word once.

WORD BANK			
play	flew	end	fly
aunt	dry	tree	
three	grew	tray	

Across

4. I like to _______ my kite.
5. My _______ came to visit.
6. I will _______ the dish.
7. I went to the _______ of the line.
8. I _______ one inch this year.
9. A leaf fell off the _______.

Down

1. We _______ a game of baseball.
2. I put food on a _______.
3. I ate _______ nuts.
4. The plane _______ in the sky.

30 • Chapter 4

Worktext page 30

C. Unscramble the Words

Below is a series of words to unscramble. The first one is done for you. Remember that each word contains either an initial consonant blend, such as *fly*, or a final consonant blend, such as *end*. When you unscramble the word, write it. Then read the word and place a check mark (✓) next to the word, indicating that you read it.

				Write the word.	Read the word.
	y	f	l	fly	☑
1.	ew	r	g	_______	☐
2.	a	ch	r	_______	☐
3.	t	ay	s	_______	☐
4.	ue	l	c	_______	☐
5.	au	t	n	_______	☐
6.	t	a	c	_______	☐
7.	ea	t	s	_______	☐
8.	r	t	ue	_______	☐
9.	ee	r	f	_______	☐
10.	g	ue	l	_______	☐
11.	ow	l	p	_______	☐
12.	y	t	r	_______	☐
13.	g	ow	l	_______	☐
14.	ew	s	t	_______	☐
15.	r	t	a	_______	☐
16.	gr	l	ow	_______	☐
17.	m	th	a	_______	☐
18.	th	ee	r	_______	☐
19.	oa	s	t	_______	☐
20.	m	r	a	_______	☐

Lesson 2 • 31

Worktext page 31

LESSON 3

OBJECTIVES

- Students will apply their decoding skills by reading newspaper articles containing three-sound, initial, and final consonants
- Students will apply their comprehension skills by writing sentences about the *who, what, where, when,* and *why* of one article
- Students will read and identify initial and final consonant blends
- Students will create their own class newspaper based on events that occur in their school

MATERIALS

Worktext, pages 32–35
Teacher's Manual, pages 36–37
Award Certificate, page 336

DECODING AND READING

A. Food Drive

Before having students read the school newspaper article, help them to decode the following words: *homeless, people, Friday.* Point out that the word *homeless* is a compound word, made up of two smaller words. Cover up *home* and have them decode *less.* Then cover up *less* so they can read *home.* Finally, have them read the compound word.

B. Who? What? Where? When? Why?

Ask students to reread the article. Then have them answer questions pertaining to the action in the article. Encourage them to write one or two sentences about the *who, what, when, where,* and *why* of the article.

C. School News

Have students read the article from Room 101. Point out any words that might give them difficulty in decoding. If they stumble over *Friday, Saturday,* and *Thursday,* write the days of the week on the board. Add any important words that students need to know, so they can become familiar with them.

D. Where Are the Consonant Blends?

Have students read the small article on Worktext page 35. Then ask them to find and circle six initial and final consonant blends. Ask them to write and read each word aloud.

E. Write Your Own Article

Assist students in writing their own articles about important class or school events or bits of news that they would find interesting. Invite a student to input the articles and create a class newspaper.

F. Write a Get Well Note

Encourage students to write a get well note to a classmate, friend, or family member.

ASSESSMENT

Dictation

Have students write down each sentence as you dictate it. Say the sentence a few times before having them write. When they're ready, say each sentence slowly and clearly. If students have difficulty thinking of how to spell a particular word, have them leave a blank or write as much of the word as they can.

1. We will have a food drive.
2. Bring a can of food to class.
3. Sal made the swim team.
4. Rob will have a car wash.
5. We will take a class trip in May.
6. Nick broke his arm.
7. Pat is sick and will not be in class.
8. You can send Pat a note.

LESSON 3

A. Food Drive
Read the following article about a food drive.

We Need Your Help! ...from Room 101

We need your help! Cody, Jane, Ned, and Kate will have a food drive for the homeless people in the city. They ask that each of you get one can of food from home. You can drop it off on Friday in Room 101. If each of you can give us one can of food, we will feed 100 people. We want to help the homeless in the city. We need your help, too!

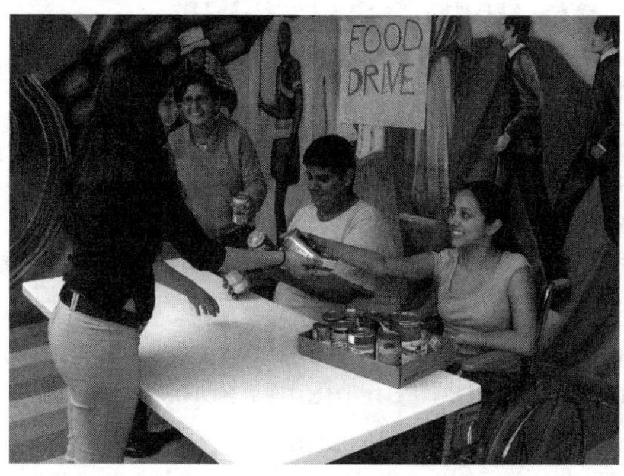

32 • Chapter 4

Worktext page 32

C. School News
Read the following article.

The News...from Room 101

- Sal, Jose, Kate, and Tom made the swim team. They will have a swim meet on Friday at 3:00 PM. Come cheer them on!
- Jay, Rob, and Maria will have a car wash on Saturday. If you can come and help, go to the lot at the back of the school. Come at 9:00 AM. The cash that we make will go to a class trip that we will take in May.
- Nick broke his arm at the track meet last week. He will help Coach Mead until his cast is off.
- Pat is sick and will be back to class next week. If you like, you can send him a get well note. You can send it to:

  Pat Van Fleet
  35 Pine Cone Road
  Oak Park, CA 91206

- Jan and Brad will sing at the class play on Thursday.

34 • Chapter 4

Worktext page 34

B. Who? What? Where? When? Why?
Reread the article about the food drive. Then answer the following five questions. Write one or two sentences explaining the *who, what, where, when,* and *why* of the article.

1. **Who** is doing the action? ______
2. **What** are they doing? ______
3. **Where** are they doing it? ______
4. **When** are they doing it? ______
5. **Why** are they doing it? ______

Lesson 3 • 33

Worktext page 33

D. Where Are the Consonant Blends?
Read the article below. Find six words that contain two consonants next to each other that make two different sounds, such as **swim**, **class**, **send**, or **last**. Circle each word that you find. Then write the words below the article.

Nick broke his arm at the track meet last week.
He will help Coach Mead until his cast is off.

1. ______ 4. ______
2. ______ 5. ______
3. ______ 6. ______

E. Write Your Own Article
Think of something that will happen or has happened in your school or class. Write a short article about it. Collect articles from other students and type them on a computer. Make up your own class newspaper.

F. Write a Get-Well Note
Reread the article about Pat Van Fleet, a student from Room 101 who is sick. Then write him a get-well note. Or, if someone is sick in your class, write a note to cheer him or her up!

Dear ______,

Sincerely,

Lesson 3 • 35

Worktext page 35

CHAPTER 5
Four-Sound Words

TOKEN LESSON A

OBJECTIVES

- Students will develop phonemic awareness as they use tokens to segment nonsense words comprised of four sounds that include initial and consonant blends
- Students will discriminate sounds through substitution and deletion routines as well as shifting the position of sounds

WORD BANK OF NONSENSE WORDS

krig	skaj	stuv	twim	slig
gesp	lusk	moft	tainz	dift
inst	umps	akst	olpt	ilps
frud	ploe	naft	sieks	onts

WORD BANK OF REAL WORDS

swim	desk	prow	stub	tusk
gasp	loft	task	soft	last
plow	plot	bump	musk	brim
raft	mask	twin	dump	jump

MATERIALS

Teacher's Manual, pages 38–39
Token cards
Additional list of nonsense words, page 337

PHONEMIC AWARENESS

Segmenting Sounds

Place four tokens on the table, such as a star, triangle, circle, and square.

- Say it slowly: ***krig.* What is the first sound you hear in *krig*?** As you say the word whole, elongating each sound, have a student point to the star and say /*k*/.
- Say it slowly: ***krig.* What is the second sound you hear in *krig*?** Ask a student to say the word, stretching each sound. Cut the student off after saying /*r*/. Ask the student to point to the token that stands for that sound. (*the triangle*)
- Say it slowly: ***krig.* What is the third sound you hear in *krig*?** The student says the word slowly and focuses on what comes after the /*r*/. When the student identifies /*i*/, have the student point to the circle.
- Say it slowly: ***krig.* What is the last sound you hear in *krig*?** Have the student say /*g*/ and point to the square.
- Rotating around the small group, invite other students to segment and sound out nonsense words from the Word Bank.

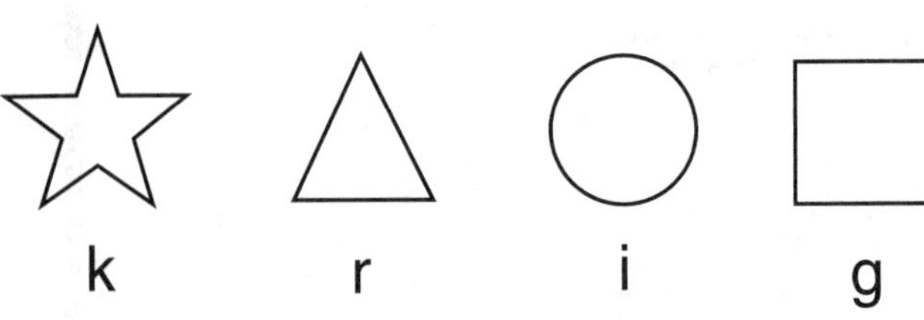

WORD-PAIR ROUTINES

Consonant Blends

Place a diamond, circle, and star on the table.

- Say: **This says *kaj*. I'm going to make *skaj*.** Add a rectangle before the diamond and circle. Say: **What new sound did I add?** Invite a student to say /*s*/ and point to the rectangle.
- Repeat this routine with other nonsense words containing initial consonant blends.
- Put a rectangle, circle, and square on the table. Say: **This says *mot*. I'm going to make *moft*.** Add a diamond in between the circle and square. Ask a volunteer to say the added sound (/*f*/) and point to the new token representing that sound.
- Place a star, circle, and diamond in front of students. Say: **This says *olp*. I'm going to make *olpt*.** Put a square at the end of the nonsense word and invite a student to say the added sound /*t*/. Have students segment each sound, elongating and emphasizing each of the three consonant sounds in the second, third, and fourth positions.
- Once students have worked with CCVC, CVCC, and VCCC patterns, invite them to make new nonsense words. Say: **If this says *ums*, make *umps*.** Students should be able to place a new token in between the second and third sounds, and identify the added sound /*p*/.

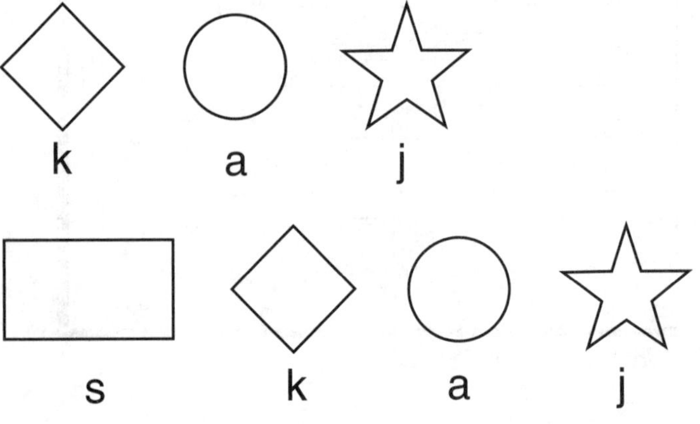

SUBSTITUTION ROUTINES

Initial Consonant Blends

On the table, place a triangle, diamond, circle, and square.

- Say: **If this says *stuv*, make *smuv*.** Invite a volunteer to replace the diamond with another token. Ask the student to sound out the new nonsense word.
- Have students substitute other consonants to form new nonsense words, such as *slig/ srig*, *frud/ flud*, and *ploe/ proe.*

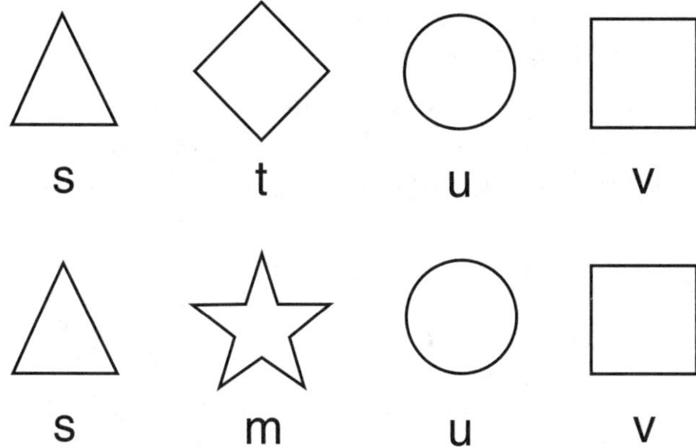

Final Consonant Blends

- Use new tokens and have students substitute consonants in the third and fourth positions, such as *dift/ difs*, *lusk/ lumk*, and *gesp/ gesk.*
- As a challenge, invite students to substitute tokens to create new nonsense words containing three consonants, such as *akst/ amst/ amsk.*

SHIFTING ROUTINES

When students are proficient at substituting initial and final consonant blends, introduce a nonsense word and shift the position of sounds within that particular word.

- Place a rectangle, circle, triangle, and star on the table. Say: **If this says *slig*, make *ligs*.** Guide a student while shifting the rectangle from the first position to the fourth position.
- Say: **If this says *ligs*, make *glis*.** Invite a volunteer to shift positions by moving the star to the first position.
- Say: **If this says *glis*, make *ilgs*.** After shifting positions, placing the triangle, circle, star, and rectangle in a row, have the student point to each token to segment the nonsense word.

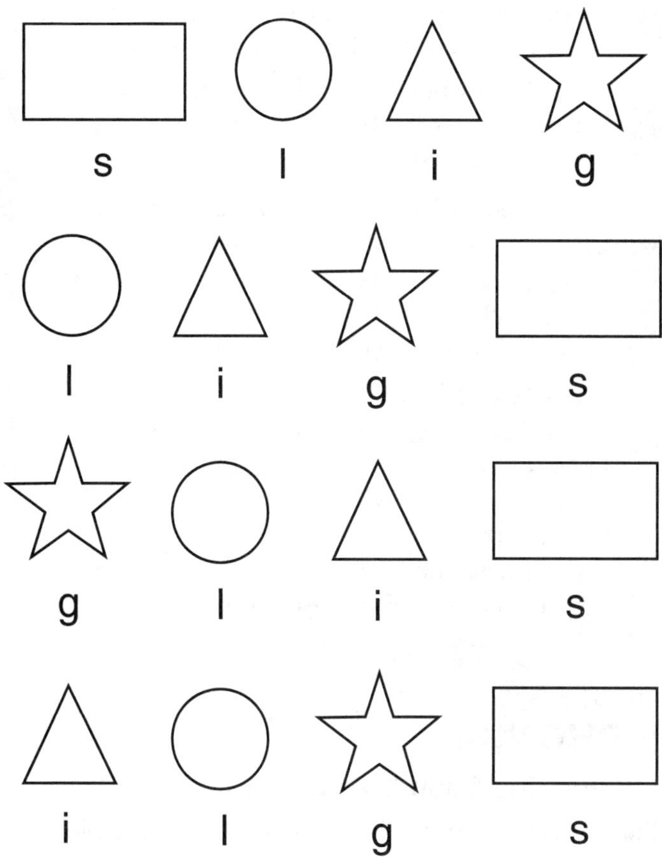

- If students have trouble with these, try *skree/ krees/ reeks/ reesk.*
- For additional four-sound nonsense words containing initial and final consonant blends, turn to page 337.
- After students have worked with four-sound nonsense words, you can use the Word Bank of Real Words with them.

TOKEN LESSON B

OBJECTIVES

- Students will segment four-sound words comprised of initial or final consonant blends by connecting sounds to letters
- Students will make and then read new nonsense words by adding, substituting, deleting, or shifting the position of letters

WORD BANK OF NONSENSE WORDS

brosh	snij	gliz	speg	troep
fiapt	dind	tanz	luft	chuvz
umps	elfth	reps	frak	soild
sploe	klech	pras	twoit	sweeth

MATERIALS

Teacher's Manual, pages 40–41
Assessment Checklist, page 62 of the *Assessment Manual*
Token cards
Letter cards, including all vowels, vowel pairs, consonants, and consonant digraphs

PHONICS

Connecting Sounds to Letters

Place three different-shaped tokens on the table. Keep a set of letter cards handy.

- Say it slowly: ***brosh.*** Point to the first token and say: **What sound does this make?** After a student responds /*b*/, say: **Find the letter that makes that sound.** Invite the student to place the letter *b* under the first token.
- Say it slowly: ***brosh.*** Point to the second token and say: **What sound does this make?** Have the student place the letter *r* below the second token and say /*r*/.
- Say it slowly: ***brosh.*** Point to the third token and say: **What sound does this make?** As the student says /*o*/, ask the student to point to the token representing that sound.
- Say it slowly: ***brosh.*** Point to the last token and say: **What sound does this make?** Coach the student to find the consonant digraph letter card that says /*sh*/.
- Using other nonsense words found in the Word Bank, repeat this routine with all of your students. Be sure to practice words containing initial and final consonant blends.

SUBSTITUTION ROUTINES

Initial Consonant Blends

Once students are able to identify and connect the sounds to letters, remove the tokens and manipulate the letter cards only. Explain that you're going to substitute consonants in the first and second position of each nonsense word.

- Say: **This says *snij.* Make *slij.*** Say the word slowly, emphasizing and elongating the first two consonant sounds. Coach a volunteer to find the letter *l* to replace the *n.*
- Say: **This says *slij.* Make *prij.*** Ask students how many sounds have been changed, coaching them to substitute *sl* with *pr.*
- Repeat this routine with other nonsense words until all students have had the opportunity to manipulate the letter cards.

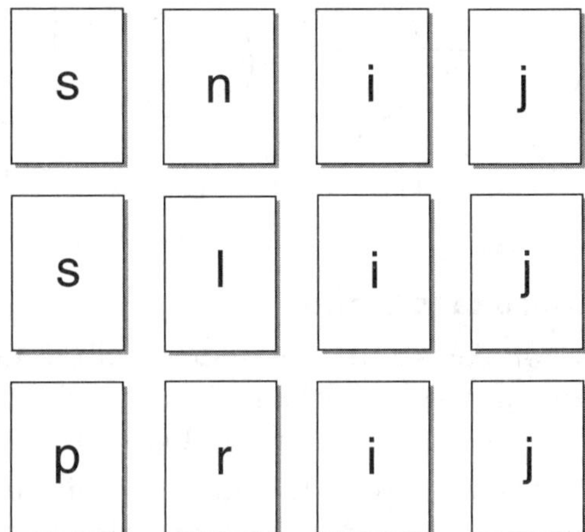

Final Consonant Blends

Mention to students that you will be substituting consonants at the end of each nonsense word. Ask them to listen carefully for those sounds.

- Say: **This says *chuvz.* Make *chuvd.*** Have a student substitute the last consonant for the letter *d.*
- Say: **This says *chuvd.* Make *chuvg.*** Have a volunteer substitute the last consonant for the letter *g.*
- Say: **This says *chuvg.* Make *chuvth.*** Invite a student to substitute *th* for *g.*

- Rotate around the small group as students work with substituting final consonant blends.

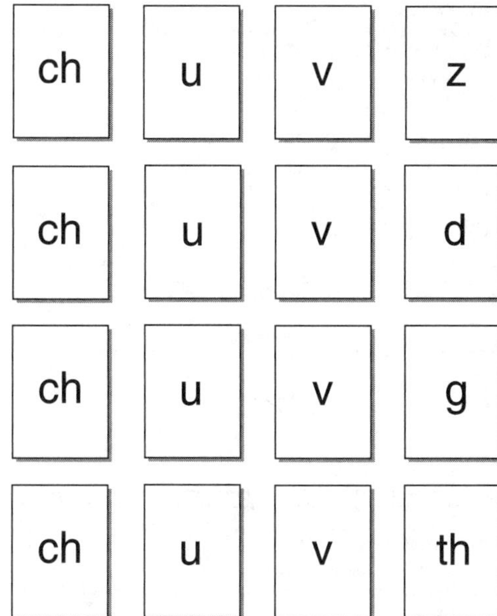

DELETION ROUTINES

Explain to students that you will be deleting a consonant somewhere in each nonsense word. Ask them to listen carefully as you elongate each sound, without segmenting the word.

- Say: **This says *twoit.* Make *toit.*** Have the student remove the *w,* and say the new nonsense word.
- Repeat this routine with other nonsense words, such as *soild/soid, pras/pas, elfth/elth,* and *sploe/spoe.*

SHIFTING ROUTINES

As you begin the next routine, mention that you will be shifting the position of letters within each word. Because this is a more challenging activity, stretch each sound as you say the nonsense word.

- Say: **This says *klech.* Make *chelk.*** Encourage a volunteer to shift the initial consonant /*k*/ with the final consonant digraph /*ch*/, as well as shifting the position of the *e* and *l.*
- Continue the routine and have students make other nonsense words, such as *kelch.*

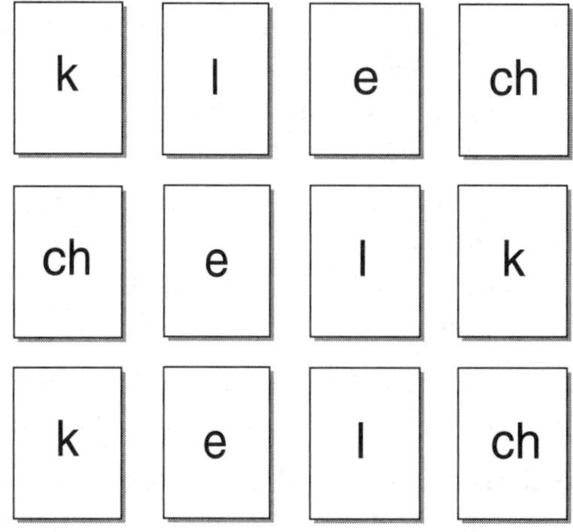

READING ROUTINES

Blending Sounds

After students have practiced manipulating and spelling nonsense words, assess their ability to read the words that they are making.

Place the word *umps* in front of a student and invite him or her to read it. If read correctly, ask the next student to read a new nonsense word.

INFORMAL ASSESSMENT

Use the Assessment Checklist found on page 62 of the *Assessment Manual* to determine whether students are able to decode and read four-sound nonsense words that contain either initial or final consonant blends.

LESSON 1 (Part 1)

OBJECTIVES

- Students will recognize that words with *kn*, *wr*, *gn*, and *mb* stand for only one sound. One of the consonants is silent, as in *know*, *write*, *sign*, and *lamb*
- Students will identify words containing silent letters
- Students will sort words according to their spelling pattern
- Students will read sentences, fill in the correct word, and identify misspelled words

WORD BANK OF REAL WORDS

knit	knob	sign	write	wrist
wreck	limb	know	climb	thumb
kneel	comb	gnaw	lamb	wrench
wren	design	knife	knot	wrap

MATERIALS

Worktext, page 36
Teacher's Manual, page 42

CHAPTER 5

LESSON 1 (Part 1)

SPELLING RULE
Words with *kn*, *wr*, *gn*, and *mb* stand for only one sound. One of the consonants is silent, as in *know*, *write*, *sign*, and *lamb*.

A. Say the Words
Say each word in the Word Bank. Remember that one of the consonants in each word is silent.

WORD BANK				
knit	knob	sign	write	wrist
wreck	limb	know	climb	thumb
kneel	comb	gnaw	lamb	wrench
wren	design	knife		

B. Sort the Words
Read the words again in the Word Bank. Sort and write each word under the correct category. Circle the silent letter in each word.

kn	wr	gn	mb
________	________	________	________
________	________	________	________
________	________	________	________
________	________		________
________	________		________

C. Proofread the Note
Read the note that Jen sent to her Aunt Sue. Find the five misspelled words and underline them. Write them correctly on the lines below.

Dear Aunt Sue,

Thank you for the get-well note. My rist and thum feel better. When I can, I will nit you a sweater made of wool from a lam. Please rite back.

Love,
Jen

1. ________ 2. ________ 3. ________ 4. ________ 5. ________

36 • Chapter 5

Worktext page 36

SPELLING

Kn, wr, gn, mb

- Write the following categories on the board: **kn**, **wr**, **gn**, and **mb**. Explain to students that each of these consonant pairs represents one sound, and in each pair, one consonant is silent. Write the following words below the correct categories: **know**, **write**, **sign**, and **lamb**.
- Rotating around the room, have students read each of the words found in the Word Bank, on Worktext page 36. Then ask students to sort the words according to their consonant pairs.
- As students proofread the note from Jen to Aunt Sue, mention that the correct spelling of words can be found in the Word Bank.

LESSON 1 (Part 2)

OBJECTIVES

- Students will recognize the sounds *r*-controlled vowels make. For example, the vowel sound in *far* can be spelled *ar.* The vowel sound in *forth* can be spelled *or.* And the vowel sound in *bird* can be spelled *ir, er,* and *ur,* as in *fir, her,* and *burn*
- Students will identify words containing *r*-controlled vowels
- Students will sort words according to their vowel sounds and identify words in sentences containing these sounds

WORD BANK OF REAL WORDS

far	forth	bird	fir	her
burn	car	girl	large	shore
form	hurt	first	church	
skirt	turn	nerve	thirst	
verb	serve	storm	march	
corn	hard	sport	germ	

MATERIALS

Worktext, page 37

Teacher's Manual, page 43

LESSON 1 (Part 2)

SPELLING RULE

The vowel sound in *far* can be spelled *ar*. The vowel sound in *forth* can be spelled *or*. The vowel sound in *bird* can be spelled *er*, *ir*, and *ur*, as in *her*, *fir*, and *burn*.

A. Say the Words

Say each word in the Word Bank and listen for the vowel sound with *r*.

WORD BANK				
car	girl	large	shore	form
hurt	first	church	skirt	turn
nerve	thirst	verb	serve	storm
march	corn	hard	sport	germ

B. Sort the Words

Read the words again in the Word Bank. Sort and write each word under the correct category. Circle the vowel plus *r*.

ar	er	ir	or	ur
______	______	______	______	______
______	______	______	______	______
______	______	______	______	______
______	______	______	______	
			______	

C. What's the Vowel Sound?

Read each sentence. Circle words that contain a vowel followed by *r*.

1. I drove my car through the storm.
2. First, we went to the shore.
3. Jay will pick corn in the large field.
4. Her skirt is red and white.
5. Please turn left at the stop sign.
6. The class will form a line.
7. I lost my nerve at the game.
8. The church is on the right.

Lesson 1 • 37

Worktext page 37

SPELLING

R-controlled Vowels

- Write the following categories on the board: **ar**, **or**, **ir**, **er**, and **ur**. Explain to students that the vowel sound in *far* can be spelled *ar,* while the vowel sound in *forth* can be spelled *or.* Mention that the sound in *bird* can be spelled *ir, er,* and *ur,* as in *fir, her,* and *burn.* Ask students to think of words they know that end in those sounds. Have volunteers write each of the words under the correct category on the board. Invite them to think of other words where the *r* controls the vowel sound.
- Have students turn to page 37 in the Worktext. Ask volunteers to read each word aloud. Then have them work individually, sorting the words according to their sound and spelling pattern.
- As students complete "What's the Vowel Sound?" have them circle words that contain a vowel followed by *r.* Remind them that there may be more than one word in each sentence to circle.

LESSON 1 (Part 3)

OBJECTIVES

- Students will recognize that words with *ch, tch,* and *ng* stand for one consonant sound, and that words with *nk* stand for two consonant sounds
- Students will identify words containing *ch, tch, ng,* and *nk*
- Students will sort words according to their sounds and read sentences to fill in words containing these sounds

WORD BANK OF REAL WORDS

much	hatch	ring	rink
watch	think	sing	church
pink	long	pitch	march
wrong	drink	which	crutch
reach	song	thank	catch

MATERIALS

Worktext, page 38
Teacher's Manual, page 44

LESSON 1 (Part 3)

SPELLING RULE
Words with *ch* and *tch* can stand for one-consonant sound, as in *much* and *hatch*. Words with *ng* can stand for one-consonant sound, as in *ring*. Words with *nk* can stand for two-consonant sounds, as in *rink*.

A. Say the Words
Say each word in the Word Bank. Remember that *ch, tch,* and *ng* can stand for one sound, and *nk* can stand for two sounds.

WORD BANK			
watch	think	sing	reach
pink	long	pitch	march
wrong	drink	which	catch

B. Sort the Words
Read the words again in the Word Bank. Sort and write each word under the correct category. Circle *ch, tch, ng,* or *nk* in each of the words.

ch	tch	ng	nk
________	________	________	________
________	________	________	________
________	________	________	________

C. Fill in the Blanks
Read the sentences and fill in the correct words. The words can be found in the Word Bank.

1. Jess will __________ first in the game.
2. __________ student would like to sing last?
3. Will you play __________ with me?
4. My shirt is __________.

D. Name That Word
Make words, using *ch, tch, ng,* or *nk*. You can make words not found in the Word Bank. Use a dictionary to check your answers.

1. si _ _
2. pi _ _ _
3. mar _ _
4. wro _ _
5. dri _ _
6. whi _ _
7. thi _ _
8. ri _ _

38 • Chapter 5

Worktext page 38

SPELLING

Ch, tch, ng, nk

- Chart the following categories on the board: **ch**, **tch**, **ng**, and **nk**. Explain to students that words with *ch, tch,* and *ng* stand for one consonant sound, while *nk* has two consonant sounds. When you put a *k* after an *n*, the *n* really sounds like an *ngk*. Say each word slowly and invite volunteers to write them below the correct category: **much**, **hatch**, **ring**, **rink**.
- Rotating around the room, ask students to read each word found in the Word Bank on Worktext page 38. Then have students sort each word according to their sound and spelling pattern.
- Coach students who need additional assistance in completing "Fill in the Blanks" and "Name That Word."

LESSON 2

OBJECTIVES

- Students will decode, read, and sort four-phoneme words that contain initial and final consonant blends
- Students will write lists of rhyming words
- Students will build and spell words using letter cards
- Students will play Word Search and Bingo games, identifying and reading four-sound words

WORD BANK OF REAL WORDS

sleep	zest	mound	kind
skirt	class	stick	swing
bench	barge	brain	frown
court	swell	crowd	bind
drain	drown	quail	swerve

MATERIALS

Worktext, pages 39–41
Teacher's Manual, pages 45–46
Assessment Checklist, page 62 of the *Assessment Manual*
Award Certificate, page 336
Letter cards for each pair of students

RHYMING ROUTINES

- Write the word **mound** on the board and say it slowly, so that students hear each of the four sounds. Have them write the word on paper and ask them to brainstorm other words that rhyme with it, changing the initial consonant, as in *bound, found, hound, pound, round, sound,* and *wound.* If a volunteer says *ground,* guide students in writing all five letters. Say the word slowly, stretching the initial consonant blend, **gr**. Repeat this routine with other words found in the Word Bank.
- Invite individuals to come up to the board and spell words that you dictate from the Word Bank. Ask other students to write rhyming words beneath each one. Help students sound out and spell words that contain more than four sounds: *brain/ sprain, swing/ string.*

SORTING ROUTINES

Write each word from the Word Bank on index cards. Have students take turns sorting each word according to initial or final consonant blends. As students sort, ask them to read each word aloud. Mention that there may be words that don't fit either category.

WORD-BUILDING ROUTINES

- Provide individuals or pairs of students with a set of letter cards. Depending on what spelling pattern students need to practice, ask them to pull specific cards. For example, to work with four-sound words containing */ou/* or */ow/*, use the following cards: *b, d, f, g, m, n, o, p, r, s, u, w.* Ask them to make as many words as they can.
- Time students in the word-building activity, then award a certificate to the individual or pair that makes the most words in a five-minute time period. Be sure that the students can read each word correctly. The certificate can be found on page 336.

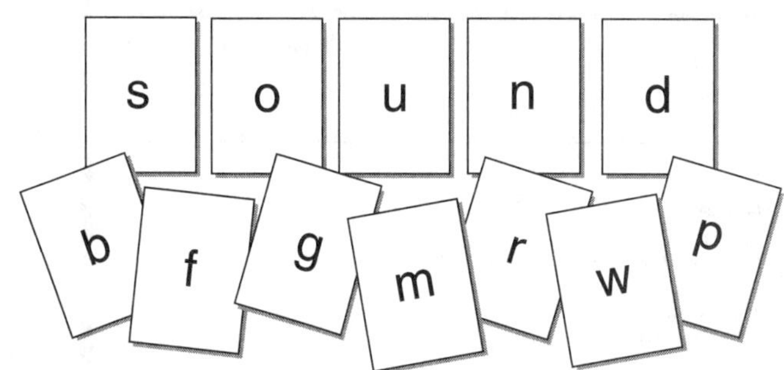

PRACTICE

A. Word Search

Have students complete the Word Search board, found on Worktext page 39. Before completing the activity, ask students to take turns reading aloud the words found in the Word Bank.

B. Bingo

Choose a more able reader to be the caller. Have the caller read words from the Word Bank as three other students play the game. Coach students if they have difficulty in identifying words on their Bingo cards.

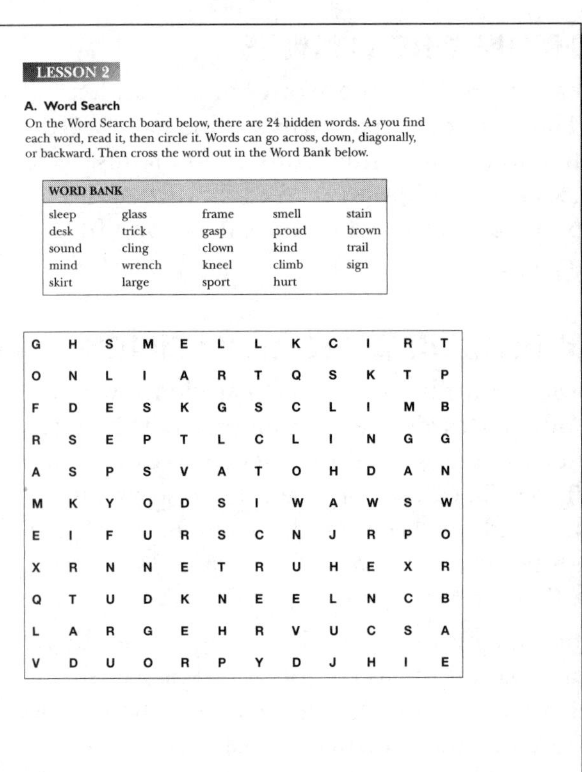

LESSON 2

A. Word Search

On the Word Search board below, there are 24 hidden words. As you find each word, read it, then circle it. Words can go across, down, diagonally, or backward. Then cross the word out in the Word Bank below.

WORD BANK				
sleep	glass	frame	smell	stain
desk	trick	gasp	proud	brown
sound	cling	clown	kind	trail
mind	wrench	kneel	climb	sign
skirt	large	sport	hurt	

G	H	S	M	E	L	L	K	C	I	R	T
O	N	L	I	A	R	T	Q	S	K	T	P
F	D	E	S	K	G	S	C	L	I	M	B
R	S	E	P	T	L	C	L	I	N	G	G
A	S	P	S	V	A	T	O	H	D	A	N
M	K	Y	O	D	S	I	W	A	W	S	W
E	I	F	U	R	S	C	N	J	R	P	O
X	R	N	N	E	T	R	U	H	E	X	R
Q	T	U	D	K	N	E	E	L	N	C	B
L	A	R	G	E	H	R	V	U	C	S	A
V	D	U	O	R	P	Y	D	J	H	I	E

Lesson 2 • 39

Worktext page 39

B. Bingo

Directions

1. Each player should use a different Bingo card.
2. Each player takes some tokens.
3. Pick a caller.
4. The caller reads a word from the Word Bank in any order.
5. The players put a token on the square that contains the word.
6. The first player to get four tokens in a row says, "Bingo!"

WORD BANK				
comb	creep	train	stick	crowd
found	last	wreck	thing	stale
find	bench	serve	grass	long
wheel	patch	blink	groom	plain
first	storm	shirt	star	next

Bingo Card 1

comb	wreck	find	blink
stale	serve	long	shirt
crowd	first	storm	creep
wheel	groom	train	thing

40 • Chapter 5

Worktext page 40

Bingo Card 2

creep	serve	grass	wreck
found	long	plain	next
stale	patch	train	crowd
last	find	wheel	blink

Bingo Card 3

stick	stale	comb	patch
grass	found	first	star
bench	creep	plain	shirt
train	find	wheel	last

Lesson 2 • 41

Worktext page 41

LESSON 3

OBJECTIVES

- Students will apply their decoding skills by reading directions to a game, an invitation, and a newspaper advertisement
- Students will apply their writing skills by writing directions from school to home, writing an invitation, and writing a newspaper advertisement
- Students will read and identify four-sound words

MATERIALS

Worktext, pages 42–45
Teacher's Manual, pages 47–49
Award Certificate, page 336

DECODING AND READING

A. Directions to the Game

- Before having students read Worktext page 42, write the following word on the board: **front**. Explain to students that the word contains five sounds and two consonant blends, *fr* and *nt*. Say the word slowly, elongating each sound, but still blending them together. Invite a volunteer to segment the sounds, then blend them together to form the word.
- Write other words on the board that students may have difficulty decoding, such as **driveway**. Tell them that the word is a compound word comprised of two words they already know. Help them decode it by covering up *way* and reading *drive*. Then cover up *drive* and read *way*. Invite a volunteer to read the two words together to form the compound word.

B. The Post-Game Party

Have students read the invitation silently, and then ask them to practice reading it a few times. Time their reading of the invitation, encouraging them to read it as fluently as possible. Award a certificate to those students who have made the most progress recently. See page 336 for the certificate.

C. Find the Consonant Blends

Ask students to reread the directions found on page 43 in their Worktexts. Tell them that each direction line contains one or more words that have initial or final consonant blends. Have them read the directions silently, and circle the words containing the blends. Mention that there may be words that contain both an initial and final consonant blend.

D. Make Up Your Own Directions

Before completing this writing activity, ask students to think of how they would give directions to a friend if they were going from school to the local movie theater. As students tell you each direction line, write it on the board. Then ask them to write directions from school to their own homes.

Teacher Tip

If . . . students have difficulty writing some of the words in their directions, tell them to leave a space or draw a blank line.

Then . . . have them come back to that direction when they're done with the activity. You can help them by asking them to sound out the word, segmenting each sound and writing each letter that they hear, until they have written the entire word.

E. Party Time!

Have students write an invitation to a party they'd like to have, filling in the particulars of *when, time, place*, and what they'd like their guests to *bring*.

F. First Come! First Served!

Before reading the newspaper advertisement, write the following words on the board: **skirt**, **slack**, **belt**, and **band**. Mention that all of the words contain four sounds, inviting volunteers to read each word. Then add an *s* to the end of each word, saying that each word now contains five sounds. Have students read the words, adding /*s*/ to the end of each.

G. Half-Off Sale! Come While It Lasts!

Invite students to write an advertisement telling about a half-off sale at their own clothing store. Ask them to come up with a title for the advertisement, the name of their store, and a brief description of the sale. Using the Word Bank and other words they know, have them list the clothing items, the original price, and the half-off price.

ASSESSMENT

Dictation

Have students write down each sentence as you dictate it. Say the sentence a few times before having them write. When they're ready, say each sentence slowly and distinctly. If students have difficulty thinking of how to spell a particular word, have them leave a blank or write as much of the word as possible.

1. All cars can form a line next to the curb.
2. Make a left on Pine Trail Road.
3. Turn into the large lot.
4. Join the team in a post-game party.
5. All price tags will say "half off."
6. We will sell three skirts.
7. Two sweatbands are for sale.
8. I sold a pair of blue jeans.

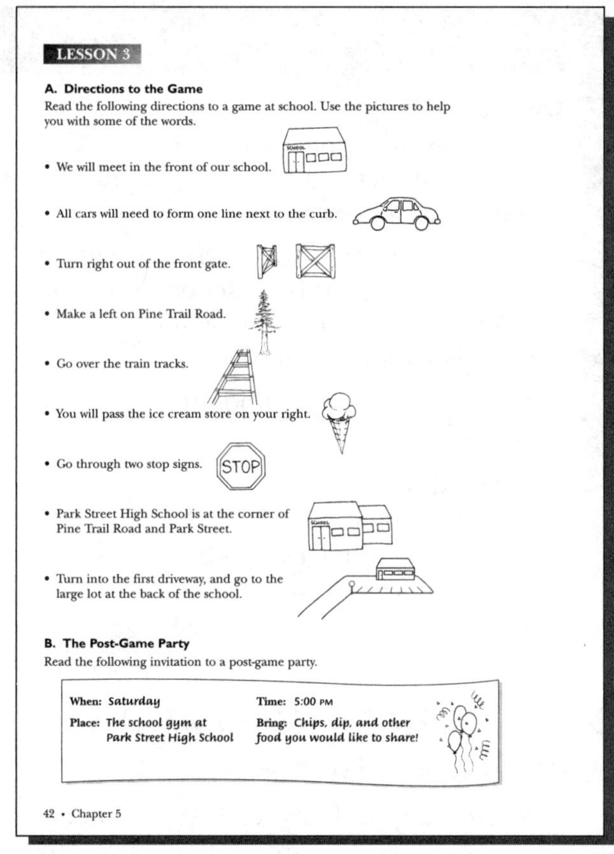

LESSON 3

A. Directions to the Game

Read the following directions to a game at school. Use the pictures to help you with some of the words.

- We will meet in the front of our school.
- All cars will need to form one line next to the curb.
- Turn right out of the front gate.
- Make a left on Pine Trail Road.
- Go over the train tracks.
- You will pass the ice cream store on your right.
- Go through two stop signs.
- Park Street High School is at the corner of Pine Trail Road and Park Street.
- Turn into the first driveway, and go to the large lot at the back of the school.

B. The Post-Game Party

Read the following invitation to a post-game party.

When: Saturday
Place: The school gym at Park Street High School
Time: 5:00 PM
Bring: Chips, dip, and other food you would like to share!

42 • Chapter 5

Worktext page 42

C. Find the Consonant Blends

Reread the directions below. Look at each word, and circle the consonant blends. Remember, they are words that contain two consonants that are next to each other and make two sounds, as in the words *last*, *desk*, and *sport*. You may find words that contain two pairs of consonant blends.

- We will meet in the front of our school.
- All cars will need to form one line next to the curb.
- Turn right out of the front gate.
- Make a left on Pine Trail Road.
- Go over the train tracks.

D. Make Up Your Own Directions

Have you ever had to give a friend directions to your home? If you were at school, how would you describe how to walk or drive to your home? Think of the streets you turn onto or pass. Picture the houses, stores, train tracks, stop signs, or traffic lights you see. Now write the directions below. Be sure to include your address in your last direction.

Directions from School to Home

____

____

____

____

____

E. Party Time!

If you were to have a party, who would you invite? What would you like your guests to bring? Make up your own invitation below.

It's Party Time!

____

____

____

When: ______________

Time: ______________

Place: ______________

Bring: ______________

Lesson 3 • 43

Worktext page 43

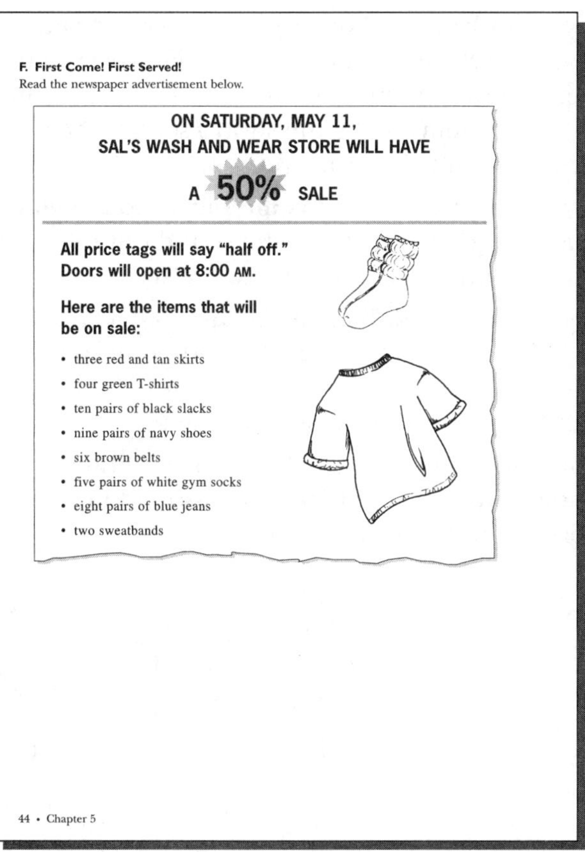

F. First Come! First Served!
Read the newspaper advertisement below.

ON SATURDAY, MAY 11,
SAL'S WASH AND WEAR STORE WILL HAVE
A 50% SALE

All price tags will say "half off." Doors will open at 8:00 AM.

Here are the items that will be on sale:

- three red and tan skirts
- four green T-shirts
- ten pairs of black slacks
- nine pairs of navy shoes
- six brown belts
- five pairs of white gym socks
- eight pairs of blue jeans
- two sweatbands

44 • Chapter 5

Worktext page 44

G. Half-Off Sale! Come While It Lasts!

Pretend that you own your own clothing store. What would you sell? How much would it cost? Suppose you had a "half-off" sale. How much would each item cost then? Write a newspaper advertisement telling about the sale. Make a list of the items that are for sale. Write the price next to each and then the sale price. Use your Word Bank for items you might like to sell. Think of other items, and add them to your list.

WORD BANK			
skirt	shirts	slacks	shoes
belts	socks	jeans	sweatbands

Title of Advertisement: ______________________________

____

____

____

Sale Items	Price	Half-Off Price
________	________	________
________	________	________
________	________	________
________	________	________
________	________	________
________	________	________
________	________	________
________	________	________
________	________	________

Lesson 3 • 45

Worktext page 45

CHAPTER 6
Five- and Six-Sound Words

TOKEN LESSON A

OBJECTIVES

- Students will develop phonemic awareness as they use tokens to segment five- and six-sound nonsense words that include initial and final consonant blends
- Students will discriminate sounds through substitution and deletion routines as well as through shifting the position of sounds in nonsense words

WORD BANK OF NONSENSE WORDS

plift	gloaft	baulps	throinch
thelkt	scrome	lowkst	flauts
skurbd	kroifs	vults	shiemps
snimps	stroilsh	proimst	troulks
kipst	bonts	fencht	skunsht

WORD BANK OF REAL WORDS

plank	crisp	springs
skimps	splint	bunts
claps	streets	trusts
clasp	strict	stump

MATERIALS

Teacher's Manual, pages 50–51
Token cards
Additional list of nonsense words, page 337

PHONEMIC AWARENESS

Segmenting Sounds

Place five tokens in front of a small group of students, such as a circle, square, triangle, star, and diamond.

- Say it slowly: ***plift*. What is the first sound you hear in *plift*?** As you stretch out each sound, be sure to emphasize each phoneme, especially the initial and final consonant blends. Invite volunteers to point to the circle and say /*p*/.
- Say it slowly: ***plift*. What is the second sound you hear in *plift*?** Ask students to sound out the nonsense word, stopping them after the /*l*/. Have them isolate that sound and point to the token that corresponds to it. (*square*)
- Say it slowly: ***plift*. What is the third sound you hear in *plift*?** Ask students to say ***plift*** slowly and focus on what their mouths are making after the /*l*/. As students make the short *i* sound, they should point to the triangle.
- Say it slowly: ***plift*. What is the fourth sound you hear in *plift*?** Students should sound out the word and stop after /*f*/, pointing to the star.
- Say it slowly: ***plift*. What is the last sound you hear in *plift*?** Have students say /*t*/ and point to the diamond. Ask them to read the nonsense word, blending all of the sounds together.
- Rotating around the small group, ask other students to segment five- and six-sound nonsense words from the Word Bank.

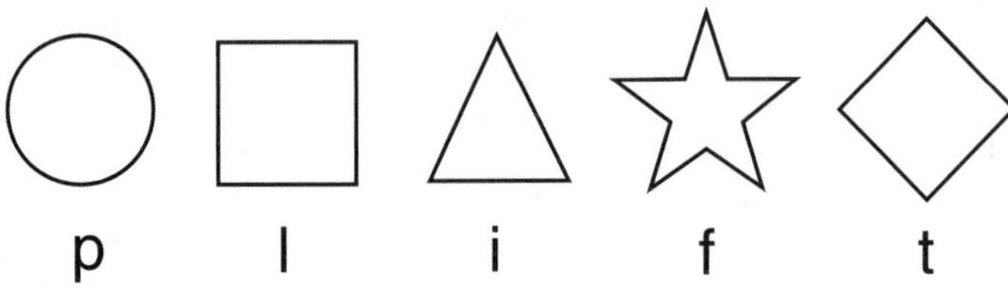

SUBSTITUTION ROUTINES

Place a diamond, star, rectangle, circle, and triangle on the table.

- Say: **If this says *gloaft*, make *gloath*.** Coach a student in taking away the circle and triangle and replacing them with a square.
- Have students substitute other sounds to form new nonsense words, such as *snimps/ shimps/ thimps*; *flauts/ flauth/ flauch*; *bonts/ bants/ banth*; *vults/ thults/ chults*.

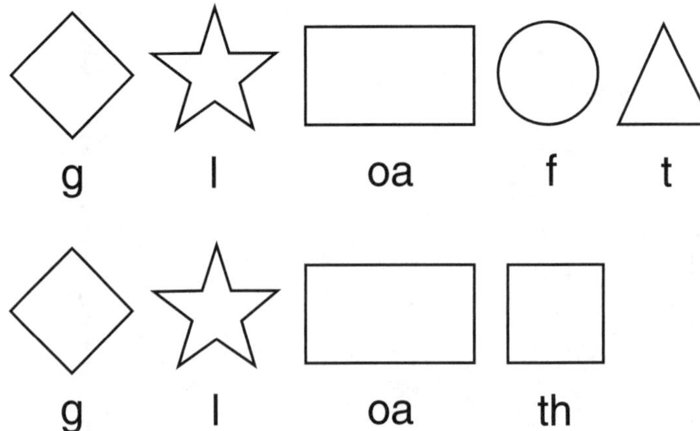

DELETION ROUTINES

On the table, place a circle, square, triangle, star, diamond, and rectangle.

- Say: **This says *proimst*. Make *poimst*.** Invite a student to remove the square, deleting /***r***/ from the nonsense word.
- Say: **This says *poimst*. Make *poimt*.** Guide the student in removing the diamond or /***s***/ from the nonsense word.
- Say: **This says *poimt*. Make *oimt*.** The student should now delete the circle or /***p***/ from the word.
- Say: **This says *oimt*. Make *oit*.** As the student hears that the /***m***/ is omitted from the word, he or she should remove the star.
- Have students work with other nonsense words from the Word Bank, deleting phonemes step by step.

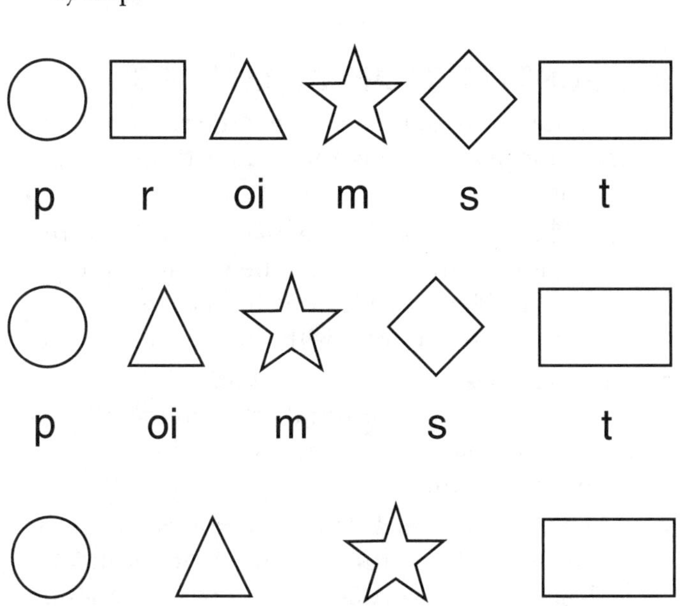

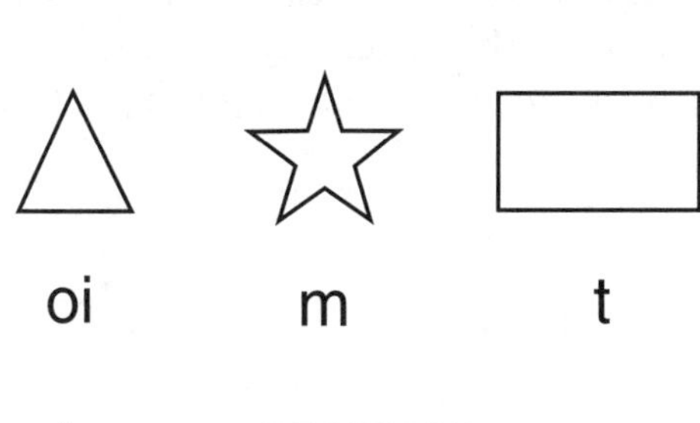

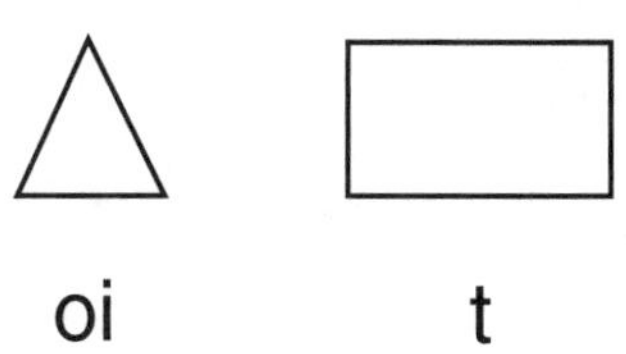

SHIFTING ROUTINES

When students are able to substitute and delete phonemes with ease, challenge them to shift the position of sounds in nonsense words. Place a star, circle, square, triangle, and diamond on the table.

- Say: **This says *kroifs*. Make *roifsk*.** Watch as students shift the star to the last position.
- Say: **This says *roifsk*. Make *froisk*.** Guide students to shift the triangle and circle into the first and second positions.
- Repeat this routine with other nonsense words.

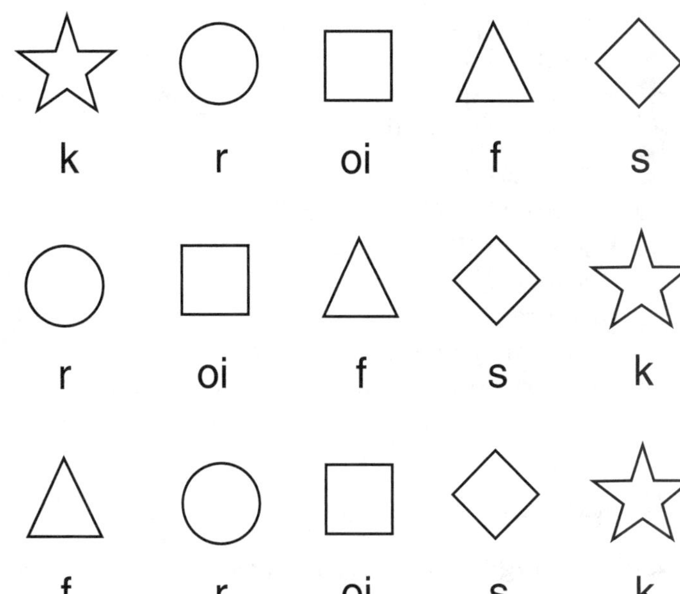

- For additional five- and six-sound words, turn to page 337.
- After students have worked with five- and six-sound nonsense words, you can use the Word Bank of Real Words with them.

TOKEN LESSON B

OBJECTIVES

- Students will segment five- and six-sound nonsense words, some comprised of two and three initial and final consonant blends
- Students will make and then read new nonsense words by adding, substituting, deleting, or shifting the position of letters

WORD BANK OF NONSENSE WORDS

klingk	spleef	naimps	gompt
prensk	blaimst	skloop	krumst
strangk	gleend	thwomps	flamst
stowpst	skreefs	swivz	snumd
sploibd	splawps	bloorch	kwanst
trolch	drowpths	twonch	frelk

MATERIALS

Teacher's Manual, pages 52–53
Assessment Checklist, page 62 of the *Assessment Manual*
Token cards
Letter cards, including all vowels, vowel pairs, consonants, and consonant digraphs

PHONICS

Connecting Sounds to Letters

Place five different tokens on the table, such as a diamond, star, circle, square, and triangle.

- Say it slowly: ***twonch.*** Point to the first token and say: **What sound does this make?** After a student responds /*t*/, say: **Find the letter that makes that sound.** Have the student find the letter *t* and place it beneath the diamond.
- Say it slowly: ***twonch.*** Point to the second token and say: **What sound does this make?** Have the student say /*w*/ and place the letter card beneath the star.
- Say it slowly: ***twonch.*** Point to the third token and say: **What sound does this make?** After the student says /*o*/, he or she should place the corresponding letter card beneath the circle.
- Say it slowly: ***twonch.*** Point to the fourth token and say: **What sound does this make?** The student should say /*n*/ and place the letter card below the square.
- Say it slowly: ***twonch.*** Point to the last token and say: **What sound does this make?** Coach the student to look for the consonant digraph /*ch*/ and place that letter card beneath the triangle.
- Using other five- and six-sound nonsense words from the Word Bank, have students connect the sounds to letters using the cards.

Teacher Tip

Pay special attention to nonsense words containing three-sound consonant blends, as in ***sploibd, strangk,*** or ***splawps.*** Be sure to stretch the sounds so students can discriminate each one.

SUBSTITUTION ROUTINES

Once students are able to connect the sounds to letters, remove the tokens and work with the letter cards only.

- Say: **This says *prensk.* Make *brensk.*** Say the word slowly, especially elongating the initial and final consonant blends. Guide a volunteer in substituting the letter *p* with the letter *b.*
- Say: **This says *brensk.* Make *breensk.*** Coach a student to substitute the letters *ee* for *e*, which now makes the nonsense word have a long-vowel sound.
- Say: **This says *breensk.* Make *breensh.*** Be sure that when the student substitutes the letters *s* and *k* with *sh,* he or she pronounces /*sh*/ as one sound, not two.
- Say: **This says *breensh.* Make *theensh.*** Guide the student in substituting the initial consonant blend /*b*/ /*r*/ with the consonant digraph /*th*/.

- Rotating around the room, have other students spell nonsense words and substitute sounds in a variety of positions.

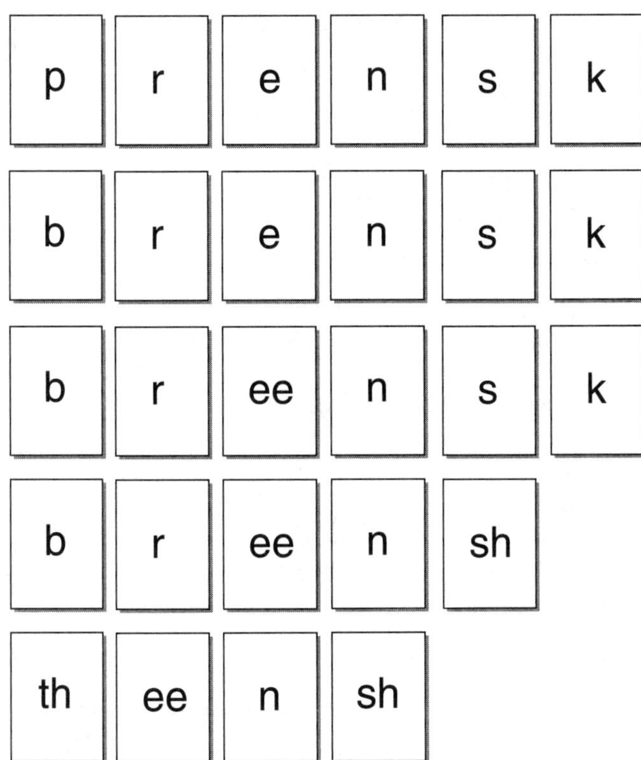

DELETION ROUTINES

Explain to students that you will be deleting single consonants, consonant blends (two letters that make two sounds), or consonant digraphs (two letters that make one sound).

- Say: **This says *gleend*. Make *geend*.** Have the student remove *l* and read the new nonsense word.
- Continue this routine with other nonsense words, such as *snumd/ snud*; *splawps/ spawps*; *kwanst/ kwant*; *thwomps/ twomps*.

SHIFTING ROUTINES

Mention to students that you will be shifting the position of letters within each word. Since this is a more challenging activity, stretch each sound as you say the nonsense word.

- Say: **This says *krumst*. Make *strumk*.** Guide a volunteer in shifting *s* and *t* to the first and second positions, and placing the *k* at the end of the word.
- Say: **This says *strumk*. Make *trumks*.** Coach the student as he or she places the *s* at the end of the word.
- Rotating around the room, have students shift positions in words, such as *frelk/ relfk*; *flamst/ lamfst*; *skloop/ loopsk*.

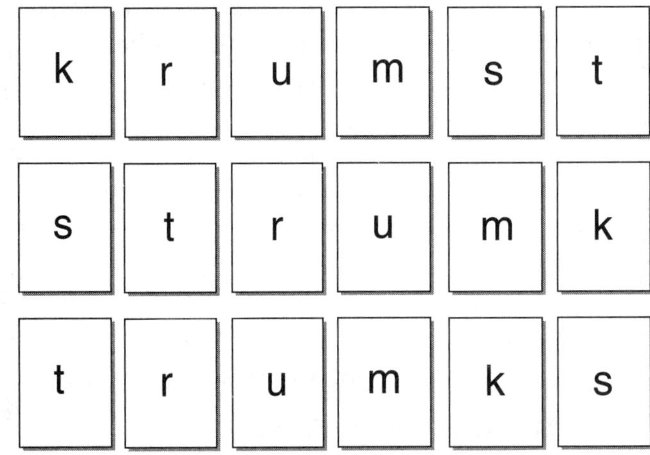

READING ROUTINES

Blending Sounds

- After students have manipulated and spelled a variety of words, have them practice reading them.
- Write each of the words in the Word Bank on index cards. Rotating around the small group, ask each student to read a word. If students are having difficulty, say the word slowly, stretching each sound; then ask them to segment each phoneme. When they can do this successfully, have them say the word slowly, blending the sounds together. Ask them to say the sounds more quickly, forming the word.

INFORMAL ASSESSMENT

- Use the Assessment Checklist found on page 62 of the *Assessment Manual* to determine whether students are able to decode and read five- and six-sound nonsense words.
- Working in pairs, have students test each other by asking their partners to read a nonsense word they've created. In addition, students can have their partners listen as they substitute, add, or delete sounds, and then invite them to make the new word.

LESSON 1 (Part 1)

OBJECTIVES

- Students will recognize that some base words do not change when adding the suffixes *ed* or *ing*, as in *clean, cleaned, cleaning*
- Students will recognize that the final consonant is doubled in single-syllable base words that end in consonant-vowel-consonant, as in *step, stepped, stepping*
- Students will sort words according to their spelling pattern
- Students will read sentences, fill in the correct word, and identify misspelled words

WORD BANK OF REAL WORDS

pitched	jumping	swimming	splashing
running	grabbed	cleaned	tripped
cooking	shopping	talked	stopped
loaded	walking	slipping	chirping

MATERIALS

Worktext, page 46
Teacher's Manual, page 54

CHAPTER 6

LESSON 1 (Part 1)

SPELLING RULE
Some base words do not change when adding the suffixes *ed* or *ing*, as in *clean, cleaned,* and *cleaning*. The final consonant is doubled in single-syllable base words that end in consonant-vowel-consonant, as in *step, stepped,* and *stepping*.

A. Say the Words
Say each word in the Word Bank. If you have trouble reading the words, cover up *ed* or *ing* and read each base word first. Then blend the whole word together.

WORD BANK			
pitched	jumping	swimming	splashing
running	grabbed	cleaned	tripped
cooking	shopping	talked	stopped
loaded	walking	slipping	chirping

B. Sort the Words
Read the words again in the Word Bank. Sort and write each word under the correct category.

No change when adding *ed/ing*

The final consonant is doubled when adding *ed/ing*

C. Fill in the Blanks
Read the sentences and fill in the correct words. The words can be found in the Word Bank. Use each word once.

1. I __________ to go __________ in the lake.
2. Pat __________ on the phone with Jake.
3. "Let's go __________," said Maria.
4. Meg __________ her room.
5. Sam __________ on the tip of the rug.

46 • Chapter 6

Worktext page 46

SPELLING

Ed and *ing*

- Explain to students that some base words don't change when adding ***ed*** or ***ing***, as in the words *clean, cleaned, cleaning*. Mention that the final consonant is doubled in single-syllable base words that end in consonant-vowel-consonant, as in *step, stepped, stepping*. Write these words on the board and have students brainstorm other words to put in each category. Keep some dictionaries handy so that students can check their spelling.
- Have students turn to page 46 in their Worktext. Rotating around the room, ask students to read each word found in the Word Bank. Have students sort the words in the categories listed on the page.
- Ask students to "Fill in the Blanks" by finding a word in the Word Bank to complete each sentence.

LESSON 1 (Part 2)

OBJECTIVES

- Students will recognize that words with double consonants sometimes stand for one sound, such as /n/ in *dinner*
- Students will identify words containing double consonants
- Students will sort words according to the one sound each double consonant makes
- Students will read sentences, fill in the correct word, and proofread a passage

WORD BANK OF REAL WORDS

happy	slipper	ridden	hobby
bubble	written	follow	ladder
carry	balloon	berry	bottle
puppy	saddle	supper	lettuce
button	hidden	borrow	parrot

MATERIALS

Worktext, page 47

Teacher's Manual, page 55

LESSON 1 (Part 2)

SPELLING RULE
Words with double consonants sometimes stand for one sound, like /n/ in *dinner*.

A. Say the Words
Say each word in the Word Bank.

WORD BANK			
bubble	written	follow	ladder
carry	balloon	berry	rubber
puppy	saddle	supper	lettuce
button	hidden	borrow	happy

B. Sort the Words
Sort and write each word under the correct double-consonant sound category. Circle the double consonants found in each word.

/p/	/b/	/r/	/t/	/d/	/l/
______	______	______	______	______	______
______	______	______	______	______	______
______		______	______	______	

C. Proofread a Note
Read the note. Find the five misspelled words and underline them. Write them correctly on the lines below.

Dear Sal,

My pupy is very small, but cute. She likes to sit by me when I have super. I cary her when I go to the store. She likes to folow me to school. She is hapy all the time. Please stop by and meet her!

Love,
Deb

1. ______ 2. ______ 3. ______ 4. ______ 5. ______

Lesson 1 • 47

Worktext page 47

SPELLING

Medial Double Consonants

- Write the word **dinner** on the board. Explain to students that words with double consonants sometimes stand for one sound. Say the words **slipper**, **ridden**, **hobby**, and **happy**. Have volunteers sound them out and spell them on the board.
- Have students take turns reading each of the words found in the Word Bank on Worktext page 47. Then have them sort each word according to the one sound each double consonant makes, such as /b/, /r/, /t/, /d/, and /l/.
- Have students proofread the note at the bottom of the page.

LESSON 2

OBJECTIVES

- Students will decode and read five- and six-sound words
- Students will write lists of rhyming words
- Students will build and spell words using letter cards
- Students will read clues and find words that contain five and six sounds
- Students will practice sorting three-, four-, five-, and six-sound words
- Students will play Word Search, locating five- and six-sound words

WORD BANK OF REAL WORDS

shrimp	stream	ground	float
streets	desks	skipped	lamps
plunk	splint	clasp	

MATERIALS

Worktext, pages 48–49
Teacher's Manual, pages 56–57
Award Certificate, page 336
Letter cards for each pair of students

RHYMING ROUTINES

- Write one of the words from the Word Bank on the board, such as **stream**. Ask students to write the word on their papers. Have them brainstorm and write down other words that have the same spelling pattern and that rhyme with it, such as **beam**, **cream**, **dream**, **gleam**, **team**. If students have difficulty spelling the words, have them practice stretching out each sound as they write.
- Invite volunteers to come up to the board and write words that you dictate from the Word Bank. Ask them to think of a rhyming word for each, such as *float/ goat/ moat/ coat/ boat*; *skipped/ dipped/ tripped*; *lamps/ stamps/ camps*; *streets/ meet/ feet.*

WORD-BUILDING ROUTINES

- Provide individuals or pairs of students with a set of letter cards. Depending on what spelling pattern students need to practice, you may wish to pull specific letter cards. Or you may wish to give them a word, such as *stream*, and ask them to make as many little words as they can using only those letter cards.
- Time students in this word-building activity, then award a certificate to the individual who makes the most words in a ten-minute time period. Ask each student to read each word. The certificate is found on page 336.

PRACTICE

A. Guess the Word

Have students complete the activity on page 48 in the Worktext. Students can work in pairs to read each clue and find the mystery word found in the Word Bank.

B. Sort the Words

Invite students to sort three-, four-, five-, and six-sound words found in the Word Bank.

C. Word Search

Have students locate and circle the words found in the Word Bank on the Word Search board.

LESSON 2

A. Guess the Word

With a partner, take turns reading each word in the Word Bank. Then read the clues below and guess which mystery word answers the clue. Use each word once.

WORD BANK		
paddle	skunk	shrimp
guppy	carrot	stream
claps	bottle	ground
flippers	street	lamps
floats	desks	skipped

Clues — **Mystery Words**

1. They need light bulbs to work. __________
2. They are found in the water and are good to eat. __________
3. We sit at them each day in school. __________
4. It is a good snack to eat. __________
5. It is black and white. __________
6. It is a small fish. __________
7. This word makes the long *o* sound. __________
8. It rhymes with *dream.* __________
9. You row with it. __________
10. You can put water in it. __________
11. It rhymes with *sound.* __________
12. The first three letters begin like *string.* __________
13. It rhymes with *taps.* __________
14. When you unscramble k-p-p-s-e-d-i, you make this word. __________
15. It rhymes with *zippers.* __________

48 • Chapter 6

Worktext page 48

B. Sort the Words

Congratulations! You have learned a lot about three-, four-, five-, and six-sound words. Read each word in the Word Bank. Sound out each one carefully. How many sounds does each word have? Sort the words in the correct category below.

WORD BANK			
theme	gruff	streets	plunk
strict	spring	trick	rule
mill	clasp	lunged	wished
found	check	splint	crisp

Three-Sound Words	Four-Sound Words	Five-Sound Words	Six-Sound Words
__________	__________	__________	__________
__________	__________	__________	__________
__________	__________	__________	__________
		__________	__________
		__________	__________

C. Word Search

On the Word Search board below, there are 24 hidden words. As you find each word, read it, then circle it. The words can go across, down, diagonally, or backward. Then cross the word out in the Word Bank above.

J	L	K	B	G	N	I	R	P	S
B	H	P	T	R	U	L	E	F	T
S	V	S	L	U	N	G	E	D	R
P	T	I	D	F	I	T	C	F	I
P	K	R	T	F	E	N	H	O	C
S	C	C	E	M	F	I	E	U	T
A	I	J	E	E	S	L	C	N	S
L	R	H	D	K	T	P	K	D	H
C	T	J	Y	W	I	S	H	E	D
J	K	N	U	L	P	M	I	L	L

Lesson 2 • 49

Worktext page 49

LESSON 3

OBJECTIVES

- Students will apply decoding skills by reading a travel diary entry and a music review
- Students will apply their writing skills by using five- and six-sound words to write a diary entry and a music review
- Students will apply comprehension skills by answering questions about a music review

MATERIALS

Worktext, pages 50–54
Teacher's Manual, pages 58–59
Award Certificate, page 336

DECODING AND READING

A. Let's Go Camping!

- Have students open to page 50 in the Worktext. Read the title "Let's Go Camping!" Mention that the word ***Let's*** means the same thing as ***Let us***, and is called a contraction. Explain that when we talk, we often use contractions.
- Have students read aloud, taking turns reading each travel diary entry.

B. Oh, What a Trip!

Have students read the words found in the Word Bank. Ask them to pretend they've just come back from a camping trip. Brainstorm what might have happened using the words from the Word Bank. Then have students write some diary entries using these words.

C. Good Times

- Before reading the music review, write the following words on the board: **Saturday**, **people**, **guitar**, **keyboard**, **player**, and **drummer**. Ask volunteers to read the words. See if the volunteers can demonstrate on the board to the rest of the class how to decode a word if they are having difficulty, such as covering up ***er*** in the word *player*, and decoding *play* first. Make note of those students who have difficulty using their decoding strategies.
- Write the phrase **hot riffs** on the board. Explain that the term *riffs* means a repeated melody and that when combined with *hot* (a slang term), it means that the player executed some outstanding melodic phrases on the guitar.
- Have students read the review, coaching students if they need help decoding a challenging word.

D. Think About It

Have students read the music review and answer the questions. Remind them to answer the questions using complete sentences.

E. A Music Review

- Brainstorm music groups that students find to be their favorite and least favorite. Then have them write their own music review, describing the *who, what, where, when,* and *why* of the event.
- Give Award Certificates, found on page 336, to students who write the most creative reviews.

ASSESSMENT

Dictation

Ask students to write down the following sentences as you dictate them. Be sure to say each sentence a few times before having them write. Say each sentence slowly and distinctly. If students have difficulty spelling a word, have them leave a blank or write as much of the word as they can.

1. Matt and his dad pitched the tent.
2. Pip jumped into the stream and splashed around.
3. Matt made a splint for my sprained thumb.
4. We made a fire and cooked the fish.
5. The crowd screamed, danced, and clapped to the beat.

LESSON 3

A. Let's Go Camping!
Read the travel diary entry below.

Day 1: Saturday

3:00 PM We got to our campsite by midday. Matt and his dad pitched the tent, while I went to the store to buy food.

4:00 PM When I got back from the store, my dog, Pip, jumped out of the truck and ran to the stream. He jumped into the stream, splashing and swimming with joy. Then Pip saw a black-and-white striped skunk! He started to run near the skunk, but I grabbed his collar to stop him. When I did, I tripped on a rock and fell. I hurt my thumb. Matt and his dad saw me fall and ran to me. We looked at my thumb and thought it might be sprained. Matt made a splint out of a small stick and tape.

5:00 PM While Matt and his dad went looking for wood to make a fire, I fished in the stream. Pip helped too! I caught two striped bass. Then I cleaned them so we could have a fish dinner.

6:30 PM When Matt and his dad got back to our camp, Matt made a fire, and we cooked the fish. I put some black beans in a pot and cooked them too. We ate the fish and dipped some bread in the beans and its sauce. Our meal was so good! As we were cleaning up, we gave Pip the food scraps. He licked his dish clean and barked for more!

8:45 PM When it got dark, we put our sleeping bags in the tent. We made sure there was no food in the tent. I had seen a sign at the store that said, "WATCH OUT FOR BEARS." We knew that the bears would leave us alone if we left our food in the truck, not in the tent. Then we talked and talked and started to fall asleep.

50 • Chapter 6

Worktext page 50

Day 2: Sunday

6:00 AM Pip and I woke up when we heard the birds chirping. Matt and his dad started to stir. We took a quick dip in the stream and ate some fruit. We took down the tent and rolled up our sleeping bags. We loaded them into the truck.

7:45 AM We took a three-mile hike, with Pip leading the way. While we were walking, we saw a deer running in the woods. When we got back to camp, we ate a snack and headed for home. Next month, we want to come back and camp here for three days. But next time, I do not want to sprain my thumb!

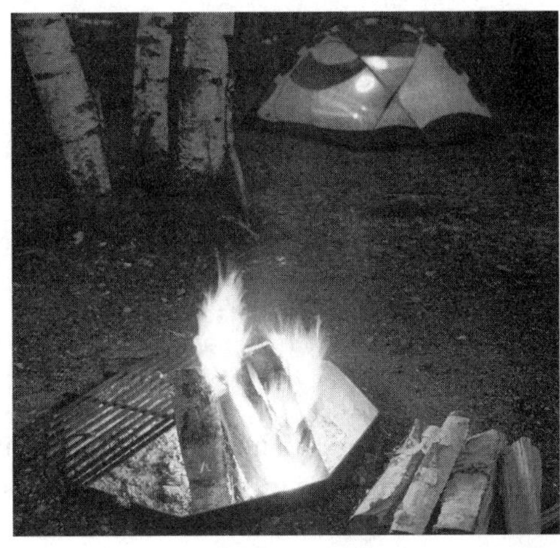

Lesson 3 • 51

Worktext page 51

C. Good Times
Read the following article.

Rock 'n' Roll in the Park

Last Saturday, the Good Time Rockers, a group from Los Angeles, played to a crowd of more than 1,000 people at Stone Park. The crowd sat on the ground and ate food as the group played old rock tunes from the 1960s and 1970s. The crowd screamed and sang along. Some people got up and danced as they snapped and clapped to the beat. The guitar player made up some hot riffs on a slow song. When it ended, the crowd shouted for more. Then the keyboard player started a new tune, with the bass player singing lead. On one song, the drummer played a 20-minute solo and had the crowd cheering. All in all, the Good Time Rockers is the best rock group that has ever played at Stone Park.

Lesson 3 • 53

Worktext page 53

B. Oh, What a Trip!
Pretend that you and your friends just came home from a camping trip. Lots of things happened, some good and some not so good! With a partner, take turns reading the words in the Word Bank. Talk with each other about what might have happened if the two of you went on a camping trip. Write some travel diary entries about what happened, using as many of the words in the Word Bank as you can.

WORD BANK			
scratched	tents	splashing	swimming
skunks	tripped	bears	screamed
drenched	shivered	cooked	camping
jumped	stream	fished	running
slipped	sprained	grabbed	pitched

My Diary

Day 1: ____________

Day 2: ____________

Day 3: ____________

Day 4: ____________

Day 5: ____________

52 • Chapter 6

Worktext page 52

D. Think About It
Reread "Rock 'n' Roll in the Park." Then answer the questions below.

1. On what day did the Good Time Rockers perform? ____________
2. Where does this music group live? ____________
3. What kind of music do they play? ____________
4. How many players are in the group? ____________
5. What instruments do they play? ____________
6. How did the crowd react to the music? ____________
7. Who played a solo? ____________
8. What did the music reviewer think of the group? ____________

E. Music Review
Write your own music review about your favorite or least favorite music group. Be sure to include the following:

- *Who* performed?
- *What* kind of music did the group perform?
- *Where* did they perform?
- *When* did they perform?
- *Why* did you like the group? Why didn't you like the group?

54 • Chapter 6

Worktext page 54

CHAPTER 7
Two-Syllable, Compound, and Multisyllabic Words

LESSON 1

OBJECTIVES

- Students will develop phonemic awareness as they identify words containing more than one syllable
- Students will connect sounds to letters by identifying the number of vowel sounds in two-syllable words
- Students will decode, read, and spell words containing two syllables

WORD BANK OF TWO-SYLLABLE WORDS

visit	almost	pencil	lemon
barrel	chicken	orchard	respect
welcome	zebra	doctor	either
feather	gallon	machine	quarter
travel	unite	harbor	invite
jelly	kitten	never	shoulder

MATERIALS

Worktext, page 55
Teacher's Manual, page 60
Letter cards

PHONEMIC AWARENESS

Clapping Syllable Patterns

- Introduce the concept that words can have more than one syllable by asking students to repeat each of the following words after you: **money**, **imagination**, **grocery**, **invitation**, **encyclopedia**. Ask them to say the words again, this time clapping the rhythm or counting the syllables on their fingers. Have volunteers say the number of syllables in each word.
- Invite students to think of big words to share with classmates, and have them clap and count the syllables.

PHONICS

Connecting Sounds to Letters

- Mention that a lot of words are made up of syllables, or smaller parts. Write **gallon** on the board. Recall that in Chapter 6, students learned about words that contain double consonants, such as the /*l*/ in *gallon.* Point out that this word contains a vowel in each syllable, the /*a*/ and /*o*/. Write **welcome** on the board and invite a student to come up to the board and circle each vowel. Then ask the student to decode each syllable and blend the sounds together to form the word.
- Have students brainstorm other two-syllable words, inviting them to sound out and spell the words on the board.

WORD-BUILDING ROUTINES

Using letter cards, ask students to build the word *lemon.* Students can work independently or in pairs for this activity. After they've spelled the word successfully, have them think of two-syllable words for the class to spell. Using a checklist, record the types of errors students make, identifying whether they're making mistakes with vowel sounds, or initial, medial, or final consonants.

PRACTICE

- Have students turn to page 55 in the Worktext and take turns reading the words in the Word Bank. Then ask them to circle the vowels contained in the first and second syllable of each word.
- Ask students to read the sentences and fill in the missing words. Each word can be found in the Word Bank.
- Students then read and underline each two-syllable word in the passage.

CHAPTER 7

LESSON 1

A. Say the Words

Working with a partner, take turns reading each word in the Word Bank. Then circle the two vowels found in the first and second syllable of each word.

WORD BANK			
visit	almost	pencil	lemon
barrel	chicken	orchard	respect
welcome	zebra	doctor	either
feather	gallon	machine	quarter
travel	unite	harbor	invite
jelly	kitten	never	shoulder

B. Fill in the Blanks

Read each sentence, and fill in the missing word. Use your Word Bank for help. Use each word once.

1. "__________ home," said Joe to his father.
2. I have a __________ tree in my front yard.
3. Jenny wanted to __________ a friend to her house after school.
4. Let's have __________ for dinner.
5. I need a __________ to write my paper.
6. Marge went to the store to buy a __________ jug of milk.
7. Nick's __________ walked through the apple __________.
8. We like to __________ by either plane or train.
9. I paid a __________ for a small pack of gum.
10. On Saturday, I'm going to __________ my friend Sam.

C. Read and Underline

Read the following passage and underline all the two-syllable words. Some of these words will not be found in the Word Bank. Good luck!

On Sunday, Mark will invite his friends Peg and Steven to supper. He will serve lemon chicken, rice, and soda. After supper, they will go into the apple orchard and pick apples, filling up an entire barrel. When it gets dark, they will go inside and make gallons of apple cider and seven apple pies.

Lesson 1 • 55

Worktext page 55

LESSON 2

OBJECTIVES

- Students will develop phonemic awareness as they identify the similarities in compound words
- Students will connect sounds to letters by recognizing that compound words are made up of smaller words
- Students will decode, read, and spell compound words

WORD BANK OF COMPOUND WORDS

basketball	baseball	football	birthday
outhouse	lighthouse	inside	softball
beside	sunflower	snowball	today
carport	raincoat	sunshine	
snowflake	airport	raindrop	
seaport	snowplow	Sunday	
fireball	sunlight	rainbow	
sunset	snowsuit	outside	

MATERIALS

Worktext, page 56
Teacher's Manual, page 61

PHONEMIC AWARENESS

Compound Words

- Ask students what the following words have in common: **basketball**, **baseball**, **football**. If students say that they are all types of sports, praise them. Then ask them if the words sound similar in any way. Students should say that they all end in *ball*.
- Say another set of words, such as **outhouse** and **lighthouse**. Ask students to determine the similarities in these words.

PHONICS

Connecting Sounds to Letters

- Mention that all of these are compound words, which are made up of smaller words. Using paper and pencils, have students write the words **basketball**, **baseball**, and **football**. If they have difficulty, have them write the similar part in each word first, then add on the parts that are different. Do the same routine with *outhouse, lighthouse*, *inside*, *outside*, and *beside*.

PRACTICE

- Have students turn to page 56 in their Worktexts and take turns reading the compound words found in the Word Bank.
- Ask them to sort the words according to similar smaller words contained in each compound word.
- Invite students to match up small words to make compound words.
- Have students read the sentences and underline the compound words that don't make sense. Ask them to write the correct word in the space provided.

LESSON 2

A. Say and Sort the Words

Read the compound words found in the Word Bank. Then sort each word according to similar smaller words contained in each compound word. Two words are used twice.

WORD BANK			
sunflower	snowball	birthday	carport
raincoat	sunshine	softball	snowflake
airport	raindrop	today	seaport
snowplow	Sunday	fireball	sunlight
rainbow	snowsuit		

sun-	snow-	rain-	-ball	-port	-day
________	________	________	________	________	________
________	________	________	________	________	________
________	________	________	________	________	________
________	________				

B. Make a Bigger Word

Look at the words in each box. Combine a word in the first box with a word in the second box to make a bigger word. Write each compound word below.

butter	snake
good	fly
rattle	stand
under	bye

1. ________ 2. ________ 3. ________ 4. ________

C. Make Sense!

Read each sentence. Find and underline the compound word that does not make sense as written in the sentence. Write the correct word after each sentence. Use the Word Bank for help.

1. The child wore a snowsuit when it rained. ________
2. The raindrop bloomed in spring. ________
3. I pitched a snowball to the player who was batting for the home team. ________
4. I parked my boat in the carport. ________

56 • Chapter 7

Worktext page 56

LESSON 3

OBJECTIVES

- Students will develop phonemic awareness as they identify words containing prefixes
- Students will decode by analogy as they identify similar word parts or chunks
- Students will decode, read, and spell words containing prefixes

WORD BANK OF WORDS CONTAINING PREFIXES

exchange	export	exhale	express
depart	deport	deplane	decrease
disappoint	disapprove	disagree	disinterest
unfair	unlike	unpack	unwrap
unhappy	untie	unfold	unlucky
reread	rework	return	replace
refill	rebuild	rewrite	rebound

MATERIALS

Worktext, page 57
Teacher's Manual, page 62

PHONEMIC AWARENESS

Similar Word Parts

- Say the following words to students: **exchange**, **export**, **exhale**, **express**. Ask them to decide what feature is similar among the words. When students say that the words begin the same way, repeat each word and invite them to echo you. Do the same routine with other words in the Word Bank.
- Say the following words to students: **disagree**, **disinterest**, **depart**, **disapprove**. Ask them to name the word that isn't the same. Do this routine with other words.

PHONICS

Decoding by Analogy

- Write the words **exchange**, **export**, **exhale**, and **express** on the board. Have a volunteer circle the word part that is similar in each word and underline the word parts that are different. Explain that *ex* is a prefix or word chunk that is added at the beginning of a base word. Mention that prefixes change the meaning of the word. In this case, *ex* means *out of* or *from*.
- Do this routine with other words found in the Word Bank.
- You may want to mention that *un* usually means *not*; *dis* usually means *the opposite of*; *re* usually means *do again* or *back*; *de* usually means *go away from* or *step down*.

PRACTICE

- Have students turn to page 57 in the Worktext. Rotating around the room, have students read the words in the Word Bank. Ask them to circle each prefix and underline the base words.
- Ask students to complete the sentences by filling in the blanks with words found in the Word Bank.
- Have students proofread the passage and write the correct spellings for each word.

LESSON 3

A. Say the Words

Read the words found in the Word Bank. Then circle each prefix and underline the base words. Remember that the prefix is the word part or chunk found at the beginning of each word.

WORD BANK			
exchange	deport	disinterest	rebuild
unfair	reread	unlike	disapprove
exhale	deplane	re-write	unhappy
disappoint	depart	express	unwrap
rebound	untie	refill	unpack
export	unlucky	replace	rework
unfold	return	disagree	decrease

B. Fill in the Blanks

Read each sentence and fill in the missing word. Use your Word Bank for help.

1. I think that it is ____________ that we only have 20 minutes to eat lunch.
2. Pat was very ____________ with her spelling grade.
3. Jay ____________ the poem before he wrote his own.
4. I ____________ with the law that was just put into effect.
5. Sally and Rob are going to ____________ the car's engine.

C. Proofread It

Read the following paragraph and circle the five words that are misspelled. Write the correct spellings below.

I was unhapy when I came home from my trip because I had such a good time. The first thing I did was unpak my suitcase. Then I wrote my friend a note to expres to her how much fun I had. I told her that I would like to retirn to her town for a visit during spring break. I rered my note before sending it to her.

1. __________ 2. __________ 3. __________ 4. __________ 5. __________

Lesson 3 • 57

Worktext page 57

LESSON 4

OBJECTIVES

- Students will develop phonemic awareness as they identify words containing suffixes
- Students will decode by analogy as they identify similar word parts or chunks
- Students will decode, read, and spell words containing suffixes

WORD BANK OF WORDS CONTAINING SUFFIXES

careful	thankful	painful	helpful
hopeful	harmful	useful	thoughtful
careless	thankless	painless	helpless
hopeless	harmless	useless	thoughtless
washable	dependable	breakable	reliable
sinkable	honorable		

MATERIALS

Worktext, page 58
Teacher's Manual, page 63

PHONEMIC AWARENESS

Suffixes

- Say the words **washable**, **breakable**, and **sinkable**. Ask students to name the word chunk that is similar in each word. (*able*) Explain to students that *able* means *able to* or *full of*. Tell them that a suffix is a word part that is attached at the end of a base word.
- Do this routine with other words found in the Word Bank. Explain that *ful* means *full of*; *less* means *without*.

PHONICS

Decoding by Analogy

- Write **careful** on the board. Ask students to think of other words that they know that end in *ful*, such as *useful*, *thoughtful*, *hopeful*, and *painful*. Have them write these words as students brainstorm each.
- Have students spell other words found in the Word Bank by asking them to think of other words that have similar word chunks.

PRACTICE

- Ask students to turn to page 58 in the Worktext. Have them take turns reading each of the words. Afterward, they can circle the suffixes and underline each base word.
- Have students reread the words in the Word Bank and sort them according to their endings.
- Ask students to complete the sentences by filling in the appropriate words.

LESSON 4

A. Say the Words

Read each word found in the Word Bank. Then circle the suffixes and underline the base words. Remember that suffixes are the word parts or chunks found at the end of each word.

WORD BANK			
careful	harmless	washable	reliable
helpless	thankful	hopeless	helpful
honorable	painless	thoughtful	breakable
sinkable	thankless	useless	thoughtless
hopeful	careless	painful	useful
dependable	harmful		

B. Sort the Words

Reread each word and sort them according to their endings.

-ful	-less	-able
______	______	______
______	______	______
______	______	______
______	______	______
______	______	______
______	______	______
______	______	
______	______	

C. Fill in the Blanks

Read each sentence, and fill in the missing word. Use the Word Bank if you need help. More than one word may complete some of the sentences.

1. I felt very __________ when I could help Mom set the table.
2. I have to be careful because the dishes are __________.
3. Randy was __________ when the car did not hit him.
4. She is a very __________ sister.
5. I am very __________ when I hold my baby brother.

58 • Chapter 7

Worktext page 58

LESSON 5

OBJECTIVES

- Students will apply their decoding skills by reading poems that contain compound, two-syllable, and multisyllabic words
- Students will apply their writing skills by writing a poem and a paragraph about themselves

MATERIALS

Worktext, page 59–62
Teacher's Manual, pages 64–65
Award Certificate, page 336

DECODING AND READING

A. Compound Raps

Have students turn to page 59 in their Worktexts. Mention that "Seasons" and "What's the Score?" are two poems or raps that have a steady, toe-tapping, finger-snapping rhythm. Explain that each of them contains compound words. Ask students to scan the text silently to see if there are words they have difficulty decoding. Write them on the board and have volunteers help the class to read them, demonstrating their decoding strategies. Then have students read the text.

B. Find the Compound Words

Invite students to reread "Seasons." Then ask them to underline all of the compound words. Afterward, have them draw a line in between the two smaller words that make up each compound word. Encourage them to check their answers using a dictionary.

C. Write Your Own

Ask students to write their own poem or rap using some of the words found in the Word Bank. Students can also brainstorm some compound words of their own or use some that are found in the two raps they just read.

D. Beginnings and Endings

I Am Able

- Review prefixes and suffixes with students; then have them scan the text for words that may be difficult to decode. Write the words on the board and guide students as they employ their decoding strategies. First, have them look at the base word and decode it. Then move to the prefix or suffix.
- If a word has both a prefix and suffix, decode the suffix first; then move to the prefix. When students are able to decode all of the word parts or chunks, then ask them to blend the parts together to form the word. Finally, have students read the poem, "I Am Able."

E. Count the Syllables

Ask students to reread the poem. Have pairs of students look for words that contain more than one syllable. Have them draw lines in between each syllable; then have them check their answers using a dictionary.

F. Sorting the Words

Invite students to read the poem again. Have them find and sort four words for each category, according to how many syllables the words contain.

G. I Am ______________

With lots of enthusiasm, tell your students "Congratulations—for a job well done!" Mention that they have just completed *Getting Ready* and have the skills necessary to move forward into the *Caught Reading* Worktexts. As a celebration, award each student a certificate, found on page 336. Then ask them to write a short paragraph about themselves, describing all the positive qualities that they possess. Brainstorm a list of words and have them spell and write each one on the board. Ask students to think of one word that sums them up and to use it in the title.

ASSESSMENT

Dictation

As a final dictation activity, use some of the sentences that students wrote to describe themselves, such as *I am a person worthy of love. I am helpful and reliable in class. I am thoughtful to my family and friends. I am interested in listening to what my brother has to say. I am cheerful and happy—and it rubs off onto others!*

LESSON 5

A. Compound Raps

Read the following poems.

Seasons

Winter, spring, summer, and fall.
Tell me the season that's best of all.
Raincoats, raindrops, rainbows, too.
Spring has rain showers that rain on you!
Spring turns to summer. Did you know?
Buttercups bloom and sunflowers grow.
Summertime is fun at the sunny seashore.
Let's find seashells. Time to explore!
Fall is the time for a football game.
Cheerleaders cheer each player's name.
Wintertime is cold with lots of snowflakes,
Snowballs, snowsuits, and icy lakes.

What's the Score?

Baseball and basketball can be fun.
Football is the sport where you kick,
  throw, and run!
Fullback, quarterback, linebacker, too.
Root for the team in red and blue.
Watch the scoreboard. What's the score?
Make a touchdown. We want more!

Lesson 5 • 59

Worktext page 59

B. Find the Compound Words

Reread the rap below. Find each compound word and underline it. Then draw a line in between the two smaller words that make up each compound word.

Seasons

Winter, spring, summer, and fall.
Tell me the season that's best of all.
Raincoats, raindrops, rainbows, too.
Spring has rain showers that rain on you!
Spring turns to summer. Did you know?
Buttercups bloom and sunflowers grow.
Summertime is fun at the sunny seashore.
Let's find seashells. Time to explore!
Fall is the time for a football game.
Cheerleaders cheer each player's name.
Wintertime is cold with lots of snowflakes,
Snowballs, snowsuits, and icy lakes.

C. Write Your Own Rap or Poem

Write your own rap or poem using some of the words in the Word Bank. You can use a dictionary or brainstorm other words that you would like to use.

WORD BANK		
newspaper	goldfish	sweatshirt
breakfast	grapefruit	strawberry
doorbell	seashell	flashlight
something	anywhere	volleyball
inside	outside	weekend
sailboat	sunset	football

____
____
____
____
____
____

60 • Chapter 7

Worktext page 60

D. Beginnings and Endings

Read the following poem.

I Am Able

Un can begin some words you see.
Unbeatable and unafraid can describe me.
Inactive and intolerant are just not "in."
Be involved and interested. You'll fit right in!
Able can end some words for you,
Like reliable, dependable, and honorable, too.
Thankful and bashful are sometimes me.
Thoughtful and helpful are always me!
Foolish and childish, I am not.
Admirable qualities are what I've got!

Lesson 5 • 61

Worktext page 61

E. Count the Syllables

Reread "I Am Able." Then look for words that contain more than one syllable. Draw a line between each syllable. Check your answers by looking up the words in the dictionary.

I Am Able

Un can begin some words you see.
Unbeatable and unafraid can describe me.
Inactive and intolerant are just not "in."
Be involved and interested. You'll fit right in!
Able can end some words for you,
Like reliable, dependable, and honorable, too.
Thankful and bashful are sometimes me.
Thoughtful and helpful are always me!
Foolish and childish, I am not.
Admirable qualities are what I've got!

F. Sorting the Words

As you read the poem again, find and sort four words for each category, according to how many syllables the words contain.

One syllable	Two syllables	Three syllables	Four syllables
________	________	________	________
________	________	________	________
________	________	________	________
________	________	________	________

G. I Am ________

Write a paragraph that describes what you are like as a person. Think about all of the positive qualities that you have. Then choose one word that sums you up and use it in the title of this activity.

Title: ________________

____
____
____
____
____

62 • Chapter 7

Worktext page 62

LEVEL 1

ORGANIZER

Level 1 of the *Caught Reading* program includes the following components:

Worktext 1

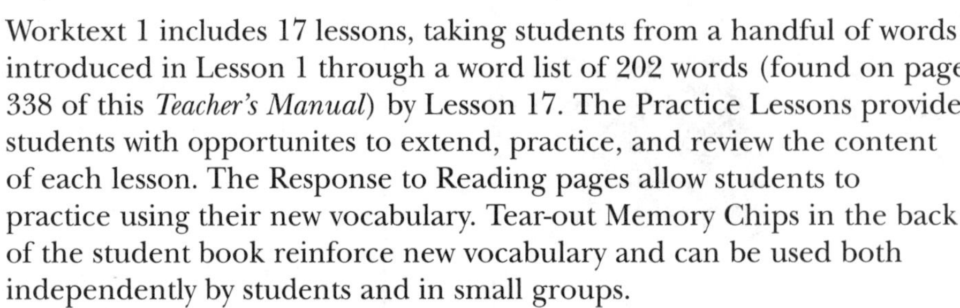

Worktext 1 includes 17 lessons, taking students from a handful of words introduced in Lesson 1 through a word list of 202 words (found on page 338 of this *Teacher's Manual*) by Lesson 17. The Practice Lessons provide students with opportunites to extend, practice, and review the content of each lesson. The Response to Reading pages allow students to practice using their new vocabulary. Tear-out Memory Chips in the back of the student book reinforce new vocabulary and can be used both independently by students and in small groups.

Midway and Final Novels 1

These novels are designed to reinforce learned vocabulary and give students the opportunity to read for meaning. Their high-interest plots encourage successful reading experiences and an appreciation for literature.

- *Hit and Run* includes only vocabulary students have learned up to the midway point of the level.
- *Crash!* includes all vocabulary learned in Level 1.

Teacher's Manual

The *Teacher's Manual* provides detailed objectives and instruction for each skill taught in the Worktext, as well as additional teaching suggestions for meaningful practice and reinforcement. The *Teacher's Manual* provides choices for flexible instruction. Comprehension questions for the Midway and Final novels are included, as well as Answer Keys for the Worktext activities and the Practice Lessons.

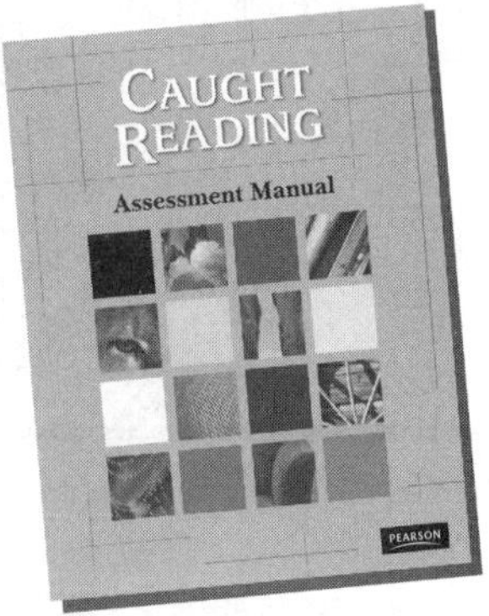

Assessment Manual

The *Assessment Manual* provides preassessment, ongoing assessment, and postassessment to administer to students throughout their work in *Caught Reading*. Within this Manual you will also find Midway and Final Assessments to determine the students' comprehension of the Midway and Final Novels.

OBJECTIVES

Vocabulary Development

- Read a base vocabulary of words, plus additional words made up of base words and endings.
- Use the word learning sequence to remember and spell words correctly.
- Review vocabulary independently, both in and out of context, using the Memory Chips.

Phonics

- Learn to recognize words with *s, er, ing, 's, es, ed, est,* and *th* endings.
- Combine familiar words into compound words.
- Recognize the letter groups *ay, ot, alk, all, an, ike, ake, ad, eep, ight,* and *eam* at the ends of words.
- Combine initial letter sounds and initial consonant blends with letter groups.

Reading Comprehension

- Remember details from a story.
- Identify the main idea of a story.
- Determine plot sequences.

Literary Analysis

- Identify characters, settings, and key events.
- Identify the main problem or conflict of the plot and how it is resolved.

Writing

- Write brief narratives that move through a logical sequence of events.
- Write descriptions of setting, character, objects, and events in detail.

Speaking and Listening

- Discuss issues presented in stories.
- Listen attentively as others read aloud.
- Describe plot sequences.

INTRODUCTION & LESSON 1.1

OBJECTIVES

- Students will learn new words containing the *ay* phonogram
- Students will apply endings *s* and *er* to base words to form new words

PHONICS VOCABULARY

play	say	wants	says
day	player	makes	

WORDS TO KNOW

in	to	go	get	make
Jake	want	money	mom	Tom
have	we	school	need	she
the	about	hall	your	find
who	lost	can	MP3	job
dog	say	think	I	a
Jen	play			

MATERIALS

Worktext 1, pages 6–13
Teacher's Manual, pages 68–71
Practice Lesson 1.1, pages 64–66 of the Worktext

TEACH

- Using Worktext pages 6–8, begin to introduce students to the vocabulary words in this lesson. Give them an opportunity to practice writing words on page 7.
- Students can organize their Memory Chips, found in the back of the Worktext. You may wish to say each word, having students repeat it after you.

Worktext page 7 can also be used to reinforce spelling. Use the five-step process detailed on page 71 of this *Teacher's Manual*.

Phonogram *ay*

Write this sentence on the board and read it aloud: **I say I want to go.** Ask a volunteer to point to *say*.

Blending Circle *ay*, modeling how to blend the sounds: **Listen as I pronounce this vowel sound for you: /*a*/. The letters *ay* make the long *a* vowel sound. If I put /*s*/ in front of the letters *ay*, it will make the word *say*.** Write **say** on the board. Make a word ladder with students, having them add other beginning consonant and consonant blends to *ay*, such as *bay, lay, may, pay, ray, way, play*. Write each new word on the board as it is suggested. Students can pronounce the new word, blending each sound.

Ending *s*

Write this sentence on the board and read it aloud: **Tom says he has the cans.** Point to *says* and *cans* and ask students how these words are alike. (They end in *s.*) Ask students what sound they hear at the end of *cans* and *says*. (/*z*/)

Make New Words Write these words on the board and invite students to add *s* to the end of each word: **job**, **think**, **dog**, **play**, **say**, **want**, **make**, **can**, **need**. Have them use each new word in a sentence.

Ending *er*

Write this sentence on the board and read it aloud: **We need an MP3 player.** Ask a volunteer to point to *player*. Cover the ending *er* and ask students what word they see. Tell them that when *er* is added to words, it sometimes means "one who" or "something that." *Player* means "something that plays."

Make New Words Write **think** on the board and have a volunteer add *er*. Ask students what *thinker* means. (*One who thinks.*)

PRACTICE

- Let students practice the new words they have learned and formed by completing the activities found on pages 9–10 of the Worktext.
- If students are experiencing difficulty with the Words to Know section on pages 9–10, you may have groups of students place two sets of Memory Chips on a table with the words facing up. Students can take turns finding two that match. Have them say the words and keep the cards.

For further practice, have students complete Practice Lessons 1.1 on pages 64–66 of the Worktext. Answers can be found in the Answer Key on page 347 of this *Teacher's Manual*.

APPLY

- Have students talk about the story concept by discussing things they have experienced. Ask: **Have you ever found money? What did you do with it?** Tell them they are going to use the words they have learned to read a short story.
- Ask students to read the story on page 12 in the Worktext. Offer assistance if necessary, but encourage students to decode the words independently, using the clues and patterns they have learned.
- After students have completed reading the story, have them complete the Cooperative Group Activity (What Do You Think?) and Comprehension Exercise (Remembering Details) on page 13 in their Worktext. Answers can be found in the Answer Key on page 347 of this *Teacher's Manual.*

CONNECTION

Strategy for Reading Have students reread the selection "Money" on page 12 to correct comprehension breakdowns. Students may achieve understanding by reprocessing the same text with greater attention focused on its meaning.

Speaking/Listening Have student partners read aloud the selection "Money." The partners can alternate being speaker and listener.

Writing Students should be encouraged to keep a journal of their writings. They can use these journals to record responses to their reading, list new words they have learned, or record their thoughts and feelings about the reading selections.

Strategy for Reading After students finish reading the selection, ask them to summarize it either aloud or in writing.

Five Steps to Learn a Word

The following five steps are the best way to learn new words.

1. **Find out what the word is.** Later, you will learn ways to figure out new words on your own. But you can always ask your teacher or a friend what a word is. Find out what this word is: **job**.
2. **Look at the word very carefully.** Note its shape, length, and anything unusual about the way it looks. Then look at each letter: **j-o-b**.
3. **Say the word.** Say the word out loud several times. Listen carefully to the sounds. What is the first letter? How does the **j** sound in **job**? What is the last letter? Can you hear the **b** sound? Can you hear every letter in **job**?
4. **Picture the word.** You've looked hard at **job**. You've listened to the sounds in **job**. Now close your eyes. Try to picture the word in your mind. Try to see the shape of the whole word as well as each letter. If you can't, keep practicing steps 2 and 3 until you can.
5. **Write the word.** Without looking at the word, write it on a piece of paper. Did you write **j-o-b**? If not, practice steps 2, 3, and 4 until you can write **job** without looking at it. Don't worry if you have to go over the steps several times to learn a word.

6

Worktext page 6

Words to Know

Every time you see **Words to Know** you will use the five steps to learn some new words. You will see a chart like this.

	Look	Say	Picture	Write
job	☐	☐	☐	________

As you complete each step in learning a new word, put a check (√) in the box. When you can write the word without looking, write it on the line below the word **Write.** When you have learned a word, your chart will look like this:

	Look	Say	Picture	Write
job	√	√	√	job

Practice Learning New Words

Use the five steps to practice learning the following new words.

	Look	Say	Picture	Write
dog	☐	☐	☐	________
say	☐	☐	☐	________
think	☐	☐	☐	________

7

Worktext page 7

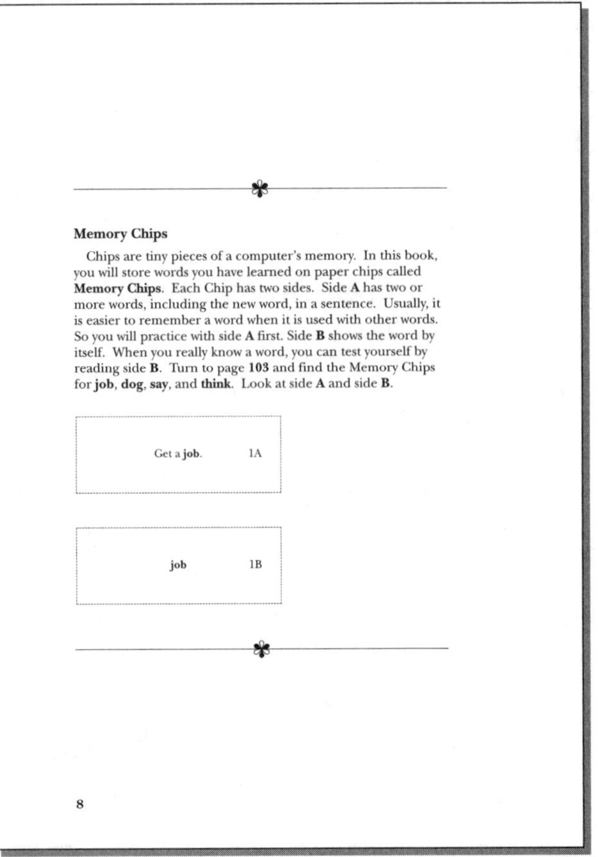

Memory Chips

Chips are tiny pieces of a computer's memory. In this book, you will store words you have learned on paper chips called **Memory Chips**. Each Chip has two sides. Side **A** has two or more words, including the new word, in a sentence. Usually, it is easier to remember a word when it is used with other words. So you will practice with side **A** first. Side **B** shows the word by itself. When you really know a word, you can test yourself by reading side **B**. Turn to page **103** and find the Memory Chips for **job**, **dog**, **say**, and **think**. Look at side **A** and side **B**.

Get a **job**. 1A

job 1B

8

Worktext page 8

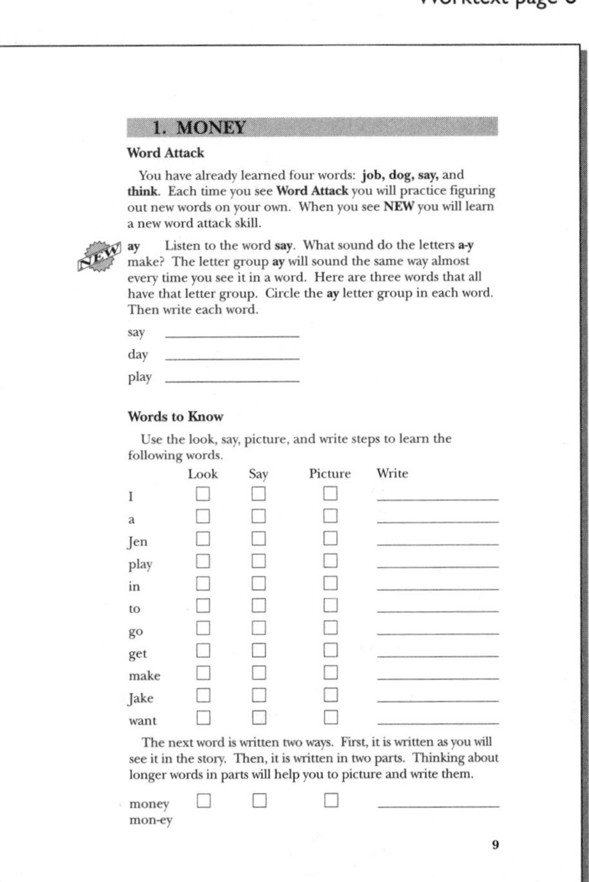

1. MONEY

Word Attack

You have already learned four words: **job, dog, say,** and **think**. Each time you see **Word Attack** you will practice figuring out new words on your own. When you see **NEW** you will learn a new word attack skill.

NEW **ay** Listen to the word **say**. What sound do the letters **a-y** make? The letter group **ay** will sound the same way almost every time you see it in a word. Here are three words that all have that letter group. Circle the **ay** letter group in each word. Then write each word.

say ______________

day ______________

play ______________

Words to Know

Use the look, say, picture, and write steps to learn the following words.

	Look	Say	Picture	Write
I	☐	☐	☐	______
a	☐	☐	☐	______
Jen	☐	☐	☐	______
play	☐	☐	☐	______
in	☐	☐	☐	______
to	☐	☐	☐	______
go	☐	☐	☐	______
get	☐	☐	☐	______
make	☐	☐	☐	______
Jake	☐	☐	☐	______
want	☐	☐	☐	______

The next word is written two ways. First, it is written as you will see it in the story. Then, it is written in two parts. Thinking about longer words in parts will help you to picture and write them.

	Look	Say	Picture	Write
money mon-ey	☐	☐	☐	______

9

Worktext page 9

Work Attack

NEW **+s** Three of the words you just learned can be changed by adding an **s**.

I say. She **says**.

The word **say** is called a base word. The letter **s** is an ending. Write each of the words below and add an **s** ending.

say ______________ want ______________ make ______________

NEW **+er** The letters **er** are another ending. Write the following base word, adding an **er** ending.

play ______________ Now circle the base word.

Words to Know

Here are the rest of the words you need to know to read the first story. You may already know some of them. Learn the rest so you can enjoy the story.

	Look	Say	Picture	Write
mom	☐	☐	☐	______
Tom	☐	☐	☐	______
have	☐	☐	☐	______
we	☐	☐	☐	______
school	☐	☐	☐	______
need	☐	☐	☐	______
she	☐	☐	☐	______
the	☐	☐	☐	______
about a-bout	☐	☐	☐	______
MP3	☐	☐	☐	______
hall	☐	☐	☐	______
your	☐	☐	☐	______
find	☐	☐	☐	______
who	☐	☐	☐	______
lost	☐	☐	☐	______
can	☐	☐	☐	______

10

Worktext page 10

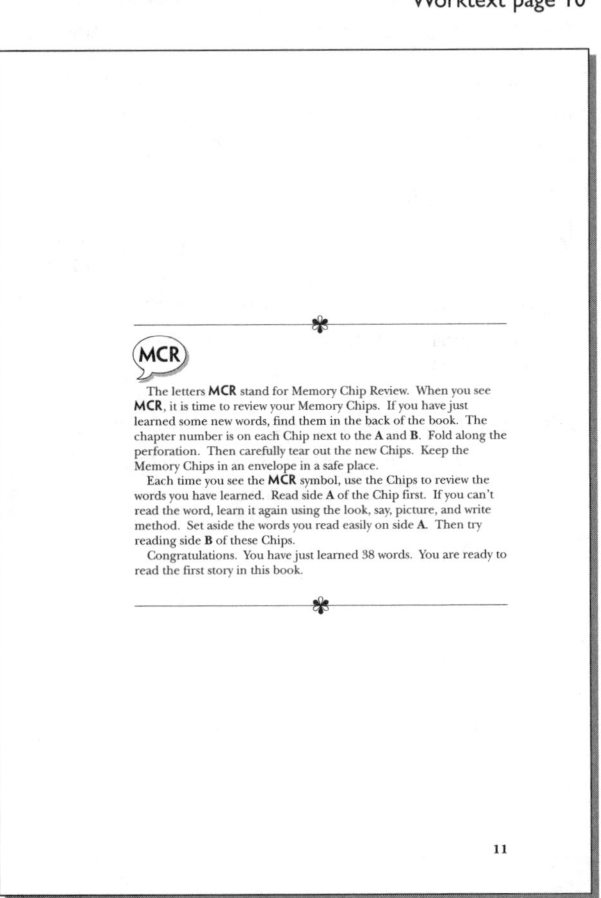

MCR

The letters **MCR** stand for Memory Chip Review. When you see **MCR**, it is time to review your Memory Chips. If you have just learned some new words, find them in the back of the book. The chapter number is on each Chip next to the **A** and **B**. Fold along the perforation. Then carefully tear out the new Chips. Keep the Memory Chips in an envelope in a safe place.

Each time you see the **MCR** symbol, use the Chips to review the words you have learned. Read side **A** of the Chip first. If you can't read the word, learn it again using the look, say, picture, and write method. Set aside the words you read easily on side **A**. Then try reading side **B** of these Chips.

Congratulations. You have just learned 38 words. You are ready to read the first story in this book.

11

Worktext page 11

Worktext Pages 12–13

1. MONEY

"I want a job," I say to Mom.

She says, "Go to school."

I say, "We need money."

She says, "I make the money. Go to school!"

In school, I think about money. Mom wants a dog. I want a MP3 player. I need a job!

In the school hall, I find money. $200! I think about the dog Mom wants. I think about a MP3 player. I have the money. I can get a MP3 player. I can get a dog.

I find Jen. She says, "Get the MP3 player."

I find Jake. Jake says, "Get your mom a dog."

I find Tom. Tom says, "Find who lost the money."

The money makes me think.

12

Worktext page 12

What Do You Think?

Meet with a friend or in a small group. Talk about what you think the person in this story should do with the money. Give your reasons why.

Remembering Details

Here are some sentences from the story. Write the word that goes in each blank. Look back at the story if you need to.

I want a ____________________.

Mom wants a ____________________.

In the school hall, I find ____________________.

Tom says, "Find out who ____________________ the money."

The ____________________ makes me think.

13

Worktext page 13

CONNECTION

Spelling You may use the following five-step process to reinforce spelling and word recognition for your students throughout this program. Encourage your students to follow this process as they complete the Words to Know sections in their Worktext pages.

Step 1
Find out what the word is.

Step 2
Look carefully at the word. First look at the word as a whole. What shape does it have? Do any letters go above or below the line? Next, look carefully at each letter in the word.

Step 3
Say the word out loud several times. Listen to all the sounds in the word as you say it again.

Step 4
Picture the word. Try to see each letter and the shape of the whole word. Practice looking at the word and saying it until you get a good mental picture of it.

Step 5
Write the word.

LESSON 1.2

OBJECTIVES

- Students will apply endings *s* and *ing* to base words to form new words
- Students will learn the possessive ('s) form of words

PHONICS VOCABULARY

going	finds	says	walks	Tom's
MP3s	Mom's	Jen's	Jake's	

WORDS TO KNOW

he	am	is	me	my
lot	like	but	off	sick
you	home	walk	coach	game
what	Saturday	grandma	CD	

MATERIALS

Worktext 1, pages 14–17
Teacher's Manual, pages 72–73
Practice Lesson 1.2, pages 67–69 of the Worktext

TEACH

- Using Worktext page 14, introduce students to the vocabulary words. Give them an opportunity to practice writing the words.
- Students can organize their Memory Chips, found in the back of the Worktext. Have students divide them into groups of words they know and words they don't recognize. Then say each word, having students repeat it after you.

Worktext page 14 can also be used to reinforce spelling. Use the five-step process detailed on page 71 of this *Teacher's Manual.*

Ending *s*

Write this sentence on the board and read it aloud: **Mom has two CDs.** Point to *has* and *CDs* and ask students how these words are alike. (*They both end in* s.) Ask students what sound they hear at the end of *has* and *CDs.* (/*z*/)

Make New Words Write these words on the board and invite students to add *s* to the end of each word: **find**, **think**, **say**, **player**, **dog**, **hall**, **play**, **home**, **game**, **school**, **need**, **job**. They can use each word they make in a sentence.

Ending *ing*

Write these sentences on the board and read them aloud: **I go to school. I am going to school.** Ask a volunteer to point to *go* and *going* and tell how the words are different. (Going *ends in* ing.)

Make New Words Make word cards for these words: **walk**, **find**, **go**, **need**. Make a card for **ing**. Have students take turns using the cards to make new words using *ing*. Have them use the new word in a sentence. Write each new word on the board.

Possessives

Write this sentence on the board and read it aloud: **I have Jake's money.** Ask students who the money belongs to. (*Jake*) Circle the apostrophe and *s* and tell students when they see an apostrophe and *s* after the name of a person or thing, it means that person or thing owns something.

Make New Words Write these words on the board and have students add an apostrophe and an *s* after each name: **Mom**, **school**, **dog**, **Jen**, **Tom**. Then have them dictate or write the new word in a sentence.

PRACTICE

- Let students practice the new words they have learned and formed by completing the activities on page 15 of the Worktext.
- If students are experiencing difficulty with the Words to Know section on page 14, you may wish to play a Memory Chip Bingo game. Have students write 16 of the words in a 16-square Bingo grid. Use the Memory Chips to read the words and have students mark the squares as you call out each word. The first student to get all 16 squares filled in yells "Bingo!"

For further practice, have students complete Practice Lesson 1.2 on pages 67–69 of the Worktext. Answers can be found in the Answer Key on page 347 of this *Teacher's Manual.*

APPLY

- Have students talk about the story concept by sharing their personal experiences. Ask: **Have two or more people ever wanted you to do something at the same time? How did you decide what you needed to do?** Tell them they are going to use the words they have learned to read a short story.
- Ask students to read the story on page 16 in the Worktext. Encourage students to decode the words independently, using the clues and patterns they have learned.
- After students have completed reading the story, have them complete the Cooperative Group Activity (What Do You Think?) and Comprehension Exercises (Remembering Details and Finding the Main Idea) on page 17 in their Worktext. Answers can be found in the Answer Key on page 347 of this *Teacher's Manual.*

2. SATURDAY

Words to Know

Take the time to learn these words well. You will enjoy the reading a lot more.

	Look	Say	Picture	Write
he	☐	☐	☐	______
am	☐	☐	☐	______
is	☐	☐	☐	______
me	☐	☐	☐	______
my	☐	☐	☐	______
lot	☐	☐	☐	______
like	☐	☐	☐	______
but	☐	☐	☐	______
off	☐	☐	☐	______
sick	☐	☐	☐	______
you	☐	☐	☐	______
home	☐	☐	☐	______
walk	☐	☐	☐	______
coach	☐	☐	☐	______
game	☐	☐	☐	______
what	☐	☐	☐	______
Saturday Sat-ur-day	☐	☐	☐	______
grandma grand-ma	☐	☐	☐	______
CD	☐	☐	☐	______

14

Worktext page 14

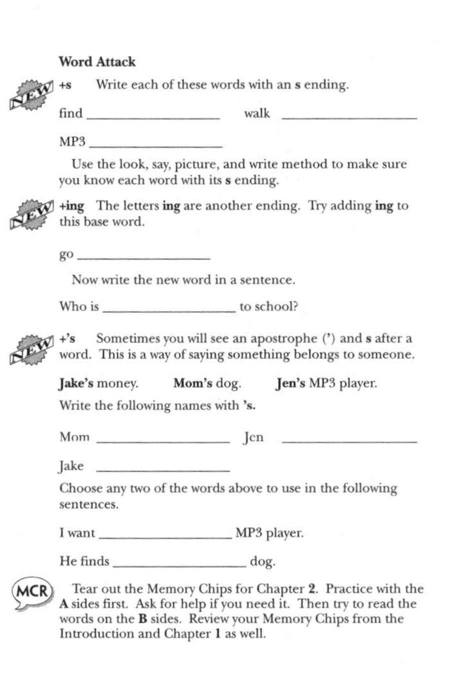

Word Attack

NEW **+s** Write each of these words with an **s** ending.

find ______ walk ______

MP3 ______

Use the look, say, picture, and write method to make sure you know each word with its **s** ending.

NEW **+ing** The letters **ing** are another ending. Try adding **ing** to this base word.

go ______

Now write the new word in a sentence.

Who is ______ to school?

NEW **+'s** Sometimes you will see an apostrophe (') and **s** after a word. This is a way of saying something belongs to someone.

Jake's money. **Mom's** dog. **Jen's** MP3 player.

Write the following names with **'s**.

Mom ______ Jen ______

Jake ______

Choose any two of the words above to use in the following sentences.

I want ______ MP3 player.

He finds ______ dog.

MCR Tear out the Memory Chips for Chapter **2**. Practice with the **A** sides first. Ask for help if you need it. Then try to read the words on the **B** sides. Review your Memory Chips from the Introduction and Chapter **1** as well.

15

Worktext page 15

2. SATURDAY

On Saturday, I am going to Tom's to play CDs. I like Tom a lot.

But my coach finds me in the school hall. She says, "We have a game Saturday."

"What?" I say.

"We have a game Saturday. You have to play."

"But —"

Coach walks off.

I go home. I think about Saturday. I want to play in the game. I want to go to Tom's.

Grandma walks in. She says, "I need you Saturday. I am sick."

I say, "But Grandma!"

She says, "What?"

I think, *My grandma is sick.* I say, "OK."

But I think, *What about the game? What about Tom?*

16

Worktext page 16

What Do You Think?

Meet with a friend or in a small group. Talk about what you think the person in this story should do about Saturday. Try to think of more than one good way she could handle the situation. Give your reasons why.

Remembering Details

Write a word from the story in each space. You can look back at the story if you need to.

I like Tom a ______.

But my coach finds me in the ______ hall.

"We have a game ______."

I think, *My grandma is* ______.

Finding the Main Idea

It is important to remember details from your reading. It is also important to think about the main idea. The main idea is what the whole story is about. Each of the groups of words below says something about the story. But one of them best describes the story's main idea. Write that group of words on the line.

I like Tom.

what to do on Saturday

Grandma is sick.

______

Take a Breather

From now on, after each story you get a free story. That means you don't have to learn any new words to read it. The free stories give you more practice reading the words you have already learned. However, you should still review your Memory Chips before reading the free stories. Find the **MCR** on the next page.

17

Worktext page 17

LESSON 1.3

OBJECTIVE

- Students will practice and apply skills to extended passages

MATERIALS

Worktext, pages 18–19
Teacher's Manual, page 74
Practice Lesson 1.3, page 70 of the Worktext

SKILLS REVIEW

- Before reading, you may wish to review these words that apply phonics skills: *says, makes, going.* Have students review the Memory Chips they have learned so far. Then ask: **What kinds of friends do you like to be around?**
- While reading, have students think about which character in the story they would like to have as a friend and why.
- After reading, have students complete the exercises on Worktext page 19.

For further practice, have students complete Practice Lesson 1.3 on page 70 of the Worktext. Answers can be found in the Answer Key on page 347 of this *Teacher's Manual.*

RETEACH

If students need further review of phonics skills, you may wish to use the following activity:

Phonogram *ay*

Moving Letters Write letters **K**, **s**, **p**, **l**, **s**, **a**, and **y** on large index cards. Distribute one card to each student. Then have students with cards *s, a,* and *y* stand up. Tell them to stand in the sequence that spells the word *say.* Then tell them you want to make the word *says.* Ask the student who has the missing letter to stand up and make the word. Continue by forming new words by substituting beginning letters or adding *s.* You can make these words: *say, says, Kay, pay, play, pays, plays, lay, lays.*

CONNECTION

Writing Students can write a few sentences in which they describe the two characters in the story. They can compare how the characters are different and how they are alike.

Worktext Pages 18–19

3. THINK ABOUT WHAT YOU WANT

"Coach makes me sick," says Tom.

"I like Coach," I say.

"But you get to play a lot," Tom says.

"My job makes me sick," Tom says.

"I like my job," I say.

"But you make money," Tom says. "A lot."

"School makes me sick," Tom says.

"I like Saturday," I say. "I am lost in school. But we need school."

"What is school going to get me?" Tom says.

"A job," I say.

"Who says?" Tom says.

"Tom," I say, "you make me sick. Think about what you want. You want money? Get a job. You want a job you like? Go to school. Think about what you want. I am going home."

18

Worktext page 18

What Do You Think?

Meet with a friend or in a small group. Talk about the two people in this story. How are they different? Are there ways they are alike? Which person are you most like and why?

Remembering Details

Write a word from the story in each space. You may look back at the story if you need to.

"Coach makes me ________," says Tom.

"I like my ________," I say.

Think about what you ________.

I am going ________.

Finding the Main Idea

Write the group of words that best says what the whole story is about.

what makes Tom sick

Tom likes school.

who makes money

____

____

____

19

Worktext page 19

LESSON 1.4

OBJECTIVES

- Students will learn new words containing the *ot* phonogram
- Students will apply endings *s* and *ing* to base words to form new words

PHONICS VOCABULARY

says	fire	trucks	gets	not
needs	thinking	waiting	goes	firetrucks

WORDS TO KNOW

of	it	not	on	fire
see	her	car	truck	wait
out	back	hide	house	boss
happy	sister			

MATERIALS

Worktext 1, pages 20–23
Teacher's Manual, pages 75–76
Practice Lesson 1.4, pages 71–73 of the Worktext

TEACH

- Using Worktext page 20, introduce students to the vocabulary words. Have them complete the page.
- Students can organize their Memory Chips, found in the back of the Worktext. Have them sort the words into known and unknown words. Then say each unfamiliar word, having students repeat it after you.

Worktext page 20 can also be used to reinforce spelling. Use the five-step process detailed on page 71 of this *Teacher's Manual.*

Phonogram *ot*

Write this sentence on the board and read it aloud: **A truck is not a car.** Ask a volunteer to point to *not.*

Blending Circle *not,* modeling how to blend the sounds: /n/ /o/ /t/. **When I see *o* surrounded by two consonants, the *o* has a short vowel sound. If I put *p* in front of the letters *ot*, it will make the word *pot*.** Write **pot** on the board. Make a word ladder with students, having them add other beginning consonant and consonant blends to *ot,* such as *cot, lot, hot, jot.* Write each new word on the board as it is suggested. Students can pronounce the new word, blending each sound.

Endings *s, ing*

Review with students how they can add *s* and *ing* to words. Have them find the Memory Chips that have the endings *s* and *ing.*

Make New Words Write these words on the board and invite volunteers to add *s* and *ing* to the end of each word: **need, think, wait**. As they write each new word, have them pronounce it and use it in a sentence.

PRACTICE

- Let students practice the new words they have learned and formed by completing the activities on page 21 of the Worktext.
- If students are experiencing difficulty with the Words to Know section on page 20, help them sort the words into categories like these: beginning sounds; endings *s, es,* and *ing*; number of letters in each word; words that name people; words that name things; words that show action.

For further practice, have students complete Practice Lesson 1.4 on pages 71–73 of the Worktext. Answers can be found in the Answer Key on page 348 of this *Teacher's Manual.*

APPLY

- Have students talk about the story concept by sharing their personal experiences. Ask: **What is the most important thing in your life? Why is that?** Tell them they are going to use the words they have learned to read a short story about a character who experiences a tragedy at home and realizes what is important in life.
- Ask students to read the story on page 22 in the Worktext. Offer assistance if necessary, but encourage students to decode the words independently, using the clues and patterns they have learned.
- After students have completed reading the story, have them complete the Cooperative Group Activity (What Do You Think?) and Comprehension Exercises (Remembering Details and Putting Ideas in Order) on page 23 in their Worktext. Answers can be found in the Answer Key on page 347 of this *Teacher's Manual.*

4. FIRE

Good job. You have learned 64 words. You have read three stories. You have also learned about base words, endings, and letter groups.

Word Attack

NEW **ot** You know the word **lot**. Change **l** to **n** and you have **not**. Write **not** on the line. Then circle the letter group **ot**.

not ________________

Write the word **not** in a sentence.

I am ________________ going.

Words to Know

	Look	Say	Picture	Write
of	☐	☐	☐	________
it	☐	☐	☐	________
not	☐	☐	☐	________
on	☐	☐	☐	________
fire	☐	☐	☐	________
see	☐	☐	☐	________
her	☐	☐	☐	________
car	☐	☐	☐	________
truck	☐	☐	☐	________
wait	☐	☐	☐	________
out	☐	☐	☐	________
back	☐	☐	☐	________
hide	☐	☐	☐	________
house	☐	☐	☐	________
boss	☐	☐	☐	________
happy hap-py	☐	☐	☐	________
sister sis-ter	☐	☐	☐	________

20

Worktext page 20

4. FIRE

I have a job. I like my boss. I make OK money. I hide my money at home. I want to get a car.

My boss says, "You hide your money at home?"

I say, "I like to see my money."

"It is your money," he says.

On Saturday, I get off my job. I walk home thinking about the car I want. I see my house. My house is on fire!

I see firetrucks, but I do not wait. I go into the house. I find my mom. I make her get up. I find Grandma. I get her out of the house. I go back in. The fire is now in the hall. I find my sister. I get her out of the house. My mom gets the dog. We get out.

We lost the house. I lost my money. But I am happy. I have my grandma. I have my mom. I have my sister. I have my dog.

22

Worktext page 22

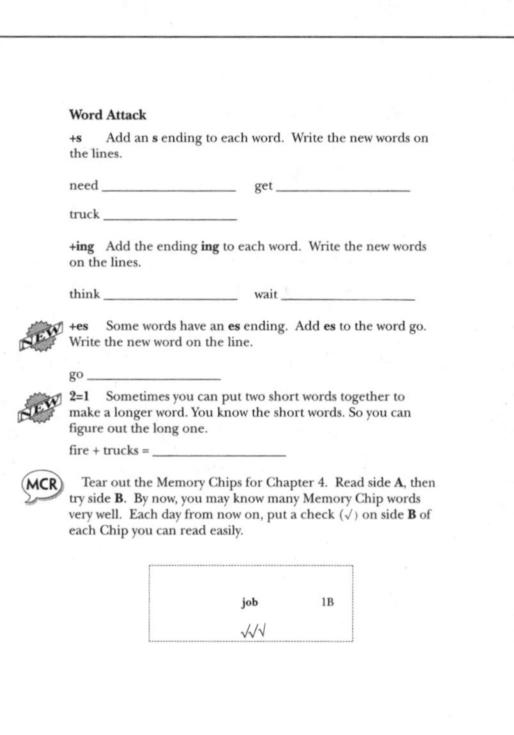

Word Attack

+s Add an **s** ending to each word. Write the new words on the lines.

need ________________ get ________________

truck ________________

+ing Add the ending **ing** to each word. Write the new words on the lines.

think ________________ wait ________________

NEW **+es** Some words have an **es** ending. Add **es** to the word go. Write the new word on the line.

go ________________

NEW **2=1** Sometimes you can put two short words together to make a longer word. You know the short words. So you can figure out the long one.

fire + trucks = ________________

MCR Tear out the Memory Chips for Chapter 4. Read side **A**, then try side **B**. By now, you may know many Memory Chip words very well. Each day from now on, put a check (√) on side **B** of each Chip you can read easily.

job 1B

√√√

21

Worktext page 21

What Do You Think?

Meet with a friend or in a small group. Something bad just hit this boy and his family. Talk about what you think he meant when he said, "But I am happy."

Remembering Details

Write a word from the story in each blank.

I hide my ________________ at home.

I see fire ________________.

I get her out of the ________________.

But I am ________________. I have my grandma.

Putting Ideas in Order

Here are three sentences from the story. Write the sentences in the order that they happened. Read the story again if you need to.

My house is on fire!

I lost my money.

My mom gets the dog.

____

____

____

23

Worktext page 23

LESSON 1.5

OBJECTIVE

- Students will practice and apply skills to extended passages

MATERIALS

Worktext 1, pages 24–25
Teacher's Manual, page 77
Practice Lesson 1.5, page 74 of the Worktext
Tagboard, brad/fastener (Reteach)

SKILLS REVIEW

- Before reading, you may wish to review these story words that apply phonics skills: *not, walks, waiting, Jen's, needs.* Have students review the Memory Chips they have learned so far. Then ask: **What do you do when someone is lost or missing?**
- While reading, have students think about what they would do if they were Jen's sister.
- After reading, have students complete the exercises on Worktext page 25.

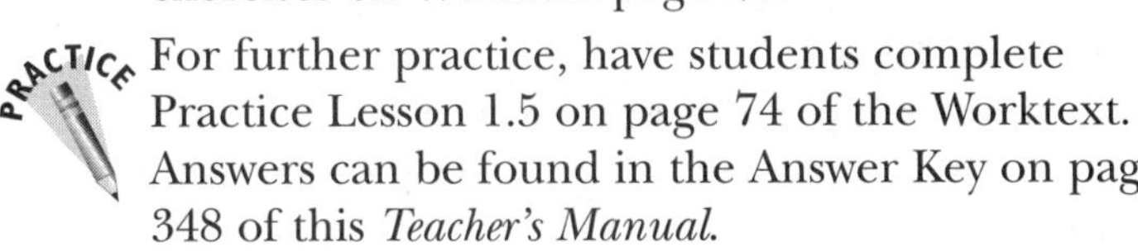

For further practice, have students complete Practice Lesson 1.5 on page 74 of the Worktext. Answers can be found in the Answer Key on page 348 of this *Teacher's Manual.*

RETEACH

If students need further review of phonics skills, you may wish to use the following activity:

Phonograms *ot, ay*

Spin It! Make a spinner and arrow out of tagboard and a brad, and divide the wheel into 10 sections. Write these consonants on different sections of the wheel: **h, n, l, c, g, p, s, w, r, m.** Write **ot** on the board seven times. Write **ay** on the board eight times. Then have students take turns spinning the spinner. Have students add the consonant to the beginning of *ot* or *ay* and write it on the board. Then have the students use the word in a sentence. Continue until all the words have been made. (*hot, not, lot, cot, got, pot, rot; hay, lay, gay, pay, say, way, ray, may*)

CONNECTION

Writing Students can write a few sentences describing how they would feel if their sister or brother were missing. Have student volunteers share their writing with the class.

MCR

5. MY SISTER IS LOST

It is 9:00. My sister is not in school.
It is 4:00. She is not at her job.
It is 11:00. She is not home.
My Mom is not happy. She walks about the house. She is waiting.
I say, "Mom, I think Jen is lost. Think about what to do!"
"Wait," she says. "We have to wait."
"I am going out to find her," I say. I get the car. I go out.
I find Jen's boss. I say, "My sister is not home."
"What about the game? Is she at the game?"
I go to school. I go in to the game. Jen is not at the game.
My sister needs me! She is lost!
I go home. I say to Mom, "Think about what to do!"
But Mom walks about the house. I see she is not happy. But I want her to say, "Jen is home." I want my sister back home.

24

Worktext page 24

What Do You Think?

Meet with a friend or in a small group. Tell how the girl and the mother are the same and different. Compare their two personalities. Then, say what you would do if your sister was missing.

Remembering Details

Write a word from the story in each space.

It is 9:00. My sister is not in ________.

"I am going out to ________ her," I say.

But ________ walks about the house.

I see she is not ________.

But I want her to ________, "Jen is home."

Read It Again

The more you practice reading, the better you will get. Stories are usually easier to read the second time. So for practice, read again **Money** on page **12**. Then read these sentences. Choose the best answer (**a**, **b**, or **c**), and write it on the line.

In school I think about ________.
(a) Mom (b) a dog (c) money

I ________ a job!
(a) need (b) have (c) find

The money makes me ________.
(a) find Mom (b) think (c) get a job

25

Worktext page 25

LESSON 1.6

OBJECTIVES

- Students will learn new words containing the *alk* and *ay* phonograms
- Students will learn to recognize and form compound words
- Students will apply endings *er*, *s*, and *ing* to base words to form new words

PHONICS VOCABULARY

talking	talk	walk	says	cannot
hitting	bigger	may	kidding	

WORDS TO KNOW

day	did	next	big	then
girl	are	new	dad	little
do	stop	hit	kid	problem

MATERIALS

Worktext 1, pages 26–29
Teacher's Manual, pages 78–79
Practice Lesson 1.6, pages 75–77 of the Worktext

TEACH

- Using Worktext page 26, introduce students to the vocabulary words at the bottom of the page. Have them complete the Words to Know section.
- Students can organize their Memory Chips, found in the back of the Worktext. Have them sort the words into known and unknown words. Then say each unfamiliar word, having students repeat it after you.

Worktext page 26 can also be used to reinforce spelling. Use the five-step process detailed on page 71 of this *Teacher's Manual.*

Phonograms *alk, ay*

Write this sentence on the board and read it aloud: **I talk and say a lot.** Ask a volunteer to point to *talk* and *say.*

Blending Remind students they can make new words by changing the beginning sounds of words with phonograms. Write **talk** on the board, say the word, and ask them what new word they can make if they replace the *t* with a *w*. Help them blend the sounds in the new word. Repeat, using **say**.

talk	say
walk	day
chalk	way

Compound Words

Remind students they can often find two smaller words in one larger word. Write this sentence on the board and have them find the compound word: **I cannot go.** (*cannot*)

Make New Words Write these words on cards and have students put them together to make new words: **can**, **not**, **grand**, **ma**, **fire**, **truck**, **dog**, **house**.

Endings *er, s, ing*

Remind students they can add *er*, *s*, and *ing* to words. Have them find the Memory Chips that have the endings *er*, *s*, and *ing*. Then write this sentence on the board: **I am bigger than Tom.** Circle *bigger.* Cover *ger* and ask students to read the word. Tell them that when a word has a short vowel sound like *big*, and you add an ending like *er*, you double the consonant before you add the ending. Repeat, using *hit* and *hitting.*

Make New Words Write these words on the board and invite volunteers to add *er*, *s*, or *ing* to the end of each word: **kid**, **hit**, **sit**. As they say each new word, have them use it in a sentence.

PRACTICE

- Let students practice the new words they have learned and formed by completing the activities on pages 26–27 of the Worktext.
- If students are experiencing difficulty with the Words to Know section on page 26, you may wish to display the Memory Chips on a table. Say incomplete sentences like the one below, having students choose a Memory Chip to complete the sentence: **I went to school the _____ day.** (*next*)

For further practice, have students complete Practice Lesson 1.6 on pages 75–77 of the Worktext. Answers can be found in the Answer Key on page 348 of this *Teacher's Manual.*

APPLY

- Have students talk about the story concept by sharing their personal experiences. Ask: **How do you make new friends at school?** Tell them they are going to use the words they have learned to read a short story about a boy's first days at a new school.
- Ask students to read the story on page 28 in the Worktext.
- After students have completed reading the story, have them complete the Cooperative Group Activity (What Do You Think?) and Comprehension Exercises (Remembering Details and Putting Ideas in Order) on page 29 in their Worktext. Answers can be found in the Answer Key on page 347 of this *Teacher's Manual.*

6. NEW KID AT SCHOOL

Word Attack

ay You know the words **play** and **say**. Change the first letter of either word to **m** and you have **may**. Then write the words.

say ________________ play ________________

may ________________

NEW **alk** You know the word **walk**. Change the first letter to **t** and you have **talk**. Circle the letter group **alk** in each word. Then write the words.

walk ________________ talk ________________

2=1 Sometimes two short words are put together to make a longer word. You know the short words. So you can figure out the long one. **can + not = cannot**

Write the word **cannot**. ________________ Now circle the two short words in the word you wrote.

Words to Know

	Look	Say	Picture	Write
day	☐	☐	☐	________________
talk	☐	☐	☐	________________
did	☐	☐	☐	________________
next	☐	☐	☐	________________
stop	☐	☐	☐	________________
hit	☐	☐	☐	________________
big	☐	☐	☐	________________
then	☐	☐	☐	________________
girl	☐	☐	☐	________________
are	☐	☐	☐	________________
do	☐	☐	☐	________________
kid	☐	☐	☐	________________
new	☐	☐	☐	________________
dad	☐	☐	☐	________________
little lit-tle	☐	☐	☐	________________
problem prob-lem	☐	☐	☐	________________

26

Worktext page 26

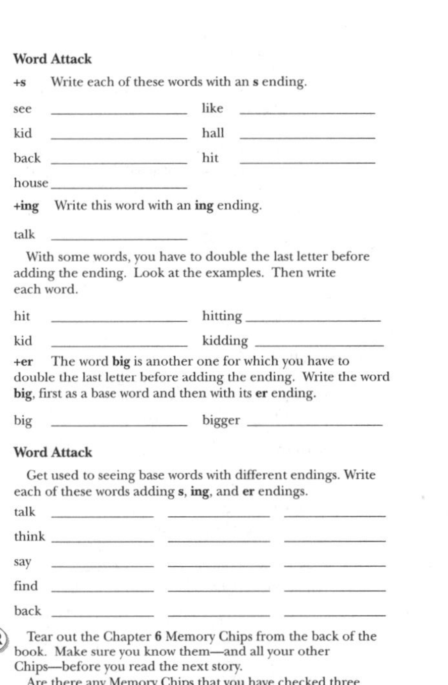

Word Attack

+s Write each of these words with an **s** ending.

see ________________ like ________________

kid ________________ hall ________________

back ________________ hit ________________

house ________________

+ing Write this word with an **ing** ending.

talk ________________

With some words, you have to double the last letter before adding the ending. Look at the examples. Then write each word.

hit ________________ hitting ________________

kid ________________ kidding ________________

+er The word **big** is another one for which you have to double the last letter before adding the ending. Write the word **big**, first as a base word and then with its **er** ending.

big ________________ bigger ________________

Word Attack

Get used to seeing base words with different endings. Write each of these words adding **s**, **ing**, and **er** endings.

talk ____________ ____________ ____________

think ____________ ____________ ____________

say ____________ ____________ ____________

find ____________ ____________ ____________

back ____________ ____________ ____________

MCR Tear out the Chapter **6** Memory Chips from the back of the book. Make sure you know them—and all your other Chips—before you read the next story.

Are there any Memory Chips that you have checked three times or more? That means you really know those words. Take any you have checked three times or more and put them in a separate envelope labeled **Words I Know**. Once in a while, we will ask you to take them out for a review.

27

Worktext page 27

6. NEW KID AT SCHOOL

I am at a new school. The kids are talking in the halls. I want to hide. I walk in the hall, and I am not happy.

At home, I say I am sick. I do not go to school the next day.

The next day, my dad says, "You are not sick! You have to go to school."

I go to school. In the hall I think about talking to a girl I see. But I cannot think what to say.

Then I see a big kid hit a little kid. I do not like to see big kids hitting little kids. I think about what to do. I want to stop the big kid. But I do not want to get hit.

Then, I see the girl walk up to the boys. "Stop!" she says. "What is your problem?" she says to the big kid. "You are bigger."

The big kid backs off.

I walk up to the girl. "I like what you did," I say.

She says, "Are you a new kid at school?"

We talk. Then I walk her home. I am happy. I am not sick the next day.

28

Worktext page 28

What Do You Think?

Meet with a friend or in a small group. What do you think is the best thing to do when you see a fight? Try to think of more than one solution.

Remembering Details

Write a word from the story in each space.

The kids are ________________ in the halls.

At home, I say I am ________________.

Then, I see the ________________ walk up to the boys.

"What is your ________________?" she says to the big kid.

Putting Ideas in Order

Here are four sentences from the story. Write them in the order that they happened.

Then I walk her home.

Then I see a big kid hit a little kid.

At home, I say I am sick.

The big kid backs off.

____

____

____

____

29

Worktext page 29

LESSON 1.7

OBJECTIVE

- Students will practice and apply skills to extended passages

MATERIALS

Worktext 1, pages 30–31
Teacher's Manual, page 80
Practice Lesson 1.7, page 78 of the Worktext
Egg timer (Reteach)

SKILLS REVIEW

- Before reading, you may wish to review these story words that apply phonics skills: *CDs, says, kidding, talk, say, going.* Have students review the Memory Chips they have learned so far. Then ask: **What would you do if you saw a big fire?**
- While reading, have students think about what they would do if they were one of the characters in the truck.
- After reading, have students complete the exercises on Worktext page 31.

For further practice, have students complete Practice Lesson 1.7 on page 78 of the Worktext. Answers can be found in the Answer Key on page 348 of this *Teacher's Manual.*

RETEACH

If students need further review of phonics skills, you may wish to use the following activity:

Endings *s, ing, er*

Make a List Make word cards for these words: **think**, **wait**, **get**, **need**, **truck**, **see**, **kid**, **back**, **house**, **hall**, **hit**, **talk**. Make word cards for endings *s, ing,* and *er.* Set the timer and have students use the cards to form new words. One player records the words on a sheet of paper. Teams earn one point for each word. When the time is up, each team reads aloud the words in their list. Possible word combinations include: *thinks, thinking, thinker, waits, waiting, waiter, gets, getting, needs, needing, trucks, trucking, trucker, sees, seeing, kids, kidding, kidder, backs, backing, houses, housing, halls, hits, hitting, hitter, talks, talking, talker.*

CONNECTION

Speaking/Listening Student partners can read aloud the selection "A Big Problem" on Worktext page 30. The partners can alternate being speaker and listener.

Worktext Pages 30–31

7. A BIG PROBLEM

Jake and I like to go out in my truck. We talk and talk and talk. And then we play CDs. He likes my CDs.

On Saturday, Jake says, "I want to go see the big fire."

I say, "Are you kidding?"

"I want to see it," he says.

We get in my truck. We talk. We play CDs. Then, I see the fire.

"Jake," I say. "The fire."

I stop the truck. I see firetrucks. I see houses on fire. We have to get out.

"I want to go back," I say. I get the truck going.

Then, Jake says, "Stop!"

I do not see what he sees. My truck hits a big dog.

"Jake," I say, "I hit a dog."

"What are we going to do?" Jake says.

We have a big, big problem.

30

Worktext page 30

What Do You Think?

Talk with a friend or in a small group. If you were one of the people in this story, what would you do about the problem? Try to think of more than one good answer.

Finding the Main Idea

Write the group of words that best says what the whole story is about.

My truck hits a dog.

We do not go to school.

Jake is my problem.

____

____

Read It Again

Read again the story on page **16** called **Saturday**. Then read these sentences. Choose the best answer (**a**, **b**, or **c**), and write it on the line.

But my coach ________________ me in the school hall.
(a) hits (b) finds (c) walks

I think, my ________________ *is sick.*
(a) grandma (b) sister (c) coach

She says, "I need you on Saturday. I am ________________."
(a) happy (b) kidding (c) sick

31

Worktext page 31

LESSON 1.8

OBJECTIVES

- Students will learn new words containing the *all* and *an* phonograms
- Students will apply endings *s, ing, er,* and *ed* to base words to form new words
- Students will learn the possessive form of words
- Students will learn contractions by shortening two words

PHONICS VOCABULARY

friends	Dan's	Dad's	don't	can't
Jake's	wanted	gets	sees	I'm
drinker	finds	says	Dan	call
problems				

WORDS TO KNOW

by	call	Dan	drink	his
does	with	that	own	sorry
people	friend			

MATERIALS

Worktext 1, pages 32–35
Teacher's Manual, pages 81–82
Practice Lesson 1.8, pages 79-81 of the Worktext

TEACH

- Using Worktext pages 32–33, introduce students to the vocabulary words in the Words to Know sections.
- Students can organize their Memory Chips, found in the back of the Worktext. Have them sort the words into known and unknown words. Help students figure out unknown words with decoding and context clues.

Worktext pages 32–33 can also be used to reinforce spelling. Use the five-step process detailed on page 71 of this *Teacher's Manual.*

Phonograms *all, an*

Write this sentence on the board and read it aloud: **I call Dan at home.** Ask a volunteer to point to *Dan* and *call.*

Blending Remind students they can make new words by changing the beginning sounds of words with phonograms. Write **call** on the board, say the word, and ask them what new word they can make if they replace the *c* with a *b*. Then have them suggest other words that rhyme, replacing the first consonant sound. Repeat, using **Dan**.

call	Dan
ball	fan
tall	ran

Endings *s, ing, er, ed*

Remind students they can add *s, ing, er,* and *ed* to words. Have them find the new Memory Chips that have these endings.

Make New Words Write these endings and words on index cards and have students put them together to make new words: **s, ing, er, ed, drink, friend, own, call.** Record the words on the board.

Possessives and Contractions

Write this sentence on the board: **I'm going to Dan's house.** Have students point to the word that tells Dan owns something. (*Dan's*) Then have them point to *I'm.* Tell them *I'm* is a short way of writing *I am.* Write **I am** on the board and cross out the *a*, replacing it with the apostrophe.

Make New Words Work with students to use an apostrophe to make new words with these examples:

a house that belongs to Dan (*Dan's house*)

cannot (*can't*)

PRACTICE

- Let students practice the new words they have learned and formed by completing the activities on pages 32–33 of the Worktext.
- If students are experiencing difficulty with the Words to Know sections on pages 32–33, you may wish to display the Memory Chips on a table. Say a riddle for each and have students choose the appropriate card. For example: **What word ends in *ing* and is something you could be doing with milk?** (*drinking*)

For further practice, have students complete Practice Lesson 1.8 on pages 79–81 of the Worktext. Answers can be found in the Answer Key on page 348 of this *Teacher's Manual.*

APPLY

- Have students talk about the story concept by asking: **Has someone ever told you not to speak to someone else? What did you do?** Tell them they are going to use the words they have learned to read a short story.
- Ask students to read the story on page 34 in the Worktext.
- After students have completed reading the story, have them complete the Cooperative Group Activity (What Do You Think?) and Comprehension Exercises (Remembering Details and Putting Ideas in Order) on page 35 in their Worktext. Answers can be found in the Answer Key on page 347 of this *Teacher's Manual.*

8. DAN'S SISTER

Word Attack

NEW **all** Add the letter **c** to the word **all** and you have **call**. Then write the words.

hall ________________ call ________________

NEW **an** Add the letter **D** to the word **an** and you have **Dan**. Then write the words.

can ________________ Dan ________________

Words to Know

	Look	Say	Picture	Write
by	☐	☐	☐	________
call	☐	☐	☐	________
Dan	☐	☐	☐	________
drink	☐	☐	☐	________
his	☐	☐	☐	________
does	☐	☐	☐	________
with	☐	☐	☐	________
that	☐	☐	☐	________
own	☐	☐	☐	________
sorry sor-ry	☐	☐	☐	________
people peo-ple	☐	☐	☐	________
friend	☐	☐	☐	________

Word Attack

+s Write each of these words with an **s** ending.

friend________________ problem ________________

+'s Write each of these words with an **'s** ending.

Dan ________________ Dad ________________

+ing Write **drink** with an **ing** ending. ________________

Double the last letter in **get** before adding the **ing** ending. Write **get** and **getting** on the lines.

get ________________ getting ________________

NEW **+ed** Write the word **want** with an **ed** ending. ____________

32

Worktext page 32

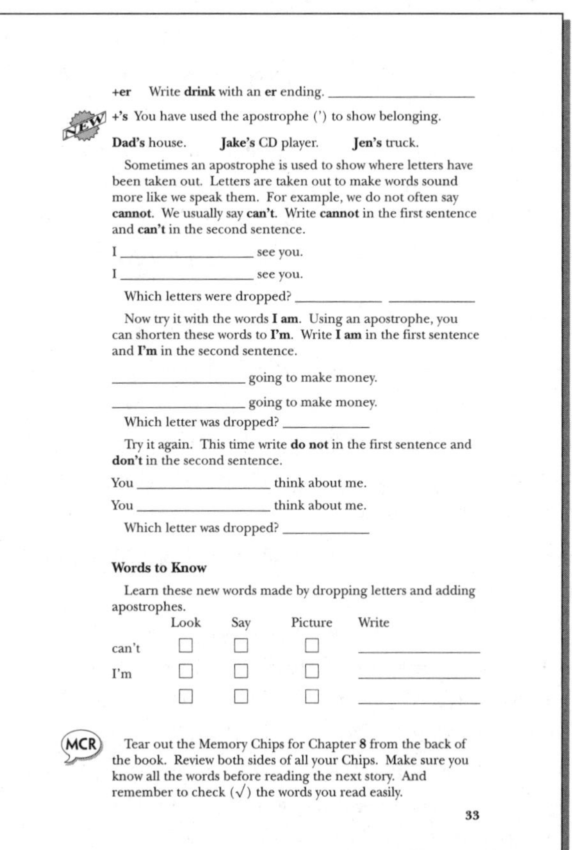

+er Write **drink** with an **er** ending. ________________

NEW **+'s** You have used the apostrophe (') to show belonging.

Dad's house. **Jake's** CD player. **Jen's** truck.

Sometimes an apostrophe is used to show where letters have been taken out. Letters are taken out to make words sound more like we speak them. For example, we do not often say **cannot**. We usually say **can't**. Write **cannot** in the first sentence and **can't** in the second sentence.

I ________________ see you.

I ________________ see you.

Which letters were dropped? __________ __________

Now try it with the words **I am**. Using an apostrophe, you can shorten these words to **I'm**. Write **I am** in the first sentence and **I'm** in the second sentence.

________________ going to make money.

________________ going to make money.

Which letter was dropped? __________

Try it again. This time write **do not** in the first sentence and **don't** in the second sentence.

You ________________ think about me.

You ________________ think about me.

Which letter was dropped? __________

Words to Know

Learn these new words made by dropping letters and adding apostrophes.

	Look	Say	Picture	Write
can't	☐	☐	☐	________
I'm	☐	☐	☐	________
	☐	☐	☐	________

MCR Tear out the Memory Chips for Chapter **8** from the back of the book. Review both sides of all your Chips. Make sure you know all the words before reading the next story. And remember to check (√) the words you read easily.

33

Worktext page 33

8. DAN'S SISTER

Dan, Tom, Jake, and I are friends. I like going to Dan's house. I like talking to his sister.

Jake says, "My dad says, 'Don't talk to Dan.'"

I say, "I don't get it."

Jake says, "I don't need friends like Dan."

I say, "What did Dan do?"

Jake says, "I can't talk. I have to go to my job."

I talk to Tom. I say, "What is Jake's problem about Dan?"

Tom says, "It is about Dan's dad. His drinking problem."

I think about that. "What does that have to do with Dan?"

Tom says, "I don't like people with problems."

I think, *Who does not have problems? I have my own problems.* But I don't say that.

I talk to my mom at home. I say, "Jake says Dan's dad is a problem drinker."

Mom says, "People like to talk."

The next day, I see Dan's sister in school. Jake is with me. I don't talk to her. She sees me. But I just walk by.

Then she finds me after school. "I'm sorry to see that you are like Tom and Jake."

"Wait," I call out.

But she gets into her car and goes.

34

Worktext page 34

What Do You Think?

Talk with a friend or in a small group. Why do you think the person in this story didn't talk to Dan's sister? How do you think he feels? How do you think Dan's sister feels?

Remembering Details

Write a word from the story in each space.

I like going to Dan's ________________.

Jake says, "I don't need ________________ like Dan."

I say, "Jake says Dan's dad is a ________________ drinker."

"I'm ________________ to see that you are like Tom and Jake."

Putting Ideas in Order

Here are four sentences from the story. Write them in the order that they happened.

Mom says, "People like to talk."

Jake says, "I don't need friends like Dan."

But I just walk by.

Dan, Tom, Jake, and I are friends.

____

____

____

____

____

35

Worktext page 35

LESSON 1.9

OBJECTIVE

- Students will practice and apply skills to extended passages

MATERIALS

Worktext 1, pages 36–37
Teacher's Manual, page 83
Practice Lesson 1.9, page 82 of the Worktext

SKILLS REVIEW

- Before reading, you may wish to review these story words that apply phonics skills: *Dad's, Dan, don't, drinking, says, wanted, Jake's, talking, getting, wants, call, hall.* Have students review the Memory Chips they have learned so far. Then ask: **What would you do if a friend asked you not to talk to someone else but wouldn't tell you the reason?**
- While reading, have students think how the main character solves the problem.
- After reading, have students complete the exercises on Worktext page 37.

For further practice, have students complete Practice Lesson 1.9 on page 82 of the Worktext. Answers can be found in the Answer Key on page 348 of this *Teacher's Manual.*

RETEACH

If students need further review of phonics skills, you may wish to use the following activity:

Phonograms *all, an, alk;* Possessives *'s*

What Word Goes There? Pass out index cards, one to each student, with the following words written on them: **Dan's, an, Dan, call, all, talk, walk.** Say these sentences and have students hold up their card when their word completes the sentence. Pause when you come to each blank so the student can hold up the card and say the word.

My best friend's name is ______. I had tried to ____ him earlier in the day. I really had to _______ to him. My car is in the shop, and I didn't want to _____ to school. Dan has ___ incredibly cool car. The phone rang. I listened and heard ______ voice. I will ___ to him. We can ____ ride to school together! (Answers: *Dan, call, talk, walk, an, Dan's, talk, all*)

Worktext Pages 36–37

MCR

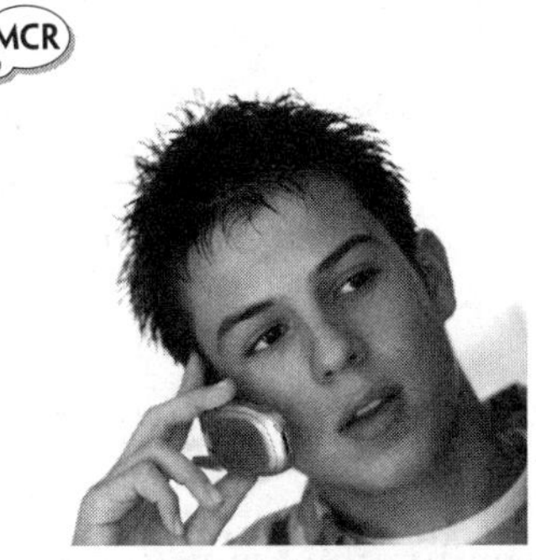

9. PEOPLE LIKE TO TALK

I call Jake. I say, "What does Dan's dad have to do with Dan?"

Jake says, "I don't want to talk about that."

Then I call Tom. I say, "What does Dan's dad's drinking problem have to do with Dan?"

"Talk to Dan's sister about that."

I call Dan's sister. She says, "I did not think you wanted to talk to me."

"I do want to talk to you," I say. "What is Jake's problem?"

She says, "He is talking about my dad at school."

"I don't get it," I say.

"Jake wanted me to go out on Saturday. I did not want to. So he is getting back by talking about my dad."

"What a dog," I say.

"People like to talk," she says.

"That is what my mom says. But what about Tom?" I say, "What is his problem?"

"His problem is he does what Jake says."

"I'm sorry I did not talk to you in the hall," I say. "Jake can say what he wants. Tom can do what he wants. But I want to do my own thinking."

36

Worktext page 36

What Do You Think?

Meet with a friend or in a small group. Talk about why the person in this story says he wants to do his own thinking. Think of examples in your own life where you had to go against what other people thought.

Finding the Main Idea

Write the sentence that best says what the whole story is about.

Dan's sister likes to talk.

Dan's dad is a drinker.

I want to do my own thinking.

____

____

Read It Again

Read again the story on page 18 called **Think About What You Want**. Then read these sentences. Choose the best answer (**a**, **b**, or **c**), and write it on the line.

"Coach makes me ________________," says Tom.
(a) happy (b) want to hide (c) sick

"What is ________________ going to get me?" Tom says.
(a) a dog (b) school (c) a job

"You want money? Get a ________________."
(a) job (b) dog (c) kid

37

Worktext page 37

MIDWAY NOVEL Hit and Run

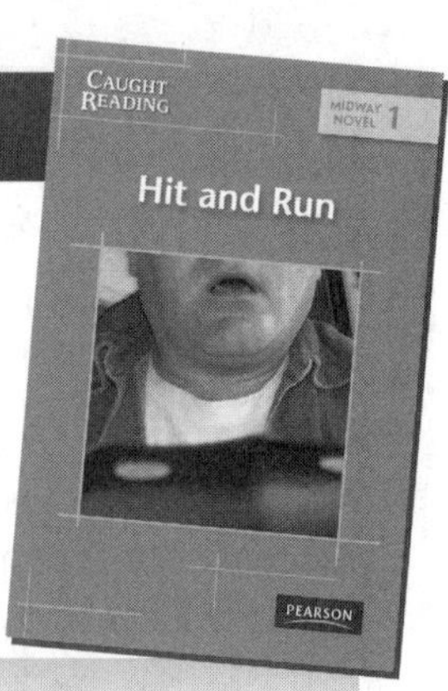

MATERIALS

Midway Novel 1, *Hit and Run*
Teacher's Manual, page 84
Assessment Manual, Midway Assessment 1, pages 63–65

Summary *Dan moves to a new school, where he tries to make friends. He has some problems with Jake, the class bully. Then Big Dog, Dan's dog, disappears. Finally, Jake returns the dog. His dad, a drinker, almost ran over Big Dog. Jake and Dan will start over and try to be friends.*

REVIEW AND ASSESSMENT

- Have students review their Memory Chips with a partner. Depending on your students' needs, review the following skills covered by Lessons 1–9: phonograms *ay, ot, alk, all, an*; compound words; possessives with apostrophe and *s*; contractions; and endings with *s, ed, er,* and *ing.*

If you wish to assess students' progress at this point, use the *Assessment Manual,* pages 63–65. For students who need additional support, you may use the Reteach activities from previous lessons.

INTRODUCE THE NOVEL

Invite students to preview the book by reading the title, looking at the illustrations, and reading aloud the captions. Begin a discussion of story concepts by asking:

- **How does it feel to be a new kid at school?**
- **How do you go about making friends?**
- **What would you do if someone didn't like you for no good reason?**

CHECK COMPREHENSION

Chapter 1 What is the narrator's problem at the beginning of the story? (*The narrator is new at school, and he hasn't made any friends. Jake has taken a dislike to him.*)

Chapter 2 Why is Grandma unhappy? (*She misses her friends in D.C.*)

Chapter 3 What happens to make Dan feel better at school? (*Tom sides with Dan when Jake bullies Dan.*)

Chapter 4 Why doesn't Dan buy the Lost Fire CD? (*Because a girl wants it, and he likes the girl.*)

Chapter 5 Why does Dan leave the CD store happy? (*Because he has a date with Jen.*)

Chapter 6 What happens to Big Dog? (*He is hit by a car. Then he runs away.*)

Chapter 7 How does Dan try to find Big Dog? (*He looks in the lot, behind Boss CD, and behind the house by the lot. Then he goes home to see if the dog went back home.*)

Chapter 8 How does Big Dog get back home? (*The people in the truck bring him back.*)

Chapter 9 What does Jen say that upsets Dan? (*Jake has a truck that is like the one that hit Big Dog.*)

Chapter 10 Why do you think Jake wants to talk to Dan? (*Students may suggest: He wants to tell him he's sorry for hitting Big Dog; he wants to thank him for encouraging him to hit the ball.*)

Chapter 11 What problem does Jake have? (*His father drinks; his father hit Big Dog.*)
What do you think will happen next? (*Jake and Dan will become friends.*)

Chapter 12 Why is Dan happy at the end of the book? (*Dan makes a new friend, his dog is OK, he went to a big school game, and he gets a girlfriend.*)

CONNECTION

Home/School Encourage students to bring home a copy of *Hit and Run.* They might read the novel, or sections of the novel, to family members.

LESSON 1.10

OBJECTIVES

- Students will learn new words containing the *ike* phonogram
- Students will apply endings *er, s, ing, ed,* and *est* to base words to form new words
- Students will apply the final digraph /*th*/ to base words to form new words
- Students will learn to recognize and form compound words

PHONICS VOCABULARY

friends	with	talks	says	makes
kids	laughing	bike	lots	girls
trying	faster	fastest	waiting	calls
helps	comes	9th	10th	helped
outs	fired	tryouts		

WORDS TO KNOW

bike	try	fast	class	team
help	race	come	Kate	one
laugh				

MATERIALS

Worktext 1, pages 38–41
Teacher's Manual, pages 85–86
Practice Lesson 1.10, pages 83–85 of the Worktext

TEACH

- Using Worktext page 38, introduce students to the vocabulary words in the Words to Know section.
- Students can organize their Memory Chips, found in the back of the Worktext. Have them say each word and read the sentence on the back with a partner.

Worktext page 38 can also be used to reinforce spelling. Use the five-step process detailed on page 71 of this *Teacher's Manual.*

Phonogram *ike*

Write this sentence on the board and read it aloud: **I like my bike.** Circle the phonogram *ike* and ask students how *bike* and *like* are alike and different.

Blending Remind students they can make new words by changing the beginning sounds of words with phonograms. Write **bike** on the board, say the word, and ask them what other words rhyme with *bike.* Write their responses on the board.

Endings *er, s, ing, ed, est*

Review with students how they can add *er, s, ing, ed,* and *est* to words. Have them find the new Memory Chips that have these endings. Write this sentence on the board: **I biked to school.** Point to *biked* and tell students when you add *ed* to a word that ends in *e,* you drop the *e* and add *ed.*

Then write these sentences on the board: **I am bigger than Tom. Jake is the biggest boy in class.** Point out that the ending *er* compares two people or things; the ending *est* compares at least three people or things.

Make New Words Write these endings and words on index cards and have students put them together to make new words: **er**, **s**, **ing**, **ed**, **est**, **fast**, **tall**, **help**, **fire**, **bike**, **laugh**. Have them use each word in a sentence.

Final Digraph /*th*/

Write this sentence on the board: **I'm the 9th girl.** Point to the number. Tell students the *th* makes the /*th*/ sound. When *th* is added to a number, you say the number and add /*th*/.

Make New Words Have students add *th* to these numbers: *5, 10, 20, 4, 8.* (*5th, 10th, 20th, 4th, 8th*)

PRACTICE

- Let students practice the new words they have learned and formed by completing the activities found on pages 38–39 of the Worktext.
- If students are experiencing difficulty with the Words to Know section on page 38, you may wish to display the Memory Chips on a table. With a separate set of cards, read aloud the sentence on the back of each card, leaving out the Memory Chip word. Have students choose the correct card.

For further practice, have students complete Practice Lesson 1.10 on pages 83–85 of the Worktext. Answers can be found in the Answer Key on page 348 of this *Teacher's Manual.*

APPLY

- Have students talk about the story concept by asking: **Have you ever tried out for a team at school? What happened?** Tell them they are going to use the words they have learned to read a short story about a girl who tries out for the biking team at school.
- Ask students to read the story on page 40 in the Worktext. Encourage students to decode the words independently, using the clues and patterns they have learned.
- After students have completed reading the story, have them complete the Cooperative Group Activity (What Do You Think?) and Comprehension Exercises (Remembering Details and Putting Ideas in Order) on page 41 in their Worktext. Answers can be found in the Answer Key on page 347 of this *Teacher's Manual.*

10. BIKE TEAM TRYOUTS

Word Attack

NEW **ike** You know the word **like**. Change **l** to **b** and you have **bike**. Circle the letter group **ike** in both words. Then write the words.

like ________________ bike ________________

Words to Know

	Look	Say	Picture	Write
bike	☐	☐	☐	________________
try	☐	☐	☐	________________
fast	☐	☐	☐	________________
class	☐	☐	☐	________________
team	☐	☐	☐	________________
help	☐	☐	☐	________________
race	☐	☐	☐	________________
come	☐	☐	☐	________________
Kate	☐	☐	☐	________________
one	☐	☐	☐	________________
laugh	☐	☐	☐	________________

Word Attack

+s Write each of these words with an **s** ending.

out ________________ make ________________

girl ________________ lot ________________

call ________________ come ________________

38

Worktext page 38

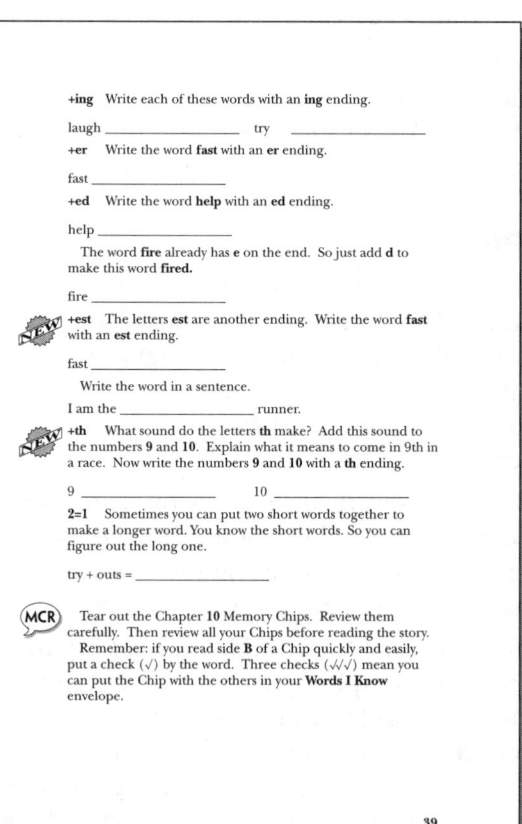

+ing Write each of these words with an **ing** ending.

laugh ________________ try ________________

+er Write the word **fast** with an **er** ending.

fast ________________

+ed Write the word **help** with an **ed** ending.

help ________________

The word **fire** already has **e** on the end. So just add **d** to make this word **fired.**

fire ________________

NEW **+est** The letters **est** are another ending. Write the word **fast** with an **est** ending.

fast ________________

Write the word in a sentence.

I am the ________________ runner.

NEW **+th** What sound do the letters **th** make? Add this sound to the numbers **9** and **10**. Explain what it means to come in 9th in a race. Now write the numbers **9** and **10** with a **th** ending.

9 ________________ 10 ________________

2=1 Sometimes you can put two short words together to make a longer word. You know the short words. So you can figure out the long one.

try + outs = ________________

MCR Tear out the Chapter **10** Memory Chips. Review them carefully. Then review all your Chips before reading the story.

Remember: if you read side **B** of a Chip quickly and easily, put a check (√) by the word. Three checks (√√√) mean you can put the Chip with the others in your **Words I Know** envelope.

39

Worktext page 39

10. BIKE TEAM TRYOUTS

Kate and I are not friends. But she goes to my school. She is in a class with me.

One day, she talks in class. What she says makes the kids laugh at her.

I say to the class, "What is your problem? Stop laughing. What makes you think you can laugh?"

Then the kids laugh at me.

The next day is bike team tryouts. I want to make the team. The coach says that just 10 girls can make the team. Lots of girls are trying out. Kate is trying out.

The tryout is a race. Coach says, "Go."

I bike fast. But lots of girls bike faster. Kate is one of the fastest. I try to go faster. But I'm in back of the race.

Then, I see Kate waiting for me. She calls out, "Bike in back of me. It helps you go faster." I bike in back of Kate. We race faster and faster. We go by lots of girls. Kate comes in 9th. I come in 10th.

"You make the team," the coach says to me.

"You did not have to help me," I say to Kate. "You are one of the fastest."

"You helped me in class. I helped you in tryouts."

I'm happy to have a new friend.

40

Worktext page 40

What Do You Think?

Meet with a friend or in a small group. Think about your skills. What could you give someone in exchange for help in something else?

Remembering Details

Write a word from the story in each space.

Lots of girls are ________________ out.

Kate is one of the ________________.

"You make the ________________," the coach says to me.

"You ________________ me in class."

"I ________________ you in tryouts."

Putting Ideas in Order

Here are three sentences from the story. Write them in the order that they happened.

The next day is bike team tryouts.

I'm happy to have a new friend.

One day, she talks in class.

____

____

____

____

____

____

____

____

41

Worktext page 41

LESSON 1.11

OBJECTIVE

- Students will practice and apply skills to extended passages

MATERIALS

Worktext 1, pages 42–43
Teacher's Manual, page 87
Practice Lesson 1.11, page 86 of the Worktext
Common classroom materials, pictures of different vehicles (Reteach)

SKILLS REVIEW

- Before reading, you may wish to review these story words that apply phonics skills: *says, needs, friends, problems, faster, call, fired.* Have students review the Memory Chips they have learned so far. Then ask: **How does it feel not to have money? How might it feel if you lost your job?**
- While reading, ask students what they think the main character will do to solve each problem.
- After reading, have students complete the exercises on Worktext page 43.

For further practice, have students complete Practice Lesson 1.11 on page 86 of the Worktext. Answers can be found in the Answer Key on page 348 of this *Teacher's Manual.*

RETEACH

If students need further review of phonics skills, you may wish to use the following activity:

Endings *er, est*

What's Bigger and Faster? Make index cards with labels **big**, **bigger**, **biggest**, **fast**, **faster**, and **fastest**. Then collect common classroom materials. Have students choose three materials that are alike. For example, a pencil, a crayon, and a piece of chalk. Place the cards *big, bigger,* and *biggest* on the table and have students put the items under the card to show the relative size of each item. Then show pictures of different vehicles. Display the index cards for *fast, faster,* and *fastest.* Have students read the label for each card. Then have them choose which car is fast, which is faster, and which is fastest.

CONNECTION

Writing Students can record in their journals responses to their reading, list new words they have learned, or record their feelings.

Worktext Pages 42–43

11. ONE SORRY DAY

I do not want to go to school. But I have to go.

Then, my mom says, "Dad needs money. Do you have $10?"

"I need that $10," I say.

"Sorry," Mom says, "Dad needs it to get to his job."

I go to school. My friends are going out on Saturday. "Want to go out?" they say.

"With what?" I say. "I don't have money."

"Sorry," they say. My friends walk off talking about what they are going to do on Saturday.

In class, I can't think. I want my problems to stop. But the problems do not stop. The problems come faster and faster.

At home, my mom says, "I'm happy you are home. Your sister is sick. I have to go to my job."

"What about my job?" I say.

"Sorry," Mom says, "call your boss."

I call my boss. He says, "I need people who don't have problems at home. You are fired."

I lost my job. My sister is sick. I don't have money to go out with my friends on Saturday. I can't think in class. What a sorry day.

42

Worktext page 42

What Do You Think?

Meet with a friend or in a small group. Everyone has bad days. Describe one you have had. Talk about good ways to get over bad days.

Finding the Main Idea

Write the group of words that best says what the whole story is about.

You are fired.

What a sorry day!

Dad needs money.

My friends are going out on Saturday.

____

____

Read It Again

Read again the story on page **28** called **New Kid at School.** Then read these sentences. Choose the best answer (**a**, **b**, or **c**), and write it on the line.

At home, I say I am ________________.
(a) sick (b) happy (c) lost

Then I see a big kid hit a ________________.
(a) little kid (b) girl (c) dog

I want to ________________ the big kid.
(a) hit (b) fire (c) stop

43

Worktext page 43

LESSON 1.12

OBJECTIVES

- Students will learn new words containing the *ad*, *ake*, and *an* phonograms
- Students will apply endings *s* and *ing* to base words to form new words
- Students will learn to recognize and form compound words

PHONICS VOCABULARY

going	make	Dan	teamwork	ad
take	thinking	can	man	takes
drives	CDs	girls	Jake	dad
weeks	plays	thinks	keeping	driving
selling				

WORDS TO KNOW

take	man	ad	keep	week
sell	car	drive	for	work
put	was			

MATERIALS

Worktext 1, pages 44–47
Teacher's Manual, pages 88–89
Practice Lesson 1.12, pages 87–89 of the Worktext

TEACH

- Using Worktext page 44, introduce students to the vocabulary words in the Words to Know section.
- Students can organize their Memory Chips, found in the back of the Worktext. Have them say each word and read the sentence on the back with a partner. Then have them arrange the cards in alphabetical order.

Worktext page 44 can also be used to reinforce spelling. Use the five-step process detailed on page 71 of this *Teacher's Manual*.

Phonograms *ad*, *ake*, *an*

Write this sentence on the board and read it aloud: **Tad will take out an ad.** Ask students which words rhyme. (*Tad*, *ad*) Then ask them which words rhyme with *cake* and *fan*. (*take*, *an*)

Blending Remind students they can make new words by changing the beginning sounds of words with phonograms. Write **Tad** on the board, say the word, and replace the *T* with *s*. Have them say the new word. Repeat with **make** and **can**.

Endings *s*, *ing*

Review with students how they can add *s* and *ing* to words. Write these words on word cards and have students take turns choosing a word, telling other students how the word ends, and pantomiming the action: **thinking**, **takes**, **drives**, **keeping**, **selling**.

Make New Words Write these base words and have students make new words by adding *ing* or *s*: **keep**, **week**, **sell**, **car**, **work**, **ad**, **play**. Have them use each new word in a sentence.

Compound Words

Remind students that sometimes long words are made up of two smaller words. Write these words on the board and ask students to identify the two smaller words in each: **teamwork**, **tryout**, **schoolhouse**, **driveway**.

Make New Words Write these words on index cards and have students put them together to make new words: **house**, **school**, **way**, **drive**, **out**, **work**, **home**, **team**, **sick**, **hall**.

PRACTICE

- Let students practice the new words they have learned and formed by completing the activities on pages 44–45 of the Worktext.
- If students are experiencing difficulty with the Words to Know section on page 44, you may wish to display the Memory Chips on a table. Say a riddle for each word and have students choose the appropriate card. For example: **This word begins like cake. It is something you drive.** (*car*)

For further practice, have students complete Practice Lesson 1.12 on pages 87–89 of the Worktext. Answers can be found in the Answer Key on page 348 of this *Teacher's Manual*.

APPLY

- Have students talk about the story concept by asking: **Have you ever been on a team? What do we mean by teamwork?** Tell them they are going to use the words they have learned to read a short story about two boys who work very hard to repair a car so they can sell it.
- Ask students to read the story on page 46 in the Worktext. Offer assistance if necessary, but encourage students to decode the words independently, using the clues and patterns they have learned.
- After students have completed reading the story, have them complete the Cooperative Group Activity (What Do You Think?) and Comprehension Exercises (Remembering Details and Putting Ideas in Order) on page 47 in their Worktext. Answers can be found in the Answer Key on page 347 of this *Teacher's Manual*.

12. WORKING ON THE CAR

Word Attack

an You know the words **can** and **Dan.** Change the first letter to **m** and you have **man.** Circle the letter group **an** in each word. Then write the words.

can ________________ Dan ________________

man ________________

NEW **ake** You know the words **Jake** and **make.** Change the first letter to **t** and you have **take.** Circle the letter group **ake** in each word. Then write the words.

Jake ________________ make ________________

take ________________

NEW **ad** You know the word **dad.** Take away the first letter and you have **ad.** Circle the letter group **ad** in both words. Then write the words.

dad ________________ ad ________________

Words to Know

	Look	Say	Picture	Write
take	☐	☐	☐	________________
man	☐	☐	☐	________________
ad	☐	☐	☐	________________
keep	☐	☐	☐	________________
week	☐	☐	☐	________________
sell	☐	☐	☐	________________
car	☐	☐	☐	________________
drive	☐	☐	☐	________________
for	☐	☐	☐	________________
work	☐	☐	☐	________________
put	☐	☐	☐	________________
was	☐	☐	☐	________________

44

Worktext page 44

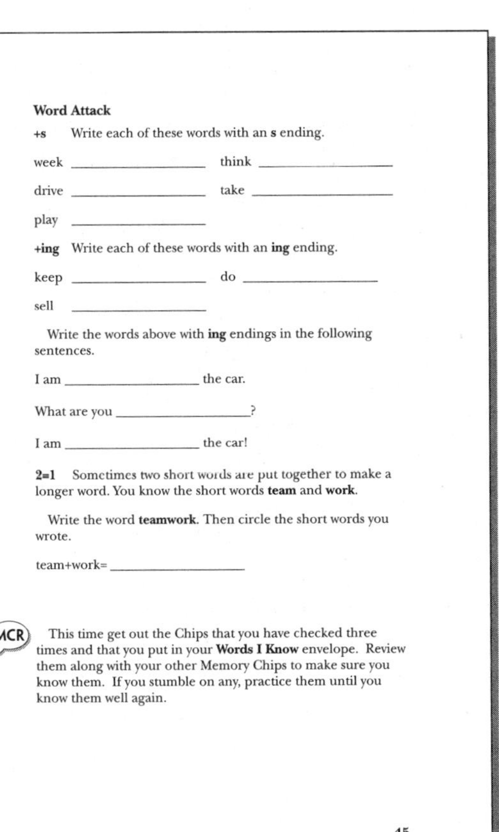

Word Attack

+s Write each of these words with an **s** ending.

week ________________ think ________________

drive ________________ take ________________

play ________________

+ing Write each of these words with an **ing** ending.

keep ________________ do ________________

sell ________________

Write the words above with **ing** endings in the following sentences.

I am ________________ the car.

What are you ________________?

I am ________________ the car!

2=1 Sometimes two short words are put together to make a longer word. You know the short words **team** and **work.**

Write the word **teamwork.** Then circle the short words you wrote.

team+work= ________________

MCR This time get out the Chips that you have checked three times and that you put in your **Words I Know** envelope. Review them along with your other Memory Chips to make sure you know them. If you stumble on any, practice them until you know them well again.

45

Worktext page 45

1998 Neptune XE
Blue, 2-dr. auto, A/C, CD, 77K mi,
looks good and runs great,
good transp. $1500
201-555-5555

12. WORKING ON THE CAR

I get a car for $300. That is a lot of money. Dan and I are going to make that money back.

I put in the $300, but Dan does the work with me. We work on the car for weeks and weeks. We put in a CD player. *This is teamwork* I think.

Then I say, "I'm going to take out the ad."

Dan says, "I was thinking about keeping the car. We can take girls out."

"But what about the money!" I say. "We can get $1,500 for that car."

Dan says, "Man, think about the work we put in. I want to keep it."

"I want to sell it," I say. "I want the money."

"I want the car," Dan says.

"Find $750 for me," I say. "Then you can keep it."

Dan thinks. Then he says, "I want to drive it for one week. Then we can sell it."

"OK," I say. "One week."

That week, Dan drives the car to school. He takes lots of girls out for drives. He plays CDs for the girls.

But then Dan says, "Next Saturday, Kate is going out with me. I have to have the car."

"I want my $750," I say. "Then you can keep the car."

He says, "We can sell it next week."

"What about me?" I say. "It is your car **and** my car."

46

Worktext page 46

What Do You Think?

Meet with a friend or in a small group. Talk about what you would do if you were the person telling this story? Then talk about what you predict he is going to do.

Remembering Details

Write a word from the story in each space.

Dan and I are going to make that money ________________.

Dan says, "I was thinking about ________________ the car.

"I want to ________________ it," I say. "I want the money."

He takes lots of girls out for ________________.

Putting Ideas in Order

Here are three sentences from the story. Write them in the order that they happened.

We work on the car for weeks and weeks.

"What about me?" I say. "It is your car **and** my car."

"I want the car," Dan says.

____

____

____

____

____

____

____

47

Worktext page 47

LESSON 1.13

OBJECTIVE

- Students will practice and apply skills to extended passages

MATERIALS

Worktext 1, pages 48–49
Teacher's Manual, page 90
Practice Lesson 1.13, page 90 of the Worktext
Tagboard, brad/fastener (Reteach)

SKILLS REVIEW

- Before reading, you may wish to review these story words that apply phonics skills: *Dan, drives, keep, weeks, ad, man, likes, wants, calls, says, walks, doing, selling.* Have students review the Memory Chips they have learned so far. Then ask: **How would you go about selling a car?**
- While reading, ask students if they think the narrator does the right thing in selling the car by himself.
- After reading, have students complete the exercises on Worktext page 49.

For further practice, have students complete Practice Lesson 1.13 on page 90 of the Worktext. Answers can be found in the Answer Key on page 348 of this *Teacher's Manual.*

RETEACH

If students need further review of phonics skills, you may wish to use the following activity:

Phonograms *ake, ad, ike, an, all, alk, ay, ot*

Wheel-a-Word Cut out two wheels from tagboard, one smaller than the other. Divide each wheel into eight parts. On the larger wheel, write the phonograms **ake**, **ad**, **ike**, **an**, **all**, **alk**, **ay**, and **ot** on the outer edges of the circle. On the smaller wheel, write the consonants **c**, **l**, **m**, **d**, **t**, **w**, **s**, **n**. Connect the two wheels with a brad. Then have students turn the wheel to make words with the beginning consonants and phonograms. Have them make a list of all the words they make. (*cake, lake, make, take, wake, sake, lad, mad, dad, tad, sad, like, Mike, can, man, Dan, tan, Nan, call, mall, tall, wall, talk, walk, lay, may, day, way, say, cot, lot, dot, tot, not*)

CONNECTION

Speaking/Listening After students have read "Selling the Car" silently, assign parts to two volunteers to practice for oral reading. Allow students ample time to practice their parts.

Worktext Pages 48–49

13. SELLING THE CAR

Weeks go by. Dan keeps the car. He drives it to school. I see it in the school lot.

One day, I take out an ad. I say I want $1,800 for the car. The next day, a man calls me. He wants to see the car. I say, "Go to the school lot to see it." He goes and he likes the car. He wants it.

He says, "What about $1,200?"

I say, "$1,800."

He says, "What about $1,500?"

I think about that. But I can see that the man wants the car a lot. I say, "$1,800."

"OK," he says, "I want it." He gets me the money. The man drives off in the car. I go back to school.

Dan walks out of school with Kate. "The car!" he says. "What did you do with the car?"

I say, "$750 for you. I keep $1,050. That is what I get for the weeks I waited for the car. And for doing the work of selling it."

48

Worktext page 48

What Do You Think?

Meet with a friend or in a small group. Talk about whether the person telling this story made a fair deal with Dan. Say why or why not. Explain your opinion.

Finding the Main Idea

Write the sentence that best says what the whole story is about.

Dan walks out of school with Kate.

I sell Dan's and my car.

The man likes the car a lot.

____

____

Read It Again

Read again the story on page **22** called **Fire**. Then read these sentences. Choose the best answer (**a**, **b**, or **c**), and write it on the line.

My boss says, "You hide your money at ____________?"
(a) school (b) home (c) work

My ____________ is on fire!
(a) house (b) car (c) CD player

My mom gets the ____________.
(a) dog (b) truck (c) bike

49

Worktext page 49

LESSON 1.14

OBJECTIVE

- Students will apply endings *s, ing, es,* and *ed* to base words to form new words

PHONICS VOCABULARY

says	going	talking	selling	stays
classes	cooking	cleaning	saying	sells
laughs	working	days	talked	being
taking	making			

WORDS TO KNOW

be	bus	cook	time	part
clean	more	night	careful	college

MATERIALS

Worktext 1, pages 50–53
Teacher's Manual, pages 91–92
Practice Lesson 1.14, pages 91–93 of the Worktext

TEACH

- Using Worktext page 50, introduce students to the vocabulary words in the Words to Know section.
- Students can organize their Memory Chips, found in the back of the Worktext. Have them say each word and read the sentence on the back with a partner. They can sort the words into groups of words that show action, two-syllable words, and words that begin the same.

SPELLING Worktext page 50 can also be used to reinforce spelling. Use the five-step process detailed on page 71 of this *Teacher's Manual.*

Endings *s, ing, es, ed*

Review with students how they can add *s, ing, es,* and *ed* to words. Write these words on the board and ask volunteers to say each word and circle its ending: **takes**, **working**, **stops**, **helps**, **saying**.

Then write these sentences on the board. **I will take a class. I am taking two classes.** Point to *take* and *taking.* Tell students when they add *ing* to words that end in *e,* they drop the *e* and add *ing.* Then have a volunteer point to *class* and *classes.* Tell them when words end in *ss,* you add *es* to the ending to make it mean more than one.

Make New Words Make a chart on the board like the one below and have students take turns adding *s, ing, es,* or *ed* to each word.

Base Word	+ s	+ ing	+ es	+ed
class			classes	
make	makes	making		
like	likes	liking		liked
boss		bossing	bosses	bossed

PRACTICE

- Let students practice the new words they have learned and formed by completing the activities on pages 50–51 of the Worktext.
- If students are experiencing difficulty with the Words to Know section on page 50, display the Memory Chips on a table. Say a sentence, leaving out the Memory Chip word, and have students choose the appropriate card. For example*:* **I will wash and _____ the car.** (*clean*)

For further practice, have students complete Practice Lesson 1.14 on pages 91–93 of the Worktext. Answers can be found in the Answer Key on pages 348–349 of this *Teacher's Manual.*

APPLY

- Have students talk about the story concept by asking: **What do you think it would be like if one of your parents took a second job or went back to school?** Tell them they are going to use the words they have learned to read a story about a family that has to make changes when the mother goes to college.
- Ask students to read the story on page 52 in the Worktext. Offer assistance if necessary, but encourage students to decode the words independently, using the clues and patterns they have learned.
- After students have completed reading the story, have them complete the Cooperative Group Activity (What Do You Think?) and Comprehension Exercises (Remembering Details and Putting Ideas in Order) on page 53 in their Worktext. Answers can be found in the Answer Key on page 347 of this *Teacher's Manual.*

Worktext Pages 50–53

14. DAD STOPS TALKING TO MOM

Words to Know

	Look	Say	Picture	Write
be	☐	☐	☐	____________
bus	☐	☐	☐	____________
cook	☐	☐	☐	____________
time	☐	☐	☐	____________
part	☐	☐	☐	____________
clean	☐	☐	☐	____________
more	☐	☐	☐	____________
night	☐	☐	☐	____________
careful care-ful	☐	☐	☐	____________
college col-lege	☐	☐	☐	____________

Word Attack

+s Write each of these words with an **s** ending.

stop ______________ sell ______________

laugh ______________ day ______________

+es Remember how the word **go** has an **es** ending to make **goes**. The word **class** also has an **es** ending to make **classes**. Write **class** with an **es** ending.

class ______________

Write the word in a sentence.

I am going to take ______________ in school.

50

Worktext page 50

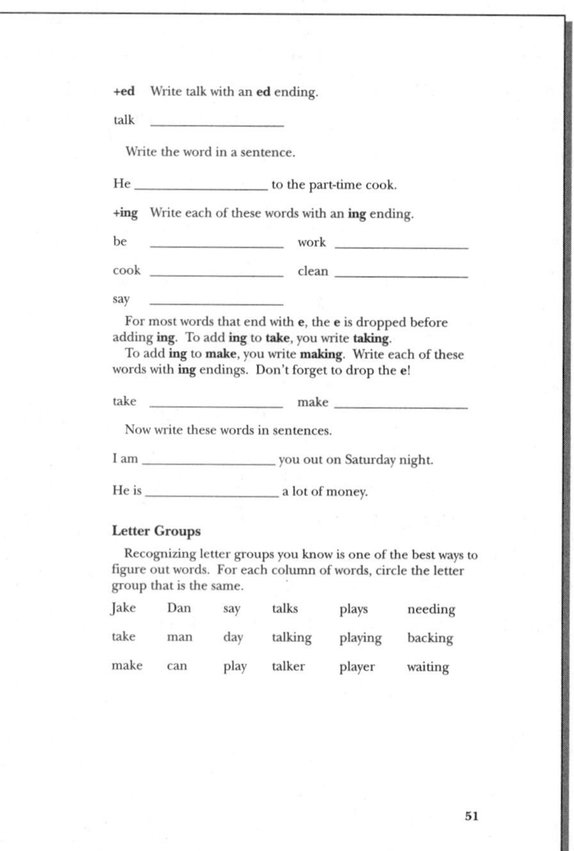

+ed Write talk with an **ed** ending.

talk ______________

Write the word in a sentence.

He ______________ to the part-time cook.

+ing Write each of these words with an **ing** ending.

be ______________ work ______________

cook ______________ clean ______________

say ______________

For most words that end with **e**, the **e** is dropped before adding **ing**. To add **ing** to **take**, you write **taking**.

To add **ing** to **make**, you write **making**. Write each of these words with **ing** endings. Don't forget to drop the **e**!

take ______________ make ______________

Now write these words in sentences.

I am ______________ you out on Saturday night.

He is ______________ a lot of money.

Letter Groups

Recognizing letter groups you know is one of the best ways to figure out words. For each column of words, circle the letter group that is the same.

Jake	Dan	say	talks	plays	needing
take	man	day	talking	playing	backing
make	can	play	talker	player	waiting

51

Worktext page 51

14. DAD STOPS TALKING TO MOM

One night, Mom says, "I'm going to sell the car."

Dad says, "What are you talking about?"

Mom says, "I'm talking about selling the car. We are going to need the money. I'm going to go to college."

Dad laughs. "College!" he says, then laughs more. "What for?"

She says, "I want to take classes."

I say, "What about your job, Mom?"

She says, "My boss says I can work part-time. I can do my schoolwork at night. You can help with the house, the cooking, and the cleaning."

"Work part-time!" Dad says. "Sell the car! Think about what you are saying! What about money? How will I get to work? How will the kids get to school?"

Mom says, "You can take the bus. We can be more careful with money."

"You are not working part-time," my dad says. "We need the money. I'm not taking the bus. That is that."

My mom says, "I'm going to college. I'm going to do it."

The next week, Mom sells the car. Then she goes to her college classes. My dad stops talking to her. He does not talk to her for days. My sister and I cook. We do the cleaning. My dad does not cook, and he does not clean. The problem gets bigger and bigger. I want Mom to stop going to college.

52

Worktext page 52

What Do You Think?

Meet with a friend or in a small group. Think about the problem that this family has. Talk about possible solutions.

Remembering Details

Write a word from the story in each space.

She say, "My boss says I can work ______________ -time."

"We can be more ______________ with money."

My dad stops ______________ to her.

I want Mom to stop going to ______________.

Putting Ideas in Order

Here are three sentences from the story. Write them in the order that they happened.

The next week, Mom sells the car.

"You are not working part-time," my dad says.

My dad stops talking to her.

53

Worktext page 53

LESSON 1.15

OBJECTIVE

- Students will practice and apply skills to extended passages

MATERIALS

Worktext 1, pages 54–55
Teacher's Manual, page 93
Practice Lesson 1.15, page 94 of the Worktext

SKILLS REVIEW

- Before reading, you may wish to review these story words that apply phonics skills: *weeks, classes, talks, going, doing, cooking, cleaning, helps, says, laughs, making, makes, wants, laughing, getting, gets.* Have students review the Memory Chips they have learned so far. Then ask: **How do you think the family will adjust to Mom going to college?**
- While reading, ask students how the characters change from the beginning of the story to the end.
- After reading, have students complete the exercises on Worktext page 55.

For further practice, have students complete Practice Lesson 1.15 on page 94 of the Worktext. Answers can be found in the Answer Key on page 349 of this *Teacher's Manual.*

RETEACH

If students need further review of phonics skills, you may wish to use the following activity:

Adding *ing*

Dropping the *e* Give each student a sheet of paper, and have each student write one of these letters on the paper: **m, a, k, e, t, a, c, o, o, s, e, l, l, i, i, n, g**. Then call out the letters *m, a, k, e* and have those students stand up and display their letters. Tell them they are going to make the word *making*. Have students with the letters *i, n, g* come up. Then ask them what letter is dropped to make *making*. (*e*) Repeat, using the words *take/taking, like/liking, sell/selling, talk/talking*, and *cook/cooking*.

CONNECTION

Speaking/Listening Invite student volunteers to take turns reading aloud the selection "Mom Gets an 'A'." Other students can follow along in their Worktext.

15. MOM GETS AN "A"

Weeks go by. Mom goes to her classes. She talks to Dad, but Dad does not talk back. He does not like her going to college. But he does take the bus to work.

I don't like doing the cooking and cleaning. But I keep doing it. My sister helps.

One day, my sister says, "Mom laughs more. She is happy."

I say, "What is making her happy? I'm not happy. Dad is not happy. Are you happy?"

She says, "I'm OK. Mom is doing what she wants to do. That makes her happy. I think it is going to make Dad happy. Wait and see."

I think about Mom being happy. I see that she does laugh more. And she talks more to me and my sister.

I say to Dad, "I think school makes Mom happy. I like cooking OK. I don't like the cleaning. But I can do it."

Dad says, "But we don't have a car to drive."

"But Mom is happy," I say. "She wants to go to college."

Dad says, "I do like to see her laughing more. That job was getting to her."

I'm happy I talked to Dad. He talks to Mom more.

One day, Mom gets an "A" in a class.

Dad sees the "A". "You did that?" he says. "An 'A'?"

"I did that," Mom says, laughing. "An 'A'."

Dad laughs with her. Then my sister laughs. Then I laugh. That night, Dad helps with the cooking.

54

Worktext page 54

What Do You Think?

Meet with a friend or in a small group. Do you think the dad in this story changed his mind? If yes, what made him change his mind? If no, why not?

Finding the Main Idea

Write the sentence that best says what the whole story is about.

I don't like doing the cooking and cleaning.

Then my sister laughs.

Mom gets an "A", and we are happy.

____

____

Read It Again

Read again the story on page **24** called **My Sister Is Lost**. Then read these sentences. Choose the best answer (**a**, **b**, or **c**), and write it on the line.

My sister is not ______________.
(a) sick (b) happy (c) in school

My sister needs me! She is ______________!
(a) a problem (b) lost (c) working

I say to Mom, "Think about what to ______________!"
(a) do (b) say (c) make

I see she is not ______________.
(a) kidding (b) drinking (c) happy

55

Worktext page 55

LESSON 1.16

OBJECTIVES

- Students will learn new words containing the *eep, ight, eam,* and *ot* phonograms
- Students will apply endings *s, ed,* and *ing* to base words to form new words
- Students will learn to recognize and form compound words

PHONICS VOCABULARY

woods	going	says	scared	sleeping
bags	bikes	comes	dogs	doing
saying	making	gets	thinking	coming
screams	boyfriend			

WORDS TO KNOW

hot	sleep	light	scream	if
bag	boy	wood	hear	us
scared				

MATERIALS

Worktext 1, pages 56–61
Teacher's Manual, pages 94–96
Practice Lesson 1.16, pages 95–97 of the Worktext

TEACH

- Using Worktext pages 56–57, introduce students to the vocabulary words in the Words to Know section.
- Students can organize their Memory Chips, found in the back of the Worktext. Have them say each word and read the sentence on the back with a partner. They can sort the words into groups by number of letters and beginning sounds.

Worktext pages 56–57 can also be used to reinforce spelling. Use the five-step process detailed on page 71 of this *Teacher's Manual.*

Phonograms *eep, ight, eam, ot*

Write this sentence on the board and read it aloud: **Keep my jeep when I sleep.** Ask students which words rhyme. (*keep, jeep, sleep*) Ask them how the words are the same and different. (*They all begin differently; all end in* eep.) Repeat, using these sentences:

I might keep the light on at night. (*might, light, night*)

I am not hot on the cot. (*not, hot, cot*)

The team will scream. (*team, scream*)

Blending Remind students they can make new words by changing the beginning sounds of words with phonograms. Write **light** on the board, say the word, and have students brainstorm new words by substituting beginning sounds. Repeat with **hot**, **team**, and **keep**.

Endings *s, ed, ing*

Review with students how they can add *s, ed,* and *ing* to words. Remind them that when a word ends in *e,* they drop the *e* and add the ending *ing.*

Make New Words Make a chart on the board like the following one and have students take turns adding *s, ed,* or *ing* to each word.

Base Word	+ s	+ ed	+ ing
race	races	raced	racing
bike	bikes	biked	biking
dog	dogs		
call	calls	called	calling

Compound Words

Remind students that sometimes longer words are made up of two smaller words. Write these equations on the board and ask students to identify the two words they make: **team + work = ______, school + house = ____, drive + way = ____, for + get = ______.**

Make New Words Write these words on index cards and have students put them together to make new words: **boy**, **friend**, **team**, **work**, **in**, **to**, **light**, **house**, **with**, **out**. (*boyfriend, housework, teamwork, into, lighthouse, without, within*)

PRACTICE

- Let students practice the new words they have learned and formed by completing the activities found on pages 56–58 of the Worktext.
- If students are experiencing difficulty with the Words to Know section on pages 56–57, display the Memory Chips on a table. Say a rhyming riddle and have them choose the word that answers it. For example: **This word rhymes with good. It begins like will.** (*wood*)

For further practice, have students complete Practice Lesson 1.16 on pages 95–97 of the Worktext. Answers can be found in the Answer Key on page 349 of this *Teacher's Manual.*

APPLY

- Have students talk about the story concept by asking: **How would you feel about going camping overnight with just a friend? What would you bring on the camping trip?** Tell them they are going to use the words they have learned to read a short story about two girls who go on a camping trip and forget one important thing.
- Ask students to read the story on pages 59–60 in the Worktext. Offer assistance if necessary, but encourage students to decode the words independently, using the clues and patterns they have learned.
- After students have completed reading the story, have them complete the Cooperative Group Activity (What Do You Think?) and Comprehension Exercises (Remembering Details and Putting Ideas in Order) on page 61 in their Worktext. Answers can be found in the Answer Key on page 347 of this *Teacher's Manual.*

16. A NIGHT IN THE WOODS

Word Attack

NEW **eep** You know the word **keep**. Change the **k** to **sl** and you have **sleep**. Circle the letter group **eep** in each word. Then write the words.

keep ________ sleep ________

NEW **ight** You know the word **night**. Change **n** to **l** and you have **light**. Circle the letter group **ight** in each word. Then write the words.

night ________ light ________

NEW **eam** You know the word **team**. Put **scr** instead of **t** in front of the letter group **eam** and you have **scream**. Circle the letter group **eam** in each word. Then write the words.

team ________ scream ________

ot You know the words **lot** and **not.** Change the first letter to **h** and you have **hot.** Circle the letter group **ot** in each word. Then write the words.

lot ________ not ________

hot ________

Words to Know

	Look	Say	Picture	Write
hot	☐	☐	☐	________
sleep	☐	☐	☐	________
light	☐	☐	☐	________
scream	☐	☐	☐	________
if	☐	☐	☐	________
bag	☐	☐	☐	________
boy	☐	☐	☐	________

56

Worktext page 56

	Look	Say	Picture	Write
wood	☐	☐	☐	________
hear	☐	☐	☐	________
us	☐	☐	☐	________
scared	☐	☐	☐	________

Word Attack ________

+s Write each of these words with an **s** ending.

wood ________ bag ________

bike ________ dog ________

scream ________

+ed The word **race** already has **e** on the end. So instead of adding **ed**, you just add **d**. Write **race** with a **d** ending.

race ________

+ing Write both of these words with **ing** endings.

call ________ sleep ________

The word **come** ends with **e**. So you drop the **e** before adding the **ing** ending: **coming**. Write **come** with an **ing** ending.

come ________

57

Worktext page 57

2=1 Sometimes two short words are put together to make a longer word. You know the short words. So you can figure out the long ones.

in + to = into **with + out = without**

for + get = forget **boy + friend = boyfriend**

Write each of these words.

into ________ forget ________

without ________ boyfriend ________

Now, circle the two short words in each long word you wrote. Look carefully at each word. Say it. Picture it. Then, write it until you have learned it.

Write each of these words in a sentence. Choose the word that best goes in each sentence.

into forget

without boyfriend

Dan is my ________.

I cannot go ________ my bike.

Do not ________ the hot dogs!

I am scared to go ________ the woods.

58

Worktext page 58

16. A NIGHT IN THE WOODS

I'm at Kate's house. We are about to go out to cook and sleep in the woods. We can't wait to get going.

"Do you have what you need?" her mom says.

We say we do.

"Be careful," her mom's boyfriend says.

"Don't say that," Kate says. "You are going to make us scared."

"Don't forget the sleeping bags," Kate's mom says. "And call if you get scared."

"Mom!" Kate says, "We can't call. We are going to be in the woods."

Kate and I get on bikes. We go out to the woods. We put out the sleeping bags.

Night comes fast. We make a fire.

"Time to cook," I say. "Get the hot dogs."

"You have the hot dogs," Kate says.

59

Worktext page 59

I stop what I'm doing. "Are you saying you don't have the hot dogs?"

"That is what I'm saying," Kate says.

The fire is making a lot of light. I can see that Kate is not happy. I say, "Want to go back?"

"It is night!" Kate says. "We can't go on bikes at night."

"Then I'm going to get in my sleeping bag. If we can't have hot dogs, I'm going to sleep."

We put out the fire. Then we get in the sleeping bags.

"I'm not scared, are you?" Kate says.

"I'm not scared," I say.

"What are you thinking about?" Kate says.

"Hot dogs," I say. "What are you thinking about?"

"Hot dogs," she says.

"But I'm not scared," I say.

"Scared?" Kate says. "Not me."

"Do you see that?" I say.

We see a light in the night. It is coming.

Kate screams.

"Hide!" I say. We get the sleeping bags. We go back into the woods. Then we wait as the light gets bigger and bigger.

60

Worktext page 60

What Do You Think?

Meet with a friend or in a small group. Talk about what you think the light is. Do you think the girls are in danger? If yes, of what? If no, why not?

Remembering Details

Write a word from the story in each space.

"We are going to be in the ________________."

"What are you ________________ about?" Kate says.

"But I'm not ________________," I say.

We see a ________________ in the night.

Then we wait as the light gets __________ and __________.

Putting Ideas in Order

Here are three sentences from the story. Write them in the order that they happened.

We go out to the woods.

Kate screams.

Then we get in the sleeping bags.

____

____

____

____

____

____

____

____

61

Worktext page 61

LESSON 1.17

OBJECTIVE

- Students will practice and apply skills to extended passages

MATERIALS

Worktext 1, pages 62–63
Teacher's Manual, page 97
Practice Lesson 1.17, page 98 of the Worktext
Long piece of butcher paper, markers (Reteach)

SKILLS REVIEW

- Before reading, you may wish to review these story words that apply phonics skills: *light, says, scared, finds, girls, talking, calls, calling, boyfriend, makes, scream, screams, woods, doing, raced, without, hot, dogs.* Have students review the Memory Chips they have learned so far. Then ask: **What do you think will happen to the girls next? Who do you think is holding the light?**
- While reading, ask students to think about how all the characters are feeling.
- After reading, have students complete the exercises on Worktext page 63.

For further practice, have students complete Practice Lesson 1.17 on page 98 of the Worktext. Answers can be found in the Answer Key on page 349 of this *Teacher's Manual.*

RETEACH

If students need further review of phonics skills, you may wish to use the following activity:

Phonograms *ot, ay, alk, all, an, ike, ake, ad, eep, ight, eam*

Twist It! Secure a six-foot long piece of butcher paper to the floor. Draw large circles on the paper and write these words in each circle: **not**, **say**, **walk**, **all**, **an**, **like**, **make**, **ad**, **call**, **jeep**, **cake**, **talk**, **day**, **hot**, **keep**, **night**, **team**. Then have two students play "Twist It!" One student places one part of his or her body on one circle and says the word and a word that rhymes with it. Then the other student chooses a circle on the mat to touch and says the word on that circle along with a rhyming word. (The student must keep touching that circle with that body part or the game is over.) Students continue taking turns placing hands, feet, elbows, and knees on the circles until they cannot move. The last student to touch a new circle wins the game.

Worktext Pages 62–63

Level I

MCR

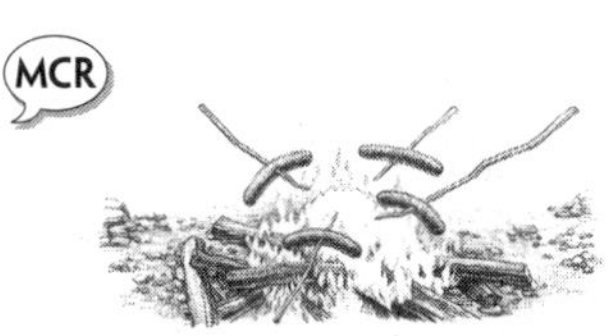

17. WHO IS SCARED?

The light stops. Then I hear a man talking.
"Who is it?" Kate says to me.
"A man," I say. "What does he want?"
"I'm scared," Kate says.
"Don't talk," I say. "What if he finds us!"
I can hear the man say, "I don't see the girls."
"Is he talking about you and me?" Kate says.
Then the man calls out, "Kate! Jen!"
"He is calling us!" I say.
"Wait," Kate says. "That man. It is Mom's boyfriend!"
Then I hear Kate's mom. She calls, "Kate! Jen!"
"Mom!" Kate calls out.
That makes Kate's mom scream. Then her mom's boyfriend screams.
We come out of the woods.
"Kate!" her mom says. "What are you doing?"
"What are you doing?" Kate says.
"You raced off without the hot dogs. I did not want you to go to sleep without your hot dogs."
"You scared me, and you scared Jen!" I say.
"I'm sorry," Kate's mom says. "But you scared me."
"And me," Kate's mom's boyfriend says.
We laugh. Then we make a fire. Kate's mom and her boyfriend cook hot dogs with us. Then Kate's mom and her boyfriend go back home. Kate and I sleep out in the woods. We go to sleep fast. We do not have time to be scared.

62

Worktext page 62

What Do You Think?

Meet with a friend or in a small group. Take turns telling stories about times when you were really scared by something. Be as descriptive as you can.

Finding the Main Idea

Write the group of words that best says what the whole story is about.

We go to sleep fast.

We laugh.

We get scared in the woods.

____

____

____

Read It Again

Read again the story on page **34** called **Dan's Sister.** Then read these sentences. Choose the best answer (**a**, **b**, or **c**), and write it on the line.

Dan, Tom, Jake, and I are __________.
(a) friends (b) on the team (c) in a car

Tom says, "I don't like people with __________."
(a) cars (b) sisters (c) problems

Mom says, "People like to __________."
(a) drink (b) talk (c) scream

The next day, I see Dan's __________ in school.
(a) friend (b) mom (c) sister

63

Worktext page 63

FINAL NOVEL Crash!

MATERIALS
Final Novel 1, *Crash!*
Teacher's Manual, page 98
Assessment Manual, Final Assessment 1, pages 66–70

Summary *The basketball team isn't playing like a team. After a game, a truck hits the team's bus. Now the teens are forced to work together to get help. After the accident, the teens become closer. They have learned the importance of working as a team.*

REVIEW AND ASSESSMENT

- Have students review their Memory Chips for Lessons 1–17 with a partner. Depending on your students' needs, review the following skills covered by Lessons 10–17: compound words; final digraph /*th*/; phonograms *ike, an, ake, ad, eep, ight, eam, ot*; and endings *s, ed, er, est, ing*.

If you wish to assess students' progress at this point, use the *Assessment Manual*, pages 66–70. For students who need additional support, you may use the Reteach activities from previous lessons.

INTRODUCE THE NOVEL

Invite students to preview the book by reading the title, looking at the illustrations, and reading aloud the captions. Begin a discussion of story concepts by asking:

- **What does it take to have a good team?**
- **What is teamwork?**
- **How can teamwork help a team win games?**

CHECK COMPREHENSION

Chapter 1 Why does Coach quit the team? (*The players won't work together as a team.*)

Chapter 2 Why is Coach knocked out? (*A truck hit the bus. Coach got injured.*)

Chapter 3 How do the kids decide to get help for Coach? (*They split into teams. One team stays with Coach, and the other goes to find help.*)

Chapter 4 Why does the team going for help come back to the bus? (*A dog is scaring Jen.*)

Chapter 5 What happens after the team follows the dog? (*The dog leads them to a house. A man is there, but he runs them off.*)

Chapter 6 What happens after the team leaves the house? (*They find people in the woods. They agree to help.*)

Chapter 7 Why do you think Kate wants to find the man in the truck? (*She thinks he was drinking, and a man who was drinking and driving killed her father.*)

Chapter 8 Why does Jen disappear? (*She is scared.*)

Chapter 9 How do you think Dan and Kate feel to be back at school? (*They feel relieved and happy to be back; they are also probably very tired.*)

Chapter 10 Why does Kate call Dan? (*She wants him to help her find the driver of the truck that made the bus crash.*)

Chapter 11 Why does Kate think she found the man who hit the bus? (*His truck is in the shop getting fixed. She thinks it is being fixed after hitting the bus.*)

Chapter 12 Why is everyone so surprised that Tom has a plan for making Coach come back? (*He is usually not a team player.*)

Chapter 13 Why doesn't the man remember what happened to his truck? (*He was drinking.*)

Chapter 14 What does the man who hit the bus say when he comes to school? (*He is sorry he hit the bus, and he is getting help for his drinking problem. He wants to help the kids if he can.*)

Chapter 15 What do Tom, Dan, and Jake do to get Kate back on the team? (*They go to Kate's house to talk to her new father.*)

Chapter 16 Do you think the team will convince Coach to come back and coach them? (*Possible answer: Yes, because he will see how they work as a team.*)

Chapter 17 If the team lost, why did Coach decide to coach the team again? (*He saw they all worked together as a team.*)

CONNECTION

Home/School Encourage students to bring home a copy of *Crash!* They might read the novel, or sections of the novel, to family members.

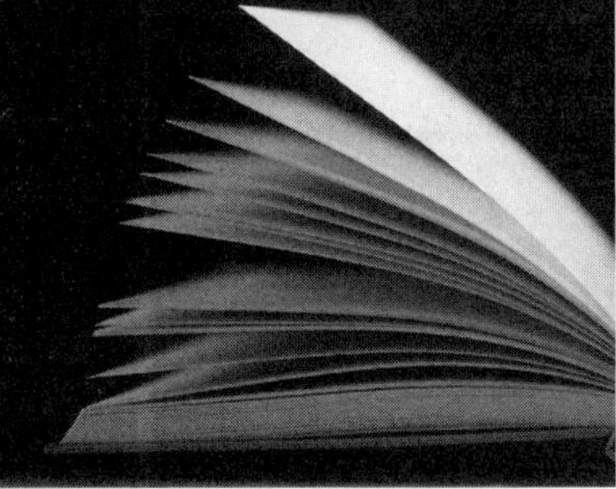

LEVEL 2

ORGANIZER

Level 2 of the *Caught Reading* program includes the following components:

Worktext 2

Worktext 2 includes 16 lessons, taking students from those words introduced in Level 1 through a word list of 147 words (found on page 339 of this *Teacher's Manual*) by Lesson 16. The Practice Lessons provide students with opportunites to extend practice, and review the content of each lesson. The Response to Reading pages allow students to practice using their new vocabulary. Tear-out Memory Chips in the back of the student book reinforce new vocabulary and can be used both independently by students and in small groups.

Midway and Final Novels 2

These novels are designed to reinforce learned vocabulary and give students the opportunity to read for meaning. Their high-interest plots encourage successful reading experiences and an appreciation for literature.

- *Playing With Fire* includes only vocabulary students have learned up to the midway point of this level.
- *Stolen Chances* includes all vocabulary learned through Level 2.

Teacher's Manual

The *Teacher's Manual* provides detailed objectives and instruction for each skill taught in the Worktext, as well as additional teaching suggestions for meaningful practice and reinforcement. The *Teacher's Manual* provides choices for flexible instruction. Comprehension questions for the Midway and Final novels are included, as well as Answer Keys for the Worktext activities and the Practice Lessons.

Assessment Manual

The *Assessment Manual* provides preassessment, ongoing assessment, and postassessment to administer to students throughout their work in *Caught Reading*. Within this Manual you will also find Midway and Final Assessments to determine the students' comprehension of the Midway and Final Novels.

OBJECTIVES

Vocabulary Development

- Read a base vocabulary of words, plus additional words made up of base words and endings.
- Use the word-learning sequence to remember and spell words correctly.
- Review vocabulary independently, both in and out of context, using the Memory Chips.

Phonics

- Recognize base words with *ly*, *en*, and *less* endings.
- Read the contractions *it's*, *I'll*, *didn't*, *doesn't*, *you're*, and *what's*.
- Recognize the letter groups *ook*, *ell*, *op*, *old*, *ack*, *un*, *art*, *and*, *ow*, and *ave* in words.
- Use the vowel generalization: When two vowels come together in a word, usually the first one has the long sound and the second vowel is silent.

Reading Comprehension

- Remember the main idea and details from a story.
- Make predictions based on information in the story.

Literary Analysis

- Identify characters, settings, and key events.
- Identify the main incidents of the plot, their causes, and how they influence future action.

Writing

- Write brief descriptions of people, places, or events using sensory details.
- Write brief narratives describing experiences.

Speaking and Listening

- Share information, opinions, and questions in coherent, complete sentences.
- Retell stories, including characters, setting, and plot.

INTRODUCTION & LESSON 2.1

OBJECTIVES

- Students will learn new words containing the *ay*, *all*, *ook*, and *ell* phonograms
- Students will apply endings *ly*, *er*, *s*, and *ing* to base words to form new words
- Students will recognize and form compound words

PHONICS VOCABULARY

boys	ideas	clears	puts	may
selling	talking	tells	getting	say
going	takes	working	looks	friendly
walls	painter	maybe	Kay	keeps
wall	look	sell	painting	finding
putting	painters	paintings		

WORDS TO KNOW

may	wall	look	tell	up
will	Mrs.	Jared	idea	paint
after	principal	graffiti	Kay	

MATERIALS

Worktext 2, pages 5–10
Teacher's Manual, pages 102–104
Practice Lesson 2.1, pages 66–67 of the Worktext

TEACH

- Using Worktext page 7, introduce students to the vocabulary words. Give them an opportunity to practice writing the words.
- Students can organize their Memory Chips, found in the back of the Worktext. You may wish to say each word, having students repeat it after you.

Worktext page 7 can be used to reinforce spelling. Use the five-step process detailed on page 71 of this *Teacher's Manual.*

Phonogram *ay, all, ook, ell*

Write this sentence on the board and read it aloud: **All the boys say they cook well.** Ask a volunteer to point to *cook.*

Blending Circle *cook*, modeling how to blend the sounds: /*k*/ /*oo*/ /*k*/, then say the word naturally. Write **cook** on the board. Have students take turns substituting *b*, *l*, and *t* for the *c*, blending each word. Write each new word on the board as it is suggested. Repeat, using **all**, **say**, and **well** from the sentence above.

cook	say	all	well
book	way	ball	tell
look	hay	tall	bell
took	Kay	fall	sell

Endings *ly, er, s, ing*

Write these sentences on the board: **Tom is my friend. Tom is friendly.** Point to *friend* and *friendly* and ask students how these words are different. (Friendly *ends in* ly.) Tell students *ly* is an ending that is added to *friend* to help describe Tom. Write this sentence on the board: **The teacher says we are going.** Have students circle the endings *er*, *s*, and *ing* in the words *teacher*, *says*, and *going*.

Make New Words Write a chart like the one below on the board and have students add the endings *ly*, *er*, *s*, and *ing* to the words.

Base Word	+ ly	+ er	+ s	+ ing
friend	friendly		friends	
talk		talker	talks	talking
paint		painter	paints	painting
boy			boys	
tell		teller	tells	telling
week	weekly		weeks	

Compound Words

Remind students that two smaller words can be put together to make a new word. Write these two words on the board: **may**, **be**. Have students put the two words together to make a new word. (*maybe*)

Make New Words Write these words on index cards and have students put them together to make new words: **up**, **on**, **hall**, **way**, **day**, **time**. (*upon*, *hallway*, *daytime*) They can write the words on a separate piece of paper.

PRACTICE

- Let students practice the new words they have learned and formed by completing the activities on pages 6–8 of the Worktext.
- If students are experiencing difficulty with the Words to Know section on page 7, place the Memory Chips on the table. Pose riddles like this for each word: **This word begins like ice and is something I get in my mind.** (*idea*)

For further practice, have students complete Practice Lesson 2.1 on pages 66–67 of the Worktext. Answers can be found in the Answer Key on page 350 of this *Teacher's Manual.*

APPLY

- Have students talk about the story concept by discussing things they have experienced. Ask: **Have you ever been asked to go to the principal's office? What happened?** Tell them they are going to use the words they have learned to read a short story about a boy who is called in to see the principal.
- Ask students to read the story on page 9 in the Worktext. Offer assistance if necessary, but encourage students to decode the words independently, using the clues and patterns they have learned.
- After students have completed reading the story, have them complete the Cooperative Group Activity (What Do You Think?) and Comprehension Exercises (Remembering Details and Putting Ideas in Order) on page 10 in their Worktext. Answers can be found in the Answer Key on page 349 of this *Teacher's Manual.*

CONNECTION

Strategy for Reading Have students reread the selection "Graffiti" on Worktext page 9 to correct comprehension breakdowns. Students may achieve understanding by reprocessing the same text with greater attention focused on its meaning.

Speaking/Listening Have student partners read aloud the selection "Graffiti" on Worktext page 9. The partners can alternate being speaker and listener.

Level 2

1. GRAFFITI

Word Attack

ay You know the words **say**, **play**, and **day**. Put **m** before the letter group **ay**, and you have **may**. Put **K** before the letter group, and you have **Kay**. Write the words on the lines. Then circle the letter group **ay**.

may ________________ Kay ________________

all You know the words **hall** and **call**. Change the first letter to **w**, and you have **wall**. Write **wall** on the line. Then circle the letter group **all.**

wall ________________

ook You know the word **cook**. Change the first letter to **l**, and you have **look**. Write both words. Then circle the letter group **ook** in each.

cook ________________ look ________________

ell You know the word **tell**. Change the first letter to **s**, and you have **sell**. Write both words. Then circle the letter group **ell** in each.

tell ________________ sell ________________

Letter Groups

Circle the letter groups that are the same in each list of words.

say	cook	sell	hall
Kay	look	tell	call
may			wall

6

Worktext page 6

Words to Know

	Look	Say	Picture	Write
may	☐	☐	☐	________
Kay	☐	☐	☐	________
wall	☐	☐	☐	________
look	☐	☐	☐	________
tell	☐	☐	☐	________
up	☐	☐	☐	________
will	☐	☐	☐	________
Mrs.	☐	☐	☐	________
Jared Ja-red	☐	☐	☐	________
idea	☐	☐	☐	________
paint	☐	☐	☐	________
after af-ter	☐	☐	☐	________
principal prin-ci-pal	☐	☐	☐	________
graffiti graf-fi-ti	☐	☐	☐	________

Word Attack

+er Write this word with an **er** ending.

paint ________________

NEW **+ly** The letters **ly** are another ending. Write the following base word with an **ly** ending.

friend ________________

7

Worktext page 7

+ing Write these words with **ing** endings.

paint ________________ find ________________

When you write **put** with an **ing** ending, you have to double the **t**. Write the base word, then the base word with an **ing** ending.

put ________________ putting ________________

+s Write each of these words with an **s** ending.

tell ________________ wall ________________

put ________________ keep ________________

boy ________________ idea ________________

clean ________________ painter ________________

painting ________________

2=1 The word **maybe** is made of two short words you know. Circle each of the two short words. Then write the whole word.

maybe ________________

MCR Tear out the Memory Chips for Chapter **1** from the back of the book. Review them with those you are saving from **Caught Reading Level 1**. Make sure you know them before you read the story.

8

Worktext page 8

1. GRAFFITI

Mrs. Selling says, "Jared, the principal wants to see you after school."

Boy, I think, *what did I do?*

Then, I am talking to Kate in the hall. My coach comes up to me. He tells me, "Jared, the principal wants to see you after school."

I am getting scared. What is the big idea?

After school, Kate comes up to me. "Don't forget to go see the principal, Jared!" she says, then laughs.

"Come with me," I say.

"To see the principal? Forget it!" Kate takes off fast.

I go see the principal. She is working. I walk in, and she looks up. "You wanted to see me?" I say.

She does not look friendly.

I want to scream, *What did I do?*

She tells me, "I want to talk to you about that wall out by the lot. That graffiti is a big problem."

"I don't do graffiti!" I tell her.

The principal says, "Mrs. Selling says you are a painter."

"But I did not paint on that wall!" I get up. I am about to go.

The principal says, "Wait, Jared."

I think, *What is going on?*

9

Worktext page 9

What Do You Think?

Meet with a friend or in a small group. Talk about what you would do now if you were Jared. What do you think is about to happen to him? Explain why you think so.

Remembering Details

Write a word from the story in each space.

"Jared, the ________________ wants to see you after school."

What is the big ________________?

She does not look ________________.

"I don't do ________________!" I tell her.

Putting Ideas in Order

Here are four sentences from the story. Write them in the order that they happened.

The principal says, "Mrs. Selling says you are a painter."

I am getting scared.

I want to scream, *What did I do?*

The principal says, "Wait, Jared."

____

____

____

____

____

____

10

Worktext page 10

LESSON 2.2

OBJECTIVE

- Students will practice and apply skills to an extended passage

MATERIALS

Worktext 2, pages 11–12
Teacher's Manual, page 105
Practice Lesson 2.2, pages 68–69 of the Worktext

SKILLS REVIEW

- Before reading, you may wish to review these words that apply phonics skills: *selling, laughs, painters, ideas, painting, weeks, helps, says, forget, puts, putting, finding, kids, paintings, cleans.* Have students review the Memory Chips they have learned so far. Then ask: **How could you solve the problem of graffiti on a school wall?**
- While reading, have students think about how the principal and kids solve the problem.
- After reading, have students complete the exercises on Worktext page 12.

For further practice, have students complete Practice Lesson 2.2 on pages 68–69 of the Worktext. Answers to these questions can be found in the Answer Key on page 350 of this *Teacher's Manual.*

RETEACH

If students need further review of phonics skills, you may wish to use the following activity:

Compound Words

Compound Get-Togethers Write these words on index cards and pass them out, one to each student: **fire**, **truck**, **can**, **not**, **team**, **work**, **with**, **out**, **boy**, **friend**, **in**, **to**, **for**, **get**, **may**, **be**. Then have students search for a partner with whom they can put the two words together to make a compound word. Then they can raise their hands, say the word, and use it in a sentence.

2. PAINTING THE SCHOOL

Mrs. Selling laughs. "Hear me out. I want you to get a team of painters. You and your team can paint the wall. Maybe that will stop the graffiti."

I like that idea. I get a team of painters. We work on ideas for the wall. Then we work on painting the wall for weeks. The painting is all I can think about. We do careful work.

Then one day, I find graffiti on the painting. I get out more paint. I clean up the painting. The next day, I find more graffiti. My team helps me clean it up.

Kate says, "I want to find out who is putting graffiti on the painting."

The next night, we hide in the back of a truck. We wait. Then I see one, no, two, boys come with paint. One boy puts graffiti on the wall painting.

The next day, I go see the principal. I say, "I can tell you who is putting graffiti on the painting."

"Who?" she says.

"I don't want to say," I say. "Will you think about my idea if I tell you?"

"OK," she says.

"I want you to find a wall for the kid doing the graffiti. So he can do a painting of his own."

The principal says, "If Mrs. Selling says it is OK, he can paint the wall in her class."

The graffiti problem at my school does not stop. But the principal keeps finding walls for kids to paint. We have paintings on three walls. I like the paintings a lot. If I find graffiti on a painting, my team cleans it up with more painting. We get to paint a lot.

11

Worktext page 11

What Do You Think?

Meet with a friend or in a small group. Talk about how you feel about graffiti. What do you think about how Jared handled the situation with the boy who was putting graffiti on his painting? Do you think he did the right or wrong thing? Why?

Remembering Details

Write a word from the story in each space.

I get a team of ________________.

"Will you think about my ________________ if I tell you?"

The graffiti ________________ at my school does not stop.

If I find graffiti on a painting, my team ________________ it up with more painting.

Finding the Main Idea

Write the sentence that best says what the whole story is about.

We do careful work.

We have paintings on three walls.

Jared paints walls at school to help stop graffiti.

____

____

____

____

____

____

12

Worktext page 12

LESSON 2.3

OBJECTIVES

- Students will learn new words containing the *ad* and *op* phonograms
- Students will apply endings *er, s,* and *ing* to base words to form new words
- Students will recognize and form contractions
- Students will learn new words containing vowel pairs

PHONICS VOCABULARY

dad	shop	it's	can't	says
looking	makes	comes	gives	going
gets	looks	tells	wanting	longer
bad	drives	hears		

WORDS TO KNOW

bad	shop	no	at	him
ring	just	give	long	feel
sold	alive	they		

MATERIALS

Worktext 2, pages 13–16
Teacher's Manual, pages 106–107
Practice Lesson 2.3, pages 70–71 of the Worktext

TEACH

- Using Worktext page 13, introduce students to the vocabulary words. Give them an opportunity to practice writing the words.
- Students can organize their Memory Chips, found in the back of the Worktext. They can divide them into groups of words they know and words they don't recognize.

Worktext page 13 can also be used to reinforce spelling. Use the five-step process detailed on page 71 of this *Teacher's Manual.*

Phonograms *ad, op*

Write this sentence on the board: **My dad has a shop.** Have a volunteer point to the word *dad.* Blend the sounds with students, /*d*/ /*a*/ /*d*/. Point out how the vowel *a* is surrounded by two consonants. Tell them that when this happens, the vowel has the short sound. Repeat, using *shop.*

Make New Words Students can substitute beginning sounds and letters to make word ladders with *dad* and *shop.*

dad	sad	shop	hop
mad	had	mop	stop

Endings *er, s, ing*

Write this sentence on the board and read it aloud: **The painter paints.** Have a volunteer point to *painter* and *paints* and ask students how these words are alike and different. (*They both have the base word* paint*; one ends in* er *and the other in* s.)

Make New Words Write these words on the chalkboard, and invite students to add *er, s,* and *ing* to the end of each word: **find**, **think**, and **play**. (*finder, finds, finding*; *thinker, thinks, thinking*; *player, plays, playing*)

Contractions

Write this sentence on the board, and read it aloud: **I can't go to school.** Point to *can't,* and ask students what two words *can't* stands for. (*can, not*)

Make New Words Write these words on the board, and have students write contractions for them: **it/is**, **can/not**, **do/not**. (*it's, can't, don't*)

Vowels

Write this sentence on the board and read it aloud: **Kay sees Coach.** Circle the vowels *ay, ee,* and *oa.* Tell students when they see two vowels together in a word, the first one usually has the long sound, and the second one is silent. Have students identify each long vowel sound in the sentence.

Make New Words Write these incomplete words on the board. Have students fill in the blanks with *oa, ee, ea, ay, ai,* or *oe* to make a word: **c l _ _ n**, **c _ _ c h**, **s l _ _ p**; **f _ _ d**; **g _ _ t**; **m _ _ l**, **p _ _ n t**, **g _ _ s**, **t _ _**, **t _ _ m**, **pl _ _**, **w _ _ t**.

PRACTICE

- Let students practice the new words they have learned and formed by completing the activities on pages 13–14 of the Worktext.

For further practice, have students complete Practice Lesson 2.3 on pages 70–71 of the Worktext. Answers to these questions can be found in the Answer Key on page 350 of this *Teacher's Manual.*

APPLY

- Ask students to read the story on page 15 in the Worktext. Encourage students to decode the words independently, using the clues and patterns they have learned.
- After students have completed reading the story, have them complete the Making Predictions Exercise on page 16 in their Worktext. Answers can be found in the Answer Key on page 349 of this *Teacher's Manual.*

3. SELLING THE RING

Word Attack

ad You know the word **dad**. Change the first letter to **b**, and you have **bad**. Circle the letter group **ad** in both words. Then write the words.

dad ________________ bad ________________

op You know the word **stop**. Change the first two letters to **sh**, and you have **shop**. Circle the letter group **op** in both words. Then write the words.

stop ________________ shop ________________

Words to Know

	Look	Say	Picture	Write
bad	☐	☐	☐	__________
shop	☐	☐	☐	__________
no	☐	☐	☐	__________
at	☐	☐	☐	__________
him	☐	☐	☐	__________
feel	☐	☐	☐	__________
ring	☐	☐	☐	__________
just	☐	☐	☐	__________
give	☐	☐	☐	__________
long	☐	☐	☐	__________
sold	☐	☐	☐	__________
alive a-live	☐	☐	☐	__________
they	☐	☐	☐	__________

13

Worktext page 13

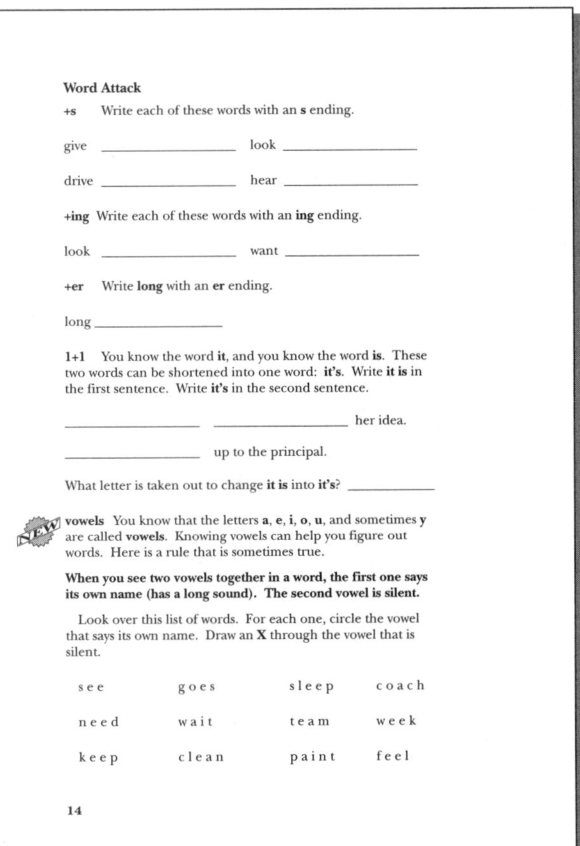

Word Attack

+s Write each of these words with an **s** ending.

give ________________ look ________________

drive ________________ hear ________________

+ing Write each of these words with an **ing** ending.

look ________________ want ________________

+er Write **long** with an **er** ending.

long ________________

1+1 You know the word **it**, and you know the word **is**. These two words can be shortened into one word: **it's**. Write **it is** in the first sentence. Write **it's** in the second sentence.

________________ ________________ her idea.

________________ up to the principal.

What letter is taken out to change **it is** into **it's**? ____________

NEW **vowels** You know that the letters **a**, **e**, **i**, **o**, **u**, and sometimes **y** are called **vowels**. Knowing vowels can help you figure out words. Here is a rule that is sometimes true.

When you see two vowels together in a word, the first one says its own name (has a long sound). The second vowel is silent.

Look over this list of words. For each one, circle the vowel that says its own name. Draw an **X** through the vowel that is silent.

see	goes	sleep	coach
need	wait	team	week
keep	clean	paint	feel

14

Worktext page 14

3. SELLING THE RING

My mom is no longer alive. It's just my dad and I at home. One day, my dad is not happy. He says, "I have lost my job."

We are OK for about ten weeks. Then we need money.

Dad gives me Mom's ring. "Go sell it," he tells me.

"Mom's ring?" I say, looking at it.

"We need the money. Sell the ring and come back with the money. I can't do it. It makes me feel bad."

My boyfriend comes with me. We go to a shop. We sell the ring. The man gives me $500 for it.

Back at home, my dad says, "$500? Is that all?"

I feel bad. I say to him, "I can go get it back."

Dad says, "That was your mom's ring. And it was Grandma's ring. Next, it was going to be your ring."

I look at my boyfriend. He says, "If we go fast, maybe we can get it back."

"No," my dad says. "It's sold. And we need the money."

My dad gets a call. He looks happy. Then he tells us, "My boss wants me back at work. They want me next week!"

We laugh. Then my boyfriend says, "Wait! What about the ring?"

Dad gives us the $500. We drive back to the shop. Maybe we can get to the shop in time.

15

Worktext page 15

Making Predictions

When you **predict**, you say what you think will happen. The best predictions are backed up by thoughtful reasons. Circle **YES** or **NO** below this question.

Do you think the people in this story will get the ring back?

YES NO

Now back up your prediction with some sentences from the story. Find all the sentences below that support your prediction. Write them on the lines.

"If we go fast, maybe we can get it back."

Dad gives us the $500.

The man gives me $500 for it.

"No," my dad says. "It's sold."

____

____

____

____

____

____

____

____

____

____

____

16

Worktext page 16

LESSON 2.4

OBJECTIVE

- Students will practice and apply skills to an extended passage

MATERIALS

Worktext 2, pages 17–18
Teacher's Manual, page 108
Practice Lesson 2.4, pages 72–73 of the Worktext

SKILLS REVIEW

- Before reading, you may wish to review these words that apply phonics skills: *shop, says, getting, it's, can't, don't, drives, takes, stops, gets, goes, hears, dad, longer.* Have students review the Memory Chips they have learned so far. Then ask: **Do you think the girl and her boyfriend will get the ring back? Why or why not?**
- While reading, have students think about what they would say to the man who has the ring.
- After reading, have students complete the exercises on Worktext page 18.

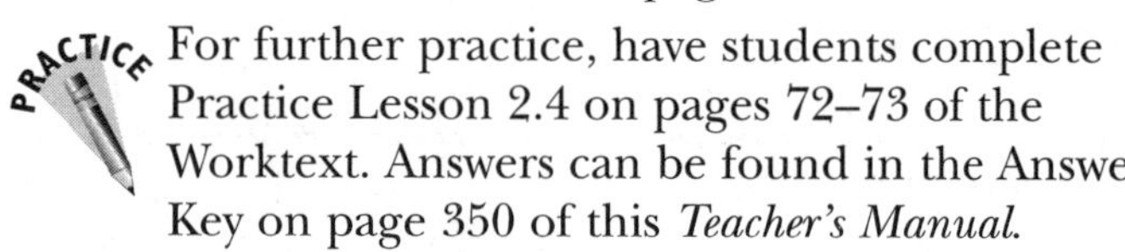

For further practice, have students complete Practice Lesson 2.4 on pages 72–73 of the Worktext. Answers can be found in the Answer Key on page 350 of this *Teacher's Manual.*

RETEACH

If students need further review of phonics skills, you may wish to use the following activity:

Silent Vowels

Silent Letter Riddles Write these words on the board: **see, need, keep, goes, wait, clean, sleep, team, paint, coach, week, feel.** Say riddles like the ones below, one for each word:

- **I am what you do when you go to bed. What word am I?** (*sleep*)
- **I have seven days in me. What am I?** (*week*)
- **I rhyme with sleep. What word am I?** (*keep*)
- **I am something you do with your eyes. What word am I?** (*see*)
- **I tell my players what to do. Who am I?** (*coach*)

Have the students point to the word on the board that answers the riddle. Then have the students tell what vowel sound they hear and draw a line through the silent vowel.

Worktext Pages 17–18

MCR

4. WANTING THE RING BACK

The man in the shop says, "See that car? I just sold the ring to the man getting in it."

"Come on," my boyfriend says.

"It's sold," I say. "We can't get it back."

"Don't say that without trying."

My boyfriend drives. But we can't keep up with the man with the ring. He drives fast. We are about to give up.

But then we come to a stop light. I see the man! I get out of my boyfriend's car. I go up to the man's car. But just then, the man takes off. I get back in my boyfriend's car. He drives after the man.

After a long time, the man stops. He gets out of the car and goes up to a house. I get out of my boyfriend's car and go after him.

The man stops and hears what I have to say. I tell him, "That ring was my grandma's and my mom's. They are no longer alive. My dad and I did not want to sell the ring. You can have the $500. Can we have the ring back?"

The man looks at my money. He says, "The man in the shop sold me the ring for $800. Sorry. It's no longer your ring." He goes in his house.

17

Worktext page 17

Remembering Details

Write a word from the story in each space.

"It's ________________," I say. "We can't get it back."

My ________________ drives.

"That ring was my ________________ and my ________________."

"They are no longer ________________."

Putting Ideas in Order

Here are three sentences from the story. Write them in the order that they happened.

The man stops and hears what I have to say.

He drives after the man.

"Sorry. It's no longer your ring."

____

____

____

____

____

____

____

____

____

18

Worktext page 18

LESSON 2.5

OBJECTIVES

- Students will learn new words containing the *old, ad,* and *op* phonograms
- Students will apply endings *s, ing, ed,* and *er* to base words to form new words
- Students will recognize and form compound words
- Students will recognize and form contractions

PHONICS VOCABULARY

sold	dad	bad	hold	job
shop	cops	says	old	boyfriend
going	don't	I'll	needed	looks
kidding	anymore	thinks	longer	comes
talks	feels	wanted	didn't	gives
wearing	sees	mad	cop	screams
races	feeling	teller		

WORDS TO KNOW

mad	hold	cop	has	any
most	bank	gave	wear	woman
because				

MATERIALS

Worktext 2, pages 19–23
Teacher's Manual, pages 109–111
Practice Lesson 2.5, pages 74–75 of the Worktext

TEACH

- Using Worktext page 20, introduce students to the vocabulary words. Give them an opportunity to practice writing the words.
- Students can organize their Memory Chips, found in the back of the Worktext. They can divide them into groups of words they know and words they don't recognize. Then say each word, having students repeat it after you.

Worktext page 20 can also be used to reinforce spelling. Use the five-step process detailed on page 71 of this *Teacher's Manual.*

Phonograms *old, ad, op*

Write this sentence on the board: **My dad sold the shop.** Have a volunteer point to the word *sold.* Blend the word with students, /s/ /o/ /ld/. Circle the *old* phonogram and tell them when they see *old,* the *o* has the long sound. Then have students find words in the sentence that rhyme with *had* and *top.* Have volunteers circle the phonograms *ad* and *op.* Remind students of the CVC pattern, which gives the short vowel sounds in *dad* and *shop.*

Make New Words Make letter cards for the consonants **h**, **s**, **t**, and **c**. Have students take turns placing the consonants in front of the phonograms *old, ad,* and *op* to make new words. (*hold, sold, told, cold; sad, had; hop, top, cop*)

Endings *s, ing, ed, er*

Remind students that words can end in *s, ing, ed,* and *er.* Write this sentence on the board and read it aloud: **The teacher holds a painting I wanted.** Look at each word and have students look for a base word and the endings *s, ing, ed,* and *er.* Have them circle the base word and underline the endings.

Make New Words Write these words on the board, and invite students to add *s, ing, ed,* or *er* to the end of each word: **bank**, **hold**, **talk**, **scream**. (*banks, banking, banked, banker; holds, holding, holder; talks, talking, talked, talker; screams, screaming, screamed, screamer*) They can use each word they make in a sentence.

Compound Words

Write this sentence on the board, and read it aloud: **I am not mad anymore.** Point to *anymore* and ask what two words they see. (*any, more*) Remind students when they see a word like *anymore,* they can look for two smaller words to help them figure out the word.

Make New Words Write these words on the board, and have students tell what two smaller words they find in each: **boyfriend**, **homework**, **cleanup**, **forget**, **maybe**. (*boy, friend; home, work; clean, up; for, get; may, be*)

Contractions

Write this sentence on the board and read it aloud: **I will go to school.** Point to *I will* and ask students how they can shorten the words to make one word, or a contraction. Guide them to remove the *wi* and add an apostrophe. Remind students when two words are shortened into one, one or more letters are taken out, and an apostrophe is added.

Make New Words Write these words on the board, and have students write contractions for them: **can not**, **it is**, **did not**, **do not**. (*can't, it's, didn't, don't*)

PRACTICE

- Let students practice the new words they have learned and formed by completing the activities on pages 19–21 of the Worktext.
- If students are experiencing difficulty with the Words to Know section on page 20, you may wish to play a riddle game. Read a riddle like this one and have students choose the correct word from their Memory Chips: **I begin like *boy* and rhyme with *tank.*** (*bank*)

For further practice, have students complete Practice Lesson 2.5 on pages 74–75 of the Worktext. Answers can be found in the Answer Key on page 350 of this *Teacher's Manual.*

APPLY

- Have students talk about the story concept by sharing their personal experiences. Ask: **Have you ever had a problem that was solved in an unusual way?** Tell them they are going to use the words they have learned to read a short story that tells how a problem was solved quite unexpectedly.
- Ask students to read the story on page 22 in the Worktext. Offer assistance if necessary, but encourage students to decode the words independently, using the clues and patterns they have learned.
- After students have completed reading the story, have them complete the Cooperative Group Activity (What Do You Think?) and Comprehension Exercises (Remembering Details and Finding the Main Idea) on page 23 in their Worktext. Answers can be found in the Answer Key on page 349 of this *Teacher's Manual.*

CONNECTION

Strategy for Reading After students finish reading the selection "The Ring Is Sold—One More Time" on Worktext page 22, ask them to summarize it either aloud or in writing.

Writing Students can write a few sentences describing how they would feel if they had to sell something important to them because they needed money. Have student volunteers share their writing with the class.

Worktext Pages 19–20

5. THE RING IS SOLD—ONE MORE TIME

Word Attack

ad You know the words **dad**, **ad**, and **bad**. Most of the times you see the letter group **ad**, it will sound the same way it does in these words. Try putting the letter **m** in front of the letter group **ad**. You get the word **mad**. Circle the letter group **ad** in each word. Then write the words.

dad ________ ad ________

bad ________ mad ________

old You know the word **sold**. Change the **s** to an **h** and you have **hold**. Circle the letter group **old** in both words. Then write the words.

sold ________ hold ________

The letter group **old** is a word all by itself. What does that word mean? Write **old** in the sentence below.

She is an ________ woman.

op You know the letter group **op**, as in **stop** and **shop**. What do you get when you put **c** in front of the letters **op**? You get the word **cop**. Circle the letter group **op** in each word. Then write the words.

stop ________ shop ________

cop ________

19

Worktext page 19

Words to Know

	Look	Say	Picture	Write
mad	☐	☐	☐	________
hold	☐	☐	☐	________
cop	☐	☐	☐	________
has	☐	☐	☐	________
any	☐	☐	☐	________
most	☐	☐	☐	________
bank	☐	☐	☐	________
gave	☐	☐	☐	________
wear	☐	☐	☐	________
woman wo-man	☐	☐	☐	________
because be-cause	☐	☐	☐	________

Word Attack

+s Write each of these words with an **s** ending.

feel ________ talk ________

cop ________ scream ________

race ________

+ing Write each of these words with an **ing** ending.

wear ________ feel ________

+ed Write **need** with an **ed** ending. ________

+er Write **tell** with an **er** ending. ________

20

Worktext page 20

2=1 You know the two short words **any** and **more**. These two words can be written together to make one longer word: **anymore**. Write the word **anymore** in the sentence.

I don't want to go to work ________________.

Circle each of the two short words in the word you just wrote.

1+1 You know the word **I**, and you know the word **will**. These two words can be shortened into one word: **I'll**. Write **I will** in the first sentence. Write **I'll** in the second sentence.

________________ ________________ get the call.

________________ get the call.

What two letters are taken out to change **I will** into **I'll**?

________________ ________________

You know the words **did not**. These two words can be shortened into one word: **didn't**. Write **did not** in the first sentence. Write **didn't** in the second sentence.

You ________________ ________________ clean the car.

You ________________ clean the car.

What letter is taken out to change **did not** into **didn't**? ________

21

Worktext page 21

What Do You Think?

Meet with a friend or in a small group. Talk about how this family handled money problems. Do you think they handled them well? Why or why not? What would you do if you needed some cash right away?

Remembering Details

Write a word from the story in each space.

My dad ________________ bad about the ring.

"Don't call the ________________!" she says.

So is my dad when I give the ____________ to him that night.

Finding the Main Idea

Write the sentence that best says what the whole story is about.

She gets her mom's and grandma's ring back.

"Sold," the woman says.

I see that she is wearing Mom's ring!

____

____

____

____

23

Worktext page 23

5. THE RING IS SOLD—ONE MORE TIME

My dad feels bad about the ring. He wanted it because it was Mom's. He wanted me to have it. He is sorry that he didn't hold out a little longer.

But we are happy he has his job back.

One day, I go to see my boyfriend at work. He has a job in a car shop. A woman comes in. She talks to my boyfriend about her car. She gives him money for his work on the car.

I see she is wearing Mom's ring!

My boyfriend sees it. He says, "That is your mom's ring!"

The woman says, "What are you talking about?"

I say, "That ring was my mom's and my grandma's."

"Don't call the cops!" she says. "My old boyfriend gave it to me!"

"The cops?" I say. "I'm not going to call the cops. We sold the ring to a shop because we needed money."

The woman looks at the ring. "Do you want it back? What will you give me for it?"

"Are you kidding?" I say.

"I don't see my old boyfriend anymore. He is the one who gave me the ring. I will sell it back to you. I need the money. What about $300?"

I can see that she thinks $300 is a lot for Mom's ring. I am about to scream, *I'll take it!*

But my boyfriend says, "$300? Forget it. We can give you $200."

"Sold," the woman says.

I drive fast to the bank. I get the $200. I drive back and give the money to the woman. She is happy to have my money. I am happy to have Mom's ring. So is my dad when I give the ring to him that night.

22

Worktext page 22

LESSON 2.6

OBJECTIVE

- Students will practice and apply skills to an extended passage

MATERIALS

Worktext 2, pages 24–25
Teacher's Manual, page 112
Practice Lesson 2.6, pages 76–77 of the Worktext
Markers (Reteach)

SKILLS REVIEW

- Before reading, you may wish to review these words that apply phonics skills: *waiting, teller, gets, gives, feeling, says, forget, didn't, maybe, takes, sees, doing, talking, taking, screams, makes, races, calls, cops, hold, hold-up, bad.* Have students review the Memory Chips they have learned so far. Then ask: **What do you think it would be like if your bank was held up while you were in it?**
- While reading, have students think about what they would have said and done if they had been in the bank during the hold-up.
- After reading, have students complete the exercises on Worktext page 25.

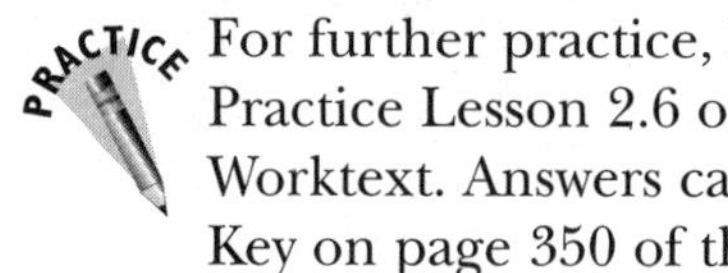

For further practice, have students complete Practice Lesson 2.6 on pages 76–77 of the Worktext. Answers can be found in the Answer Key on page 350 of this *Teacher's Manual.*

RETEACH

If students need further review of phonics skills, you may wish to use the following activity:

Contractions

Contraction Stand Up Write each of these letters and this symbol on a separate sheet of paper: **n, o, o, t, I, w, i, l, l, d, d, s,** and an apostrophe. Give one paper to each student. Then have students take turns standing up in front of the class to make words with their letters. First, they will make two words, such as *do not.* Then have the student with the second *o* sit down and have the student with the apostrophe stand in his or her place. Have the class read the new word. Repeat with **don't, did not/didn't, will not/won't, I will/I'll, is not/isn't, it is/it's.**

Worktext Pages 24–25

6. THE BANK HOLD-UP

I am at the bank. I am waiting to see a bank teller. A man gets in back of me. He gives me a bad feeling. Just as I look at him one more time, he says, "Give me your money."

"Forget it," I say. "Who do you think you are?"

The man says, "Maybe you didn't hear me. Give me your money."

The man takes my money. No one sees him doing it. I try to get the bank teller to look. She can call for help. But she is talking to a woman. She does not see the man taking my money.

Next, the man says to the bank teller, "Give me all your money."

The woman who was talking to the bank teller screams.

That makes the man mad. He takes the money the bank teller gives him. He races out of the bank.

But the bank teller calls the cops. They come in no time. The cops hold the man and his truck out by the school. He has $4,000.

The next day at school, all the kids want to hear about the hold-up. I am just happy to be alive.

24

Worktext page 24

What Do You Think?

Meet with a friend or in a small group. Talk about the following sentences from the story: **"Forget it," I say. "Who do you think you are?"** Do you think this was a good thing for the person to say to the bank robber? Why or why not? What would you have done?

Remembering Details

Write a word from the story in each space.

I am ________________ to see a bank teller.

The man takes my ________________.

All the kids want to hear about the ________________.

I am just ________________ to be alive.

Read It Again

Read again the stories on pages **9** and **11** called **Graffiti** and **Painting the School**. Then read these sentences. Choose the best answer (**a**, **b**, or **c**), and write the words on the line.

"Jared, ________________ wants to see you after school."

(a) Mrs. Selling (b) the principal (c) your coach

"I don't do ________________!" I tell her.

(a) painting (b) work (c) graffiti

"He can do a ________________ of his own."

(a) job (b) painting (c) game

25

Worktext page 25

LESSON 2.7

OBJECTIVES

- Students will learn new words containing the *ay*, *all*, *old*, and *ack* phonograms
- Students will apply endings *en*, *ing*, *s*, and *ed* to base words to form new words
- Students will recognize and form contractions

PHONICS VOCABULARY

woods	packs	snowing	says	knows
going	wooden	getting	doesn't	having
cold	lighten	walked	tells	wants
longer	stop	looks	walking	coming
don't	screams	screaming	all	pack
snowballs	say	way	back	ball
cooking	ways	mountain	cars	others

WORDS TO KNOW

way	cold	pack	sun	snow
know	where	there	other	dinner
over	shelter	mountain	snowball	

MATERIALS

Worktext 2, pages 26–31
Teacher's Manual, pages 113–115
Practice Lesson 2.7, pages 78–79 of the Worktext

TEACH

- Using Worktext page 27, introduce students to the vocabulary words. Give them an opportunity to practice writing the words.
- Students can organize their Memory Chips, found in the back of the Worktext. Say each word, having students repeat it after you. Then have them sort the words according to words with one and two syllables and words that have the same vowel sound as in *hold*.

Worktext page 27 can also be used to reinforce spelling. Use the five-step process detailed on page 71 of this *Teacher's Manual*.

Phonograms *ay, all, old, ack*

Write these words on the board and say them aloud: **say**, **all**, **old**, and **sack**. Then have students brainstorm words that rhyme with each word. Write their suggestions on the board.

Make New Words Make letter cards for consonants **s**, **b**, **g**, **c**, and **m** and phonograms **ay**, **all**, **old**, and **ack**. Have students take turns placing the consonants in front of phonograms to make new words. (*say, bay, gay, may*; *ball, gall, call, mall*; *sold, bold, gold, cold, mold*; *sack, back, Mack*)

Endings *en, ing, s, ed*

Write these sentences on the board: **The paint is light. I will lighten the paint.** Point to *light* and *lighten* and ask students how the words are alike. (They both have the word *light*.) Tell them *light* is the base word and *en* is an ending. Write these sentences on the board: **I take the bus. I am taking the bus.** Have volunteers circle *take* and *taking*. Tell them that *take* is the base word. When a base word ends in *e*, you drop the *e* and add *ing*.

Make New Words Write these words on the board, and invite students to add *en*, *ing*, *s*, or *ed* to the end of each word: **light**, **wood**, **have**, **take**, **paint**. (*lighten, lighting, lights, lighted*; *wooden, woods, wooded*; *having*; *taken, taking, takes*; *painting, paints, painted*) They can use each word they make in a sentence.

Contractions

Write this sentence on the board and read it aloud: **Tom does not play.** Point to *does not* and ask students how they can make the two words into one by creating a contraction. Guide them to remove the *o* in *not* and add an apostrophe. Remind students when two words are shortened into one, one or more letters is taken out and an apostrophe is added.

Make New Words Write these words on the board and have students write contractions for them: **is not**, **did not**, **do not**. (*isn't, didn't, don't*)

PRACTICE

- Let students practice the new words they have learned and formed by completing the activities on pages 26–28 of the Worktext.
- If students are experiencing difficulty with the Words to Know section on page 27, put the Memory Chip cards down on the table, word side up. Say a sentence, leaving out a word. Have students choose the correct card for the missing word. Use sentences like this: **Let's go _____ there.** (*over*)

For further practice, have students complete Practice Lesson 2.7 on pages 78–79 of the Worktext. Answers can be found in the Answer Key on page 350 of this *Teacher's Manual*.

APPLY

- Have students talk about the story concept by sharing their personal experiences. Ask: **Have you ever lost your way in the woods? How did you get lost? How did you find your way?** Tell them they are going to use the words they have learned to read a short story about three boys who get lost in the woods on a camping trip.
- Ask students to read the story on pages 29–30 in the Worktext. Offer assistance if necessary, but encourage students to decode the words independently, using the clues and patterns they have learned.
- After students have completed reading the story, have them complete the Making Predictions Activity on page 31 in their Worktext. Answers can be found in the Answer Key on page 349 of this *Teacher's Manual.*

CONNECTION

Speaking/Listening Student partners can read aloud the selection "Getting Lost in the Woods" on Worktext pages 29–30. The partners can alternate being speaker and listener.

Writing Give students an opportunity to write in their journals, recording how they would feel if they were the main character in "Getting Lost in the Woods."

Worktext Pages 26–27

7. GETTING LOST IN THE WOODS

Word Attack

ay You have learned a lot of words that have the letter group **ay**. What word do you get when you put a **w** in front of **ay**? You get the word **way**. Circle the letter group **ay** in each word. Then write the words.

say ______________ play ______________

day ______________ may ______________

way ______________

all You know the words **hall**, **call**, and **wall**. Change the first letter of any of these words to **b**, and you have **ball**. Circle the letter group **all** in each word. Then write the words.

hall ______________ call ______________

wall ______________ ball ______________

old You know the words **sold** and **hold**. Change the first letter of either word to **c**, and you have **cold**. Circle the letter group **old** in each word. Then write the words.

sold ______________ hold ______________

cold ______________

ack You know the word **back**. Change the **b** to **p**, and you have **pack**. Circle the letter group **ack** in each word. Then write the words.

back ______________ pack ______________

26

Worktext page 26

Words to Know

	Look	Say	Picture	Write
way	☐	☐	☐	______________
cold	☐	☐	☐	______________
pack	☐	☐	☐	______________
sun	☐	☐	☐	______________
snow	☐	☐	☐	______________
know	☐	☐	☐	______________
where	☐	☐	☐	______________
there	☐	☐	☐	______________
other oth-er	☐	☐	☐	______________
dinner din-ner	☐	☐	☐	______________
over o-ver	☐	☐	☐	______________
shelter shel-ter	☐	☐	☐	______________
mountain moun-tain	☐	☐	☐	______________
snowball snow-ball	☐	☐	☐	______________

Word Attack

+ing Write each of these words with an **ing** ending.

snow ______________ walk ______________

scream ______________ cook ______________

27

Worktext page 27

+s Write each of these words with an **s** ending.

pack __________ know __________

way __________ snowball __________

other __________ car __________

mountain __________

You have to drop the **e** in **have** before adding an **ing** ending to it: **having**. Write **have** in the first sentence. Writing **having** in the second sentence.

I __________ sold the paint.

I am __________ a bad time.

+ed Write **walk** with an **ed** ending.

walk __________

NEW **+en** The letters **en** are another ending. Write each of these base words with an **en** ending.

wood __________ light __________

1+1 You know the words **does** and **not**. These can be written together as one word: **doesn't**. Write **does not** in the first sentence. Write **doesn't** in the second sentence.

She __________ __________ want dinner.

She __________ want your help.

28

Worktext page 28

7. GETTING LOST IN THE WOODS

Dan, Tom, and I walk out into the woods with packs. It is snowing a lot. But Tom says he knows where he is going. He knows about a little wooden shelter in the woods. We are going to sleep in the shelter. Tom says he goes to it all the time.

We walk and walk, but we do not get there.

I can tell Dan is getting mad. He doesn't like having a pack. He doesn't like the cold snow. I make a snowball. I hit Dan with one. I am trying to get him to lighten up. But he will not laugh.

"Where is the shelter?" Dan says.

"Just over the next mountain," Tom says.

"It was just over **that** mountain," Dan says, looking at the one we just walked over.

"One more," Tom tells him.

"I'm cold," I say.

"Walk faster," Tom says. "You will work off the cold."

"Can we make a fire in the shelter?" Dan wants to know.

Tom says, "In the shelter, we will have a hot fire. We will cook a hot dinner."

"If we get there," Dan says.

29

Worktext page 29

We walk and walk. I look up. It is going to be night in no time. There is more and more snow. It just takes longer and longer to walk in the snow.

Then Tom stops. He looks one way. Then he looks the other way. "I think we go that way," he says.

"You **think**?" Dan says.

"It has to be over there," Tom says. But he is not walking fast. The snow keeps coming. I am cold. I want a hot dinner.

"I want to go back," I say.

"I don't know the way back," Tom says.

"Then find the shelter!" Dan screams.

"Screaming will not help," I say. "Tom, do you know where we are?"

Tom does not talk for a long time. Then he says, "No, I don't."

I want my dinner. I am cold. The snow is coming down. Night is coming. We are out in the woods.

"Help!" Dan screams. "HELP! HELP!"

30

Worktext page 30

Making Predictions

Remember that to predict means to say what you think will happen. The best predictions are backed up by thoughtful reasons. Circle **YES** or **NO** below this question.

Do you think the boys will find shelter by nighttime?

YES NO

Now back up your prediction with some sentences from the story. Find all the sentences below that support your prediction. Write them on the lines.

Tom says he knows where he is going.

The snow is coming down.

Tom says he goes to the shelter all the time.

Night is coming on fast.

"I don't know the way back," Tom says.

It just takes longer and longer to walk in the snow.

____

____

____

____

____

____

____

____

____

____

31

Worktext page 31

LESSON 2.8

OBJECTIVE

- Students will practice and apply skills to an extended passage

MATERIALS

Worktext 2, pages 32–33
Teacher's Manual, page 116
Practice Lesson 2.8, pages 80–81 of the Worktext
Checkerboard, small stick-on notes (Reteach)

SKILLS REVIEW

- Before reading, you may wish to review these words that apply phonics skills: *screaming, stops, all, pack, say, way, snowball, snowballs, others, takes, gets, helps, back, woods, scared, making, cooking.* Have students review the Memory Chips they have learned so far. Then ask: **What would you do if you had to sleep outside in the snow without shelter?**
- While reading, have students decide who uses good judgment in the story.
- After reading, have students complete the exercises on Worktext page 33.

For further practice, have students complete Practice Lesson 2.8 on pages 80–81 of the Worktext. Answers can be found in the Answer Key on page 350 of this *Teacher's Manual.*

RETEACH

If students need further review of phonics skills, you may wish to use the following activity:

Phonograms *ack, old, all, ay*

Phonogram Checkers Write words with phonograms **ack**, **old**, **all**, and **ay** and with other phonograms you wish to review on the stick-on notes and post them on the black squares of a checkerboard. Then have students play checkers, except each player must read the word on each space he or she lands on. If a player cannot read the word, he or she returns to the original space. Words you may wish to use are: *back, pack, sold, told, cold, hold, fold, gold, hall, wall, call, ball, fall, tall, play, may, say, ray, hay, lay, Kay, day, way, stay, sack, tack, rack, Mack, Zack.*

Worktext Pages 32–33

MCR

8. THE SNOW SHELTER

Night is coming fast. I think about what to do.

"Stop screaming," I tell Dan.

He stops screaming. But he is mad and scared. We all are.

I take off my pack. I think about making a shelter with snow. I know people can keep alive in a snow shelter for a long time.

I say to Dan and Tom, "I know what we have to do. Night is on the way. Then there will be no light. We have to work fast."

I make a big snowball. Then I make more big snowballs. I pack the snow. We put more snowballs on the others. I pack snow in where we need it. It takes a long time. But we make a little snow shelter.

Then we get in it. No one is happy. But we are not cold. We eat the dinner without cooking it. All night long, I sleep off and on.

After a long, long time, it gets light out. We get out of the snow shelter. I look up at the sun. That helps me tell where we are. I tell Dan and Tom to come with me. We go back over the mountains.

After a long time, I hear cars. We come out of the woods. We have a long way to go to get to my truck. But we are alive. All I want is a hot dinner and sleep.

32

Worktext page 32

What Do You Think?

Meet with a friend or in a small group. Talk about how the three boys in this story reacted in different ways to the situation. Describe how each of their reactions was different from the other boys' reaction.

Remembering Details

Write a word from the story in each space.

"Stop ______________," I tell Dan.

I pack the ______________.

We make a little snow ______________.

All I want is a hot ______________ and sleep.

Putting Ideas in Order

Here are four sentences from the story. Write them in the order that they happened.

We come out of the woods.

We eat the dinner without cooking it.

I think about making a shelter with snow.

I make a big snowball.

____

____

____

____

____

____

33

Worktext page 33

MIDWAY NOVEL Playing With Fire

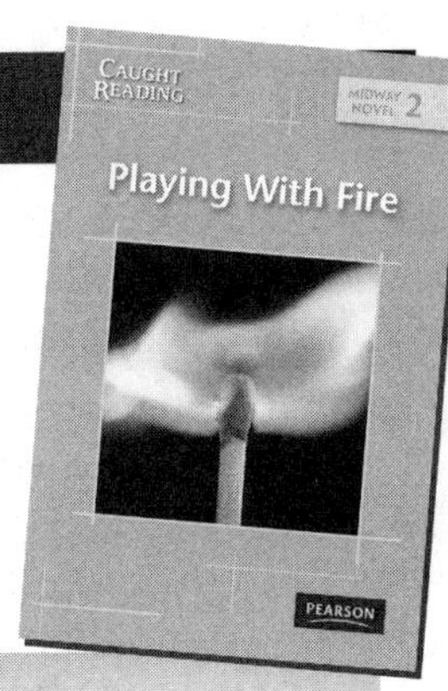

MATERIALS
Midway Novel 2, *Playing With Fire*
Teacher's Manual, page 117
Assessment Manual, Midway Assessment 2, pages 71–73

Summary *The high school is putting on a play. Tom, Jared, Kate, and Jen get parts in the play. Then things start to go wrong. First there's a fire, then the set is ruined by graffiti, and finally, Jen gets sick. They are able to overcome the obstacles, and the play will go on as scheduled.*

Level 2

REVIEW AND ASSESSMENT

- Have students review their Memory Chips with a partner. Depending on your students' needs, review the following skills covered in Lessons 1–8: phonograms *ell, ook, all, ad, op, old, ack,* and *ay*; vowel pairs; compound words; contractions; and endings with *s, ed, ly, er, en,* and *ing* (dropping the *e* and adding *ing*; doubling the consonant and adding *ing*).

If you wish to assess students' progress at this point, use *Assessment Manual,* pages 71–73. For students who need additional support, you may use the Reteach activities from previous lessons.

INTRODUCE THE NOVEL

Invite students to preview the book by reading the title, looking at the illustrations, and reading the captions aloud. Begin a discussion of story concepts by asking:

- **Have you ever seen a play or been to one?**
- **How do you try out for a part in a play?**
- **What do you think it would be like to be in a play?**

CHECK COMPREHENSION

Chapter 1 Why does Dan Ringover get mad at Jared? (*He thinks Jared is making fun of his girlfriend, Kate.*)

Chapter 2 Who gets the main parts in the play? (*Jen is playing the lost girl, and Jared is the painter.*)

Chapter 3 What problem does Tom have? (*He likes Kate, but she already has a boyfriend.*)

Chapter 4 Why is Dan unhappy? (*He thinks Kate should have gotten the part of the lost girl.*)

Chapter 5 What do you think Kate wants to tell Tom? (*Possible answer: She likes him; she wants to break up with Dan.*)

Chapter 6 Who do you think set the fire? (*Students will probably say Dan Ringover did.*)

Chapter 7 Would you like to have Dan Ringover for a friend? Why or why not? (*Most will say no because he is possessive with his friends, he gets mad a lot, and he is sneaky.*)

Chapter 8 What is the second thing that threatens to postpone the play? (*Graffiti is found all over the wall in back of the shelter.*)

Chapter 9 Why does Jared suspect Kate of setting the fire and painting the wall with graffiti? (*She wanted the part of the lost girl and she didn't get it.*)

Chapter 10 Who helps solve the problem of the graffiti? (*Principal Walls and Mrs. Newman*)

Chapter 11 What do you think will happen now that Jen is sick? (*Kate will play the part of the lost girl.*)

Chapter 12 Why do you think Dan Ringover set a fire and painted graffiti over the wall at the shelter? (*He was angry that Kate didn't get the part.*)

Chapter 13 Why didn't Kate say something about Dan's behavior before now? (*She was scared. He told her not to say anything and threatened her.*)

Chapter 14 What does Kate mean when she says she wants to be the girl Tom finds? (*She wants to be his girlfriend.*)

CONNECTION

Home/School Encourage students to bring home a copy of *Playing With Fire.* They might read the novel, or sections of the novel, to family members.

LESSON 2.9

OBJECTIVES

- Students will learn new words containing the *art* and *un* phonograms
- Students will apply endings *less, s, ing,* and *ed* to base words to form new words
- Students will recognize and form compound words

PHONICS VOCABULARY

says	baseball	looked	laughs
fires	sleeping	smashed	gets
running	doing	homeless	talks
holds	thinking	apartment	run
start	smashing	art	jobs
telling			

WORDS TO KNOW

start	apartment	base	field
when	smash	should	family
window	already	Mu Lan	

MATERIALS

Worktext 2, pages 34–39
Teacher's Manual, pages 118–120
Practice Lesson 2.9, pages 82–83 of the Worktext

TEACH

- Using Worktext page 35, introduce students to the vocabulary words. Give them an opportunity to practice writing the words.
- Students can organize their Memory Chips, found in the back of the Worktext. Say each word, having students repeat it after you. Then have them sort the words according to words they know and those that are unfamiliar. Say each unfamiliar word and have students use it in a sentence.

Worktext page 35 can also be used to reinforce spelling. Use the five-step process detailed on page 71 of this *Teacher's Manual.*

Phonograms *art, un*

Write this sentence on the board and read it aloud: **Art is fun.** Have a volunteer point to the word *Art.* Ask students to brainstorm other words that rhyme with *art.* (*part, dart, Bart, cart*) Repeat with *fun.*

Make New Words Make letter cards for the consonants **p**, **d**, **c**, **s**, **b**, and **r** and phonograms **art** and **un**. Have students take turns placing the consonants in front of the phonograms to make new words. (*part, dart, cart, Bart; pun, sun, bun, run*)

Endings *less, s, ing, ed*

Write these sentences on the board: **I have a home. The man is homeless.** Point to *home* and *homeless* and ask students how the words are alike. (*They both have the word* home.) Tell them *home* is the base word and *less* is an ending that means "without." Ask them what *homeless* means. (*without a home*) Remind students they can also make new words with the endings *s, ing,* and *ed.*

Make New Words Write these words on the board, and invite students to add *less, s, ing,* or *ed* to the end of each word: **home**, **job**, **work**, **friend**. (*homeless, homes; jobless, jobs; works, working, worked; friendless, friends*) They can use each word they make in a sentence.

Compound Words

Write this sentence on the board and read it aloud: **Tom is my boyfriend.** Point to *boyfriend* and ask students what two smaller words they see in the larger word. Remind them that finding smaller words inside compound words can help them read unfamiliar words.

Make New Words Write these words on the board and have students use them to make compound words: **for**, **friend**, **get**, **boy**, **ball**, **base**. (*forget, boyfriend, baseball*)

PRACTICE

- Let students practice the new words they have learned and formed by completing the activities on pages 34–36 of the Worktext.
- If students are experiencing difficulty with the Words to Know section on page 35, you can write the beginnings and endings of the words on the board, leaving out the middle letters. Have students use their Memory Chips to write the whole words. Then have them use each word in a sentence.

For further practice, have students complete Practice Lesson 2.9 on pages 82–83 of the Worktext. Answers can be found in the Answer Key on page 351 of this *Teacher's Manual.*

APPLY

- Have students talk about the story concept by sharing their personal experiences. Ask: **Have you ever seen a homeless person or family? Where did they sleep? Why were they homeless?** Tell them they are going to use the words they have learned to read a short story about some kids who discover a homeless family in a most unusual place.

- Ask students to read the story on pages 37–38 in the Worktext. Offer assistance if necessary, but encourage students to decode the words independently, using the clues and patterns they have learned.
- After students have completed reading the story, have them complete the Cooperative Group Activity (What Do You Think?) and Comprehension Exercises (Finding the Main Idea and Read It Again) on page 39 in their Worktext. Answers can be found in the Answer Key on page 349 of this *Teacher's Manual.*

CONNECTION

Strategy for Reading After students read the selection "Sleeping in the Baseball Field" on Worktext pages 37–38, have them summarize it either aloud or in writing.

Worktext Pages 34–36

9. SLEEPING IN THE BASEBALL FIELD

Word Attack

un You know the word **sun**. If you change the **s** to **r**, you have the word **run**. Write the words **sun** and **run** on the lines below. Then circle the letter group **un** in both words.

sun ________________ run ________________

art You know the word **part**. Change the **p** to **st**, and you have the word **start**. Write the words **part** and **start** on the lines below. Then circle the letter group **art** in both words.

part ________________ start ________________

The letter group **art** is a word all by itself. What does the word **art** mean? Write the word in the sentence below.

I want to get an "A" in ________________ class.

You are about to learn a new word that is quite long. But it has two shorter words that you know in it. Find the word **a** and the word **part** in this word. Circle both words.

a p a r t m e n t

Now write the word **apartment** in a sentence.

I have a big ________________.

34

Worktext page 34

Words to Know

	Look	Say	Picture	Write
start	☐	☐	☐	________
apartment apart-ment	☐	☐	☐	________
base	☐	☐	☐	________
field	☐	☐	☐	________
when	☐	☐	☐	________
smash	☐	☐	☐	________
should	☐	☐	☐	________
family fam-i-ly	☐	☐	☐	________
window win-dow	☐	☐	☐	________
already al-ready	☐	☐	☐	________
Mu Lan	☐	☐	☐	________

Word Attack

+s Write these words with **s** endings.

fire ________________ hold ________________

job ________________

35

Worktext page 35

+ing Write these words with **ing** endings.

sleep ________________ tell ________________

+ed Write these word with **ed** endings.

look ________________ smash ________________

+less The letters **less** are another ending. Write the following word with a **less** ending.

home ________________

Write the word **home** in the first sentence. Write the word **homeless** in the second sentence.

He lives in his grandma's ________________.

She has been ________________ for weeks.

2=1 You know the word **base**, and you know the word **ball**. You can write these two words together to make one word: **baseball**. Write the new word in the following sentence.

All he wants is to play ________________.

Now circle each of the two shorter words in the word you wrote.

36

Worktext page 36

9. SLEEPING IN THE BASEBALL FIELD

"I have an idea," Kate says. "I want to play baseball in that big field in back of the bank."

"At night?" Dan says, looking out the window. "It's cold!"

"It's already after 9:00," I say.

"I'll play!" Jared says. He laughs at the idea.

"I'm in," Mu Lan says.

We run over to the field in back of the bank. We start to play. Jared fires the baseball at me. It goes by me. I run to get it.

Then I see people. A family is sleeping in the field. The baseball just about smashed the woman.

"Sorry," I say. "We didn't see you there."

The dad says to his little boy, "Go back to sleep." But the little boy gets up and gets the baseball.

Jared, Dan, and Mu Lan come running.

"What are you all looking at?" the man says.

"What are you doing sleeping out in a cold field?" Jared says.

37

Worktext page 37

"Don't you know there is a homeless shelter?"

I don't like the way Jared talks to the family.

"Come on," I say. "I want to go home."

"What about the baseball?" Jared says. "Kid, give back the ball."

But the little boy holds on to the baseball.

The boy's mom says, "Give it back."

The boy says, "No."

Jared goes to get the ball. But I say, "Stop! He can have the baseball. Come on, Jared. It's time to go home."

"People can't sleep in a field!" Jared says. "They should get an apartment!"

"What is it to you?" Dan says. "Come on."

We start to walk home. Jared says, "We can't play baseball because of homeless people. That man should get a job. What does he think he is doing sleeping in a field?"

No one talks back to Jared. I am thinking about that family. They looked cold. Did they have dinner? I say, "Maybe the man and the woman are just out of work."

38

Worktext page 38

What Do You Think?

Meet with a friend or in a small group. Talk about the disagreement between the person telling this story and Jared. From the way they talk and act, what differences do you see in how they view homeless people? What are your own views on homelessness?

Finding the Main Idea

Write the sentence that best says what the whole story is about.

The kids in the story find a family sleeping in the field.

Jared doesn't like homeless people.

No one wants to play baseball.

____

____

____

Read It Again

Read again the story on page **24** called **The Bank Hold-Up**. Then read these sentences. Choose the best answer (**a**, **b**, or **c**), and write the words on the line.

The man takes my ______________.

(a) money (b) sister (c) dinner

The next day at school, all the kids want to hear about the ______________.

(a) art class (b) baseball game (c) hold-up

I am just happy to be ______________.

(a) in school (b) alive (c) at home

39

Worktext page 39

LESSON 2.10

OBJECTIVE
- Students will practice and apply skills to an extended passage

MATERIALS
Worktext 2, pages 40–42
Teacher's Manual, pages 121–122, 330–331
Practice Lesson 2.10, pages 84–85 of the Worktext
Three-minute egg timer (Reteach)

SKILLS REVIEW

- Before reading, you may wish to review these words that apply phonics skills: *comes, smashed, baseball, going, sleeping, telling, talked, homeless, says, takes, gives, doing, looks, jobs, tells, saying, start.* Have students review the Memory Chips they have learned so far. Then ask: **Is it your problem if a homeless family has no money and no place to sleep? Why or why not?**
- While reading, have students compare and contrast the way Jared and the narrator think about the homeless family.
- After reading, have students complete the exercises on Worktext page 42.

For further practice, have students complete Practice Lesson 2.10 on pages 84–85 of the Worktext. Answers can be found in the Answer Key on page 351 of this *Teacher's Manual.*

RETEACH

If students need further review of phonics skills, you may wish to use the following activity:

Endings *less, ed, ing, s*

Three-Minute Word Race Write the following words and endings on index cards: **home**, **less**, **look**, **smash**, **sleep**, **tell**, **say**, **fire**, **job**, **hold**, **friend**, **s**, **ing**, and **ed**. Then put the timer right side up and have students make as many words as they can in the three minutes. One student can record the words as the other students form them.

CONNECTION

Response to Reading

- To reinforce students' understanding of the literary elements found in their reading material, have them complete the Story Map and Character Cluster reproducibles found on pages 330–331.
- Students will demonstrate an understanding of setting, characters, and plot by filling out the organizers.
- Students may share their completed organizers with the class.

Independent Reading

- Encourage students to read for pleasure. Pearson's *Uptown, Downtown* series consists of eight short, easy-to-read novels that allow students to easily relate to the main character and learn valuable life lessons. See page xvii of this *Teacher's Manual* for additional titles.
- After reading, students may form small groups to informally critique and discuss their books. You may also ask students to write a brief three-line summary of what they have read.

10. THE BANK WINDOW

The next day, Jared comes up to me at school. "Did you hear about the bank window?" he says.

"No," I say.

"Smashed by a baseball." He laughs. "I'm going to tell the bank who did it. That family should not be sleeping in that field."

I feel sick. It was bad of that family to smash the bank window. But Jared does not have to tell on the family.

The next day, I see Jared. "Did you tell the people at the bank?" I say.

"I did," Jared says.

"And?" I say.

Jared says, "The family already talked to the bank people about it. They already gave the bank money for the window, just like they should have."

40

Worktext page 40

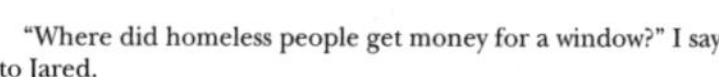

"Where did homeless people get money for a window?" I say to Jared.

"Not my problem," he says.

That night, I go back to the field. I take a hot dinner with me. The man will not talk to me. But the woman takes the hot dinner. She gives it to her little boy.

Then she says, "Did you come to find out about the bank window? We already gave the bank money for it. My boy was just playing with the baseball. He didn't try to do that to the window."

"What do you want?" the man says to me. "What are you doing here?"

The woman looks at him, then at me. She says, "He is mad because the money we gave the bank was going to go to an apartment. We will have to start over."

"Do you have jobs?" I say.

"He has a job," the woman tells me. "I don't. But it takes a long time to get the money for an apartment."

I can just hear Jared saying, "Not my problem."

But it does feel like **my** problem. I don't think people should have to sleep in the cold. I don't think people should have to sleep in a field.

41

Worktext page 41

What Do You Think?

Meet with a friend or in a small group. Talk about what you would do if you were the person in this story. Do you think she should have gone back to the field? Why or why not? What do you think she should do now, if anything?

Remembering Details

Write a word from the story in each space.

"That ________________ should not be sleeping in that field."

"My boy was just ________________ with the baseball."

"But it takes a long time to get the money for an ________________."

Putting Ideas in Order

Here are three sentences from the story. Write them in the order that they happened.

Jared says, "The family already talked to the bank people about it."

"We will have to start over."

"I'm going to tell the bank who did it."

____

____

____

____

____

____

42

Worktext page 42

LESSON 2.11

OBJECTIVES

- Students will learn new words containing the *and* phonogram and vowel pairs
- Students will apply endings *s, ed, ing,* and *n* to base words to form new words

PHONICS VOCABULARY

meet	band	raise	seen	raises
holds	says	raised	cougars	uses
lots	worked	kids	votes	going

WORDS TO KNOW

band	meet	raise	won	vote
use	this	hard	close	believe
cougar				

MATERIALS

Worktext 2, pages 43–46
Teacher's Manual, pages 123–124
Practice Lesson 2.11, pages 86–87 of the Worktext

TEACH

- Using Worktext page 43, introduce students to the vocabulary words. Give them an opportunity to practice writing the words.
- Students can organize their Memory Chips, found in the back of the Worktext. You may wish to say each word, having students repeat it after you. Students can find different ways to sort the words, such as words they know and don't know, words with one and two syllables, and so on.

Worktext page 43 can also be used to reinforce spelling. Use the five-step process detailed on page 71 of this *Teacher's Manual.*

Phonogram *and*

Write this sentence on the board and read it aloud: **The band plays at the game.** Ask a volunteer to point to *band.*

Blending Circle *band,* modeling how to blend the sounds /b/ /a/ /nd/, then say the word naturally. Write **band** on the board. Have students take turns substituting *l, s,* and *h* for *b,* blending each word. Write each new word on the board as it is suggested.

band land sand hand

Vowel Pairs

Write this sentence on the board: **I raise my hand.** Have a volunteer point to *raise.* Ask them to circle the first two vowels in the word. Tell them that when they see two vowels together, the word has the long vowel sound of the first vowel. Repeat, using **week** and **meat**.

Blending Give students letter cards for *w, k, m, p, t, l, ee, ea,* and *ai.* As you say each word, have them find the letter cards that make the word: **meat**, **week**, **mail**, **wait**, **tail**, **keep**.

Endings *s, ed, ing*

Remind students that words can end in *s, ed, ing,* and *n.* Write **use** and **uses** on the board. Say the words and have students repeat them after you. Tell them when the *s* is added to *uses,* it makes another syllable. Repeat the procedure, using **vote** and **voted**.

Make New Words Write a chart like the one below on the board and have students add the endings *s, ed,* and *ing* to the words. Remind them when a word ends in *e,* the *e* is dropped and then the ending *ing* or *ed* is added. If the word ends in a consonant, they may need to double the consonant and add the ending.

Base Word	+ s	+ ed	+ ing	+n
vote	votes	voted	voting	
meet	meets		meeting	
run	runs		running	
see	sees		seeing	seen

PRACTICE

- Let students practice the new words they have learned and formed by completing the activities on pages 43–44 of the Worktext.
- If students are experiencing difficulty with the Words to Know section on page 43, place the Memory Chips on the table. Pose riddles like this for each word: **This word begins like *boy,* and it is a group that makes music.** (*band*)

For further practice, have students complete Practice Lesson 2.11 on pages 86–87 of the Worktext. Answers can be found in the Answer Key on page 351 of this *Teacher's Manual.*

APPLY

- Have students talk about the story concept by discussing things they have experienced. Ask: **Have you ever raised money for a good cause? What happened to the money?** Tell them they are going to use the words they have learned to read a short story.
- Ask students to read the story on page 45 in the Worktext.
- After students have completed reading the story, have them complete the Cooperative Group Activity (What Do You Think?) and Comprehension Exercises (Finding the Main Idea and Read It Again) on page 46 in their Worktext. Answers can be found in the Answer Key on page 350 of this *Teacher's Manual.*

Worktext Pages 43–46

11. THE VOTE

Word Attack

and You know the word **and**. Add **b** to the beginning of that word, and you have **band**. Write the word **band**, and circle the letter group **and**.

band ________________

vowels Remember what you learned about a word that has two vowels side by side. Often, the first vowel says its own name, and the second vowel is silent. Using this rule, try to figure out what the following two words are.

meet ________________ raise ________________

Circle the vowel in each word that says its own name. Draw an **X** across the silent vowel in each word. Write each word on the line.

Words to Know

	Look	Say	Picture	Write
band	☐	☐	☐	________
meet	☐	☐	☐	________
raise	☐	☐	☐	________
won	☐	☐	☐	________
vote	☐	☐	☐	________
use	☐	☐	☐	________
this	☐	☐	☐	________
hard	☐	☐	☐	________
close	☐	☐	☐	________
believe be-lieve	☐	☐	☐	________
cougar cou-gar	☐	☐	☐	________

43

Worktext page 43

11. THE VOTE

At school I start to raise money. I get other kids to help. I want to help that homeless family to get an apartment.

After some weeks, my school raises $400. I am going to take it to the family.

But Jared holds a meeting. "I want to talk about this," he says at the meeting. "The school raised this money. We should think hard about how to use it. I think the money should go to the baseball team. The Cougars have not won a game in weeks. We need money for a coach."

Mu Lan says, "I think the money should go to the band. The baseball team already has money."

"I can't believe this," I say. "We raised this money for that homeless family. People who gave money gave it for the family."

"That is a bad idea," Jared says. "They are just one little family. If the school uses the money, lots of people will be helped. This money we raised is school money. We all get to say where it goes."

"Jared, you used to be my friend," I say. "What are you doing? I worked hard to raise this money for the family."

"The kids in this school who gave the money should say where it goes. And I say the team should get that money," Jared says. "I'm sorry."

A lot of kids are with Jared. We go to the principal. She says that we have to have a vote.

The next week, the school votes. I wait to hear what most of the kids want. Will the money go to the homeless family? Will it go to the baseball team? Will it go to the band?

I think the vote will be close.

45

Worktext page 45

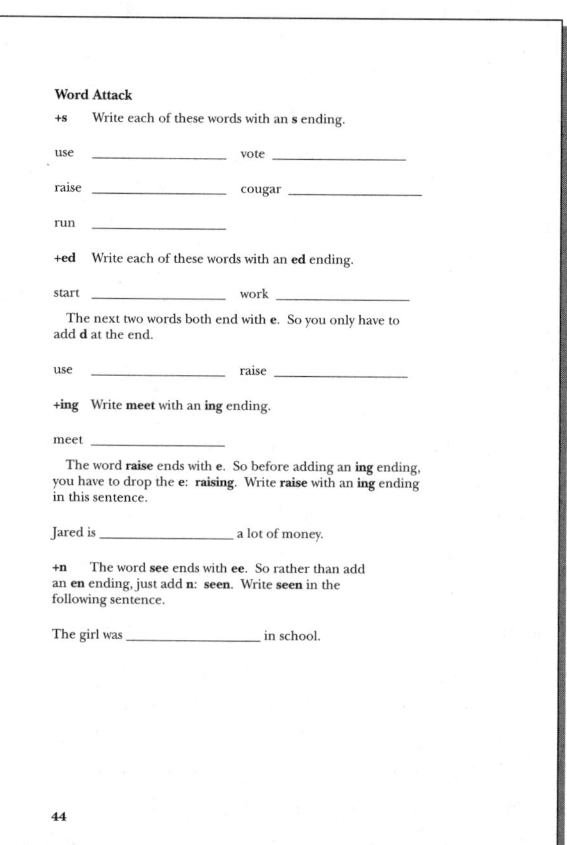

Word Attack

+s Write each of these words with an **s** ending.

use ________________ vote ________________

raise ________________ cougar ________________

run ________________

+ed Write each of these words with an **ed** ending.

start ________________ work ________________

The next two words both end with **e**. So you only have to add **d** at the end.

use ________________ raise ________________

+ing Write **meet** with an **ing** ending.

meet ________________

The word **raise** ends with **e**. So before adding an **ing** ending, you have to drop the **e**: **raising**. Write **raise** with an **ing** ending in this sentence.

Jared is ________________ a lot of money.

+n The word **see** ends with **ee**. So rather than add an **en** ending, just add **n**: **seen**. Write **seen** in the following sentence.

The girl was ________________ in school.

44

Worktext page 44

What Do You Think?

Meet with a friend or in a small group. Talk about how the principal in this story resolved the conflict. Do you think having a vote was a good way to resolve the conflict? Why or why not?

Finding the Main Idea

Write the sentence that best says what the whole story is about.

Jared takes the money to the family in the field.

The homeless family is going to get an apartment.

The kids are going to vote to say where the money goes.

____

____

____

____

____

Read It Again

Read again the stories on pages **29–30** and **32** called **Getting Lost in the Woods** and **The Snow Shelter**. Then read these sentences. Choose the best answer (**a**, **b**, or **c**), and write the words on the line.

He knows about a little ________________ in the woods.
(a) wooden shelter (b) mountain (c) apartment

Then I make more big ________________.
(a) people (b) snowballs (c) mountains

All I want is ________________ and sleep.
a) my mom b) a cold pack c) a hot dinner

46

Worktext page 46

LESSON 2.12

OBJECTIVE

- Students will practice and apply skills to an extended passage

MATERIALS

Worktext 2, pages 47–49
Teacher's Manual, pages 125–126, 330–331
Practice Lesson 2.12, pages 88–89 of the Worktext

SKILLS REVIEW

- Before reading, you may wish to review these words that apply phonics skills: *looking, doing, comes, says, homes, seen, wait, going, coming, seeing, hears, looks, drives, starts, runs, ideas, see, scream.* Have students review the Memory Chips they have learned so far. Then ask: **What would you do if there were a dangerous wild animal loose in your neighborhood?**
- While reading, have students decide if Mu Lan and the narrator make a wise decision in looking for the cougar.
- After reading, have students complete the exercises on Worktext page 49.

For further practice, have students complete Practice Lesson 2.12 on pages 88–89 of the Worktext. Answers can be found in the Answer Key on page 351 of this *Teacher's Manual.*

RETEACH

If students need further review of phonics skills, you may wish to use the following activity:

Endings *s, ed, ing*

Baseball With Endings Play a baseball game with word endings. Divide the class into two teams. One at a time, each player is up at bat. Display an index card with the following words written, one to a card: **meet**, **start**, **work**, **use**, **raise**, **run**, **cougar**, **vote**, **home**, **look**, **smash**, **tell**, **sleep**, **play**, **apartment**, **base**, **window**, **fire**, **job**, **hold**. Place index cards with the endings **s**, **ed**, and **ing** written on them face down. Have a student choose a word from the list. Then have the player choose an ending *s, ed,* or *ing.* If the word and ending make a word, the player goes to first base. If the player is unable to make a word, the team receives an out. The team at bat continues until it receives three outs. The winning team is the one that earns the most points after nine or fewer innings.

CONNECTION

Response to Reading

- To reinforce students' understanding of the literary elements found in their reading material, have them complete the Story Map and Character Cluster reproducibles found on pages 330–331.
- Students will demonstrate an understanding of setting, characters, and plot by filling out the organizers.
- Students may share their completed organizers with the class.

12. THE COUGAR

Mu Lan and I are looking at a baseball game on TV. I cook a little dinner. We are not doing a lot. I start to feel sleepy.

Then a woman comes on the TV and says, "Do not go out of your homes! A cougar is out. She was seen over by the school. Wait in your homes. We will tell you when they get the cougar."

"Did you hear that?" Mu Lan says. "I want to go find the cougar!"

"No way," I say. "Do you know how fast a cougar can run?"

"I'm going," Mu Lan says. "I want to see the cougar. Are you coming?"

I run after Mu Lan. I scream, "Think about what we are doing!"

But she is racing to the school. Then she stops fast. There in

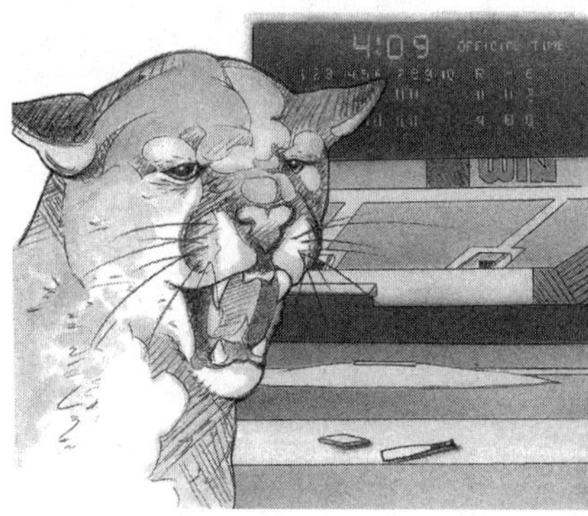

47

Worktext page 47

the baseball field is a big cougar. I can't believe I am seeing it.

"This is when I want to have a car," Mu Lan tells me.

"I hear that," I say. We start to back up.

The cougar is over at the back of the field. But she hears us. She looks over at us.

I hold Mu Lan back. I hold back my scream.

Then I say, "I think we are about to be dinner for the cougar."

"Run!" Mu Lan says.

"NO!" I tell her. "That will make the cougar run after us."

Just then, a truck drives up. A big man and a woman get out. They have dinner for the cougar. They hold the dinner out to her. She starts to come for the dinner.

Then fast, they put the dinner in the back of the truck. The cougar runs for it.

I get in back of Mu Lan. I want to scream.

But the cougar just runs into the truck after her dinner. The man and the woman close up the back of the truck fast. They drive off with the cougar.

I look at Mu Lan. "You and your big ideas," I say. Then we run all the way home.

48

Worktext page 48

Remembering Details

Write a word from the story in each space.

"Do you know how fast a ________________ can run?"

There in the ________________ field is a big cougar.

I can't ________________ I am seeing it.

They hold the ________________ out to her.

Putting Ideas in Order

Here are three sentences from the story. Write them in the order that they happened.

The man and the woman close up the back of the truck fast.

"I want to go find the cougar!"

Mu Lan and I are looking at the baseball game on TV.

____

____

____

____

____

____

____

____

____

____

49

Worktext page 49

LESSON 2.13

OBJECTIVES

- Students will learn new words containing the *ow* and *ave* phonograms and vowel pairs
- Students will apply endings *s, n, ed, ing, er,* and *est* to base words to form new words
- Students will recognize and form compound words
- Students will decode words using word parts

PHONICS VOCABULARY

fishing	closer	lighter	fished	days
looking	looks	getting	another	going
biggest	waves	gets	bigger	take
says	three	sea	throws	boat
lines	away	hitting	throw	wave
starts	thrown	smashing	throwing	
champions		championship		

WORDS TO KNOW

throw	wave	sea	boat	fish
our	line	ship	some	dark
ever	worth	three	Cruz	champion

MATERIALS

Worktext 2, pages 50–54
Teacher's Manual, pages 127–129
Practice Lesson 2.13, pages 90–91 of the Worktext

TEACH

- Using Worktext pages 50–51, introduce students to the vocabulary words. Give them an opportunity to practice writing the words.
- Students can organize their Memory Chips, found in the back of the Worktext. They can sort the words according to those words they know and those they don't. You may wish to say each word, having students repeat it after you. Then have them work with a partner, saying each word and using it in a sentence.

Worktext pages 50–51 can also be used to reinforce spelling. Use the five-step process detailed on page 71 of this *Teacher's Manual.*

Phonograms *ow, ave*

Write this sentence on the board and read it aloud: **I know I gave the football to Sam.** Ask a volunteer to point to *know.*

Blending Circle *ow,* and tell students these letters can have the sound of long *o.* Write **know** on the board. Have students take turns substituting *gr, b,* and *t* for the *kn,* blending each word. Write each new word on the board as it is suggested. Repeat the procedure with the phonogram *ave,* using the word *gave* from the sentence on the board, and substituting other consonants for *g.*

know	gave
grow	save
bow	pave
tow	Dave

Vowel Pairs

Write this sentence on the board: **We are in a boat in the sea.** Point to *boat* and *sea.* Have students circle the vowels in each word. Ask students what vowel sounds they hear in boat and sea. (*long* o, *long* e) Explain that usually when they see two vowels together, the first one is long, and the second is silent.

Blending Write these words on the board and have volunteers take turns substituting beginning and ending consonants to make new words: **sea**, **boat**. (For example: *sea, seat, beat, feat, heat*; *boat, coat, goat, goal*)

Endings *s, n, ed, ing, er, est*

Remind students they can add the endings *s, n, ed, ing, er,* and *est* to words. When a word ends in *e,* the *e* is dropped and the ending *ed, ing, er,* or *est* is added. If a word ends in a consonant, students might have to double the consonant and add the ending.

Make New Words Write a chart like the one below on the board, and have students add the endings *s, n, ed, ing, er,* and *est* to the words. Have students choose one word with an ending to use in a sentence.

Base Word	+ s	+ n	+ ed	+ ing	+ er	+est
big					bigger	biggest
close	closes		closed	closing	closer	closest
fish			fished	fishing	fisher	
take	takes	taken		taking	taker	
wave	waves		waved	waving	waver	
line	lines		lined	lining	liner	

Compound Words

Remind students that two smaller words can be put together to make a new word. Write the words **into** and **snowball** and ask students what two smaller words they see in each compound word. (*in, to, snow, ball*)

Level 2

Make New Words Write these words on index cards, and have students put them together to make new words: **a**, **way**, **may**, **be**, **champion**, **ship**, **an**, **other**, **base**, **ball**. They can use each new word in a sentence.

PRACTICE

- Let students practice the new words they have learned and formed by completing the activities on pages 50–52 of the Worktext.
- If students are experiencing difficulty with the Words to Know section on pages 50–51, place the Memory Chips on the table. Pose riddles like this for each word: **This word has four letters and ends with the sound /z/.** (*Cruz*)

For further practice, have students complete Practice Lesson 2.13 on pages 90–91 of the Worktext. Answers can be found in the Answer Key on page 351 of this *Teacher's Manual.*

APPLY

- Have students talk about the story concept by discussing things they have experienced. Ask: **How do you think it would feel to be very good at something? What would you feel if you were close to breaking a record at doing something you do well?** Tell students they are going to use the words they have learned to read a short story about a family that places itself in danger to break a record.
- Ask students to read the story on page 53 in the Worktext. Offer assistance if necessary, but encourage students to decode the words independently, using the clues and patterns they have learned.
- After students have completed reading the story, have them work together with a partner or small group to complete the Making Predictions activity on page 54 of their Worktext. Answers can be found in the Answer Key on page 350 of this *Teacher's Manual.*

CONNECTION

Writing Students should be encouraged to keep a journal of their writings. They can use these journals to record responses to their reading, list new words they have learned, or record their thoughts and feelings about the reading selections. This can be done on the Response to Reading pages in each Worktext before the Memory Chips or in a separate notebook.

Worktext Pages 50–51

13. THE FISHING CHAMPIONSHIP

Word Attack

+ow You know the words **snow** and **know**. What sound do the letters **ow** make in these words? What word do you get if you put **thr** in front of **ow**? Write the words on the lines. Then circle the letter group **ow** in each word.

snow ____________ know ____________

throw ____________

+ave You know the word **gave**. What sound do the letters **ave** make in this word? Try putting **w** in front of those letters. What word do you get? Write the words on the lines. Then circle the letter group **ave** in each word.

gave ____________ wave ____________

vowels What do you know about the sounds of two vowels when they are side by side in a word? Often, the first vowel says its own name and the second vowel is silent. Using this rule, try to figure out the following two words.

sea ____________ boat ____________

Circle the vowel in each word that says its own name. Draw an **X** across the silent vowel in each word. Write each word on the line.

Words to Know

	Look	Say	Picture	Write
throw	☐	☐	☐	____________
wave	☐	☐	☐	____________
sea	☐	☐	☐	____________
boat	☐	☐	☐	____________
fish	☐	☐	☐	____________

50

Worktext page 50

	Look	Say	Picture	Write
our	☐	☐	☐	____________
line	☐	☐	☐	____________
ship	☐	☐	☐	____________
some	☐	☐	☐	____________
dark	☐	☐	☐	____________
ever	☐	☐	☐	____________
worth	☐	☐	☐	____________
three	☐	☐	☐	____________
Cruz	☐	☐	☐	____________
champion cham-pi-on	☐	☐	☐	____________

Word Attack

+s Write each of these words with **s** endings.

day ____________ wave ____________

line ____________ start ____________

throw ____________ champion ____________

+n Write each of these words with an **n** ending.

take ____________ throw ____________

+ed Write **fish** with an **ed** ending. ____________

+ing Write each of these words with an **ing** ending.

fish ____________ smash ____________

throw ____________

+er Write **light** with an **er** ending. ____________

51

Worktext page 51

The word **close** already has **e** on the end. So just add **r**: **closer**. Write **close** with an **er** ending.

close ____________________

+est Write the word **big** with an **est** ending. First, you have to double the **g**: **biggest**.

big ____________________

Now write **big** in the first sentence and **biggest** in the second sentence.

That is a ____________________ car.

He is the ____________________ player on the team.

2=1 You know the word **a**, and you know the word **way**. Write these two words together to make one word: **away**. Write the new word in the following sentence.

He is going to go ____________________.

Now circle each of the two shorter words in the word you wrote.

You know the word **an**, and you know the word **other**. You can write these two words together to make one word: **another**. Write the new word in the following sentence.

Give her ____________________ bike.

Now circle each of the two shorter words in the word you wrote.

You know the words **champion** and **ship**. Put the two words together to make one word: **championship**. Write the new word in the sentence.

We are a ____________________ baseball team.

Now circle each of the two shorter words in the word you wrote.

52

Worktext page 52

13. THE FISHING CHAMPIONSHIP

My family, the Cruz family, is into fishing. My dad, his dad, and **his** dad all fished. We have a fishing boat. My dad goes out most days. I go out on the days I'm not in school.

One Saturday, I go out with my dad and sister. The fishing is hot. I take in fish after fish. They are all **big**. We don't want to stop fishing. But Dad keeps looking up at the sun. Then he looks out at the sea.

"It's getting dark," he says. "And it's just 1:00."

Just then, my sister takes in another big one.

"We can't stop," I say. "This is going to be one of our biggest days. **Ever**."

The sea looks dark. Waves smash up on the boat. I take in another big fish. Dad puts his line in. He gets another one.

The waves are getting bigger and bigger. I can see a small ship out on the sea. It is a long way away. The waves are hitting it hard.

"Your mom will not like this," Dad says. "We have to go in. It's just not worth it."

My sister looks over all the fish we have taken in. "Just three more fish," she says, "and it will be our biggest fishing day."

"Come on, Dad," I say. "We **have** to go for it."

"OK," Dad says. "The one who gets the most of the next three fish is the champion."

We all put in our lines. I get one. My sister gets one. My dad gets one.

"We did it!" I say. "The biggest fishing day ever! It's the fishing championship!"

"OK, we are all champions," Dad says, but he does not look happy. He is looking at the dark sea. "We have to get going," he says.

More waves smash up over the boat. The sea throws the boat one way and then the other way. Dad can't make the boat go the way he wants. I am scared we will go over.

Some champions we are!

53

Worktext page 53

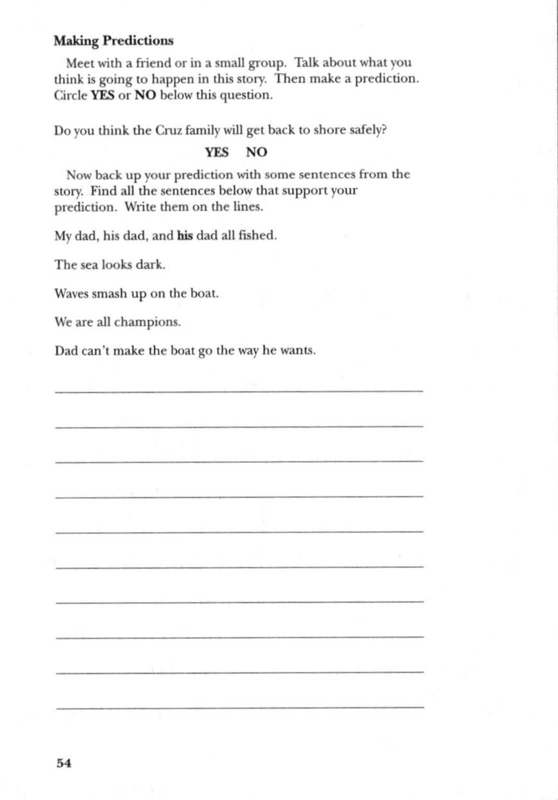

Making Predictions

Meet with a friend or in a small group. Talk about what you think is going to happen in this story. Then make a prediction. Circle **YES** or **NO** below this question.

Do you think the Cruz family will get back to shore safely?

YES NO

Now back up your prediction with some sentences from the story. Find all the sentences below that support your prediction. Write them on the lines.

My dad, his dad, and **his** dad all fished.

The sea looks dark.

Waves smash up on the boat.

We are all champions.

Dad can't make the boat go the way he wants.

____

____

____

____

____

____

____

____

____

____

54

Worktext page 54

LESSON 2.14

OBJECTIVE

- Students will practice and apply skills to an extended passage

MATERIALS

Worktext 2, pages 55–57
Teacher's Manual, pages 130–131, 330–331
Practice Lesson 2.14, pages 92–93 of the Worktext

SKILLS REVIEW

- Before reading, you may wish to review these words that apply phonics skills: *screams, comes, sea, wave, thrown, trying, boat, going, see, says, scream, waves, closer, smashing, kids, throwing, getting, wait, bigger, thinking, coming, lighter, takes, holds, championship, forget.* Then ask: **What would you do if a boat you were in was caught in a bad storm?**
- While reading, have students think about how the characters are feeling during the storm.
- After reading, have students complete the exercises on Worktext page 57.

PRACTICE For further practice, have students complete Practice Lesson 2.14 on pages 92–93 of the Worktext. Answers can be found in the Answer Key on page 351 of this *Teacher's Manual.*

RETEACH

If students need further review of phonics skills, you may wish to use the following activity:

Endings *est, er, n, s, ing, ed*

Scavenger Hunt Divide the class into small groups. Write the following clues on paper, and have groups find objects that satisfy each clue. Then gather groups together and have them identify each object with its matching clue. The group with the most objects wins.

- This likes to be thrown.
- This is lighter than a pen.
- This is the lightest thing in the class.
- This is the biggest pencil.
- This is the smallest pencil.
- This is the closest thing to the window.
- This starts a ballgame.
- You can wave this.
- This has lines on it.
- This shows the days in the week.

CONNECTION

Response to Reading

- To reinforce students' understanding of the literary elements found in their reading material, have them complete the Story Map and Character Cluster reproducibles found on pages 330–331.
- Students will demonstrate an understanding of setting, characters, and plot by filling out the organizers.
- Students may share their completed organizers with the class.

Level 2

14. THE BIG WAVE

"Get your sister!" my dad screams as a big wave comes over the boat. I get her and hold on. All of our fish get thrown back into the sea by the wave. Dad is trying to keep the boat from going over.

"We have to get that ship to see us!" my sister says. I look up at the ship. It is just a big boat. I don't think they can help us. But I try to scream to the people on it.

"They can't hear you," my dad says. He waves a big light. The people on the big boat see the light. The boat starts to come closer. I can see the people on it. They come out and scream at us. I can't hear them. The sea keeps smashing up on our little boat.

Dad says, "I think they want us to come up on the boat. You kids go. They are throwing a line to you. But I am not getting off our boat."

"Dad, you can't wait this out!" my sister says. "The waves are getting bigger."

"This boat is all I have. It was my dad's boat," he says. "I am not getting off it. Do what I tell you. Get on that big boat."

55

Worktext page 55

The people on the boat keep trying to throw us a line. But we can't get close to the other boat. The waves keep smashing us away. The line does not make it onto our boat.

"They will call for help," Dad says as the boat goes off. "All we can do is wait."

Over and over, we get hit by big waves. I keep thinking, *This is it. We are going over.* But the boat does not go over. A long time goes by. We try to take shelter where we can.

Then after a long time, the waves stop coming over the boat. I feel light on my back. I look and see the sun! The sea gets lighter.

Dad takes hold of my sister and me. He holds us close. We can't believe what a close call that was.

Then my dad says, "No championship is worth what we just did. We lost all the fish. And I just about lost you. Don't ever forget this day. Do you hear me?"

My sister and I tell him that we will not forget this day. Then we start to take the boat back home where we know Mom is going to be **mad**.

56

Worktext page 56

What Do You Think?

Meet with a friend or in a small group. Talk about the father in this story. He was not going to leave his boat, no matter what. What do you think about his position? Explain your point of view.

Finding the Main Idea

Write the sentence that best says what the whole story is about.

This boat is all he has.

I feel light on my back.

No championship is worth being thrown into the sea.

____

____

____

____

____

Read It Again

Read again the stories on pages **37–38** and **40–41** called **Sleeping in the Baseball Field** and **The Bank Window**. Then read these sentences. Choose the best answer (**a**, **b**, or **c**), and write the words on the line.

The little boy holds onto the ________________.
(a) window (b) snow bank (c) baseball

Maybe the man and the woman lost their ________________.
(a) girl (b) jobs (c) home

They already gave the bank money for the ________________.
(a) apartment (b) window (c) dinner

It takes a long time to get money for ________________.
(a) an apartment (b) a car (c) a baseball

57

Worktext page 57

LESSON 2.15

OBJECTIVES

- Students will learn new words containing the *ack* phonogram and vowel pairs
- Students will apply endings *s, es, ing, ly,* and *ed* to base words to form new words
- Students will recognize and form contractions

PHONICS VOCABULARY

I'm	getting	says	you're	screams
really	throwing	don't	making	married
can't	asks	Mack	real	looking
marrying	meet	beach	times	seen
doing	smiles	knows	hardly	telling
going	I'll	what's	runs	classes
crying	passing	waving		

WORDS TO KNOW

Mack	beach	real	marry	only
how	many	smile	cry	ask
good	pass	Robin		

MATERIALS

Worktext 2, pages 58–62
Teacher's Manual, pages 132–134
Practice Lesson 2.15, pages 94–95 of the Worktext

TEACH

- Using Worktext page 59, introduce students to the vocabulary words. Give them an opportunity to practice writing the words.
- Students can organize their Memory Chips, found in the back of the Worktext. You may wish to say each word, having students repeat it after you.

Worktext page 59 can also be used to reinforce spelling. Use the five-step process detailed on page 71 in this *Teacher's Manual.*

Phonogram *ack*

Write this sentence on the board and read it aloud: **I gave the backpack back to Mack.** Ask a volunteer to point to the words that rhyme with Mack. (*back, backpack*) Then have them circle **ack** in each word.

Blending Write **ack**, modeling how to blend the sounds: /*ak*/. Add a *b* in front of the phonogram. Then have students take turns making new words by adding different beginning consonants.

back tack sack pack rack

Vowel Pairs

Write this sentence on the board: **The beach is by the sea.** Point to *beach* and *sea.* Have students circle the vowels in each word. Ask students what vowel sounds they hear. (*long* e) Explain that often when they see two vowels together, the first one is long and the second is silent.

Blending Write **sea** on the board. Then ask a volunteer to add *t* to the end and blend the new word. Continue the word ladder, having students substitute the *b* for *s, ch* for *t,* and *p* for *b.*

sea seat beat beach peach

Endings *s, es, ing, ly, ed*

Tell students that when a word ends in *ss, s,* and *x,* they add *es* to a word instead of just *s.* Write **class**, **bus**, and **box** on the board. Have volunteers add **es** to each word. Write **marry** on the board. Cross out the **y** and add **ies**. Tell students that when some words end in *y*, the *y* is changed to *i*, and the ending is added. Ask a volunteer to form the word *married.*

Make New Words Write these endings and words on word cards, and have partners take turns making new words: **s**, **es**, **ing**, **ly**, **ed**, **carry**, **wave**, **real**, **hard**, **part**, **cry**, **pass**, **class**, **box**, **smile**. One student can make the new word with the cards and the partner can write it. Remind them to drop the *e* when they add *ing* and *ed* and to change the *y* to *i* and add *es* or *ed.*

Contractions

Remind students you can put together two words to make a shorter word. Write **you are** on the board, take out the *a*, and replace it with an apostrophe. (*you're*) Repeat with **what is**. (*what's*)

Make New Words Write these word pairs on the board and have students make contractions with each: **you are**, **what is**, **do not**, **I am**, **I will**. They can use each new word in a sentence.

PRACTICE

- Let students practice the new words they have learned and formed by completing the activities on pages 58–60 of the Worktext.
- If students are experiencing difficulty with the Words to Know section on page 59, place the Memory Chips on the table. Say a sentence with a missing word and have students choose a Memory Chip to complete it. For example: **We had a picnic at the _____.** (*beach*)

For further practice, have students complete Practice Lesson 2.15 on pages 94–95 of the Worktext. Answers can be found in the Answer Key on page 351 of this *Teacher's Manual.*

APPLY

- Have students talk about the story concept by discussing things they have experienced. Ask: **Have you ever had a friend or relative get married? How did you feel about it?** Tell them they are going to use the words they have learned to read a short story about a girl who wants to get married.
- Ask students to read the story on page 61 in the Worktext. Offer assistance if necessary, but encourage students to decode the words independently, using the clues and patterns they have learned.
- After students have completed reading the story, have them complete the Cooperative Group Activity (What Do You Think?) and Comprehension Exercises (Remembering Details and Putting Ideas in Order) on page 62 in their Worktext. Answers can be found in the Answer Key on page 350 of this *Teacher's Manual.*

CONNECTION

Speaking/Listening Student partners can read aloud the selection "Robin is Getting Married" on Worktext page 61. The partners can alternate being speaker and listener.

Strategy for Reading Have students reread the story to correct comprehension breakdowns. Students may achieve understanding by reprocessing the same text with greater attention focused on its meaning.

Worktext Pages 58–59

Level 2

15. ROBIN IS GETTING MARRIED

Word Attack

ack You know the words **back** and **pack**. What sound does the letter **m** make? What word do you make if you change the **p** in **pack** to **M**? If you said **Mack**, you were right. Circle the letter group **ack** in each word. Then write the words.

back ______ pack ______

Mack ______

vowels What do you know about the sounds of two vowels when they are side by side in a word? Often, the first vowel says its own name, and the second vowel is silent. Using this rule, try to figure out the following two words.

beach ______ real ______

Circle the vowel in each word that says its own name. Draw an **X** across the silent vowel in each word. Write each word on the line.

1+1 You know the words **you** and **are**. You can put these two words together to get the word **you're**. Write **you are** in the first sentence. Write **you're** in the second sentence.

______ ______ a real help.

______ no help at all.

Which letter is dropped to make **you are** into **you're**? ______

You also know the words **what** and **is**. Put these two words together to make **what's**. Write **what is** in the first sentence. Write **what's** in the second sentence.

______ ______ your problem?

______ going on in there?

Which letter is dropped to make **what is** into **what's**? ______

58

Worktext page 58

Words to Know

	Look	Say	Picture	Write
Mack	☐	☐	☐	______
beach	☐	☐	☐	______
real	☐	☐	☐	______
marry mar-ry	☐	☐	☐	______
only on-ly	☐	☐	☐	______
how	☐	☐	☐	______
many ma-ny	☐	☐	☐	______
smile	☐	☐	☐	______
cry	☐	☐	☐	______
ask	☐	☐	☐	______
good	☐	☐	☐	______
pass	☐	☐	☐	______
Robin Rob-in	☐	☐	☐	______

Word Attack

+s Write each of these words with an **s** ending.

time ______ ask ______

smile ______

+es Write **class** with an **es** ending.

class ______

59

Worktext page 59

+ing Write each of these words with an **ing** ending.

marry ________________ cry ________________

pass ________________

To write **wave** with an **ing** ending, you have to drop the **e**: **waving**. Write **wave** with an **ing** ending.

wave ________________

+ly Write each word with an **ly** ending. Even though the first word ends with an **l**, add another one.

real ________________ hard ________________

+ed When words end with a **y**, you have to change the **y** to an **i** before adding an ending. Look at the following endings in the word **marry**.

marry marr**ies** marr**ied**

Write **marry**, **marries**, or **married** in each sentence.

I want to ________________ her.

She ________________ him for money.

I am getting ________________ next week.

60

Worktext page 60

15. ROBIN IS GETTING MARRIED

"You're **what**?" I say to Robin, my sister.

"I'm getting married," she says.

"You're only 16," screams Kate. "That is **really** stupid!"

"You're throwing it all away!" I call out.

"Don't do it!" Kate says.

My sister Robin is 16. I am 18. It is a Saturday night. Mom is out. Kate is over, and we are making some dinner. Then Robin says she is getting married! I can't believe it!

"Who is the man?" asks Kate.

"Mack," Robin says. "And he is **real** good-looking."

"It will pass," Kate says. "Don't go marrying some boy just because he is good-looking!"

"Mack?" I say. "Where did you meet this Mack?"

"At the beach," she says.

"How many times have you seen him?" Kate asks.

"One time. What's it to you?"

"You don't know this boy," I say. "What are you doing this for?"

"I know what I'm doing," Robin says. She smiles like she is happy. But how can she be happy about marrying a man she hardly knows?

"I'm telling Mom," I say. "Then I'm going to call Dad and tell him." Our dad does not live with us, but I call him all the time.

"Try it," my sister says. "I'll already be married. We are doing it next Saturday."

Kate and I look at each other. "Robin," I say, "do you need our help? What's going on?"

"What's going on," says Robin, "is that I'm getting married. No one can stop me."

Then she starts to cry and runs out of the apartment.

61

Worktext page 61

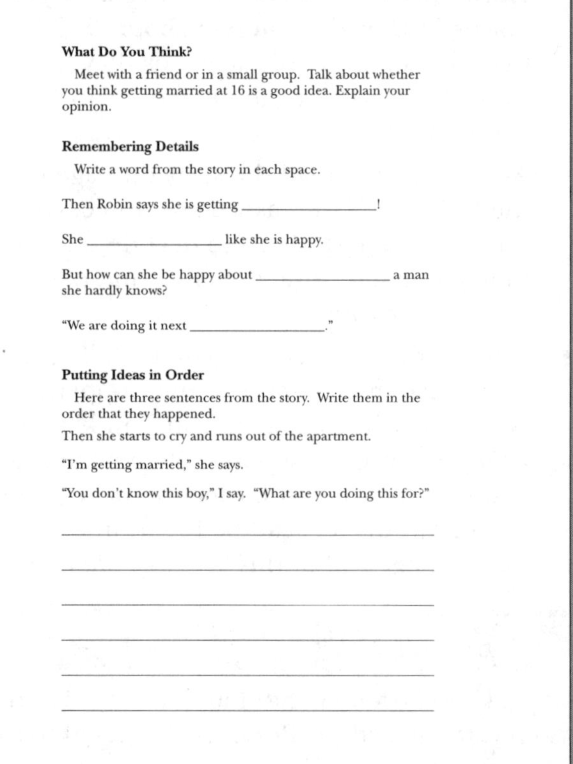

What Do You Think?

Meet with a friend or in a small group. Talk about whether you think getting married at 16 is a good idea. Explain your opinion.

Remembering Details

Write a word from the story in each space.

Then Robin says she is getting ________________!

She ________________ like she is happy.

But how can she be happy about ________________ a man she hardly knows?

"We are doing it next ________________."

Putting Ideas in Order

Here are three sentences from the story. Write them in the order that they happened.

Then she starts to cry and runs out of the apartment.

"I'm getting married," she says.

"You don't know this boy," I say. "What are you doing this for?"

____

____

____

____

____

____

62

Worktext page 62

LESSON 2.16

OBJECTIVE

- Students will practice and apply skills to an extended passage

MATERIALS

Worktext 2, pages 63–65
Teacher's Manual, pages 135–136, 330–331
Practice Lesson 2.16, pages 96–97 of the Worktext
Tagboard, brad/fastener (Reteach)

SKILLS REVIEW

- Before reading, you may wish to review these words that apply phonics skills: *taking, Mack, meet, meeting, beach, feel, don't, sea, wait, coming, smiles, says, looking, waves, looks, waving, tells, wanted, walking, doesn't, walks, starts, crying, didn't, classes, real, married, trying, passing, getting, passed, I'll, going.* Have students review the Memory Chips they have learned so far. Then ask: **Why do you think Robin wants to get married?**
- While reading, have students think about which character they would like to have for a friend, Robin or her sibling.
- After reading, have students complete the exercises on Worktext page 65.

For further practice, have students complete Practice Lesson 2.16 on pages 96–97 of the Worktext. Answers can be found in the Answer Key on page 351 of this *Teacher's Manual.*

RETEACH

If students need further review of phonics skills, you may wish to use the following activity:

Endings *ing, ly, ed, ing, es, s*

It All Adds Up: Make a spinner out of tagboard that has a wheel and an arrow. Write the following endings on the wheel: **s**, **es**, **ing**, **ly**, **ed**. Write these words on index cards, and place in a stack face down: **marry**, **real**, **hard**, **wave**, **pass**, **cry**, **time**, **smile**, **ask**, **class**. Have students take turns spinning the wheel and choosing a card from the top of the stack. If the word card they choose makes a word with the ending from the wheel, they write the word and get a point. If not, they lose a turn. At the end of the game, the student with the most words wins.

CONNECTION

Response to Reading

- To reinforce students' understanding of the literary elements found in their reading material, have them complete the Story Map and Character Cluster reproducibles found on pages 330–331.
- Students will demonstrate an understanding of setting, characters, and plot by filling out the organizers.
- Students may share their completed organizers with the class.

Independent Reading

- Encourage students to read for pleasure. Pearson's *Reading Explorations,* Levels A and B, cover social studies, science, math, and life-skills topics in an easy-to-read format. For ESL students, vocabulary words are listed and defined before each reading. Comprehension and critical thinking questions appear throughout the texts to encourage active reading. See page xvii of this *Teacher's Manual* for additional titles.
- After reading, students may form small groups to informally share what they learned.

16. MEETING MACK

The next day, I talk Robin into taking me to meet Mack. She says she is meeting him at the beach.

I go to the beach with my sister. I feel a little scared. *Who is this Mack? What if I don't like him?* It is a hot day. We walk by the sea and wait for Mack.

I see a man coming up the beach. He looks old, about 60. He smiles at us. "Is that Mack?" I ask Robin.

She smiles, and I think, *It is Mack*!

But then she says, "No."

More time goes by. Then I see a big, good-looking man coming up the beach. This man waves at us. Robin is looking out at the sea. She does not see him.

"Robin!" I say taking hold of her. "There he is! Mack is over there!" This man is really good-looking. I feel happy for Robin. I forget she is only 16.

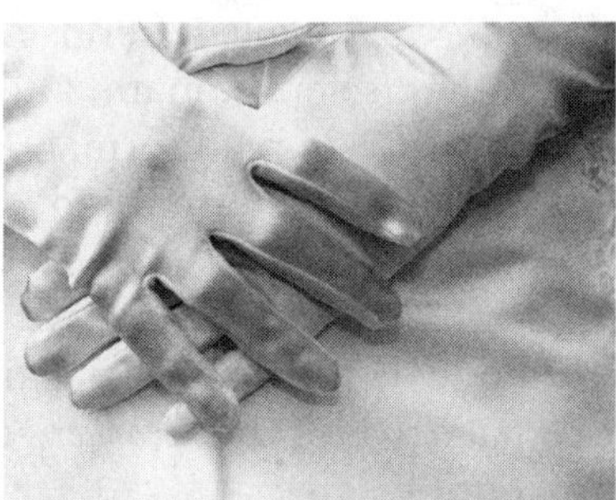

63

Worktext page 63

Robin looks at the man who is waving. "Don't wave back at that man!" she tells me. "We don't know him. That is not Mack."

I feel bad. I wanted that good-looking man to be Mack. We keep walking on the beach. "Where is Mack?" I say to Robin.

"He will be coming," Robin says. But she doesn't look at me.

Then I see a boy who looks about 16 or 17. He does not smile at us. But he is walking our way. I wait for Robin to run up to him. The boy walks on by without looking at us.

I take hold of Robin. I make her look at me. I say, "Where is Mack? I don't believe there is a Mack."

Robin starts crying.

"What is it?" I ask.

Then she tells me. "I didn't pass three of my classes. I want out of school! Mack is not real. But I wanted to believe in him. I just want to get married and run away!"

I take Robin up the beach to get a cold soft drink. I am trying to think what to say. Not passing three classes is really bad. After a long time, I say, "I know how you feel. School can be really hard. But getting married is not going to help."

"I know," Robin says. I don't know what Mom is going to say." Then she starts to cry some more. "Can you believe I only passed three of my classes!"

I hold my sister. I say, "I'll talk to Mom. We can work this out. You will see." But I know that Robin is going to feel bad for a long, long time.

64

Worktext page 64

What Do You Think?

Meet with a friend or in a small group. Talk about how it feels to fail at something. If you were Robin, how might you begin to solve the problem she has? If you were Robin's sister, how might you help her?

Finding the Main Idea

Write the sentence that best says what the whole story is about.

Robin makes up Mack because she doesn't want to think about school.

I wanted that good-looking man to be Mack.

I take Robin up the beach to get a cold soft drink.

____

____

____

____

____

65

Worktext page 65

FINAL NOVEL Stolen Chances

MATERIALS
Final Novel 2, *Stolen Chances*
Teacher's Manual, page 137
Assessment Manual, Final Assessment 2, pages 74–77

Summary *Will's baseball team is trying to win the championship, but he has to quit to get a job. His boss is trying to keep Will from playing so that his son will look better. Then Mike's sister disappears. Will and Mike are able to find her and make it back in time to win the championship.*

REVIEW AND ASSESSMENT

- Have students review their Memory Chips for Level 2 with a partner. Tell students they will also encounter the word *too* in the novel, *Stolen Chances.* Depending on your students' needs, review the following skills covered in Lessons 9–16: compound words; contractions; vowel pairs (CVVC); phonograms *un, art, and, ow, ave,* and *ack;* and endings *s, ing, ed, less, n, en, er, est,* and *ly.*

INTRODUCE THE NOVEL

Invite students to preview the book by reading the title, looking at the illustrations, and reading the captions aloud. Begin a discussion of story concepts by asking:

- **What is it like playing on a sports team?**
- **What is more important, playing on a team, or having a good-paying job?**

If you wish to assess students progress at this point, use *Assessment Manual,* pages 74–77. For students who need additional support, you may use the Reteach activities from previous lessons.

CHECK COMPREHENSION

Chapter 1 Why does Will quit the team? (*He can't play and have a job, and he needs the money to go to college.*)

Chapter 2 What do you think the note means that Will finds in the back of the shop? (*Dan Ramos wants to stop Will from playing, so the Cougars can't win the championship.*)

Chapter 3 What advice does Robin give Will? (*She says to forget the note, forget the call, and keep the job.*)

Chapter 4 What do you think Will should do now? (*Most students will say he should play in the championship game; others may say he should stay with the job.*)

Chapter 5 What does Will tell Dan Ramos? (*He tells him he is quitting because he has another job.*)

Chapter 6 What does Coach say when Will says he wants back on the team? (*He agrees to let him play, but says he has to practice a lot in the next week.*)

Chapter 7 Why is Mike feeling bad? (*His mother and father are having problems at home.*)

Chapter 8 What do Will and Mike do when Robin disappears? (*They call the cops.*)

Chapter 9 What do Will and Mike do to find Robin? (*They go to Kate's house to see if she knows where she is.*)

Chapter 10 What does Dan Ramos tell Will about Robin? (*He tells Will that Robin called and is at Snow Pass.*)

Chapter 11 What happens after Will and Mike get to Snow Pass? (*They find an empty shelter. It starts to snow, and they decide to spend the night there.*)

Chapter 12 Where do you think Robin is? (*Students will probably say she is at Mrs. Cook's beach house.*)

Chapter 13 What kind of person is Dan Ramos? How do you know? (*He lies because he told Will that Robin was at Snow Pass. He will do anything to get Will and Mike out of the championship game.*)

Chapter 14 Why is Will so happy before the game? (*His dad made it back to see the game.*)

Chapter 15 How do Will and Mike decide to get back at the Ramoses? (*They decide they will win the championship.*)

Chapter 16 Who do you think will win the championship? (*Most students might say the Cougars; others might say the Dogs will win.*)

Chapter 17 Why does Mike hit the ball to win the game? (*He hears Dan Ramos screaming that he can't hit the ball.*)

Chapter 18 What makes Will happy after the championship game? (*His dad announces that he has a new job that won't make him be away from home all the time.*)

CONNECTION

Home/School Encourage students to bring home a copy of *Stolen Chances.* They might read the novel, or sections of the novel, to family members.

LEVEL 3

ORGANIZER

Level 3 of the *Caught Reading* program includes the following components:

Worktext 3

Worktext 3 includes 17 lessons, taking students from those words introduced in previous levels through a word list of 181 words (found on page 340 of this *Teacher's Manual*) by Lesson 17. The Practice Lessons provide students with opportunites to extend practice, and review the content of each lesson. The Response to Reading pages allow students to practice using their new vocabulary. Tear-out Memory Chips in the back of the student book reinforce new vocabulary and can be used both independently by students and in small groups.

Midway and Final Novels 3

These novels are designed to reinforce learned vocabulary and give students the opportunity to read for meaning. Their high-interest plots encourage successful reading experiences and an appreciation for literature.

- *High Stakes* includes only vocabulary students have learned up to the midway point of this level.
- *The $22,000 Problem* includes all vocabulary learned through Level 3.

Teacher's Manual

The *Teacher's Manual* provides detailed objectives and instruction for each skill taught in the Worktext, as well as additional teaching suggestions for meaningful practice and reinforcement. The *Teacher's Manual* provides choices for flexible instruction. Comprehension questions for the Midway and Final novels are included, as well as Answer Keys for the Worktext activities and the Practice Lessons.

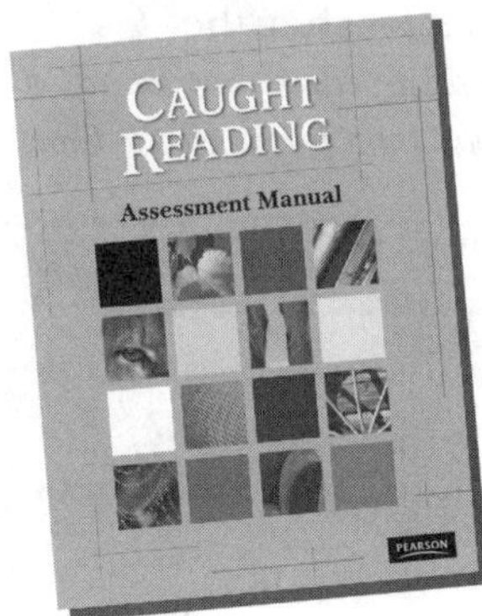

Assessment Manual

The *Assessment Manual* provides preassessment, ongoing assessment, and postassessment to administer to students throughout their work in *Caught Reading*. Within this Manual you will also find Midway and Final Assessments to determine the students' comprehension of the Midway and Final Novels.

OBJECTIVES

Vocabulary Development

- Read a base vocabulary, plus base vocabulary words with various endings, compound words, and contractions formed from base words.
- Use the word learning sequence to remember and spell words correctly.
- Review vocabulary independently, both in and out of context, using the Memory Chips.

Phonics

- Use context clues to decode words.
- Read the contractions *isn't, he's, let's, that's,* and *she's.*
- Recognize the letter groups *it, et, ast, etter, uy, ace, ind, ould, ame, ile, ust, art, ad,* and *afe.*
- Use the vowel generalization: When the last three letters in a word are a vowel, a consonant, and an *e,* then the vowel has the long sound, and the *e* is silent.

Reading Comprehension

- Remember the main idea and details from a story.
- Read instructional material independently.

Literary Analysis

- Determine the underlying theme or author's message in fiction.
- Identify the speaker or narrator in a selection.

Writing

- Write descriptions of people, places, and events in the story.
- Write responses to stories in journals.

Speaking and Listening

- Use descriptive words when speaking about people, places, things, and events.
- Retell the central ideas of simple narrative passages.

INTRODUCTION & LESSON 3.1

OBJECTIVES

- Students will learn new words containing the *old, ame, ight,* and *it* phonograms
- Students will apply endings *s* and *es* to base words to form new words
- Students will recognize and form compound words
- Students will recognize and form possessives with an apostrophe and *s*

PHONICS VOCABULARY

boxes	comes	things	sits	asks
gets	walks	leaves	calls	forget
keeps	takes	thinks	runs	needs
without	Tom's	knows	opens	something
looks	someone	letters	groups	sentences
sounds	words			

WORDS TO KNOW

as	box	down	has	here
leave	name	old	open	or
right	same	sit	thing	attack
below	circle	group	letter	read
game	sentence	sound	story	together
these	word	write	introduction	

MATERIALS

Worktext 3, pages 4–9
Teacher's Manual, pages 140–142
Practice Lesson 3.1, pages 66–67 of the Worktext

TEACH

- Before you begin Worktext pages 6–9, have students complete pages 4–5 independently.
- Using Worktext page 7, introduce students to the vocabulary words. Give them an opportunity to practice writing the words.
- Students can organize their Memory Chips, found in the back of the Worktext. You may wish to say each word, having students repeat it after you. Students can take turns using each word in a sentence.

Worktext page 7 can also be used to reinforce spelling. Use the five-step process detailed on page 71 of this *Teacher's Manual.*

Phonograms *old, ame, ight, it*

Write these sentences on the board and read them aloud: **The old man did not know his name last night. It was Tom.** Ask a volunteer to point to *night.*

Blending Circle *igh* and tell students that these letters make the long *i* sound. Ask them which letters are silent. (*gh*) Model how to blend the sounds: /n/ /ī/ /t/. Write **night** on the board. Have students take turns substituting *br, l, s,* and *t* for the *n,* blending each word. Write each new word on the board as it is suggested by the students. Repeat, using *ame* in *name, old,* and *it* from the sentences above.

old	game	night	it
gold	lame	light	fit
told	tame	tight	kit
fold	same	sight	pit

Endings *s, es*

Write this sentence on the board: **Tom sits on the boxes.** Point to *sits,* and ask students to identify the ending. (*s*) Point to *boxes,* and ask them to identify its ending. (*es*) Remind students that when words end in *s, x, ch, sh,* and *ss,* then *es* is added as the ending.

Make New Words Make a chart like the one below, and have students add the ending *s* or *es* to the words.

Base Word	+s or +es
class	classes
sit	sits
fox	foxes
leave	leaves
fish	fishes

Compound Words

Remind students that two smaller words can be put together to make a new word. Write these two words on the board: **no thing**. Have students put the two words together to make a new word. (*nothing*)

Make New Words Write these words on index cards and have students put them together to make new words: **some**, **one**, **no**, **thing**. They can write each new word on a separate piece of paper. *(someone, nothing, something)*

Possessives

Write these sentences on the board and read them aloud: **Tom has a car. The car is Tom's.** Ask students to point to *Tom* and *Tom's* and tell how they are different. Tell them that *Tom's* means something that belongs to Tom. Ask them what belongs to Tom. (*the car*) Ask them what is added to *Tom* to show possession. (*apostrophe and* s)

Make New Words Have students add an apostrophe and *s* to these words and then use each one in a sentence: *Tom, Kay, boy, teacher. (Tom's, Kay's, boy's, teacher's)*

PRACTICE

- Let students practice the new words they have learned and formed by completing the activities found on pages 6–7 of the Worktext.
- If students are experiencing difficulty with the Words to Know section on page 7, place the Memory Chips on the table. Write incomplete words on the board and have students use the Memory Chips to complete them. For example: **o _ _ n** (*open*)

For further practice, have students complete Practice Lesson 3.1 on pages 66–67 of the Worktext. Answers can be found in the Answer Key on page 352 of this *Teacher's Manual.*

APPLY

- Have students talk about the story concept by discussing things they have experienced. Ask: **Have you ever found something that didn't belong to you? What did you do with it?** Tell them they are going to use the words they have learned to read a short story about a boy who finds a mysterious box at a bus stop.
- Ask students to read the story on page 8 in the Worktext. Offer assistance if necessary, but encourage students to decode the words independently, using the clues and patterns they have learned.
- After students have completed reading the story, have them complete the Cooperative Group Activity (You Make the Call) and Comprehension Exercises (Putting Ideas in Order and Remembering Details) on page 9 in their Worktext. Answers can be found in the Answer Key on page 351 of this *Teacher's Manual.*

CONNECTION

Speaking/Listening Invite student volunteers to take turns reading aloud the selection "At a Bus Stop One Day" on Worktext page 8. Other students can follow along in their Worktext.

Worktext Pages 4–5

Level 3

INTRODUCTION

You have learned more than 400 words since you started **Caught Reading**. You have read more than 30 stories. Now, learn more words so you can read even more stories. Go right on into **Caught Reading Level 3**.

So far, your teacher or reading helper has read you the directions before and after each story. Now you will slowly take over this job. By Chapter **6** of this book, you will be reading all the directions yourself. Your teacher or a reading helper will still help you learn the **Words to Know** before each story. But you will be able to read everything else.

Words to Know

Today, you will learn some of the words you need for reading the directions. These are words you have already seen and heard. You have seen and heard them in **Caught Reading Level 1** and **Caught Reading Level 2**. If you have been following along as your teacher or a reading helper read directions, you may already be reading these words.

	Look	Say	Picture	Write
attack at-tack	☐	☐	☐	________
below be-low	☐	☐	☐	________
circle cir-cle	☐	☐	☐	________
game	☐	☐	☐	________
group	☐	☐	☐	________
introduction in-tro-duc-tion	☐	☐	☐	________
letter let-ter	☐	☐	☐	________
read	☐	☐	☐	________
sentence sen-tence	☐	☐	☐	________

4

Worktext page 4

	Look	Say	Picture	Write
sound	☐	☐	☐	________
story sto-ry	☐	☐	☐	________
these	☐	☐	☐	________
together to-geth-er	☐	☐	☐	________
word	☐	☐	☐	________
write	☐	☐	☐	________

Word Attack

+s Write **s** after the words below.

letter ________ group ________

sentence ________ sound ________

word ________ read ________

+ing Now write **ing** after **read**. ________

+er, +ing Add the endings **er** and **ing** to **write**. But first you have to take away the **e** from **write**. Write the words below.

write + er ________ write + ing ________

2=1 Put together the words below to make new words. Write them below.

a + like = ________ a + part = ________

a + long = ________

MCR Tear out the **MCR** Chips for the new words you have learned. They are on page **104** and are marked ***IA***. (***I*** stands for **Introduction**.) Tear out a new group of Chips every time you learn a new group of words. When you see **MCR**, you know it is time to program your memory to hold more words.

5

Worktext page 5

1. AT A BUS STOP ONE DAY

Word Attack

Try This

Some words end with one vowel, another letter, and then **e**. Here is something that works with many (but not all) words like this. The first vowel sounds like its own name. The **e** at the end makes no sound. Look for this in the words below. Circle the vowels that sound like their own names. Put an **X** over the vowels you cannot hear.

made time vote use these

Try it with a new word: **here**. Read it, then write it.

here ________________

it You know the word **it**. One of the new **Words to Know** is **s** + **it**. Try reading this word: **sit**. Write the word below on the line.

sit ________________

game You know how the word **game** sounds. The end sounds like the end of two of the new words. Try reading this word: **name**. And try reading this word: **same**. Now write the words below and circle the letter group that you find in all the words.

name ________________ same ________________

game ________________

night You know how the letter group **ight** sounds in the word **night**. Now read this new word: **right**. Write the words below. Circle the letter group that you find in all the words.

right ________________ night ________________

sold You know the word **sold**. Take away **s** and you have the word **old**. Write this new word in the sentence.

My grandma is ________________.

6

Worktext page 6

1. AT A BUS STOP ONE DAY

Tom is at a bus stop one day. A man with some boxes comes up. He puts his things next to Tom. He sits down.

Time goes by. Then more time goes by. "Where is that bus?" Tom asks. He finds it hard to just sit and wait. He gets up to look for the bus. The other man gets up, too. But he is giving up on the bus. He walks away. He leaves a big box next to Tom.

Tom calls after the man. "Wait!" he says. "You there! Did you forget this thing? Don't you want it?"

The man keeps walking. Tom thinks, *What **is** it about this guy? Is he **trying** to get away from the box? Should I be scared? No, the man is just old. Maybe he can't hear me.*

So Tom gets up and runs after the man. But as he runs, he sees his bus coming. He can't get to the man and back to the bus. Tom really needs to get on that bus. So back he goes.

He runs as fast as he can. But he doesn't make it! The bus leaves without him.

Tom has the box. But he doesn't know what to do with it. There is no name on it. He knows nothing about the man. If he opens the box, he can see what is in it. Maybe he will find out something about the man. But he doesn't think it is right to open a box that is not his.

Tom sits down to wait for the next bus. He thinks and thinks about the box. He thinks about the old man, too. He looked like a man with money. Tom looks at the box. What is in it? What should Tom do with it? When the next bus comes, Tom will have to get on. Should he leave the box here or what? The old man may come back for it. He will look for it where he put it. But then Tom thinks, *Lots of people go by this bus stop. Someone will get the box. But who says it will be the old man?*

Just then Tom's bus comes. So Tom gets on the bus. He takes the box along. Already he thinks of it as his box. He does not know what is in it. But he is going to find out. Then it will be his.

8

Worktext page 8

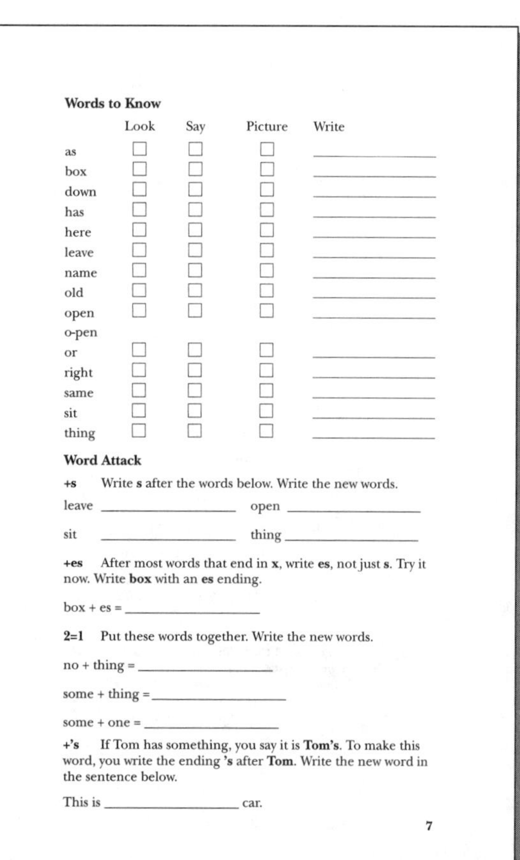

Words to Know

	Look	Say	Picture	Write
as	☐	☐	☐	________
box	☐	☐	☐	________
down	☐	☐	☐	________
has	☐	☐	☐	________
here	☐	☐	☐	________
leave	☐	☐	☐	________
name	☐	☐	☐	________
old	☐	☐	☐	________
open o-pen	☐	☐	☐	________
or	☐	☐	☐	________
right	☐	☐	☐	________
same	☐	☐	☐	________
sit	☐	☐	☐	________
thing	☐	☐	☐	________

Word Attack

+s Write **s** after the words below. Write the new words.

leave ________________ open ________________

sit ________________ thing ________________

+es After most words that end in **x**, write **es**, not just **s**. Try it now. Write **box** with an **es** ending.

box + es = ________________

2=1 Put these words together. Write the new words.

no + thing = ________________

some + thing = ________________

some + one = ________________

+'s If Tom has something, you say it is **Tom's**. To make this word, you write the ending **'s** after **Tom**. Write the new word in the sentence below.

This is ________________ car.

7

Worktext page 7

You Make the Call

Get together with a group of friends who have read the story. Talk about the problem that Tom has. What should he do with the box? Should he take it home, or should he leave it at the bus stop? What would you do if you were Tom? Why?

Putting Ideas in Order

These sentences are about the story. Write them below in the order that they come up in the story. Read the story one more time if you need to.

The bus leaves without Tom.

A man with some boxes comes up.

Tom runs after the man.

Tom gets on the bus with the box.

The man gives up and walks away.

____

____

____

____

____

Remembering Details

Write words from the story on the lines. Look back at the story if you have to.

Tom is at a ________________ stop in this story.

A man leaves a ________________ next to Tom.

The box has no ________________ on the outside.

Maybe the man can't hear Tom because the man is ________________.

9

Worktext page 9

LESSON 3.2

OBJECTIVE

- Students will practice and apply skills to an extended passage

MATERIALS

Worktext 3, pages 10–11
Teacher's Manual, page 143
Practice Lesson 3.2, pages 68–69 of the Worktext

SKILLS REVIEW

- Before reading, you may wish to review these words that apply phonics skills: *walks, says, tells, forget, gets, Tom's, looks, takes, sit, it, nothing, old, something, Grandma.* Have students review the Memory Chips they have learned so far. Then ask: **What do you predict will be in the box Tom takes home?**
- While reading, have students think about what Tom should do with whatever he finds in the box.
- After reading, have students complete the exercises on Worktext page 11.

For further practice, have students complete Practice Lesson 3.2 on pages 68–69 of the Worktext. Answers can be found in the Answer Key on page 352 of this *Teacher's Manual.*

RETEACH

If students need further review of phonics skills, you may wish to use the following activity:

Phonograms *it, ame, ight, old*

Sort It Out Write the following words on index cards: **sit, hit, name, same, game, right, light, night, old, sold, told, cold.** Spread the cards down on the table and have students sort them into groups of rhyming words. Then have students take turns choosing one group of words, using all the words in one silly sentence. Give them one point per word they use. Have each student continue with each group, and see how many points they can get with all 12 words.

Worktext Pages 10–11

2. THE THING IN THE BOX

Tom walks into his house with his box. His family has already started dinner. "Sit down," says his grandma. "What do you have in the box?"

Tom tells the story of the man at the bus stop. He tells his grandma how the man did not wait for the bus. Tom tells her how the man walked away and did not take the box with him.

"Open it," says his sister. "I want to see what's in there."

"What if it's something bad?" Tom says with a laugh.

"Good or bad, you can't keep it," says his dad. "We have to give it back to the man."

Tom says, "Forget it, Dad. We don't know where to find the man. We can't give it back to him."

Tom's sister says, "What if there is money in the box?"

"I want it to be an MP3 player," says Tom.

"No, you don't," says his sister. "If you have money, you can get an MP3 player."

"If you have an MP3 player, you can get money," Tom says. "You can always sell an MP3 player."

"What?" Tom's sister gets mad. "You're going to sell our MP3 player?"

"It's my MP3 player," says Tom. "I can do what I want with it."

"MP3 player?" Grandma asks.

Tom's dad laughs. "Kids, kids! You don't know what's in that box. But I guess it's OK to open it. We will see what is in it. Then we will talk about what to do with it."

Tom opens the box. Then he backs away—fast!

Tom's sister looks into the box. She says. "OK, Tom, I give up. You can keep this."

Grandma looks into the box. "My word!" she says. "There is nothing in this box but a really old fish!"

"You call that a fish?" says Tom.

"What do you call it?" his grandma asks.

Tom takes another careful look into the box.

"I call it—**The Thing Without a Name,**" he says.

10

Worktext page 10

What Do You Think?

Meet with a friend or in a small group. Talk about what you think Tom should do with the box. Do you think it was right for Tom to open the box? Give your reasons why.

Putting Ideas in Order

Here are four sentences from the story. Write them below in the order that they come up in the story.

"I call it—**The Thing Without a Name,**" he says.

"It's my MP3 player," says Tom.

Tom's sister looks into the box.

Tom opens the box.

Find the One Big Idea

One of the sentences below best says what the story is about. It gives the big idea of the story. Find that sentence, and write it below.

Tom finds something he has wanted for a long time.

Tom and his sister do not get along.

The thing in the box is a thing no one wants.

11

Worktext page 11

Level 3

LESSON 3.3

OBJECTIVES

- Students will learn new words containing the *et, ast, etter,* and *ade* phonograms and letter patterns
- Students will use context clues to figure out unfamiliar words
- Students will recognize and form compound words
- Students will recognize and form possessives
- Students will apply endings *s* and *ed* to base words to form new words

PHONICS VOCABULARY

what's	sits	asks	called
without	gives	don't	better
anything	good-looking	he's	leaves
says	gets	lets	starts
comes	everywhere	everything	I'm
sisters	made	let	last
kitchen	isn't	anywhere	Inez's

WORDS TO KNOW

better	Carmen	every	had
Inez	kitchen	last	let
made	show	so	too

MATERIALS

Worktext 3, pages 12–16
Teacher's Manual, pages 144–146
Practice Lesson 3.3, pages 70–71 of the Worktext

TEACH

- Using Worktext page 13, introduce students to the vocabulary words. Give them an opportunity to practice writing the words.
- Students can organize their Memory Chips, found in the back of the Worktext. They can divide them into groups of words they know and words they don't recognize. Then say each word, having students repeat it after you.

Worktext page 13 can also be used to reinforce spelling. Use the five-step process detailed on page 71 of this *Teacher's Manual.*

Phonograms and Letter Patterns *et, ast, etter, ade*
Write these sentences on the board: **I let the dog run fast. Mom made me mail the letter.** Have a volunteer point to the word *fast.* Blend the word with students, /*f*/ /*a*/ /*st*/. Point out how the vowel *a* is surrounded by two consonants. Tell them that when this happens, the vowel usually has the short sound. Repeat the blending procedure with the words *letter, made,* and *let.*

Blending Students can substitute beginning sounds and letters to make word ladders with *fast, let, made,* and *letter.*

fast	let	made	letter
last	bet	fade	better
cast	set	wade	setter

Context Clues

Write this sentence on the board: **Come into the kitchen and help me cook.** Point to the word *kitchen* and tell students that when they see an unfamiliar word like this one, they can read the words around it and use what they know about letters and sounds to help them figure out the word. Cover *kitchen* and read the sentence without it. Uncover the word, and have students look at the beginning letter. Tell them that the *k* gives us a clue as to how the word begins. Ask students what word they think goes in the sentence. (*kitchen*)

Compound Words

Remind students that they can figure out some words by finding smaller words within a big word. Write **something** on the board. Ask them what two words they see in *something.* (*some, thing*)

Make New Words Write these words on index cards, and have students put two together to make new words: **some**, **thing**, **any**, **every**, **where**. (*something, everything, everywhere, anything, anywhere, somewhere)*

Possessives

Remind students when they see a phrase like *Tom's dog* and *Jen's CD,* the apostrophe and *s* after the person's name mean that the person owns something.

Make New Words Have students pick out something a friend owns and write a sentence about it. For example: **Jane's CD is good.**

Endings *s, ed*

Write this sentence on the board, and read it aloud: **The sisters called the dog.** Have a volunteer point to *sisters* and *called.* Ask students to circle the word endings *s* and *ed* in the two words.

Make New Words Write these words on the board and invite students to add *s* or *ed* to the end of each word: **let**, **find**, and **look**. (*lets; finds; looks, looked*) They can use each new word they make in a sentence.

PRACTICE

- Let students practice the new words they have learned and formed by completing the activities found on pages 12–14 of the Worktext.
- If students are experiencing difficulty with the Words to Know section on page 13, you may wish to play a Memory Chip Bingo game. Have students write 16 of the words they have learned so far in a 16-square Bingo grid. Use the Memory Chips to read the words, and have students mark the squares as you call out each word. The first student to get all 16 squares filled in yells "Bingo!"

For further practice, have students complete Practice Lesson 3.3 on pages 70–71 of the Worktext. Answers can be found in the Answer Key on page 352 of this *Teacher's Manual.*

APPLY

- Have students talk about the story concept by sharing their personal experiences. Ask: **What is it like to have a little sister or brother?** Tell them that they are going to use the words they have learned to read a short story about two sisters.
- Ask students to read the story on page 15 in the Worktext. Offer assistance if necessary, but encourage students to decode the words independently, using the clues and patterns they have learned.
- After students have completed reading the story, have them complete the Cooperative Group Activity (What Do You Think?) and Comprehension Exercises (Remembering Details and Describe It) on page 16 in their Worktext. Answers can be found in the Answer Key on page 351 of this *Teacher's Manual.*

CONNECTION

Strategy for Reading After students finish reading the selection "What's a Little Sister For?" on page 15, ask them to summarize it either aloud or in writing.

Worktext Pages 12–13

3. WHAT'S A LITTLE SISTER FOR?

Word Attack

get One of your new **Words to Know** ends the same way as the word **get**. See if you can read this word: **let**. Now write the new word in the sentence below.

_______________ me go.

fast You know the word **fast**. Try to read this word: **last**. Now write the two words below, and circle the letter group you see in both words.

fast _______________ last _______________

letter You have seen the letter group **etter** in **letter**. It sounds the same in **better**. Read **better**. Write the two words below, and circle the letter group **etter**.

better _______________ letter _______________

NEW **made** Do you remember what works with many words that end with a vowel, another letter, and then **e**? The first vowel has a **long** sound. The **e** at the end has no sound. Use this to attack one of the new words. Try to read **made**. Now write the new word in the sentence.

Jared _______________ a good dinner.

Take a Guess

There are times when you can tell what a new word is by reading it in a sentence. The other words in the sentence can help you guess the word. Read the sentence below. Try to guess the word in dark letters. The word **cook** can help you. Think about where a cook may be.

The cook is in the **kitchen**.

What would you guess the new word to be? Maybe your guess is **kitchen**. How do you find out if you are right? Do these things:

1. Say the word you guess. Think of the sound it starts with: **k**.

12

Worktext page 12

2. Look at the sound that starts the word in the sentence. Is it the same? Yes. The word **kitchen** starts with **k**. So far, **kitchen** looks like the right word.
3. Now look at the other letters in the word. Look for sounds and letter groups that you know. Do you see an ending you have seen before?

The word is **kitchen**. Write it. _______________

Words to Know

	Look	Say	Picture	Write
better bet-ter	☐	☐	☐	________
Carmen Car-men	☐	☐	☐	________
every ev-ery	☐	☐	☐	________
had	☐	☐	☐	________
Inez I-nez	☐	☐	☐	________
kitchen kitch-en	☐	☐	☐	________
last	☐	☐	☐	________
let	☐	☐	☐	________
made	☐	☐	☐	________
show	☐	☐	☐	________
so	☐	☐	☐	________
too	☐	☐	☐	________

13

Worktext page 13

Word Attack

2=1 You know the words **any**, **every**, **thing**, and **where**. From these words, you can make four new words. Write the new words on the lines below.

any + thing = ________________

any + where = ________________

every + thing = ________________

every + where = ________________

+'s Write **'s** after **Inez** to make **Inez's**. Write the new word in the sentence.

You can walk to ________________ house from here.

+s Write **s** after these words to make two new words.

let ________________ sister ________________

+ed Write **call** with an **ed** ending. ________________

1+1 You can write **is not** as one word: **isn't**. Write an **X** over the letter you leave out of **is not** to write **isn't**. Then fill in the blanks in the sentences below with the words *is not* and *isn't*.

This ________________ ________________ my house.

________________ it your house?

Tear out the Memory Chips for Chapter **3**. Practice with the **A** side first. Ask for help if you need it. Then try to read the words on the **B** side. Review your Memory Chips from the Introduction and Chapter **1** as well.

14

Worktext page 14

What Do You Think?

Meet with a friend or in a small group. Talk about Inez and Carmen. How are they different? Are there ways they are alike? Which one are you most like, and why?

Remembering Details

Write words from the story on each line. Look back at the story if you have to.

Carmen is looking at a TV show called ________________.

Inez wants to see a show called ________________.

Carmen gives up on her show and goes into the

________________ to cook.

Describe It

To **describe** something is to give details about it. Words that describe help you picture what you are reading. Take this sentence:

Inez is 14—friendly and happy, most of the time.

Friendly and **happy** are words that describe Inez. They help you picture what Inez is like. Find two words that describe the look that Inez gives her sister. Write them on the line below.

____

____

Inez talks about two shows on TV. Here some words she uses. Write the words next to the things they describe.

sorry so good good-looking out of it

The Thing Without a Name: ________________

The people on Carmen's show: ________________

Anything for a Laugh: ________________

A boy on **Anything for a Laugh**: ________________

16

Worktext page 16

3. WHAT'S A LITTLE SISTER FOR?

Carmen is looking at the TV. Her sister Inez comes in. Inez is 14—friendly and happy, most of the time. She sits down next to Carmen. "What is this show?" Inez asks.

"It's called **The Thing Without a Name**," says Carmen.

Inez gives her sister a long, dark look. "You don't really like this sorry show, do you? I don't. The people are so out of it. There is a better show on at this time. It's a game show. Have you ever seen **Anything for a Laugh**? It's so good! There is a boy on the show who is so good-looking! There is another one—he's good-looking, too. You just have to see him. Don't you want to see them, Carmen?"

"No," says Carmen. The idea of Inez's show leaves her cold.

But Inez keeps talking about it. At last, Carmen gets up. She lets Inez have the TV. "I will start dinner," she says.

Carmen goes into the kitchen and starts to cook.

But Inez comes right after her. "What are you cooking?" she asks. "Can I help? I know another thing we can make. It's better. Let me show you. I made it just the other day."

And she comes closer.

"Inez," says Carmen, "I have had it up to here with you. Every time I look, there you are. Everywhere I go, you come after me. Everything I do, you want to try it, too. How come you will not let me be?"

"Because," says Inez, "I'm your little sister. This is what little sisters do, isn't it? I am just doing my job!"

15

Worktext page 15

LESSON 3.4

OBJECTIVE
- Students will practice and apply skills to an extended passage

MATERIALS
Worktext 3, pages 17–19
Teacher's Manual, pages 147–148
Practice Lesson 3.4, pages 72–73 in the Worktext
5-square by 5-square Bingo game boards, markers (Reteach)

SKILLS REVIEW

- Before reading, you may wish to review these words that apply phonics skills: *say, it's, stops, asks, don't, can't, starts, faster, I'm, looks, gets, sisters, wanted, without, made.* Have students review the Memory Chips they have learned so far. Then ask: **What do you know how to cook? How do you cook it?**
- While reading, have students think about what they think Inez's drink tastes like.
- After reading, have students complete the exercises on Worktext page 19.

PRACTICE For further practice, have students complete Practice Lesson 3.4 on pages 72–73 of the Worktext. Answers can be found in the Answer Key on page 352 of this *Teacher's Manual.*

RETEACH

If students need further review of phonics skills, you may wish to use the following activity:

Review Phonograms

Rhyming Bingo Have students write these words in the Bingo squares in any order: **letter**, **fast**, **get**, **snow**, **gave**, **and**, **art**, **fun**, **back**, **sold**, **shop**, **team**, **light**, **jeep**, **ad**, **make**, **bike**, **fan**, **tall**, **walk**, **say**, **hot**, **game**, **night**, **sit**. Rhyming Bingo is played like regular Bingo, except students put a marker over a word when they hear a rhyming word. As you call out the following words, have students mark one word that rhymes: *better, last, let, throw, wave, band, start, sun, pack, hold, hop, seam, bright, keep, mad, take, like, can, wall, talk, day, spot, same, fight, hit.* When they get five words in a row going across, down, or diagonally, they yell, "Bingo!" and read the words aloud. If the rhyming words match what you called out, the player wins. Repeat the game as many times as you like.

CONNECTION

Independent Reading
- Encourage students to read for pleasure. Pearson's *SporTellers*™ series is a collection of eight novels that focus on the drama of different sports. Each novel explores conflicts and challenges that confront young athletes. See page xvii of this *Teacher's Manual* for additional titles.
- After reading, students may work with a partner. Each partner can summarize his or her story for the other. Students may then write a short description of their partner's story.

4. A NEW DRINK

"OK," says Carmen, "show me what you want to cook."

"It's a—it's a—" Inez stops to think. "It's a drink," she says. "A new drink."

"Is this a hot drink?" Carmen asks. "I don't know if you should be cooking over a hot—"

"It's not hot," says Inez. "It's a cold drink."

"Is that so?" says Carmen. "What is in this drink?"

"I can't tell you about it," says Inez. "You just have to see. Let me make some." Inez starts to work on the drink. "You put in a little of this—" she says. "You put in a little of that—" She is working faster. "And a little of this—" she goes on. "And some of this—and a lot of that—"

Carmen smiles. "Inez, these things don't go together. You are making this up as you go."

"No, I'm not. I made some the other day. It's good. Believe me." She puts in one more thing and says, "There! Have some of this, Carmen."

"Not me," says Carmen. "You have some."

Inez looks at the drink for a long time. But she does not drink it. She says, "It has to sit here a little. Then it gets really good."

"I am going back to my TV show," says Carmen.

"Me, too," says Inez.

After the TV show, the sisters go back to the kitchen. They see the family dog. He is just drinking the last of Inez's drink.

"No!" Inez lets out a cry. She goes for the dog. But Carmen stops her.

"It's OK, Inez. I don't think you really wanted to drink any of that. I know I didn't. But look how happy you have made the dog."

"See?" says Inez. "What did I tell you? **The Drink Without a Name** is good!"

17

Worktext page 17

Putting Ideas in Order

Here are three things that go on in the story. Write them below in the order that they come up in the story.

Carmen goes back to the TV.

The dog has a drink.

Inez looks at the drink but does not drink it.

Inez says she will make a new drink.

____

____

____

____

____

____

____

Find the One Big Idea

One of the sentences below best says what the story is about. Find that sentence, and write it below.

Inez makes up a drink that is good—but only for dogs.

Inez shows Carmen how to make something new.

Carmen goes back to her TV show.

____

____

____

____

19

Worktext page 19

Describe It

Here is an ad for the drink Inez has made up. It needs three more words. Find three words in the story that describe **The Drink Without a Name**. Write the words on the lines.

TRY ... THE DRINK WITHOUT A NAME!

It's ___________! It's ___________! It's ___________!

People will like it! Even your dog will like it.

18

Worktext page 18

LESSON 3.5

OBJECTIVES

- Students will apply endings *s* and *ing* to base words to form new words

MATERIALS

Worktext 3, page 20
Teacher's Manual, page 149
Practice Lesson 3.5, pages 74–75 of the Worktext

TEACH

- Using Worktext page 20, introduce students to the vocabulary words. Say each word, and have students repeat it after you. Give them an opportunity to practice writing the words.
- Students can organize their Memory Chips, found in the back of the Worktext. They can divide them into groups of words that have one, two, and three syllables.

Endings *s*, *ing*

Remind students that *s* and *ing* can be added to base words as endings. Write this sentence on the board and read it aloud: **Tom remembers ordering the CD.** Have students point to *remembers* and *ordering*. Have them circle each base word and underline each ending.

Make New Words Write the endings **s** and **ing** on the board, and invite students to add *s* and *ing* to the end of these Memory Chip words: *answer, detail, end, order, remember.* They can use each word in a sentence.

PRACTICE

- Let students practice the new words they have learned and formed by completing the activities found on page 20 of the Worktext.
- If students are experiencing difficulty with the More Words to Know section on page 20, you may wish to ask questions about the words. Have students pick a Memory Chip word that answers questions such as: **Which word rhymes with peach?** (*each*) **Which word is the opposite of worst?** (*best*) **Which word has three syllables?** (*remember*)

PRACTICE

For further practice, have students complete Practice Lesson 3.5 on pages 74–75 of the Worktext. Answers can be found in the Answer Key on page 352 of this *Teacher's Manual.*

APPLY

- Students can apply the new words and word endings by reading the directions independently for the remainder of the Worktext.

CONNECTION

Writing Have students use the words they have just learned in sentences. Have volunteers share their sentences with the class.

Level 3

Worktext Page 20

5. MORE WORDS TO KNOW

After you learn these words, you will be able to read all the directions in this book—both before and after the stories.

	Look	Say	Picture	Write
again a-gain	☐	☐	☐	________
all	☐	☐	☐	________
answer an-swer	☐	☐	☐	________
best	☐	☐	☐	________
describe de-scribe	☐	☐	☐	________
detail de-tail	☐	☐	☐	________
each	☐	☐	☐	________
end	☐	☐	☐	________
guess	☐	☐	☐	________
order or-der	☐	☐	☐	________
picture pic-ture	☐	☐	☐	________
remember re-mem-ber	☐	☐	☐	________
vowel vow-el	☐	☐	☐	________

Word Attack

+ing Write **ing** after **remember**, **order**, and **end**.

remember ________ order ________

end ________

+s Write these words with the ending **s** after them.

vowel ________ detail ________

end ________ ending ________

picture ________ answer ________

20

Worktext page 20

LESSON 3.6

OBJECTIVES

- Students will learn new words containing the *ould, ind, ell,* and *ace* phonograms
- Students will recognize and form compound words
- Students will apply endings *es* and *s* to base words to form new words
- Students will recognize and form contractions

PHONICS VOCABULARY

runs	into	well	says
everywhere	asks	something	should
someone	believes	cries	walls
doesn't	everyone	didn't	today
anyway	maybe	off-base	somehow
he's	looks	let's	mind
tries	starts	things	face
find	would	wrong	everyone
that's			

WORDS TO KNOW

face	from	guy	mind	said
saw	than	well	were	why
would	wrong			

MATERIALS

Worktext 3, pages 21–25
Teacher's Manual, pages 150–152
Practice Lesson 3.6, pages 76–77 of the Worktext

TEACH

- Using Worktext page 22, introduce students to the vocabulary words. Give them an opportunity to practice writing the words.
- Students can organize their Memory Chips, found in the back of the Worktext. Say each word, having students repeat it after you. Then have them sort the words according to beginning sounds.

Worktext page 22 can also be used to reinforce spelling. Use the five-step process detailed on page 71 of this *Teacher's Manual.*

Phonograms *ould, ind, ell, ace*

Write these sentences on the board and say them aloud: **I wish I could find the bell. It is in a funny place**. Have volunteers point to words in the sentences that rhyme with *should, tell, mind,* and *race.* Write each word pair on the board, and point out that each word pair ends with the same letters.

Blending Make letter cards for the consonants **f**, **t**, **sh**, **c**, **w**, **r**, **s**, and **m** and the phonograms **ace**, **ind**, **ell**, and **ould**. Have students take turns placing the consonants in front of the phonograms to make new words. (*face, race, mace; find, wind, rind, mind; fell, tell, shell, cell, well, sell; should, could, would*)

Compound Words

Remind students that they can look for smaller words inside unfamiliar words to help them read. Write these words on the board and have students draw a line between the two smaller words inside: **everywhere**, **inside**, **into**. *(every, where; in, side; in, to)*

Make New Words Write these words on index cards, and have students mix and match to make compound words: **some**, **every**, **where**, **thing**, **how**. (*something, somewhere, somehow, everywhere, everything*) They can write the new words in a list.

Endings es, s

Remind students that the ending *s* is added to some words and the ending *es* is added to others. Write this sentence on the board: **The boy cries.** Ask students to identify the base word in *cries.* (*cry*) Write **cry** on the board, and remind them that the *y* is changed to *i* and *es* is added as the ending to make *cries.*

Make New Words Write these words on the board, and invite students to add *s* or *es* to the end of each word: **believe**, **try**, **cry**, **fry**, **mind**, **face**. (*believes, tries, cries, fries, minds, faces*) They can use each word they make in a sentence.

Contractions

Write this sentence on the board and read it aloud: **That's not the book he's got to have.** Have students point to the two contractions in the sentence. (*that's, he's*). Remind students when two words are shortened into one, one or more letters is taken out and an apostrophe is added. Ask students to name the words that *that's* and *he's* stand for. (*that is, he is*)

Make New Words Write these words on the board and have students write contractions for them: **let us**, **did not**, **is not**, **do not**. (*let's, didn't, isn't, don't*)

PRACTICE

- Let students practice the new words they have learned and formed by completing the activities found on pages 21–23 of the Worktext.
- If students are experiencing difficulty with the Words to Know section on page 22, put the Memory Chip cards down word side up. Say a sentence, leaving out a word, and have students choose the correct card to complete the sentence.

Use sentences like this: **Another word for man or boy is ____.** (*guy*)

For further practice, have students complete Practice Lesson 3.6 on pages 76–77 of the Worktext. Answers can be found in the Answer Key on page 352 of this *Teacher's Manual.*

APPLY

- Have students talk about the story concept by sharing their personal experiences. Ask: **Have you ever had to go to the principal's office because someone had blamed you for something you didn't do? How did you feel about it?** Tell them they are going to use the words they have learned to read a short story about a boy who is on his way to the principal's office.
- Ask students to read the story on page 24 in the Worktext. Offer assistance if necessary, but encourage students to decode the words independently, using the clues and patterns they have learned.
- After students have completed reading the story, have them complete the Cooperative Group Activity (What Do You Think?) and Comprehension Exercises (Read It Again and Describe It) on page 25 in their Worktext. Answers can be found in the Answer Key on page 351 of this *Teacher's Manual.*

CONNECTION

Speaking/Listening Student partners can read aloud the selection "A Problem for Tom" on Worktext page 24. The partners can alternate being speaker and listener.

Writing Students can write a few sentences describing how they would feel if they were Tom. Have student volunteers share their writings with the class.

Worktext Pages 21–22

6. A PROBLEM FOR TOM

Word Attack

race You have seen the word **race**. You will see the ending sound **ace** in one of the new words, too. It sounds the same here. Try reading this word: **face**. Now write the words below. Circle the letter group that is the same in them.

face ____________ race ____________

find You know how the letter group **ind** sounds in **find**. This letter group is in one of your new **Words to Know**, and it sounds the same as it does in **find**. Say **m** with **ind** and you have a new word. Try reading the word: **mind**. Write the two words you see below. Circle the letter group **ind** in the two words.

mind ____________ find ____________

tell You know the word **tell**. Change the first letter to **w**, and you have a new word. Read this word: **well**. Write the words below. Circle the letter group that is the same.

well ____________ tell ____________

should You can attack the new word **would**. It sounds like **should** and ends with the same letter group. Try reading the word: **would**. Now write the words below on the lines. Circle the letters that are the same in them.

would ____________ should ____________

21

Worktext page 21

Take a Guess

Maybe you can guess the word **wrong** by reading it in a sentence. The first letter in this word is one that you can't hear. So don't go by the first letter. Use the other words to help you guess. The words **not right** may help you get it.

This answer is not right. It's **wrong**.

Did you guess the new word? Write it. ____________

Words to Know

	Look	Say	Picture	Write
face	☐	☐	☐	____________
from	☐	☐	☐	____________
guy	☐	☐	☐	____________
mind	☐	☐	☐	____________
said	☐	☐	☐	____________
saw	☐	☐	☐	____________
than	☐	☐	☐	____________
well	☐	☐	☐	____________
were	☐	☐	☐	____________
why	☐	☐	☐	____________
would	☐	☐	☐	____________
wrong	☐	☐	☐	____________

22

Worktext page 22

Level 3

Word Attack

2=1 You know the words below. Write them together to make four new words.

any + way = ____________________

to + day = ____________________

every + one = ____________________

some + how = ____________________

+s You know the word **believe**. Write **s** after it.

believe ____________________

1+1 You can write **he is** as one new word: **he's**. You can write **let us** as one new word: **let's**. You can write **that is** as one new word: **that's**. Write the three new words in the sentences below. Then write an **X** over the letter in each set of two words that is not in the one word.

he is: Call Tom. I know ____________________ home.

let us: Everyone, ____________________ go see Tom.

that is: I think ____________________ his house.

+es To write **cry** with an **es** ending, change the **y** to **i**. (Do this with most words that end in **y**.) Write the new word.

cry ____________________

Now write **try** with an **es** ending. (Remember: first change **y** to **i**.)

try ____________________

23

Worktext page 23

What Do You Think?

Meet with one or more friends who have read **A Problem for Tom**. Talk about what you would do if you were Carmen. Would you try to help Tom? Why or why not? Carmen says she wants to help Tom. What do you think—can she really help him? Why or why not?

Read It Again

The sentences below ask about the story. Look back at the story to find answers. Use your own words to write the answers on the lines. The first answer is already there.

Why is the graffiti at school a problem for Tom?

The principal thinks he did it.

Why didn't Tom go in and talk to the principal?

____

Why was Tom not at school today?

____

How come Carmen is going to go with Tom?

____

Describe It

A writer may describe one thing by telling how it is like another thing. This can be a good way to tell how people in a story feel. One sentence in **A Problem for Tom** does just this. Here is the sentence.

Tom's face looks as long as a day without sun.

What is this sentence really saying about Tom? Find the answer below. Circle it. Then write it on the line.

Tom does not feel happy.

Tom is a bad boy.

Tom is really sick.

____

____

____

25

Worktext page 25

6. A PROBLEM FOR TOM

Carmen runs into a boy from her class. His name is Tom. "Well, there you are!" she says. "The principal has been looking everywhere for you."

"Why?" asks Tom. "Is something wrong?"

"I should say so!" Carmen goes up to him. "Someone put some graffiti on the wall at school. The principal believes it was you. The principal was not happy when he saw it. He was screaming."

"Me?" cries Tom. Now Tom is not happy. "How can you say a thing like that? I would not write on the school walls. I would not write on any walls—ever! Don't you know me better than that, Carmen?"

"I guess I do," says Carmen. "But the principal doesn't. He asked everyone to come in and see him today. He called the kids in one by one. He had each of us tell him what we know. But one guy did not go in and see him. That one guy was you, Tom. How come you didn't talk to the principal?"

"Because I was not at school today, that's why. I was not feeling well," says Tom. "Anyway, so what if I didn't talk to him. What does that show?"

"He said maybe it shows you have something to hide."

"Man, he's so off-base," says Tom. "I have to talk to him. Somehow, I have to show him that he's wrong about me." Tom's face looks as long as a day without sun.

"Well," says Carmen, "we will think of something on the way. Let's go."

"We?" says Tom. "Are you coming with me?"

"Why not?" says Carmen. "I want to help. Do you mind?"

Tom tries to smile. "Why should I mind? I can use all the help I can get." Tom starts to think. Maybe with some help from Carmen things will be OK. Together they will find out who did the graffiti.

24

Worktext page 24

LESSON 3.7

OBJECTIVE

- Students will practice and apply skills to an extended passage

MATERIALS

Worktext 3, pages 26–28
Teacher's Manual, pages 153–154, 330–331
Practice Lesson 3.7, pages 78–79 of the Worktext

SKILLS REVIEW

- Before reading, you may wish to review these words that apply phonics skills: *don't, says, didn't, what's, kids, screams, anyway, thinks, looks, someone, walks, baseball, it's, believes, everyone, something, can't, find, would, telling.* Have students review the Memory Chips they have learned so far. Then ask: **What would you do if someone who looked like you did something wrong, and you got blamed for it?**
- While reading, have students decide who they believe, Tom or the kids at school.
- After reading, have students complete the exercises on Worktext page 28.

For further practice, have students complete Practice Lesson 3.7 on pages 78–79 of the Worktext. Answers can be found in the Answer Key on page 353 of this *Teacher's Manual.*

RETEACH

If students need further review of phonics skills, you may wish to use the following activity:

Contractions

Contraction Concentration Write the following word pairs and contractions on index cards: **let us**, **he is**, **that is**, **cannot**, **do not**, **did not**, **does not**, **it is**, **I will**, **let's**, **he's**, **that's**, **can't**, **don't**, **didn't**, **doesn't**, **it's**, **I'll**. Turn all the cards face down and mix them up. Then have students take turns turning over two cards. If one of the two cards shows a contraction and the other shows the words the contraction stands for, the student keeps the two cards and takes another turn. If not, the player loses a turn and the next player tries. When all the cards are removed, the game is over. The student with the most cards wins.

CONNECTION

Response to Reading

- To reinforce students' understanding of the literary elements found in their reading material, have them complete the Story Map and Character Cluster reproducibles found on pages 330–331.
- Students will demonstrate an understanding of setting, characters, and plot by filling out the organizers.
- Students may share their completed organizers with the class.

7. WHAT THE KIDS SAW

"I just don't get it," says Tom. "Why does the principal think this graffiti is my work?"

Carmen and Tom are walking to the school.

Carmen says, "For one thing, you did do some graffiti another time. Didn't you?"

"Well—" says Tom, "yes."

"Didn't they call you **Graffiti Guy**?"

"Well—" says Tom, "yes, they did. OK? But that was a long time back. I was just a kid. I didn't know any better. I am not the same guy."

"And there is another thing," says Carmen.

"What's that?" Tom stops and looks at her.

"Some kids say they saw you doing it," says Carmen.

"What?" screams Tom. "When? Where? How? What did they say?"

Carmen can see that Tom is getting mad. But she goes on. "They saw some guy last Saturday. That's what they say, anyway. They were going by the school. They looked over, and there he was—writing on the wall. From what I hear, he looked like you."

Tom is walking faster. Now he is getting really hot. "Why would they say a thing like that? Who are these kids? I would like to get a hold of them!"

"And then what?" says Carmen. "What would you do? Hit someone? What good will that do? The principal already thinks of you as **Graffiti Guy**. What will they call you if you start hitting people?"

"I guess it would not look good," Tom says.

"This is not just about looks," says Carmen. "If you hit someone, it will be bad."

"I know." Tom is looking down as he walks. "I just want to know—what's the use? I study hard. I try hard. I am on the baseball team. It's all going to be for nothing. Someone does graffiti. Right away, everyone believes it was me."

26

Worktext page 26

"Not everyone," says Carmen. "I believe you. That's something, isn't it?"

"I guess."

"Tom, you can't be mad at the kids who said they saw you. They are just telling the principal what they saw. They did see someone. They are not making it up. But they did not see him up close. So you know what I think?"

"What?"

"I think the guy who did this looks like you."

"I see," says Tom. "But how does that help me?"

"It may help you look for him," says Carmen. "In the end, you will have to find the real **Graffiti Guy**. Then people will believe you."

"Yes, but where should I look?" says Tom.

"I don't know," says Carmen. And they keep walking.

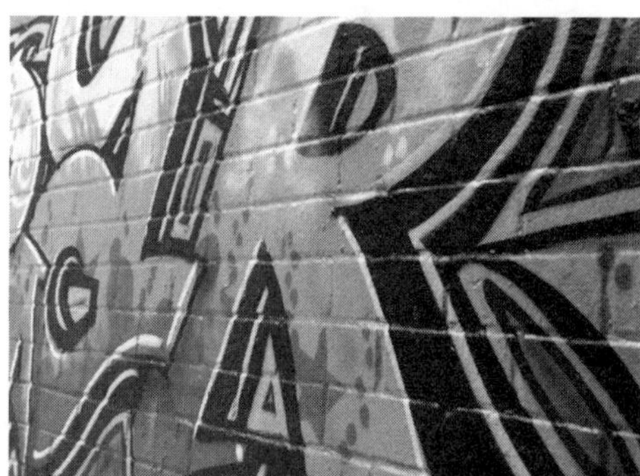

27

Worktext page 27

What Do You Think?

Carmen does not think Tom did the graffiti. What do you think? Get together with a friend or a group of friends. Talk about it. Look for details in the story that show why you think as you do.

Remembering Details

Words such as **when, where**, and **what** can get you right to the details in a story. In **What the Kids Saw**, the principal hears a story from some kids. The sentences below ask about this story. Read the sentences. Write the answers. Look back at the reading if you have to.

The kids say they saw something. **When** did they see it?

____

Where were they at the time?

____

They say they saw a guy. **What** was the guy doing?

____

What Comes Next?

The sentences below tell four things that **may** come up in the next part of this story. Circle the one thing you think **will** come up in the next part of the story. Read it. Write it on the lines. Then talk about it with a friend who has read the story, too. Why do you think as you do? What does your friend think?

Tom will get mad and scream at the principal.

Carmen will get mad and walk away from Tom.

Carmen will find out who really did the graffiti.

The principal will not believe Tom.

____

____

____

28

Worktext page 28

LESSON 3.8

OBJECTIVES

- Students will learn new words containing the *ace* phonogram
- Students will apply ending *s* to base words to form new words
- Students will recognize and form compound words

PHONICS VOCABULARY

shops	stops	points	sells	looks
says	laughs	lots	sees	words
lights	shows	takes	feelings	always
someday	games	girls	places	calls
starts	himself	place	point	moves

WORDS TO KNOW

always	else	first	Luis	move
place	point	self	them	yes

MATERIALS

Worktext 3, pages 29–32
Teacher's Manual, pages 155–156
Practice Lesson 3.8, pages 80–81 of the Worktext

TEACH

- Using Worktext page 29, introduce students to the vocabulary words. Give them an opportunity to practice writing the words.
- Students can organize their Memory Chips, found in the back of the Worktext. Say each word, having students repeat it after you. Then have them sort the words according to the number of letters.

Worktext page 29 can also be used to reinforce spelling. Use the five-step process detailed on page 71 of this *Teacher's Manual*.

Phonogram *ace*

Write this sentence on the board and have a volunteer read it: **I know a good place to go.** Ask a volunteer to point to *place*. Erase the *pl* and insert an *f*. Ask students to read the new word and use it in a sentence.

Blending Make a word ladder, beginning with *place*. Students can take turns substituting beginning letters to continue the ladder.

place
face
lace
space
race

Ending *s*

Remind students that *s* can be added to words. Explain that some words have more than one syllable when the *s* is added, such as *places*.

Make New Words Write these words in a chart, and invite students to add *s* and tell how many syllables they hear: **face**, **place**, **light**, **point**.

faces	2	lights	1
places	2	points	1

Compound Words

Remind students that they can sometimes find two smaller words inside unfamiliar words. Write these words on the board and have students find the two words that make up each word: **boyfriend**, **showtime**, **lighthouse**. *(boy, friend; show, time; light, house)*

Make New Words Write these words on index cards, and have students mix and match to make compound words: **some**, **every**, **day**, **time**, **thing**, **where**. (*something, somewhere, someday, sometime; everyday, everything; everywhere; daytime*)

PRACTICE

- Let students practice the new words they have learned and formed by completing the activities found on page 29 of the Worktext.
- If students are experiencing difficulty with the Words to Know section on page 29, write scrambled letters like these on the board: **seel** (*else*), **voem** (*move*), **cleap** (*place*), **fels** (*self*), **mteh** (*them*), **esy** (*yes*). Then have them unscramble the letters to make the words on their Memory Chips.

For further practice, have students complete Practice Lesson 3.8 on pages 80–81 of the Worktext. Answers can be found in the Answer Key on page 353 of this *Teacher's Manual*.

APPLY

- Have students talk about the story concept by sharing their experiences. Ask: **Do you know anyone who writes graffiti? Why do you think he or she does it?** Tell them they are going to use the words they have learned to read a short story.
- Ask students to read the story on pages 30–31 in the Worktext.
- After students have completed reading the story, have them complete the Cooperative Group Activity (What Do You Think?) and Comprehension Exercises (Putting Ideas in Order and Describe It) on page 32 in their Worktext. Answers can be found in the Answer Key on page 352 of this *Teacher's Manual*.

8. GRAFFITI GUY

Word Attack

face One of the new **Words to Know** has the same ending sound as **face**. Read it, then write the new word, **place**, in the sentence.

I like this ________________.

Take a Guess

Read the sentence. Guess the new word from the other words around it.

Where is your sister? **Point** to her.

Write the new word. ________________

Words to Know

	Look	Say	Picture	Write
always al-ways	☐	☐	☐	________
else	☐	☐	☐	________
first	☐	☐	☐	________
Luis Lu-is	☐	☐	☐	________
move	☐	☐	☐	________
place	☐	☐	☐	________
point	☐	☐	☐	________
self	☐	☐	☐	________
them	☐	☐	☐	________
yes	☐	☐	☐	________

Word Attack

+s Write **s** after each of the words below.

feeling ________________ game ________________

light ________________ place ________________

point ________________ shop ________________

show ________________ move ________________

2=1 Find two words you know in **someday**. Write them below.

someday = ________________ + ________________

29

Worktext page 29

MCR

8. GRAFFITI GUY

Carmen and Tom are walking by some shops. Carmen stops. She points at a shop that sells fish. "Look over there, Tom. What do you see?"

Tom sees a boy writing on the wall.

"He looks a little like me!" says Tom. "Doesn't he?"

"Wait here," says Carmen. She goes over to the boy.

"What are you doing?" she asks.

The boy laughs. "I am writing an ad. What does it look like?"

"An ad for what?" says Carmen.

30

Worktext page 30

"An ad for my self," says the boy. "Who else?"

"On a wall?" says Carmen.

"That's the point!" the boy says. "I want lots of people to see it." He goes right on working. Then he says, "There! That's that. What do you think? Move back a little. That way you can see it better."

Carmen looks up. She sees the ad. The letters are as big as people. She reads the words. They say:

Luis is the man! Luis is the best. What a hot guy!

"Are you Luis?" she asks.

"Yes, I am." His face lights up. "I am the man himself. Luis is my name. Writing on walls is my game. I have what it takes and it shows. Who are you?"

"I'm Carmen," she says. "I think I am going to be sick."

"Many people have these feelings at first," Luis tells her. "You will get over it. Already I think you like me. Yes, you do. Don't try to hide it. I know people, and I know them well. I'm good that way. I can always tell. So what do you say? Let's go out someday."

Carmen looks Luis over. She says, "How about today?"

"Man! You don't play games, do you? I like that," says Luis. "I have a lot of girls after me, Carmen. But you know what? I will always like you best. Really. Always. Where should we go? I know some good places." When Luis talks, his words come fast.

"I know just the place," says Carmen. "Come on." She calls out, "Tom! Are you coming?"

"Tom?" says Luis. "Who is Tom? And where are we going?"

"You will see," says Carmen. She starts for the school.

31

Worktext page 31

What Do You Think?

Carmen is taking Luis in to see the principal. Is she doing the right thing? Meet with one or more friends and talk about it. What would you do if you were Carmen? Why?

Putting Ideas in Order

Here are five sentences from the story. Write them below in the order that they come up in the story.

"Are you Luis?" she asks.

Carmen looks up and sees the ad.

Tom sees a boy writing on the wall.

"Tom?" says Luis. "Who is Tom?"

"I know just the place," says Carmen.

____

____

____

____

____

Describe It

Find sentences in the story that describe the things below. Write the sentences on the lines.

What does Luis's ad look like?

____

How does Luis's face look when he talks to Carmen?

____

How does Luis sound when he talks?

____

32

Worktext page 32

LESSON 3.9

OBJECTIVE

- Students will practice and apply skills to an extended passage

MATERIALS

Worktext 3, pages 33–34
Teacher's Manual, page 157
Practice Lesson 3.9, pages 82–83 of the Worktext

SKILLS REVIEW

- Before reading, you may wish to review these words that apply phonics skills: *smiles, someone, comes, says, walls, boys, looks.* Have students review the Memory Chips they have learned so far. Then ask: **Do you think Luis is the one who wrote the graffiti? Why or why not?**
- While reading the story on page 33, have students decide who they believe, Luis or Tom.
- After reading, have students complete the exercises on Worktext page 34.

For further practice, have students complete Practice Lesson 3.9 on pages 82–83 of the Worktext. Answers can be found in the Answer Key on page 353 of this *Teacher's Manual.*

RETEACH

If students need further review of phonics skills, you may wish to use the following activity:

Ending *s*; Phonogram *ace*

Scrambled Words Divide students into teams of three or four. Provide each team with the list of 10 scrambled words shown below. Have each team take five minutes to unscramble as many words as possible. Tell students these words end in *s* or rhyme with *face.*

celap (*place*)	cela (*lace*)
celaps (*places*)	voems (*moves*)
tosipn (*points*)	wossh (*shows*)
slifnege (*feelings*)	megas (*games*)
spohs (*shops*)	gilsht (*lights*)

Worktext Pages 33–34

9. LUIS TELLS A FISH STORY

"Wait," says Luis. "What are we doing here? This is the school! Is this your idea of a good time, Carmen?"

Carmen smiles. "Who said anything about a good time, Luis? I want you to meet someone."

She takes Luis to the principal. Tom comes, too. She says to the principal, "You know the graffiti on the school walls? I think you should talk to these boys. This is Tom. He is the one you wanted to see. This other boy is Luis. He goes to our school, too. I think they look alike, don't you?"

"A little," says the principal. "What's your point?"

"Some people say they saw Tom writing the graffiti. But maybe they saw Luis," says Carmen.

The principal says to Luis, "Well? Let's hear it. What do you know about this graffiti?"

"Graffiti?" says Luis. "Did someone write graffiti on the walls here?"

"Yes," says the principal. "Didn't you see it?"

"No, I didn't see it or hear about it," says Luis. "I was not at school today. Where would I hear about it? I did not do it."

"Why should we believe you?" Carmen asks.

"Because I was home at the time," says Luis. "My sister will back me up. Call her. She saw me come in at 4:00 on Saturday. She saw me leave at 6:00."

"What does that show?" asks Tom.

"It shows that I was home from 4:00 to 6:00. The graffiti was put on that wall at 5:00 on Saturday," says Luis.

The principal makes Luis sit down. "Luis," he says, "you said you didn't even hear about this graffiti. How come you know just when it was put on that wall? You say you know the day and the time. You are telling us a fish story, Luis. The one who did this graffiti is you."

Luis just looks down. He does not look at the principal. He does not look at Carmen or Tom. Luis knows he is telling a fish story. What will he do now?

33

Worktext page 33

Put Sentences in Order

The sentences below tell four things that take place in the story. Write them in the order that they take place.

Luis says he was at home from 4:00 to 6:00.

The principal asks Luis about the graffiti.

The principal says that Luis did the graffiti.

Carmen takes Luis to the principal.

____

____

____

____

Find the One Big Idea

What is this story really about? Only one group of words below makes this big point. Find this group of words. Write it on the line.

Luis tries to show that he did not do the graffiti. But what his story really shows is that ______________________

____

a. he has a sister.
b. he got home at 4:00 on Saturday.
c. he did the graffiti.

34

Worktext page 34

Level 3

MIDWAY NOVEL High Stakes

MATERIALS
Midway Novel 3, *High Stakes*
Teacher's Manual, page 158
Assessment Manual, Midway Assessment 3, pages 78–80

Summary *Mu Lan needs a tutor to help bring up her grades. Her friend, Inez, knows someone who can help her—if they can get along. Will, Inez's friend, is very different from Mu Lan, but agrees to help her. Mu Lan's grades improve, and in the process, she and Will become close friends.*

REVIEW AND ASSESSMENT

- Have students review their Memory Chips with a partner. Depending on your students' needs, review the following skills covered in Lessons 1–9: phonograms and letter patterns *et, ace, ast, ind, ame, etter, ade, ell, ight, old, ould*; compound words; contractions; possessives with apostrophe and *s*; and endings with *s, es, ed,* and *ing.*

If you wish to assess students' progress at this point, use *Assessment Manual,* pages 78–80. For students who need additional support, you may use the Reteach activities from previous lessons.

INTRODUCE THE NOVEL

Invite students to preview the book by reading the title, looking at the illustrations, and reading aloud the captions. Begin a discussion of story concepts by asking questions such as:

- **Do you think rich people are different from people who have less money? Why or why not?**
- **What kind of person makes a good friend?**
- **Have you ever been friends with someone you didn't expect to like? What happened?**

CHECK COMPREHENSION

Chapter 1 What kind of person is Will? (*He is a hard worker. He also knows how to keep his temper in check.*)

Chapter 2 Would you like a friend like Mu Lan? Why or why not? (*Possible answers: yes, because she has good parties and does fun things; or no, because she treats people poorly who have little money.*)

Chapter 3 Why are the kids upset with Mu Lan? (*She pretends they are not there.*)

Chapter 4 Why does Mu Lan need help? (*She got an "F" in Mrs. Packwood's class; she thinks she doesn't ever have to work hard in school.*)

Chapter 5 How does Mu Lan's dad react to her bad grade? (*He says she cannot have her party on the boat, and she has to get help with her grades.*)

Chapter 6 Who do you think Inez has in mind to help Mu Lan with her schoolwork? (*Students will probably say Will.*)

Chapter 7 What does Will make Mu Lan do to get him to help her? (*She has to say she needs his help so everyone in Graffiti hears.*)

Chapter 8 How does the first lesson go with Mu Lan and Will? (*The work is hard for Mu Lan; they both call each other names.*)

Chapter 9 Why does Will get mad? (*Dan Teller comes into Graffiti with Mu Lan and insults him.*)

Chapter 10 Who do you think hit Will's car? (*Students may predict it was Dan Teller.*)

Chapter 11 How were Mu Lan and Will both wrong? (*They both judged each other according to the amount of money the other had or didn't have.*)

Chapter 12 Why is Mu Lan happy? (*She made a "B+" in Mrs. Packwood's class.*)

Chapter 13 What do you think Dan Teller will do to the party on the boat? (*Students may predict he will try to overturn the boat or somehow ruin the party.*)

Chapter 14 How does Mu Lan solve the problem? (*She calls a ship-to-ship SOS and gets help from the cops.*)

Chapter 15 What are Will and Mu Lan happy about at the end of the story? (*They are going to college together.*)

CONNECTION

Home/School Encourage students to bring home a copy of *High Stakes.* They might read the novel, or sections of the novel, to family members.

LESSON 3.10

OBJECTIVES

- Students will learn new words containing the *ould*, *ave*, and *uy* phonograms and letter patterns
- Students will use context clues to recognize unfamiliar words
- Students will apply ending *s* to base words to form new words
- Students will recognize and form compound words
- Students will recognize and form possessives with apostrophe and *s*
- Students will recognize and form contractions

PHONICS VOCABULARY

likes	says	could	guy	somewhere
pulls	gets	sees	looks	stops
it's	she's	don't	buy	screams
lots	keeps	Carmen's	wants	doesn't
let's	I'm	homework	smiles	something
save	mouth	happens	moves	herself

WORDS TO KNOW

again	buy	could	door	food
hand	happen	mouth	oh	pull
save				

MATERIALS

Worktext 3, pages 35–39
Teacher's Manual, pages 159–161
Practice Lesson 3.10, pages 84–85 of the Worktext

TEACH

- Using Worktext page 36, introduce students to the vocabulary words. Give them an opportunity to practice writing the words.
- Students can organize their Memory Chips, found in the back of the Worktext. Say each word, having students repeat it after you. Then have students sort the words according to words they know and those that are unfamiliar. Say each unfamiliar word and have students use it in a sentence.

Worktext page 36 can also be used to reinforce spelling. Use the five-step process detailed on page 71 of this *Teacher's Manual.*

Phonograms and Letter Patterns *ould, ave, uy*

Write this sentence on the board, and read it aloud: **Would you save money to buy a CD?** Have a volunteer point to the word *buy*. Ask students to name a word that means *man* or *boy* and rhymes with *buy*. (*guy*) Repeat the exercise using *would* and *save*.

Blending Have students name rhyming words for *buy*, *would*, and *save*. List them on the board. If students name words like *stood* and *shy*, list them in another column and show how their spelling pattern is different.

Context Clues

Write this sentence on the board, and read it aloud: **Carmen opens her mouth and eats a big peach.** Point to *mouth* and tell students that when they don't recognize a word, they can read the words around it to figure out the unfamiliar word.

Ending *s*

Write this sentence on the board: **Tom shuts the door.** Ask students which word ends in *s*. (*shuts*)

Make New Words Write these words on the board, and invite students to add *s* to the end of each word: **pull**, **work**, **happen**, **move**. (*pulls, works, happens, moves*) They can use each word they make in a sentence.

Compound Words

Write this sentence on the board, and read it aloud: **I know my CD is here somewhere.** Point to *somewhere* and ask students what two smaller words they see. (*some, where*) Remind them that finding smaller words inside compound words can help them read unfamiliar words.

Make New Words Write these words on the board, and have students use them to make compound words: **self**, **him**, **her**, **my**, **home**, **work**, **some**, **where**, **thing**. (*himself, herself, myself, homework, somewhere, something*)

Possessives

Remind students when they see a word with an apostrophe *s*, it can also mean "belongs to." Write this sentence on the board: **Carmen's CD is on the player.** Ask them who the CD belongs to and how they know. (*Carmen; the apostrophe and* s *give a clue*)

Make New Words Have students write possessives for these phrases:
the car that belongs to Tom (*Tom's car*)
the graffiti that belongs to Mu Lan (*Mu Lan's graffiti*)

Contractions

Write this sentence on the board, and read it aloud: **Let's go to school.** Point to *Let's*, and ask students what two words it stands for. (*Let us*) Have a volunteer show how the *u* is taken out of *let us* and replaced with an apostrophe.

Level 3

Make New Words Write these word pairs on the board and have students use them to make contractions: **cannot**, **it is**, **do not**, **does not**. (*can't, it's, don't, doesn't*)

PRACTICE

- Let students practice the new words they have learned and formed by completing the activities found on pages 35–36 of the Worktext.
- If students are experiencing difficulty with the Words to Know section on page 36, you can write the beginnings and endings of the words on the board, leaving out the middle letters. Have students use their Memory Chips to spell and say the whole word. Then have them use each word in a sentence.

For further practice, have students complete Practice Lesson 3.10 on pages 84–85 of the Worktext. Answers can be found in the Answer Key on page 353 of this *Teacher's Manual.*

APPLY

- Have students talk about the story concept by sharing their personal experiences. Ask: **What do you think a first date is like? Where is a good place to go on a first date?** Tell them they are going to use the words they have learned to read a short story about two people who go out on a first date.
- Ask students to read the story on pages 37–38 in the Worktext. Offer assistance if necessary, but encourage students to decode the words independently, using the clues and patterns they have learned.
- After students have read the story, have them complete the Comprehension Exercise (Describe It) and Prediction Exercise (What Will Happen Next) on page 39 in their Worktext. Answers can be found in the Answer Key on page 352 of this *Teacher's Manual.*

CONNECTION

Strategy for Reading Have students reread the selection "At the Big Mouth Truck Stop" on pages 37–38 in their Worktext to correct comprehension breakdowns. Students may achieve understanding by reprocessing the same text with greater attention focused on its meaning.

Worktext Pages 35–36

10. AT THE BIG MOUTH TRUCK STOP

Word Attack

buy You know how the word **buy** sounds. Try reading the new word: **guy**. Write the word that goes in each sentence below. Circle the letter group that is the same in the words you write.

Tom is a good ____________. He will ____________ a car.

would You have seen the same letter group in **should** and **would**. Look for it in a new word now. Try reading this word: **could**. Write the three words below on the lines. Circle the letter group that is the same in the three words.

could ____________ would ____________

should ____________

wave The word **wave** ends with the letter group **ave**. Try reading this word: **save**. Is this a word you know? Write the words below. Circle the letter group that is the same in the two words. This letter group does not always sound the way it does in **wave** and **save**.

save ____________ wave ____________

Take a Guess

Can you guess the word in dark letters? Use the other words in the sentences to help you. Think of a word that starts with an **m** sound. It will be something people use when they talk.

Luis talks too much. He has a big **mouth**.

What word did you guess? Write the word. ____________

35

Worktext page 35

Words to Know

	Look	Say	Picture	Write
again a-gain	☐	☐	☐	____________
buy	☐	☐	☐	____________
could	☐	☐	☐	____________
door	☐	☐	☐	____________
food	☐	☐	☐	____________
hand	☐	☐	☐	____________
happen hap-pen	☐	☐	☐	____________
mouth	☐	☐	☐	____________
oh	☐	☐	☐	____________
pull	☐	☐	☐	____________
save	☐	☐	☐	____________

Word Attack

+s Write the words below with an **s** at the end.

pull ____________ happen ____________

2=1 The words **herself**, **homework**, and **somewhere** are made up of words you know. Write the two words.

herself ____________ + ____________

homework ____________ + ____________

somewhere ____________ + ____________

+'s Does **house of Carmen** sound right? Not really. Most of the time, most people would say **Carmen's house**. Write **'s** after **Carmen** to get the new word.

Carmen + ' s = ____________

1+1 You can write the two words **she is** as one word: **she's**. Write the one word in the sentence.

This is her house, but ____________ not home.

36

Worktext page 36

10. AT THE BIG MOUTH TRUCK STOP

Carmen and Tom leave the school. Tom is thinking, *I like this girl. I think she likes me.*

He says to Carmen, "Where are you going?"

"I don't know," says Carmen. "Why do you ask?"

"Well, I was thinking we could go somewhere together. It would be just you and I. I know this place we could go. They have good food. We could talk. I could get to know you better."

"Why not?" says Carmen. She's thinking, *I don't know what is going to happen, but I like this guy.*

Carmen gets into Tom's car, and they drive. Tom pulls up at the **Big Mouth Truck Stop**.

"This place has good food?" Carmen can hardly believe what she sees. "This place?" The door of the place looks like a big open mouth.

Tom just stops as he is about to pull the car door open. "You don't like this place? We don't have to go here."

37

Worktext page 37

"No, no. It's OK," says Carmen. "I just want to talk. I guess this place is as good as any to talk in."

But she is wrong about that. The **Big Mouth** is not a good place for two people to talk. There is just one big room. In this room are many, many people. All of them are talking and laughing at the same time. Carmen can hardly hear herself think. She and Tom buy some food. Then they sit down face to face.

"So what do you think of this place?" he screams.

"What?" she screams.

He says the words again.

"I like it," she screams. "It's like my house. Lots of sound."

She goes on talking. Tom cannot hear a word she is saying. He just keeps looking at Carmen's face. From time to time, he screams, "Yes, me too!" He wants to hold her hand. But he doesn't want to move too fast. He is thinking, *I don't want this to end.*

But, at last, Carmen looks up. "Oh!" she says. "Is it 4:00 already? I have to go. I have a lot of homework."

Tom gets up, too. "OK," he says. "But first, let me ask you something."

"Ask away," says Carmen.

"Well," he says, "I have got to hand it to you. You really helped me with the principal. But you hardly know me. Why did you go out of your way to help me?"

Carmen smiles at him. "Let's just say I like a good story," she says. "I really like a happy ending, too."

"If this an ending, I'm not happy," says Tom. "Tell me this is just the start, Carmen."

"All right," said Carmen. "Let's say this is just the start—of something. What happens next?"

"Next?" he says. "Let's go out. How about Saturday?"

"I'll see you at 8:00," she says. At the door, she stops. They go together out the door, hand in hand.

38

Worktext page 38

Describe It

Read the groups of words below. Only four of them tell something about the **Big Mouth Truck Stop**. Circle these groups. Then write them next to the things they describe.

Tom's car	a big, open mouth
many, many people	a good place to talk
good	laughing and talking

What the door is like? ____________

What you see in the truck stop? ____________

What you hear in the truck stop? ____________

What the food is like? ____________

What Will Happen Next?

Tom and Carmen say they are going to go out. What do you think will happen when they do? Read the four ideas below. Put a line through two things that you think will **not** happen. Circle two things that you think **may** happen. Write them on the lines. Sit down with some other kids who have read the story. Talk about why you think these things will happen.

The school principal will ask to come along.

Tom and Carmen will have a good time.

Carmen will get mad at Tom.

Tom and Luis will take Carmen out together.

____

____

____

____

____

39

Worktext page 39

Level 3

LESSON 3.11

OBJECTIVE

- Students will practice and apply skills to an extended passage

MATERIALS

Worktext 3, pages 40–42
Teacher's Manual, pages 162–163, 330–331
Practice Lesson 3.11, pages 86–87 of the Worktext

SKILLS REVIEW

- Before reading, you may wish to review these words that apply phonics skills: *shows, dad's, it's, says, don't, let's, something, looks, could, I'll, should, didn't, would, takes, someone, turns, you're, feels, somewhere, find, gets, points, sees, screams, boyfriend.* Have students review the Memory Chips they have learned so far. Then ask: **What would it be like to have a little sister come along on a date?**
- While reading, have students predict who they think will be in the back of the truck.
- After reading, have students complete the exercises on Worktext page 42.

PRACTICE For further practice, have students complete Practice Lesson 3.11 on pages 86–87 of the Worktext. Answers can be found in the Answer Key on page 353 of this *Teacher's Manual.*

RETEACH

If students need further review of phonics skills, you may wish to use the following activity:

Possessives

I'm Taking a Trip Tell students they will be taking a trip to some place like Canada, Mexico, or China. Then tell them to think of one thing they want to take with them. Sit in a circle and start a group story beginning, **"I'm taking a trip to Canada, and I'm taking my camera."** Then have the next student say, "I'm taking a trip to Canada, and I'm taking Mrs. Smith's camera and my swimming suit." The next student might say, "I'm taking a trip to Canada and I'm taking Mrs. Smith's camera, Carmen's swimming suit, and my iguana." Each student says one new thing plus the things that everyone else said before. Encourage silly and memorable objects. If a student's memory falters, encourage other students to help out. Continue until you go completely around the circle.

CONNECTION

Response to Reading

- To reinforce students' understanding of the literary elements found in their reading material, have them complete the Story Map and Character Cluster reproducibles found on pages 330–331.
- Students will demonstrate an understanding of setting, characters, and plot by filling out the organizers.
- Students may share their completed organizers with the class.

11. SATURDAY NIGHT

Tom shows up at 8:00 on Saturday. This time he has a truck.

"It's my dad's," he says. "My car is in the shop. You don't mind, do you?"

"Not at all," says Carmen. "Let's go."

After they drive for a time, the truck starts to make a bad sound. Then it stops.

"What is it?" Carmen asks.

"I don't know," says Tom. "Something is wrong with Dad's truck." He looks out. Snow is coming down. "I could walk to a shop," he says. "But I don't want to leave you here in the dark."

"I'll go with you," says Carmen.

"All right. But should we go when it's snowing like this?"

"No," says Carmen. "Let's wait."

40

Worktext page 40

They sit without talking. Then Tom says, "I didn't want this to happen, Carmen. I would not try to pull a fast one on you."

"Yes, I know, Tom. I believe you."

"But here we are," he goes on. "Just you and me, you know. We may as well get close. Don't you think?" He takes her hand. His face comes closer and closer.

Carmen pulls away. "I hear something." She sits up.

She looks back. "Tom," she says, "there is someone in the back of your truck."

Tom turns. He makes no sound. He looks through the window. At last, he says, "I think you're right." He opens the door. "I had better take a look."

"Be careful," says Carmen.

The night is cold. It is dark, too. Tom feels a little scared. Carmen looks scared, too. "I have a light somewhere," he says. He finds it and gets it out. He points the light into the back of the truck. He sees something dark and pretty big. He sees it move. Then the dark thing sits up. He can see that it is a little man. No, it is a little woman. No, that is wrong, too. It is a girl.

"Inez!" screams Carmen.

"Who?" says Tom.

"It's my sister, Inez. What are you doing here?"

"I just wanted to come along!" Inez is crying. They help her out of the back. She has snow all over her face. She says, "I just wanted to see where you were going. I didn't know it was going to be so cold back there."

Carmen says, "You had it coming." She is mad.

That night, Carmen and Tom end up at the **Big Mouth Truck Stop**. Inez is with them. It is not what Carmen wanted. It is not what Tom wanted. But Inez is as happy as can be.

"I like your new boyfriend," she tells Carmen when they get home.

41

Worktext page 41

What Do You Think?

Put yourself in Tom's or Carmen's place. Picture finding Inez in the back of the truck. How would you feel? Talk about it with a friend or a group of friends. Did anything like this ever happen to you?

Describe It

What is the night like when Carmen and Tom go out? Look for details in the story that describe that night. Write the details below. You can write one word, a group of words, or a sentence. Write three details.

____

____

____

Putting Ideas in Order

The sentences below tell five things that happen in the story. But they are not in the right order. Write them on the lines below in the order that they happen in the story.

He points the light into the back of the truck.

The truck starts to make a bad sound.

Tom shows up at 8:00 on Saturday.

Then the dark thing sits up.

His face comes closer and closer.

____

____

____

____

____

42

Worktext page 42

LESSON 3.12

OBJECTIVES

- Students will learn new words containing the *ame* and *old* phonograms, the vowel pair *ea,* and the CVCe pattern
- Students will apply ending *s* to base words to form new words
- Students will recognize and form possessives
- Students will recognize and form compound words

PHONICS VOCABULARY

again	wants	can't	sees	looks
clean	someone	what's	I'm	walls
you're	don't	takes	starts	paints
houses	owns	hears	game	name
asks	sales	lots	sounds	feels
myself	mean	told	gave	sale
smile	face	save		

WORDS TO KNOW

change	even	far	gone	mean
much	pretty	sale	side	told
came	around			

MATERIALS

Worktext 3, pages 43–47
Teacher's Manual, pages 164–166
Practice Lesson 3.12, pages 88–89 of the Worktext

TEACH

- Using Worktext pages 43–44, introduce students to the vocabulary words. Give them an opportunity to practice writing the words.
- Students can organize their Memory Chips, found in the back of the Worktext. You may wish to say each word, having them repeat it after you. Students can find different ways to sort the words, such as words they know and don't know, words that describe, words that show action, and so on.

Worktext pages 43–44 can also be used to reinforce spelling. Use the five-step process detailed on page 71 of this *Teacher's Manual.*

Phonograms *ame, old*

Write this sentence on the board and read it aloud: **I told him my name.** Ask a volunteer to point to *told* and *name.* Ask students to brainstorm words that rhyme with *told* and *name.*

Blending Circle *name,* modeling how to blend the sounds, then saying the word naturally. Erase the *n* and replace it with an *s.* Have students say the new word, blending the sounds. Continue using the consonants *f, l, c,* and *t.* Have a volunteer circle *told.* Have students take turns substituting *s, h, c,* and *b,* blending each word. Write each new word on the board as it is suggested.

name	lame	told	cold
same	came	sold	bold
fame	tame	hold	

CVCe and Vowel Pair *ea*

Write these sentences on the board and read them aloud: **I will clean the car. It is for sale.** Point to *sale* and ask students what vowel sound they hear. (*long a*) Remind students when they see a word that has a consonant-vowel-consonant-*e* pattern, the vowel has the long sound. Ask them what vowel sound they hear in *clean.* Have a student circle the vowels in *clean.* Remind them that when they see the letters *ea* together, the *e* is usually long and the *a* is silent.

Ending *s*

Remind students that words can end in *s.*

Make New Words Say these words, and have students add the ending *s*: **own**, **sale**, **one**, **paint**, **can**, **hand**. (*owns, sales, ones, paints, cans, hands*) Have a volunteer write each word on the board.

Possessives

Write this sentence on the board: **The pen is Jen's.** Ask them who the pen belongs to. (*Jen*) Remind students that to show ownership, an apostrophe and *s* are added to a word. Have a volunteer circle the apostrophe and *s.*

Make New Words Write these sentences on the board and have students fill in the blanks, using the possessive forms and names of people in their class or group:

It is _______ car.

It is ________ CD.

Give me ______ coat.

Compound Words

Write this sentence on the board, and read it aloud: **I can do it myself.** Ask students what word has two smaller words put together to make one word. (*myself*) Ask them what two words they see. (*my, self*)

Make New Words Write these two columns on the board and have students draw lines to connect two words to make new words: (*myself, boyfriend, sometime*)

my	time
boy	self
some	friend

PRACTICE

- Let students practice the new words they have learned and formed by completing the activities found on pages 43–44 of the Worktext.
- If students are experiencing difficulty with the Words to Know section on page 44, place the Memory Chips on the table. Pose riddles like this for each word: **This word begins like soap and rhymes with wide.** (*side*)

For further practice, have students complete Practice Lesson 3.12 on pages 88–89 of the Worktext. Answers can be found in the Answer Key on page 353 of this *Teacher's Manual.*

APPLY

- Have students talk about the story concept by discussing things they have experienced. Ask: **How could someone fix graffiti?** Tell them they are going to use the words they have learned to read a short story about Luis, the graffiti artist.
- Ask students to read the story on pages 45–46 in the Worktext. Offer assistance if necessary, but encourage students to decode the words independently, using the clues and patterns they have learned.
- After students have completed reading the story, have them complete the Cooperative Group Activity (What Do You Think?) and Comprehension Exercises (Putting Ideas in Order and Describe It) on page 47 in their Worktext. Answers can be found in the Answer Key on page 352 of this *Teacher's Manual.*

CONNECTION

Speaking/Listening Student partners can read aloud the selection "Luis Gets a Job" on pages 45–46 in their Worktext. The partners can alternate being listener and speaker.

Writing Students can write a few sentences in which they describe Luis and Carmen. They can compare how the characters are different and how they are alike.

Worktext Pages 43–44

12. LUIS GETS A JOB

Word Attack

game You know how **ame** sounds in **game**. Say **c** + **ame**, and you have a new word. Read this word: **came**. Write it in the sentence below.

Carmen __________ home with a big bag.

old You know the word **old**. You also know the words **sold** and **cold**. See if you can read this word: **told.** Now write the words below. Circle the letter group that is the same in all of them.

told __________ old __________

sold __________ cold __________

NEW **ea** Remember with some words, when you see two vowels together, the first one may sound like its own name. The next one may have no sound at all. Try this with a new word: **mean.** Read the new word **mean.**

Vowels You can attack the new word **sale**. It ends with **e**, so look at the last three letters. Yes, this is a word that ends with a vowel, another letter, and then **e**. Remember, in many words like this, the **e** has no sound. The other vowel sounds like its own name. Try reading the word: **sale.** Does it work? Yes—the word is **sale**. Write it in this sentence.

The car is not for __________.

Attack another word the same way. Try reading this word: **side.** The letter **i** sounds like its own name, and you can't hear the **e.** Do you know this word? Write it in the sentence.

The door is on the other __________ of the house.

43

Worktext page 43

Words to Know

	Look	Say	Picture	Write
around a-round	☐	☐	☐	______
came	☐	☐	☐	______
change	☐	☐	☐	______
even e-ven	☐	☐	☐	______
far	☐	☐	☐	______
gone	☐	☐	☐	______
mean	☐	☐	☐	______
much	☐	☐	☐	______
pretty pret-ty	☐	☐	☐	______
sale	☐	☐	☐	______
side	☐	☐	☐	______
told	☐	☐	☐	______

Word Attack

+s Write **s** after these words to make five new words.

it __________ one __________

own __________ paint __________

sale __________

+'s Write **'s** after **Luis** to get the word **Luis's**. Use this word to show that Luis has something. Write the new word in the sentence.

Did you see __________ ad?

2=1 You can put **him** and **self** together to make a new word: **himself.** Write it in the sentence.

Luis likes to talk about __________.

44

Worktext page 44

Level 3

12. LUIS GETS A JOB

Carmen wants to see Luis's ad again. She goes to the shop. She can't believe what she sees at first. The ad is gone. The wall of the shop looks like new snow—clean! Someone has just been painting it. Carmen goes around to the other side. There, she sees Luis. He is painting.

"What's up, Luis?"

"Carmen!" he says. "I'm so happy to see you. I wanted to tell you how sorry I am about the other day. I did not mean to make a problem for Tom."

"No? Well, you did. That was wrong, Luis."

"I know. I am going to change. No more writing on walls. Just look at me."

"I'm looking. As far as I can see, you're at it again."

"No, no. You don't get it. I'm working for the guy who owns this place. You see, I came back here. I told the guy what I did. I said I want to make it right. I asked what I could do. He gave me this paint. He told me to paint over the graffiti. So here I am."

"Good going, Luis. Maybe you're not a bad guy after all."

But Luis has put down his paint can. He is looking at the wall. "The guy wants it to look new," he says. "But you know what? I think I can make it look even better than new."

Luis takes out another can of paint. Then he takes out another can—and another—and another. He starts painting a picture on the wall. He paints a pretty beach. He paints little houses. He paints people walking hand in hand.

"Luis!" Carmen lets out a cry. "Don't you get it? This is not what the shop wants. They want the wall to look clean! They did not ask you for this no-good picture."

Just then, the man who owns the shop comes out.

Luis says, "Take a look. You're going to like this. I think it is some of my best work."

"Here we go again," says Carmen to herself.

But then she hears what the man is saying, "This painting is good, Luis. I like it. You really know how to paint."

45

Worktext page 45

"Luis is the name. Painting is my game."

"Well, Luis," says the man. "I have a big sale coming up this week. I want someone to paint an ad on my window. Can you do that for me? You can make some money."

"How much?" Luis asks.

"I'll give you $25 for the first one. If I like it, I will ask you to do more. I have sales every other week. So there will be lots of work. Maybe I can give you a little raise after a while. I said maybe. We will have to see. What do you say?"

"It sounds good to me," says Luis. He has a smile on his face. Carmen can see that he feels good about himself. But that is OK with her. She is happy for him.

"I will save up some money," says Luis. "Yes, that's what I'll do. I'll save up some money and get a good, fast bike for myself."

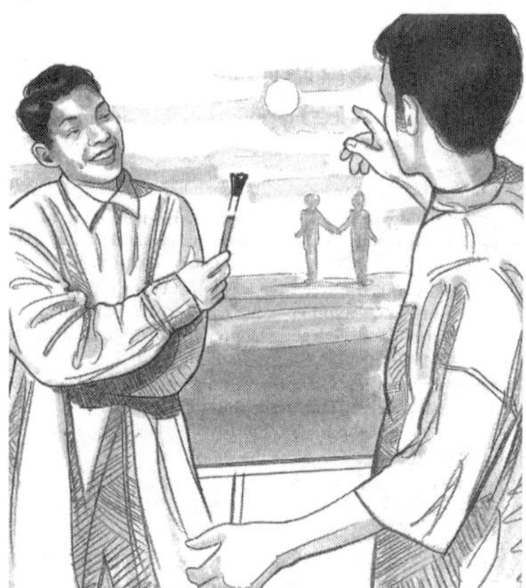

46

Worktext page 46

What Do You Think?

Luis does a painting on the wall of the shop. The man likes it. But Luis did not ask if he could do the painting before he started. Was this wrong? Why or why not? Talk about it with a friend or a group of friends.

Putting Ideas in Order

In a story, you do not always hear about things in the order that they happen. Read the sentences below. They tell three things that happen in the story in the order that you read about them. Find the thing that happens first in time. Write that sentence on the line.

Luis paints over the walls of the shop.

Luis tells the man at the shop that he did the graffiti.

Luis is asked to paint an ad for the shop.

____

____

____

Describe It

When the man comes out of the shop, he sees a painting on the wall. The words below tell three details seen in the painting. One or more words in the story describe each detail. Write these words on the lines. Look back at the story if you have to.

The painting shows a __________ beach, __________

houses, and people ____________________.

What is the painting like? All three people in this story describe it. Here are some of the words they say.

my best work   no-good   good

Who says what? Write the group of words next to the names below.

Luis: ______________________________

Carmen: ______________________________

The man who owns the shop: ____________________

47

Worktext page 47

LESSON 3.13

OBJECTIVE

- Students will practice and apply skills to an extended passage

MATERIALS

Worktext 3, pages 48–50
Teacher's Manual, pages 167–168, 330–331
Practice Lesson 3.13, pages 90–91 of the Worktext

SKILLS REVIEW

- Before reading, you may wish to review these words that apply phonics skills: *wants, bike, save, sees, sale, gets, line, takes, thinks, make, time, fire, bikes, makes, drive, really, knows, believes, himself, made-up.* Have students review the Memory Chips they have learned so far. Then ask: **What would you do if you were standing in line and got bored?**
- While reading, have students predict whether or not they think Luis will leave the line.
- After reading, have students complete the exercises on Worktext page 50.

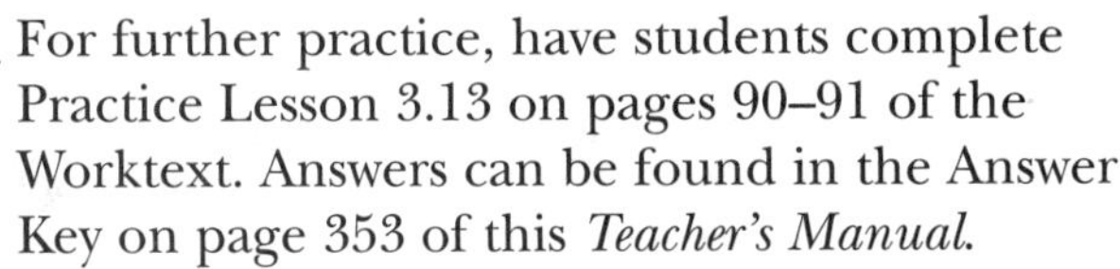

For further practice, have students complete Practice Lesson 3.13 on pages 90–91 of the Worktext. Answers can be found in the Answer Key on page 353 of this *Teacher's Manual.*

RETEACH

If students need further review of phonics skills, you may wish to use the following activity:

Long Vowel *a*: *a-consonant-e*

Climb the Ladder Draw a 10-rung ladder on the board with the word *sale* at the bottom. Then have partners take turns climbing the ladder by adding a word on the next rung. To make a new word, the student changes the beginning or ending consonant sound. When each pair is finished with the ladder, have the students read their list of long *a* words aloud. They might create a ladder like *sale, tale, tape, take, lake, wake, cake, cape, case, base.*

CONNECTION

Response to Reading

- To reinforce students' understanding of the literary elements found in their reading material, have them complete the Story Map and Character Cluster reproducibles found on pages 330–331.
- Students will demonstrate an understanding of setting, characters, and plot by filling out the organizers.
- Students may share their completed organizers with the class.

13. LUIS AND THE BIG BIKE SALE

Luis wants a bike. But he wants to save money, too. Then he sees an ad for a bike sale. *Just what I need,* he thinks. He gets to the sale as fast as he can. But there is already a long line at the shop.

Luis takes his place at the end of the line. He waits. The line does not move much. *The best bikes will be gone,* he thinks.

Then he has an idea. He will make up a story to pass the time in line. He says to himself, "What am I doing here? I should be at that other sale." He makes up a name, **Fire Mountain Bikes**. "Yes. That's it. **Fire Mountain Bikes.** They have a better sale than the one at this shop. You can get a bike for $100 there. The same bike is going for $200 here. Where is this **Fire Mountain Bikes**?" Luis makes up a place far, far away. "It's a long drive from here. But you can save $100 on a bike."

48

Worktext page 48

Really? Luis thinks. *That's worth a drive. He will not tell the other people in line or they will start talking about the sale at* ***Fire Mountain Bikes****. But one man knows about the sale at* ***Fire Mountain Bikes****. He is telling all the people in the line. When people start talking about the sale, everyone will go there.*

"Where is this **Fire Mountain Bikes**?" a girl asks.

"What's that about another sale?" a man asks.

"It's a long drive from here. But you can save $100 on a bike," says the girl.

"Really?" says the man. "That's worth a drive." Many people start talking about the sale at **Fire Mountain Bikes.**

Why am I even here? thinks Luis. *I should be at that other sale.*

But a lot more is going through his mind by this time. All this talk about another sale is getting to him. *What if there really is another sale?* he thinks. *What if there is a* ***Fire Mountain Bikes****? Everyone else believes it. Could so many people be wrong? I don't think so. They say I can get a bike there for $100. So why am I waiting to buy that same bike here for $200? I will be one sorry man if I do that. I had better get over to the other sale right away.*

Just then the line starts to move. Luis laughs to himself as he thinks, "Boy! I started to believe my own made-up story. I'll just stay in line and buy my bike." That is just what Luis did.

49

Worktext page 49

Putting Ideas in Order

Read the sentences below. They tell five things that happen in the story. Write them below in the order that they happen in the story.

People start talking about the other sale.

Luis thinks he will go to the other sale.

The line does not move much.

Luis makes up a story about another sale.

Luis sees an ad for a bike sale.

____

____

____

____

____

____

____

____

Remembering Details

Write a word from the story on each line. Look back at the story if you have to.

Luis goes to a shop to buy a ________________.

When he gets there, he finds a ________________.

Luis makes up a story about a better ________________.

He makes up a shop that he calls ________________

________________ Bikes.

50

Worktext page 50

LESSON 3.14

OBJECTIVES

- Students will learn words containing the *ind*, *ame*, and *ot* phonograms
- Students will use context clues to recognize unfamiliar words
- Students will apply endings *s* and *ing* to base words to form new words
- Students will recognize and form compound words

PHONICS VOCABULARY

behind	happens	places	takes	outside
starts	friends	news	works	lets
says	he's	showing	I'll	gives
turns	baseball	things	going	players
kidding	playing	hot	don't	can't
bases	fame	that's	let's	yourself
someone				

WORDS TO KNOW

behind	done	fame	got	now
their	through	till	turn	

MATERIALS

Worktext 3, pages 51–55
Teacher's Manual, pages 169–171
Practice Lesson 3.14, pages 92–93 of the Worktext

TEACH

- Using Worktext page 52, introduce students to the vocabulary words. Give them an opportunity to practice writing the words.
- Students can organize their Memory Chips, found in the back of the Worktext. Students can sort the words according to words they know and words they don't know. You may wish to say each word, having students repeat it after you. Then have each student work with a partner, saying each word and using it in a sentence.

Worktext page 52 can also be used to reinforce spelling. Use the five-step process detailed on page 71 of this *Teacher's Manual*.

Phonograms *ind, ame, ot*

Write this sentence on the board and read it aloud: **We are not going to find the game.** Ask a volunteer to point to *find*. Ask students what vowel sound they hear. (*long* i) Explain that when they see the letters *ind*, often the word has the long *i* sound. Then have students point to *game*. Ask them what words rhyme with *game*. (*same, fame, lame, name, tame, came*) Repeat, using *not*.

Blending Put students into three groups. Have each group work with *not, find,* or *game*. Have them substitute beginning consonants to make new words. Then have each group read their lists aloud to the rest of the class. (*find, mind, bind, kind, wind; not, cot, hot, jot, rot; game, same, lame, tame, came*)

Context Clues

Write this sentence on the board: **We ran through the woods.** Circle *through* and remind students that they can look at all the words in a sentence to figure out a word. They can look at the beginning sound and then see if the word makes sense in the sentence. Ask students what they think *through* means. (*in the middle of*)

Endings *s, ing*

Remind students that they can add the endings *s* and *ing* to make new words.

Make New Words Make a chart like the one below on the board, and have students add the endings *s* and *ing* to make new words.

Base Word	+s	+ing
turn	turns	turning
show	shows	showing
work	works	working

Compound Words

Remind students that two smaller words can be put together to make a new word. Write these words, and ask students what two smaller words they see: **yourself**, **into**, **onto**. (*your, self; in, to; on, to*)

Make New Words Write these words on index cards and have students put them together to make new words: **base**, **ball**, **in**, **to**, **on**, **your**, **my**, **self**, **him**, **boy**, **friend**. (*baseball, into, onto, yourself, myself, himself, boyfriend*) They can use each new word in a sentence.

PRACTICE

- Let students practice the new words they have learned and formed by completing the activities found on pages 51–52 of the Worktext.
- If students are experiencing difficulty with the Words to Know section on page 52, place the Memory Chips on the table. Construct incomplete sentences like the one that follows, and have students choose a Memory Chip word to finish it: **I ran fast, but I still fell _____.** (*behind*)

For further practice, have students complete Practice Lesson 3.14 on pages 92–93 of the Worktext. Answers can be found in the Answer Key on page 353 of this *Teacher's Manual*.

Level 3

APPLY

- Have students talk about the story concept by discussing things they have experienced. Ask: **Have you ever known someone who brags a lot? What did you think of that person? Why do you think people brag?** Tell them they are going to use the words they have learned to read a short story about Luis, who brags about what a great baseball player he is.
- Ask students to read the story on pages 53–54 in the Worktext. Offer assistance if necessary, but encourage students to decode the words independently, using the clues and patterns they have learned.
- After students have completed reading the story, have them complete the Cooperative Group Activity (What Do You Think?) and Comprehension Exercises (Remembering Details and What Will Happen Next?) on page 55 in their Worktext. Answers can be found in the Answer Key on page 352 of this *Teacher's Manual.*

CONNECTION

Strategy for Reading After students finish reading the selection "The Baseball Player, Part 1" on pages 53–54 of their Worktext, ask them to summarize it either aloud or in writing.

Speaking/Listening Have three student volunteers perform the play for the class. Allow students ample time to practice their parts. Encourage the rest of the class to be active, attentive listeners.

Independent Reading

- Encourage students to read for pleasure. Pearson's *SporTellers*™ books are a series of eight high-interest sports-related stories. See page xvii of this *Teacher's Manual* for additional titles.
- After reading, students may work with a partner. Each partner can summarize his or her partner's story for the class and describe his or her reaction to it.

Worktext Pages 51–52

14. THE BASEBALL PLAYER, PART 1

Word Attack

game You know the word **game**. It sounds like the new word **fame**. Try reading this word: **fame**. Write the words below on the lines. Circle the letter group that is in both of them.

fame ______________ game ______________

not The letters **ot** are in **not** and **lot**. Find the same letters in **got**. Try reading this word: **got**. Write the new word in the sentence below.

I ______________ some money at the bank.

NEW **find** You can attack the word **behind**. Just take it apart. See it as two letter groups: **be** and **hind**. You know the word **be**. And you can read **hind**. You know how the word **find** sounds. It sounds the same way here. Just take away the **f**. Say **h** with **ind**. Now try reading the word: **behind**. Then write the words below. Circle the letters that are the same in both of them.

behind ______________ find ______________

NEW **Take a Guess**

The word **through** does not sound the way it looks. But you know how the first three letters sound. You have seen them in **throw**. Now read the sentence below. See if you can guess the word in dark letters from the other words around it.

Look **through** the window.

Did you guess the word? Write it here. ______________

51

Worktext page 51

Words to Know

	Look	Say	Picture	Write
behind be-hind	☐	☐	☐	______
done	☐	☐	☐	______
fame	☐	☐	☐	______
got	☐	☐	☐	______
now	☐	☐	☐	______
their	☐	☐	☐	______
through	☐	☐	☐	______
till	☐	☐	☐	______
turn	☐	☐	☐	______

Word Attack

+s Write these words with an **s** ending. Make seven new words.

base ______________ change ______________

player ______________ write ______________

work ______________ new ______________

turn ______________

+ing Write the words below with the ending **ing**.

play ______________ show ______________

2=1 You know the words below. Put them together to make two new words. Write the new words on the line.

on + to = ______________ your + self = ______________

52

Worktext page 52

14. THE BASEBALL PLAYER, PART 1

Part 1

This two-part play happens in two places. **Part 1** takes place outside, close to Tom and Carmen's school. Carmen is with Tom when the play starts. The school can be seen behind the two friends.

Carmen: Did you hear the news, Tom? Luis got a job. He works for that fish shop now. They like the way he paints. They want him to paint an ad on their window. If he does OK, I guess they will ask him to do more.

Tom: Too much! **(He lets out a laugh.)** You mean Luis gets money to do graffiti now?

Carmen: That's one way to look at it. I don't know. Luis says he's going through a lot of changes. Maybe he's going to stop showing off so much.

Tom: I'll believe that when I see it!

(Luis comes in. He has some food in one hand. He gives Carmen a wave. Then he turns to Tom.)

Luis: Say, I hear you play baseball, Tom. How are things going with that?

Tom: **(with a cold look)** Not too bad.

Luis: Do you need some players? I'm not with a team right now.

Tom: Oh, you play baseball, too, do you?

Luis: Are you kidding? Playing baseball is what I do best. They don't call me **Hot Dog** for nothing. I have done some things that even I can't believe. You should see me going around the bases. One time, I hit this home run—well, there is no use going into it. I will be in the Hall of Fame someday. That's all I can say.

Carmen: Same old Luis.

Luis: How about it, Tom? Can I play on your team?

Tom: You ask for a lot, Luis. Maybe I can take you in to meet the coach. But that's all. I want to see you play first.

53

Worktext page 53

Luis: No problem. There is a field behind my house. Let's go play right now. You can see for yourself how good I am.

Tom: But we need one more player. We need someone to field.

Luis: **(looks at Carmen)** How about you? Don't you play a little?

Carmen: A little.

Luis: Well, then! Let's go.

54

Worktext page 54

What Do You Think?

Put yourself in Tom's place. Would you help Luis? Why or why not? Meet with one or more friends who have read **Part 1** of this play. Talk about what Tom should do. Did you ever help someone who had done a bad thing to you? Were you happy that you helped, or were you sorry? Why?

Remembering Details

The sentences below ask about details in the play so far. Write the answers on the lines. Look back at the play as much as you need to.

The kids are outside in this part of the play. What are they close to? ________________

Luis says he plays baseball so well that people have a name for him. What is the name? ________________

Who will play with Tom and Luis? ________________

Where will they play? ________________

What Will Happen Next?

All the sentences below tell things that **may** happen next. What do you think **will** happen? Write your idea on the line. Talk about it with a friend who has read **The Baseball Player, Part 1**. Tell your friend why you think this will happen. See what your friend thinks.

Tom will find that Luis plays better than he does.

Luis will talk big but will not play well.

Luis will get mad and not play at all.

____

____

____

____

____

55

Worktext page 55

LESSON 3.15

OBJECTIVE

- Students will practice and apply skills to an extended passage

MATERIALS

Worktext 3, pages 56–57
Teacher's Manual, page 172
Practice Lesson 3.15, pages 94–95 of the Worktext

SKILLS REVIEW

- Before reading, you may wish to review these words that apply phonics skills: *takes, behind, baseball, throws, moves, playing, turns, hitting, hits, runs, stop, looks, comes, sees, today, girls.* Have students review the Memory Chips they have learned so far. Then ask: **What kind of baseball player do you think Luis will turn out to be?**
- While reading, have them read to find out who Coach is watching.
- After reading, have students complete the exercises on Worktext page 57.

For further practice, have students complete Practice Lesson 3.15 on pages 94–95 of the Worktext. Answers can be found in the Answer Key on page 353 of this *Teacher's Manual.*

RETEACH

If students need further review of phonics skills, you may wish to use the following activity:

Compound Words

Compound Hide-Out Write the following words on index cards: **your**, **self**, **on**, **to**, **some**, **day**, **base**, **ball**, **may**, **be**, **for**, **get**, **in**, **to**, **boy**, **friend**, **with**, **out**, **team**, **work**, **can**, **not**, **fire**, **truck**. Then hide the cards all over the room in conspicuous places. Have partners work together to find the cards. When they find two that make a compound word, have them raise their hands and use the compound word in a sentence. Write their new word in a list under their names and give them a point for each word they make. If they find cards that don't make compound words, they can trade words with other students. When all the cards have been found, the game is over.

Worktext Pages 56–57

15. THE BASEBALL PLAYER, PART 2

Part 2

This part of the play takes place on a field behind Luis's house. Carmen, Tom, and Luis are playing baseball. Tom throws the ball to Luis. Luis throws it to Carmen.

Tom: Let's try playing for real. We can take turns hitting. Luis, you're up first.

Luis: **(He tries to hit the ball but can't.)** Oh! So close!

Tom: Close is nothing. You didn't get a hit.

Carmen: Next time, Luis.

Tom: Your turn, Carmen. I'll throw, you hit. Luis, let's see how you field.

Carmen: **(hits the ball)** All right!

Luis: **(runs back)** I have it! I have it! I have it! Oh! **(He stops and looks back.)** I had it.

(A big man comes in from the right. Tom looks up and sees him.)

Tom: Coach! What are you doing here?

Coach: I was just taking a walk. I saw you kids playing. Tom, I think you have a real player here.

Luis: That was nothing. I'm a little sick today. You should see me at my best.

Coach: I didn't mean you, guy. I'm talking about this girl. **(He looks at Carmen.)** How would you like to be part of our team?

Carmen: I hardly know what to say. How many girls will be on the team?

Coach: With you, you mean?

Carmen: Yes.

Coach: One.

Carmen: I'll have to think about it, Coach.

56

Worktext page 56

What Do You Think?

Put yourself in Carmen's place. Would you take a place on the team if you were the only girl? Meet with a friend or in a small group. Talk about what you think Carmen should do. Give your reasons why.

Remembering Details

The sentences below ask about details in the play. Write the answers. An answer can be one word, a group of words, or a sentence. Look back at the play if you need to.

Who is playing? ____________

Who gets the first hit? ____________

Who throws the ball? ____________

What does Luis do after he tries to hit? ____________

Finding the One Big Idea

The sentence below should tell the big idea of the play. Only one of the three groups of words will end the sentence in this way. Find that group of words. Write it on the line.

After Coach sees the kids playing baseball, ____________

____

a. Luis lets him know he feels a little sick.
b. he asks Carmen—not Luis—to play for the team.
c. he tells Tom he is taking a little walk.

57

Worktext page 57

LESSON 3.16

OBJECTIVES

- Students will learn new words containing the CVCe pattern and the *ook, ile, ust, ard, ad,* and *afe* phonograms
- Students will apply endings *s* and *ed* to base words to form new words
- Students will recognize and form possessives
- Students will recognize and form compound words

PHONICS VOCABULARY

cards	looks	sees	something	outside
wants	knows	holds	gets	while
just	opens	inside	says	words
thinks	must	feels	looked	puts
takes	leaves	sits	lights	card
dog's	sad	reads	happened	somewhere
Tom's	tells	stops	everything	safe
took	meets	whoever	anyone	

WORDS TO KNOW

been	before	card	must	room
sad	safe	took	under	while

MATERIALS

Worktext 3, pages 58–62
Teacher's Manual, pages 173–175
Practice Lesson 3.16, pages 96–97 of the Worktext

TEACH

- Using Worktext page 59, introduce students to the vocabulary words. Give them an opportunity to practice writing the words.
- Students can organize their Memory Chips, found in the back of the Worktext. You may wish to say each word, having them repeat it after you.

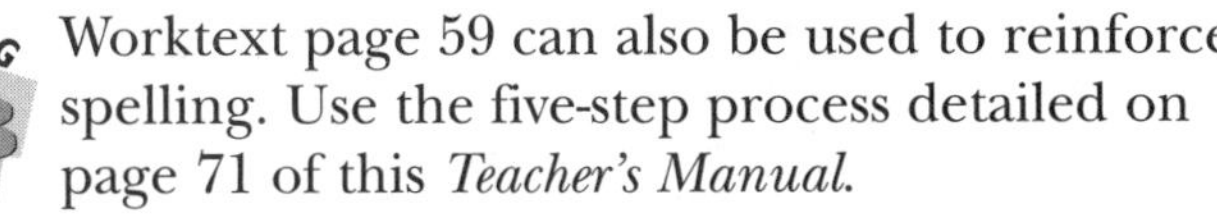

Worktext page 59 can also be used to reinforce spelling. Use the five-step process detailed on page 71 of this *Teacher's Manual.*

CVCe Pattern

Remind students that when they see a word with a consonant-vowel-consonant-*e,* the first vowel is usually long, and the *e* is silent. Write **safe** on the board, and ask students what long vowel sound they can expect to hear. (*long a*)

Blending Say *safe,* blending the sounds. Repeat with **smile** and **lake**.

Phonograms *ook, ile, ust, ard, ad, afe*

Write this sentence on the board and read it aloud: **Tom took a book.** Ask a volunteer to point to the words that rhyme. (*took, book*) Then have students circle *ook* in each word. Remind them that when they know how the ending for one word sounds, they can recognize and make new words. Write **smile**, **must**, **hard**, **mad**, and **safe** on the board. Ask students to name rhyming words for each word.

Blending Have students work in pairs. They can work together to substitute beginning consonants to make new words with *took, smile, must, hard,* and *mad.* (*cook, book, look; mile, file, tile; just, crust, rust; card; sad, had, fad*)

Endings *s, ed*

Remind students that they can add *s* and *ed* to the endings of words. Write this sentence on the board: **Good things happened today.** Ask students to circle the *s* and *ed* endings and identify the base words they see in the sentence.

Make New Words Write these endings and words on word cards and have partners take turns making new words: **s**, **ed**, **card**, **room**, **happen**. (*cards; rooms; happens, happened*)

Possessives

Remind students that ownership is shown when an apostrophe and *s* are added to the name of a person, place, or thing.

Make New Words Have students write words that show possession with these words: *dog, Tom, Luis, friend.* (*dog's, Tom's, Luis's, friend's*) They can use each new word in a sentence.

Compound Words

Remind students that two smaller words can be put together to make one word. Have students identify the smaller words in these compound words: *inside, outside, something, anything. (in, side; out, side; some, thing; any, thing)*

Make New Words Write these words on index cards and have students put them together to make compound words: **in**, **out**, **side**, **who**, **ever**, **any**, **one**, **thing**. (*inside, outside, whoever, anyone, anything*) They can use each new word in a sentence.

PRACTICE

- Let students practice the new words they have learned and formed by completing the activities found on pages 58–59 of the Worktext.
- If students are experiencing difficulty with the Words to Know section on page 59, place the Memory Chips on the table. Say each word aloud, and have students repeat it after you. Then say a

sentence with a missing word and have students choose a Memory Chip to complete it. For example: **My book is _____ the desk.** (*under*)

For further practice, have students complete Practice Lesson 3.16 on pages 96–97 of the Worktext. Answers can be found in the Answer Key on page 353 of this *Teacher's Manual.*

APPLY

- Have students talk about the story concept by discussing things they have experienced. Ask: **Have you ever read a letter that was addressed to someone else? Was it the right thing to do? How would you feel if someone read a personal letter of yours?** Tell them they are going to use the words they have learned to read a short story about a little sister who reads her older sister's mail.
- Ask students to read the story on pages 60–61 in the Worktext. Offer assistance if necessary, but encourage students to decode the words independently, using the clues and patterns they have learned.
- After students have completed reading the story, have them complete the Cooperative Group Activity (You Make the Call) and Comprehension Exercises (Describe It and Putting Ideas in Order) on page 62 in their Worktext. Answers can be found in the Answer Key on page 352 of this *Teacher's Manual.*

CONNECTION

Strategy for Reading Have students reread the selection "A Card for Carmen" on Worktext pages 60–61 to correct comprehension breakdowns. Students may achieve understanding by reprocessing the same text with greater attention focused on its meaning.

Writing Students should be encouraged to keep a journal of their writings. They can use these journals to record responses to their reading, list new words they have learned, or record their thoughts and feelings about the reading selections. This can be done on the Response to Reading pages in each Worktext or in a separate notebook.

Worktext Pages 58–59

16. A CARD FOR CARMEN

Word Attack

smile You know the word **smile**. Change the first two letters to **wh**, and you have one of your new words. Try reading this word: **while**. (Remember that **w** and **h** together make one sound.) Write the two words below. Circle the letter groups that are the same in them.

while _______________ smile _______________

just You know the word **just**. The letter group **ust** always sounds the same. Try reading this word: **must**. Write the words below. Circle the letter groups that are the same in them.

must _______________ just _______________

hard You know the word **hard**. The word **card** ends with the same letter group. The **c** in **card** has a **k** sound. Try reading the word **card**. Do you know this word? Write it in the sentence. Then circle the letter group **ard** in it.

Tom wants to buy a _______________ for his mom.

look You have seen the letter group **ook** in **look**. It has the same sound in **took**. Read this word: **took**. Write the words below. Circle the letter group that is the same in them.

took _______________ look _______________

mad You know the word **mad**. If you put **s** in place of **m** you get one of the new **Words to Know**. Try reading the word: **sad**. Write the words below. Circle the letter group they both have.

sad _______________ mad _______________

safe The word **safe** ends with a vowel, another letter, and **e**. In this word, the **e** has no sound. The **a** sounds like the letter **a**. Try to read the new word: **safe**. Write it in the sentence below.

She runs into the house. There she feels _______________.

58

Worktext page 58

Words to Know

	Look	Say	Picture	Write
been	☐	☐	☐	_______________
before be-fore	☐	☐	☐	_______________
card	☐	☐	☐	_______________
must	☐	☐	☐	_______________
room	☐	☐	☐	_______________
sad	☐	☐	☐	_______________
safe	☐	☐	☐	_______________
took	☐	☐	☐	_______________
under un-der	☐	☐	☐	_______________
while	☐	☐	☐	_______________

Word Attack

+s Write an **s** after each word below.

card _______________ meet _______________

+ed Write **happen** with **ed** at the end of the word.

happen _______________

+'s You know the word **dog**. Write **'s** after **dog**.

dog _______________

Now write this new word in the sentence below.

A _______________ mouth is not really clean.

2=1 You know the words below. Put them together to make four new words. Write the new words.

in + side = _______________

out + side = _______________

who + ever = _______________

any + one = _______________

59

Worktext page 59

16. A CARD FOR CARMEN

Many cards and letters have come to the house. Inez looks through them. She sees something for Carmen. But Carmen is not home. The outside of the letter does not say who it is from. Inez wants to open it. She knows this would be wrong, so she holds off. But after a while, she gets sick of waiting for Carmen. She just has to see who the letter is from. She opens it.

Inside, she finds a pretty card. She opens it. *I'm not going to read it,* she says to herself. But she does. She does not read much. But she can tell a lot from just the words. She can tell the card is from a boy. She can tell he likes Carmen. She does

60

Worktext page 60

not have time to see his name. But she thinks, *It must be from Tom. What other guy would write like that to Carmen?*

Now, Inez feels a little scared. Carmen will see that she has looked at her card. She will be mad about it. Inez puts the card behind a painting. Then she puts it under a box. Then she takes it out. *I have done wrong,* she thinks. *I have to face up to it.* She leaves the card where Carmen will see it.

Inez sits in her room for a long time. Carmen does not come home. At last, Inez comes out. The house is dark. She turns on some lights. The card is gone. Right away, Inez knows what has happened. The dog took it. A cold feeling goes through her. *I should have put it somewhere safe,* she thinks. She looks all over. At last, she finds the card. Yes, she was right. This card has been in a dog's mouth. It has gone through a sad change. It is no longer clean. It is not what anyone would call pretty. A dog's mouth can do that to a card. Many of the words are hard to read. Some of them are gone.

Inez does not see Tom's name. That part is inside the dog. She reads the other part. The boy writes that he wants Carmen to come over. He writes that he has something to tell her.

It must be from Tom, Inez thinks. *What other guy would ask Carmen to come over?* Inez has not been to Tom's house before. But the card tells where the house is.

I will go over there, she thinks. *I will go right now. I will tell him what happened and say I'm sorry. Everything will be all right.*

At the door, Inez stops. *I may as well wear something pretty,* she thinks.

She goes back to her room to change.

61

Worktext page 61

You Make the Call

Inez opens a letter that is for someone else. Put yourself in Inez's place. The letter is now open. You did it. You know it was wrong. But what's done is done. What should you do now? Hide the letter? Tell Carmen what you did? Talk to the writer? Get together with a group of three or four friends and talk about the story. Talk about the bigger idea, too. If you do something wrong, what should you do next? As you talk, write down some of the ideas your group comes up with.

Describe It

The groups of words below are from the story. They all describe the card. But some of them describe how the card looks at first. Some describe how it looks that night. Think where the words should go. Write them on the lines.

sad   words are gone   pretty   clean

How the card looks at first	How the card looks that night
____________	____________
____________	____________
____________	____________
____________	____________

Putting Ideas in Order

The sentences below tell four things that happen in the story. Write them below in the order that they happen in the story.

The card has gone through a sad change.

Inez opens Carmen's letter.

The card is gone.

Inez tries to hide the card behind a painting.

____

____

____

____

____

62

Worktext page 62

Level 3

LESSON 3.17

OBJECTIVE
- Students will practice and apply skills to an extended passage

MATERIALS
Worktext 3, pages 63–65
Teacher's Manual, pages 176–177
Practice Lesson 3.17, pages 98–99 of the Worktext

SKILLS REVIEW

- Before reading, you may wish to review these words that apply phonics skills: *cars, smashed, lots, looks, card, thinks, Tom's, inside, finds, walks, opens, says, Carmen's, Inez's, makes, comes, lights, wanted, wants, paintings, cards, something, likes, whoever, look, just, smile.* Have students review the Memory Chips they have learned so far. Then ask: **What do you think will happen when Inez tries to return the card to Tom?**
- While reading the story on pages 63–64, have students try to picture Luis's apartment.
- After reading, have students complete the exercises on Worktext page 65.

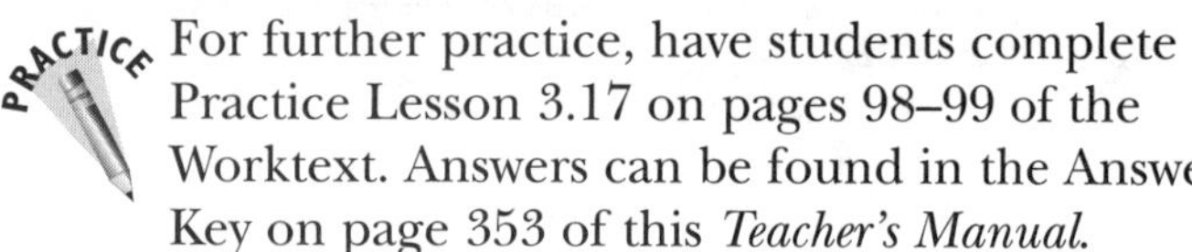

For further practice, have students complete Practice Lesson 3.17 on pages 98–99 of the Worktext. Answers can be found in the Answer Key on page 353 of this *Teacher's Manual.*

RETEACH

If students need further review of phonics skills, you may wish to use the following activity:

Phonograms *ile, use, ard, ook, ad*
Rhyming Riddles Say riddles like these and have students write the word that answers each on the chalkboard:

- **I am 5,280 feet and rhyme with *smile.*** (*mile*)
- **I rhyme with *cook* and am what you do with your eyes.** (*look*)
- **I rhyme with *hard* and am something you give someone when he or she has a birthday.** (*card*)
- **I rhyme with *just* and begin like *make.*** (*must*)
- **I rhyme with *had* and am something you feel when you get angry.** (*mad*)
- **I rhyme with *took* and you read me.** (*book*)
- **I rhyme with *sad* and am the opposite of *good.*** (*bad*)
- **I begin like *what* and rhyme with *smile.*** (*while*)

17. INEZ MEETS A BOY

Inez has come to a big apartment house. There are old cars around the place. One car has a smashed up window. There is lots of graffiti on the side of the house. It looks pretty bad here. It does not look like much of a home.

Inez looks at the card and then at the house.

Well, this must be the place, she thinks. *I guess Tom's family doesn't have much money.*

The door is open. Inez goes through it. Inside she finds a long hall. There is only one light in the hall. It is at the other end, far away. So the hall is pretty dark. Inez walks along till she finds the apartment she is looking for. *Should I ring?* she thinks. *Why not? I have come this far. I will ring.*

A boy opens the door. He looks a little like Tom. But he is not Tom.

"Yes?" the boy says.

"Is Tom home?" she asks.

"I don't know," says the boy. "Why don't you go to his house and find out? This is my house. Who are you?"

"I'm Inez. I'm Carmen's sister."

"Oh." The boy looks down. He sees the card in Inez's hand. "Well, Carmen's sister or whoever you are, what are you doing with my card?"

"Your card?" Inez throws him a look. "This is from Tom." Then she stops. She sees that she may be wrong. "Isn't it?"

"I know my own writing when I see it," says the boy.

Now Inez feels lost. "Just who are you?" she asks.

"My name is Luis."

"Luis! You mean—**The** Luis?"

"The one and only." Luis is wearing a big smile now.

"The boy who makes people laugh?" says Inez.

A change comes over Luis's face. He looks sad. "Yes. I guess that's me," he says. Then he asks Inez, "Do you like the painting on that card?"

63

Worktext page 63

"It's really pretty," says Inez. "Or should I say—it was."

His face lights up again. "I did that," says Luis. "That is what I wanted to tell Carmen. I have a new way to make money now. A card shop wants to buy my paintings. They are going to use them to make cards."

"Really? Boy, that's something. You must be a pretty good painter."

"Yes." Luis likes the way Inez is looking at him. "I am pretty good. Maybe the best that you will ever see. Would you like to see some of my paintings some time?"

"How about right now?" says Inez.

"Well!" says Luis. "I like the way you talk, Carmen's sister. Come on in."

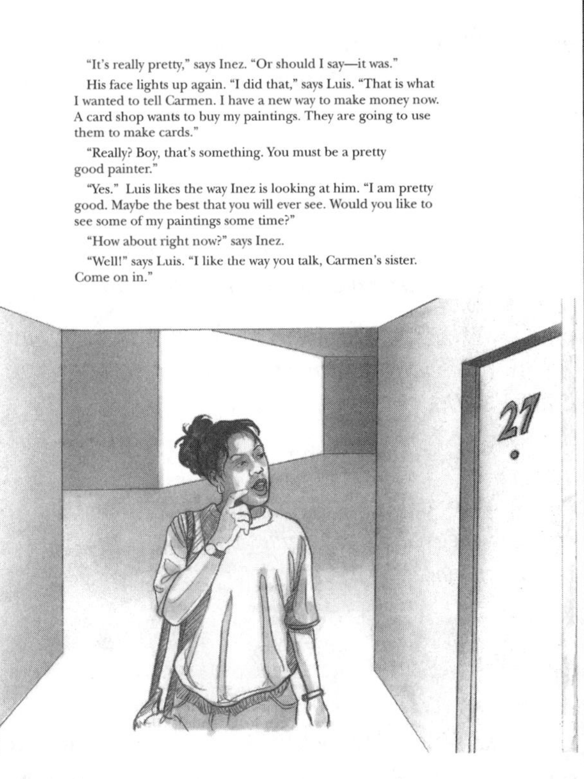

64

Worktext page 64

Describe It

The words below name things you would see around Luis's home. Find words in the story that describe these things. Write one word on every line.

__________ apartment house

__________ cars

__________ car window

__________ hall

__________ light

Remembering Details

The sentences below ask about the story. Write the answers on the line. You may write one word or more than one on a line. Look back at the story if you need to.

What is on the side of Luis's house? __________

Where is the light in the hall? __________

What does Luis see in Inez's hand? __________

What does Inez say about the painting on the card? __________

Who is now going to buy paintings from Luis? __________

Find the One Big Idea

These sentences tell about the story. One sentence tells what the story is all about. Find that sentence. Write it on the lines below.

Inez does not get to see Tom after all.

Inez meets Luis and likes him.

Luis finds out that Inez is Carmen's sister.

65

Worktext page 65

Level 3

FINAL NOVEL The $22,000 Problem

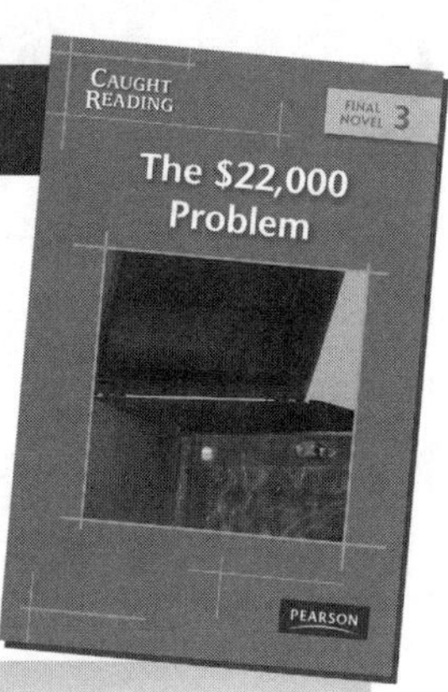

MATERIALS

Final Novel 3, *The $22,000 Problem*
Teacher's Manual, page 178
Assessment Manual, Final Assessment 3, pages 81–84

Summary *Carmen buys an old wooden box. Inside the box, she finds an expensive baseball card. She will be able to sell the card for a lot of money–if she can hold on to it. The card disappears, but Carmen finally finds it. She sells the card for a lot of money.*

REVIEW AND ASSESSMENT

- Depending on your students' needs, review the following skills covered in Lessons 9–17: context clues; possessives; compound words; contractions; vowel pairs (CVVC); vowel pair *ea*; letter patterns CVCe; phonograms *uy, ould, ave, ame, old, ot, ind, ile, ust, ard, ook,* and *ad;* and endings *s, ing,* and *ed.*
- Have students review their Memory Chips.

If you wish to assess students' progress at this point, use the *Assessment Manual*, pages 81–84. For students who need additional support, you may use the Reteach activities from previous lessons.

INTRODUCE THE NOVEL

Invite students to preview the book by reading the title, looking at the illustrations, and reading aloud the captions. Begin a discussion of story concepts by asking:

- **Have you ever bought anything at a garage or apartment sale?**
- **What kinds of things can you find to buy at a garage or apartment sale?**

CHECK COMPREHENSION

Chapter 1 Why does Carmen want to leave the house in such a hurry? (*She wants to go to a sale.*)

Chapter 2 Do you think Carmen got a good deal on the box? Why or why not? (*Students may say yes because she likes it, or no because it is a lot of money for a used box.*)

Chapter 3 How does Tom react to Carmen's purchase? (*He thinks she spent too much money on it.*)

Chapter 4 What is bothering Tom? (*His coach says he is a good ball player, but he can't afford to go to baseball school.*)

Chapter 5 What does Carmen find in the box? (*She finds an old baseball card.*)

Chapter 6 What is special about the card? (*It is a baseball card of a famous player.*)

Chapter 7 Why is Carmen feeling bad? (*She forgot to get home for supper on time, Inez's dog ate a boy's food, and the man who wanted the box at the sale showed up at the restaurant.*)

Chapter 8 What happens when Carmen takes the card to a baseball card dealer? (*She finds out it is worth $20,000.*)

Chapter 9 What do you think Carmen will do with the card? (*Possible answer: She will sell it.*)

Chapter 10 Why does Tom get upset with Carmen? (*She does not offer to pay for his baseball school.*)

Chapter 11 Why does Carmen wake up in the middle of the night? (*She hears noises and thinks someone is in the house.*)

Chapter 12 Who do you think took the baseball card? (*Possible answers: the man at the sale, the baseball card buyer, Luis, Inez*)

Chapter 13 Who was outside Carmen's house last night? (*It was Luis.*)

Chapter 14 What was Luis doing outside Carmen's house? (*He was looking out for her and the card.*)

Chapter 15 What did the man at the apartment sale really want? (*He wanted to buy the box so he could fix it and sell it for $200.*)

Chapter 16 Who took the baseball card? (*Cougar*)

Chapter 17 Why does Carmen decide Luis is her boyfriend, not Tom? (*Luis makes her laugh, and he didn't want her money.*)

CONNECTION

Home/School Encourage students to bring home a copy of *The $22,000 Problem.* They might read the novel, or sections of the novel, to family members.

LEVEL 4

ORGANIZER

Level 4 of the *Caught Reading* program includes the following components:

Worktext 4

Worktext 4 includes 15 lessons, taking students from those words introduced in previous levels through a word list of 177 words (found on page 341 of this *Teacher's Manual*) by Lesson 15. The Practice Lessons provide students with opportunites to extend practice, and review the content of each lesson. The Response to Reading pages allow students to practice using their new vocabulary. Tear-out Memory Chips in the back of the student book reinforce new vocabulary and can be used both independently by students and in small groups.

Midway and Final Novels 4

These novels are designed to reinforce learned vocabulary and give students the opportunity to read for meaning. Their high-interest plots encourage successful reading experiences and an appreciation for literature.

- *How to Shake Off a Shark* includes only vocabulary students have learned up to the midway point of this level.
- *Trapped in Space* includes all vocabulary learned through Level 4.

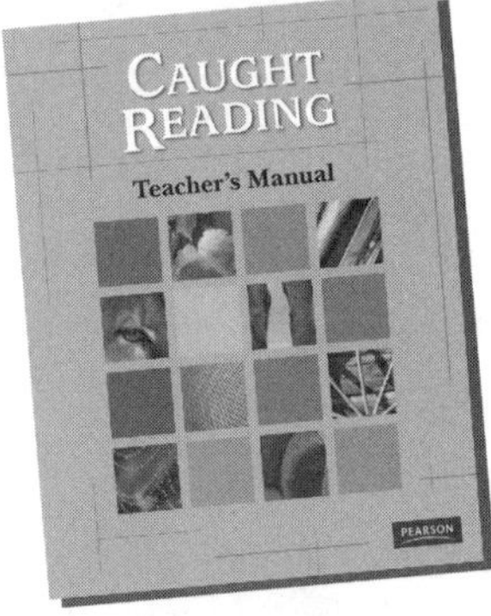

Teacher's Manual

The *Teacher's Manual* provides detailed objectives and instruction for each skill taught in the Worktext, as well as additional teaching suggestions for meaningful practice and reinforcement. The *Teacher's Manual* provides choices for flexible instruction. Comprehension questions for the Midway and Final novels are included, as well as Answer Keys for the Worktext activities and the Practice Lessons.

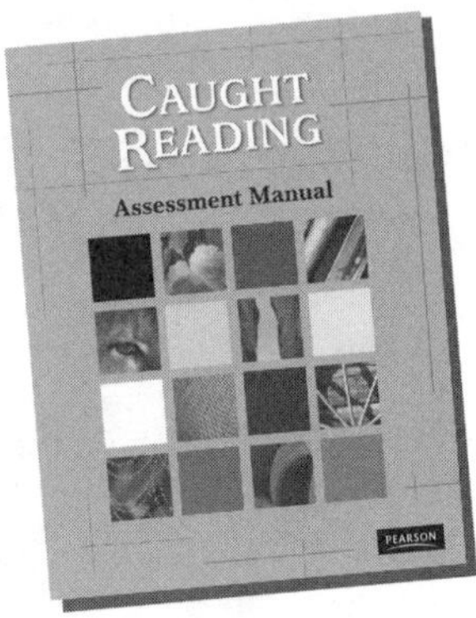

Assessment Manual

The *Assessment Manual* provides preassessment, ongoing assessment, and postassessment to administer to students throughout their work in *Caught Reading*. Within this Manual you will also find Midway and Final Assessments to determine the students' comprehension of the Midway and Final Novels.

OBJECTIVES

Vocabulary Development

- Read a base vocabulary, plus base vocabulary words with various endings, compound words, and contractions formed from base words.
- Use the word learning sequence to remember and spell words correctly.
- Review vocabulary independently, both in and out of context, using the Memory Chips.
- Learn fundamental science vocabulary.

Phonics

- Read the contractions *aren't, they're, we'll,* and *you'll.*
- Recognize the letter groups *ant, ap, ip, ut,* and *in.*

Reading Comprehension

- Use study skills to read and understand science content.
- Interpret charts and illustrations.

Literary Analysis

- Determine the underlying theme or author's message in nonfiction.
- Determine differences between fiction and nonfiction writing.

Writing

- Write summaries.
- Make headings into questions and answer them in writing.

Speaking and Listening

- Respond to questions with appropriate elaboration.
- Work in small groups to make presentations.

INTRODUCTION & LESSON 4.1

OBJECTIVES

- Students will decode and blend words containing the *ive, ind,* and *ill* phonograms
- Students will apply endings *s, ing, ed,* and *er* to base words to form new words
- Students will recognize and form contractions
- Students will recognize and form possessives

PHONICS VOCABULARY

remembers	interested	mind	sitting
talking	scientists	wants	says
studies	living	things	questions
starts	Tyrone's	sleeping	sees
parts	ones	will	can't
don't	I'll	live	kind
eyes	scientist's	tired	harder
myself	aren't	scientist	heading
headings	knowing	studying	books
maps	charts	stones	still
different			

WORDS TO KNOW

different	eat	eye	front
glass	interested	kind	life
live	scientist	still	Tyrone
book	caught	chart	fact
head	map	memory	question
science	study	summary	

MATERIALS

Worktext 4, pages 5–11
Teacher's Manual, pages 182–184
Practice Lesson 4.1, pages 67–68 of the Worktext

TEACH

- Before beginning the lesson, have students complete the exercises independently in the Introduction on Worktext page 5.
- Using Worktext page 8, introduce students to the vocabulary words. Give students an opportunity to practice writing the words.
- Students can organize their Memory Chips, found in the back of the Worktext. You may wish to say each word, having them repeat it after you. Students can take turns using each word in a sentence.

Worktext page 8 can also be used to reinforce spelling. Use the five-step process detailed on page 71 of this *Teacher's Manual.*

Phonograms *ive, ind, ill*

Write this sentence on the board and read it aloud: **I will give you everything I find.** Ask a volunteer to point to *give.*

Blending Circle the *ive* in *give* and explain that sometimes these letters have the sound of /*iv*/. Erase the *g* and write **l**. Tell students the word rhymes with *give* and ask them to blend the sounds: /*liv*/. Write **will** and **find** on the board. Have students list rhyming words for each word. (*will, kill, bill, till, sill, hill, fill; find, mind, kind*). List them on the board, blending them as you read them aloud.

Endings *s, ing, ed, er*

Write this sentence on the board: **The teacher tried to find the boys who were sitting on the bus.** Point to *tried* and ask students to identify the ending. (*ed*) Write **try** on the board and tell them *try* is the base word for *tried.* Show them how to change the *y* to *i* and add *ed.* Ask students to identify the base word in *sitting.* (*sit*) Remind them that when *ing* is added, the last consonant is doubled. Write **live** on the board. Ask a volunteer to add *ing,* reminding students to take off the *e* before adding the *ing.*

Make New Words Write these words on the board: **cry**, **hard**, **dig**, **eye**. Have students take turns adding *s, ing, ed,* or *er* to each word if it makes a new word. (*cries, crying, cried, crier; harder; digs, digging, digger; eyes, eyed*) They can write the words on the board and use each one in a sentence.

Contractions

Remind students that words like *can't, don't,* and *didn't* are other ways of saying *cannot, do not,* and *did not.* An apostrophe takes the place of letters that are taken out of the word or words.

Make New Words Have students make contractions out of these words: *are not, does not, let us.* (*aren't, doesn't, let's*)

Possessives

Remind students that they can add an apostrophe and *s* to the end of words to show that someone or something owns something else.

Make New Words Have students add an apostrophe and *s* to these words: *Inez, scientist, Tyrone, boy, car.* (*Inez's, scientist's, Tyrone's, boy's, car's*)

PRACTICE

- Let students practice the new words they have learned and formed by completing the activities found on pages 7–9 of the Worktext.
- If students are experiencing difficulty with the Words to Know section on page 8, place the

Memory Chips on the table. Write incomplete words on the board and have students use the Memory Chips to find the missing vowels. For example: **_nt_r_st_d**. (*interested*)

For further practice, have students complete Practice Lesson 4.1 on pages 67–68 of the Worktext. Answers can be found in the Answer Key on page 354 of this *Teacher's Manual.*

APPLY

- Have students talk about the story concept by discussing things they have experienced. Ask: **Have you ever had a dream that seemed to be real? What happened in the dream?** Tell students they are going to use the words they have learned to read a short story about a boy who falls asleep and has a very strange dream.
- Ask students to read the story on page 10 in the Worktext. Offer assistance if necessary, but encourage students to decode the words independently, using the clues and patterns they have learned.
- After students have completed reading the story, have them complete the Comprehension Exercise (Remembering Details) on page 11 in their Worktext. Answers can be found in the Answer Key on page 353 of this *Teacher's Manual.*

CONNECTION

Speaking/Listening Have three student volunteers read aloud the selection "The Mad Scientist" on page 10. Encourage the rest of the class to be active, attentive listeners.

Worktext Pages 5 & 7

INTRODUCTION: GET CAUGHT READING SCIENCE

Words to Know

	Look	Say	Picture	Write
book	☐	☐	☐	________
caught	☐	☐	☐	________
chart	☐	☐	☐	________
fact	☐	☐	☐	________
head	☐	☐	☐	________
map	☐	☐	☐	________
memory mem-o-ry	☐	☐	☐	________
question ques-tion	☐	☐	☐	________
science sci-ence	☐	☐	☐	________
study stud-y	☐	☐	☐	________
summary sum-ma-ry	☐	☐	☐	________

Word Attack

+ing, +s Write **head** with an **ing** ending. ________

Now write **heading** with an **s** ending. ________

+ing Write the words below with **ing** endings.

know ________ study ________

+s Write an **s** ending after these words.

book ________ map ________

chart ________ question ________

+es Write both words with **es** endings. (Change the **y** into an i.)

story ________ study ________

5

Worktext page 5

1. THE MAD SCIENTIST

Word Attack

find, mind You know the words **find** and **mind**. Try reading this word: **kind**. Write the words you see below. Circle the letter group that is the same in all of them.

kind ________ find ________

mind ________

give You know the word **give**. One of the new words sounds the same and ends the same as **give**. This letter group does not always sound like it does in **give**. But try it in this word: **live**. Do you know this word? Write it in the sentence.

I ________ in a big house.

Sometimes, the letter group **ive** sounds as it does in the word **alive**. When you see this letter group at the end of a word, try one sound. Then try the other sound. See if one of them is a word you know.

will You know how the word **will** sounds. You know, too, how **st** sounds in **stop.** Now try reading this word: **still.** Write the words below. Circle the letter group that is the same.

still ________ will ________

Take a Guess

Sometimes, you can guess a word when you see it in a sentence. See if you can guess the word in dark letters. What word works in the sentence? Think of one that starts with a **d** sound. Sound out letters to see if you are right.

A bike and a car are **different**.

Did you guess the word? Write it. ________

7

Worktext page 7

Worktext Pages 8–11

Sometimes, you can guess a word by trying two ways together. You can look at other words in the sentence. You can look for parts that you know inside the word. Try the two ways with the word in dark letters below.

A **scientist** is someone who knows about science.

The new word is made from a word you know—**science**. The first five letters are the same. Now think, *Who would know about science?* Can you guess the word? Write it in the sentence.

Luis wants to work as a ________________.

Words to Know

	Look	Say	Picture	Write
different dif-fer-ent	☐	☐	☐	________________
eat	☐	☐	☐	________________
eye	☐	☐	☐	________________
front	☐	☐	☐	________________
glass	☐	☐	☐	________________
interested in-ter-est-ed	☐	☐	☐	________________
kind	☐	☐	☐	________________
life	☐	☐	☐	________________
live	☐	☐	☐	________________
scientist sci-en-tist	☐	☐	☐	________________
still	☐	☐	☐	________________
Tyrone Ty-rone	☐	☐	☐	________________

8

Worktext page 8

1. THE MAD SCIENTIST

Tyrone remembers the night he got interested in science. He can see it in his mind. He is sitting in front of the TV. A man is talking about science. Tyrone can hardly keep his eyes open. But he wants to see this show.

The man says, "A scientist is interested in just about everything. How does sound work? What is light? These are just some of the questions a scientist asks. He or she studies living things, too. A scientist wants to know how life starts and how different things live."

As the man goes on, Tyrone's eyes start to close. Then he goes to sleep. But he does not know he is sleeping. In his mind, he still sees the TV. And in his mind, the man on TV is now a mad scientist. He comes right up to the glass of the TV. He looks out at Tyrone. "You out there," he says.

"Who? Me?" says Tyrone.

"Yes, you," says the scientist. "Why are you just sitting there? Did you forget you work for me? Go out and get me some parts." The scientist has a really mad look in his eye.

"What kind of parts?" Tyrone asks.

"Fish parts! What kind do you think? I want to put them together and make some new people. The ones I make will do what I say. The people I make will help me take over!"

"But," cries Tyrone, "you can't make people out of fish parts!"

"Don't talk back or I'll fire you," says the mad scientist. "You just get me the parts." Then he says, "All right, if you can't get fish parts, get me some fish. I'll take them apart myself. Oh, and Tyrone—"

"Yes?" says Tyrone.

"On your way back, get me some fish food," says the mad scientist. "I have not had anything to eat all day."

10

Worktext page 10

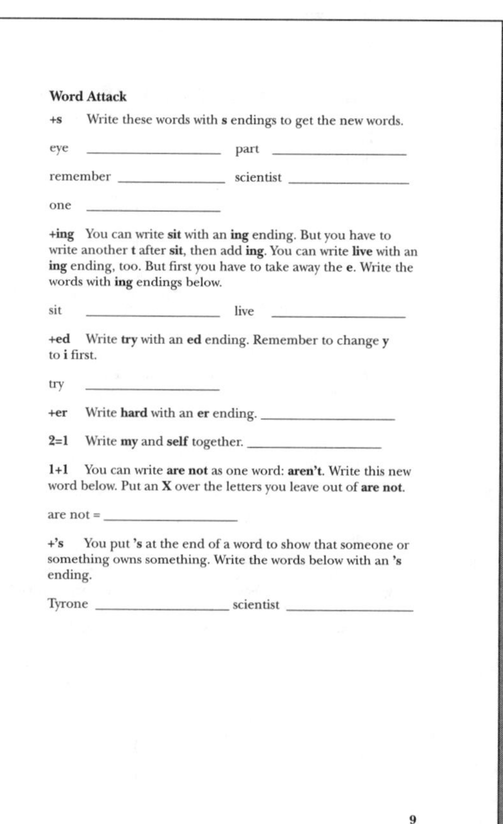

Word Attack

+s Write these words with **s** endings to get the new words.

eye ________________ part ________________

remember ________________ scientist ________________

one ________________

+ing You can write **sit** with an **ing** ending. But you have to write another **t** after **sit**, then add **ing**. You can write **live** with an **ing** ending, too. But first you have to take away the **e**. Write the words with **ing** endings below.

sit ________________ live ________________

+ed Write **try** with an **ed** ending. Remember to change **y** to **i** first.

try ________________

+er Write **hard** with an **er** ending. ________________

2=1 Write **my** and **self** together. ________________

1+1 You can write **are not** as one word: **aren't**. Write this new word below. Put an **X** over the letters you leave out of **are not**.

are not = ________________

+'s You put **'s** at the end of a word to show that someone or something owns something. Write the words below with an **'s** ending.

Tyrone ________________ scientist ________________

9

Worktext page 9

Remembering Details

This is a game to help you remember details about the story. Find words in the story to fill in the crossword. Write one letter to a box. Use the clues to help find the correct word.

Across

3. The man on TV says he wants to make some new _______.
4. In his sleep, Tyrone thinks he works for a mad _______.
6. It all starts one night when Tyrone is looking at a show about _______.

Down

1. The last thing the scientist says to Tyrone is to get him fish _______.
2. The scientist comes up to the _______ of the TV and talks to Tyrone.
3. The scientist wants Tyrone to get him some fish _______.
5. If Tyrone talks back, the scientist will _______ him.

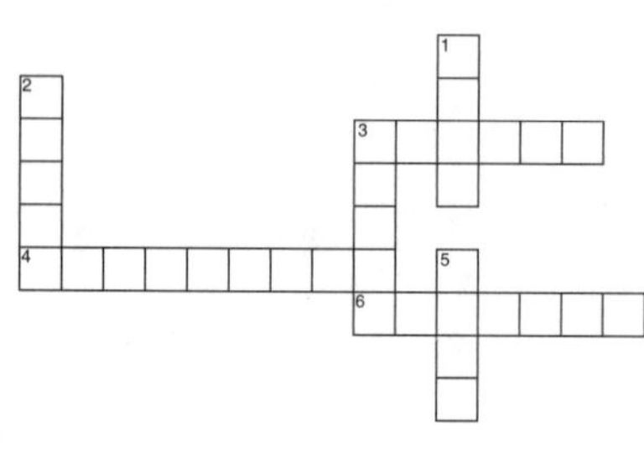

11

Worktext page 11

LESSON 4.2

OBJECTIVE

- Students will practice and apply skills to an extended passage

MATERIALS

Worktext 4, pages 12–13
Teacher's Manual, page 185
Practice Lesson 4.2, pages 69–70 of the Worktext
Two boxes (Reteach)

SKILLS REVIEW

- Before reading, you may wish to review these words that apply phonics skills: *looking, find, parts, thinks, don't, fired, will, stops, that's, it's, jobs, sleeping, taking, feels, things, looks, comes, didn't, walks, he's, says, always.* Have students review the Memory Chips they have learned so far. Then ask: **What do you think Tyrone will do next?**
- While reading, have students ask themselves if they have ever had a dream similar to Tyrone's.
- After reading, have students complete Writing a Summary on Worktext page 13.

For further practice, have students complete Practice Lesson 4.2 on pages 69–70 of the Worktext. Answers can be found in the Answer Key on page 355 of this *Teacher's Manual.*

RETEACH

If students need further review of phonics skills, you may wish to use the following activity:

Phonograms *ive, ill, ind*

Words in a Box Write phonograms **ive**, **ill**, and **ind** on index cards and place in a box on the right. Then write consonants **g**, **l**, **w**, **p**, **f**, **m**, and **k** on cards and place in a box on the left. Have students choose a card from each box and blend the two sounds together to make a word. Help students pronounce both the short and long *i* sounds for phonograms *ind* in *wind* and for *ive* in *live.* Have students use each word they make in a sentence. You may also wish to expand this activity and review phonograms such as *ook, ill, ard, ile, ell, ace, ast, et, ight, ame, it, ave, ow, and, art, un, ack, old, op, eam, eep, ad, ake, ike, an, all, alk, ay,* and *ot.*

Worktext Pages 12–13

2. LOOKING FOR FISH PARTS

Tyrone is out looking for fish parts. He has to take them back to the mad scientist.

I better find some fish parts fast, he thinks. *If I don't, then I may be fired from my job. What will I do then? How will I ever find another job in science?*

Then Tyrone stops. *Something is wrong with all this,* he thinks. *Here I am, looking for fish parts. What kind of job is that? That's not a science job. It's not any kind of job. There are no jobs like that—not in real life. Could it be that this is not real life? Could it be that I am sleeping? Could all this be taking place in my sleep?*

At first, he can't believe it. Everything feels so real. But then he thinks, *Wait. If I am sleeping, I will not know that I am sleeping. Things will feel real. So how can I tell if I am sleeping or not?* This looks like a problem. Tyrone thinks and thinks about it, and then an idea comes to him. *Why didn't I think of it before?* he asks himself. *If I am sleeping, I will be at home. So I will just go home and look. I will see if I am sleeping.*

Tyrone goes home. He walks into his living room, and there he is! He's in front of the TV—sleeping!

"But wait!" he says. "If that is Tyrone—who am I?"

As he says this, his eyes open. He find himself in front of the TV. The other Tyrone is gone. There is a real scientist on TV. "So," says this scientist, "I will say it again. There will always be good jobs in science."

Tyrone sits up. *Good jobs in science,* he thinks. *Yes, that's it. I will study science, and one day, I will get a job in science. But it will be a real job.*

12

Worktext page 12

Writing a Summary

A **summary** is a way to tell a long story in just four or five sentences. It gives only the big things that happen in a story. A summary tells the story in the same order that it happens.

Read these sentences about the story you just read. Some of them tell about big things. Some give details. The sentences are in the right order. To make a summary, write four of the sentences on the lines below. Write only the sentences that tell the big things that happened.

In his sleep, Tyrone thinks he works for a mad scientist.

The scientist has had nothing to eat all day.

Tyrone goes out to find fish parts for the scientist.

He comes home and sees himself sleeping.

Tyrone's sleeping self is in the living room.

Tyrone opens his eyes and sees a real scientist on TV.

____

____

____

____

____

13

Worktext page 13

LESSON 4.3

OBJECTIVES

- Students will learn new words containing the phonograms and letter patterns *ut, all, ever,* and *ark,* and vowel pairs *ee* and *ea*
- Students will use context clues to recognize an unfamiliar word
- Students will apply endings *er, est, s, ed,* and *ing* to base words to form new words
- Students will recognize and form plural possessives

PHONICS VOCABULARY

sharks'	biggest	sharks	but	shark
lines	teeth	opens	all	never
coming	gets	weeks	eat	small
creatures	darkest	using	makes	feel
making	hiding	keep	faster	works
keeps	clean	eats	attacks	times
turn	run	shark's	moving	cut
fall	monster	year	animals	eats
smaller	monsters	closed	attacked	

WORDS TO KNOW

animal	creature	cut	die	fall
monster	never	shark	small	teeth
water	year			

MATERIALS

Worktext 4, pages 14–19
Teacher's Manual, pages 186–188
Practice Lesson 4.3, pages 71–72 of the Worktext

TEACH

- Using Worktext page 15, introduce students to the vocabulary words. Give students an opportunity to practice writing the words.
- Students can organize their Memory Chips, found in the back of the Worktext. They can divide them into groups of words they know and words they don't recognize.

Worktext page 15 can also be used to reinforce spelling. Use the five-step process detailed on page 71 of this *Teacher's Manual.*

Phonograms and Letter Patterns *ut, all, ever, ark*

Write these sentences on the board: **But are all the dogs out? Will it ever be dark?** Have a volunteer point to the word *dark.* Blend the word with the help of students, /*d*/ /*âr*/ /*k*/. Tell students that when they see *ar* together, the *r* gives *a* the sound of /*âr*/. Have them point to the words *but, ever,* and *all.*

Blending Write **but**, **ever**, **all**, and **dark** on the board. Have students name rhyming words for each word.

As each word is suggested, volunteers can substitute beginning letters and blends to make new words.

but	ever	all	dark
cut	never	ball	park
rut	clever	fall	shark

Vowel Pairs

Write this sentence on the board, and have a volunteer read it aloud: **During a year, a shark loses a lot of teeth.** Ask a volunteer to point to *year.* Ask the volunteer to circle the vowels that make the long *e* sound in *year.* Repeat with *teeth.* Remind students that when they see words with the *ee* or *ea* vowel pair, the long *e* sound is usually made.

Blending Write the words **neat**, **fear**, **deer**, and **feet** on the board. Say the word *neat* pointing to the letters as you segment the word: /*n*/ /*ē*/ /*t*/. Repeat, using the words *fear, deer,* and *feet.*

Context Clues

Write this sentence on the board: **I was shocked to see a monster standing in the kitchen.** Cover the word *monster,* and tell students that when they see an unfamiliar word like this one, they can read the words around it and use what they know about letters and sounds to help them figure out the word. Read the sentence without *monster.* Uncover the word, and have students look at the beginning letter. Tell them that the *m* gives us a clue as to how the word begins. Ask them what word they think goes in the sentence. (*monster*)

Endings *er, est, s, ed, ing*

Write these sentences on the board, and read them aloud: **My dog is smaller than your dog. Tom's dog is the smallest.** Ask students to circle the endings *er* and *est* in *smaller* and *smallest.* Tell them the ending *er* is used to compare two people, places, or things; the ending *est* is used to compare three or more people, places, or things. Then remind students that they have learned to add *s, ed,* and *ing* to words. Ask them what they do when a word ends in *e* and they add an ending *ed* or *ing.* (*They drop the* e *and add the ending.*)

Make New Words Write these words on the board, and invite students to add *er* or *est* to the end of each word: **tall**, **short**, and **dark**. (*taller, tallest*; *shorter, shortest*; *darker, darkest*) They can use each new word they make in a sentence. Then have them add endings *ed, s,* and *ing* to these words (not all words will work with each ending): *close, attack, creature, shark, hide, move, turn.* (*closed, closes, closing*; *attacked, attacks, attacking*; *creatures*; *sharks*; *hides, hiding*; *moved, moves, moving*; *turned, turns, turning*)

Possessives

Write this sentence on the board, and read it aloud: **The boys' coats are lost.** Ask students if the sentence is about one boy or more than one. (*more than one*) Tell them that when ownership needs to be indicated in a word ending in *s*, most of the time just an apostrophe is added.

Make New Words Have students add an apostrophe to show ownership in these words: *sharks, girls, teachers, painters, cars.* (*sharks', girls', teachers', painters', cars'*)

PRACTICE

- Let students practice the new words they have learned and formed by completing the activities found on pages 14–16 of the Worktext.
- If students are experiencing difficulty with the Words to Know section on page 15, you may wish to have students draw pictures to help them remember words like *animal, creature, monster, shark, small, teeth, water,* and *year.*

For further practice, have students complete Practice Lesson 4.3 on pages 71–72 of the Worktext. Answers can be found in the Answer Key on page 355 of this *Teacher's Manual.*

APPLY

- Have students talk about the story concept by sharing their prior knowledge. Ask: **What do you know about sharks?** Tell them they are going to use the words they have learned to read a short article about sharks.
- Ask students to read the article on pages 17–18 in the Worktext. Offer assistance if necessary, but encourage students to decode the words independently, using the clues and patterns they have learned.
- After students have completed reading the article, have them complete the Comprehension Exercises (Make Headings into Questions and Now Find the Facts) on page 19 in their Worktext. Answers can be found in the Answer Key on page 354 of this *Teacher's Manual.*

CONNECTION

Strategy for Reading After students finish reading the selection, "Monsters of the Sea" on Worktext pages 17–18, ask them to summarize it either aloud or in writing.

Writing Students can write a few sentences on what they think about sharks. Have student volunteers share their writing with the class.

Worktext Pages 14–15

3. MONSTERS OF THE SEA

Word Attack

but You know the word **but**. Try reading this word: **cut**. Write the words below.

cut ______________ but ______________

all, hall You know the words **all** and **hall**. Try reading this word: **fall**. Now attack another word with the same letter group: **small**. Write the words below. Circle the letter group that is the same in them.

fall ______________ small ______________

all ______________ hall ______________

ever You know the word **ever**. The new word **never** is **n + ever**. Trying reading **never**. Write it in the sentence.

Tom has ______________ seen Carmen's sister.

dark You know the word **dark**. The letter group **ark** sounds the same at the end of any word. Try to read this new word: **shark**. Write it in the sentence below.

A ______________ is a fish.

ea, ee Remember what may work at times: when two vowels are side by side, the first one may have a **long** sound. The next one may have no sound. Try using this to attack the word **year**. Now use it to attack the word **teeth**. Write the two words in the sentences below.

A ______________ is a long time.

Is it hard to eat if you have no ______________?

Take a Guess

You can guess one new word by reading it in the sentence below. Think of a word that starts with an **m** sound and works in the sentence.

I am scared of a **monster** I see in the dark.

Did you guess the word? Write it. ______________

14

Worktext page 14

Words to Know

	Look	Say	Picture	Write
animal an-i-mal	☐	☐	☐	______________
creature crea-ture	☐	☐	☐	______________
cut	☐	☐	☐	______________
die	☐	☐	☐	______________
fall	☐	☐	☐	______________
monster mon-ster	☐	☐	☐	______________
never ne-ver	☐	☐	☐	______________
shark	☐	☐	☐	______________
small	☐	☐	☐	______________
teeth	☐	☐	☐	______________
water wa-ter	☐	☐	☐	______________
year	☐	☐	☐	______________

Word Attack

+s You know the words below. Write them with **s** endings.

animal ______________ attack ______________

creature ______________ eat ______________

monster ______________ shark ______________

+ed Write the words below with **ed** endings. Remember to take away the **e** at the end of **close** before you write **ed**.

attack ______________ close ______________

+est Write **dark** with the ending **est**. ______________

+er Write **small** with the ending **er**. ______________

15

Worktext page 15

Level 4

+ing The words **hide**, **move**, and **use** all end with **e**. Take away the **e**, then write **ing**. You get the new words: **hiding**, **moving**, and **using**. Write these words with **ing** endings.

hide __________________ move __________________

use __________________

+s' A word for many things already ends with an **s**, as in one **shark**; many **sharks**. To show that sharks have something, just add (') after the **s**: the **sharks'** home. Write this new word in the sentence below.

All the __________________ eyes were open.

–s You know the words **turns** and **runs**. Take away the **s**, and you have the base words: **turn** and **run**. Write these words in the sentence below.

I ________ around, I see the dog, and I start to _________.

16

Worktext page 16

The Things Sharks Eat

Most sharks live on fish. But they will eat any animal they can find. In fact, sharks may even take in things that are not alive. One shark had a bike inside it when it was caught and cut open!

Most sharks eat live fish. They even eat other sharks. Big sharks eat small ones. Sharks also eat fish that are not alive.

How Sharks Find Food

It is hard to get away from a shark in the water. For one thing, sharks can see really well. Their eyes do not need much light. In fact, sharks see best after the sun goes down. Many sharks are creatures of the night.

Sharks can get around even in the darkest night. They don't need to see to find animals. They can do this without using their eyes. When a fish goes through the water, it makes the water move. Sharks can feel the water move. They can tell what is making the water move and where the fish is. So even if a fish is hiding, a shark can find it.

How Sharks Attack

Sharks cannot stop moving. If they stop moving, they die. So even in their sleep, sharks keep moving. Sharks circle a fish before they attack it. At first, they make a big circle. Then they move in, going even faster. At last, they turn in and hit the fish.

Many sharks have a little fish that goes with them everywhere. The little fish works for the shark. It keeps the shark clean. When the shark attacks something, the little fish eats some of it, too. The shark does not attack this little fish.

Now and again, you hear about a shark that attacks people. Scientists do not know why sharks at times attack people and at other times leave them be.

18

Worktext page 18

3. MONSTERS OF THE SEA

The biggest fish in the sea are sharks. But when most people think of sharks, they don't think **big**. They think **monster**. Why are people scared of this creature? Look into the mouth of one, and you'll see why.

What Sharks' Teeth Are Like

People have only two lines of teeth. A shark has many lines of teeth. When its mouth is closed, its teeth point to the back. But when the mouth opens, all the teeth point to the front. Sharks never run out of teeth. As the front teeth wear down, they fall out. The next line of teeth then moves to the front. New teeth are always coming in at the back. A shark gets a new line of teeth every one to two weeks.

17

Worktext page 17

For Better Studying

You have just read some facts about sharks. These facts were under headings. When you read, headings let you know what kinds of facts are coming next. All the facts below one heading go together.

Make Headings into Questions

A good way to remember the facts below a heading is to turn the heading into a question. Words like **what**, **how**, **why**, **where**, and **when** before a heading can help turn it into a question. You may have to move words around a little to make a heading read like a question. A question word may be in the heading already: **How Sharks Attack**. Then you may need to put in another word or two to make a question: **How do sharks attack**?

Below are the headings from the story. Make them into questions. The first one is done for you. The next one has been started for you. Do the last one by yourself.

1. Heading: **What Sharks' Teeth Are Like**

Question: *What are sharks' teeth like?*

2. Heading: **How Sharks Find Food**

Question: *How do* ________________

3. Heading: **The Things Sharks Eat**

Question: ________________________________

Now Find the Facts

Now that you have questions, you can look for facts that answer them. Look at the question below. Find facts in the story that answer it. Write the facts on the lines below.

Question 1: *What Are Sharks' Teeth Like?*

Facts: ________________________________

____

____

____

19

Worktext page 19

LESSON 4.4

OBJECTIVE

- Students will practice and apply skills to an extended passage

MATERIALS

Worktext 4, pages 20–22
Teacher's Manual, pages 189–190, 330–331, 333
Practice Lesson 4.4, pages 73–74 of the Worktext

SKILLS REVIEW

- Before reading, you may wish to review these words that apply phonics skills: *fishing, throws, happens, likes, being, feels, sits, knows, pulls, closer, gets, sees, ever, bigger, thinks, comes, hits, starts, shark, faster, going, tells, happened, friends, believes.* Have students review the Memory Chips they have learned so far. Then ask: **Has something ever happened to you that no one would believe?**
- While reading, have students think about how Tom must have felt when he saw the shark.
- After reading, have students complete the summarizing activity on Worktext page 21 and the chart activities on page 22.

For further practice, have students complete Practice Lesson 4.4 on pages 73–74 of the Worktext. Answers can be found in the Answer Key on page 355 of this *Teacher's Manual.*

RETEACH

If students need further review of phonics skills, you may wish to use the following activity:

Phonograms *ut, ark, all*; **Long e**: *ee, ea*

Charades Write these words on slips of paper: **cut**, **fall**, **tall**, **hall**, **small**, **dark**, **shark**, **teeth**, **eat**, **year**, **fear**, **wall**, **mall**. Have students take turns choosing one slip of paper and pantomiming actions that represent the actions for that word. Have students guess the word's identity and spell it. Remind them that when they play charades, the person giving the clues cannot speak—he or she can only act out clues to the word's identity. Tell them that holding up the number of fingers tells how many letters the word is.

CONNECTION

Response to Reading

- To reinforce students' understanding of the literary elements found in their reading material, have them complete the Story Map and Character Cluster reproducibles found on pages 330–331.
- Students will demonstrate an understanding of setting, characters, and plot by filling out the organizers.
- Students may share their completed organizers with the class.

Literature

- Students may enjoy reading or listening to other books about the sea. *Moby Dick* and *20,000 Leagues Under the Sea* are available in softcover texts and on audiocassette from Pearson's *Pacemaker™ Classics.*
- Students may use the Book Report reproducible found on page 333 of this *Teacher's Manual* to record their responses to the book they read.

4. A FISH STORY

Tom has his own boat. One day he goes out by himself to do a little fishing. He throws out his line. Not much happens. That is all right with Tom. He just likes being out in the water under the hot sun. He goes to sleep. Then he feels his line move. Tom sits up. He has no idea how much time has gone by. But he knows he has caught something really big. He pulls on his line. The fish pulls back. Tom pulls really hard. So does the fish. Now Tom really goes to work. He knows how to fish when he has to. He lets the line out. Then he pulls it in. He makes that fish work. Little by little, he pulls it closer. At last, he gets it right next to his boat. Then he sees it, and his eyes get big. No one will ever laugh at Tom again. The fish is bigger than he is. How can he even get it into his boat?

He thinks hard about this problem.

Then it happens. A shark comes out of the water. Tom can feel it when the shark hits his fish. Just like that, a big part of his fish is gone. Tom starts his boat. He has to get away. But the shark can move much faster than his boat. Tom sees it going around him in a circle. He is scared. Maybe the shark will come after him. Maybe he will not get out of this alive. Again and again, the shark hits Tom's fish. There is nothing Tom can do. Before he knows it, the fish is all gone.

Then the shark goes away.

Tom gets back as the sun is going down. He tells everyone what happened. "I caught a fish that was bigger than I am! But a shark got it on the way back!"

But his friends just smile. "I caught one bigger than a bus," says his friend Will.

"I caught one bigger than a house one time," says his friend Mike. "Too bad a shark got it before anyone could see it."

No one believes the story about Tom and the really big fish.

20

Worktext page 20

Write a Summary

The sentences below all tell things that happen in the story. Find the four that give the best summary of the story. Write the four sentences on the lines below.

Tom goes out in a boat by himself to fish.

He goes to sleep for a while under the hot sun.

Then he pulls in a really big fish.

A shark eats the fish on his way back.

The shark moves faster than his boat.

No one believes his story about the big fish.

____

____

____

____

____

____

____

____

____

____

____

21

Worktext page 21

Making a Chart

Tom and his friends say they have caught big fish. If all the stories are right, who got the biggest fish? One way to find out is to make a chart. Find sentences in the story that tell how big the fish were. Next to each name in the chart, write words that tell how big that guy's fish was. The first one is done for you.

	How Big His Fish Was
Tom	bigger than he is
Will	
Mike	

Reading a Chart

Now use the chart to answer this question: Who tells the biggest fish story? ________________________________

22

Worktext page 22

LESSON 4.5

OBJECTIVES

- Students will learn new words containing the *ow* phonogram and CVCe pattern with the long *o*
- Students will apply endings *s, er, n, ful,* and *ness* to base words to form new words
- Students will recognize and form contractions
- Students will read a chart

PHONICS VOCABULARY

scientists	kinds	insects	known	given
names	close	harmful	hope	makes
eats	falls	plants	animals	things
legs	parts	feelers	ants	they're
sickness	wooden	grow	those	hole
feeler	known			

WORDS TO KNOW

ant	body	grow	harm	hole
hope	insect	legs	page	plants
spider	those			

MATERIALS

Worktext 4, pages 23–27
Teacher's Manual, pages 191–193
Practice lesson 4.5, pages 75–76 of the Worktext

TEACH

- Using Worktext page 23, introduce students to the vocabulary words. Say each word, and have students repeat it after you. Give them an opportunity to practice writing the words.
- Students can organize their Memory Chips, found in the back of the Worktext. They can divide them into groups of words that have the same vowel sounds. Then have them say the words in each group and use the words in a sentence.

Worktext page 23 can also be used to reinforce spelling. Use the five-step process detailed on page 71 of this *Teacher's Manual.*

Phonogram *ow and CVCe: long o*

Write this sentence on the board: **I hope I grow tall.** Have a volunteer point to the words *grow* and *hope.* Ask students what long vowel sound they hear in both words. (*long* o) Explain that *ow* makes the long *o* sound. Then point out the *o*-consonant-*e* pattern. Explain that when they see an *o* followed by a consonant and *e*, the *o* is long, and the *e* is silent.

Blending Blend *grow* and *hope* with the help of students, segmenting each sound they hear: */gr/ /o/, /h/ /o/ /p/*. Then have students name rhyming words for *grow.* Make a word ladder with *hope,* having students take turns substituting the beginning and ending consonant sounds to make new words.

grow	hope
know	hole
show	pole
row	pose

Endings *s, er, n, ful, ness*

Remind students that they can add *s, er, n (en), ful,* and *ness* to the ending of words. Write these sentences on the board and read them aloud: **The painter does a wonderful job. He paints the wooden door. The insect is harmless.** Have students point to *painter, wonderful, paints, wooden,* and *harmless.* Have them circle the base word and underline the ending in each word.

Make New Words Write these endings and words on index cards: **s**, **er**, **n**, **ful**, **ness**, **harm**, **sick**, **teach**, **give**, **know**, **kind**, **feel**. Students can put two cards together to make a new word. (*harms, harmful; sicker, sickness; teacher; given, giver, gives; knows; feels, feeler*) Have them use each word in a sentence.

Contractions

Remind students that two words are made into one word in a contraction. Read this sentence, and have students raise their hands when they hear a contraction: **Bob can't go if they're not finished with the homework.** (*can't, they're*)

Make New Words Write these words on the board, and have volunteers take turns making one word out of two words: **they are**, **we are**, **is not**, **I will**. Remind them to replace the missing letters with an apostrophe. (*they're, we're, isn't, I'll*)

PRACTICE

- Let students practice the new words they have learned and formed by completing the activities found on pages 23–24 of the Worktext.
- If students are experiencing difficulty with the Words to Know section on page 23, you may wish to write the problematic words in a Tic-Tac-Toe grid. Have partners play Tic-Tac-Toe, saying each word before they mark the space with an X or O.

For further practice, have students complete Practice Lesson 4.5 on pages 75–76 of the Worktext. Answers can be found in the Answer Key on page 355 of this *Teacher's Manual.*

APPLY

- Have students talk about the story concept by sharing their prior knowledge. Ask: **What do you know about insects?** Tell them they are going to use the words they have learned to read a short article about insects.
- Ask students to read the article on pages 25–26 in the Worktext. Offer assistance if necessary, but encourage students to decode the words independently, using the clues and patterns they have learned.
- After students have completed reading the story, have them complete the Comprehension Exercises (Make a Heading into a Question, Now Find the Facts, and Reading a Chart) on page 27 in their Worktext. Answers can be found in the Answer Key on page 354 of this *Teacher's Manual.*

CONNECTION

Strategy for Reading Have students reread the selection "Insects" on Worktext pages 25–26 to correct comprehension breakdowns. Students may achieve understanding by reprocessing the same text with greater attention focused on its meaning.

Writing Students should be encouraged to keep a journal of their writings. They can use these journals to record responses to their reading, list new words they have learned, or record their thoughts and feelings about the reading selections. This can be done on the Response to Reading pages in each Worktext before the Memory Chips or in a separate notebook.

Worktext Pages 23–24

5. INSECTS

Word Attack

show, know The new word **grow** sounds like the words **show** and **know**. Try reading the word: **grow**. Now write the words below. Circle the letter group that is the same in them.

grow ______ show ______

know ______

close Remember what may work in words that end with a vowel, another letter, and an **e**, as in **close**. The first vowel sounds like its own name. You can't hear the **e**. This idea can help you attack the new words: **those**, **hope**, and **hole**. Try reading the words below. Write the words.

those ______ hope ______

hole ______ close ______

Words to Know

	Look	Say	Picture	Write
ant	☐	☐	☐	______
body bod-y	☐	☐	☐	______
grow	☐	☐	☐	______
harm	☐	☐	☐	______
hole	☐	☐	☐	______
hope	☐	☐	☐	______
insect in-sect	☐	☐	☐	______
legs	☐	☐	☐	______
page	☐	☐	☐	______
plants	☐	☐	☐	______
spider spi-der	☐	☐	☐	______
those	☐	☐	☐	______

23

Worktext page 23

Word Attack

+er Write **feel** with the ending **er**. ______

+s Write these words with **s** to make new words.

ant ______ fall ______

feeler ______ kind ______

name ______ insect ______

+n You can write **give** and **know** with **n** at the end to make two new words. Write the new words on the lines.

give ______ know ______

+ful The ending **ful** may be added to some words. Write **harm** with **ful** to make a new word.

harm + ful = ______

+ness The letter group **ness** is another ending. Write **sick** with **ness** to make a new word.

sick + ness = ______

Write the new word in this sentence.

Bad food gave her this ______.

1+1 The words **they are** can be said as one word: **they're**. Write the one word in the sentence below. Put an **X** over the letter in **they are** that is not in **they're**.

These people are my friends, ______ not in my family.

MCR You now have more than 500 Memory Chips. There is a big group of them that you have marked off three times (√√√) and put aside. You have come a long way! Get them all out again one more time. Study them with your other Memory Chips—just to see that you know them for good. If you know them, you can put them out of the way again.

24

Worktext page 25

5. INSECTS

Scientists say there are more than 2,000,000 kinds of insects. Most of them are not known to science. They have not even been given names. The next time you see an insect, take a really close look. It may be a kind of insect no one has seen before!

How Insects Harm and Help Us

Some people think insects are harmful creatures. They hope that people will do away with them. They say that insects take sickness from place to place. They are right. They say that insects eat our food. They are right about this, too. There is an insect that eats wood. It makes a hole in the wood as it eats. This kind of insect can get into a wooden house. It can eat so much wood that the house falls down.

But most insects do not harm people. In fact, they help us. Many plants could not grow without help from insects. Insects are food for many animals, too. If insects were gone, those animals would die. Then the animals that eat those animals would die. Insects are a part of life. It would be harmful to do away with them.

What Every Insect Looks Like

How can you tell that a creature is an insect? There are three things to look for. First, every insect has six legs. Next, its body has three parts. Last, every insect has two feelers on its head.

Ants have all these parts. So an ant is an insect. A spider, on the other hand, is not. Take a close look at a spider. You will see that a spider has eight legs. Its body has two parts. A spider has no feelers. It does have two things in front that look like feelers. But they point down, not up. They're part of the mouth. The chart is a fast way to see how a spider is different from an ant.

25

Worktext page 25

What Every Insect Looks Like		
	Spider	Ant
legs	8	6
body	2 parts	3 parts
head	no feelers	2 feelers

26

Worktext page 26

Make a Heading into a Question

Make this heading from **Insects** into a question.

Heading: **How Insects Harm and Help Us**

Question: ______________________________

Now Find the Facts

Now that you have a question, write the answers on the lines below. Look for facts under the first heading in **Insects**. Write your facts next to the right headings below.

Harm

____

____

____

Help

____

____

____

Reading a Chart

A chart can help you see facts and remember them. Look back at the chart on page **26**. It shows facts that are under the heading **What Every Insect Looks Like**. Use the chart to answer the questions below. Write the answers on the lines.

What has more legs, an ant or a spider? ______________

How many body parts does a spider have? ______________

What creature has feelers? ______________

27

Worktext page 27

LESSON 4.6

OBJECTIVE
- Students will practice and apply skills to an extended passage

MATERIALS
Worktext 4, pages 28–30
Teacher's Manual, pages 194–195, 330–331, 333
Practice Lesson 4.6, pages 77–78 of the Worktext
Chart paper (Reteach)

SKILLS REVIEW

- Before reading, you may wish to review these words that apply phonics skills: *facts, gives, writes, turns, hole, ants, feelers, keeps, comes, sees, grow, balls, knows, know, remembers, walls, feels.* Have students review the Memory Chips they have learned so far. Then ask: **What do you think it would be like to be an ant?**
- While reading, have students imagine that they are with Mu Lan in the ant hole.
- After reading, have students complete the Comprehension Exercises (Remembering Details and What's in a Picture?) on Worktext pages 29–30.

For further practice, have students complete Practice Lesson 4.6 on pages 77–78 of the Worktext. Answers can be found in the Answer Key on page 355 of this *Teacher's Manual.*

RETEACH

If students need further review of phonics skills, you may wish to use the following activity:

Phonogram *ow* and *o-e*

Picture Charades Students will enjoy playing a picture charades game. Write these words on slips of paper: **rose**, **hope**, **hole**, **close**, **show**, **grow**, **know**, **mope**, **pole**, **mole**, **sole**, **rope**, **smoke**. Then have volunteers take turns choosing a word and giving the group clues to the word's identity by drawing pictures on the chart paper. Remind students that when they play picture charades, they cannot speak—they can only draw.

CONNECTION

Response to Reading
- To reinforce students' understanding of the literary elements found in their reading material, have them complete the Story Map and Character Cluster reproducibles found on pages 330–331.
- Students will demonstrate an understanding of setting, characters, and plot by filling out the organizers.
- Students may share their completed organizers with the class.

Literature
- Students may enjoy reading or listening to other books relating to science fiction themes. *The Time Machine* and *Dr. Jeckyl and Mr. Hyde* are available in softcover texts and on audiocassette from Pearson's *Pacemaker*™ *Classics.*
- Students may use the Book Report reproducible found on page 333 of this *Teacher's Manual* to record their response to the book they read.

6. MU LAN AND THE ANTS

Mu Lan has to write a story for science class. She has been asked to use science facts in a made-up story.

She is thinking about what to write. Just then, an ant goes by. That gives her an idea. Mu Lan writes a story about herself. In the story, she can turn into anything she wants. So she turns into an ant.

She goes after the ant she has just seen. The ant goes into a hole. Mu Lan goes into the hole, too. She finds herself in a long, dark hall. There must be 1,000 ants in there. They are all moving as fast as they can. Some are going in. Some are coming out. But they are all going somewhere.

From time to time, ants stop. They put out their feelers. They feel one another. Then they move on.

Mu Lan keeps going. Way down inside the hole, she comes to a long room. Every ant going into this room has a little ball in its mouth. It puts the ball into a hole. Mu Lan sees that this is where the little ants will grow.

Mu Lan keeps going. Way down inside the hole she comes to a room. Here, she sees a big creature. It does not look like an ant. It does not look like it can move. Other ants are coming up to this creature with food. All around the creature are little balls. Some ants are working hard. They are taking the little balls away. Little ants will come out of these.

Then an ant comes up to Mu Lan. Mu Lan does what she has seen other ants do. She puts out her feelers. The other ant does the same. But when the feelers come together, Mu Lan knows something is wrong. The other ant backs away. It can tell that Mu Lan is not really an ant.

Somehow it lets the other ants know.

Then Mu Lan remembers that she can turn into anything she wants! She turns back into a girl. The hole is too small for her now. She goes right through the walls. She finds herself outside, under the sun. She can see the light. She feels so happy.

There is just one problem.

She has ants all over her body.

28

Worktext page 28

Remembering Details

Here again is the crossword game that can help you remember details from a story. Find the right word for each line below. Write the word in the boxes of the game. Only one letter goes in a box.

Across

1. Every ant in the hole is going ________________.
3. Some ants are taking little ________________ into a room where the little ants are to grow.
4. The big creature does not look like it can ____________.
5. All the ants work to get food to the ________________.

Down

1. Mu Lan has to write a story for ________________ class.
2. In the story, Mu Lan goes into an ant ________________.
3. In one room, Mu Lan finds a ________________ creature.

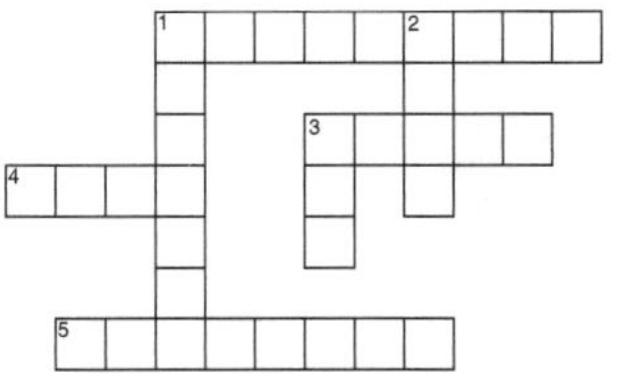

29

Worktext page 29

What's in a Picture?

Pictures and words can work together. A picture can help you know more about what you are reading. The picture below is a map of the ant hole in the story. The words above the picture tell what the letters and lines mean. Use the map to answer the questions. Write the answers on the lines.

A. mouth of the ant hole
B. room where ants keep food
C. room where little ants grow
D. room where the big creature lives
E. place where Mu Lan turns back into a girl

What is in the room Mu Lan does not go into? ____________

When Mu Lan is on her way to the room of the big creature, is she going up or down? ________________

At what point does Mu Lan write that she turns back into a girl? ________________

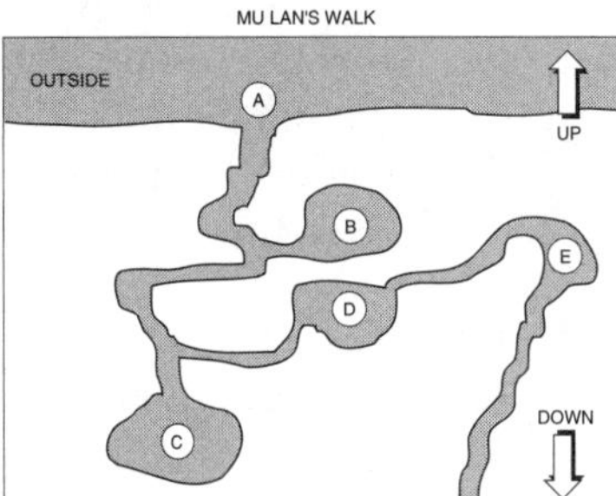

30

Worktext page 30

Level 4

LESSON 4.7

OBJECTIVES

- Students will decode and make new words containing the *een, ant,* and *ap* phonograms
- Students will use context clues to recognize an unfamiliar word
- Students will apply endings *s, less,* and *ed* to base words to form new words
- Students will recognize and read homographs
- Students will recognize and form compound words

PHONICS VOCABULARY

animals	plants	closes	flytrap	green
leaves	hands	outside	inside	pointed
parts	gets	makes	something	sits
sticks	plant	changed	opens	scared
looks	harmless	spiders	things	trap
fight	grows	sometimes		

WORDS TO KNOW

cage	course	enough	fight	fly
drug	green	liquid	plant	red
sticks	trap	Venus		

MATERIALS

Worktext 4, pages 31–34
Teacher's Manual, pages 196–197
Practice Lesson 4.7, pages 79–80 of the Worktext

TEACH

- Using Worktext pages 31–32, introduce students to the vocabulary words. Give students an opportunity to practice writing the words.
- Students can organize their Memory Chips, found in the back of the Worktext. Say each word, having students repeat it after you.

Worktext pages 31–32 can also be used to reinforce spelling. Use the five-step process detailed on page 71 of this *Teacher's Manual.*

Phonograms *een, ant, ap*

Write these sentences on the board and have a volunteer read them: **I have a green cap. We water the plant.** Ask a volunteer to point to *green.* Ask students to name words that rhyme with *green.* Repeat with *cap* and *plant.*

Blending Say the word **green**, pointing to the letters as you segment the word: */gr/ /e/ /n/*. Repeat, using the words **cap** and **plant**. Have students work in groups to make word ladders. If students have trouble thinking of new words to blend, suggest beginning letters *s* and *qu* for *green; ch* and *p* for *plant;* and *t* and *cl,* for *cap.*

green	plant	cap
seen	chant	tap
queen	pant	clap

Endings *s, less, ed*

Remind students that *s, less,* and *ed* can be added to words. Remind them that in some words, the *e* is taken off when the *ed* is added.

Make New Words Write *close* and *harm* in a chart, and invite students to add *s, less,* and *ed* to them to make new words. (*closes, closed, harms, harmless, harmed*)

Homographs

Write these sentences on the board and read them aloud: **The dog will live for fifteen years. That is a live plant.** Point to *live* in both sentences, and explain that sometimes a word is spelled the same but has two different meanings and is pronounced different ways. Have students underline and pronounce the homographs and tell what each word means.

Compound Words

Remind students that they can sometimes find two smaller words inside unfamiliar words. Write these words on the board and have students find the two words that make up each word: **outside**, **inside**, **boyfriend**, **everything**, **something**, **sometime**.

Make New Words Write these words on index cards, and have students mix and match to make compound words: **some**, **every**, **day**, **side**, **in**, **thing**, **where**. (*something, somewhere, someday; everyday, everything, everywhere; inside*)

PRACTICE

- Let students practice the new words they have learned and formed by completing the activities found on pages 31–32 of the Worktext.

For further practice, have students complete Practice Lesson 4.7 on pages 79–80 of the Worktext. Answers can be found in the Answer Key on page 355 of this *Teacher's Manual.*

APPLY

- Have students talk about the story concept by sharing their prior knowledge. Ask: **Do you think it is possible for plants to eat animals? Why or why not?** Tell students they are going to use the words they have learned to read an article.
- After students have completed reading the article, have them complete the Comprehension Exercises (Remembering Details, Make Headings into Questions, and Now Find the Facts) on page 34 in their Worktext. Answers can be found in the Answer Key on page 354 of this *Teacher's Manual.*

7. PLANTS THAT EAT ANIMALS

Word Attack

seen You know the word **seen**. One of the new words sounds and ends like the word **seen**. Try reading this word: **green**. Now write the words you see below. Circle the letter group that is the same in them.

green ________________ seen ________________

ant You know the word **ant**. One of the new words ends like the word **ant**. Read this word: **plant**. Now write them.

plant ________________ ant ________________

map You can read **map**. Put **tr** in place of the **m**. Now you have one of the new words. Trying reading this word: **trap**. Now write the words below. Circle the letter group that is the same in them.

trap ________________ map ________________

Take a Guess

Attack one new word by reading it in a sentence. It is the word in dark letters below. Use other words in the sentence to help you guess what it is. What word would work in the sentence. Think of a word that starts with the same sound.

If an ant is attacked, it will **fight** back.

Did you guess the word? Write it. ________________

Words to Know

	Look	Say	Picture	Write
cage	☐	☐	☐	________________
course	☐	☐	☐	________________
drug	☐	☐	☐	________________
enough e-nough	☐	☐	☐	________________
fight	☐	☐	☐	________________

31

Worktext page 31

	Look	Say	Picture	Write
fly	☐	☐	☐	________________
green	☐	☐	☐	________________
liquid liq-uid	☐	☐	☐	________________
plant	☐	☐	☐	________________
red	☐	☐	☐	________________
sticks	☐	☐	☐	________________
trap	☐	☐	☐	________________
Venus Ve-nus	☐	☐	☐	________________

Word Attack

+s Write the words below with an **s** ending.

close ________________ grow ________________

spider________________

close The word **close** is really one word that can be said two ways. One way to say the word is to make the **s** sound like the **s** in **fast**. The other way to say the word is to make the **s** sound like the **s** in **those**. Read these words in the sentences below.

Close the door. The door is **close** to the window.

+less Write **less** after **harm** to make a new word: **harmless**. Write the new word in this sentence.

Don't be scared; the dog is ________________.

+ed Write the words below with the ending **ed**. Remember to take the **e** off **change** before you write the ending.

point ________________ change ________________

2=1 Put the words below together to make a new word.

some + times = ________________

32

Worktext page 32

7. PLANTS THAT EAT ANIMALS

Many animals eat plants. That is a well-known fact. But do plants ever eat animals? The answer is—yes! The best known of these plants is the Venus Flytrap. This plant grows in places with lots of water and some sun.

What the Venus Flytrap Looks Like

The Venus Flytrap does not look like much at first. It has green leaves like most plants. But two of the leaves are bigger. They look like two hands. They are green on the outside. They are light red on the inside. Study the picture. Close to the outside of the hands, you can see some pointed parts.

How the Venus Flytrap Gets Its Food

The red part of the Venus Flytrap puts out a liquid. It makes the fly want to come close. It is something like a drug to the fly. But when a fly sits on the red part, it sticks there. The plant closes. The fly is caught as if in a cage. It may fight, but the plant does not open. While it is closed, it makes more liquid. This liquid gets all over the fly. Much of the fly is changed into a liquid. The liquid goes back into the plant.

After many days, the plant opens again. Some hard parts of the fly fall out. Most of it is gone, and the plant looks just as harmless as before.

Other Plants that Eat Animals

The Venus Flytrap is too little to eat anything bigger than a fly. But there are some bigger plants that eat animals. These plants, of course, can eat bigger animals. They may eat big spiders. Sometimes, they eat even bigger things. But there is no need to be scared. No plant is big enough to eat people.

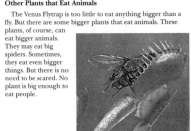

33

Worktext page 33

Remembering Details

The sentences below give facts about the reading. Find a word to write on every line. Look back at the reading if you need to.

Some kinds of ________________ eat animals. The Venus Flytrap is one that grows in places with a lot of ________________ and some sun. If a fly comes down on the red part of a Venus Flytrap, it ________________ there. After the plant closes, a ________________ comes out. A bigger plant can eat a big ________________.

Make Headings into Questions

Here are three headings from the reading. Write them as questions. The first one is already done for you. You write the next two headings.

1. Heading: **What the Venus Flytrap Looks Like**
Question: What does the Venus Flytrap look like?

2. Heading: **How the Venus Flytrap Gets Its Food**
Question: ________________________________

3. Heading: **Other Plants That Eat Animals**
Question: ________________________________

Now Find the Facts

Find facts in the reading that answer the question below. Write the facts on the lines. You will find the facts under the heading **What the Venus Flytrap Looks Like**.

Question: What does the Venus Flytrap look like?

____

____

____

____

34

Worktext page 34

Level 4

LESSON 4.8

OBJECTIVE

- Students will practice and apply skills to an extended passage

MATERIALS

Worktext 4, pages 35–37
Teacher's Manual, pages 198–199, 333
Practice Lesson 4.8, pages 81–82 of the Worktext

SKILLS REVIEW

- Before reading, you may wish to review these words that apply phonics skills: *plant, thinks, things, grows, gets, needs, puts, sees, hits, gives, plants, leaves, writes, weeks.* Have students review the Memory Chips they have learned so far. Then ask: **What does a plant need to live?**
- While reading, have students predict which plant will grow faster.
- After reading, have students complete the Comprehension Exercises (Putting Ideas in Order and What's in a Chart) on Worktext page 37.

PRACTICE For further practice, have students complete Practice Lesson 4.8 on pages 81–82 of the Worktext. Answers can be found in the Answer Key on page 355 of this *Teacher's Manual.*

RETEACH

If students need further review of phonics skills, you may wish to use the following activity:

Phonograms *een, ant, ap*

The Missing Word Write these words on index cards: **green, seen, ant, plant, map, trap**. Say each word and have students say it after you. Then have students group the words into rhyming words and suggest other rhyming words. List them on the board. Then read this story, pausing for each blank. Have students point to the word that goes in each blank:

> Once there was a tiny, tiny, tiny ______ (*ant*) who decided to take his tiny, tiny legs and walk up a very tall ________. (*plant*) He walked and walked, and said, "I have never _______ (*seen*) anything like this! All I see is the color _______! (*green*) I would know where I was going if I had a _______. (*map*) I hope I don't get lost or fall into a _______." (*trap*)

Then encourage students to choose one set of rhyming words. Have them write or dictate their own story.

CONNECTION

Response to Reading

- Discuss with students the differences between the non-fiction selection "Studying a Plant" and fiction selections they have read.

Literature

- Students may enjoy reading or listening to other non-fiction books. *Anne Frank: The Diary of a Young Girl* is available in softcover text and on audiocassette from Pearson's *Pacemaker™ Classics.*
- Students may use the Book Report reproducible found on page 333 of this *Teacher's Manual* to record their responses to the book they read.

8. STUDYING A PLANT

Kate has a new house plant. It is not doing well. She does not know why. Is it getting too much water? Or not enough? Should it get more sun? She just doesn't know.

But I know what a scientist would do to find out. A scientist would make a careful study, she thinks. *A scientist would take one thing at a time and look at it. I will write down all the things that can change how a plant grows. How much water it gets is one thing. How much light it gets is another. Then there is the question of what kind of plant food to give it. There are all these things to think about. I will write them all down in some kind of order, then I will do my study. I think I will find out how much water my plant needs first. Then I will study how much light it needs. I will find out all about my plant.*

Let's say I'm going to find out about water. I get two plants that look just the same. I put them in my house. I give one plant more water than the other. But I keep everything else the same. Then I just keep an eye on them. If one of the plants starts to do better than the other, I will know why. It will be because of the water. But I won't just go on memory. I will keep a chart. I will write down what I see when I look at the plants, and I will look at them at the same time. I could take a close look at the start of every week. After four weeks, the chart should show me what I want to know.

So Kate gets two plants. She puts them in the same place. She sees to it that the sun hits them at the same time every day. She gives them the same kind of plant food. But she gives one plant a can of water **every** day. She gives the other plant a can of water every **other** day. Each week, she looks to see how big and how green the plants are. She writes down how many new leaves have come in. She writes down how many old leaves have come off—if any. Her chart after three weeks is on page 36.

35

Worktext page 35

	Plant A (gets water every day)	Plant B (gets water every other day)
Week 1	2 new leaves	2 new leaves
Week 2	3 new leaves	no new leaves
Week 3	6 new leaves	lost 2 leaves

36

Worktext page 36

Putting Ideas in Order

Kate wants to find out how much water her plant needs. She studies the plant by doing five things. These things are given below—but not in the right order. Write them in the order that they should be done.

After three weeks, see what the chart shows.

Put the plants in the same place in the house.

Look at the plants every week and write what I see.

Give one plant more water than the other.

Find two plants that look just the same.

____

____

____

____

____

What's in a Chart

A good science chart shows facts. Look again at the chart on page **36**. Write **A** or **B** on the lines below.

Plant __________ gets more water than Plant __________.

Plant __________ gets new leaves every week.

Plant __________ has lost some leaves by Week 3.

Plant __________ is growing every week.

A scientist can look at the facts in a chart and see where they point. In this way, a scientist can use a chart to answer a science question. Think about the facts in Kate's chart. Now look at the science question Kate wanted to answer. Use the chart to write in the answer for her.

Question: Should I water my plant every day or every other day?

Answer: I should water my plant ________________.

37

Worktext page 37

Level 4

MIDWAY NOVEL How to Shake Off a Shark

MATERIALS
Midway Novel 4, *How to Shake Off a Shark*
Teacher' Manual, page 200
Assessment Manual, Midway Assessment 4, pages 85–89

Summary *Tyrone goes to live with his grandma. At first, he is not happy with the idea. He meets Carmen, and together they find a map that leads them to stolen money. The bad guys catch them, but the police show up to save the day.*

REVIEW AND ASSESSMENT

- Have students review their Memory Chips with a partner. Depending on your students' needs, review the following skills covered in Lessons 1–8: phonograms and letter patterns *ive, ill, all, ever, ark, ee, ea, ow, ut, een, ant,* and *ap*; CVCe letter patterns; compound words; context clues; homographs; contractions; and endings with *s, ing, er, ed, est, ful, less,* and *ness.*

If you wish to assess students' progress at this point, use *Assessment Manual,* pages 85–89. Answers can be found in the Answer Key on page 355. If students need additional support, you may use the Reteach activities from previous lessons.

INTRODUCE THE NOVEL

Invite students to preview the book by reading the title, looking at the illustrations, and reading aloud the captions. Begin a discussion of story concepts by asking questions such as:

- **Have you ever had something happen that you didn't expect? Did it turn out better or worse than you expected?**
- **How do you make a new friend in a new place?**

CHECK COMPREHENSION

Chapter 1 Why does Tyrone have an unpleasant journey on the *Sea Spider*? (*He isn't used to the sea, and he gets seasick; he is also going to a place he does not want to go.*)

Chapter 2 What does Gran tell Tyrone he can do that excites him? (*She tells him he can fix the* Venus Light, *a boat his father used to race.*)

Chapter 3 Why doesn't Tyrone like Carmen? (*Possible answer: Because she found out that he threw up on the boat.*)

Chapter 4 Who is Tom Champion? (*He runs an animal shelter; he is also Carmen's father.*)

Chapter 5 What does Tom Champion do for a living? (*He helps sick cats and dogs and studies sharks.*)

Chapter 6 Why do Tyrone and Carmen think they have found a map to money? (*Because there's an X on the map and a picture of something that looks like money.*)

Chapter 7 Why did Tyrone come to Spider's Point? (*Because his mother and father are having problems.*)

Chapter 8 Why is Tyrone scared of the two men who are fighting? (*Because he thinks that they are the ones who the map belongs to and that they are up to no good.*)

Chapter 9 Why do Tyrone and Carmen have to ask Tom Champion if they can take out the *Venus Light*? (*Because Tyrone doesn't know how to sail a boat.*)

Chapter 10 What do Tyrone and Carmen find under the red boat? (*They discover money that was stolen from a bank.*)

Chapter 11 What happens when Tyrone and Carmen return to Spider's Point? (*Tyrone's grandmother is missing, and the shelter has been ransacked.*)

Chapter 12 What does Tyrone do next? (*He goes back out in the boat to find the money.*)

Chapter 13 What happens after Tyrone finds Carmen and her dad? (*The mean men find them all.*)

Chapter 14 How do you think the cops knew to come and rescue Tyrone, Carmen, and her dad? (*They came because Tyrone left a note for his grandmother.*)

Chapter 15 Why do you think Gran wants Tyrone back by 6:30? (*His parents are there to visit.*)

Chapter 16 How does the story end? (*Tyrone's parents are moving in with Gran at Spider's Point.*)

CONNECTION

Home/School Encourage students to bring home copies of *How to Shake Off a Shark.* They might read the novel, or sections of the novel, to family members.

LESSON 4.9

OBJECTIVES

- Students will use context and decoding clues to read unfamiliar words
- Students will decode words containing the *ake, ack,* and *and* phonograms
- Students will apply endings *s, ed, en, n,* and *ing* to base words to form new words
- Students will recognize and form compound words

PHONICS VOCABULARY

working	stops	eyes	sees	gets
coming	inside	outside	parts	sitting
pushed	shake	shakes	houses	something
things	pushes	holds	cracks	running
comes	turns	circles	years	mountains
crack	land	back	and	crash
balls	rocks	gotten	shown	anywhere
shaking				

WORDS TO KNOW

against	ball	crack	crash	Earth
ground	land	metal	push	rock
shake	solid			

MATERIALS

Worktext 4, pages 38–42
Teacher's Manual, pages 201–203
Practice Lesson 4.9, pages 83–84 of the Worktext

TEACH

- Using Worktext pages 38–39, introduce students to the vocabulary words. Give students an opportunity to practice writing the words.
- Students can organize their Memory Chips, found in the back of the Worktext. Say each word, having students repeat it after you. Then have them sort the words according to words they know and those that are unfamiliar. Say each unfamiliar word and have students use it in a sentence.

Worktext pages 38–39 can also be used to reinforce spelling. Use the five-step process detailed on page 71 of this *Teacher's Manual.*

Context Clues

Write this sentence on the board: **Don't crash into anything when you drive.** Cover *crash,* and ask students how they would read this word if they did not know it. (Read the sentence and use clues from the sentence along with decoding clues.) Read the sentence, leaving out *crash.* Ask students what they think the word might be and how they figured it out.

Phonograms *ack, ake, and*

Write this sentence on the board and read it aloud: **Take this sack, and shake it.** Have a volunteer find the two words that rhyme. (*take, shake*) Ask what letters he or she sees in both *take* and *shake.* (*ake*) Have a volunteer point to the word *sack.* Ask students to name a word that rhymes with *sack.* Repeat with *and.*

Blending Have students name other rhyming words for *take, sack,* and *and.* List them on the board, blending the sounds as you write each word. (*shake, bake, lake, cake, make, rake; tack, rack, back, pack; and, land, sand, band*)

Endings *s, ed, en, n, ing*

Remind students that they can add *s, ed, en, n,* and *ing* to the endings of words. Tell them when a word ends in a consonant, the consonant may need to be doubled before the ending is added.

Make New Words Write these words on the board, and invite students to add endings *s, ed, en, n,* or *ing* to the end of each word: **got**, **crack**, **shake**, **run**, **land, show**. (*gotten; cracks, cracked, cracking; shakes, shaken, shaking; runs, running; lands, landed, landing; shows, showed, shown, showing*) They can use each word they make in a sentence.

Compound Words

Write this sentence on the board, and read it aloud: **I can go anywhere I want.** Point to *anywhere,* and ask students what two smaller words they see. Remind them that finding smaller words inside compound words can help them read unfamiliar words.

Make New Words Write these words on the board, and have students use them to make compound words: **any**, **where**, **thing**, **some**. (*anywhere, anything, somewhere, something*)

PRACTICE

- Let students practice the new words they have learned and formed by completing the activities found on pages 38–39 of the Worktext.
- If students are experiencing difficulty with the Words to Know section on pages 38–39, you can write the beginning and endings of the words on the board, leaving out the middle letters. Have students use their Memory Chips to spell and say the whole word. Then have them use each word in a sentence.

For further practice, have students complete Practice Lesson 4.9 on pages 83–84 of the Worktext. Answers can be found in the Answer Key on page 355 of this *Teacher's Manual.*

Level 4

APPLY

- Have students talk about the story concept by sharing their prior knowledge about what Earth is like inside its core. Ask: **What is under Earth's crust? How are mountains made?** Tell them they are going to use the words they have learned to read an article about how mountains are made from hot liquid rock inside Earth.
- Ask students to read the article on pages 40–41 in the Worktext. Offer assistance if necessary, but encourage students to decode the words independently, using the clues and patterns they have learned.
- After students have completed reading the article, have them complete the Comprehension Exercises (Use a Picture and Remembering Details) on page 42 in their Worktext. Answers can be found in the Answer Key on page 354 of this *Teacher's Manual.*

CONNECTION

Strategy for Reading After students finish reading the selection "Fire Inside Earth" on Worktext pages 40–41, ask them to summarize it aloud or in writing.

Speaking/Listening Have student partners read the selection aloud. The partners can alternate being speaker and listener.

Writing Ask students to write a few sentences about what they learned about the Ring of Fire.

Worktext Pages 38–39

9. FIRE INSIDE EARTH

Take a Guess

See if you can guess one of the new words by reading it in a sentence. It is the word in dark letters below. What word works in this sentence? Think of a word that starts with the **k** sound that **c** sometimes has.

Be careful on your bike, or you may **crash** into something.

Did you guess the word? Write it. ________________

Word Attack

band You know the word **band.** One of the new words is **land.** Read this word: **land.** Now write the words below. Circle the letter group that is the same in them.

land ________________ band ________________

take, make You know the words **take** and **make.** Try reading this word: **shake.** Write the words below. Circle the letter group that is the same in all of them.

shake ________________ take ________________

make ________________

back, pack You know how the words **back** and **pack** sound. Try reading this word: **crack.** Now write the words below. Circle the letters that are the same in all of them.

crack ________________ back ________________

pack ________________

Words to Know

	Look	Say	Picture	Write
against a-gainst	☐	☐	☐	________
ball	☐	☐	☐	________
crack	☐	☐	☐	________

38

Worktext page 38

	Look	Say	Picture	Write
crash	☐	☐	☐	________
earth	☐	☐	☐	________
ground	☐	☐	☐	________
land	☐	☐	☐	________
metal met-al	☐	☐	☐	________
push	☐	☐	☐	________
rock	☐	☐	☐	________
shake	☐	☐	☐	________
solid sol-id	☐	☐	☐	________

Word Attack

+s Write these words with an **s** ending. (Write **e** after **push,** and then write the **s.**)

crack ________________ ball ________________

push ________________ rock ________________

shake ________________ year ________________

+ed Write **ed** after **push.** ________________

2=1 Circle and write the two words you know in **anywhere.**

anywhere = ________________ + ________________

+en Write **got** with an **en** ending. But first write another **t** after **got.** Then write the ending.

got ________________

+n Write **show** with **n** after it. ________________

+ing Write these words with an **ing** ending. But write another **n** after **run,** and take away the **e** after **shake.**

run ________________ shake ________________

39

Worktext page 39

9. FIRE INSIDE EARTH

A man is working in his field. He stops. His eyes get big. He sees the earth crack in front of him. The crack gets bigger—and bigger—and bigger. Something red is coming out. It is hot!

This is something that really happened. It took place in the year 1943. What the man saw coming out of the crack was red-hot liquid rock. The hot rock is there all the time. It is under the ground. You see, the earth is not just one solid ball. It is like a ball inside a ball inside a ball. On the outside is the land we see every day (the crust). Under this is solid rock (the mantle). Under the solid rock is hot liquid rock (the core). Under the liquid rock is a ball of red-hot metal. The outside of this red-hot metal ball is liquid (the outer core). The inside of this red-hot metal ball is solid (the inner core). Take a look at the picture.

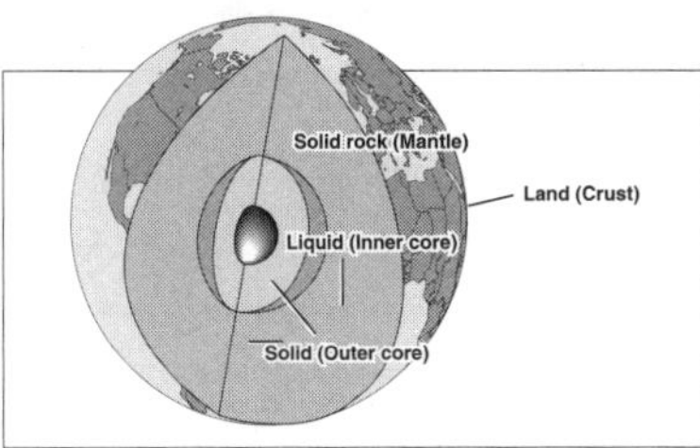

The solid rock is not all one rock. It is in parts. These parts sit on the liquid rock. Each one is like a boat sitting on water. It could move if there were room to move. But there is hardly any room. All around Earth, all the rock parts are pushed together. But from time to time, some part of the solid rock does move—just a little. This makes the ground shake. When the ground shakes, houses can fall down. People may die.

40

Worktext page 40

Here is something you may not know. When things get hot, they get bigger. They try to take up more room. The liquid rock inside Earth is hot. So it is always trying to take up more room. But there is no more room in there. So it pushes against the solid rock. Most of the time, the solid rock holds it back. But the solid rock has cracks. Anywhere that one part of the rock is pushed against another part, there is a crack. Now and again, hot liquid rock pushes up through one of these cracks. Then it may crash out in a big ball of fire, or it may come running out like water. As it comes out, the rock gets cold and turns solid. But after the first rock has gotten cold, more hot rock may come out. This rock gets solid, too. In this way, little by little, a new mountain may come to be. You could call this a **fire mountain**. Earth has many fire mountains, and many of them are still alive. That is, hot rock still comes out of them at times.

Some parts of Earth have more cracks than other parts. These places make a kind of big circle. The circle is called the **Ring of Fire**. The Ring of Fire is shown on the map below.

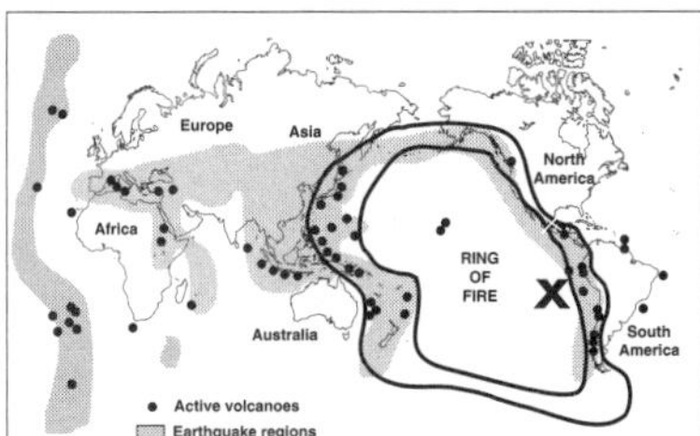

On the map, the circles show where some of the big fire mountains are. These mountains are alive. Fire has come out from them in the last 100 years. Find the **X** on the map. This is where the story of the man and his field took place. The field you read about is gone now. Where it used to be, there is now a big mountain.

41

Worktext page 41

Use a Picture

A picture can be a fast way to get facts. The picture shows it. Use the picture on page **40** to answer the questions below. Write the parts of the earth in the order that you would go through them.

__________ Next? __________ Next?

__________ Next? __________

Remembering Details

How well do you remember details from the reading? Find the right words for the sentences below. Write the words in the boxes of the crossword game.

Across

3. The rock inside Earth is liquid because it is __________.
4. The __________ of Fire looks like a big circle.
5. When the rock under us moves, the ground __________.
7. When liquid rock gets cold, it turns __________.

Down

1. Hot rock may still come out of some __________.
2. The liquid rock __________ against the solid rock.
6. Most ________ mountains are somewhere along the Ring of Fire.

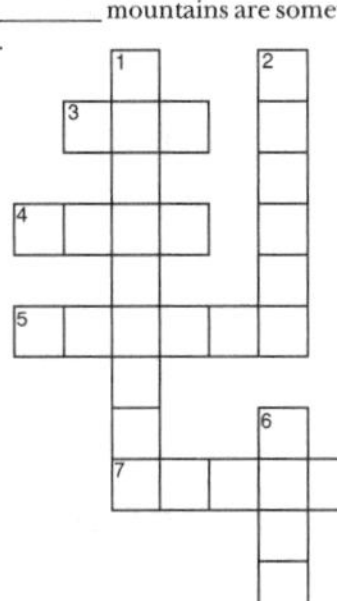

42

Worktext page 42

Level 4

LESSON 4.10

OBJECTIVE

- Students will practice and apply skills to an extended passage

MATERIALS

Worktext 4, pages 43–44
Teacher's Manual, page 204
Practice Lesson 4.10, pages 85–86 of the Worktext

SKILLS REVIEW

- Before reading, you may wish to review these words that apply phonics skills: *working, tells, something, always, going, days, anything, says, looks, comes, turns, runs, gets, parts, keeps, walking, things, puts, moves, works, back, and.* Have students review the Memory Chips they have learned so far. Then ask: **What is a car made of?**
- While reading, have students make pictures in their mind when Tyrone explains how glass and metal are made.
- After reading, have students complete the Comprehension Exercises (Read it Again and Putting Ideas in Order) on Worktext page 44.

For further practice, have students complete Practice Lesson 4.10 on pages 85–86 of the Worktext. Answers can be found in the Answer Key on pages 354–355 of this *Teacher's Manual.*

RETEACH

If students need further review of phonics skills, you may wish to use the following activity:

Phonograms *ad, ake, ack*

What's Wrong with This Sentence? Write sentences on the board like the ones below, but without the underlining. Each sentence should have a misspelled phonogram word. Read each sentence aloud as it should be read. Have volunteers take turns finding out what is wrong with the sentence and correcting the misspellings.

- **I like to drive an ride in a car.** (*and*)
- **Jeff plays in a bend.** (*band*)
- **There is a crick in that CD.** (*crack*)
- **Did you pak the lunch?** (*pack*)
- **I put the CDs in the beck seat.** (*back*)
- **I want to mak a lot of money.** (*make*)
- **It will tack me a week to save for a CD.** (*take*)
- **Don't shack that sack.** (*shake*)
- **We grow plants on the lind.** (*land*)

Worktext Pages 43–44

10. JARED'S CAR

Jared is working on his car again. "Man," he tells Tyrone, "I don't know about this car. Something is always going wrong. You know, in the old days, people did not have much. But what they had was made from rock. Hardly anything could go wrong. I think those days were better."

"Those days are not really gone," says Tyrone.

Jared looks at him. "What do you mean?"

"Just look at your car," says Tyrone. "Most of it is made from metal—right? Where do you think metal comes from? People can't make it out of nothing. Metal comes from rock. It's a kind of rock, really. People go out and find the kind of rock that has metal in it. They get the rock really, really hot. The metal turns to liquid and runs out. After it gets cold, it turns solid again. Then people make car parts out of it."

Jared gives him a look and just keeps on working.

"What about this window?" Tyrone goes on. "It's made of glass. Well, go down to the beach and look down. What are you walking on? It's rock, really. But water and other things have ground it up. Right?"

"So?" says Jared. "What does ground up rock from a beach have to do with glass?"

"That's where glass comes from. Don't you know? People take the ground-up rock and get it hot. The rock turns to liquid and runs out. When it gets cold, it's glass. Here is that glass now." Tyrone puts his hand on the window again.

"I see," says Jared. "So my car is really made of rock. Is that what you're telling me?"

"That's what it comes down to," Tyrone says.

Jared moves back with a smile on his face. "Now I know why it never works right," he says.

43

Worktext page 43

Read It Again

Did you get the point Tyrone is making in this story? The sentences below are a summary of his ideas. Write the words that should go on the lines. You can look back at the story if you want.

Jared says that people used to make things from ______________.

Tyrone says that they still do. He points out that ______________ and ______________ are made from rocks.

Much of Jared's car is made of ______________.

Every window in the car is made of ______________.

So, in a way, Jared's car is made from ______________.

Putting Ideas in Order

The sentences below tell how to make metal. But they are not in the right order. Write the sentences on the lines in the order that they should be done. If you need help, look back at the story.

Make what you want out of the metal.

Let the liquid metal run into something.

Wait for the metal to get cold and turn solid.

Find the kind of rock that has metal in it.

Get the rock really hot.

____

____

____

____

____

44

Worktext page 44

LESSON 4.11

OBJECTIVES

- Students will decode and blend words containing the *and* and *ace* phonograms
- Students will use context clues to figure out unfamiliar words
- Students will apply endings *s*, *er*, and *ness* to base words to form new words
- Students will recognize and form compound words

PHONICS VOCABULARY

seems	hits	comes	waves	answers
space	moves	ways	keeps	balls
something	changes	stand	leaves	place
happens	faster	places	years	outer
takes	longer	stars	toward	darkness
direction	ahead	itself	understand	

WORDS TO KNOW

air	each	corner	direction	seem
space	stand	star	toward	yet

MATERIALS

Worktext 4, pages 45–49
Teacher's Manual, pages 205–207
Practice Lesson 4.11, pages 87–88 of the Worktext

TEACH

- Using Worktext page 46, introduce students to the vocabulary words. Give students an opportunity to practice writing the words.
- Students can organize their Memory Chips, found in the back of the Worktext. You may wish to say each word, having them repeat it after you. Students can find different ways to sort the words, such as by beginning letters, number of letters, and number of syllables.

Worktext page 46 can also be used to reinforce spelling. Use the five-step process detailed on page 71 of this *Teacher's Manual*.

Phonograms *and, ace*

Write this sentence on the board, and read it aloud: **Look at the sand in this place!** Ask a volunteer to point to *sand*. Blend the word with students: /*s*/ /*a*/ /*nd*/. Repeat, using *place*.

Blending Write **sand** on the board; erase the *s* and replace it with a *b*. Have students say the new word, blending the sounds. Continue with *l, st, h,* and *gr*. Have a volunteer circle *place*. Erase the *pl* and have students take turns substituting *sp, f, l,* and *br*, blending each word. Have students make a sentence with each new word.

sand	place
land	space
stand	face
hand	lace
grand	brace

Context Clues

Remind students that when they see an unfamiliar word, they can look at the words and sentences around the word and then look at the way the word begins to help them. Write this sentence on the board and ask students what they think the underlined word means: **I called the dog, and now it is coming <u>toward</u> me.** (*coming in my direction*) Guide students to understand that because the speaker calls the dog, it is probably coming in the speaker's direction.

Endings *s, er, ness*

Remind students that they can add *s, er,* and *ness* to the endings of words.

Make New Words Say these words, and have students add the ending *s*: **seem**, **answer**, **light**. (*seems, answers, lights*) Have a volunteer write each word on the board. Repeat, having students add *er* to **paint**, **out**, and **fast**. (*painter, outer, faster*) Then have students add *ness* to **dark**. (*darkness*) Assist students with spelling as necessary.

Compound Words

Write this sentence on the board, and read it aloud: **I understand the problem.** Ask students what word has two smaller words put together to make one word. (*understand*) Ask them what two words they see. (*under, stand*)

Make New Words Write these two columns on the board and have students draw lines to connect two words to make new words:

under	time
out	stand
some	side

PRACTICE

- Let students practice the new words they have learned and formed by completing the activities found on pages 45–46 of the Worktext.
- If students are experiencing difficulty with the Words to Know section on page 46, place the Memory Chips on the table. Pose riddles like this for each word: **This word begins like *stand* and rhymes with *car*.** (*star*)

For further practice, have students complete Practice Lesson 4.11 on pages 87–88 of the Worktext. Answers can be found in the Answer Key on page 355 of this *Teacher's Manual*.

APPLY

- Have students talk about the story concept by discussing things they already know. Ask: **What do you know about light?** Tell students they are going to use the words they have learned to read a short article that gives them facts about light.
- Ask students to read the article on pages 47–48 in the Worktext. Offer assistance if necessary, but encourage students to decode the words independently, using the clues and patterns they have learned.
- After students have completed reading the article, have them complete the Comprehension Exercises (Make Headings into Questions and Now Find the Facts) on page 49 in their Worktext. Answers can be found in the Answer Key on page 354 of this *Teacher's Manual*.

CONNECTION

Strategy for Reading Have students reread the article "What Is Light?" on Worktext pages 47–48 to correct comprehension breakdowns. Students may achieve understanding by reprocessing the same text with greater attention focused on its meaning.

Worktext Pages 45–46

11. WHAT IS LIGHT?

Word Attack

face You know the word **face**. One of the new words sounds the same and ends the same as **face**. Try reading this word: **space**. Write the word in this sentence.

The room is big. It has a lot of ________.

and, land You know the word **and**. It sounds the same in **land**. It is also in one of the new words. Try to read this word: **stand**. Write the words below. Circle the word that is the same in them.

stand ________ and ________

land ________

Take a Guess

Attack one of your new words by reading it in a sentence. Use other words in the sentence (like **not away from**) to help you guess. Think of a word that starts with the sound of **t**.

The ball comes **toward** me, not away from me.

Did you guess the word? Write it. ________

Try another one. What is the word in dark letters?

The ball is coming in my **direction**.

Did you guess it? Write the word. ________

45

Worktext page 45

Words to Know

	Look	Say	Picture	Write
air	☐	☐	☐	________
corner cor-ner	☐	☐	☐	________
direction di-rec-tion	☐	☐	☐	________
each	☐	☐	☐	________
seem	☐	☐	☐	________
space	☐	☐	☐	________
stand	☐	☐	☐	________
star	☐	☐	☐	________
toward to-ward	☐	☐	☐	________
yet	☐	☐	☐	________

Word Attack

+s Write an **s** ending after **seem**. ________

+er Write **er** after **out**. ________

+ness Write **ness** after **dark**. ________

2=1 You know the words below. Put them together to make new words.

a + head = ________ it + self = ________

under + stand = ________

46

Worktext page 46

11. WHAT IS LIGHT?

We all need light in order to see. Here is how it seems to work: light hits something, then it comes to your eye. A picture of that thing comes with the light. The light goes into your eye, and that is when you see it.

But what is light?

Scientists have asked that question for a long, long time. They have no real answer. They can only say what light is **like**. They still cannot say what light **is**.

What Is Light Like?

Scientists have two answers to this question. In some ways, they say, light is like waves in the sea. There is just one problem. Waves in the sea are made of water. What are light waves made of? They can't be made of air. There is no air in space. In fact, there is nothing in space. Yet, light somehow moves through that nothing. In some ways, then, light must be something in itself.

One Way That Light Is Like a Thing

Here is one way that light is like a thing. When you throw a ball, it just keeps going. If it comes to a corner, it does not turn—not by itself anyway. Light is the same way. You can picture light as many, many little balls. All of them are moving. They move ahead till they hit something. Then they go off in some other direction. They do just what a lot of little balls would do.

Another Way That Light Changes Direction

Light changes direction in another way, too. It changes direction when it goes from water to air. Here is something you can try. Put a small rock in a can. Stand where you can see it. Then move back till you can't see it.

47

Worktext page 47

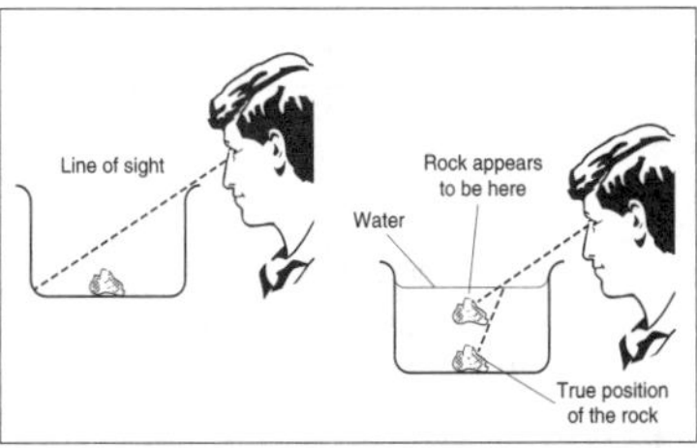

Have a friend put water in the can. Now you can see the rock again. Why? Because the light coming from the rock changes direction. In the water, it is going one way. As it leaves the water, it turns. It goes in a new direction. Now it is coming toward you. The picture may help you understand this idea better.

How Does Light Move?

You already know some things about the way light moves. You know that it moves in a line. You know that light does not turn at a corner. You know that when light hits something, it goes off again in another direction. Light also changes direction when it goes from water to air. (It changes direction when it goes from air to water, too.)

But here is something you may not know. Light takes time to get from place to place. It does not seem to. When you turn on a light, it seems to get to you right away. But that is not what really happens. Light does take time to move, but it moves really, really fast. It moves about 1,000,000 times faster than sound. Nothing can go faster than light—nothing. And Earth is small. All places are close together. So light gets from place to place on Earth fast.

Outer space is different. There, things are far apart. How long does light take to get here from the sun? Count to 500. (Don't count fast.) That is about how long it takes. It takes even longer for light to get here from the sun and stars. (The sun is a star, too.) In fact, light from the star closest to Earth (not the sun) takes four years to get here.

48

Worktext page 48

Make Headings into Questions

Here are four headings from the reading. Write them again as questions. Remember, some headings may already be questions.

1. Heading: **What Is Light Like?**

Question: ______________________

2. Heading: **One Way That Light Is Like a Thing**

Question: ______________________

3. Heading: **Another Way That Light Changes Direction**

Question: ______________________

4. Heading: **How Does Light Move?**

Question: ______________________

Now Find the Facts

Here are questions about Headings 1 and 4. Find facts in the reading that answer the questions. Write two facts for the question about Heading 1. Write five facts (or more) for the question about Heading 4.

Question about Heading 1: **What is light like?**

____
____
____
____

Question about Heading 4: **How does light move?**

____
____
____
____
____

49

Worktext page 49

Level 4

LESSON 4.12

OBJECTIVE

- Students will practice and apply skills to an extended passage

MATERIALS

Worktext 4, pages 50–51
Teacher's Manual, page 208
Practice Lesson 4.12, pages 89–90 of the Worktext

SKILLS REVIEW

- Before reading, you may wish to review these words that apply phonics skills: *says, hand, holds, sticks, points, looks, laughs, yourself, mirrors, shows.* Have students review the Memory Chips they have learned so far. Then ask: **How is it possible to see around a corner?**
- While reading, have students use the illustration to help them comprehend the text.
- After reading, have students complete the exercise on Worktext page 51.

For further practice, have students complete Practice Lesson 4.12 on pages 89–90 of the Worktext. Answers can be found in the Answer Key on page 355 of this *Teacher's Manual.*

RETEACH

If students need further review of phonics skills, you may wish to use the following activity:

Phonograms *ace, and;* **Endings** *s, er, ness*

Make Crossword Puzzles Brainstorm words that rhyme with *face* and *and. (space, lace, grace; land, stand, grand, hand, sand, band)* Then model how to make a crossword puzzle with two of the words, such as *face* and *space.* (For example: Across: This is what you put a mask over. Down: Spaceships go up into this.) Then have students make a puzzle of their own. They may also use these story words: *outer, darkness, stars, air.*

Worktext Pages 50–51

12. HOW TO SEE AROUND A CORNER

"I can see around a corner," says Kate.

"No you can't," says Tyrone.

"Yes, I can," says Kate. "I do it with this box." She has a long box in her hand. She holds it against the wall so that one end sticks out from the corner. She points to a hole at the other end. "Look through this window," she says.

Tyrone looks.

"What do you see?" she asks.

"I see what is around the corner," Tyrone says. "How does it work?"

Kate laughs. "It's all done with a looking glass, as my grandma would say. You can make one of these yourself. Let me show you a picture."

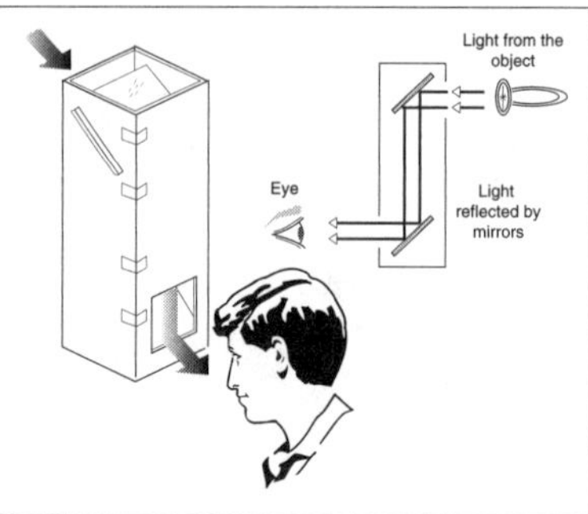

This is the picture that Kate shows Tyrone.

50

Worktext page 50

Why the Box Works

Remember the idea that light is like a lot of little balls? Think about what a ball does when it hits a wall. If it goes right toward the wall, it comes right back along the same line. But what if the ball comes in from the side? It goes off on the other side.

Kate's box uses this idea. Light comes from something. Let's say it comes from a ring. The light goes into the top of the box. The light hits the top looking glass. That looking glass sends the light down to the bottom looking glass. And that looking glass sends the light out through the bottom window and into your eyes. Then you see the ring.

You Tell How the Box Works

You read **Why the Box Works.** Now you tell how the box works to a friend. Use the picture in this book or draw your own.

51

Worktext page 51

LESSON 4.13

OBJECTIVES

- Students will decode words with two syllables
- Students will decode and blend words containing the *in* and *ip* phonograms
- Students will use context clues to recognize unfamiliar words
- Students will apply endings *s*, *ed*, and *ing* to base words to form new words

PHONICS VOCABULARY

planets	sometimes	used	can	in
creatures	thinking	stories	lots	plants
fights	harmed	fighting	saved	things
lives	spaceship	pictures	machines	lets
sits	gets	planet	trip	win
break	cooked	stands	means	stars

WORDS TO KNOW

between	break	gang	gas	machine
planet	sky	steal	trip	win

MATERIALS

Worktext 4, pages 52–57
Teacher's Manual, pages 209–211
Practice Lesson 4.13, pages 91–92 of the Worktext

TEACH

- Using Worktext pages 52–53, introduce students to the vocabulary words. Give students an opportunity to practice writing the words.
- Students can organize their Memory Chips, found in the back of the Worktext. Students can sort the words according to words they know and words they don't know. You may wish to say each word, having them repeat it after you. Then have them work with a partner, saying each word and using it in a sentence.

Worktext pages 52–53 can also be used to reinforce spelling. Use the five-step process detailed on page 71 of this *Teacher's Manual.*

Two-Syllable Words

Write this word on the board: **planet**. Say the word, and then have students say it after you. Tell them that sometimes words have two parts. Cover *et* and have students read the word part *plan.* Then cover *plan* and have them read the word part *et.* Then have them put the two parts together.

Blending Write these words on the board, and have students take turns reading the two parts of the words: **pic•tures**, **ma•chine**, **be•tween**, **Ty•rone**. Help them blend the two parts together.

Phonograms *in, ip*

Write this sentence on the board, and read it aloud: **We can win a trip.** Ask a volunteer to point to *win.* Ask them what vowel sound they hear. (*short i*) Then have students point to another word in the sentence that has the short *i* sound. (*trip*)

Blending Put students into two groups. Have one group work with *win* and one group work with *trip.* Have them substitute beginning consonants to make new words. Then have them read their lists. (*bin, fin, gin, sin, grin, tin; ship, lip, flip, sip, grip, hip, zip, tip*)

Context Clues

Write this sentence on the board: **If you drop a glass, it will break.** Circle *break*, and remind students they can look at all the other words in the sentence to figure out this word. They can look at the beginning sound and then see if the word makes sense in the sentence. Ask students to read the sentence and tell what they think *break* means. (*smash*)

Endings *s, ed, ing*

Remind students they can add the endings *s*, *ed*, and *ing* to make new words. Remind them if a word ends in an *e*, the *e* is taken off before *ed* or *ing* is added.

Make New Words Write a chart like the one below on the board, and have students add the endings *s*, *ed*, and *ing* to make new words. Have students choose one word with an ending to use in a sentence.

Base Word	+ s	+ ed	+ ing
live	lives	lived	living
harm	harms	harmed	harming
fight	fights		fighting

PRACTICE

- Let students practice the new words they have learned and formed by completing the activities found on pages 52–53 of the Worktext.
- If students are experiencing difficulty with the Words to Know section on pages 52–53, place the Memory Chips on the table. Say incomplete sentences like the one following and have students choose a Memory Chip word to finish it: **A scared little dog was _______ the boy and girl.** (*between*)

For further practice, have students complete Practice Lesson 4.13 on pages 91–92 of the Worktext. Answers can be found in the Answer Key on page 355 of this *Teacher's Manual.*

Level 4

APPLY

- Have students talk about the story concept by discussing things they already know. Ask: **What do you know about the planet Venus?** Tell them they are going to use the words they have learned to read a short article about the planet Venus.
- Ask students to read the article on pages 54–55 in the Worktext. Offer assistance if necessary, but encourage students to decode the words independently, using the clues and patterns they have learned.
- After students have completed reading the article, have them complete the Comprehension Exercises (Make Headings into Questions, Now Find the Facts, and What Are the Facts?) on pages 56–57 in their Worktext. Answers can be found in the Answer Key on page 354 of this *Teacher's Manual.*

CONNECTION

Strategy for Reading After students finish reading the selection "Our Sister Planet" on Worktext pages 54–55, ask them to summarize it either aloud or in writing.

Speaking/Listening Divide students into four groups. Assign each group to one of the four sections in the selection "Our Sister Planet." Have each group read their section and choose a group member to summarize the section for the rest of the class. Encourage students to be active, attentive listeners.

Worktext Pages 52–53

13. OUR SISTER PLANET

Word Attack

NEW **an** You can attack the word **planet**. Look at it as two parts: **plan** and **et.** Say **pl** (as in **place**) with **an**. You have seen the letter group **et** in **get**. It sounds the same here. Say **plan** and **et** together. Now try reading the word: **planet**. Write it in the sentence.

We live on ________________ Earth.

ship You know the word **ship**. Now try reading a new word: **trip**. Write the words you see below. Circle the letter group that is the same in them.

trip ________________ ship ________________

in You know the word **in**. A new word is **w** + **in**. Try reading this word: **win**. Write it in the sentence below.

Kate plays well. She will ________________ the game for us.

Take a Guess

Try to guess one of the new words by using other words in a sentence. Read the sentence below. What is it saying? What word would work in this sentence? Think of a word that starts with a **b** sound.

If you hit the glass with a rock, it will **break**.

Did you guess the word? Write it here. ________________

Words to Know

	Look	Say	Picture	Write
between be-tween	☐	☐	☐	________
break	☐	☐	☐	________
gang	☐	☐	☐	________
gas	☐	☐	☐	________

52

Worktext page 52

	Look	Say	Picture	Write
machine ma-chine	☐	☐	☐	________
planet plan-et	☐	☐	☐	________
sky	☐	☐	☐	________
steal	☐	☐	☐	________
trip	☐	☐	☐	________
win	☐	☐	☐	________

Word Attack

+s Put **s** endings on the words below. Write the new words.

live ________________ fight ________________

mean ________________ stand ________________

star ________________ planet ________________

machine ________________

+ed Write these words with an **ed** ending. (Take off the **e** from **save** before you write the ending.)

harm ________________ save ________________

cook ________________

+ing Write **fight** with an **ing** ending to get a new word: **fighting**. Write the new word in the sentence.

The boys are ________________ again.

53

Worktext page 53

13. OUR SISTER PLANET

There are nine planets that go around our sun. Two of them are between Earth and the sun. The planet that is closer to us is called Venus. People sometimes call Venus our sister planet.

Why Venus Is Called Our Sister Planet

Many years back, people used to think that Earth and Venus were alike. After all, Venus is just about as big as Earth, and it is close to us. We can see Venus from Earth. It stands out in the night sky like a big star. There is one other thing. Venus has some kind of gas all around it. Earth has gas around it, too. The gas around Earth is air. Air is something that all living creatures need. So people said, "Maybe Venus has air, too. If so, maybe people can live on Venus. In fact, maybe creatures of some kind already live on Venus."

Stories About Life on Venus

This got people to thinking. What would creatures from Venus be like? They made up stories. In most of these stories, Venus is a place with lots of plants. Thinking creatures live on the planet. In some stories, these creatures are good. In some, they are bad. Anything can happen in these stories. Creatures from Venus may attack Earth and try to take over. In this kind of story, Earth fights back. Much of our planet is harmed in the fighting. But at last, we win, and Earth is saved. Or maybe a gang from Earth goes to Venus. They steal and smash and break things. Why not? Anything can happen in a story.

Why There Is No Life on Venus

But in real life, these things cannot happen. Why? Because nothing really lives on Venus. We know that now. A real spaceship has gone close to Venus. No people were on that trip. But a machine that was on the ship took pictures. We have seen the pictures. Scientists can tell much from these pictures. Here is one thing they can tell. The gas around Venus is not like the air on Earth. In fact, it is a harmful gas. It would make any plant or animal die.

54

Worktext page 54

People cannot even land on Venus. The gas is not the biggest problem. Machines could keep us safe from the gas, and maybe someday our machines will land on Venus. But for people, there is a bigger problem. Venus is just too hot. It is about as hot as any fire.

Why Venus Is So Hot

Venus is closer to the sun than we are. But that is not why Venus is so hot. Another planet is even closer to the sun. But it is not as hot as Venus. In fact, no other planet that goes around our sun is as hot as Venus. Why is Venus so hot?

The answer is the harmful gas around the planet. The gas lets in light from the sun. It does not let the light back out. Anything that sits in the light of the sun gets hot. So Venus keeps getting more and more hot. People who land on Venus will get cooked!

55

Worktext page 55

Make Headings into Questions

Here are two headings from the reading. Write them as questions. Do some careful thinking about Heading 2 before you write the question. You will have to put in more words.

1. Heading: **Why Venus Is Called Our Sister Planet**

Question: ______________________________

____

2. Heading: **Stories About Life on Venus**

Question: ______________________________

____

Now Find the Facts

The questions below were made from Headings 3 and 4 of the reading. Find facts that answer the questions. Look for them under the last two headings. Write the facts on the lines.

Question: **Why is there no life on Venus?**

____

____

Question: **Why is Venus so hot?**

____

____

What Are the Facts?

A fact is what people know to be so. It is not just what someone thinks or believes. When you read about science, most of the sentences will give facts. But some may not. Sometimes, a sentence that is not a fact has a word like **maybe** in it—but not always. A sentence is not a fact just because you see the word **fact** in it.

56

Worktext page 56

Here are six sentences from the reading about Venus. Only three of them are facts. Look back at the reading for help, to find the three sentences that are facts. Write them on the lines below.

Venus is closer to the sun than we are.

In fact, maybe creatures of some kind already live on Venus.

We can see Venus from Earth.

Creatures from Venus may attack Earth and try to take over.

Thinking creatures live on Venus.

The gas around Venus is not like the air on Earth.

____

____

____

____

____

____

____

57

Worktext page 57

Level 4

LESSON 4.14

OBJECTIVE
- Students will practice and apply skills to an extended passage

MATERIALS
Worktext 4, pages 58–60
Teacher's Manual, pages 212–213, 330–331, 333
Practice Lesson 4.14, pages 93–94 of the Worktext

SKILLS REVIEW

- Before reading, you may wish to review these words that apply phonics skills: *gets, wants, looking, sees, stars, looks, spaceship, comes, hits, feeling, thinks, waiting, sitting, asks, says, cooking, wanted, happens, thinking, snowing, stops, works, screams, hits, falls, happened, sits, knows, starts, telling, in.* Have students review the Memory Chips they have learned so far. Then ask: **What do you think it would be like to get everything you wanted just by thinking about having it?**
- While reading, have students read to find out how Kate gets everything she wants.
- After reading, have students complete the summarizing exercise on Worktext page 60.

For further practice, have students complete Practice Lesson 4.14 on pages 93–94 of the Worktext. Answers can be found in the Answer Key on page 355 of this *Teacher's Manual.*

RETEACH

If students need further review of phonics skills, you may wish to use the following activity:

Syllables

Syllable Race Draw a large game board with a start and finish, with squares that connect both on a large area. Have players take turns drawing a card with one or two syllables. If the player says the word correctly, he or she can advance the number of spaces on the game board as there are syllables in the word. Use words like these: **planet**, **machine**, **between**, **metal**, **solid**, **Earth**, **close**, **closes**, **harmless**, **insect**, **spider**, **shark**, **spaceship**, **space**.

CONNECTION

Response to Reading
- To reinforce students' understanding of the literary elements found in their reading material, have them complete the Story Map and Character Cluster reproducibles found on pages 330–331.
- Students will demonstrate an understanding of setting, characters, and plot by filling out the organizers.
- Students may share their completed organizers with the class.

Literature
- Students may enjoy reading or listening to other books with a fantasy theme. *Gulliver's Travels* and *A Midsummer Night's Dream* are available in softcover texts and on audiocassette from Pearson's *Pacemaker*™ *Classics.*
- Students may use the Book Report reproducible found on page 333 of this *Teacher's Manual* to record their responses to the book they read.

Independent Reading
- Encourage students to read for pleasure. Pearson's *World Myths and Legends I* series is a set of eight culturally-diverse myths and legends that have developed around the world. See page xvii of the *Teacher's Manual* for additional titles.
- After reading, students may form small groups. Students can rate their stories on a scale of 1–10. Each group can then prepare a brief presentation explaining their ratings.

14. THE GIRL WHO GETS EVERYTHING SHE WANTS

One night, Kate is outside looking up at the stars. She sees something that looks like a spaceship. A green light comes from it. The light hits Kate in the face. She feels as if she is about to fall over. Then the feeling goes away.

Boy, she thinks, *what was that? I hope I'm OK.*

Right away she does feel OK—not bad and not good. Just OK.

Kate goes home. On the way, she is thinking, *I hope dinner is waiting.* She doesn't think it will happen. But when she gets home, dinner is hot. Her family is just sitting down.

"What's going on?" she asks. "We hardly ever eat till 8:00."

"I know," says her dad. "But this time I did the cooking. I don't know why. I just got a feeling that I wanted to cook."

Just before she goes to sleep that night, Kate thinks, *I hope it will snow in the night.*

The next day, Kate gets up. She looks out the window. She sees snow coming down. *What is this?* she thinks. *Every time I hope for something, it happens. Can it be? Can I really make things happen just by thinking?*

She tries it. She says, "I hope it stops snowing."

The snow stops, just like that.

"Oh my," says Kate, "this really works." Now she wants to tell her boyfriend about it. She gets on her bike. She will see him at school. But she can hardly wait that long. *I hope I run into him on the way to school,* she says to herself.

She goes toward the school on her bike as fast as she can. Someone screams. "Kate! Look out!" But Kate is going too fast to hear it. Crash! Her bike hits another bike. Kate falls over. When she gets up, she sees her boyfriend.

"Oh no!" Only now does she remember what she said on the way out of the house. It has happened. She has run into her boyfriend on the way.

58

Worktext page 58

He says, "Kate, are you OK?"

"I think so." She sits up. She holds her head. "I feel good, but—"

"But what?"

But something is different. She thinks she knows what it could be. She looks up. "I hope it starts to snow," she says, "right now!"

Nothing happens.

"Oh, well," says Kate, "I guess it was too good to last."

"What was too good to last?" asks her boyfriend.

But Kate does not tell him. There is no use in telling anyone now.

59

Worktext page 59

Write a Summary

The sentences below tell things that happen in the story. Some of the sentences tell details. Some tell big things that happen. Find five sentences that tell big things. Use them to write a summary of the story. Write the sentences on the lines below.

Kate is looking at the stars one night.

A light from a spaceship hits Kate.

After that, everything she wants to happen does.

She wants dinner, and there it is, waiting for her.

She says, "I hope I will run into my boyfriend."

She goes to school on her bike.

On her way to school, she does crash into her boyfriend.

Her boyfriend asks how she feels.

After the crash, she can't make things happen just by wanting them to happen.

60

Worktext page 60

Level 4

LESSON 4.15

OBJECTIVES

- Students will decode and blend words containing the *arm, ay,* and *ot* phonograms
- Students will use context clues to recognize unfamiliar words
- Students will apply endings *s, ing, less,* and *ly* to base words to form new words
- Students will recognize and form possessives
- Students will recognize and form contractions
- Students will recognize and form compound words

PHONICS VOCABULARY

robot	computers	robots	machines	helps
lets	radios	voices	always	ways
things	ones	getting	places	making
parts	you'll	comes	arm	can't
helpless	working	talking	taking	cars
robot's	someone	jobs	helping	belongs
say	housework	scientists	pay	partly
today's	we'll	isn't	spaceship	count
orders	computer	breaks	belong	losing

WORDS TO KNOW

arm	computer	count	fix	lose
oil	pay	radio	robot	voice

MATERIALS

Worktext 4, pages 61–66
Teacher's Manual, pages 214–216
Practice Lesson 4.15, pages 95–96 of the Worktext

TEACH

- Using Worktext page 62, introduce students to the vocabulary words. Give students an opportunity to practice writing the words.
- Students can organize their Memory Chips, found in the back of the Worktext. You may wish to say each word, having them repeat it after you.

Worktext page 62 can also be used to reinforce spelling. Use the five-step process detailed on page 71 of this *Teacher's Manual.*

Phonograms *arm, ay, ot*

Write these words on the board, and have volunteers read them aloud: **arm**, **say**, **not**. Circle the phonogram in each word. Remind students that when they know how the ending for one word sounds, they can recognize and make new words. Ask students to name rhyming words for each word.

Blending Have students work in pairs. They can work together to substitute beginning consonants to make new words with *arm, say,* and *not.* (*harm, farm, charm; pay, play, Fay, Kay, lay, gray, day; hot, dot, cot, pot, rot*)

Context Clues

Remind students that they can figure out a new word by reading all the other words in the sentence and seeing what word makes sense. They can look at the beginning sound of the word for another clue. Write this sentence on the board, underlining *computer,* and have students figure out the underlined word: **We can type the letter on the <u>computer</u>.**

Endings *s, ing, less, ly*

Remind students that they can add *s, ing, less,* and *ly* to the endings of words. Write these sentences on the board: **I gladly took the books. Walking in the dark is harmless.** Ask students to circle the endings and identify the base words they see in each sentence.

Make New Words Write these endings and words on word cards and have partners take turns making new words*:* **s**, **ing**, **less**, **ly**, **belong**, **voice**, **robot**, **lose**, **help**, **harm**, **part**. (*belongs, voices, robots, loses, helps, harms, parts; belonging, losing, helping, harming, parting; voiceless, helpless, harmless; partly*)

Possessives

Remind students that ownership can be shown when an apostrophe and *s* are added to a name of a person, place, or thing.

Make New Words Have students write words that show possession with these words: **robot**, **today**, **computer**. (*robot's, today's, computer's*) They can use each new word in a sentence.

Contractions

Remind students that words like *we will* can be said as one word: *we'll.* Show them how the *wi* is taken out and replaced with an apostrophe.

Make New Words Write these words on the board, and have students take turns rewriting the two words into one word: **is not**, **we will**, **you will**. (*isn't, we'll, you'll*)

Compound Words

Remind students that two smaller words can be put together to make one word. Have students identify the smaller words in these compound words: *inside, somewhere. (in, side; some, where)*

Make New Words Write these words on index cards, and have students put them together to make compound words: **space**, **ship**, **some**, **thing**, **where**, **snow**, **flake**. (*spaceship, something, somewhere, snowflake*) They can use each new word in a sentence.

PRACTICE

- Let students practice the new words they have learned and formed by completing the activities found on pages 61–63 of the Worktext.
- If students are experiencing difficulty with the Words to Know section on page 62, place the Memory Chips on the table. Say each word aloud and have students repeat it after you. Then say a sentence with a missing word, and have students choose a Memory Chip to complete it. For example: **Turn on the ____ to find out what time it is.** (*radio*)

For further practice, have students complete Practice Lesson 4.15 on pages 95–96 of the Worktext. Answers can be found in the Answer Key on page 355 of this *Teacher's Manual.*

APPLY

- Have students talk about the story concept by discussing things they have experienced. Ask: **Do you think computers and robots are good things? Why or why not?** Tell students they are going to use the words they have learned to read an essay that gives an opinion about the usefulness of robots and computers.
- Ask students to read the article on pages 64–65 in the Worktext. Offer assistance if necessary, but encourage students to decode the words independently, using the clues and patterns they have learned.
- After students have completed reading the article, have them complete the Cooperative Group Activity (What Do You Think?) and Comprehension Exercise (What Are the Facts?) on page 66 in their Worktext. Answers can be found in the Answer Key on page 354 of this *Teacher's Manual.*

CONNECTION

Writing Give students an opportunity to write in their journals, recording how they feel about computers and robots.

Worktext Pages 61–62

15. COMPUTERS AND ROBOTS

Word Attack

2=1 You know the words **be** and **long**. Together they make a new word. Read this word: **belong**. Write it in the sentence.

A dog does not ________________ in school.

harm You know the word **harm**. One of the new words is just **harm** without the **h**. Try reading this word: **arm**. Write the word in the sentence.

You move your ________________ when you wave.

say The letter group **ay** is in **say**. It sounds the same in the word **pay**. Read this word: **pay**. Write it in the sentence.

You have to ________________ to see this game.

got, not You can attack the new word **robot**. Look at it as two parts: **ro** and **bot**. If you can read **no**, you can read **ro**. If you can read **got** and **not**, you can read **bot**. Say **ro** and **bot** together. Now try reading this word: **robot**. Write it in the sentence below.

A ________________ is a machine.

Take a Guess

Try to get one of the new words by reading it in a sentence. It is the word in dark letters below. What word would work here? Think of a word that starts with the **k** sound that **c** sometimes has.

How many boys are in the class? Let's **count** them.

Did you guess the word? Write it here. ________________

Now try another one. Can you guess the word in dark letters?

A **computer** is a machine that can work out hard math.

What is the word? Write it here. ________________

61

Worktext page 61

Words to Know

	Look	Say	Picture	Write
arm	☐	☐	☐	________
belong	☐	☐	☐	________
computer com-put-er	☐	☐	☐	________
count	☐	☐	☐	________
fix	☐	☐	☐	________
lose	☐	☐	☐	________
oil	☐	☐	☐	________
pay	☐	☐	☐	________
radio ra-di-o	☐	☐	☐	________
robot ro-bot	☐	☐	☐	________
voice	☐	☐	☐	________

Word Attack

+s Write the words below with an **s** ending to get the new word.

belong ________________ computer ________________

order ________________ radio ________________

break ________________ robot ________________

voice ________________

+ing Write **ing** after **help**. ________________

Write **ing** after **lose**. First take off the **e**.

lose ________________

+less Write **help** with a **less** ending to get a new word.

help+less= ________________

62

Worktext page 62

+ly Write **part** with an **ly** ending. ____________

+'s You can write **'s** after a word to show that something else belongs to it. Write the words below with the ending **'s**.

today ____________ robot ____________

1+1 The words **we will** can be said as one word: **we'll**.

The words **you will** can be said as one word: **you'll**.

The words **is not** can be said as one word: **isn't**.

Write the one word that can take the place of each two words below. Put **X** over every letter you leave out when you write each new word.

we will ____________ you will ____________

is not ____________

2=1 Try reading this word: **spaceship**. It is made up of two words that you know. Write the two words below:

spaceship = ____________ + ____________

63

Worktext page 63

Could Robots Take the Place of People?

Some people say machines no longer just help us. They say machines are taking the place of people. When robots make cars, some people lose their jobs. You never hear of anyone taking away a robot's job! Of course, some people get new jobs because of robots. Someone has to fix the robots when they break. People should not be helping machines. It should be the other way around.

Most of us would pay a lot for a robot that does housework. But do you know what? No robot can do this job. Scientists have been trying to make one, and they can't! Housework is too hard for robots. A day may come when Earth belongs to robots and computers. Guess what people will be doing on that day? You got it: we will be doing housework!

65

Worktext page 65

15. COMPUTERS AND ROBOTS

Machines help us live better and do more. The car helps us get around faster. The radio lets us hear a voice from far away. With car radios, we can get around fast and hear voices, too. Just look at all the machines that help us cook and clean! Yes, machines help us. But they change us, too—and the change is not always good. Look at the car. In some ways, life was better before the car came along.

Now, we have computers. Computers may change life even more than cars did. The computer is a machine that helps us think. The first computers could not do much more than count. Today's computers can do many things. Now, you need a computer just to count the things a computer can do! Every year, new computers come out. The new computers are better and faster than the old ones. At the same time, computers keep getting smaller.

Then there are robots. Robots are machines that can move like people. Do you think robots belong only in stories? Think again. Robots are a part of real life now. Already, in some places, robots are making cars, and there is talk of people getting more and more robot parts someday. When that day comes, you'll get a new arm just like your old one. A robot arm may work better than your old arm.

Robots and computers work together. Already they can do things that are hard to believe. A well-known scientist got sick some years back. He could no longer move or talk. He still can't. But he is far from helpless. In fact, he is still working. He has a computer that can sound out words. He makes it do the talking for him.

64

Worktext page 64

What Do You Think?

Meet with a small group of friends. Talk about the new machines people are making. Do you think some machines are bad? What do you think of computers? Do you think robots may ever take the place of people? Why or why not?

What Are the Facts?

One kind of sentence tells a **fact**. A fact is something people know. But some sentences do not tell facts. They tell what someone thinks, feels, or believes. Most sentences that say what **will** or **may** happen are **not** facts. The sentences below do not give facts. Words such as **good** and **should** show up in many sentences of this kind.

Cars are a good thing. People should not drive so much.

Write **Fact** or **Not Fact** after each sentence below.

Computers may change life even more than cars did.

____

Already, in some places, robots are making cars.

____

In some ways, life was better before the car came along.

____

People should not be helping machines.

____

The first computers could not do much more than count.

____

66

Worktext page 66

FINAL NOVEL Trapped in Space

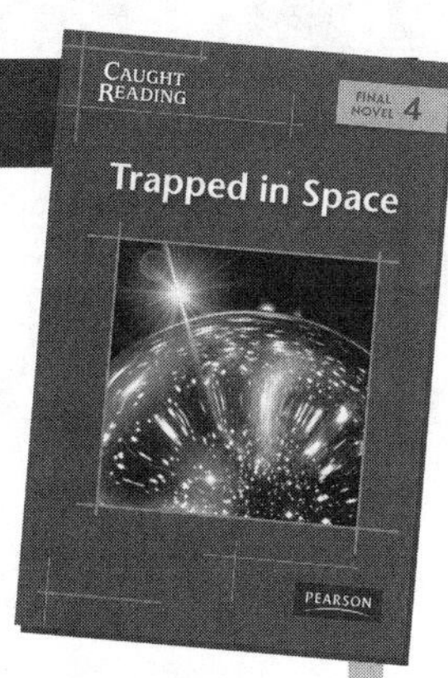

MATERIALS

Final Novel 4, *Trapped in Space*
Teacher's Manual, page 217
Assessment Manual, Final Assessment 4, pages 90–94

Summary Mars One *is sent into outer space. The spaceship is captured by aliens that turn out to be robots.* Mars One *crew tries to escape so that they can save Earth from the robots. One crew member realizes that the robots love computer games. The crew uses the computer games to distract the robots. Earth is saved.*

REVIEW AND ASSESSMENT

- Have students review their Memory Chips with a small group or a partner.
- Depending on your students' needs, review the following skills covered in Lessons 9–15: context clues; possessives; compound words; contractions; phonograms *and, ake, ack, ip, an, ace, arm,* and *ay*; syllabication; and endings *s, ing, less, ly, ness, en, n,* and *ed.*

If you wish to assess students' progress at this point, use the *Assessment Manual,* pages 90–94. If students need additional support, you may use the Reteach activities from previous lessons.

INTRODUCE THE NOVEL

Invite students to preview the book by reading the title, looking at the illustrations, and reading aloud the captions. Begin a discussion of story concepts by asking:

- **What do you think it would be like to go on a trip to Mars?**
- **What kinds of creatures do you think might exist in outer space?**

CHECK COMPREHENSION

Chapter 1 Who is on the spaceship, and where are they going? (*Mu Lan, Tyrone, Jake, and Kate are on* Mars One *and are on their way to Mars.*)

Chapter 2 What is the first problem the crew has on its way to Mars? How does the crew solve it? (*The crew members get on each other's nerves, so the crew begins taking turns playing a computer game that Tyrone invented.*)

Chapter 3 What three problems are the characters having now? (*The spaceship won't go where they want it to; they have lost contact with Earth; they are in a place they don't recognize.*)

Chapter 4 What happened to the crew of *Mars One*? (*They crashed and have been captured and put into boxes.*)

Chapter 5 How do the creatures look and how do they act? (*They are big and red and look like giant spiders with one giant eye; they copy everything people say.*)

Chapter 6 Who do the creatures want? (*They want the boss of the group to come with them.*)

Chapter 7 What do the creatures want Kate to do? (*They want her to fix the broken machines.*)

Chapter 8 What does Tyrone plan to do to get the monsters to listen to reason? (*He is going to tap into their feelings, so they will listen to him.*)

Chapter 9 How does the plan work to get the creatures to feel sorry for the crew members of *Mars One*? (*It doesn't work because the creature is not interested in Tyrone or his family.*)

Chapter 10 What does Tyrone discover about the creatures after the big fight? (*They are actually machines, not animals. They don't have feelings.*)

Chapter 11 What are the creatures planning to do? (*They want to take over Earth and steal everything.*)

Chapter 12 What do you think Tyrone's plan might be to save Earth? (*Possible answers: It has something to do with computer games; possibly he will get the robots to play a game and destroy themselves.*)

Chapter 13 How does Tyrone solve the problem? (*He gets the robots addicted to playing computer games; they won't stop playing the games.*)

Chapter 14 Why is Tyrone famous? (*He saved Earth from the creatures.*)

CONNECTION

Home/School Encourage students to bring home a copy of *Trapped in Space.* They might read the novel, or sections of the novel, to family members.

Level 4

LEVEL 5

ORGANIZER

Level 5 of the *Caught Reading* program includes the following components:

Worktext 5

Worktext 5 includes 14 lessons, taking students from those words introduced in previous levels through a word list of 172 words (found on page 342 of this *Teacher's Manual*) by Lesson 14. The Practice Lessons provide students with opportunites to extend practice, and review the content of each lesson. The Response to Reading pages allow students to practice using their new vocabulary. Tear-out Memory Chips in the back of the student book reinforce new vocabulary and can be used both independently by students and in small groups.

Midway and Final Novels 5

These novels are designed to reinforce learned vocabulary and give students the opportunity to read for meaning. Their high-interest plots encourage successful reading experiences and an appreciation for literature.

- *A Fight for Life* includes only vocabulary students have learned up to the midway point of this level.
- *Running Out of Time* includes all vocabulary learned through Level 5.

Teacher's Manual

The *Teacher's Manual* provides detailed objectives and instruction for each skill taught in the Worktext, as well as additional teaching suggestions for meaningful practice and reinforcement. The *Teacher's Manual* provides choices for flexible instruction. Comprehension questions for the Midway and Final novels are included, as well as Answer Keys for the Worktext activities and the Practice Lessons.

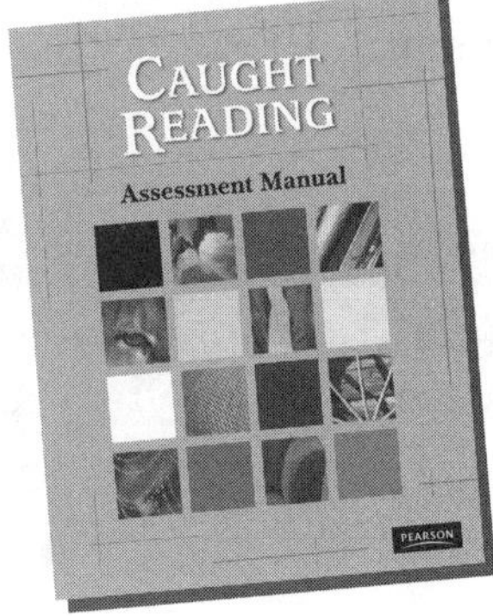

Assessment Manual

The *Assessment Manual* provides preassessment, ongoing assessment, and postassessment to administer to students throughout their work in *Caught Reading*. Within this Manual you will also find Midway and Final Assessments to determine the students' comprehension of the Midway and Final Novels.

OBJECTIVES

Vocabulary Development

- Read a base vocabulary, plus base vocabulary words with various endings, compound words, and contractions formed from base words.
- Use the word learning sequence to remember and spell words correctly.
- Review vocabulary independently, both in and out of context, using the Memory Chips.
- Learn fundamental social studies vocabulary.

Phonics

- Read the contractions *I'd, wasn't,* and *couldn't.*
- Recognize the letter groups *eat, ood, ean, ong, ike,* and *air.*
- Use a new vowel generalization: If a word has only one vowel, that vowel usually has the short sound.

Reading Comprehension

- Use study skills to read and understand social studies content.
- Make a timeline.
- Make comparisons.

Literary Analysis

- Determine the underlying theme or author's message in nonfiction.
- Determine what characters are like by what they say or do and by how the author portrays them.

Writing

- Write narratives that relate observations and ideas using narrative strategies.
- Write reports that include facts and details that illuminate the main ideas.

Speaking and Listening

- Answer *who, what, where, when,* and *why* about readings.
- Summarize major ideas and supporting evidence about readings.

INTRODUCTION & LESSON 5.1

OBJECTIVES

- Students will decode and blend words containing the *op, eat,* and *ill* phonograms
- Students will apply endings *s, en, ing, ly, ed,* and *er* to base words to form new words
- Students will recognize and form compound words
- Students will recognize and form possessives
- Students will use context clues to recognize unfamiliar words

PHONICS VOCABULARY

having	law	voting	bill	sometimes
harder	whites	beat	started	Americans
worked	owned	crops	married	fields
animals	killed	asked	years	cleaned
meeting	reading	wanted	passed	given
stopped	writing	raised	laws	questions
driver	tried	looked	kids	registering
taken	Hamer's	farm	friends	problems
test	living	sharecropper's		outlawed
badly	sharecropping		happily	willing
cropping	whatever	however	outlaw	yourself
bills	farms	kill	voter	cropper
rights	crop	laws	beat	learning
born	voters	tests	sharecropper	

WORDS TO KNOW

beat	kill	born	went	yellow
police	white	south	African	share
husband	register	politics	act	Mississippi
social	learn	bill	crop	American
law	test	farm	Fannie Lou Hamer	

MATERIALS

Worktext 5, pages 5–12
Teacher's Manual, pages 220–222
Practice Lesson 5.1, pages 66–67 of the Worktext

TEACH

- Before beginning the lesson, have students complete the exercises independently in the Introduction beginning on Worktext page 5.
- Using Worktext pages 7–8, introduce students to the vocabulary words. Give students an opportunity to practice writing the words.
- Students can organize their Memory Chips, found in the back of the Worktext. You may wish to say each word, having students repeat it after you. Students can take turns using each word in a sentence.

Worktext pages 7–8 can also be used to reinforce spelling. Use the five-step process detailed on page 71 of this *Teacher's Manual.*

Phonograms *eat, ill*

Write this sentence on the board and read it aloud: **I will beat the drum.** Ask a volunteer to point to *beat.*

Blending Circle the letters *ea* in *beat,* and explain that sometimes these letters have the long *e* sound. Say *beat,* segmenting the sounds: /*bbbbb ēēēēēttt*/. Then say the word naturally. Erase the *b* and write *h.* Have students blend the sounds: /*hēt*/. Have a student point to *will.* Ask him or her to list rhyming words for *will.* (*kill, bill, till, sill, hill, fill*) List them on the board, blending them as you read them aloud.

Endings *s, en, ing, ly, ed, er*

Remind students that they can add the endings *s, en, ing, ly, ed,* and *er* to words. Write this sentence on the board: **Those seats are taken.** Have students find two words with *s* or *en* endings. (*seats, taken*) Have them identify the base words. Then remind students that when they add *ing* to some words, the consonant is doubled and *ing* is added. Remind them that when a word ends in *e,* the *e* is dropped, and *er* or *en* is added.

Make New Words Write these words on the board: **take**, **crop**, **kill**, **bad**. Have students take turns adding *s, en, ing, ly, ed,* or *er* to each word if it makes a new word. (*takes, taken, taking, taker; crops, cropping, cropped, cropper; kills, killing, killed, killer; badly*) They can write the words on the board and use each one in a sentence.

Compound Words

Remind students that words like *sometimes* and *anything* are made up of two smaller words.

Make New Words Write these words on index cards, and have students put two words together to make new words: **share**, **what**, **how**, **out**, **your**, **self**, **law**, **ever**, **cropping**. (*sharecropping, whatever, however, outlaw, yourself*)

Possessives

Remind students that they can add an apostrophe and *s* to the end of some words to show that someone or something owns something.

Make New Words Have students add an apostrophe and *s* to these words: *sharecropper, Hamer, field.* (*sharecropper's, Hamer's, field's*)

PRACTICE

- Let students practice the new words they have learned and formed by completing the activities found on pages 7–9 of the Worktext.
- If students are experiencing difficulty with the Words to Know section on pages 7–8, place the Memory Chips on the table. Pose riddles like this,

and have students use the Memory Chips to answer the clues: **I am a color. I am the color of a school bus.** (*yellow*)

For further practice, have students complete Practice Lesson 5.1 on pages 66–67 of the Worktext. Answers can be found in the Answer Key on page 357 of this *Teacher's Manual.*

APPLY

- Have students talk about the story concept by discussing things they already know. Ask: **What do you know about Fannie Lou Hamer? What do you know about sharecropping?** Tell students they are going to use the words they have learned to read an article about Fannie Lou Hamer, an African American woman who was determined to vote.
- Ask students to read the article on pages 10–11 in the Worktext. Offer assistance if necessary, but encourage students to decode the words independently, using the clues and patterns they have learned.
- After students have completed reading the story, have them complete the Cooperative Group Activity (What Do You Think?) and Comprehension Exercises (Describe It and What Will Happen Next?) on page 12 in their Worktext. Answers can be found in the Answer Key on pages 355–356 of this *Teacher's Manual.*

INTRODUCTION: GET CAUGHT READING SOCIAL STUDIES

Word Attack

till You know the words **till**, **will**, and **still**. Put a **b** before the word **ill** and you get **bill**. Write it.

bill ________________

stop You know the words **stop**, **shop**, and **cop**. Change the **st** in **stop** to **cr**. Write the new word **crop**.

crop ________________

Words to Know

	Look	Say	Picture	Write
act	☐	☐	☐	________
American Amer-i-can	☐	☐	☐	________
bill	☐	☐	☐	________
crop	☐	☐	☐	________
farm	☐	☐	☐	________
law	☐	☐	☐	________
learn	☐	☐	☐	________
politics pol-i-tics	☐	☐	☐	________
social so-cial	☐	☐	☐	________
test	☐	☐	☐	________

Word Attack

+s Write each word with an **s** ending.

bill ________________ law ________________

farm ________________ crop ________________

+ing Write **learn** with an **ing** ending. ________________

5

Worktext page 5

1. FANNIE LOU HAMER, THE SHARECROPPER

Word Attack

eat You know the word **eat**. Put a **b** before the word **eat** and you get **beat**. Write it.

beat ________________

till You know the words **till**, **will**, **still**, and **bill**. Put a **k** before the word **ill**, and you get **kill**. Write it.

kill ________________

Take a Guess

Try to guess this new word by reading the other words in the sentences. Think of a word that starts with **b**.

He is an old man. He was **born** in 1914.

Did you guess the word? Write it. ________________

Words to Know

	Look	Say	Picture	Write
African Af-ri-can	☐	☐	☐	________
beat	☐	☐	☐	________
born	☐	☐	☐	________
Fannie Lou Hamer Fan-nie Lou Ham-er	☐	☐	☐	________
husband hus-band	☐	☐	☐	________
kill	☐	☐	☐	________
Mississippi Mis-sis-sip-pi	☐	☐	☐	________
police po-lice	☐	☐	☐	________

7

Worktext page 7

	Look	Say	Picture	Write
register reg-is-ter	☐	☐	☐	________
share	☐	☐	☐	________
south	☐	☐	☐	________
went	☐	☐	☐	________
white	☐	☐	☐	________
yellow yel-low	☐	☐	☐	________

Word Attack

+er Write **crop** with an **er** ending. You have to add another **p**: **cropper.**

crop ________________

Write **drive** and **vote** with **er** endings. These words already have an **e** on the end. So just add **r**: **driver, voter.**

drive ________________ vote ________________

+s Write each word with an **s** ending.

American ________________ white ________________

field ________________ right ________________

voter ________________ test ________________

+ing Write each word with an **ing** ending.

will ________________ register ________________

Write **crop** with an **ing** ending. You have to add another **p**: **cropping.**

crop ________________

Write **vote** with an **ing** ending. You have to take away the **e**, then add the **ing**: **voting.**

vote ________________

8

Worktext page 8

2=1 Below are words that you already know. Put them together to make new words. Write the new, longer word.

Then circle the two smaller words in each longer word you wrote.

share + cropper = ________________

share + cropping = ________________

what + ever = ________________

how + ever = ________________

out + law = ________________

your + self = ________________

+ed Write an **ed** ending after each word.

kill ________________ own ________________

pass ________________ ask ________________

clean ________________ outlaw ________________

+n Write an **n** ending after the word **take**.

take ________________

+ly Write an **ly** ending after the word **bad**.

bad ________________

Write an **ly** ending after the word **happy**. Remember to change the **y** at the end of **happy** to an **i** first.

happy ________________

+'s Write each word with an **'s** ending.

sharecropper ________________

Hamer ________________

9

Worktext page 9

1. FANNIE LOU HAMER, THE SHARECROPPER

Sometimes, people would try to kill Fannie Lou Hamer. Why? Only because she wanted to vote.

From around 1877 to 1964, many African Americans could not vote in the South. By law, African Americans had the right to vote. Many white people in the South did not want African Americans to have a say. So they made laws to stop people from voting. One law made people pay money to vote. Most African Americans in the South did not have much money. Another law made people show they could read and write before voting. A much harder test was given to African Americans than was given to whites. Sometimes, African Americans were even beat up for trying to vote.

Fannie Lou Hamer's life started in 1917 in Mississippi. There were 14 boys and six girls in her family. She was the last one born. Her family worked on a farm owned by a white man. They had to give him a lot of their crops because he owned the land. This is called sharecropping.

When Fannie was 12, her dad got his own land and some farm animals. Some white people in Mississippi didn't like this. They killed his farm animals. The family had to go back to sharecropping.

In 1944, Hamer married. Her husband worked for another sharecropper. She went to work and live with her new husband. She worked in the fields in the day. At night, she cleaned the sharecropper's house. The years passed by.

Then, in 1962, she went to a meeting. A man asked who wanted to register to vote. Fannie Lou Hamer raised her hand.

A group of African Americans got on a bus to go to register to vote. They were all given a reading and writing test. Not one man or woman passed the test. It had really hard questions about the laws of Mississippi.

On the way home, the bus was stopped by police. The bus driver and another man were taken in. The police said they had to pay $100 because the bus was too yellow. They said the

10

Worktext page 10

Fannie Lou Hamer in 1964.

bus could be taken for a real school bus. What law said a bus could not be yellow? So what if it looked like a school bus? This was just one way the police tried to stop African Americans from registering to vote.

Hamer's problems had only started. She and her husband had worked for the same man for 18 years. She had worked on his farm, taken care of his kids, and cleaned his house. This man made Hamer leave her home and job because she tried to register to vote.

Some friends put her up, but she still was not safe. People fired at the house where Hamer was now living. Her husband lost his job. The family lost their car and house. What did Fannie Lou Hamer do? Did she say she would never again try to vote? Did she say she would never again speak out? No. Fannie Lou Hamer tried one more time to register to vote. Again, she did not pass the test.

"You'll see me every 30 days till the day I pass," she said. That is only the start of Fannie Lou Hamer's story.

11

Worktext page 11

What Do You Think?

Meet with a friend or in a small group. Talk about what you know about Fannie Lou Hamer. Do you think what she was doing was a good idea? Why or why not? Do you think you would ever put yourself on the line like that? Why or why not?

Describe It

Circle each sentence below that describe Hamer's life.

She tried to register to vote.

She was a sharecropper.

She came from a big family.

She came from a small family.

She was not interested in voting.

She gave up.

She would not give up.

What Will Happen Next?

Do you think Fannie Lou Hamer will ever get to vote? Circle one answer.

YES **NO**

Write two sentences that back up what you think. You can use these sentences or make up your own.

Fannie Lou Hamer did not give up.

African Americans will never get to vote in Mississippi.

She will never have enough money.

They will keep finding ways to stop her from voting.

She no longer had anything to lose.

By law, African Americans had the right to vote.

____

____

____

____

____

12

Worktext page 12

LESSON 5.2

OBJECTIVE
- Students will practice and apply skills to an extended passage

MATERIALS
Worktext 5, pages 13–15
Teacher's Manual, pages 223–224, 331, 333
Practice Lesson 5.2, pages 68–69 of the Worktext

SKILLS REVIEW

- Before reading, you may wish to review these words that apply phonics skills: *going, nothing, longer, started, Americans, everywhere, doing, Hamer, running, living, badly, trying, voting, helped, friends, willing, passed, studied, laws, questions, waited, happily, however, rights, making, outlawed, voters, reading, writing, Hamer's, politics, talks, years, everyone.* Have students review the Memory Chips they have learned so far. Then ask: **What do you think will happen to Fannie Lou Hamer next?**
- While reading, have students take note of what Fannie Lou Hamer did to win the right to vote.
- After reading, have students complete the comprehension exercises on Worktext page 15.

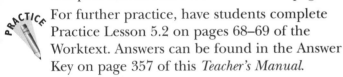

For further practice, have students complete Practice Lesson 5.2 on pages 68–69 of the Worktext. Answers can be found in the Answer Key on page 357 of this *Teacher's Manual.*

RETEACH

If students need further review of phonics skills, you may wish to use the following activity:

Ending *er*

Pantomimes Write the following words on index cards: **drive**, **vote**, **hit**, **grow**, **teach**, **help**, **clean**, **speak**, **work**, **rob**. Remind students that when they add *er* to the end of words it means "one who." Have students add *er* to each word and tell what the new word means. Guide them to drop the *e* after *vote* and *drive* before they add the ending; help them double the final consonant in *hit* and *rob.* Then place the index cards in a box. Have students take turns choosing a card, pantomiming the action while the group guesses who the person is. (*driver, voter, hitter, grower, teacher, helper, cleaner, speaker, worker, robber*)

CONNECTION

Response to Reading
- Have students complete the Character Cluster reproducible found on page 331 of this *Teacher's Manual.* Students can fill in words that describe character traits of Fannie Lou Hamer.
- Have student volunteers share their completed organizers with the class.

Literature
- Students may enjoy reading or listening to another book about an African American hero. *Narrative of the Life of Frederick Douglass* is available in softcover text and on audiocassette from Pearson's *Pacemaker*™ *Classics.*
- Students may use the Book Report reproducible found on page 333 of this *Teacher's Manual* to record their responses to the book they read.

Independent Reading
- If students wish to read more about Fannie Lou Hamer, Pearson publishes a series of biographies entitled *Freedom Fighters.* Students may choose the biography of Fannie Lou Hamer or another freedom fighter.
- After reading, students may work with a partner. Each partner can summarize and explain how they feel about their book. Students may then orally summarize their partner's story for the class and describe their reaction to it.

2. FANNIE LOU HAMER IN POLITICS

Fannie Lou Hamer was not going to stop now. She said, "There was nothing they could do to me. They could not fire me because I didn't have a job. They could not put me out of my house because I didn't have one. There was nothing they could take from me any longer."

Hamer started to talk to African Americans everywhere. She told them they had the right to vote.

Fannie Lou Hamer in 1964.

13

Worktext page 13

Many white people didn't like her doing this. One time, the police came and went through her house. Another time, the Hamers got a water bill for $9,000. They didn't even have running water in the house where they were living. Another time, Fannie Lou Hamer was badly beaten.

Even this didn't stop Hamer from trying to get African Americans to take their voting rights. Friends helped the Hamers out with money and food. Fannie Lou Hamer was willing to do whatever it took. She was even willing to die for the right to vote.

Then, in 1963, Fannie Lou Hamer took the voting test again. This time she passed. She had studied the laws of Mississippi so that she could answer the questions. She waited happily for voting day. On that day, however, they said she had to pay money before she could vote. She didn't have the money. Fannie Lou Hamer didn't get to vote.

Hamer and her friends worked and worked to get their voting rights. At long last, making people pay to vote was outlawed. Then, in 1965, the Voting Rights Act was passed. The Voting Rights Act said voters did not have to take reading and writing tests. It said no one could stop other people from voting. Fannie Lou Hamer's work helped get this law passed.

She was not done. She went into politics and won some of her races. She gave talks on TV. She gave talks to other people in politics. Hamer worked in politics for many more years. People said that Fannie Lou Hamer had made Mississippi and the U.S. a better place for everyone. She died in 1977.

14

Worktext page 14

Remembering Details

Write a word from the story in each space.

Hamer started to talk to ________________ American people everywhere.

She was even willing to die for the right to ______________

Then, in 1965, the Voting ________________ Act was passed.

Who? What? Where? When? Why?

Who, **what**, **where**, **when**, and **why** are five question words. These questions all start with the letter **W**. Some people call them the **5 Ws**. When you read social studies, it is a good idea to ask these questions as you read.

You just read about Fannie Lou Hamer's life. Get together with a friend or in a small group. Talk about the 5 W questions. Then write an answer to each question.

1. **Who** was Fannie Lou Hamer? ________________
2. **What** did she do? ________________
3. **Where** did she do it? ________________
4. **When** did she do it? ________________
5. **Why** did she do it? ________________

15

Worktext page 15

LESSON 5.3

OBJECTIVES

- Students will decode words containing the *ood* phonogram
- Students will use context clues to read unfamiliar words
- Students will apply endings *s*, *ed*, *en*, and *ing* to base words to form new words
- Students will recognize and form compound words

PHONICS VOCABULARY

opened	stood	neighborhood	cooking
called	talking	neighbors	waited
freeway	going	buildings	says
always	something	running	wants
wins	asking	started	stopped
guys	voting	counts	anything
good	building	walked	closed
cares	hood	joke	build
moved	voted	winning	seen
named			

WORDS TO KNOW

hood	stood	joke	build	free
hurt	ruin	office	neighbor	poor

MATERIALS

Worktext 5, pages 16–20
Teacher's Manual, pages 225–227
Practice Lesson 5.3, pages 70–71 of the Worktext

TEACH

- Using Worktext pages 16–17, introduce students to the vocabulary words. Give students an opportunity to practice writing the words.
- Students can organize their Memory Chips, found in the back of the Worktext. They can divide them into groups of words they know and words they don't recognize. Then say each word, having students repeat each one after you.

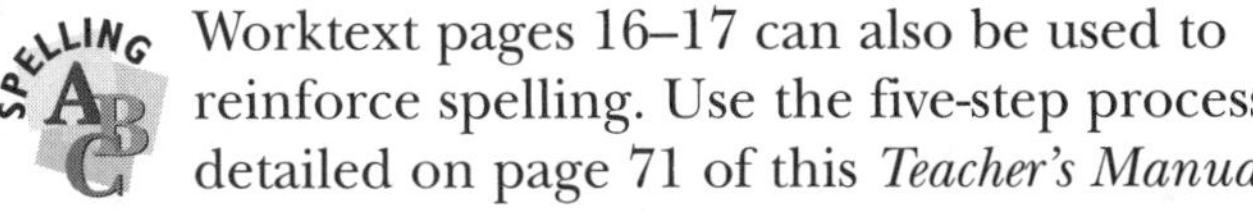

Worktext pages 16–17 can also be used to reinforce spelling. Use the five-step process detailed on page 71 of this *Teacher's Manual.*

Phonogram *ood*

Write this sentence on the board: **The boy stood on the hood.** Ask students what two words rhyme. (*stood, hood*) Ask them what letters are the same in both words. (*ood*)

Blending Write **stood** on the board. Have students name rhyming words for each word. As each word is suggested, volunteers can substitute beginning letters and blend the new words. If students suggest other spellings like *could* and *should,* list these words in another column.

stood
hood
wood

Context Clues

Write this sentence on the board: **I live in the brick building.** Cover the word *building* and tell students that when they see an unfamiliar word like this one, they can read the words around it and use what they know about letters and sounds to help them figure out the word. Read the sentence without *building.* Uncover the word and have them look at the beginning letter. Tell students that the *b* gives us a clue as to how the word begins. Ask them what word they think goes in the sentence. (*building*)

Endings *s, ed, ing*

Remind students that when *ing* is added to some words, the ending consonant is doubled; when *ed* and *ing* are added to some words, the *e* is dropped and the *ed* or *ing* ending is added.

Make New Words Write these words on the board and invite students to add *s, ed,* and *ing* to the end of each: **care**, **open**, **move**, **win**, **ask**, **build**. (*cares, cared, caring*; *opens, opened, opening*; *moves, moved, moving*; *wins, winning*; *asks, asked, asking*; *builds, building*) They can use each new word they make in a sentence.

Compound Words

Write this sentence on the board, and read it aloud: **This is my neighborhood.** Draw a line between *neighbor* and *hood,* and ask students what they notice about *neighborhood.* (*It is made up of two words.*)

Make New Words Write these words on index cards, and have students make new words by putting two of the words together: **free**, **way**, **neighbor**, **hood**, **boy**, **friend**. (*freeway, neighborhood, boyfriend*)

PRACTICE

- Let students practice the new words they have learned and formed by completing the activities found on pages 16–17 of the Worktext.
- If students are experiencing difficulty with the Words to Know section on pages 16–17, you may wish to scramble the letters in each word on the board. Then have partners look at the Memory Chips, unscramble the words, and read them aloud.

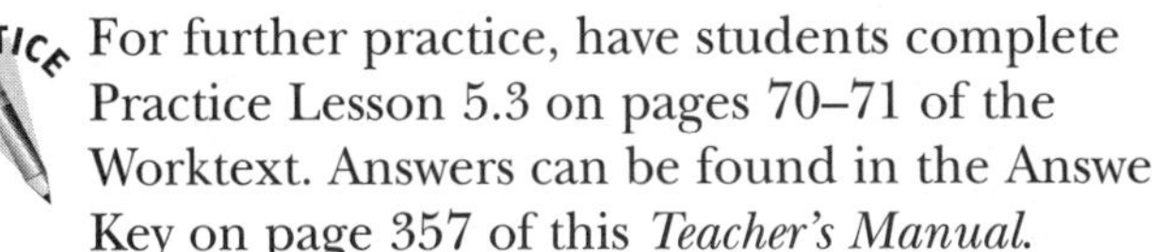

For further practice, have students complete Practice Lesson 5.3 on pages 70–71 of the Worktext. Answers can be found in the Answer Key on page 357 of this *Teacher's Manual.*

Level 5

APPLY

- Have students talk about the story concept by sharing their prior knowledge. Ask: **Why is it important to vote?** Tell them they are going to use the words they have learned to read a short story about a boy who is trying to get people to vote to save the neighborhood from being destroyed by a new freeway.
- Ask students to read the story on pages 18–19 in the Worktext. Offer assistance if necessary, but encourage students to decode the words independently, using the clues and patterns they have learned.
- After students have completed reading the story, have them complete the Comprehension Exercises (How Are People Alike and Different? and Putting Ideas in Order) on page 20 in their Worktext. Answers can be found in the Answer Key on page 356 of this *Teacher's Manual.*

CONNECTION

Strategy for Reading Have students reread the selection "Who Cares About Politics?" on Worktext pages 18–19 to correct comprehension breakdowns. Students may achieve understanding by reprocessing the same text with greater attention focused on its meaning.

Speaking/Listening Have students read aloud the selection "Who Cares About Politics?" on Worktext pages 18–19. The partners can alternate being speaker and listener.

Worktext Pages 16–17

3. WHO CARES ABOUT POLITICS?

Word Attack

wood You know the words **wood** and **good**. Change the **w** in **wood** to **h**. What word do you get? Write it.

hood ________________

Now change the **h** in **hood** to **st**. What new word do you get? Write it.

stood ________________

Take a Guess

Try to guess this new word by reading the other words in the sentences. Think of a word that starts with **j**.

Tyrone really knows how to tell a **joke**. He always makes me laugh.

Did you guess the word? Write it. ________________

Try another one. Read this sentence. Then guess what the new word is.

My family is going to **build** our own house by hand.

Did you guess the word? Write it. ________________

Words to Know

	Look	Say	Picture	Write
build	☐	☐	☐	________
free	☐	☐	☐	________
hood	☐	☐	☐	________
hurt	☐	☐	☐	________
joke	☐	☐	☐	________
neighbor neigh-bor	☐	☐	☐	________
office of-fice	☐	☐	☐	________

16

Worktext page 16

	Look	Say	Picture	Write
poor	☐	☐	☐	________
ruin	☐	☐	☐	________
stood	☐	☐	☐	________

Word Attack

+ing Write each word with an **ing** ending.

build ________________ ask ________________

To add **ing** to **win** you have to add another **n**: **winning**.

win ________________

+s Write each word with an **s** ending.

care ________________ neighbor ________________

building ________________ win ________________

count ________________ guy ________________

build ________________

+ed Write **open** with an **ed** ending. ________________

These next words all end with **e**. So you only have to add a **d**.

name ________________ move ________________

vote ________________ open ________________

+n Write **see** with an **n** ending. ________________

2=1 Below are words that you already know. Put them together to make new words. Write the new, longer words.

free + way = ________________

neighbor + hood = ________________

Now circle the two small words in each longer word you wrote.

17

Worktext page 17

3. WHO CARES ABOUT POLITICS?

I opened the door. An African American kid stood there. I had seen him around the neighborhood. His name was Jared.

My friend, Beth, and I were cooking. She called out, "Who is it?"

"My name is Jared," the kid said. "I am talking to all our neighbors. Did you hear what they want to do to the neighborhood?"

Beth came to the door and stood next to me. She waited for Jared to go on.

"They want to put in a freeway. They are going to take down a lot of buildings. This one, the one you live in, is going to be taken down."

"**Our** building?" I say.

"So?" Beth says. "What else is new? They are always doing **something** to ruin what we have."

18

Worktext page 18

"We can stop this," Jared said. "A man named Will Glass is running for office. He wants the freeway. If he wins, they will do it. They will take down your building, my building, and most of our neighborhood. I am asking you to vote **against** Will Glass."

"Look, politics are not my thing," Beth said. She started to close the door. Jared stopped her.

"How old are you?" he said to her.

Beth said, "18."

"What about you?" he asked me.

"18."

"Me, too. So we are old enough to vote. I think we should. Those guys in politics think they can do what they want with our neighborhood because poor people live here. We can make them think again."

"Forget it," Beth said. "What does voting get us? One little vote. As if my vote counts for anything!"

"Your name is Mu Lan," Jared said to me.

"Yes. How did you know?"

"I have seen you around. What do you think about voting?"

"I don't know. I don't think voting does much good."

"Think about it," he said. "Voting day is next week. Be there. If you aren't, your building will not be here next year."

Then Jared walked away. I closed the door.

"What a joke," Beth said.

"It can't hurt to vote," I said. "Why not try?"

"I don't have time for politics," Beth said. "Who cares about politics?"

19

Worktext page 19

How are People Alike and Different?

Jared, Beth, and Mu Lan are all different people. They have different ideas. Are there any ways in which they are alike? Read these sentences. Then write the sentences that say how Jared, Beth, and Mu Lan are alike.

They all believe in voting.

They are all 18 years old.

They are all African American.

They all live in the same neighborhood.

They all live in the same building.

They all can vote.

They all like Will Glass.

____

____

____

____

____

____

____

Putting Ideas in Order

Here are sentences from the story. Write them in the order that they happened.

"We can stop this," Jared said. "I am asking you to vote **against** Will Glass."

Beth came to the door and stood next to me.

"It can't hurt to vote," I said. "Why not try?"

____

____

____

____

20

Worktext page 20

LESSON 5.4

OBJECTIVE

- Students will practice and apply skills to an extended passage

MATERIALS

Worktext 5, pages 21–22
Teacher's Manual, page 228
Practice Lesson 5.4, pages 72–73 of the Worktext

SKILLS REVIEW

- Before reading, you may wish to review these words that apply phonics skills: *moving, moved, building, helping, taking, turned, winning, freeway, good, voted, voting, lots, looked, stood, helped, worked, neighbors, stopped, feeling, politics, guys, whatever, neighborhood, without.* Have students review the Memory Chips they have learned so far. Then ask: **Do you think Jared got enough people to vote against Will Glass?**
- While reading, have students think about the importance of voting.
- After reading, have students complete the Cooperative Group Activity (What Do You Think?) and the Comprehension Exercise (Write a Summary) on Worktext page 22.

For further practice, have students complete Practice Lesson 5.4 on pages 72–73 of the Worktext. Answers can be found in the Answer Key on pages 356–357 of this *Teacher's Manual.*

RETEACH

If students need further review of phonics skills, you may wish to use the following activity:

Compound Words

Find a Partner! Write the following words on index cards, and give one or more cards to each student: **some**, **times**, **day**, **on**, **to**, **your**, **self**, **in**, **side**, **out**, **who**, **ever**, **any**, **one**, **where**, **under**, **stand**, **it**, **law**, **how**, **what**, **neighbor**, **hood**, **free**, **way**, **friend**, **boy**, **with**. Then time students for five minutes. Have them find as many partners as they can to make as many compound words as they can in the time allowed. As they make a word, have them write the word on the board. Possible combinations include: *sometimes, someday, without, outside, inside, outlaw, however, wherever, whatever, neighborhood, freeway, boyfriend, onto, into, yourself, itself, anyone, anywhere, anyhow, somehow, within, understand, whoever.*

Worktext Pages 21–22

4. MOVING OUT OF THE NEIGHBORHOOD

I was so sick of moving. My mom and dad and I just moved into this building. Now we have to move again. Beth was helping us out. Dad and I were taking the TV out the door.

That's when I saw Jared walk up. I turned my back. I didn't want to talk to him. He would just say, "I told you so." He came up to me.

"I'm sorry about Will Glass winning," he said. "It's really bad. Who needs a freeway?"

"I hear that," my dad said.

Jared said, "I have to move next week, too."

"Well," I said, "I'll have you know that I **did** vote. Look what good it did."

"I voted, too," Jared said. "I guess you are right. What good does voting do?"

Beth put down a radio she was taking to the truck. "I told you so," she said. "Politics are for people with lots of money. What did voting get you? Nothing at all."

Jared and I looked at each other. Beth just stood there shaking her head like Jared and I didn't know anything. Then Jared took an end of the TV and helped my dad take it to the truck.

"It could have worked," I said to Beth. "What if you and I had helped Jared talk to the neighbors? Maybe we could have talked more people into voting. Maybe we could have stopped the freeway." I could tell Jared was feeling bad. He had worked so hard to try to stop this freeway.

"No way," Beth said. "That's politics. The big guys do whatever they want. You can't stop them."

"Only about 50% of the people in our neighborhood voted," Jared said. "What if 100% voted? Will Glass would not be in office. He would not be able to put in the freeway."

I didn't want to hear what Beth had to say to that. I went back into the building to see if we had gotten everything. My room looked sad without anything in it. I was sick of moving. I didn't like the idea of a freeway taking the place of my room. I just didn't know: Was Jared right, or was Beth right?

21

Worktext page 21

What Do You Think?

Meet with a friend or in a small group. Talk about the different ideas of Jared, Beth, and Mu Lan. What do **you** think? Do you think voting does any good? Why or why not? If you could talk to these people, what would you say?

Write a Summary

Read these sentences. Which ones are about the big ideas in the two stories you just read? Circle these. Which ones are about details? Put a line through each of these.

Jared tried to get Mu Lan and Beth to vote.

My friend, Beth, and I were cooking.

My room looked sad without anything in it.

Will Glass won the race.

They are taking down our neighborhood to put in a freeway.

Dad and I were taking the TV out the door.

Now write a summary. Write the big-idea sentences in the order that they happened in the story.

22

Worktext page 22

LESSON 5.5

OBJECTIVES

- Students will decode and blend words with the *ean, old,* and *ong* phonograms
- Students will apply endings *y, s, er, ing,* and *ed* to base words to form new words
- Students will recognize and form compound words

PHONICS VOCABULARY

jeans	finding	mountains	named	others
miners	used	tents	wagons	pants
lasted	hopes	becoming	wanted	stronger
putting	however	underwear	burns	rivets
changes	days	gold	strong	sold
sunny	heard	become	moving	flying
jean	miner	stronger	guys	headed
mined				

WORDS TO KNOW

jeans	gold	strong	burn	pants
tent	hope	mine	cloth	wagon
rivet	California	history	Levi Strauss	

MATERIALS

Worktext 5, pages 23–26
Teacher's Manual, pages 229–230
Practice Lesson 5.5, pages 74–75 of the Worktext

TEACH

- Using Worktext page 23, introduce students to the vocabulary words. Say each word and have students repeat it after you. Give students an opportunity to practice writing the words.
- Students can organize their Memory Chips, found in the back of the Worktext. They can divide them into groups of words with one, two, three, or four syllables. Then have students put the words in alphabetical order.

Worktext page 23 can also be used to reinforce spelling. Use the five-step process detailed on page 71 of this *Teacher's Manual.*

Phonograms *ean, old, ong*

Write this sentence on the board: **My jeans are clean, old, and long.** Ask students what they notice about *jeans* and *clean.* (They both have the letters *ean.*) Ask students what long vowel sound they hear. (*long* e) Have a volunteer point to *old.* Ask him or her to name a word that rhymes with *old.* Repeat, using *long.*

Blending Work with students to make word ladders with *old, long,* and *clean.* Have students take turns substituting the beginning consonant sound to make new words.

clean	old	long
lean	gold	strong
bean	sold	song

Endings *y, s, er, ing, ed*

Write this sentence on the board and read it aloud: **It is sunny today.** Ask a volunteer to point to *sunny.* Circle *sun* and tell students *sun* is the base word. Tell them that to make the word *sunny,* the consonant *n* is doubled and the *y* is added. Remind students that they can add *s, er, ing,* and *ed* to words. If a word ends in *e,* the *e* is dropped and *er, ing,* or *ed* is added.

Make New Words Write these words on the board, and have students add *y* to them: **sun**, **jump**, **fun**. (*sunny, jumpy, funny*) Then write these words, and have students add *s, er, ing,* and *ed* to make new words: **mine**, **use**, **last**, **wagon**, **hope**. (*mines, miner, mining, mined; uses, user, using, used; lasts, lasting, lasted; wagons; hopes, hoping, hoped*)

Compound Words

Remind students that they can sometimes find two words in longer words. Write **boyfriend** on the board, and ask students what two smaller words they see.

Make New Words Write these words on the board, and have volunteers take turns putting together two words to make new words: **be**, **come**, **under**, **wear**, **out**, **side**, **in**. (*become, underwear, outside, inside*)

PRACTICE

- Let students practice the new words they have learned and formed by completing the activities found on pages 23–24 of the Worktext.

For further practice, have students complete Practice Lesson 5.5 on pages 74–75 of the Worktext. Answers can be found in the Answer Key on page 357 of this *Teacher's Manual.*

APPLY

- Have students talk about the story concept by sharing their prior knowledge. Ask: **What do you know about blue jeans? Who invented them and why were they invented?**
- Ask students to read the article on page 25 in the Worktext. Encourage students to decode the words independently, using the clues and patterns they have learned.
- After students have completed reading the story, have them complete the Cooperative Group Activity (What Do You Think?) and Comprehension Exercise (Who? What? Where? When? Why?) on page 26 in their Worktext. Answers can be found in the Answer Key on page 356 of this *Teacher's Manual.*

5. THE HISTORY OF JEANS

Word Attack

clean What word do you get when you change the **cl** in **clean** to **j**? Write the word on the line.

jean ______________

old Put a **g** in front of the letter group **old**, and you get **gold**. Write it.

gold ______________

long Write the letters **str** in place of the **l** in **long**, and you have **strong**.

strong ______________

Words to Know

	Look	Say	Picture	Write
burn	☐	☐	☐	______
California Cal-i-for-nia	☐	☐	☐	______
cloth	☐	☐	☐	______
gold	☐	☐	☐	______
history his-to-ry	☐	☐	☐	______
hope	☐	☐	☐	______
Levi Strauss Le-vi Strauss	☐	☐	☐	______
mine	☐	☐	☐	______
pants	☐	☐	☐	______
rivet riv-et	☐	☐	☐	______
strong	☐	☐	☐	______
tent	☐	☐	☐	______
wagon wag-on	☐	☐	☐	______

23

Worktext page 23

Word Attack

+er Write these words with **er** endings. The first word already has an **e**, so you only have to put an **r**.

mine ______________ strong ______________

+s Write these words with **s** endings.

miner ______________ tent ______________

burn ______________ jean ______________

rivet ______________ wagon ______________

hope ______________

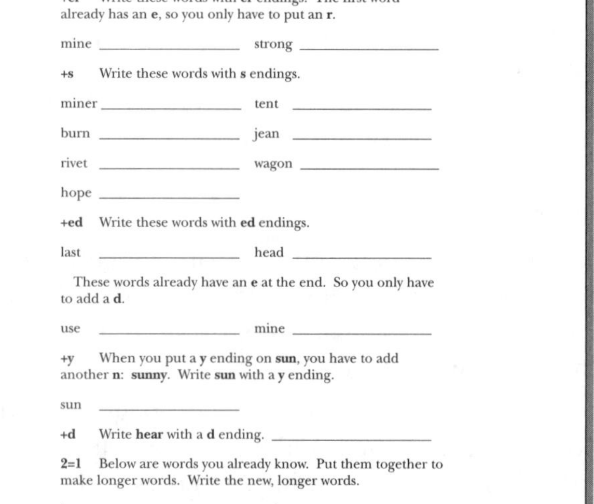

+ed Write these words with **ed** endings.

last ______________ head ______________

These words already have an **e** at the end. So you only have to add a **d**.

use ______________ mine ______________

+y When you put a **y** ending on **sun**, you have to add another **n**: **sunny**. Write **sun** with a **y** ending.

sun ______________

+d Write **hear** with a **d** ending. ______________

2=1 Below are words you already know. Put them together to make longer words. Write the new, longer words.

be + come = ______________ under + wear = ______________

+ing Write each of these words with an **ing** ending. Remember if the word ends with an **e**, leave the **e** off before writing the ending.

mine ______________ become ______________

fly ______________

24

Worktext page 24

5. THE HISTORY OF JEANS

In 1850, a 17-year-old boy went to California. He went to make a lot of money. People were finding gold all over the mountains in California.

This boy was named Levi Strauss. He was not going to make his money by finding gold like the others. He had another idea. Levi Strauss took some strong cloth to California. He sold the strong cloth to the gold miners. The miners used the cloth to make tents and to put over their wagons.

Then Strauss had a good idea. He saw that the miners did a lot of hard work. He saw that their pants didn't last long. He made some pants out of the strong cloth. The pants lasted a long time. He sold a lot of pants. His hopes for making big money were becoming real.

Strauss wanted to sell even more pants. He wanted to make them better. He made the cloth even stronger by putting in metal rivets. These metal rivets were a problem, however. Many miners did not wear underwear. When they got too close to the fire, the metal rivets got too hot. The miners got bad burns!

Strauss took the rivets off the jeans. Over time, he made other changes to his jeans. Many of the jeans you see today are much like those he made back in the days of California gold.

Levi Strauss

25

Worktext page 25

The Levi Strauss & Company store in San Francisco, California about 1880.

What Do You Think?

Meet with a friend or in a small group. In the story, Levi Strauss was a 17-year-old who wanted to make a lot of money fast. How can a 17-year-old make money today? Which are the best ways? Why do you think so?

Who? What? Where? When? Why?

Remember the 5 Ws: **who, what, where, when,** and **why**. Find an answer to each of these questions in the story about Levi Strauss. Write the answers on the lines.

1. **Who** was Levi Strauss? ______________
2. **What** did he do? ______________
3. **Where** did he do it? ______________
4. **When** did he do it? ______________
5. **Why** did he do it? ______________

26

Worktext page 26

LESSON 5.6

OBJECTIVE

- Students will practice and apply skills to an extended passage

MATERIALS

Worktext 5, pages 27–30
Teacher's Manual, pages 231–232, 333
Practice Lesson 5.6, pages 76–77 of the Worktext
Tagboard, brad/fastener, scissors (Reteach)

SKILLS REVIEW

- Before reading, you may wish to review these words that apply phonics skills: *faster, calls, driving, laughs, thinks, gold, going, fields, mined, ahead, years, old, knows, died, remembers, sunny, wanted, likes, weeks, mountains, asks, says, walks, falling, hers, miners, married, ideas, wants, plants, grows, hears, looks, flying, screams, jumps, owned.* Have students review the Memory Chips they have learned so far. Then ask: **What do you think it was like for the early settlers who went to California?**
- While reading, have students imagine they are on the trip with Mack, Robin, and her dad.
- After reading, have students complete the Comprehension Exercises (What Will Happen Next? and Describe It) on Worktext pages 29–30.

For further practice, have students complete Practice Lesson 5.6 on pages 76–77 of the Worktext. Answers can be found in the Answer Key on pages 356–357 of this *Teacher's Manual.*

RETEACH

If students need further review of phonics skills, you may wish to use the following activity:

Phonograms *ean, old, ong*

Phonogram Wheel Cut two wheels out of tagboard, one larger than the other. On the larger wheel write the following phonograms on the edges: **ean**, **old**, **ong**. On the smaller wheel, write these consonants and consonant blends on the edges: **cl**, **j**, **b**, **l**, **g**, **t**, **f**, **h**, **str**. Connect the two wheels with a brad. Then have students turn the wheels to make words with the phonograms. If you wish, you may also want to add these phonograms to the outer wheel: **eat**, **in**, **ip**, **ap**, **een**, **ant**, **ill**, **ook**, **ard**, **ile**.

CONNECTION

Strategy for Reading After students finish reading the selection "Gold in California!" on Worktext pages 27–28, ask them to summarize it either aloud or in writing.

Speaking/Listening Invite student volunteers to take turns reading aloud the selection "Gold in California!" Other students can follow along in their Worktext. Encourage students to be active, attentive listeners.

Writing Students should be encouraged to keep a journal of their writings. They can use these journals to record responses to their reading, list new words they have learned, or record their thoughts and feelings about the reading selections.

Response to Reading

- Have students write a short paragraph predicting what will happen next in the story "Gold in California!"
- Students should share their prediction with the class.

Literature

- Students may enjoy reading or listening to books sets in other times in history. *Adventures of Huckleberry Finn* and *The Last of the Mohicans* are available in softcover texts and on audiocassette from Pearson's *Pacemaker*™ *Classics.*
- Students may use the Book Report reproducible found on page 333 of this *Teacher's Manual* to record their responses to the books they read.

6. GOLD IN CALIFORNIA!

"Go faster!" Mack calls out to his dad, who is driving the wagon.

"This is as fast as it goes," his dad, Bill, laughs.

Robin laughs, too. Mack thinks all of life is a race. This time, he is right. The family is going to the gold fields of California. They want to get there fast to make money. They also want to go there to get free. Most of the best gold fields have been mined already.

Little Mack, just 10 years old, can't wait. Robin is 18 years old. She knows there is still a long trip ahead of them.

The year is 1849. Robin and Mack's mom died a long time back. Robin remembers her mom. She knows that she would have wanted to go on this trip, too!

Robin likes the trip. For weeks and weeks, they went over land with no mountains. Now they are way up in the

27

Worktext page 27

mountains, and they are going up even more mountains. That is why they can't go fast. When they get past these mountains, they will be almost there.

"Can I drive?" Mack asks for about the 100th time.

"When we get out of the mountains," his dad says, "we will see."

Robin walks next to the wagon. She doesn't want Mack to drive. On one side of the wagon is the mountain. On the other side of the wagon, there is a big bank falling off into open space.

She hears Mack and her dad talk as she walks. She thinks about what she is going to do in California. All her friends said, "You can find a gold miner with lots of money and get married!"

Robin has other ideas. She wants to make her own money. California, they say, is hot and sunny. She wants to grow plants for food. Then she will sell what she grows. She has heard that you can make more money from selling to the miners than finding gold in the gold fields.

"Look out!" she hears her dad scream.

Robin looks up. A big rock is flying right at their wagon. Robin screams. She pulls Mack off the wagon just in time. Dad jumps just in time, too. They run far behind the wagon.

The big rock smashes into the wagon. They can't do a thing as they see the rock push their wagon off the bank into space. Every last thing they owned was in that wagon.

28

Worktext page 28

What Will Happen Next?

Do you think Bill, Robin, and Mack will ever get to California? Circle one answer.

YES **NO**

Write two sentences that back up what you think. You can use these sentences or make up your own.

The family wants to get there fast.

There is still a long trip ahead of them.

They have no wagon.

They have lost everything they own.

After they get over the mountains, they will be almost there.

Robin, Mack, and Bill all seem strong.

____

____

____

____

____

____

____

Describe It

Robin, Bill, and Mack are going to the gold fields of California. Circle the words below that describe California in 1849.

hot and sunny	cold with lots of snow
people are very poor	lots of gold
high mountains	politics are big
no mountains	miners live there

29

Worktext page 29

Now say that you are Robin or Mack. Write a letter home about what California is going to be like. Use the words you circled.

Dear ______________,

I can't wait to get to California! ______________

____

____

____

____

____

____

____

____

____

____

____

____

Your friend,

____

30

Worktext page 30

LESSON 5.7

OBJECTIVES

- Students will use context clues to figure out unfamiliar words
- Students will decode and make new words containing vowel pairs and words with the CVCe pattern
- Students will recognize and form compound words
- Students will apply endings *s, ing, er, est,* and *es* to base words to form new words
- Students will recognize and form possessives

PHONICS VOCABULARY

families	take	worker	heads	shake
running	miles	mountains	camps	gives
coming	without	going	cannot	shakes
getting	walks	takes	screams	guys
everyone	else's	anything	runs	sleep
handouts	throws	says	needed	pushed
looks	scared	highest	lots	winter
smiles	cuts	dies	thief	late
accident	mile	firewood	roaming	

WORDS TO KNOW

winter	thief	accident	mile	late
swim	high	camp	blanket	found

MATERIALS

Worktext 5, pages 31–35
Teacher's Manual, pages 233–235
Practice Lesson 5.7, pages 78–79 of the Worktext

TEACH

- Using Worktext page 32, introduce students to the vocabulary words. Give them an opportunity to practice writing the words.
- Students can organize their Memory Chips, found in the back of the Worktext. Say each word, having students repeat it after you. Then have students sort the words according to words that name persons, places, and things and words that show action.

Worktext page 32 can also be used to reinforce spelling. Use the five-step process detailed on page 71 of this *Teacher's Manual.*

Context Clues

Remind students that when they see an unfamiliar word, they can guess how to read the word by looking at the other words in the sentence and looking at the beginning sound. Write this sentence on the board, and read it aloud, leaving out the word *thief*: **The ______ took the money and ran away.** Have students figure out the word from the other words around it.

Vowel Pairs and Words with the CVCe Pattern

Write this sentence on the board, and have a volunteer read it aloud: **I hope we keep the same coach.** Ask a volunteer to point to *keep.* Ask a volunteer to circle the vowels that make the long *e* sound in *keep.* Repeat with *coach,* focusing on the long *o* sound made by *oa.* Then point to *hope.* Ask students what vowel sound they hear in *hope.* Remind students when they see a word that has a consonant-vowel-consonant-e pattern, the first vowel is long, and the *e* is silent. Have them find another word in the sentence that has the consonant-vowel-consonant-e pattern. (*same*)

Blending Write the words **team**, **boat**, **joke**, and **mine** on the board. Say the word *team,* pointing to the letters as you segment the word: /t/ /ē/ /m/. Repeat, using the words *boat, joke,* and *mine.*

Compound Words

Remind students that they can sometimes find two smaller words inside unfamiliar words. Write these words on the board and have students find the two words that make up each word: **anything**, **sometimes**, **boyfriend**. (*any, thing; some, times; boy, friend*)

Make New Words Write these words on index cards, and have students say them aloud: **fire**, **wood**, **place**. Then have them mix and match the words to make compound words. (*fireplace, firewood*) They can use each compound word in a sentence.

Endings *s, ing, er, est, es*

Remind students that *s, ing, er, est,* and *es* can be added to words. Remind them that when a word ends in *y,* the *y* is changed to *i,* and *es* is added. Also remind them that the ending *est* compares three or more things.

Make New Words Write these words in a chart, and invite students to add *s, ing, er, est,* and *es* to the words to make new ones.

Base Word	+ s	+ ing	+ er	+ est	+ es
room	rooms	rooming			
work	works	working	worker		
high			higher	highest	
smile	smiles	smiling	smiler		
family					families

PRACTICE

- Let students practice the new words they have learned and formed by completing the activities found on pages 31–32 of the Worktext.
- If students are experiencing difficulty with the Words to Know section on page 32, write scrambled letters like these on the board: **gihh** (*high*), **wims** (*swim*), **dunof** (*found*), **macp** (*camp*). Then have them unscramble the letters to make the words on their Memory Chips. They can write each word.

For further practice, have students complete Practice Lesson 5.7 on pages 78–79 of the Worktext. Answers can be found in the Answer Key on page 357 of this *Teacher's Manual.*

APPLY

- Have students predict what they think will happen next. Ask: **What do you think will happen to Robin, Mack, and their dad?** Tell them that they are going to use the words they have learned to read what happens next to this pioneer family.
- Ask students to read the story on pages 33–34 in the Worktext. Offer assistance if necessary, but encourage students to decode the words independently, using the clues and patterns they have learned.
- After students have completed reading the story, have them complete the Cooperative Group Activity (What Do You Think?) and Comprehension Exercise (Remembering Details) on page 35 in their Worktext. Answers can be found in the Answer Key on page 356 of this *Teacher's Manual.*

CONNECTION

Writing Give students an opportunity to write in their journals, recording how they would feel if they were going to California in search of gold like the characters in the selection "High in the Mountains" on Worktext pages 33–34.

Worktext Pages 31–32

7. HIGH IN THE MOUNTAINS

Take a Guess

Try to guess this new word by reading the other words in the sentences. Think of a word that starts with a **w**.

In the **winter** it grows very cold and sometimes snows.

Did you guess the word? Write it. ________________

Try another one. This word starts with the letters **th**.

Stop that man! He took my radio! He is a **thief**.

Did you guess the word? Write it. ________________

Try one more. This word starts with **a**.

She can't walk because she was hurt in a car **accident**.

Did you guess the word? Write it. ________________

NEW **Vowels** What have you learned about words that have two vowels together? Circle the vowels below that say their own names. Put an **X** over each vowel that you can't hear when you say the word.

keep coach team boat

Try the long vowel sound another time when you see a word that ends with **e**. Say these words you know:

joke mine take close

You don't hear the ending **e**. The other vowel has the long sound.

Look at these new words. Circle the vowel that has the long sound. Put an **X** over the **e** you can't hear.

mile late

Write one of these new words in each sentence below.

I had to walk a ________________ to get home.

If I don't run, I will be ________________.

31

Worktext page 31

Words to Know

	Look	Say	Picture	Write
accident ac-ci-dent	☐	☐	☐	________
blanket blan-ket	☐	☐	☐	________
camp	☐	☐	☐	________
found	☐	☐	☐	________
high	☐	☐	☐	________
late	☐	☐	☐	________
mile	☐	☐	☐	________
swim	☐	☐	☐	________
thief	☐	☐	☐	________
winter win-ter	☐	☐	☐	________

Word Attack

2=1 You know the words **fire** and **wood.** Put them together to make one word: **firewood.** Write it in the sentence.

I went into the woods to cut some ________________.

+'s Write this word with an **'s** ending.
else ________________

+ing Write **room** with an **ing** ending. ________________

+er Write **work** with an **er** ending. ________________

+est Write **high** with an **est** ending. ________________

+s Write these words with **s** endings.

head ________________ camp ________________
smile ________________ cut ________________
die ________________ mile ________________

+es Write **family** with an **es** ending. You have to change the **y** to an **i** first: **families.**

family ________________

32

Worktext page 32

MCR

7. HIGH IN THE MOUNTAINS

Robin, Mack, and their dad, Bill, try to get help. They ask other families to take them along to California.

"I'm a good worker," Bill says. "So are Mack and Robin." Family after family just shake their heads no. It is getting late in the year. People are running out of food for their own families. No one has enough to take along another family.

Robin, Mack, and Bill walk miles and miles through the mountains. At night, they sleep in the big camps of other people going to California. Some people give them a little food. One family gives them each a blanket, but they are still cold at night. They need more food. Winter is coming. Without a wagon, they are not going to make it.

One day, they have to swim through some very cold water. Bill cannot get warm after that. He shakes and shakes and shakes. Robin can see that her dad is getting sick.

33

Worktext page 33

That night, she walks all over camp asking for food. A kind family gives her a little. She takes it back to her dad and Mack.

The next morning, a big man shakes Bill awake. "What did you do with it?" the man screams. "You took our food. You good for nothing. You thief!"

"I did not take your food," Dad yells back. "I am not a thief!"

"Oh, I know guys like you. You want to live off everyone else's hard work. Where is your wagon? Why did you come out here if you don't have anything?"

Just then, a woman runs over to the man. "I found it!" she calls out. "I found our food. It was under the wagon. Luis must have put it there before we went to sleep."

The man lets go of Bill. "You still should not be out here looking for handouts all the time."

Robin throws off her blanket. She says, "You say you're sorry to my dad. How can you say he took your food! He is not a thief. We **did** have a wagon. We **did** have food. We had all we needed. A big rock pushed our wagon off the mountain. We can't help the accident!"

The man looks a little sorry, but he just walks away. Everyone in the camp is scared. Winter is coming.

Some people are not as mean as that man. "Come with us," says the kind woman who gave Robin food. "We are almost over the mountains. It is not many more miles. Then we are close to the gold country. We can use the help."

Robin and Mack work very hard. They want to make up for Bill who is too sick to work. The woman and her family are kind.

Then one day, they get to the highest place in the mountains. They look down into California. "Look, Dad!" Robin says. "We are going to make it. We will find lots of gold then. We will get another wagon."

Bill smiles, but Robin can see that he does not believe it. That night, Bill dies in his sleep.

34

Worktext page 34

What Do You Think?

Meet with a friend or in a small group. Pick a person to be Mack and another person to be Robin. Have a talk. Try to think about what you are going to do. Should you go back home? Should you go to California? How are you going to live now?

Remembering Details

Write a word from the story in each space.

They ask other families to take them along to ______________.

"I did not take your food," Dad yells back. "I am not a ________________ !"

"I found our food. It was under the ________________."

Then one day, they get to the ________________ place in the mountains.

Wagon train out West

35

Worktext page 35

Level 5

LESSON 5.8

OBJECTIVE

- Students will practice and apply skills to an extended passage

MATERIALS

Worktext 5, pages 36–38
Teacher's Manual, pages 236–237, 330–331, 333
Practice Lesson 5.8, pages 80–81 of the Worktext

SKILLS REVIEW

- Before reading, you may wish to review these words that apply phonics skills: *says, smile, died, cuts, firewood, keep, tells, stories, losing, jobs, lots, somewhere, mine, need, real, mines, see, sleep, mining, leaves, moves, clean, mean, holds, close, runs, calls, puts, himself, between, laughs, rooming, asks, opens, same, time, hours, waiting, walks, looks, feels, starting, place.* Have students review the Memory Chips they have learned so far. Then ask: **What do you think will happen to Robin and Mack in California?**
- While reading, have students think about how Robin and Mack feel about what is happening.
- After reading, have students complete the Comprehension Exercises (Write a Summary and How Are People Alike and Different?) on Worktext page 38.

For further practice, have students complete Practice Lesson 5.8 on pages 80–81 of the Worktext. Answers can be found in the Answer Key on pages 356–357 of this *Teacher's Manual.*

RETEACH

If students need further review of phonics skills, you may wish to use the following activity:

Silent Vowels

Silent Vowel Riddles Ask students riddles like the ones below. When they guess the word, have a volunteer write the answer on the board. Ask students to circle the vowel they hear and make an *X* over the vowel that is silent.

- **This is a person who tells a team what to do.** (*coach*)
- **This is the opposite of far.** (*close*)
- **This is what I tell to make people laugh.** (*joke*)
- **This is the opposite of "give away".** (*keep*)
- **It takes nine people to make this in baseball.** (*team*)
- **This keeps me out of the water.** (*boat*)
- **This is how far I can run without stopping.** (*mile*)
- **This is the opposite of early.** (*late*)
- **This is the opposite of dirty.** (*clean*)

CONNECTION

Response to Reading

- To reinforce students' understanding of the literary elements found in their reading material, have them complete the Story Map and Character Cluster reproducibles found on pages 330–331.
- Students will demonstrate an understanding of setting, characters, and plot by filling out the organizers.
- Students may share their completed organizers with the class.

Literature

- Students may enjoy reading or listening to other books about adventure. *The Adventures of Tom Sawyer* and *The Call of the Wild* are available in softcover texts and on audiocassette from Pearson's *Pacemaker™ Classics.*
- Students may use the Book Report reproducible found on page 333 of this *Teacher's Manual* to record their responses to the books they read.

8. ROBIN AND MACK IN CALIFORNIA

"It's just you and me now," Robin says to Mack the day after their dad died.

"I guess that makes me the man in the family," 10-year-old Mack says.

Robin smiles sadly. She says, "I guess so."

They go with the kind family on to California. Mack cuts firewood for his keep. Robin cooks for the family.

At night, she tells Mack stories to keep his mind off losing their dad. "In California," she tells him, "we can get good jobs. There is lots of money in California. We'll have all the food we want. We'll find a little farm somewhere. I'll grow all our food. We will be free."

"I'll get Dad's gold mine," Mack says. "I'll find lots of gold."

"I don't know," Robin says. "I think we'll need real jobs first."

"All the mines will be gone!"

"We'll see," Robin says. "Now go to sleep."

At long last, they come to the California mining town where they were headed. The kind family leaves Robin and Mack. Then the family moves on.

"I don't like this town," Robin says. "The people do not look clean. Some of them look mean." Robin holds Mack close to her.

Right away, a man runs up to them.

"A woman!" the man calls out.

"You keep away from my sister!" Little Mack puts himself between the man and Robin.

The man laughs. "Look," he says, "you have my word I'll not hurt your sister. You look like you just got here. I run the rooming house over there. My cook has just run out on me. Need work? You look like you can cut wood. Can your sister cook?" the man asks Mack.

Robin's face opens in a big smile.

"She sure can!" Mack calls out.

36

Worktext page 36

"If you don't mind having one small room together," the man says, "I can let you have one in the rooming house."

"Yes!" Robin and Mack say at the same time.

"Well, no time to stand around talking. I have to have dinner for a lot of hungry people in two hours."

"What are you waiting for, then?" Robin says. She walks in front of him toward the rooming house. Mack runs along behind.

The work will be hard, but the man looks kind. Best of all, they will have a room and food. Robin feels so sad about losing her dad. She knows he would be happy she is starting to make a new home for Mack and herself. California may turn out to be a good place, after all.

37

Worktext page 37

Write a Summary

Read these sentences. Which ones are about the big ideas in the stories you read about going to California. Circle these. Which ones are about details? Put a line through each of these.

Robin, Mack, and Bill are going to the California gold fields.

Robin walks next to the wagon.

A rock pushes their wagon off the mountain.

Bill dies.

Robin throws off her blanket.

Mack and Robin make it to California and get jobs.

The man laughs.

Now write a summary. Write the big-idea sentences in the order that they happened in the story.

____

____

____

____

____

____

____

How Are People Alike and Different?

How are Levi Strauss and Robin alike? How are they different? Read these sentences. Then circle the sentences that say how Levi Strauss and Robin are alike.

They went to California.

They had ideas about making money in California.

Their dads die.

They do not want to mine for gold.

They are girls.

They make lots and lots of money.

38

Worktext page 38

MIDWAY NOVEL A Fight for Life

MATERIALS
Midway Novel 5, *A Fight for Life*
Teacher's Manual, page 238
Assessment Manual, Midway Assessment 5, pages 95–99

Summary *Carmen, a South American girl, loses her family. The Driver family brings Carmen to California. Carmen has trouble fitting in with Jen and her friends. After a while, Carmen begins to help Jen and her friends with their charity work. Jen starts a group called Friends of South America.*

REVIEW AND ASSESSMENT

- Have students review their Memory Chips with a partner. Depending on your students' needs, review the following skills covered in Lessons 1–8: phonograms *ill*, *op*, *eat*, *ood*, *ean*, *old*, and *ong*; CVCe letter patterns; vowel pairs; compound words; context clues; singular possessives; and endings with *s*, *ing*, *er*, *ed*, *es*, *est*, *en*, *ly*, and *y*.

If you wish to assess students' progress at this point, use *Assessment Manual*, pages 95–99. For students who need additional support, you may use the Reteach activities from previous lessons.

INTRODUCE THE NOVEL

Invite students to preview the book by reading the title, looking at the illustrations, and reading aloud the captions. Begin a discussion of story concepts by asking questions such as:

- **Have you ever worked to help other people? What did you do, and what was it like?**
- **Why is it a good idea to get active when things need to be done?**
- **How can helping others help yourself?**

CHECK COMPREHENSION

Chapter 1 Where does this story begin, and who is the main character? (*Carmen is the main character; she is in some kind of camp in South America.*)

Chapter 2 What happened the day the men came to Carmen's house? (*They knocked down the door and took Carmen's father. When the men grabbed Carmen, she ran into the woods.*)

Chapter 3 How does Carmen know the Driver family? (*They are friends of the Cruz family.*)

Chapter 4 How does Carmen get to leave the camp? (*Mrs. Driver comes and gets her.*)

Chapter 5 How does Carmen like being in California? (*She is happy to be safe, but she is still scared.*)

Chapter 6 How do Jen and Robin get Carmen to leave the house? (*They ask her to help clean cars for Friends 4 Life.*)

Chapter 7 Why does Mr. Goldman think Jared and Carmen will be good friends? (*They both have been through hard times.*)

Chapter 8 How does Jared explain how things get better? (*He says that when you help someone else, you end up helping yourself.*)

Chapter 9 Why is Carmen looking forward to school? (*She is going to be in Jared's classes.*)

Chapter 10 Why do the KTVN people want Carmen on TV? (*They want her to tell her story and tell how she got through a bad part of her life and now helps others.*)

Chapter 11 What does Carmen say on TV? (*She tells about what happened in South America and how much working at the shelter has helped her get over her hard times.*)

Chapter 12 Why does Carmen think Jen is like a sister? (*Jen wants to help people in South America.*)

Chapter 13 How did Inez find Carmen? (*She saw Carmen on TV.*)

Chapter 14 How does Carmen feel about herself now? (*She feels that she will go far and do big things.*)

CONNECTION

Home/School Encourage students to bring home a copy of *A Fight for Life*. They might read the novel, or sections of the novel, to family members.

LESSON 5.9

OBJECTIVES

- Students will decode words containing the *ay* phonogram and words with the CVCe pattern
- Students will use context and decoding clues to read unfamiliar words
- Students will apply endings *er, s, ed,* and *ing* to base words to form new words
- Students will recognize and form possessives
- Students will recognize and form compound words

PHONICS VOCABULARY

Mankiller	Cherokee	Cherokees	growing
becoming	name	hoped	home
leave	married	politics	girls
going	problems	getting	life
stayed	working	starting	wanted
thinking	farming	homes	building
pipeline	doing	hanged	looked
making	things	talks	lived
become	dying	stay	pipe
town	ideas	killer	swimmer
people's	finished	died	believed

WORDS TO KNOW

stay	town	two	ready
chief	pipe	finish	nation
Wilma	Oklahoma	Cherokee	

MATERIALS

Worktext 5, pages 39–43
Teacher's Manual, pages 239–241
Practice Lesson 5.9, pages 82–83 of the Worktext

TEACH

- Using Worktext pages 39–40, introduce students to the vocabulary words. Give them an opportunity to practice writing the words.
- Students can organize their Memory Chips, found in the back of the Worktext. Say each word, having students repeat it after you. Then have them sort the words according to words they know and those that are unfamiliar. Have the students say each unfamiliar word and use it in a sentence.

Worktext pages 39–40 can also be used to reinforce spelling. Use the five-step process detailed on page 71 of this *Teacher's Manual.*

Phonogram *ay* and Letter Pattern *CVCe*

Write this sentence on the board and read it aloud: **Kay will tell a joke.** Have a student point to *Kay*. Ask students what vowel sound they hear. (*long* a) Ask them what two letters make the vowel sound. (*ay*) Point to the word *joke* and remind students that when they see a consonant-vowel-consonant-e pattern, the first vowel is usually long, and the *e* is silent.

Blending Have students name words that rhyme with *Kay*. List them on the board, blending the sounds as you write each word. (*bay, say, ray, stay*) Then write **joke** on the board. Have students take turns substituting vowels and beginning and ending consonants to make new words in the CVCe pattern. Help them blend each word. For example: *joke, Jake; lake, lane, line.*

Context Clues

Write these sentences on the board: **That man is 80 years old. He was born in 1930.** Cover *born*, and ask students how they would read this word if they did not know it. (*Read the sentence and use clues from the sentence along with decoding clues.*) Read the sentences, leaving out *born*. Ask students what they think the word might be and how they figured it out.

Endings *s, er, ed, ing*

Remind students they can add *s, er, ed,* and *ing* to the endings of words. Tell them that when a word ends in *e*, the *e* is dropped, and the ending is added. Write the word **die** on the board. Tell them when they add *ing* to *die*, they change the *ie* to *y* and add *ing*.

Make New Words Write these words on the board, and invite students to add the endings *s, er, ing,* and *ed* to the end of each word: **die, stay, live, kill, home.** (*dies, dying died; stays, staying, stayed; lives, living, lived; kills, killer, killing, killed; homes*) They can use each word they make in a sentence.

Possessives

Write this sentence on the board, and read it aloud: **Don't take other people's word.** Point to *people's*, and have students point out the ending. Tell them "people's word" means "the word that belongs to the people." Remind them that an apostrophe and *s* show ownership.

Make New Words Write these words on the board and have students add an apostrophe and *s* to each one: **girl, people, children.** (*girl's, people's, children's*)

Compound Words

Remind students that two words can be put together to make another word.

Make New Words Write these words on the board in random order, and have students use them to make compound words: **man, killer, pipe, line, boy, friend, some, time.** (*mankiller, pipeline, boyfriend, sometime*)

PRACTICE

- Let students practice the new words they have learned and formed by completing the activities found on pages 39–40 of the Worktext.
- If students are experiencing difficulty with the Words to Know section on pages 39–40, you can pose riddles like the one below and have students choose a Memory Chip to answer each one: **This word is the name of a state. It begins like "open."** (*Oklahoma*)

For further practice, have students complete Practice Lesson 5.9 on pages 82–83 of the Worktext. Answers can be found in the Answer Key on page 357 of this *Teacher's Manual.*

APPLY

- Have students talk about the story concept by sharing their prior knowledge about the Cherokee nation. Ask: **What is the Cherokee nation? Where do the Cherokees live?** Tell them they are going to use the words they have learned to read an article about Wilma Mankiller, a Cherokee chief.
- Ask students to read the article on pages 41–42 in the Worktext. Offer assistance if necessary, but encourage students to decode the words independently, using the clues and patterns they have learned.
- After students have completed reading the article, have them complete the Comprehension Exercises (Remembering Details and What is the Main Idea?) on page 43 in their Worktext. Answers can be found in the Answer Key on page 356 of this *Teacher's Manual.*

CONNECTION

Strategy for Reading Have students reread the selection "Wilma Mankiller: The Woman Who Lived Before" on Worktext pages 41–42 to correct comprehension breakdowns. Students may achieve understanding by reprocessing the same text with greater attention focused on its meaning.

Writing Students can write a few sentences in which they describe Wilma Mankiller. Have student volunteers share their writing with the class.

Worktext Pages 39–40

9. WILMA MANKILLER: THE WOMAN WHO LIVED BEFORE

Word Attack

say What word do you get if you changed the **s** in **say** to **st**? Write the new word below.

stay ______________

Vowels Remember what you learned about words that end with an **e** that you can't hear, like **mine**, **like**, **joke**, and **take**. The other vowel has the long sound.

Look at this new word. Circle the vowel that has the long sound. Put an **X** over the **e** you can't hear.

p i p e

Write the new word in the sentence.

He has to ______________ water into his home.

Take a Guess

Try to guess this new word by reading the other words in the sentences. Think of a word that starts with **t**.

I would not want to live on a farm. I want to live in **town**.

Did you guess the word? Write it. ______________

Words to Know

	Look	Say	Picture	Write
Cherokee Cher-o-kee	☐	☐	☐	______
chief	☐	☐	☐	______
finish fin-ish	☐	☐	☐	______
nation na-tion	☐	☐	☐	______
Oklahoma Okla-ho-ma	☐	☐	☐	______
pipe	☐	☐	☐	______
ready	☐	☐	☐	______

39

Worktext page 39

	Look	Say	Picture	Write
stay	☐	☐	☐	______
town	☐	☐	☐	______
two	☐	☐	☐	______
Wilma Wil-ma	☐	☐	☐	______

Word Attack

+s Write each word with an **s** ending.

idea ______________ home ______________

Cherokee ______________

+er Write each word with an **er** ending.

kill ______________ swim ______________

+ing Write **farm** with an **ing** ending. ______________

Write **die** with an **ing** ending. To do this, you have to change the **i** to a **y** and leave off the **e**: **dying**. Write **dying** in the sentence. She was ______________ to go home.

+'s Write **people** with an **'s**. ______________

+ed Write these words with **ed** endings.

stay ______________ finish ______________

The next words already have an **e** at the end. So you just have to add **d**.

live ______________ hope ______________

die ______________ believe ______________

2=1 Below are words you already know. Put them together to make longer words. Write the new, longer words.

man + killer = ______________ pipe + line = ______________

40

Worktext page 40

9. WILMA MANKILLER: THE WOMAN WHO LIVED BEFORE

Wilma Mankiller was the principal chief of the Cherokee Nation from 1985–1995. She was the first woman to be chief of the Cherokees. There are more than 120,000 Cherokee people.

Growing up, Wilma Mankiller did not think about becoming chief. She was born in 1945 in a small Oklahoma town. There were 11 kids in her family. The name **Mankiller** is her family name.

When she was 11, her family moved to California. Her dad hoped he could get a better job. Wilma didn't want to leave Oklahoma. To her, the small town in Oklahoma was home.

Wilma got married after going to high school in California. Then she had two girls. She had no ideas about going into politics at that time. In 1972, she started college.

Wilma Mankiller meets with President Ronald Reagan in 1988.

41

Worktext page 41

Wilma did not finish college. In 1976, she went home to her small town in Oklahoma. She could not find any work there. So back she went to California, and then back again to Oklahoma. Wilma was having problems getting her life together, but this time she stayed in Oklahoma. She got a job working for the Cherokee Nation. She went back to school, too. In 1979, she finished college.

Then she went on to even more school! Wilma Mankiller was starting to find out who she was and what she wanted to do with her life. She was thinking a lot about the Cherokee people. Some were so poor they did not have water for farming or to use in their homes. She had an idea about building a water pipeline, but she didn't know how to go about doing it.

Then Wilma was in a bad car accident. She almost died. That did it for Wilma Mankiller. Almost dying changed the way she looked at life. She now knew that she wanted to give her life to making things better for the Cherokee Nation.

Today, Wilma Mankiller talks of the "woman who lived before and the woman who lived after" the car accident. The woman who lived before didn't know what she wanted. The woman who lived after was ready to become chief of the Cherokee Nation.

42

Worktext page 42

Remembering Details

Write a word from the story in each space.

Wilma Mankiller is the principal chief of the

________________ Nation.

She had an idea about building a water ________________.

Then Wilma Mankiller was in a bad car ________________.

The woman who lived after was ready to become

________________ of the Cherokee Nation.

What Is the Main Idea?

Write the sentence that best says the main idea of the reading.

When she was 11, Wilma Mankiller moved to California.

The name **Mankiller** is her family name.

After living through a bad car accident, Wilma Mankiller knew what she wanted to do with her life.

____

____

____

____

43

Worktext page 43

Level 5

LESSON 5.10

OBJECTIVE

- Students will practice and apply skills to an extended passage

MATERIALS

Worktext 5, pages 44–47
Teacher's Manual, pages 242–243, 333
Practice Lesson 5.10, pages 84–85 of the Worktext
Egg timer (Reteach)

SKILLS REVIEW

- Before reading, you may wish to review these words that apply phonics skills: *Mankiller, believed, having, hope, wanted, lives, answers, problems, running, homes, pipeline, helped, hands, farming, changed, people's, lives, learned, building, working, named, swimmer, leader, everyone, however, things, voted, time, added, rights, makes, likes.* Have students review the Memory Chips they have learned so far. Then ask: **How do you think Wilma Mankiller became chief of the Cherokee nation?**
- While reading, have students think about what made Wilma Mankiller a good leader of the Cherokee nation.
- After reading, have students complete the Cooperative Group Activity (What Do You Think?) and Comprehension Exercise (Who? What? Where? When? Why?) on Worktext pages 46–47.

For further practice, have students complete Practice Lesson 5.10 on pages 84–85 of the Worktext. Answers can be found in the Answer Key on pages 356–357 of this *Teacher's Manual*.

RETEACH

If students need further review of phonics skills, you may wish to use the following activity:

Endings *s, ing, er, ed*

Time Out! Make word cards for these words: **kill**, **idea**, **home**, **Cherokee**, **swim**, **farm**, **stay**, **finish**, **live**, **hope**, **die**, **believe**. Make word cards for **s**, **ing**, **er**, and **ed**. Set the timer and have students use the cards to form new words. One player records the words on a sheet of paper. Teams earn one point for each word. When the time is up, each team reads aloud the words in their list. Possible word combinations include: *kills, killing, killer, killed; ideas; homes; Cherokees; swims, swimming, swimmer; farms, farming, farmer, farmed; stays, staying, stayed; finishes, finishing, finisher, finished; lives, living, lived; hopes, hoping, hoped; dies, dying, died; believes, believing, believer, believed.*

CONNECTION

Strategy for Reading After students finish reading the selection "Wilma Mankiller: Chief of the Cherokee Nation" on Worktext pages 44–45, ask them to summarize it either aloud or in writing.

Writing Students should be encouraged to keep a journal of their writings. They can use these journals to record responses to their reading, list new words they have learned, or record their thoughts about the reading selection.

Speaking/Listening Student partners can read aloud the selection. The partners can alternate being speaker and listener.

Literature

- Students may enjoy reading or listening to books about other leaders who fought for a cause. *César Chávez* and *Fannie Lou Hamer* are available in softcover texts as part of Pearson's *Freedom Fighters* series.
- Students may use the Book Report reproducible found on page 333 of this *Teacher's Manual* to record their responses to the books they read.

10. WILMA MANKILLER: CHIEF OF THE CHEROKEE NATION

Wilma Mankiller believed that the biggest problem with her people was not having hope. She wanted to show people that they could change their own lives. She wanted them to see that they could find answers to their own problems.

Wilma went to a Cherokee town that was very, very poor. They had no running water. She asked the people there if they wanted water in their homes. They said yes. She told them they could build a water pipeline.

Together, with their own hands, Wilma helped the people build a 16-mile water pipeline. This pipeline gave the people water for farming and for their homes. Having water changed the people's lives. It helped them to find answers to their own problems. Best of all, the people learned that they could change their own lives. They found out they could build a 16-mile water pipeline with their own hands.

Wilma did not think about running for office. She was happy building things and working with people. People all over the Cherokee Nation heard about her pipeline. A man named Swimmer was running for the office of principal chief. He asked her to run with him. She said she would do it.

Some people were against Wilma Mankiller being a Cherokee leader. They said a woman could not hold a big office in the Cherokee Nation, but Swimmer and Mankiller won the race!

Then, in 1985, Swimmer went off to another job. That made Wilma Mankiller principal chief of the Cherokee Nation. She did more and more for her people. She made the Cherokee Nation a better place to live for everyone.

44

Worktext page 44

In 1987, if she wanted to keep the job, Mankiller had to run for office herself. By then, however, she had shown what she could do. She had done many things to make life better for the Cherokee people. Some people still didn't like a woman being chief, but she had done too much good not to win. The people voted her in. In 1991, she was voted in again. This time she got 83% of the vote!

During her time as chief, the Cherokee Nation added more than 100,000 people. And she has met with three presidents and become a champion for her people's rights.

In 1995, Mankiller was ready to be done as chief. She said it was time to make a change in her life. But Mankiller will keep on doing the work that makes her happy. Most of all, she likes doing things she can feel and see like building a pipeline or a house.

Wilma Mankiller in 2004.

45

Worktext page 45

What Do You Think?

Meet with a friend or in a small group. Imagine that you are leaders in your neighborhood. What would you do to help the people in your neighborhood if you had the money and power to do it?

Who? What? Where? When? Why?

Remember the 5 Ws: **who**, **what**, **where**, **when**, and **why**. Find an answer to each of these questions in the two stories about Wilma Mankiller. Write the answers on the lines.

1. **Who** is Wilma Mankiller? ____________________
2. **What** did she do? ____________________
3. **Where** did she do it? ____________________
4. **When** did she do it? ____________________
5. **Why** did she do it? ____________________

46

Worktext page 46

How Are People Alike and Different?

People change. How was Wilma Mankiller **different** before the car accident than she was after the car accident? Write each of these groups of words under one of the headings below.

did not think about being a chief

was ready to become chief of the Cherokees

had problems getting her life together

believed people could find answers to their own problems

didn't know what she wanted

liked building houses and pipelines

Before the car accident:

____

After the car accident:

____

47

Worktext page 47

Level 5

LESSON 5.11

OBJECTIVES

- Students will decode and blend words containing the *ike* and *air* phonograms and CVCe letter pattern
- Students will apply endings *s, er, ing, ed,* and *ly* to base words to form new words
- Students will recognize and form compound words
- Students will recognize and form contractions

PHONICS VOCABULARY

farmworker	years	crops	farmers
lots	stopped	home	married
started	living	working	fields
problems	grape	pickers	made
growers	paying	workers	needed
badly	sending	others	outhouse
sometimes	worked	wanted	believed
everyone	fair	without	strongly
drive	talked	meeting	strike
grapes	listened	gave	willing
holding	fights	eating	pulled
showed	five	farmer	picker
grower	couldn't	picking	buying
girlfriend	picked	I'd	wasn't

WORDS TO KNOW

fair	strike	pick	grape
Navy	hour	union	violence
religious	Arizona	César Chávez	

MATERIALS

Worktext 5, pages 48–54
Teacher's Manual, pages 244–246
Practice Lesson 5.11, pages 86–87 of the Worktext

TEACH

- Using Worktext pages 48–49, introduce students to the vocabulary words. Give students an opportunity to practice writing the words.
- Students can organize their Memory Chips, found in the back of the Worktext. You may wish to say each word, having them repeat it after you. Students can find different ways to sort the words, such as by beginning letters, number of letters, and number of syllables.

Worktext pages 48–49 can also be used to reinforce spelling. Use the five-step process detailed on page 71 of this *Teacher's Manual.*

Phonograms *ike, air* and Letter Pattern *CVCe*

Write this sentence on the board and read it aloud: **I like her hair.** Ask a volunteer to point to *hair.* Ask students what words rhyme with *hair.* Have a volunteer point to *like.* Write **bike** on the board, and ask students how *like* and *bike* are alike. (*They rhyme and both end in* ike.) Write **grape** on the board. Ask students what long vowel they would expect to hear in *grape.* Point out the CVCe pattern and have students say the word.

Blending Work with three groups of students to make word ladders, blending each word as they substitute letters. Have the first group write a list of words that rhyme with *hair,* the second group write a list of words that rhyme with *like,* and the third group make a list of CVCe words (beginning with *grape*). Tell the third group that they can substitute beginning and ending consonants or the first vowel.

hair	like	grape
chair	bike	tape
stair	hike	tale
fair	strike	tile

Endings *er, s, ing, ed, ly*

Remind students that they can add *er, s, ing, ed,* and *ly* to the endings of words. Tell students that when *er* is added to the end of a word, it can mean "one who."

Make New Words Say these words, and have students add the ending *er* and then *s*: **farm**, **grow**, **pick**. (*farmer, farmers; grower, growers; picker, pickers*) Have a volunteer write each word on the board. Repeat, having students add *ing* and *ed* to *pull* and *pay.* (*pulling, pulled; paying, paid*) Then have students add *ly* to *strong* and *firm.* (*strongly, firmly*) Assist students with spelling as necessary.

Compound Words

Write this sentence on the board, and read it aloud: **The farmworker is paid.** Ask students what word has two smaller words put together to make one word. (*farmworker*) Ask them what two words they see. (*farm, worker*)

Make New Words Write these two columns on the board, and have students draw lines to connect two words to make new words:

girl	worker
out	house
farm	friend

Contractions

Remind students that they can make two words into one. Write **I would** on the board. Show students how to erase the letters *woul* and replace them with an apostrophe. (*I'd*)

Make New Words Work together with students to make contractions out of these words: *was not, could not, you would.* (*wasn't, couldn't, you'd*)

PRACTICE

- Let students practice the new words they have learned and formed by completing the activities found on pages 48–50 of the Worktext.

For further practice, have students complete Practice Lesson 5.11 on pages 86–87 of the Worktext. Answers can be found in the Answer Key on page 357 of this *Teacher's Manual.*

APPLY

- Have students talk about the story concept by tapping their prior knowledge. Ask: **Who was César Chávez?** Tell them they are going to use the words they have learned to read a short article about this famous man.
- Ask students to read the article on pages 51–52 in the Worktext.
- After students have completed reading the article, have them complete the Cooperative Group Activity (What Do You Think?) and Comprehension Exercises (Who? What? Where? When? Why? and Making a Timeline) on pages 53–54 in their Worktext. Answers can be found in the Answer Key on page 356 of this *Teacher's Manual.*

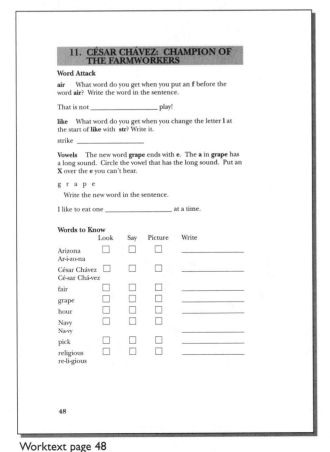

11. CÉSAR CHÁVEZ: CHAMPION OF THE FARMWORKERS

Word Attack

air What word do you get when you put an **f** before the word **air**? Write the word in the sentence.

That is not ________________ play!

like What word do you get when you change the letter **l** at the start of **like** with **str**? Write it.

strike ________________

Vowels The new word **grape** ends with **e**. The **a** in **grape** has a long sound. Circle the vowel that has the long sound. Put an **X** over the **e** you can't hear.

g r a p e

Write the new word in the sentence.

I like to eat one ________________ at a time.

Words to Know

	Look	Say	Picture	Write
Arizona Ar-i-zo-na	☐	☐	☐	________________
César Chávez Cé-sar Chá-vez	☐	☐	☐	________________
fair	☐	☐	☐	________________
grape	☐	☐	☐	________________
hour	☐	☐	☐	________________
Navy Na-vy	☐	☐	☐	________________
pick	☐	☐	☐	________________
religious re-li-gious	☐	☐	☐	________________

48

Worktext page 48

Worktext Pages 48–50

	Look	Say	Picture	Write
strike	☐	☐	☐	________________
union	☐	☐	☐	________________
violence vi-o-lence	☐	☐	☐	________________

Word Attack

+er Write each word with an **er** ending.

farm ________________ pick ________________

grow ________________

+s Write each word with an **s** ending.

farmer ________________ picker ________________

grower ________________ worker ________________

grape ________________

+ing Write each word with an **ing** ending.

pick ________________ pay ________________

hold ________________ eat ________________

buy ________________

+ed Write each word with an **ed** ending.

pull ________________ show ________________

pick ________________

+ly Write **strong** with an **ly** ending in the sentence.

I ________________ believe in playing fair.

49

Worktext page 49

2=1 Below are words that you already know. Put them together to make new words. Write the new, longer word.

out + house = ________________

farm + worker = ________________

girl + friend = ________________

Now circle the two small words in each longer word you wrote.

1+1 You know the words **I** and **would**. These two words can be made into one word: **I'd**. Write **I would** in the first sentence. Write **I'd** in the second sentence.

________________ ________________ leave if I were you.

________________ give him the money now.

What letters are taken out to change **I would** into **I'd**?

____

You know the words **was** and **not**. These two words can be made into one word: **wasn't**. Write **was not** in the first sentence. Write **wasn't** in the second sentence.

I ________________ ________________ going to school today.

She ________________ any help at all.

What letters are taken out to change **was not** into **wasn't**?

____

You know the words **could** and **not**. Put these together to make **couldn't**. Write **could not** in the first sentence. Write **couldn't** in the second sentence.

He ________________ ________________ work that week.

Dad ________________ stop talking.

50

Worktext page 50

Level 5

11. CÉSAR CHÁVEZ: CHAMPION OF THE FARMWORKERS

César Chávez was born on an Arizona farm in 1927. Not many years after that, his family lost their farm. The family then started to pick crops for farmers with lots of land. César stopped going to school when he was 15. He had to help his family make a living.

When he was 18, Chávez went into the Navy and off to World War II. Then he came home, got married, and started a family of his own. Just like his mom and dad, Chávez made his living by working in the fields.

Over the years, Chávez saw that farmworkers had a lot of problems. Grape pickers made as little as $1 an hour. Families made as little as $1,500 a year. Growers could get away with paying so little because of the way they got workers. Some growers put out a call for workers. Far too many workers would come for the work. All these workers needed jobs badly. So the growers could get away with sending most home and paying the others very little.

There were other problems on the job. Many growers did not even have outhouses for the workers to use. Sometimes,

César Chávez leads farm workers in California in 1969. Chávez asked Americans not to buy grapes.

51

Worktext page 51

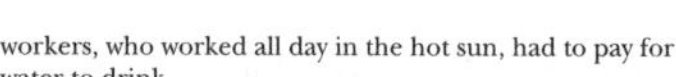

workers, who worked all day in the hot sun, had to pay for water to drink.

César Chávez wanted to change all this. He was a very religious man. He believed that everyone had a right to make a fair living. He believed that real change could only be made without violence. He was strongly against violence.

In 1962, Chávez worked to start a farmworkers' union. A **union** is a group of workers who work together for the good of the group. Chávez would drive from town to town in his old car. He talked to workers in the fields. He told them about his idea for a union. By the fall of 1964, enough workers had become part of the union to hold a meeting.

Then, in 1965, the union went on strike against the grape growers. Chávez asked Americans not to buy grapes. He told people about the problems farmworkers had. People listened. They stopped buying grapes. The next year, one big grape grower gave up. The grower said he was willing to talk with Chávez and the union.

The other big grape growers were holding out. They did not want to change how they ran their grape fields. Fights started to break out between workers and growers. Chávez could not stand violence. He did not believe anything good could ever come of violence.

So, to stop the violence, he stopped eating. Chávez went on a 25-day fast. This means he did not eat for 25 days.The fast worked. It pulled the workers in the union together. It showed them that Chávez was willing to die if the violence went on.

By 1969, the growers were starting to break down. Just five years before, there were 200 grape growers. Now there were only 60. They could not sell grapes. They said they had lost $25,000,000 because of people not buying grapes.

At last, in 1970, 23 growers said that they were ready to talk with Chávez and the union. Chávez told the American people they could buy grapes again!

Chávez worked all his life for the rights of farm workers. Sometimes he won. Sometimes he lost, but he never stopped believing in people. He died in 1993.

52

Worktext page 52

What Do You Think?

Meet with a friend or in a small group. Talk about Chávez's belief that nothing could be won with violence. Do you think he was right or wrong? Why?

Who? What? Where? When? Why?

Find an answer to each of these questions in the story about César Chávez. Write the answers on the lines.

1. **Who** was César Chávez? ____________________
2. **What** did he do? ____________________
3. **Where** did he do it? ____________________
4. **When** did he do it? ____________________
5. **Why** did he do it? ____________________

53

Worktext page 53

Making a Timeline

When you study history, you are looking back in time. Sometimes, it helps to make a timeline. That helps you remember what happened when. Next to each year, write what happened in Chávez's life.

Timeline for the Life of César Chávez

1920	1930	1940	1950	1960	1970	1980	1990	2000

1927: ____________________

1945: ____________________

1962: ____________________

1964: ____________________

1965: ____________________

1970: ____________________

1993: ____________________

César Chávez talks about grapes in 1990.

54

Worktext page 54

LESSON 5.12

OBJECTIVE

- Students will practice and apply skills to an extended passage

MATERIALS

Worktext 5, pages 55–57
Teacher's Manual, pages 247–248, 333
Practice Lesson 5.12, pages 88–89 of the Worktext

SKILLS REVIEW

- Before reading, you may wish to review these words that apply phonics skills: *used, like, drive, home, boys, I'd, girlfriend, sometimes, looked, guys, everything, changed, going, whatever, wanted, neighborhood, didn't, anymore, started, seeing, anyway, liked, don't, started, getting, makes, screamed, picked, aren't, something, I'm, couldn't, anything, always, wasn't, mine, anyone, while, I'll, called, can't, made, you're.* Have students review the Memory Chips they have learned so far. Then ask: **What do you think would happen if a kid hangs around another kid who gets into a lot of trouble?**
- While reading, have students read to see what kind of character they think the narrator is.
- After reading, have students complete the Cooperative Group Activity (What Do You Think?) and the Comprehension Exercise (What Will Happen Next?) on Worktext page 57.

For further practice, have students complete Practice Lesson 5.12 on pages 88–89 of the Worktext. Answers can be found in the Answer Key on pages 356–357 of this *Teacher's Manual.*

RETEACH

If students need further review of phonics skills, you may wish to use the following activity:

Phonograms *air, ike*

Putting It Back Together Write these words on index cards, and say them with students: **stair, strike, like, bike, hair, hike, chair, fair**. Then cut the cards in two, separating the phonogram from the beginning consonant, consonant blend, or digraph. Then have students put the words back together. Have them use each completed word in a sentence.

CONNECTION

Response to Reading

- Have students write a short paragraph predicting what will happen next in the story "Mom Lost Her Job."
- Students should share their prediction with the class.

Literature

- Students may enjoy reading or listening to other adventure books. *Adventures of Huckleberry Finn* and *The Adventures of Tom Sawyer* are available in softcover texts and on audiocassette from Pearson's *Pacemaker™ Classics.*
- Students may use the Book Report reproducible found on page 333 of this *Teacher's Manual* to record responses to the books they read.

Independent Reading

- If students wish to read more about César Chávez, Pearson publishes a series of biographies entitled *Freedom Fighters.* Students may choose the biography about Chávez or another freedom fighter.
- After reading, students may work with a partner. Each partner can summarize and explain how they feel about their book. Students may then write a brief summary of their partner's story and their reaction to it.

12. MOM LOST HER JOB

I live in L.A. This is a big town. I used to like it here. I'd drive around with my friends. I'd go out with my girlfriend. I'd go to school. Sometimes, I looked for a job, but there is no work in this town for 16-year-old guys like me.

Last year, everything changed. My mom lost her job. I said I was going to leave school. I could find **some** kind of job, but Mom said, "no way." Whatever it took, she wanted me to finish school.

We had to move to another neighborhood. I went to a new school. So I didn't get to see my girlfriend much anymore. Then she started seeing another guy. Before long, even my friends didn't remember me much. Anyway, I had to take a bus a long way to see them.

So I started to go around with another kid in my new school. He liked to fight a lot. I don't fight, but every time he got in a fight, I'd be with him. So people started to think of me like that.

55

Worktext page 55

I used to get all "B"s and "C"s. At the new school, I was getting "D"s and even "F"s.

Every day, Mom looked for work. She said we could move back to our old neighborhood if she got a job. What good would that do? My girlfriend already had another guy. My friends didn't remember me. Next year would be my last year in school, anyway. Then I could get a good job and make a lot of money.

"What makes you think you can make a lot of money when you are getting 'D's and 'F's in school?" my mom screamed at me.

Then my new friend was picked up by the police. The police called me in, too. They said, "You are his friend, aren't you? Aren't you with him all the time?"

The police said a thief had taken something from the principal's office. They said that the thief was my friend. They said that I must have been in on it because I'm his friend.

In the end, they couldn't find anything against me. So they let me go. I don't always do the right thing, but I'm not a thief. I never took anything that wasn't mine from anyone.

That week, my mom found a new job. I was really happy. So was she — about the job. She wasn't happy with me.

"I want you to get out of L.A. for a while," she said. "I'll make some money at my new job. Then I'm going to put you in a better school for your last year."

"Out of L.A.?" I asked. "Where am I going to go?"

"I have made a call to my sister, Inez," she said.

My mom's sister, Inez, lives on a farm here in California. She has a husband, César, and a kid, Luis. Luis is 16, like me.

"No way, Mom!" I called out. "I can't live on a farm. I'll get all 'A's from now on. I promise. I'll keep away from that other kid."

"I have made up my mind," Mom said. "You're going."

56

Worktext page 56

What Do You Think?

Meet with a friend or in a small group. Talk about where you live. If you live in a big town, do you like it? Why or why not? If you live in a little town or on a farm, do you like it? Why or why not? If you could live anywhere, where would you live?

What Will Happen Next?

Do you think the boy in this story will be happy on the farm? Circle **YES** or **NO**.

YES **NO**

Write two sentences that back up what you think. You can use these sentences or make up your own.

He was having problems in L.A.

He is used to a big place like L.A.

He didn't have his good friends anymore.

Luis, who lives on the farm, is 16, like him.

He will not have problems with the police on the farm.

He will miss his mom.

He will miss driving around with friends.

____

____

____

____

____

____

____

____

57

Worktext page 57

LESSON 5.13

OBJECTIVES

- Students will decode and blend words with short vowels
- Students will use context clues to recognize unfamiliar words
- Students will apply endings *s*, *ed*, and *ing* to base words to form new words

PHONICS VOCABULARY

had	land	crops	worked	on
picked	liked	talked	always	asking
questions	getting	fights	fighting	job
got	screamed	left	walked	back
called	mom	stand	want	send
bus	can	stars	listened	will
but	just	going	asked	wanted
went	bank	bills	looked	hand
counted	smiling	changed	hanging	went
that	jump	at	missed	still
guessed	answered	circled	miss	dollar
summer	pocket	sides	happening	

WORDS TO KNOW

miss	left	send	summer	dollar
pocket	city	hang	listen	quiet
lettuce	thought			

MATERIALS

Worktext 5, pages 58–62
Teacher's Manual, pages 249–251
Practice Lesson 5.13, pages 90–91 of the Worktext

TEACH

- Using Worktext pages 58–59, introduce students to the vocabulary words. Give students an opportunity to practice writing the words.
- Students can organize their Memory Chips, found in the back of the Worktext. Students can sort the words according to words they know and words they don't. You may also wish to have them sort the words into words with one and two syllables.

Worktext pages 58–59 can also be used to reinforce spelling. Use the five-step process detailed on page 71 of this *Teacher's Manual.*

Short Vowels

Write this sentence on the board and read it aloud: **We can send a card.** Ask a volunteer to point to *send.* Ask them what vowel sound they hear. (*short* e) Point out the CVC letter pattern in *send*, and explain when they see a word with only one vowel, they should try the short vowel sound first.

Blending Say the word **send** aloud, blending the word slowly as you point to each letter you say: /s/ /e/ /nd/. Repeat, using words like *test, camp, cut,* and *swim.* Ask students what vowel sound they hear in each word.

Context Clues

Write this sentence on the board: **I needed to find money to pay for my ticket, but I only had a dollar.** Circle *dollar,* and remind students that they can look at all the other words in the sentence to figure out this word. They can look at the beginning sound and then see if the word makes sense in the sentence. Ask students to read the sentence and tell why they think the last word is *dollar.*

Endings *s, ed, ing*

Remind students that they can add the endings *s, ed,* and *ing* to make new words. Remind them that if the word ends in an *e*, the *e* is taken off before *ed* or *ing* is added.

Make New Words Write a chart like the one below on the board and have students add the endings *s, ed,* and *ing* to make new words. Have students choose one word with an ending to use in a sentence.

Base Word	+ s	+ ed	+ ing
smile	smiles	smiled	smiling
scream	screams	screamed	screaming
circle	circles	circled	circling
answer	answers	answered	answering

PRACTICE

- Let students practice the new words they have learned and formed by completing the activities found on pages 58–59 of the Worktext.
- If students are experiencing difficulty with the Words to Know section on pages 58–59, have students write each word on an index card and draw a picture on the back of the card to illustrate it.

For further practice, have students complete Practice Lesson 5.13 on pages 90–91 of the Worktext. Answers can be found in the Answer Key on page 357 of this *Teacher's Manual.*

APPLY

- Have students talk about what they think will happen next to the boy who is sent away from L.A. Ask: **What do you think will happen to the boy who had to go to the farm in California?** Tell them they are going to use the words they have learned to read a short story that tells them what will happen to the boy.
- Ask students to read the story on pages 60–61 in the Worktext. Offer assistance if necessary, but encourage students to decode the words independently, using the clues and patterns they have learned.
- After students have completed reading the story, have them complete the Comprehension Exercises (Remembering Details and What Is the Main Idea?) on page 62 in their Worktext. Answers can be found in the Answer Key on page 356 of this *Teacher's Manual.*

Worktext Pages 58–59

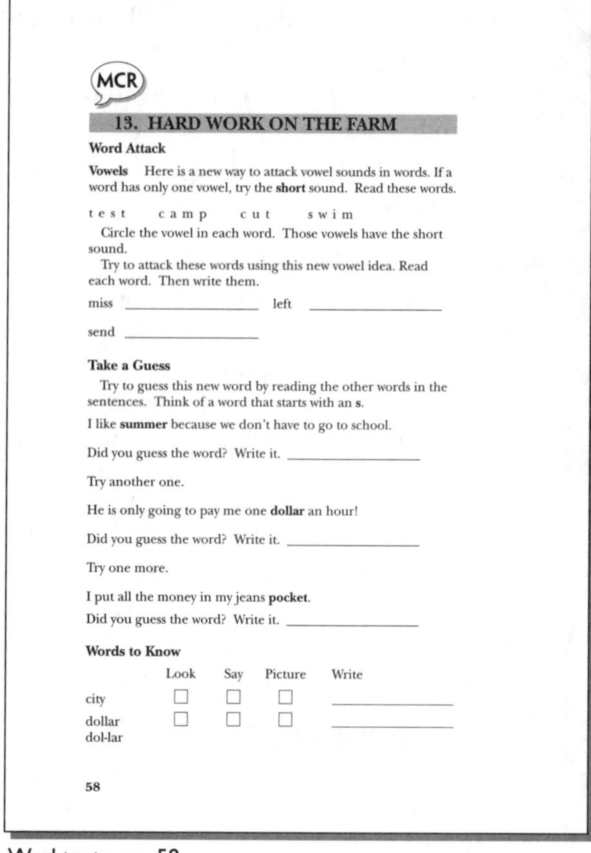
MCR

13. HARD WORK ON THE FARM

Word Attack

Vowels Here is a new way to attack vowel sounds in words. If a word has only one vowel, try the **short** sound. Read these words.

test camp cut swim

Circle the vowel in each word. Those vowels have the short sound.

Try to attack these words using this new vowel idea. Read each word. Then write them.

miss ________ left ________

send ________

Take a Guess

Try to guess this new word by reading the other words in the sentences. Think of a word that starts with an **s**.

I like **summer** because we don't have to go to school.

Did you guess the word? Write it. ________

Try another one.

He is only going to pay me one **dollar** an hour!

Did you guess the word? Write it. ________

Try one more.

I put all the money in my jeans **pocket**.

Did you guess the word? Write it. ________

Words to Know

	Look	Say	Picture	Write
city	☐	☐	☐	________
dollar dol-lar	☐	☐	☐	________

58

Worktext page 58

	Look	Say	Picture	Write
hang	☐	☐	☐	________
left	☐	☐	☐	________
lettuce let-tuce	☐	☐	☐	________
listen lis-ten	☐	☐	☐	________
miss	☐	☐	☐	________
pocket pock-et	☐	☐	☐	________
quiet qui-et	☐	☐	☐	________
send	☐	☐	☐	________
summer sum-mer	☐	☐	☐	________
thought	☐	☐	☐	________

Word Attack

+s Write **side** with an **s** ending. ________

+ing Write each word with an **ing** ending.

hang ________ happen ________

Write **smile** with an **ing** ending. Take off the **e** first.

smile ________

+ed Write each word with an **ed** ending.

scream ________ listen ________

miss ________ guess ________

count ________ answer ________

Write **circle** with an **ed** ending. It already ends with an **e**, so you just have to add **d**. circle ________

59

Worktext page 59

13. HARD WORK ON THE FARM

Inez and her husband, César, had their own land in California. They raised different crops. In the summer, Inez, César, and Luis all worked on the farm.

They put me right to work when I got there. We picked lettuce. I liked Inez and César all right. Luis talked too much. He was always asking me questions as we worked.

"What's L.A. like?"

"Do you have a girlfriend?"

"Did you have a job?"

"Is there a lot of violence there?"

"My mom said you were getting into fights. What were you fighting about?"

At last, I had to say, "Look, Luis. Don't talk so much."

"Why not?"

"**Stop asking questions**!" I screamed. Then I left the lettuce field. I walked all the way back to their house. I called my mom at her new job.

"I can't stand Luis," I said to her. "I want to come home. Please send me bus money. It is too quiet here. You can hear every little insect. The night is so dark. There are too many stars."

My mom listened to me. Then she said, "You have to stay there for the summer. I'm sorry. The air and hard work will be good for you. Try to like Luis."

"But Mom —"

"Just try."

On Saturday, César and Luis were going into town. They asked if I wanted to come. What else was there to do? So I went. We went to the bank. Then César gave me a lot of bills.

I looked at the money in my hand for a long time. Then I counted the money. I had never had this much at one time in my life.

60

Worktext page 60

"Two weeks of hard work," César said smiling. "That's your pay."

"I didn't know I was going to get **pay**," I said.

That changed everything. I had $400 in my pocket!

That night, I went out with Luis and some of his friends. It wasn't like hanging out in the city with my friends, but we had a pretty good time. We went to see some friends. I couldn't believe all that money in the back pocket of my jeans. I thought I should hide it somewhere. Then I thought, *This isn't L.A. No one is going to jump me for my money.*

That night we got back to the house at around 1:00. Luis went right to sleep, but I went back outside. I looked at the dark sky and all those stars. It **was** too quiet here. I liked having all that money. It wasn't so bad hanging out on a Saturday night and not having to think about anything bad happening. I missed my mom. I missed the city still, but I guessed I could get through the summer here.

61

Worktext page 61

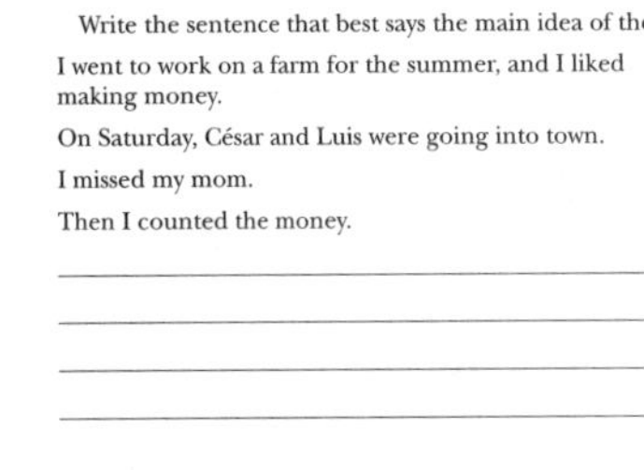

Remembering Details

Write a word from the story in each space.

They raised __________ crops.

In the __________, Inez, César, and Luis all worked on the farm.

We picked __________.

"Stop asking __________!"

I couldn't believe all that money in the back __________ of my jeans.

What Is the Main Idea?

Write the sentence that best says the main idea of the story.

I went to work on a farm for the summer, and I liked making money.

On Saturday, César and Luis were going into town.

I missed my mom.

Then I counted the money.

____

____

____

____

62

Worktext page 62

Level 5

LESSON 5.14

OBJECTIVE

- Students will practice and apply skills to an extended passage

MATERIALS

Worktext 5, pages 63–65
Teacher's Manual, pages 252–253, 330–331
Practice Lesson 5.14, pages 92–93 of the Worktext

SKILLS REVIEW

- Before reading, you may wish to review these words that apply phonics skills: *changed, questions, used, asked, had, bad, having, problems, last, back, looked, guys, bank, going, next, jobs, class, laughing, circled, him, mom, working, want, kid, not, still, pushed, stand, jumped, hit, pulled, started, making, stayed, laughed, remembered, went, got, stop, asking, when.* Have students review the Memory Chips they have learned so far. Then ask: **What do you think would happen if Luis went to L.A.?**
- While reading, have students read to find out how the narrator's feelings change toward Luis.
- After reading, have students complete the Cooperative Group Activity (What Do You Think?) and Comprehension Exercise (Write a Summary) on Worktext page 65.

For further practice, have students complete Practice Lesson 5.14 on pages 92–93 of the Worktext. Answers can be found in the Answer Key on pages 356–357 of this *Teacher's Manual.*

RETEACH

If students need further review of phonics skills, you may wish to use the following activity:

Short Vowels

The Missing Letter To review short vowel sounds, write these sentences on the board. Have students fill in the blanks with the missing vowel. Next have them read the word they made and tell why they chose the vowel they did. Then have students read the sentence to make sure the word makes sense.

- **I made a "B+" on my math t _ st.** (*test*)
- **Mom and Dad say I can go to baseball c _ mp this summer.** (*camp*)
- **I don't like to m_ss a day of school.** (*miss*)
- **I think you need to turn l_ft here.** (*left*)
- **I will s_nd a letter to Grandma.** (*send*)
- **I c_t my hair. Do you like it?** (*cut*)
- **I wish I could sw_m well.** (*swim*)

CONNECTION

Response to Reading

- To reinforce students' understanding of the stories about Luis and the boy from L.A., have them complete the Story Map and Character Cluster reproducibles found on pages 330–331.
- Students will demonstrate an understanding of setting, characters, and plot by filling out the organizers.
- Students may share their completed organizers with the class.

14. LUIS IN L.A.

Luis never changed. Questions, questions, questions. But I got used to him. Then, at the end of the summer, he asked if he could come back to L.A. with me.

I didn't like the idea at first, but Mom had not moved yet. I didn't really have friends at the new school. Luis was OK. It would not be so bad having him with us in L.A.

César and Inez were not so happy about the idea. They didn't want Luis having the same kind of problems I had. At last, they gave in. So, in the fall, Luis came back with me to L.A.

At school, some of the guys gave him a hard time for asking so many questions in class. The way I looked at it, we had it over those guys. Luis and I had a lot of money in the bank from our summer work. I was going back to the farm next summer, too. Those guys were all talk. Luis and I had good jobs and money in the bank.

63

Worktext page 63

Then one day, Luis asked one too many questions in class. I could see all the kids laughing at him. After class, a group of guys circled around him. They gave him a pretty hard time.

My mom said if I got in **any** fights, she was going to send me to Inez and César's farm for **good**. I didn't mind working there in the summer. But no way did I want to live there all the time!

Then one kid pushed Luis. Not very hard, but still he pushed him.

I couldn't stand by while someone pushed my family. I jumped in and was about to hit the guy. Luis caught my arm and pulled me away.

"Forget it," he said.

"You can't just walk away from a fight," I told him.

"Why not?" Luis said. He started to walk away. All the guys started to laugh at him.

"Oh, man," I said to myself. Luis was making problems for me.

So I stayed there in the hall with the guys. I laughed at Luis with them. Then I remembered that Luis was family. You can't turn your back on family.

I went and caught up with Luis.

"Man, you have **got** to keep your mouth closed," I said. "Stop asking questions all the time. You aren't on the farm anymore. This is L.A."

"What's wrong with questions? Are people in L.A. really that different from people back home? Why do those guys want to fight all the time? Don't they have anything better to do?"

I gave up. Luis was **never** going to stop asking questions. The thing was, his questions were not all that bad. Sometimes, he had a point.

"OK, OK," I said. "I guess I'm just going to have to keep an eye on you."

"What for?" he asked.

Another question!

"Because you're a problem," I said.

"Then I guess we are even," he answered. "When you came to the farm, **you** were the problem."

Then we both laughed.

64

Worktext page 64

What Do You Think?

Meet with a friend or a small group. Talk about what you would do if you were the guy in this story. Would you be friends with Luis? Why or why not? What would you say to him?

Write a Summary

Read these sentences. Which ones are about the big ideas in the story you just read? Circle these. Which ones are about details? Put a line through each of these.

I gave up and started being friends with him.

"Forget it," he said.

In the fall, Luis came back with me to L.A.

At school, some of the guys gave him a hard time for asking so many questions in class.

Then we both laughed.

Sometimes, he had a point.

Now write a summary. Write the big-idea sentences in the order that they happened in the story.

____

____

____

____

____

____

65

Worktext page 65

Level 5

FINAL NOVEL Running Out of Time

MATERIALS
Final Novel 5, *Running Out of Time*
Teacher's Manual, page 254
Assessment Manual, Final Assessment 5, pages 100–105

Summary *Wilma doesn't like school—until the day she finds out they are closing down her high school. Wilma organizes a group to save the school. They need to raise a lot of money. Wilma and her friends are able to save the school.*

REVIEW AND ASSESSMENT

- Have students review their Memory Chips for Level 5 in small groups or with partners. Depending on your students' needs, review the following skills covered in Lessons 9–14: context clues; possessives; compound words; contractions; phonograms *ay, air,* and *ike;* letter pattern CVCe; short vowels; and endings *s, ing, er, ly,* and *ed.*

If you wish to assess students' progress at this point, use *Assessment Manual,* pages 100–105. For students who need additional support, you may use the Reteach activities from previous lessons.

INTRODUCE THE NOVEL

Invite students to preview the book by reading the title, looking at the illustrations, and reading aloud the captions. Begin a discussion of story concepts by asking:

- **Why is a school important to students?**
- **What do you think the saying "Don't get mad, get even" means?**

CHECK COMPREHENSION

Chapter 1 Why does Wilma have to stay after school? (*She is not doing her homework.*)

Chapter 2 Why doesn't Wilma do her homework when she gets home? (*Levi used to help her.*)

Chapter 3 Why does the school have an all-school meeting? (*to tell the students that the school is closing*)

Chapter 4 What do you think Levi means in his letter to Wilma? (*Possible answer: He thinks she should do something instead of just getting mad and quitting.*)

Chapter 5 Why does Wilma feel bad? (*She put ads all over the school for the meeting, but no one came.*)

Chapter 6 What does Wilma plan to do since no one came to the meeting? (*She plans to quit school.*)

Chapter 7 What do the other kids want to do the next day? (*They want to have another meeting.*)

Chapter 8 What do the students have to do to save the school? (*They have to raise $150,000 for repairs.*)

Chapter 9 How do you think Wilma plans to fight for her school? (*Possible answers: She could raise money; she could ask for donations.*)

Chapter 10 What do the students do first to save the school? (*They strike or have a picket march.*)

Chapter 11 Why does Mr. Singer call Wilma? (*He calls to tell her that if the students try to save the school, he will back them up.*)

Chapter 12 What does Mrs. Wells suggest Wilma do about her failing grades? (*She suggests she make up the classes in summer school.*)

Chapter 13 What do the kids plan to do with the money they have made so far? (*They plan to use it for materials, so volunteer workers can begin fixing the school.*)

Chapter 14 What does Wilma have to be happy about now? (*She is on TV once again, and Luis and she go out together and have a good time.*)

Chapter 15 Who do you think took the money? (*Some students might suggest César.*)

Chapter 16 What happened to the money? (*Jen's father put it in the bank.*)

Chapter 17 How much money do the students still need to keep the school open? (*$20,000*)

Chapter 18 How do they plan to get the final $20,000? (*César agrees to sell his car.*)

Chapter 19 What happens when César tries to sell his car? (*He gets $20,000.*)

Chapter 20 Why is KXED interested in Wilma? (*She looks and sounds good on TV.*)

Chapter 21 How does the story end? (*Wilma goes on TV to tell everyone the story of how the school was saved, and her brother Levi returns and sees her.*)

CONNECTION

Home/School Encourage students to bring home a copy of *Running Out of Time.* They might read the novel, or sections of the novel, to family members.

LEVEL 6

ORGANIZER

Level 6 of the *Caught Reading* program includes the following components:

Worktext 6

Worktext 6 includes 12 lessons, taking students from those words introduced in previous levels through a word list of 163 words (found on page 343 of this *Teacher's Manual*) by Lesson 12. The Practice Lessons provide students with opportunites to extend practice, and review the content of each lesson. The Response to Reading pages allow students to practice using their new vocabulary. Tear-out Memory Chips in the back of the student book reinforce new vocabulary and can be used both independently by students and in small groups.

Midway and Final Novels 6

These novels are designed to reinforce learned vocabulary and give students the opportunity to read for meaning. Their high-interest plots encourage successful reading experiences and an appreciation for literature.

- *Caged* includes only vocabulary students have learned up to the midway point of this level.
- *Under Fire* includes all vocabulary learned through Level 6.

Teacher's Manual

The *Teacher's Manual* provides detailed objectives and instruction for each skill taught in the Worktext, as well as additional teaching suggestions for meaningful practice and reinforcement. The *Teacher's Manual* provides choices for flexible instruction. Comprehension questions for the Midway and Final novels are included, as well as Answer Keys for the Worktext activities and the Practice Lessons.

Assessment Manual

The *Assessment Manual* provides preassessment, ongoing assessment, and postassessment to administer to students throughout their work in *Caught Reading*. Within this Manual you will also find Midway and Final Assessments to determine the students' comprehension of the Midway and Final Novels.

OBJECTIVES

Vocabulary Development

- Read a base vocabulary, plus base vocabulary words with various endings, compound words, and contractions formed from base words.
- Use the word learning sequence to remember and spell words correctly.
- Review vocabulary independently, both in and out of context, using the Memory Chips.
- Learn vocabulary to talk and write about literature.

Phonics

- Read the contractions *we're, won't, hasn't, wouldn't, you've, I'm, she'll, they'll, they've,* and *we've.*
- Recognize the letter groups *ool, oor,* and *ark.*
- Use a new vowel generalization: If a word has only one vowel, that vowel usually has the short sound.

Reading Comprehension

- Read plays, short stories, and a biography.
- Read poetry and understand its rhythm.

Literary Analysis

- Distinguish among common forms of fiction and describe the major characteristics of each.
- Define how mood or meaning is conveyed in poetry.

Writing

- Write responses to literature that demonstrate an understanding of the literary work.
- Write brief descriptions that identify setting and conflict in a story.

Speaking and Listening

- Listen to the beat, or rhythm, in poetry.
- Match words that rhyme.

INTRODUCTION & LESSON 6.1

OBJECTIVES

- Students will decode and blend words containing the *eat* and *ool* phonograms
- Students will use context clues to figure out unfamiliar words
- Students will apply endings *ity, s, ing, est,* and *y* to base words to form new words
- Students will recognize and form compound words

PHONICS VOCABULARY

lines	excites	feelings	kinds	poems
pictures	longest	words	rhymes	beat
sound	points	letters	cool	electricity
dirty	falling	looking	meat	sometime
eat	bones	runs	heat	exciting
moving	setting	poems	sets	beginning
settings	electric	wand	care	dogs
characters		upon	everywhere	

WORDS TO KNOW

alone	bones	dirt	electric	fancy
fat	hat	hey	cool	heat
love	music	meat	noise	pole
street	world	add	begin	biography
excite	which	middle	often	character
plot	poem	rhyme	set	short
literature				

MATERIALS

Worktext 6, pages 5–11
Teacher's Manual, pages 258–260
Practice Lesson 6.1, pages 67–68 of the Worktext

TEACH

- Before beginning the lesson, have students complete the exercises independently in the Introduction on Worktext pages 5–6.
- Using Worktext pages 7–8, introduce students to the vocabulary words. Give them an opportunity to practice writing the words.
- Students can organize their Memory Chips, found in the back of the Worktext. You may wish to say each word, having them repeat it after you.

Worktext pages 7–8 can also be used to reinforce spelling. Use the five-step process detailed on page 71 of this *Teacher's Manual.*

Phonograms *eat, ool*

Write this sentence on the board and read it aloud: **The sun will heat the pool.** Ask a volunteer to point to *pool.* Ask students what words rhyme with *pool.* (*school, tool, cool*) Point to the letters *ool.* Tell students that when they see these letters, they can expect to hear the /o͝ol/ sound. Ask a volunteer to point to *heat.* Remind students that *heat* has the long *e* sound and is made by the letters *ea.* Say /hēt/, emphasizing the sounds.

Blending Write **pool** on the board. Erase the *p*, and write *c*. Have students blend the sounds: /kool/. Then ask them to list rhyming words for *heat* and *pool.* (*beat, seat, cheat; tool, cool, school*) List them on the board, and blend them as you read them aloud.

Context Clues

Remind students that when they see a word they do not know, they can read the words around it to help them figure it out. Write these sentences on the board: **The man went on a long trip. He went all around the world.** Read the sentences, leaving out the word *world.* Ask students what they think the word is and what other words give them clues.

Endings *ity, s, ing, est, y*

Write **electricity** on the board. Cover the *ity* and read *electric.* Tell students that this is a base word. Uncover *ity* and tell them that this ending can be added to make new words. Then remind students that they can add other endings such as *s, ing, est,* and *y* to words.

Make New Words Write these words and endings on index cards: **dirt**, **chill**, **long**, **fall**, **electric**, **ity**, **s**, **ing**, **est**, **y**. Have students take turns putting two cards together to make a new word. (*dirty; chilly, chills, chilling; longest; falls, falling; electricity*) They can write the words on the board and use each in a sentence.

Compound Words

Remind students that words like *everything* and *onto* are made up of two smaller words.

Make New Words Write these words on index cards and have students put two of them together to make new words: **up**, **on**, **some**, **time**, **any**, **where**. (*upon, anytime, sometime, anywhere, somewhere*)

PRACTICE

- Let students practice the new words they have learned and formed by completing the activities found on pages 7–8 of the Worktext.
- If students are experiencing difficulty with the Words to Know section on pages 7–8, place the Memory Chips on the table. Say each of the Memory Chip words and use them in sentences. Have students choose the word you say from the table.

For further practice, have students complete Practice Lesson 6.1 on pages 67–68 of the Worktext. Answers can be found in the Answer Key on page 358 of this *Teacher's Manual.*

APPLY

- Have students talk about the story concept by discussing things they already know. Ask: **What is a poem? Why are poems fun to read?** Tell them they are going to use the words they have learned to read an article about poems and to read three short poems.
- Ask students to read the article and poems on pages 9–10 in the Worktext. Offer assistance if necessary, but encourage students to decode the words independently, using the clues and patterns they have learned.
- After students have completed reading the article and poems, have them complete the Comprehension Exercises (Remembering Details, Writing the Rhymes, and Finding the Beat) on page 11 in their Worktext. Answers can be found in the Answer Key on page 358 of this *Teacher's Manual.*

CONNECTION

Strategy for Reading Have students reread the poems on Worktext page 10 to correct comprehension breakdowns. Students may achieve understanding by reprocessing the same text with greater attention focused on its meaning.

Worktext Pages 5–7

INTRODUCTION: GET CAUGHT READING LITERATURE

Words to Know

	Look	Say	Picture	Write
add	☐	☐	☐	______
begin be-gin	☐	☐	☐	______
biography bi-og-ra-phy	☐	☐	☐	______
character char-ac-ter	☐	☐	☐	______
excite ex-cite	☐	☐	☐	______
literature lit-er-a-ture	☐	☐	☐	______
middle mid-dle	☐	☐	☐	______
often of-ten	☐	☐	☐	______
plot	☐	☐	☐	______
poem po-em	☐	☐	☐	______
rhyme	☐	☐	☐	______
set	☐	☐	☐	______
short	☐	☐	☐	______
which	☐	☐	☐	______

Word Attack

+ing Write the words below with **ing** at the end to make new words. Before the ending, add one more **n** to **begin**. Add one more **t** to **set**. Take away the **e** at the end of **excite**.

begin ______ set ______

excite ______

5

Worktext page 5

+s Write the words below with an **s** ending.

character ______ poem ______

rhyme ______ excite ______

set ______ setting ______

You are moving along through **Caught Reading**. So far you have learned about 900 words. Now you are about to begin Level 6. In this book, you will learn how to get the most out of literature.

Literature is good writing that makes you think and feel. Often, a work of literature sets out exciting ideas and uses words in exciting ways. Literature can tell a story. It can give facts. It can make you laugh, cry, become angry, or do all these things at the same time.

In **Caught Reading Level 6**, you will read four different kinds of literature. First, you will read some poems. You will hear rhymes and other sounds that set a poem apart from other kinds of writing. Then you will read a short story. You will see how a story moves from the beginning to the middle to the end. You will see how setting, characters, and plot work together to make a story exciting. Next, you will read a play, which is just a different way of setting out a story. Last, you will read a biography, the story of a person's life.

Happy reading!

MCR Each time you see **MCR**, it is time for a Memory Chip Review. Remember: practice first with side **A**, then with side **B**. Check (√) the ones you read easily on side **B**. When a Memory Chip has three checks (√√√), put it in the **Words I Know** envelope.

6

Worktext page 6

1. WHAT IS A POEM?

Letter Groups

school Take away **sch** from **school**, and put **c** in its place. Now you have the word **cool**. Read this new word. Write it in the sentence below.

The water was hot, but it's ______ now.

eat You know the word **eat**. Two of your new words end with this word. Read the words. Write them below.

heat ______ meat ______

Take a Guess

Read the sentences below. See if you can guess the words in dark letters.

Turn on the **electric** light.
This is the biggest mountain in the **world**.

Write the words. ______ ______

Word Attack

Base Word You have a Memory Chip for the word **cares**. Take away the **s**, and you have the base word **care**. Write this word in the sentence below.

I don't ______ if I lose the game.

Words to Know

	Look	Say	Picture	Write
alone a-lone	☐	☐	☐	______
bones	☐	☐	☐	______
cool	☐	☐	☐	______
dirt	☐	☐	☐	______
electric e-lec-tric	☐	☐	☐	______
fancy fan-cy	☐	☐	☐	______

7

Worktext page 7

Level 6

	Look	Say	Picture	Write
fat	☐	☐	☐	______
hat	☐	☐	☐	______
heat	☐	☐	☐	______
hey	☐	☐	☐	______
love	☐	☐	☐	______
meat	☐	☐	☐	______
music mu-sic	☐	☐	☐	______
noise	☐	☐	☐	______
pole	☐	☐	☐	______
street	☐	☐	☐	______
world	☐	☐	☐	______

Word Attack

+s Write **s** after **dog** to get a new word. ______

+ing Write **fall** with an **ing** ending. ______

+est Write **long** with an **est** ending. ______

+y Write **dirt** with the ending **y**. ______

+ity The letters **ity** are an ending you can add to some words. Write them after **electric** to make a new word. In the new word, the **c** sounds like **s**. Read the new word.

electric + ity = ______

2=1 Look for two words you know in each word below. Write the two words that you find in each word.

upon = ______+ ______ sometime = ______+ ______

8

Worktext page 8

Snow in the City

It was cold last night; the sky was dark.
My window looked out upon a dirty street.
Cars screamed, going by. The city
Was electricity with a beat.

Snow started falling
Sometime in that long, dark night.
I was looking through a different window
In the first yellow light.

Every pole had a small, white hat,
And the street was clean.
Cars went by without a noise
In this city that I had never seen.

Two Dogs

Fancy dog has meat to eat;
lives in a fancy home.
Mean dog is a street dog;
Runs alone, lives on bones.

One is fat; and one is free.
Each dog has its way.
Which one is the happy dog?
Who can say? Who can say?

Summer

Heat.
People in the street.
Electric music in the air.

Moving to the beat,
Boy and girl
Meet.

Hey!
Love is everywhere.

10

Worktext page 10

1. WHAT IS A POEM?

Some would say a poem is a short set of lines that excites strong feelings in you when you read it. That is one kind of poem. But there are many other kinds. Some poems paint pictures with words. Some make you laugh. Some even tell stories. The longest story in the world is, in fact, a poem.

Any set of lines can be a poem. Each line may or may not be a sentence. Often, some lines in a poem rhyme. That is, they end with words that rhyme, or sound alike. Yet, not all poems have rhymes. The lines of a poem often have a beat, too. The beat is made by strong sounds that fall at set points. In the lines below, the strong sounds are shown in dark letters. Read these lines. Can you hear the beat?

The **sun** was **hot**, the **woods** were **cool**,
and **waves** of **light** came **off** the **sea**.

The beat may be the same in every line of a poem. Or it may be different from line to line. In fact, there may be only one thing you can say about every poem. The words have a kind of music to them. Read the poems on the next page and listen for that music. Try to hear the beat and the rhymes. Think about the feelings these poems give you and the pictures they paint in your mind.

And if you want to, read the poems you like again and again. You may get a new picture or idea each time.

9

Worktext page 9

Remembering Details

The questions below are about the poem **Summer**. Write the answer to each question.

Who is in the street? ______

What is in the air? ______

Who meets? ______

What is everywhere? ______

Writing the Rhymes

Find the lines that rhyme in the poem **Snow in the City**. Write the words that rhyme.

______ rhymes with ______

______ rhymes with ______

______ rhymes with ______

Finding the Beat

Write lines one and three from the poem **Two Dogs**. Circle the strong sounds that give these lines their **beat**.

Write line one. ______

______

Write line three. ______

______

Is the beat in these two lines the same or different?

______

11

Worktext page 11

LESSON 6.2

OBJECTIVE

- Students will practice and apply skills as they read poetry

MATERIALS

Worktext 6, pages 12–14
Teacher's Manual, pages 261–262
Practice Lesson 6.2, pages 69–70 of the Worktext
Chart paper, markers (Reteach)

SKILLS REVIEW

- Before reading, you may wish to review these words that apply phonics skills: *pulls, heat, waves, cracks, someone, feelings, inside, cool, something, working, anywhere, names, wants, coming, eat, turns.* Have students review the Memory Chips they have learned so far. Then ask: **What can poems be about?**
- While reading, have students make pictures in their minds about what the poems are saying.
- After reading, have students complete the Comprehension Exercises (Finding Rhymes, Hearing the Beat, and Finding the Main Idea) on Worktext page 14.

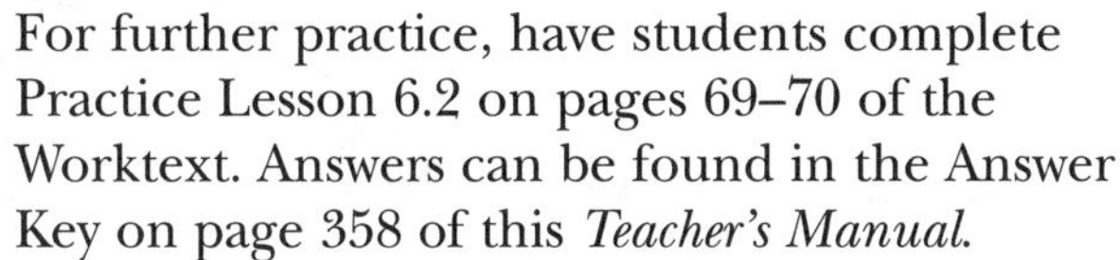

For further practice, have students complete Practice Lesson 6.2 on pages 69–70 of the Worktext. Answers can be found in the Answer Key on page 358 of this *Teacher's Manual.*

RETEACH

If students need further review of phonics skills, you may wish to use the following activity:

Phonograms *ool, eat*

Picture Mysteries Have students take turns making new words by substituting the beginning consonants in *school* and adding consonants and consonant blends to the beginning of *eat.* (*school, cool, pool, fool; beat, meat, heat, neat, feat*) Write the words on the board. Then have students take turns choosing one word. Have them draw a picture that represents each word. The class can guess each mystery word.

CONNECTION

Response to Reading

- Have students work in cooperative groups to write two short poems in which the rhyming patterns and the beat evoke different sets of feelings.
- Have student groups share their poetry with the class.

Literature

- Students may enjoy reading other poems. *Latino Poetry* and *African American Poetry* are available from Pearson. Both books offer a wide range of poets and forms of poetry.

2. POEMS

On a Day Like This

On a day like this
summer in the city
pulls people out.
You can see the heat
come up in waves
from the street
where people push,
push one another.
One wrong word.
One wrong word
cracks the air
and violence is born.

A Friend

A friend, I hear them say,
Is someone you can talk to,
Someone you can tell about
the feelings that you hide
inside.

OK. I buy that, but–

I just want to say,
A friend is someone, too,
Who leaves you alone till you
Want to talk. And then
If you still want to hide
the feelings that you have inside
Says, "Cool.

Let's find something else to do."

12

Worktext page 12

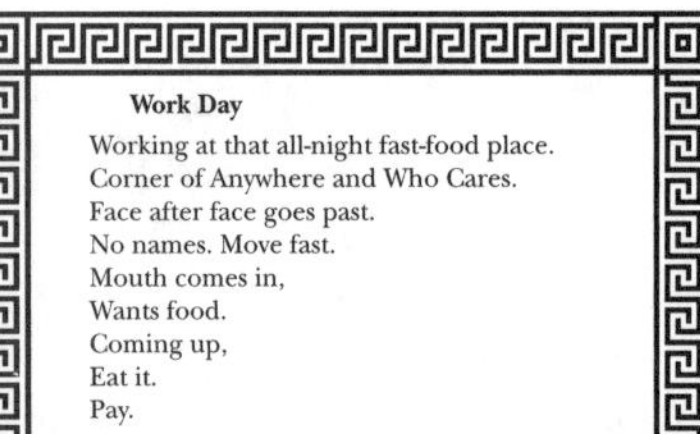

Work Day

Working at that all-night fast-food place.
Corner of Anywhere and Who Cares.
Face after face goes past.
No names. Move fast.
Mouth comes in,
Wants food.
Coming up,
Eat it.
Pay.

Next!

Day
turns into night:
Liquid noise. White light.

13

Worktext page 13

Finding Rhymes

Which poem has only two lines that rhyme? Write the name of the poem. Below it, write the words that rhyme.

Poem: ______________________

__________ rhymes with __________

Which poem has four lines that rhyme? Write the name of the poem. Below it, write the words that rhyme.

Poem: ______________________

__________ rhymes with __________

__________ rhymes with __________

Hearing the Beat

You have just read three poems. Each has a different kind of beat. In each poem, a different feeling comes from the beat. Which of the words below describe which poem? Write the name of the poem next to the words that describe it best.

On a Day Like This **Work Day** **A Friend**

sounds like people just talking __________

has a hard, fast beat __________

gets faster and faster __________

Finding the Main Idea

What does **Work Day** say? Finish the sentence below with the ending that best tells the main idea of this poem. Use ending **a**, ending **b**, or ending **c** below.

After you work at the fast-food place for awhile,

____

____

a. everything you see and hear starts to run together.
b. some of the noises start to sound like water.
c. you meet some really cool people.

14

Worktext page 14

LESSON 6.3

OBJECTIVES

- Students will decode words containing the *oor* and *ark* phonograms
- Students will use context clues to read unfamiliar words
- Students will apply endings *s, ed, ing,* and *er* to base words to form new words
- Students will recognize and form possessives
- Students will recognize and form compound words

PHONICS VOCABULARY

years	wanted	something	whatever
feeling	glasses	stopped	looked
everything	that's	scared	nothing
wasn't	friends	kids	used
baseball	park	liked	cars
sometimes	girls	guys	boys
neighborhood	someday	talked	jobs
didn't	building	doors	anyone
apartments	lots	hiding	started
lives	thinking	maybe	cops
don't	news	into	you're
going	kidding	bones	dark
César's	it's	finds	working
things	won't	banks	camping
meeting	they're	I'll	we'll
outlaw	asking	restaurants	floor
locked	parked	starting	panting
describing	owner	later	tonight
we're	stolen	stick	steal
join	windows	restaurant	

WORDS TO KNOW

both	floor	full	handle	lock
might	park	rent	shut	watch
restaurant	great	rich	ride	stolen

MATERIALS

Worktext 6, pages 15–21
Teacher's Manual, pages 263–265
Practice Lesson 6.3, pages 71–72 of the Worktext

TEACH

- Using Worktext pages 15–16, introduce students to the vocabulary words. Give them an opportunity to practice writing the words.
- Students can organize their Memory Chips, found in the back of the Worktext. They can divide them into groups of words they know and words they don't recognize.

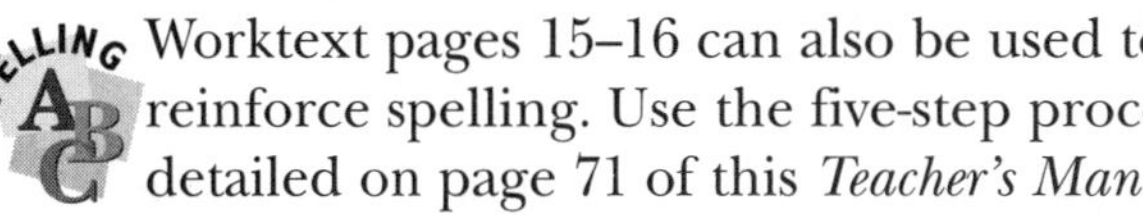

Worktext pages 15–16 can also be used to reinforce spelling. Use the five-step process detailed on page 71 of this *Teacher's Manual.*

Phonograms *oor, ark*

Write this sentence on the board: **I could not see the door or the floor in the dark.** Ask students what two words rhyme. (*door, floor*) Ask them what letters are the same in both words. (*oor*) Have a volunteer point to *dark.* Tell students when *a* is followed by *r, a* has the sound of /â/.

Blending Write **door** and **floor** on the board. Blend the word *door* with students as you pass your finger underneath the letters: /dôr/. Then repeat for *floor*: /flôr/. Repeat the procedure using *dark* and *park.* (/dârk/, /pârk/)

Context Clues

Write these sentences on the board: **I'm hungry. Let's go out to a restaurant and eat.** Cover the word *restaurant,* and tell students that when they see an unfamiliar word, they can read the words around it and use what they know about letters and sounds to help them figure out the word. Read the sentences without *restaurant.* Uncover the word and have students look at the beginning letter. Tell them that the *r* gives us a clue as to how the word begins. Ask them what word they think goes in the sentence.

Endings *s, ed, ing, er*

Remind students that when *ed, ing,* and *er* are added to some words, the ending consonant is doubled; when *ed, ing,* and *er* are added to words that end in *e,* the *e* is dropped and the ending is added.

Make New Words Write these words on the board, and invite students to add *s, ed, ing,* and *er* to the end of each: **stop**, **camp**, **like**, **own**. (*stops, stopped, stopping, stopper; camps, camped, camping, camper; likes, liked, liking; owns, owned, owning, owner*)

Possessives

Remind students that when they want to show ownership in a person or thing, they add an apostrophe and *s.*

Make New Words Have students add an apostrophe and *s* to each of these words and use them in a sentence: *boy, Kay, César.* (*boy's, Kay's, César's*)

Compound Words

Remind students that words like *neighborhood* are made up of two words. Write **neighborhood** on the board and have a student draw a line between the two words.

Make New Words Write these words on index cards and have students make new words by putting two of them together: **to**, **day**, **night**, **neighbor**, **hood**, **free**, **way**. (*today, tonight, neighborhood, freeway*)

PRACTICE

- Let students practice the new words they have learned and formed by completing the activities found on pages 15–17 of the Worktext.
- If students are experiencing difficulty with the Words to Know section on pages 15–16, you may wish to scramble the letters of each word and write them on the board. Then have students unscramble the words, and read the words aloud.

For further practice, have students complete Practice Lesson 6.3 on pages 71–72 of the Worktext. Answers can be found in the Answer Key on page 358 of this *Teacher's Manual.*

APPLY

- Have students talk about the story concept by sharing their experiences. Ask: **Has someone ever asked you to do something that you were scared to do? What happened?**
- Ask students to read the story on pages 18–20 in the Worktext. Encourage students to decode the words independently, using the clues and patterns they have learned.
- After students have completed reading the story, have them complete the Comprehension Exercises (Meeting Characters and Describing the Setting) on page 21 in their Worktext. Answers can be found in the Answer Key on page 358 of this *Teacher's Manual.*

Worktext Pages 15–17

3. THE OLD GREEN BUILDING, PART 1

Letter Groups

oor You know how **oor** sounds in **door**? It sounds the same in **floor**. Write this new word in the sentence below.

Don't walk on that clean ____________.

ark You know how **ark** sounds in **dark**. Read it the same way in **park**. Write the new word below.

park ____________

Take a Guess

Read the sentences below. See if you can guess the words in dark letters.

Let's go out to a **restaurant** to eat.
Call the cops! My money has been **stolen**!

Write the new words below. Then read each one again.

____________ ____________

Word Attack

Base words You know the words **sticks**, **steals**, and **joined**. Take away the **s** or **ed** endings. Now you have the base words **stick**, **steal**, and **join**. Write these words below.

____________ ____________ ____________

Words to Know

	Look	Say	Picture	Write
both	☐	☐	☐	____________
floor	☐	☐	☐	____________
full	☐	☐	☐	____________
great	☐	☐	☐	____________
handle han-dle	☐	☐	☐	____________

15

Worktext page 15

	Look	Say	Picture	Write
lock	☐	☐	☐	____________
might	☐	☐	☐	____________
park	☐	☐	☐	____________
rent	☐	☐	☐	____________
restaurant res-tau-rant	☐	☐	☐	____________
rich	☐	☐	☐	____________
ride	☐	☐	☐	____________
shut	☐	☐	☐	____________
stolen sto-len	☐	☐	☐	____________
watch	☐	☐	☐	____________

Word Attack

+s Add **s** to each word below to make the new words. Add **e** to **glass** before you write the **s**.

apartment ____________ bank ____________

door ____________ restaurant ____________

glass ____________ window ____________

+ed Write the words below with the ending **ed**. Add one more **p** to **stop** before the ending. The word **like** already has an **e**, so just add **d** to this word.

stop ____________ lock ____________

like ____________ park ____________

+ing Write these words with an **ing** ending. Take the **e** away from **describe** before you add **ing**.

camp ____________ start ____________

park ____________ describe ____________

16

Worktext page 16

+er Write the words below with an **er** ending. Because **late** already has an **e**, just add **r**.

own ____________ late ____________

+'s Write **César** with **'s** to show that something belongs to César. Write the new word in the sentence below.

Give to César what is ____________.

2=1 You know the words **to** and **night**. Write them together to make a new word.

to + night = ____________

1+1 You can write the words **we are** as one word: **we're**. You can write the words **will not** as one word: **won't**. Write each of these as one word and then as two.

we're ____________ = ____________ ____________

won't ____________ = ____________ ____________

17

Worktext page 17

3. THE OLD GREEN BUILDING, PART 1

Mike was 17 years old. He was strong and fast and full of life. When he wanted to do something, he just did it. Why stop to think? Whatever came up, he could handle it. That was the feeling Mike had about himself. Most of the time, he was right.

César was 16 years old. He was short and had glasses. Most people used the word **careful** to describe him. When César came to a room, he stopped at the door and looked the place over. He thought about everything that might happen and what he would do and say. That's just the kind of guy he was. He wanted to be like Mike—scared of nothing. But he just wasn't.

Even so, the boys were good friends. So what if they were different? As kids, they used to play baseball together in the park next to the school. These days, they liked to hang at the corner close to César's house. There, they would watch cars, talk to girls, and listen to a big radio. Sometimes, other guys would come by, and they would all listen to music together.

Both boys wanted to get out of the neighborhood someday. They talked about good jobs they might get and the money they might make. But, of course, you need money to make money. Money was one thing Mike and César didn't have.

Then one day, the two were alone on the corner. Mike said, "Hey, César, you know about that old green building up on 9th and Page?"

"Of course I know it."

César could picture the place. It used to have restaurants on the ground floor and apartments for rent on the next two stories. Then the city shut it down. There were lots of things wrong with the place. By law, the owner had to fix it, but he never had the money. So the doors stayed locked.

"What about it?" said César. He could tell Mike was up to something.

18

Worktext page 18

"Did you ever see anyone going in or out of it?" Mike asked.

"No."

"Anyone in the windows?"

"Of course not. No one lives there."

"Right. That's what got me thinking—" Mike put one hand in his pocket.

"Yes?" said César. "Thinking what?"

"That it might be a good hiding place."

César started to laugh. "What do you want to hide?"

"I don't want to hide anything. I want to find something." Mike stopped and looked César in the face. "Didn't you hear about that guy last week? The one in the news? You must have seen something about it on TV. He hit a bank on the south side. They say he got away with $100,000."

"I don't remember," said César. "Maybe."

"The cops caught him right up here on Page Street."

"So he didn't really get away with anything," César pointed out.

"Oh, but he did," said Mike. "You see, the money wasn't on him when he got caught. The cops think he has a hiding place in this neighborhood. That's the word on the street. The cops are going around looking for people he might know. So far, they have not found any. You know what I think?"

"I don't even want to guess," says César.

"I don't think he knows anyone in this neighborhood. I think he might have put his stolen money in that old building."

"You're kidding. The green one?"

"Why not? You are right when you say no one lives there. No one ever goes into that place. He was right by it when he got caught. The old green building would be a great place to hide something. That's where the money must be. I was thinking—"

"I can guess. You want to go into that building and look for money."

"Hey! You're way ahead of me! Good going, César!" Mike tried to shake César's hand.

But César pulled back. "I never said—"

"Now here is the thing," Mike cut in. "We can't go in by day. Other guys will see us and want to get in on this. It's best to go in at night. See? We—"

19

Worktext page 19

César could feel the cold going right to his bones. The thought of going into that old building scared him. The dark scared him. The two together scared him. But he didn't want to say anything. He didn't want Mike to start kidding him about these things. "Mike," he said, "even if we find the money, it won't belong to us."

"Of course not. But the bank will give $10,000 to anyone who finds the money. That's enough for a new car!"

"But what if the guy was not working alone? What if we break into that building and find a gang meeting going on?"

"That's why we go in at night! See? They're not going to be there at night. Guys that steal from banks are rich. They're not into camping in some dirty old building. They hide their money and go home to a fancy apartment. But look, if you don't want to come with me, César—"

"Well, I just think we should—"

"If you're scared of the dark—" said Mike.

"Don't make me laugh!" César cut in fast.

"If you want to stay home where it's safe, just say so," Mike went on. "You can hide in your house and watch TV, OK? But me? I want to be the guy they show on TV. I can hear it now: **Neighborhood boy finds outlaw hiding place. Details at 10:00.** Well, if I get money out of this, don't be asking for any. You know? I'll let you ride in my new car. That's all."

"I'm not scared." César got the words in at last. "I never said I was scared. I just said—"

"Good! Then it's you and me together! César, César, I can always count on you," said Mike. "You're a real friend."

"I guess," said César.

"So I'll come by around 8:00," said Mike. "Be ready, OK? We'll get something to eat and hang around for awhile. Then at 11:00, we'll go over to this place, OK?"

"I'll be ready," said César.

20

Worktext page 20

Meeting Characters

In the beginning of a story, you meet the characters. These are the people in the story. **The Old Green Building** is about two characters. Write their names below. Under each name, write three details that describe the character. Use details from below.

____________	____________
____________	____________
____________	____________
____________	____________
____________	____________
____________	____________
____________	____________

thinks he can handle whatever comes up	is careful
is strong, fast, and full of life	is 16 years old
wants to be more like his friend	is 17 years old

Describing the Setting

Every story takes place somewhere at some time. This is called the **setting**. Most stories let you know something about time and place right from the beginning. When and where is **The Old Green Building** set? Pick one of the settings below. Write it on the line.

1492, an African country
Today, some American city
Today, a farm somewhere

____

What made you pick this setting? Get together with a friend who is reading the story, too. Talk about the story. What details point to the setting? See if you can write down one or more details below.

Time: ____________________

Place: ____________________

21

Worktext page 21

Level 6

LESSON 6.4

OBJECTIVE

- Students practice and apply skills to an extended passage

MATERIALS

Worktext 6, pages 22–24
Teacher's Manual, pages 266–267, 333
Practice Lesson 6.4, pages 73–74 of the Worktext
Egg timer (Reteach)

SKILLS REVIEW

- Before reading, you may wish to review these words that apply phonics skills: *walked, called, going, don't, waiting, pointed, lets, sometimes, bags, camping, it's, going, dark, building, César's, we're, anything, nothing, waited, let's, bigger, somehow, windows, doors, boys, words, laughing, someone, pushed, helped, looked, stars.* Have students review the Memory Chips they have learned so far. Then ask: **What do you think will happen when the boys go to the old green building?**
- While reading, have students make pictures in their minds of what is happening in the story.
- After reading, have students complete the Comprehension Exercises (What's the Problem? and Looking Ahead) on Worktext page 24.

For further practice, have students complete Practice Lesson 6.4 on pages 73–74 of the Worktext. Answers can be found in the Answer Key on pages 358–359 of this *Teacher's Manual.*

RETEACH

If students need further review of phonics skills, you may wish to use the following activity:

Base Words and Endings *s, ed, ing, er, 's*

Base Word Match-up Write the following words and endings on index cards: **Mack**, **Kay**, **own**, **late**, **camp**, **park**, **start**, **describe**, **stop**, **like**, **lock**, **window**, **restaurant**, **bank**, **apartment**, **door**, **glass**, **stick**, **steak**, **join**, **door**, **s**, **es**, **ed**, **ing**, **er**, **'s**. Lay the cards face up on a table. Begin the timer and have partners work together. One partner makes a new word with a base word and ending, and the other partner writes the word, making any necessary spelling changes. At the end of three minutes, check the spelling for each word, and count the number of new words made. Then have partners exchange roles.

CONNECTION

Response to Reading

- Have students write predictions of what they think will happen next in the story.
- Student volunteers can share their predictions with the class.

Literature

- Students may enjoy reading or listening to books about other adventures. *Robinson Crusoe* and *The Three Musketeers* are available in softcover texts and on audiocassette from Pearson's *Pacemaker™ Classics.*
- Students may use the Book Report reproducible found on page 333 of this *Teacher's Manual* to record their responses to the books they read.

Independent Reading

- Encourage students to read for pleasure. Pearson's *BesTellers I, II, III,* and *IV* series is a collection of 40 easy-to-read, high-interest books. The series covers a wide variety of genres, including mystery, suspense, science fiction, and adventure. The controlled vocabulary and concept level make the books ideal for ESL students as well. See page xvii of the *Teacher's Manual* for additional titles.
- After reading, you may ask students to describe the characters, setting, and plot as they learned in Lessons 6.3 and 6.4.

4. THE OLD GREEN BUILDING, PART 2

"Good night, Mom," César called out as he walked through the door.

"Where are you going?" she called back.

"Out with Mike."

"Don't stay out too late," she said.

Mike was waiting for César down the street. "Look what I got," he said. He pointed to a long red car.

"Where did you get that?" César asked.

"My dad lets me drive it sometimes. I got some bags to put the money in."

"I got a camping light," said César. "It's going to be dark in that building."

"Good," said Mike. Then Mike saw the look on César's face. "Hey, lighten up. We're not out to break the law or anything. We're going to do some good."

César said nothing more. He just let Mike drive through the darkness. They ate at a restaurant. Then they got to the old green building a little after 11:00. Mike found a place to park in front of the building. They waited for a car to go by.

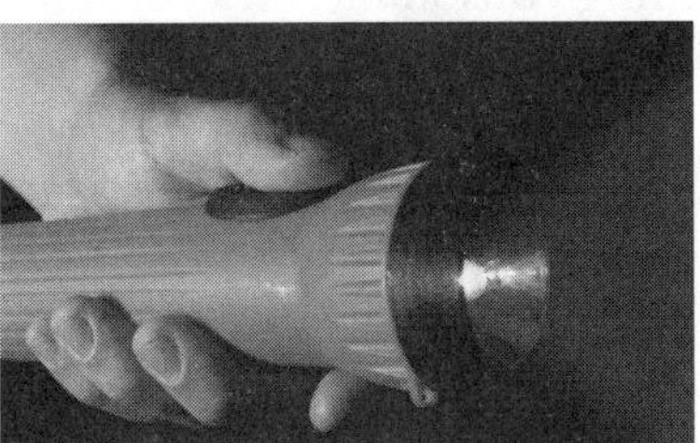

22

Worktext page 22

Another car came along, and they waited for that one, too—and another one. After that, they were alone.

"Let's go," said Mike.

Somehow, the building looked bigger in the dark. There was wood over the front windows and doors. The boys could not get into the building from this side. César pointed his light at the door and saw some words. "Keep Out," they said. "Building is not safe."

Mike let out a little laugh. "Right," he said, "as if words can keep us out."

These words could keep me out, César thought. But he said nothing to Mike. He didn't want his friend laughing at him.

Mike said, "Come around to the back. Turn off that light for now. Someone is going to see it. Wait till we get in."

They made their way along the side of the building. There was water on the ground. The air was dark. Behind the building they found a big lot with 20 or 30 cars in it. The back windows of the building had no wood over them. Mike found one that was not even locked. He pushed it up and went in. Then he helped César get in, too. The boys looked around. They were in a long dark room. The front windows were big, but the wood over them shut out the light from the street. The back windows were small. But a little light came through them. It was only the light from the stars and from other buildings far away.

23

Worktext page 23

What's the Problem?

The things that happen in a story are called the **plot**. Often, there is a problem that drives the plot along. The characters are scared of something. Or they want something that is hard to get. Or they face something that could hurt them. We keep reading to find out what they are going to do about the problem. What is the problem in **The Old Green Building**? Read the sentences below. Circle the one that tells what the real problem is in this story. Write the sentence on the lines.

César is scared to go into the green building.
Mike has to get the money before César does.
The cops are after Mike and César.

____

____

____

____

____

Looking Ahead

Some details in a story make you look ahead. They make you think about bad things that could happen. Here are some details from **The Old Green Building**. Do any of them make you think something bad will happen? Which ones? Circle them.

The building is locked.
No light comes in through the front windows.
The night is dark and cold.
The building is green.
Words on the front door say that the building is not safe.
There is a parking lot behind the building.

Talk the story over with a friend. Would you both circle the same details? Do you think something bad is going to happen to Mike and César? What might happen? Why do you think so?

24

Worktext page 24

LESSON 6.5

OBJECTIVES

- Students will decode and blend words containing the *ow*, *eet*, and *op* phonograms
- Students will apply endings *s*, *ing*, *ly*, *en*, and *ed* to base words to form new words
- Students will recognize and form contractions
- Students will use context clues to read unfamiliar words

PHONICS VOCABULARY

don't	scared	feeling	couldn't	pushed
boys	eyes	stairs	going	started
follow	didn't	it's	voices	wanted
they're	wouldn't	we're	thinking	hands
stopped	moved	suddenly	pulled	walked
what's	means	slowly	you've	hearing
building	let's	spiders	can't	looking
walking	windows	breaking	turned	feet
called	happened	I'm	sticks	lines
fallen	knees	pointed	webs	slow
ones	lots	rocks	moving	street
hasn't	sounded	written	follows	meet
following	secret	top	giving	pushing
standing				

WORDS TO KNOW

feet	follow	gun	main	paper
slow	secret	soon	stairs	storm
sudden	top	very	web	

MATERIALS

Worktext 6, pages 25–31
Teacher's Manual, pages 268–270
Practice Lesson 6.5, pages 75–76 of the Worktext

TEACH

- Using Worktext pages 25–26, introduce students to the vocabulary words. Say each word, and have students repeat it after you. Give students an opportunity to practice writing the words.
- Students can organize their Memory Chips, found in the back of the Worktext. They can divide them into words that have one and two syllables. Then have them sort the words by beginning sounds.

Worktext pages 25–26 can also be used to reinforce spelling. Use the five-step process detailed on page 71 of this *Teacher's Manual.*

Phonograms *ow, eet, op*

Write this sentence on the board, and read it aloud: **I know the clock is slow.** Ask students what two words rhyme. (*know, slow*) Ask students what long vowel sound they hear. (*long* o) Point to the letters *ow* and tell students that these letters can have the long *o* sound. Then write these sentences on the board: **A beet is sweet. I will stop and mop.** Have students identify the two words that rhyme in each sentence and circle the letters that are the same in each of the two words. Make sure students understand that the letters *ee* make the long *e* sound.

Blending Write the word **slow** on the board. Point your finger to the letters in *slow* as you say the word, segmenting the sounds: /*sl*/ /*o*/. Repeat, using *feet* and *stop*. (/*f*/ /*e*/ /*t*/, /*st*/ /*o*/ /*p*/) Then work with students to make word ladders with each phonogram, substituting beginning consonants and consonant blends to make new words.

slow	feet	stop
know	sweet	mop
low	tweet	chop
grow	beet	hop

Endings *s, ing, ly, en, ed*

Remind students that they can add *s*, *ing*, *ly*, *en*, and *ed* as endings to words.

Make New Words Write these words on the board, and have students take turns adding the endings *s*, *ing*, *ly*, *en*, and *ed* to them to make new words: **break**, **follow**, **fall**, **slow**, **sudden**. (*breaks, breaking; follows, following, followed; falls, falling, fallen; slows, slowing, slowly, slowed; suddenly*) Have them use each word in a sentence.

Contractions

Remind students that they can sometimes shorten two words into one word. Write **wasn't** on the board, and ask students what two words it stands for. (*was not*)

Make New Words Write these word pairs on the board and have volunteers take turns making contractions of each: **has not**, **would not**, **you have**, **you are**. (*hasn't, wouldn't, you've, you're*)

PRACTICE

- Let students practice the new words they have learned and formed by completing the activities found on pages 25–27 of the Worktext.
- If students are experiencing difficulty with the Words to Know section on pages 25–26, you may wish to have them write the troublesome words on laminated Tic-Tac-Toe grids. Have each student play Tic-Tac-Toe with a partner, saying each word before marking an O or X.

For further practice, have students complete Practice Lesson 6.5 on pages 75–76 of the Worktext. Answers can be found in the Answer Key on page 359 of this *Teacher's Manual.*

APPLY

- Have students talk about the story concept in Lesson 6.4. Have them predict what they think will happen next. Ask: **What do you think will happen next?** Tell students they are going to use the words they have learned to find out.
- Ask students to read the story on pages 28–30 in the Worktext. Offer assistance if necessary, but encourage students to decode the words independently, using the clues and patterns they have learned.
- After students have completed reading the story, have them complete the Comprehension Exercises (Following the Plot and What Will Happen Next?) on page 31 in their Worktext. Answers can be found in the Answer Key on page 358 of this *Teacher's Manual.*

CONNECTION

Writing Give students an opportunity to write in their journals, recording how they would feel if they were in a strange, new place in total darkness like the characters in the selection "The Old Green Building, Part 3" on Worktext pages 28–30.

5. THE OLD GREEN BUILDING, PART 3

Try This

The ending sound in **how** is different from the ending sound in **know**, even though they are spelled the same. When you hear this ending sound, spelled **ow**, at the end of a word, sound it out both ways to see which one works. Try it with the words below. You know the first word. The other two rhyme with it. Write the new words after you read them.

throw ________ slow ________ follow ________

Letter Groups

feet The word **feet** sounds like **street** and **meet**. Write all three words, and circle the letter group that is the same in all of them.

feet ________ street ________ meet ________

stop You know the first two words below. The last one is new. Can you read it? Write all the words, and circle the letters that are in all of them.

stop ________ cop ________ top ________

Take a Guess

Read the sentence below, and see if you can guess the word in dark letters. Then write the word.

If you can keep a **secret**, I will tell you one. ________

Words to Know

	Look	Say	Picture	Write
feet	☐	☐	☐	________
follow fol-low	☐	☐	☐	________
gun	☐	☐	☐	________
main	☐	☐	☐	________

25

Worktext page 25

Worktext Pages 25–27

	Look	Say	Picture	Write
paper pa-per	☐	☐	☐	________
secret se-cret	☐	☐	☐	________
slow	☐	☐	☐	________
soon	☐	☐	☐	________
stairs	☐	☐	☐	________
storm	☐	☐	☐	________
sudden sud-den	☐	☐	☐	________
top	☐	☐	☐	________
very ver-y	☐	☐	☐	________
web	☐	☐	☐	________

Word Attack

+ing Make new words by adding the ending **ing** to the words below. Remember to take the **e** away from **give** before you write the ending.

break________ follow ________

give________ hear ________

push ________ stand ________

+ed Write **sound** with **ed** as an ending. ________

Write **turn** with **ed** as an ending. ________

+en Write **en** after **fall** to make a new word. ________

Add the ending **en** to the word **write**. First, take away the **e**. Then, add another **t**. Last, add **en**. (write **-e +t +en**) In the new word, the first part rhymes with **hit**. Read the new word.

write + en ________

26

Worktext page 26

+ly The letter group **ly** is an ending. Add **ly** to the words **slow** and **sudden**. Write the new words, and read them.

slow ________ sudden ________

+s Write **web** and **follow** with an **s** ending. Read the new words.

web ________ follow ________

1+1 You can write **has not** as one word: **hasn't**. You can write **would not** as one word: **wouldn't**. You can write **you have** as one word: **you've**. Write each set of words below as one word.

has not = ________would not = ________

you have = ________

27

Worktext page 27

Level 6

5. THE OLD GREEN BUILDING, PART 3

"Don't turn on that light," Mike said. "Someone on the outside might see it."

Or someone on the inside, thought César, giving his friend a look. *Someone with a gun.* He was scared, but he had to keep the feeling secret. He couldn't have Mike laughing at him. He just pushed the light into his pocket. Both boys stood in place. Soon, their eyes got used to the darkness. But they saw nothing. There was nothing in the room to see. Through an open door in the side wall, César could make out a dark hall. There were stairs in that hall, going up.

Mike started to move. "Follow me," he said.

But César raised his hand. "Wait! Listen!"

Mike waited. "Well?" he said at last. "What?"

"Didn't you hear it?" César said. "That noise?"

"It's the storm," said Mike. "The radio said there would be a storm tonight."

"No," said César, "I heard voices." Had it come from the hall? Or from another room? He tried to see into the darkness. He wanted so much to turn on his light.

Mike said, "That was someone in the parking lot. I heard a car door shut before. They're coming this way. They wouldn't come in here. I think we're alone in this building."

"Oh, good," said César. *Oh, bad,* he was thinking. He made his way toward the open door. His hands were out so that he could feel his way through the darkness. At the door, he stopped. Something very, very light had moved against his hand. Then—suddenly—he could tell what it was. He pulled his hand back as if from hot water.

"Mike," he said, "come here!"

Mike walked up to join him. "Keep your voice down. What is it?"

"Never mind about my voice. No one is going to hear us," said César. "Feel what's in the door."

28

Worktext page 28

Mike put out his hand. "A spider web?" he said.

"From side to side," César said. "From the floor all the way up. Anyone who goes through this door would break the web. Don't you see what this means?"

"I guess I do," said Mike slowly. "No one has gone through this door in awhile."

"Right. So those stories you've been thinking were wrong. No one has been inside this building. There is no money here. There is nothing to find. So let's get out of here."

"Spiders!" said Mike. "I can't stand them. You're right. Let's go."

César had his back to Mike and was still looking into the hall. He could hear his friend walking toward the front windows. Suddenly, he heard wood breaking. A scream cut through the air.

The scream had come from Mike. César turned. His friend was gone. He started to race to the place where Mike had been. But he pulled up short. He could not see two feet in front of him. Running in this darkness was the wrong thing to do. "Mike!" he called out. "Where are you?"

"César! Down here!"

"What happened?" Just then, César saw what looked like a dark place on the floor. It was a hole. "Did you fall through?"

"Like a rock. Watch yourself up there. The wood is just like paper."

"Are you OK?"

29

Worktext page 29

"I'm not hurt too badly. But I don't know if I can move."

"Why not? Did you break—"

"No, but I'm caught in something. I don't know what. It's all around me. It kind of sticks to me. You got that light? Turn it on. Point it down here, and let me see where I'm at."

César pulled the light out of his pocket and turned it on. He could see just where Mike had fallen through the floor. He must be in a room below the ground. César got down on his knees and started to move to the hole. He tried to be careful. The floor could give way at any time.

At last, he got close enough to see into the hole. He pointed his light down.

What he saw made a sick feeling well up inside him. The room down there was full of spider webs. It was so full of them that the air looked white. Yet, César saw little lines of yellow where the web caught the light. There was a hole through the middle of the webs, where Mike had fallen through.

There, way down below, was Mike. César could see that his friend was scared. His eyes were so big. Then César saw why his friend was scared. It wasn't just that the room was full of webs. The webs were full of spiders—big ones—lots of them. They looked like dark rocks. There was one really big spider on Mike. It was on his body. But it was moving toward his head.

30

Worktext page 30

Following the Plot

In most stories, the plot keeps building all through the middle part. New problems come up. Old problems become harder. Little problems give way to bigger ones. The plot keeps moving toward a point of highest excitement—a **turning point.** The sentences below describe what has happened in **The Old Green Building** so far. Put these sentences in the order they happened.

Mike falls through the floor.
César hears voices somewhere.
The room below is full of spider webs.
César sees a big spider on Mike.
César finds a spider web in an open door.

____

____

____

____

____

Now look at the sentences in the order that you have written them. Talk about the plot of this story with a friend. Is the excitement building up? Do you think the turning point has come yet? Why or why not?

What Will Happen Next?

Here are some things that could happen next. Which one do you think will happen? Circle the sentence. After you read the next part, look back at this page to see if you were right.

The spider will kill Mike.

César will run away.

César will learn something new about Mike.

31

Worktext page 31

LESSON 6.6

OBJECTIVE

- Students will practice and apply skills to an extended passage

MATERIALS

Worktext 6, pages 32–34
Teacher's Manual, pages 271–272, 330–331, 333
Practice Lesson 6.6, pages 77–78 of the Worktext
Tagboard, brad/fastener (Reteach)

SKILLS REVIEW

- Before reading, you may wish to review these words that apply phonics skills: *called, I'm, going, don't, words, shaking, isn't, it's, killer, spiders, likes, really, doesn't, gets, won't, you've, coming, I'll, locked, pushed, webs, bags, going, eyes, started, turned, moved, hands, feet, pointed, pulled, follow, didn't, following, stairs, window, turned, feeling.* Have students review the Memory Chips they have learned so far. Then ask: **What do you think happened to Mike?**
- While reading, encourage students to make pictures in their minds of what happens in the story.
- After reading, have students complete the Comprehension Exercise (Following the Plot) on Worktext page 34.

For further practice, have students complete Practice Lesson 6.6 on pages 77–78 of the Worktext. Answers can be found in the Answer Key on pages 358–359 of this *Teacher's Manual.*

RETEACH

If students need further review of phonics skills, you may wish to use the following activity:

Endings *ing, ed, en, ly, s*

Words on a Wheel Make two word wheels out of tagboard, one larger than the other. On the larger one, write the following endings: **ing**, **ed**, **en**, **ly**, **s**. On the smaller one, write the following base words: **web**, **follow**, **slow**, **sudden**, **write**, **turn**, **fall**, **sound**, **break**, **give**, **push**, **hear**, **stand**. Connect the two wheels with a brad. Then have students take turns turning the word wheel to make new words. They can write each word on a separate piece of paper.

CONNECTION

Response to Reading

- To reinforce students' understanding of the literary elements found in their reading material, have them complete the Story Map and Character Cluster reproducibles found on pages 330–331.
- Students will demonstrate an understanding of setting, characters, and plot by filling out the organizers.
- Students may share their completed organizers with the class.

Literature

- Students may enjoy reading or listening to other books with mystery themes. *Tales of Edgar Allan Poe* and *Frankenstein* are available in softcover texts and on audiocassette from Pearson's *Pacemaker*™ *Classics.*
- Students may use the Book Report reproducible found on page 333 of this *Teacher's Manual* to record their responses to the books they read.

Level 6

6. THE OLD GREEN BUILDING, PART 4

"Mike," César called out, "I'm going for help!"

"No! Don't go." Mike said the words in a small shaking voice. "There isn't time. This spider will be on my face soon. It's going to kill me, César."

"What? No way, man. There are no killer spiders in this part of the country. That thing is harmless."

"César?"

"What?"

"I have to tell you something. A secret. This is just between you and me."

"I don't think this is the time—"

"Believe me, César. This is the time to tell you. I'm scared of spiders."

"So am I. No one really **likes** spiders, do they?"

"No, I mean really scared. It's like a sickness. Even a picture of a spider does it to me. I mean, it doesn't have to be a killer spider—just any spider. If this thing gets on my face, it's all over. I won't make it. You've got to help me, César."

"OK, OK. I'm coming down. I'll find a way into that room somehow."

César went into the hall. He saw a door. It was locked. But he found a way to break it. He pushed the door open. He found himself face to face with a wall of spider webs. He would have to wear something over his face to go through this. But what? Then he thought of the paper bags that Mike was going to put money in. He got the bags. He cut a hole for his eyes in one of them. He put the bag over his head and started into the room. But the eye hole was of no use. He could not see through the spider webs anyway. He turned the bag around so that the hole was in back. "Mike!" he called. "Where are you?"

"Over here!" The sound came as if through a cloth. César moved toward the sound. He put his hands out to feel his way. At any time, he thought he might feel a spider. But all he could feel were the webs. Then his feet came up against something. He pointed the light down and saw a hand.

32

Worktext page 32

"Mike!"

The hand moved. It was Mike. César pulled his friend to his feet. Then he pushed a paper bag into his hand. "Put this over your head and follow me."

He didn't have to say the words. Mike was already following. They went up the stairs. They went through the room and through the window. Then, at last, they were out. Mike just stood there for a long time with his face turned up toward the sky. He could not get enough of the cold, clean air.

"You OK?" said César after a long while.

"I'll live," said Mike.

"Ready to go back inside and look for that money?" César said with a smile.

Mike said, "Not for all the gold in California."

Somehow, César had a feeling his friend would never again laugh at him for being too careful.

33

Worktext page 33

Following the Plot

The beginning of a story tells you about characters and setting. In the middle, the plot really takes off. It comes to a point of highest excitement—a turning point. Then comes the ending, which shows how the characters get past the problem. This is where you find out how everything comes out.

The sentences below give a summary of the plot in **The Old Green Building**. Write the words that go on the lines. You may write one word on each line or a group of words. Look back at the story as much as you need to.

BEGINNING: This story is about two boys named _________ and _____________. The boys make up their minds to look for money in _____________________________. Mike thinks the best time to go in would be _______________.

MIDDLE: The front door is _____________, so the boys get in through _____________________. Inside, they see an open _____________ in a side wall. César finds a ____________ that runs from side to side. Just then, ____________ falls through the floor into a room full of _________________. One big _______________ ends up on his body.

TURNING POINT: Mike tells César a big _____________. He is scared of ______________.

ENDING: ___________ puts a ___________ over his head and helps _______________ get out of the building. He knows that Mike will never again ____________________ for being too _________________.

34

Worktext page 34

LESSON 6.7

OBJECTIVES

- Students will decode and make new words containing the phonograms *ish*, *ing*, and *ong*
- Students will use context clues to figure out unfamiliar words
- Students will apply endings *s*, *es*, *ing*, *ed*, and *er* to base words to form new words
- Students will recognize and form contractions

PHONICS VOCABULARY

parts	woods	Ana's	washing	dishes
packing	bursts	turning	what's	happens
lived	miles	coming	you're	names
isn't	bigger	takes	she'll	screaming
she's	married	that's	news	things
turns	telling	knows	getting	laughs
burning	stops	breaks	playing	started
sings	plays	says	singing	placing
leaves	closes	makes	places	won't
played	washed	singer	they'll	I've
they've	picks	dish	sing	directions
sang	guitar	bands	describes	telephone

WORDS TO KNOW

Ana	dish	early	Mr.	young
guitar	since	sing	song	such
hi	ice	telephone	war	wash

MATERIALS

Worktext 6, pages 35–41
Teacher's Manual, pages 273–275
Practice Lesson 6.7, pages 79–80 of the Worktext

TEACH

- Using Worktext pages 35–36, introduce students to the vocabulary words. Give students an opportunity to practice writing the words.
- Students can organize their Memory Chips, found in the back of the Worktext. Say each word, having students repeat it after you. Then have students sort the words according to words that name persons, places, and things; words that show action; and words of greeting.

Worktext pages 35–36 can also be used to reinforce spelling. Use the five-step process detailed on page 71 of this *Teacher's Manual*.

Phonograms *ish*, *ing*, *ong*

Write these sentences on the board, and have a volunteer read them aloud: **I will finish washing the dish. Then I will sing a song.** Ask a volunteer to find the two words in the first sentence that rhyme. (*finish*, *dish*) Then have another volunteer circle *ish* in both words. Have students point to *sing*. Ask them to name a word that rhymes with *sing*. (*ring*, *thing*) Repeat with *song*.

Blending Have three groups work together to make a list of rhyming words for *sing*, *dish*, and *song*. Have them read their lists when they finish. (*sing*, *ring*, *fling*, *ding*, *wing*, *ping*; *song*, *long*, *strong*, *wrong*; *dish*, *wish*, *fish*, *finish*, *swish*)

Context Clues

Remind students that when they see an unfamiliar word, they can guess how to read the word by looking at the other words in the sentence and by looking at the beginning sound of the word. Write this sentence on the board and read it aloud, leaving out the word *guitar*: **Tom plays the guitar in a band.** Have students figure out the word from the other words around it.

Endings *s*, *es*, *ing*, *ed*, *er*

Remind students that *s*, *es*, *ing*, *ed*, and *er* can be added to words. Tell students that when a word ends in *ss*, *x*, *ch*, *sh*, or *s*, the ending *es* is added instead of *s*.

Make New Words Write these words in a chart and invite students to add *s*, *es*, *ing*, *ed*, and *er* to the words to make new words.

Base Word	+ s or + es	+ ing	+ ed	+ er
dish	dishes	dishing	dished	
sing	sings	singing		singer
pack	packs	packing	packed	packer
describe	describes	describing	described	

Contractions

Remind students that they can make a smaller word out of two words. Write these words on the board, and have students tell what two words they stand for: **wasn't**, **aren't**, **didn't**. (*was not*, *are not*, *did not*)

Make New Words Write these words on the board, and have students write contractions for each set: **they are**, **we will**, **she will**, **they have**, **they will**. (*they're*, *we'll*, *she'll*, *they've*, *they'll*)

PRACTICE

- Let students practice the new words they have learned and formed by completing the activities found on pages 35–36 of the Worktext.
- If students are experiencing difficulty with the Words to Know section on pages 35–36, write scrambled letters like these on the board: **hids** (*dish*), **gunoy** (*young*), **chus** (*such*), **peeltehno** (*telephone*). Then have students unscramble the

Level 6

letters to make the words on their Memory Chips. They can then write each word.

For further practice, have students complete Practice Lesson 6.7 on pages 79–80 of the Worktext. Answers can be found in the Answer Key on page 359 of this *Teacher's Manual.*

APPLY

- Have students discuss the story concept. Ask: **Have you ever had something really important to do that you couldn't do because you had to go to a family function? What happened?** Tell students they are going to use the words they have learned to read a play about a girl who wants to go out with her friends, but her mother insists she go to her great grandma's birthday party instead.
- Ask students to read the play on pages 37–40 in the Worktext. If you wish, have partners work together to read aloud the parts of Ana and her mother. Offer assistance if necessary, but encourage students to decode the words independently, using the clues and patterns they have learned.
- After students have completed reading the play, have them complete the Comprehension Exercises (Finding the Parts of a Play and What's the Problem?) on page 41 in their Worktext. Answers can be found in the Answer Key on page 358 of this *Teacher's Manual.*

7. YOUNG AND OLD, PART 1

Letter Groups

Look at the words in each group below. Circle the letter group that is in all the words. Read the new word that is in dark letters. Write it in the sentence.

fish	finish	**dish**	Finish the fish on your ________.
thing	ring	**sing**	They ________ an ad for a ring.
long	strong	**song**	What a long ________ they sing!

Take a Guess

Use the other words in the sentences to help you guess the words in dark letters. Test your guess by looking at the first letter in the word. What sound does it make?

Tom plays electric **guitar** in a band.
Call me on the **telephone** some time.

Words to Know

	Look	Say	Picture	Write
Ana	☐	☐	☐	________
dish	☐	☐	☐	________
early ear-ly	☐	☐	☐	________
guitar gui-tar	☐	☐	☐	________
hi	☐	☐	☐	________
ice	☐	☐	☐	________
Mr.	☐	☐	☐	________
since	☐	☐	☐	________
sing	☐	☐	☐	________
song	☐	☐	☐	________
such	☐	☐	☐	________
telephone tel-e-phone	☐	☐	☐	________

35

Worktext page 35

Worktext Pages 35–37

	Look	Say	Picture	Write
war	☐	☐	☐	________
wash	☐	☐	☐	________
young	☐	☐	☐	________

Word Attack

+s Write these words with an **s** ending. Add an **e** to **dish** before you add **s**.

band ________ dish ________
describe ________ mile ________
pick ________ sing ________
direction ________

+ing Write **ing** after the words below to make new words.

pack ________ sing ________
wash ________ turn ________

+ed Write these words with the ending **ed**.

play ________ wash ________

+'s To show that something belongs to **Ana**, write **'s** after **Ana**. Write this new word in the sentence below.

The box was left at ________ house.

+er Write the word **sing** with the ending **er**. ________

1+1 Two words can sometimes be written as one. Some words of this kind are shown below. Write the one word that can take the place of each two words. Circle the letters that you left out of the two words.

I have = I've ________
she will = she'll ________
they will = they'll ________
they have = they've ________

36

Worktext page 36

7. YOUNG AND OLD, PART 1

CHARACTERS:
Ana Teller, a 16-year-old girl
Mrs. Teller, Ana's mom
Wilma, Ana's great-grandma
Mark Cage, an 18-year-old boy
Inez Cruz, a 43-year-old woman

SETTING:
This play has two parts. Part 1 is set in the home of Mr. and Mrs. Teller. Part 2 is set at Green Woods Park, a home for old people. This is where Ana's great-grandma, Wilma, lives.

Part 1
(Saturday, around 9 AM. Mrs. Teller is alone in the kitchen. She is washing dishes and packing food into a box. Suddenly, Ana bursts into the room.)

ANA: Mom! Do I really have to go?

MRS. TELLER: (turning) Have to? You should want to. What's wrong with you? Your great-grandma is going to be 100 years old today! You think that happens every day? How many people do you know who lived to be 100?

ANA: I know. It's a great day, Mom. But—

MRS. TELLER: But nothing. Everyone in the family is going to be there. And not just the ones from these parts. Family will be coming from miles around. Why, there are some coming from California and Mississippi. You're going to see people you never even heard the names of.

ANA: How can they be family if we don't even know their names?

MRS. TELLER: Family isn't just a name. It's who you come from—what you're part of. Your great-grandma had eight kids. They all got married, had kids of their own, and—well! This family is bigger than you can shake a stick at. You ask if I know their names? I can't even count them all. But they're all going

37

Worktext page 37

to be out there at Green Woods. So don't tell me this is not a big day.

ANA: I know it's a big day. I don't mind about the day—really, Mom. But the night? Why can't we come back early? Do I have to be out there with no one to even talk to on a Saturday night—just me and a lot of screaming little kids and a lot of—

MRS. TELLER: A lot of what?

ANA: Well, old people.

MRS. TELLER: Ana! Your dad and I will be there, and we are not old!

ANA: Oh, Mom—you know what I mean! You're not kids!

MRS. TELLER: What about that Inez Cruz—that woman who takes care of your great-grandma? You get along with her, don't you? She'll be there.

ANA: She's 43, Mom! She's your age! She's married! Really! Why can't we get home by 6:00 or something.

MRS. TELLER: Ana, I don't know how to break this news to you: the world is not here to give you a good time. There are things you just have to do in life. And when your great-grandma turns 100, you have to be there. That's just the way it is. Why are you making such a noise about this?

ANA: It's not that I don't care about Great-grandma—

MRS. TELLER: But?

ANA: But this is the biggest Saturday night of the year. And if we don't get back till 9:00, it will be too late for the show.

MRS. TELLER: What show?

ANA: Don't you remember? At the Gold Circle! Mom, I've been telling you for weeks. All my friends are going. Kate can get us in for free. She knows this guy at the door. She's getting all the girls in for free. And—

MRS. TELLER: What do you mean, show? A play?

ANA: **(laughs)** Mom, the things you say! No, it's a band called the Burning Scream—

38

Worktext page 38

MRS. TELLER: Called what? **(She stops washing and turns to Ana, her mouth in a frown.)** Burning Scream? What kind of band would have a name like that? Is that one of those bands that uses dirty words and breaks things?

ANA: Mom, you ask that about every band. The answer is no—they don't. You act like there has not been one good band since you were 16. You—

MRS. TELLER: Young woman, in those days, bands played music! They didn't—

ANA: Burning Scream plays music. Good music with a hot beat. And their words are so cool. They're against war and violence and things like that. They don't even have a CD out, but they have a hit playing on the radio. They have never been on TV. Isn't that cool? Because the guy that started this band—Ice Machine, they call him—sings and plays guitar. He says music has to be live to be real. He says—

Ice Machine
and the
Burning Scream
Gold Circle 9:00 PM Saturday

39

Worktext page 39

MRS. TELLER: Ice Machine?

ANA: That's just what people call him. It's just a name, Mom. He got some friends together and just started singing on a street corner. Then the word got around. Now, everyone in California is talking about them. They're only going to be here for one night. How can I miss them?

MRS. TELLER: Somehow, you will have to, Ana. People are going to ask about you, and how will it look if you're not there? What am I going to tell them? "Oh, Ana couldn't be here. She had to see Ice Scream and his Burning Machine." Grow up. I'm off to get ready now. You had better do the same. Dad is packing the car. We want to be on the freeway by 11:00.

(Mrs. Teller leaves. The door closes. Ana makes a face.)

ANA: OK, Mom— **(Ana picks up a telephone and places a call.)** Hi, Jen? This is Ana. She won't go for it. I did talk to her, but she said no. I should never have told her the name of the band. That's what did me in. I guess you had better count me out. I know. Me, too.

40

Worktext page 40

Finding the Parts of a Play

A play is a way of **showing** a story. People take the parts of characters and act out the story. When you read a play, you are really reading directions for putting on a play. Some parts of these directions tell you about the setting. Some parts tell you what the characters do. But most parts of a play give the words for the characters.

Here are four groups of words from the play **Young and Old**. Write each group under the heading that tells what it is.

Ana makes a face.
Saturday, around 9 AM.
"Young woman, in those days bands played music!"
"Oh, Mom! Do I have to go?"

Something that Mrs. Teller says: ____________________

____

Something that Ana says: ____________________

____

Something that a character does: ____________________

____

A detail about the setting: ____________________

____

What's the Problem?

A play has all the same parts as a short story: characters, setting, and plot. In a short story, the plot often comes out of problems for the characters. The same can be said of plays. Think about the problem in this play. Which of the sentences below would you use to describe it? Circle that sentence.

Ana doesn't have enough money to see Burning Scream.

Ana can't see Burning Scream because she has to go to Green Woods.

Ana and her friend Jen are interested in the same boy.

41

Worktext page 41

Level 6

LESSON 6.8

OBJECTIVE

- Students will practice and apply skills as they read a play

MATERIALS

Worktext 6, pages 42–47
Teacher's Manual, pages 276–278, 330–331, 333
Practice Lesson 6.8, pages 81–82 of the Worktext
Two bags (numbered 1 and 2) (Reteach)

SKILLS REVIEW

- Before reading, you may wish to review these words that apply phonics skills: *doors, woods, building, talking, drinks, sitting, things, looking, steals, turns, looks, smiles, doesn't, don't, Teller, always, what's, eyes, you're, walking, talked, she's, friends, interested, I'm, comes, pushing, legs, shaking, feeling, ways, likes, wants, missing, turning, holds, strong, called, didn't, saying, wanted, wouldn't, killed, faster, that's, worked, trying, you'll, hasn't, burning, ring, heading, falls, pushing, it's, he's, runs, stops, I've, hanging.* Have students review the Memory Chips they have learned so far. Then ask: **What do you think is going to happen to Ana at her great-grandma's party?**
- While reading, have students predict what they think will happen next.
- After reading, have students complete the Comprehension Exercise (Following the Plot) on Worktext page 47.

For further practice, have students complete Practice Lesson 6.8 on pages 81–82 of the Worktext. Answers can be found in the Answer Key on pages 358–359 of this *Teacher's Manual.*

RETEACH

If students need further review of phonics skills, you may wish to use the following activity:

Contractions

Bag It Up! Write the following words on index cards, and put them in one bag: **I**, **she**, **he**, **they**, **can**, **do**, **did**, **you**. In a second bag, place these words, each written on one card: **will**, **have**, **are**, **not**. Have students take turns choosing a card from Bag 1. Then have them choose a card from Bag 2. Have them read both words and see if they can make a contraction with them. If they can, write the word on the board and have the student choose another card in Bag 2. Repeat, until no contraction can be made. Return all cards to Bag 2. Then have another student choose a word from Bag 1, and repeat the process.

CONNECTION

Response to Reading

- To reinforce students' understanding of the literary elements found in their reading material, have them complete the Story Map and Character Cluster reproducibles found on pages 330–331.
- Students will demonstrate an understanding of setting, characters, and plot by filling out the organizers.
- Students may share their completed organizers with the class.

Literature

- Students may enjoy reading or listening to other plays. *A Doll's House* and *Macbeth* are available in softcover texts and on audiocassette from Pearson's *Pacemaker*™ *Classics.*
- Students may use the Book Report reproducible found on page 333 of this *Teacher's Manual* to record their responses to the plays.

8. YOUNG AND OLD, PART 2

Part 2
(This part of the play takes place outdoors at Green Woods. A big building and some woods can be seen in the back. People are sitting around with drinks talking. Ana is sitting next to the mountain of things that people have given to her great-grandma, Wilma. Close by is Mark Cage, a good-looking young man, about 18 years old.

Ana steals a look at Mark. But when he turns his head, she looks away. Then he steals a look at her. But just as she turns to him, he looks away. Ana steals another look at Mark—and finds him looking right at her. He smiles. She doesn't.)

42

Worktext page 42

ANA: What are you looking at?

MARK: Come on. We were both looking.

ANA: Do I know you from somewhere?

MARK: I don't think so. My name is Mark Cage. Who are you?

ANA: Ana Teller. I do know you. I have seen your face somewhere.

MARK: People always say that. I just have that kind of face. You don't look too happy. What's wrong?

ANA: What's wrong? What do you think? You and I must be the only young people at this place. I can hardly keep my eyes open. Well, you must understand. How come you're here, anyway? Did your mom and dad make you come?

MARK: Well, no. My great-grandma asked me to stop in. I had no idea I was going to be walking into such a thing. But I talked to Wilma a little—is that her name? She's really interesting to talk to—your great-grandma.

ANA: My great-grandma? Isn't she your great-grandma, too?

MARK: No, she and my great-grandma were best friends as girls. My great-grandma is kind of sick now. She can hardly talk. But Wilma! She's a real ball of fire.

ANA: (more interested now) So you're not part of my family?

MARK: No, I'm a friend of the family, you might say.

ANA: You're not from these parts?

MARK: No, I—oh, here comes your great-grandma now.

(Inez Cruz comes in, pushing Wilma.)

WILMA: (in a high, shaky voice) Ana! You made time for an old woman, did you? I see you found the boy.

ANA: Yes, I did, Great-grandma. How are you feeling today?

WILMA: How do you think? I'm 100 years old. How would you feel in my place? Old, girl! No two ways about it. Old!

43

Worktext page 43

INEZ: (to Mark, smiling) Don't mind her. She always sounds mad when she's talking to people she likes.

WILMA: (to Mark) Ana is put out, young man. She wants to be in the city, but she had to come out here. I hear she's missing a good music show tonight.

ANA: (turning red) Great-grandma, I—

WILMA: (holds up her hand to stop Ana) Not another word, Ana. I know how you feel. Believe it or not, I was young in my day. I told your mom and dad, "Let the young be young!" I said, "It only comes one time! I should know!" **(turns to Mark)** When I was 15, like Ana here—

ANA: I'm 16, Great-grandma.

WILMA: As I said, when I was 16, I had a boyfriend. Oh, he looked very much like you, young man. Strong! Good-looking! He was 16, too, just like you.

MARK: I'm 18.

WILMA: Whatever. This was at the time of the Great War. I mean World War I. They called it the Great War, see? Because it was the biggest war anyone had heard of. They didn't know World War II was coming up, made the first one look like a dog show. Anyway, what was I saying? Oh, yes—my Tom wanted to join the Navy, but they wouldn't let him because he was only 16. So Tom went back and told them he was 18, and they let him in. Two days after he got on his ship, he was killed. I still remember that boy. That's why I always say, **Don't grow up any faster than you have to.** I'm here to tell you young people. Life is not a race to see who can get old first. That's what I told your mom, Ana. She wouldn't listen. But here you are, talking to this good-looking boy now. So maybe it worked out for the best. Can I tell you something, Mark?

INEZ: Wilma, we have to get going. We—

WILMA: (turning back to look at Inez) Now, you just keep your teeth in your mouth, Miss Cruz. I am trying to have a word with this boy. Now, Mark.

MARK: Yes?

44

Worktext page 44

Level 6

WILMA: You hold on to this girl. You'll be sorry if you let her get away. She's a good one.

ANA: (very red now) Great-grandma!

WILMA: OK, Inez. Let's move on.

(Inez and Wilma go on. Wilma has a happy smile on her face. Ana and Mark can hardly look each other in the eye. Both are red in the face.)

ANA: Well, that was my great-grandma. As you can see—

MARK: She hasn't lost much.

ANA: That's one way to look at it.

MARK: Life is not a race to see who can get old first. I like that line. What was that about a show you're going to miss?

ANA: Oh, there is this band that all my friends are going to see. They're only going to be in town for one show. Ice Machine and the the Burning Scream—they are so cool! Did you ever hear of them?

MARK: (smiles) I believe that name has a ring to it. But why do you have to miss it? The show doesn't start till 9:00.

ANA: My mom and dad won't leave till 9:00. They made up their mind, and nothing is going to make them change it. You know how old people are—set in their ways.

MARK: Do you have to stay till they leave? Why can't you leave before?

ANA: Get real. We're 20 miles from the city. How am I going to get back on my own?

MARK: Well— **(looks at Ana, then looks away)** you could ride with me. I'm heading back around 6:00.

ANA: You have a car? **(then her face falls)** Oh!

MARK: What?

ANA: It's no use. Forget it.

MARK: What's no use?

45

Worktext page 45

ANA: The show is sold out. How could I forget? My friends have a pass. But I already told them to count me out. They must have gotten someone to take my place by now.

MARK: Is that all? I can get you through the door.

ANA: What? How?

MARK: Well, I know some people.

ANA: At the Gold Circle? How could that be? You're from California. Oh, wait. I get it. No—it can't be. Do you mean—no. You don't mean you know someone in the band! Do you?

MARK: I know them all.

ANA: Even Ice Machine?

MARK: I know him like I know myself.

ANA: Do you think I could meet him or something? Oh, look at me, always pushing. I'm sorry. If he's your friend, I guess the last thing he wants is for you—

MARK: No, no, it's not that. You could meet him. It's just that—well, the thing is, Ana, he might not be the way you think. I mean, what he does up there when he's playing—that's a show. Outside the band, he's just a guy.

(His voice runs down. He stops talking.)

ANA: (looking hard at Mark) What did you say your name was again?

MARK: Well, my name is Mark Cage, but—

ANA: Oh, no. Oh, wait. Suddenly I think I—yes! I know where I've seen you before! I'm going to die. You're him, aren't you?

MARK: (hanging his head) I play under the name of Ice Machine, yes. But I am not him. I like to think that he is me—Mark Cage.

46

Worktext page 46

Following the Plot

Here are some things that happen in the play **Young and Old**. Write the sentences in the order that they happened.

Mark says he will give Ana a ride back to the city.
Ana is made to go to Green Woods.
Ana finds out that Mark Cage is really Ice Machine.
Ana meets Mark Cage at Green Woods.
Great-grandma Wilma tells a story about an old boyfriend.

____
____
____
____
____
____
____
____
____
____

Which sentence tells about the turning point in the play? Circle the sentence. Then get together with a group of friends or others in your class who have read the play. Do you all see the same turning point? Why or why not?

47

Worktext page 47

MIDWAY NOVEL Caged

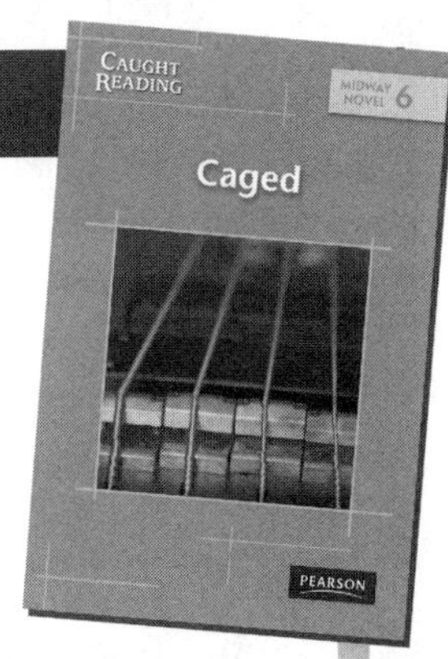

MATERIALS
Midway Novel 6, *Caged*
Teacher's Manual, page 279
Assessment Manual, Midway Assessment 6, pages 106–111

Summary *Cruz Cage, a rock star, falls for Venus Standwell. She is unlike any other woman he knows. Cruz and Venus go out together. At the end of the date, someone tries to kill them. The bad guy is caught by the police. After what they have been through together, Cruz and Venus become a couple.*

REVIEW AND ASSESSMENT

- Have students review their Memory Chips with a partner. Depending on your students' needs, review the following skills covered in Lessons 1–8: phonograms *ool, eat, oor, ark, ow, eet, op, ish, ing,* and *ong;* compound words; contractions; context clues; singular possessives; and endings with *s, ing, er, ed, est, en, ity, es, ly,* and *y.*

If you wish to assess students' progress at this point, use the *Assessment Manual,* pages 106–111. For students who need additional support, you may use the Reteach activities from previous lessons.

INTRODUCE THE NOVEL

Invite students to preview the book by reading the title, looking at the illustrations, and reading aloud the captions. Begin a discussion of story concepts by asking questions such as:

- **What do you think it would be like to be a rock star?**
- **Would you date a rock star? Why or why not?**

CHECK COMPREHENSION

Chapter 1 Who is Cruz Cage? (*He is a rock star in the band CAGE.*)

Chapter 2 How did Cruz become a star? (*Tyrone Miles heard him play at the Cherokee House, and he became a star.*)

Chapter 3 Why did the Cruz's car crash? (*A green FX-7 ran Cruz's car off the road, and it crashed into a building.*)

Chapter 4 What kind of person is Venus? (*She works hard, she studies hard, and she is conscientious. She is not impressed by rock stars.*)

Chapter 5 Why doesn't Venus jump at the chance to go out with Cruz? (*She thinks he is rich and good-looking but doesn't have much in his head.*)

Chapter 6 What happens when Cruz comes to see Venus again? (*The fans spot Cruz, and they push Venus out of the way to get to him.*)

Chapter 7 What do you think Spider Banks wants to do? (*He wants to hurt Cruz.*)

Chapter 8 Do you think Venus will fall for Cruz? Why or why not? (*Possible answers: Yes, because she goes out with him, and he's good-looking; no, because they are too different. He likes rock music, and she likes literature.*)

Chapter 9 Why is Fame and Fancy a good place to go on a date? (*Everyone thinks Cruz is impersonating himself.*)

Chapter 10 Why does Cruz envy Venus's way of life? (*He wishes he could do things without being recognized; he wants a quieter life.*)

Chapter 11 What happens after Cruz and Venus return to Rhymes? (*Spider Banks tries to run them over.*)

Chapter 12 Why do the reporters show up at Rhymes after the accident? (*Cruz Cage is big news, and everyone wants to know what happened.*)

Chapter 13 Why did Spider Banks want to harm Cruz? (*Spider Banks had written songs for the band, but Cruz wouldn't buy them.*)

Chapter 14 Why was Cruz without his bodyguards the night before? (*He wanted to be alone with Venus.*)

Chapter 15 How does Cruz show that he has changed during his concert in Arizona? (*He sings a love song that's different, and he is not drinking.*)

CONNECTION

Home/School Encourage students to bring home a copy of *Caged.* They might read the novel, or sections of the novel, to family members.

LESSON 6.9

OBJECTIVES

- Students will divide words into syllables
- Students will use context clues to figure out unfamiliar words
- Students will apply endings *ous, ment, s, er,* and *ing* to base words to form new words
- Students will recognize and form compound words

PHONICS VOCABULARY

Henson	standing	needs	years
talking	older	liking	looking
helper	someone	willing	remembers
explorer	trips	Greenland	parts
lands	eyes	books	friends
washing	dishes	miles	working
however	workers	Americans	feeling
always	excitement	places	something
freezing	country	frozen	explore
freezer	prove	helper	explorers
sleds	driving	famous	

WORDS TO KNOW

adventures	country	explore	freeze
frozen	Inuit	prove	sled
musk ox	north	Robert Peary	
Matthew Henson			

MATERIALS

Worktext 6, pages 48–53
Teacher's Manual, pages 280–282
Practice Lesson 6.9, pages 83–84 of the Worktext

TEACH

- Using Worktext pages 48–49, introduce students to the vocabulary words. Give students an opportunity to practice writing the words.
- Students can organize their Memory Chips, found in the back of the Worktext. Say each word, having students repeat it after you. Then have them sort the words according to words they know and those that are unfamiliar. Have the students say each unfamiliar word together and then use the words in sentences.

Worktext pages 48–49 can also be used to reinforce spelling. Use the five-step process detailed on page 71 of this *Teacher's Manual.*

Syllables

Write this word on the board, and say it aloud: **explore**. Tell students that when they see a word like this, they can break it into parts and say each part by itself. Cover *plore,* and say *ex.* Then cover *ex,* and say *plore.* Then say the word naturally. Repeat, using a three-syllable word like *excitement.* Have students decode each syllable before they say the whole word.

Context Clues

Write this sentence on the board: **Frozen ice cream is sweet and cold.** Cover *frozen,* and ask students how they would read this word if they did not know it. (*Read the sentence and use clues from the sentence along with decoding clues.*)

Endings *ous, ment, s, er, ing*

Write this sentence on the board, and read it aloud: **The famous rock star lost his hat in the excitement.** Point to *famous.* Tell students this word has the ending *ous. Fame* is the base word. Then have students point to *excitement.* Put your finger under *ment* and tell them this is another ending. Ask a volunteer to read the base word. Remind students that they can add *s, er,* and *ing* to the endings of words. Tell them that when a word ends in *e,* they drop the *e* and add the ending.

Make New Words Write these words on the board, and invite students to add endings *ous, ment, s, er,* and *ing* to the end of each: **explore**, **freeze**, **excite**, **fame**. (*explores, explorer, exploring; freezes, freezer, freezing; excitement, excites, exciting; famous*) They can use each word they make in a sentence.

Compound Words

Remind students that two words can be put together to make one longer word.

Make New Words Write these words on the board in random order and have students use them to make compound words: **Green**, **land**, **some**, **where**, **time**, **how**, **ever**. (*Greenland, somewhere, sometime, somehow, however, wherever*)

PRACTICE

- Let students practice the new words they have learned and formed by completing the activities found on pages 48–49 of the Worktext.
- If students are experiencing difficulty with the Words to Know section on pages 48–49, you can pose riddles like the one below, and have students choose a Memory Chip to answer each one: **This word is what we call the United States.** (*country*)

For further practice, have students complete Practice Lesson 6.9 on pages 83–84 of the Worktext. Answers can be found in the Answer Key on page 359 of this *Teacher's Manual.*

APPLY

- Have students talk about the story concept by sharing their prior knowledge about Matthew Henson. Ask: **Who was Matthew Henson? What famous thing did he do?** Tell students they are going to use the words they have learned to read an article about a famous African American explorer, Matthew Henson.
- Ask students to read the article on pages 50–52 in the Worktext. Offer assistance if necessary, but encourage students to decode the words independently, using the clues and patterns they have learned.
- After students have completed reading the article, have them complete the Comprehension Exercises (What Is a Biography? and Read It Again) on page 53 in their Worktext. Answers can be found in the Answer Key on page 358 of this *Teacher's Manual.*

CONNECTION

Strategy for Reading After students finish reading the selection "Matthew Henson, Explorer, Part 1" on Worktext pages 50–52, ask them to summarize it either aloud or in writing.

Speaking/Listening Student partners can read the selection aloud. The partners can alternate being speaker and listener.

Writing Students should be encouraged to keep a journal of their writings. They can use the journal to record responses to their reading, list new words they have learned, or record their thoughts about the reading selection.

Worktext Pages 48–49

9. MATTHEW HENSON, EXPLORER, PART 1

Try This

Often, you can break a long word into parts and read the parts. Then you can put the parts together to read the word. Try it with the word **explore**. First, break up the word: **explore = ex + plore**. You can read these parts: **ex** sounds like **x**, and **plore** rhymes with **more**. Put the parts together, and you have the word: **explore**. Read the new word. Write it in the sentence below:

The boys __________ the new house.

Take a Guess

The words in dark letters below are new **Words to Know**. Can you guess them from the other words around them? Think about the sound of the first two letters in each word. Use these letters to test your guess.

Ice is **frozen** water.
The cops can **prove** he is a thief.

Now write the words: __________ __________

Words to Know

	Look	Say	Picture	Write
adventures ad-ven-tures	☐	☐	☐	__________
country coun-try	☐	☐	☐	__________
explore ex-plore	☐	☐	☐	__________
freeze	☐	☐	☐	__________
frozen fro-zen	☐	☐	☐	__________
Inuit In-u-it	☐	☐	☐	__________

48

Worktext page 48

	Look	Say	Picture	Write
Matthew Henson Mat-thew Hen-son	☐	☐	☐	__________
musk ox	☐	☐	☐	__________
north	☐	☐	☐	__________
prove	☐	☐	☐	__________
Robert Peary Rob-ert Pea-ry	☐	☐	☐	__________
sled	☐	☐	☐	__________

Word Attack

+er Give these words an **er** ending. The words **explore** and **freeze** already have an **e** at the end, so just add **r**.

explore __________ freeze __________

hard __________ help __________

+s Give these words an **s** ending. Read the new words.

explorer __________ land __________

sled __________ trip __________

+ing Take the **e** away from the end of these words. Then write each one with an **ing** ending. Read the new words.

drive __________ freeze __________

+ment The letters **ment** are an ending that can go on some words. Write **excite** with the ending **ment**.

excite + ment = __________

+ous The letters **ous** are another ending. Write **fame** with **ous** after it (but first take away **e**). Read the new word.

fame (- e) + ous = __________

2=1 Put the words **Green** and **land** together to make the name of a place.

Green + land = __________

49

Worktext page 49

Level 6

9. MATTHEW HENSON, EXPLORER, PART 1

The year was 1887. Matthew Henson was in the back room of the hat shop where he worked. Suddenly, his boss called to him. Matthew walked out front with a box in his hand. He saw a man standing by the door. "Matthew," said his boss, "this is Mr. Robert Peary. He's going south on a job for the U.S. Navy. He needs a good sun hat. See what you can find for him."

Henson, who was just 20 years old at this time, got to talking with the older man. Peary took a liking to the young African American. Soon, he told Henson he was looking for a helper—someone who was strong and willing to work hard. "Would Henson be interested in the job?" he asked.

Henson thought about it and said, "Yes." Little did he know how that little "yes" would change his life.

History remembers Robert Peary as a great explorer. Peary made six trips to Greenland and other parts of the far north. He found frozen lands that no one had ever set eyes on before. Books tell us that Peary was the first man ever to get to the North Pole.

But was he?

Matthew Henson went with Peary on every trip. It was Henson who made friends with the Inuit. These people of the far north helped Peary. Henson made the sleds that took Peary to the Pole. Henson was driving the sled on the last trip. He and Peary stood together at the North Pole on that famous day. Matthew Henson was a great explorer in his own right. Only now is the world coming to know the full story of his life.

Henson was born in 1866. His mom died when he was only seven years old. His dad died six years later. Matthew Henson found himself alone in the world at 13. He got a job washing dishes, but he didn't like it much. So he walked 40 miles to a city by the sea where he found work on a ship. For the next five years, Matthew Henson went all over the world working on one ship after another.

These, however, were hard years for young Matthew. The problem was not the work. It was other workers. The great war between the North and South had ended just one year before Matthew was born. That war had set African

50

Worktext page 50

Matthew Henson

Robert Peary

52

Worktext page 52

Americans free. But in the U.S., many white people still wanted to keep African Americans down. Some of the people Matthew worked with had such feelings. Matthew was just a boy when he started to work on his first ship. Yet, an older man beat him up—just because he was African American. At first, Matthew was so mad about this that he could hardly work. Then he made up his mind not to let some know-nothing break him. He started working harder than ever just to prove himself.

About two years after Matthew left the sea, he started to work for Peary. He and Peary stayed together for 22 years. Side by side, they went through one of the great adventures in history. They never really got to be friends, however. Peary always saw himself as the boss. He always saw the other man as his helper—nothing more.

Yet, Peary and Henson were alike in many ways. Both were hard-driving. Both liked excitement. Both were ready to face any test, any problem. Most of all, both were explorers to their very bones. They liked going to places that were hard to get to. Both wanted to be the first to see something new.

One day in 1888, Peary called Henson to his room. He told Henson about something he had long wanted to do. Peary wanted to map the far north. This part of the world is freezing cold. Little-known animals, such as the musk ox, live there. But people had never been to the places Peary wanted to explore. Peary asked Henson if he would like to join him in this adventure. Henson did not have to give the question much thought. "Yes," he said. Peary could count on him. Henson wanted to go.

51

Worktext page 51

What Is a Biography?

The story you have started is a biography. A **biography** is the story of a life. It tells about someone real from today or from history. Two names have come up so far. Which of them is this biography about? Circle the name and write it on the line.

Matthew Henson Robert Peary

____

Read It Again

A biography gives facts. Find the fact that answers each question below. Write it on the line.

When was Matthew Henson born? ______________

What was his first job? ______________

What did he do from the time he was 13 to the time he was 18? ______________

Who beat up Henson on his first ship? ______________

____

What did this man have against Henson? ______________

____

When did Henson meet Robert Peary? ______________

____

Where did he meet Peary? ______________

____

What was Henson doing in this place? ______________

____

53

Worktext page 53

LESSON 6.10

OBJECTIVE

- Students will practice and apply skills to an extended passage

MATERIALS

Worktext 6, pages 54–57
Teacher's Manual, pages 283–284, 333
Practice Lesson 6.10, pages 85–86 of the Worktext

SKILLS REVIEW

- Before reading, you may wish to review these words that apply phonics skills: *Greenland, anything, questions, friends, sleds, dogs, miles, everything, others, scientists, jobs, cooking, going, driving, sleeping, days, freezing, parts, closer, happening, rocks, explore, willing, coming.* Have students review the Memory Chips they have learned so far. Then ask: **What do you think it would be like to explore Greenland during the coldest time of the year?**
- While reading, have students write down interesting facts they wish to remember about Matthew Henson.
- After reading, have students complete the Comprehension Exercises (Finding the Main Idea and Putting Facts in Time Order) on Worktext page 57.

For further practice, have students complete Practice Lesson 6.10 on pages 85–86 of the Worktext. Answers can be found in the Answer Key on pages 358–359 of this *Teacher's Manual*..

RETEACH

If students need further review of phonics skills, you may wish to use the following activity:

Word Parts

Putting It Back Together Write the following words on word cards: **explore**, **excitement**, **frozen**, **always**, **helper**, **something**, **adventure**, **question**, **between**, **because**, **remembers**, **problem**, **Greenland**, **answer**, **however**, **scientists**, **animals**, **awhile**, **happened**, **attacked**, **Henson**, **fallen**, **started**. Cut the cards between the syllables. Then have students match the cards back together, say each word, and write it on paper.

CONNECTION

Strategy for Reading Have students reread the selection "Matthew Henson, Explorer, Part 2" on Worktext pages 54–56 to correct comprehension breakdowns. Students may achieve understanding by reprocessing the same text with greater attention focused on its meaning.

Speaking/Listening Have students read aloud the selection "Matthew Henson, Explorer, Part 2" on Worktext pages 54–56. The partners can alternate being speaker and listener.

Response to Reading

- Have students discuss differences between fiction selections they have read and this selection, which is a nonfiction article.
- As a class, students can complete a chart with the headings "Fiction" and "Nonfiction."

Literature

- Students may enjoy reading other biographies about famous African Americans. Pearson publishes a series of biographies entitled *Freedom Fighters.* Students may choose to read *Martin Luther King, Jr., Fannie Lou Hamer,* or another biography.
- Students may use the Book Report reproducible found on page 333 of this *Teacher's Manual* to record their responses to the biographies.

10. MATTHEW HENSON, EXPLORER, PART 2

Between 1891 and 1897, Henson and Peary made three trips to Greenland. Greenland is a big land far north of the U.S. People called the Inuit live in the south of Greenland. In 1891, no one had been to the north end of Greenland. It is too cold. There is snow and ice on the ground all year. No one had any idea how big Greenland was. Did anything live up there? How far north did it go? Where did the land end and sea begin? These were some of the questions Peary wanted to answer.

On his first trip to this cold land, Peary took along a team of six people. Matthew Henson was part of the team. A ship took them to Greenland and let them out. Then the ship went home. It would not come back for a year. Till then, the group was on its own.

Henson got to work right away. He put together a house for the group to use as its home base. Then Henson made friends with the Inuit who lived there. He learned how to talk with them. He even moved in with an Inuit family for awhile. The Inuit saw Henson as one of them. They showed him how to make sleds and how to drive a dog team. They sold him some dogs. From the Inuit, Henson learned how to build a house out of snow.

All these things were a great help to Peary and his group. The first trip was a good one. Peary and another man took off on a dog sled. They went about 600 miles north.

On the next trip, however, just about everything went wrong. This time, Peary had put together a group of 15. Only Henson, Peary, and two others had been on the last trip. Most of the new people were scientists who had never been in really cold country. They were good scientists, but they could not help much with the hard jobs.

Early on, some of the sleds came apart and food was lost. Then a big wave from the sea hit the house that Henson had made. It washed away gas that was needed for cooking and heat. Later, Peary, Henson, and one other man tried to drive a

54

Worktext page 54

dog team north. They were caught in a storm and had to go back to camp.

The next year, they tried again. Some of the Inuits went with them at first, but they turned back after a while. They could see no point in going on. They said there were no animals up north. Why would people want to go where there was nothing to eat?

It was a hard question. Henson could only tell them he wanted to see what was there. He would be back, he said. They did not believe him.

Henson was driving a big sled pulled by 28 dogs. For awhile, things went well. Then snow started to fall. Peary and Henson had to get way down into their sleeping bags. They could not move for two days. They could only sit and wait and try to keep from freezing. They had no idea what had happened to the other man. After the snow let up, Henson went out to look for him. He found the poor man sitting on his sled with parts of his body frozen. He could no longer walk, but he was still alive. Henson put him on his own sled and took him back to Peary.

In 36 days, this little group went 600 miles. They came to a place close to the sea. Peary had already been this far on his first trip. But this time, many of the dogs died. The group was just about out of food. They set up camp and left the sick man there. Peary and Henson went down to the water to see if they could get some fish.

Close to the water, Peary saw a musk ox, a big animal of the far north. Peary killed it. But just as he moved toward this animal, another one showed up. Peary could tell he was going to be attacked. He turned to run, but the musk ox came after him. Peary could not run fast enough. The musk ox got closer and closer to him.

Then, Henson came along. Right away, Henson saw what was happening. There was no time to think. He just had time to raise his gun and fire. There was only time for one try.

One was all Henson needed. Crack went the gun. Down went the animal. Henson had saved the life of Robert Peary.

Now, the three started back. They had meat from the animals that Peary and Henson had killed. But the base camp was far away. They ran out of meat. After that, they had to start to eat their dogs. By the time they got back to the base camp, they had only one dog left.

55

Worktext page 55

One good thing came out of the trip. Peary and Henson found some big rocks that had fallen from the sky. In 1897, they went back to Greenland. They came back with one of those rocks. It was about 30 times as big as a car. The rock got many people interested in the far north. Some of these people wanted Peary to go back and explore some more. They were willing to help him. Money started to come in to pay for another trip.

Now, however, Peary had a new idea. He told Henson about it first. He wanted to know that his right-hand man would be coming with him. After Henson said yes, Peary told the world. On his next trip north, he would strike for the North Pole itself. This time, Peary said, he was going to stand at the very top of Earth.

56

Worktext page 56

Finding the Main Idea

Part 2 of **Matthew Henson, Explorer** tells about Henson's life from 1891 to 1897. The writer groups these years together because Henson was doing one main thing at this time. How would you describe this one main thing? Finish the sentence below about Henson's life. Use one of the endings shown under it. Write in the ending that best describes everything Henson was doing.

Between 1891 and 1897, Henson ____________________

____

a. learned the ways of the Inuit
b. and Peary got to be fast friends.
c. explored Greenland with Robert Peary.

Putting Facts in Time Order

Here are five things that happened in the life of Henson between 1891 and 1897. Put them in time order.

Henson killed a musk ox.
Henson stayed with an Inuit family.
Henson said he would go with Peary to the North Pole.
Peary and Henson had to eat their dogs.
Peary and Henson took a big rock to the U.S.

____
____
____
____
____
____
____
____

57

Worktext page 57

LESSON 6.11

OBJECTIVES

- Students will decode and blend words containing medial consonants and the *ell* and *en* phonograms
- Students will use context clues to figure out unfamiliar words
- Students will apply endings *s, en, ed, ing, er,* and *est* to base words to form new words
- Students will recognize and form possessives
- Students will recognize and form contractions

PHONICS VOCABULARY

beginning	frozen	started	miles
everyone	things	years	needed
coldest	Henson's	wearing	arms
freezing	didn't	waited	eaten
mountains	cracks	dogs	falling
explorers	worked	pushing	driving
moved	charts	excited	Inuits
boys	thinking	couldn't	men
tell	then	feeling	pictures
leaving	reaching	colder	older
oldest	Mathew's	we've	medal
either	trouble	whole	ended

WORDS TO KNOW

across	either	men	reach	fell
few	hero	medal	rest	sure
trouble	whole			

MATERIALS

Worktext 6, pages 58–63
Teacher's Manual, pages 285–287
Practice Lesson 6.11, pages 87–88 of the Worktext

TEACH

- Using Worktext pages 58–59, introduce students to the vocabulary words. Give students an opportunity to practice writing the words.
- Students can organize their Memory Chips, found in the back of the Worktext. You may wish to say each word, having students repeat it after you. Students can find different ways to sort the words, such as by beginning letters, number of letters, and those with one or two syllables.

Worktext pages 58–59 can also be used to reinforce spelling. Use the five-step process detailed on page 71 of this *Teacher's Manual.*

Medial Consonants

Write these words on the board, and say them aloud: **metal**, **medal**. Ask students to tell how the words are alike and different. (*They sound the same but they have a different consonant in the middle.*)

Blending Say **metal** and **medal** slowly, blending each word and pointing to the letters as you say them: */m//e//t//ə//l/; /m//e//d//ə//l/.*

Phonograms *ell, en*

Write this sentence on the board, and read it aloud: **I can tell when we are there.** Ask a volunteer to point to *tell.* Ask students what words rhyme with *tell.* (*bell, sell, well*) Have a volunteer point to *when.* Write **hen** on the board, and ask students how *hen* and *when* are alike. (*They rhyme and both end in* en.)

Blending Create letter cards for **l**, **l**, **w**, **n**, **t**, **h**, **b**, **w**, **f**, **s**, **th**, and **e**. Say these words: **when**, **hen**, **then**, **tell**, **bell**, **sell**, **fell**, **well**. Have students use the letter cards to make the words, then have them blend the sounds and say each word.

Context Clues

Remind students that they can figure out an unfamiliar word by reading all the words in the sentence around it and by using what they know about decoding. Write this sentence on the board, leaving out *trouble.* Have students figure out what the missing word is: **I will get into _______ if I hang out with people who break the law.** (*trouble*)

Endings *s, en, ed, ing, er, est*

Remind students that they can add *s, en, ed, ing, er,* and *est* to the endings of words. Tell students that when *er* is added to the end of a word, it compares two people or things. When *est* is added, it compares three or more people or things. Remind students that when a word ends in *e,* the *e* is dropped, and the ending is added.

Make New Words Say these words, and have students add the ending *er* and *est* to them: **old**, **cold**. (*older, oldest; colder, coldest*) Have a volunteer write each word on the board. Repeat, having students add *ing* and *en* to *eat.* (*eating, eaten*) Then have students add *ed* and *s* to *excite.* (*excited, excites*) Assist students with spelling as necessary.

Possessives

Write this sentence on the board, and read it aloud: **Matthew's sled is broken.** Ask students whose sled is broken. (*Matthew's*) Circle the apostrophe and *s,* and remind students that this tells us the sled belongs to Matthew.

Make New Words Write these words and have students add an apostrophe and *s* to them: **Henson**,

Level 6

Peary. (*Henson's, Peary's*) Then have them use each word in a sentence.

Contractions

Remind students that they can make two words into one. Write **I have** on the board. Show students how to erase the letters *ha* and replace them with an apostrophe to make *I've.*

Make New Words Work together with students to make contractions out of these words: *we have, you have.* (*we've, you've*)

PRACTICE

- Let students practice the new words they have learned and formed by completing the activities found on pages 58–59 of the Worktext.
- If students are experiencing difficulty with the Words to Know section on pages 58–59, place the Memory Chips on the table. Say cloze sentences like this, and have students choose a Memory Chip to complete each one: **I live ______ the street from my friend.** (*across*)

For further practice, have students complete Practice Lesson 6.11 on pages 87–88 of the Worktext. Answers can be found in the Answer Key on page 359 of this *Teacher's Manual.*

APPLY

- Have students talk about the story concept by predicting what they think will happen next in the story about Matthew Henson. Ask: **Who do you think will reach the North Pole first, Henson or Peary?** Tell students they are going to use the words they have learned to read an article that answers the question.
- Ask students to read the article on pages 60–62 in the Worktext. Offer assistance if necessary, but encourage students to decode the words independently, using the clues and patterns they have learned.
- After students have completed reading the article, have them complete the Comprehension Exercises (Finding Facts to Back Up Ideas and What Do You Think?) on page 63 in their Worktext. Answers can be found in the Answer Key on page 358 of this *Teacher's Manual.*

CONNECTION

Strategy for Reading After students finish reading the selection "Matthew Henson, Explorer, Part 3" on Worktext pages 60–62, ask them to summarize it either aloud or in writing.

Worktext Pages 58–59

11. MATTHEW HENSON, EXPLORER, PART 3

Try This

You know the word on the left. Can you read the other word? Only one letter is different. Circle the letter that is different in each word. Read the new word, and then write it in the sentence.

metal **medal** That man should get a ______________.

Letter Groups

Look at the words in each line. The words in dark type are new words. Circle a letter group that is in all the words in each line. Read and write the new word.

then when **men** ____________

tell well **fell** ____________

Take a Guess

Each sentence below has a new word. It is the one in dark letters. See if you can guess the new words from the other words around them.

You can have **either** one, but not both.
If it is dark outside, you may have **trouble**.
Did you eat the **whole** thing or just part of it?

Write the new words below.

____________ ____________ ____________

Words to Know

	Look	Say	Picture	Write
across a-cross	☐	☐	☐	____________
either ei-ther	☐	☐	☐	____________
fell	☐	☐	☐	____________
few	☐	☐	☐	____________
hero he-ro	☐	☐	☐	____________

58

Worktext page 58

	Look	Say	Picture	Write
medal med-al	☐	☐	☐	____________
men	☐	☐	☐	____________
reach	☐	☐	☐	____________
rest	☐	☐	☐	____________
sure	☐	☐	☐	____________
trouble trou-ble	☐	☐	☐	____________
whole	☐	☐	☐	____________

Word Attack

+s Write an **s** after **arm**. ____________

+en Write the ending **en** after **eat**. ____________

+ed Give these words an **ed** ending. Because **excite** already ends in **e**, you only need to add a letter **d**.

excite ______________ end ______________

+ing Write **leave** and **reach** with the ending **ing**. Remember to take away the **e** from **leave** before you write **ing**.

leave ______________ reach ______________

+er Write **cold** and **old** with an **er** ending.

cold + er ______________ old + er ______________

+est Now write **cold** and **old** with an **est** ending.

cold + est ______________ old + est ______________

+'s Write each word below with **'s**.

Matthew ______________ Henson ______________

1+1 The word **we've** can take the place of the two words: **we have**. Both ways mean the same thing. Write **we've**, then write **we have**. Circle the letters that are left out of the two words.

____________ = ____________ + ____________

59

Worktext page 59

11. MATTHEW HENSON, EXPLORER, PART 3

It took Peary and Henson three tries to reach the North Pole. On the first trip, they made it to the north end of Greenland—the beginning of a frozen sea. On the next trip, the men started across that sea and got as close as 175 miles to the Pole. But Peary could hardly walk by then. So they all had to turn back.

Peary and Henson went home in 1906. They told everyone they were just there to buy some things they needed. They said they were going right back to try again. This time, they were sure they would reach the Pole. It was big talk—but could they do it? Peary was now 50 years old. This would have to be his last trip. Henson was 39 and still strong. But he could not raise the money for a trip like this on his own. He needed Peary as much as Peary needed him. If this was the last trip for Peary, then it was the last one for Henson. This time it was really do or die.

It was 1908 by the time Henson and Peary set out. The group that left the U.S. was made up of seven men. In Greenland, they picked up six young Inuit men. Their ship set off in summer. But it was getting to the cold part of the year by the time they got to north Greenland. But that was good. To reach the Pole, they would have to walk across the frozen sea. They wanted to start that walk at the coldest time, when the ice would be really hard.

On the first day, Henson's sled came apart. He had to fix it out in the cold, wearing nothing on his hands. By night, the team had gone only 12 miles. They still had 400 to go! All through that first night, Henson had to get up from time to time. It was so cold. He had to beat his arms against his body to keep himself from freezing.

After many days, they came to the end of the land. From here to the Pole was a frozen sea. But again, there was trouble. Peary didn't think the water was hard enough. Henson didn't think so, either. If they went onto the ice now, they might fall through. So they had to make camp and wait. While they waited, they had to eat. Days went by in this way.

At last, the ice was good and hard, and they could start north. But by then, they had eaten too much food. Peary could

60

Worktext page 60

see that there was not enough left to get them all to the Pole and back. So every few days, he had one man start back.

Food was not the only problem. In some places, the group had to go over mountains of ice. In other places, the ice had cracks in it. Sometimes, a big crack would show up right where people were walking. The ice would come apart. People and dogs had to race to keep from falling into the water.

After 26 days, the group was down to Peary, Henson, one other American, and six Inuits. Peary now told the other American and two of the Inuits to start back. He and Henson would go on with four Inuits. The American who was going back said to Henson, "We've done all we can. The rest is up to you. History will be made in these next few days."

The little group of explorers was now just 130 miles from the Pole. Peary was too old and sick to do much work. He had to sit in the sled much of the time. So Henson now took over. He worked as never before—pushing the team, driving the dogs, and driving himself. He moved the group about 26 miles a day. Then at last, one night, he and Peary read their charts. They were just 35 miles from the North Pole! They might reach it the very next day! Henson was too excited to sleep that night. So was Peary. At last, they all got up. Peary told Henson to go on ahead with two Inuits. Peary would follow.

But, as Henson was getting ready to leave, Peary called him over. He told Henson to stop when he got close to the Pole. He wanted Henson to wait for him. Peary said, "I'll take one of the boys and go on from there."

Henson couldn't believe it. Was Peary really thinking of leaving him behind? After he had come so far and worked so hard? Would he never get to see the North Pole after all? "What about me?" he said.

"I mean we," said Peary. "We will go on."

Henson had a bad feeling. He thought maybe Peary did not want him to get to the Pole. It looked like Peary wanted to go to the North Pole all by himself.

Henson set out. He had gone just a few miles when the ice came apart under him. Down he went, into freezing cold water. One of his Inuit friends pulled him out. But it is hard to know why he didn't die. Remember that the air here was –50 F°! Yet, Henson just went on and on and on.

Suddenly, he stopped. He looked around and up at the stars. He could tell, then, that he had gone too far. He must have

61

Worktext page 61

gone right over the North Pole without knowing it. To meet up with Peary now, he would have to go back.

So when Peary caught up with Henson, the man was not close to the North Pole. He was already at the Pole. Henson had gotten there ahead of Peary.

Peary said nothing to Henson. They had worked together for 22 years to get to this place. Now, here they were at the top of the world. Peary, however, did not seem happy. Maybe he was mad at Henson for getting there first. Maybe he was just run down and feeling sick. Anyway, the men took some pictures to show where they had been. Then they started south.

On the way back, Henson was full of high hopes. He had done what no one had done before. He had stood at the North Pole.

At the top of an icy hill near the North Pole in 1909, Henson (center) and the Inuit raise the American flag.

62

Worktext page 62

Finding Facts to Back Up Ideas

In Part 1 of this biography, the writer says that Henson was a great explorer. This is not a fact; it is what the writer thinks. Facts, however, can be used to back up an idea of this kind. Here are some facts from Part 3 of the biography. Do any of them back up the idea that Henson was a great explorer? Circle four facts. Write them on the lines under the heading **Facts that back it up.**

Peary was 10 years older than Henson.
Henson was one of six men who made it to the North Pole.
Henson took over at the end of the last trip.
One man told Henson, "The rest is up to you."
Henson couldn't sleep when he got close to the Pole.
Peary told Henson to wait for him close to the Pole.
Henson fell into ice cold water, but he wouldn't turn back.
Henson got to the North Pole ahead of Peary.

Idea: Henson was a great explorer and had much to do with Peary getting to the North Pole.

Facts that back it up:

____
____
____
____
____
____
____

What Do You Think?

Look over the facts you have picked out. Talk about this biography with someone else who is reading it. What do you think of Matthew Henson? Why?

63

Worktext page 63

Level 6

LESSON 6.12

OBJECTIVE

- Students will practice and apply skills to an extended passage

MATERIALS

Worktext 6, pages 64–66
Teacher's Manual, pages 288–289, 330–331, 333
Practice Lesson 6.12, pages 89–90 of the Worktext

SKILLS REVIEW

- Before reading, you may wish to review these words that apply phonics skills: *frozen, asked, taken, wanted, ways, news, called, talks, adventures, pictures, attacked, screamed, always, taking, letters, building, moved, men, coming, medal, explorer, bigger, points.* Have students review the Memory Chips they have learned so far. Then ask: **What do you think happened after Peary and Henson got back from the North Pole?**
- While reading, have students think about how Henson might have felt to be treated the way he was after he returned from the North Pole.
- After reading, have students complete the Comprehension Exercise (Making a Timeline) on Worktext page 66.

For further practice, have students complete Practice Lesson 6.12 on pages 89–90 of the Worktext. Answers can be found in the Answer Key on pages 358–359 of this *Teacher's Manual.*

RETEACH

If students need further review of phonics skills, you may wish to use the following activity:

Endings *s, en, ed, ing, er, est, 's*

Ending Match-ups Write the following words on word cards: **arm**, **eat**, **excited**, **leave**, **reach**, **cold**, **old**, **Matthew**, **Henson**. Write these endings on word cards: **s**, **en**, **ed**, **ing**, **er**, **est**, **'s**. Turn the cards face down. Mix all the cards and then have students take turns turning over two cards at a time. If the two cards make a new word with an ending, the student writes the word on his or her list. If not, the next student takes a turn. After each turn, turn the cards over in their original position.

CONNECTION

Response to Reading

- To reinforce students' understanding of the literary elements found in their reading material, have them complete the Story Map and Character Cluster reproducibles found on pages 330–331.
- Students will demonstrate an understanding of setting, characters, and plot by filling out the organizers.
- Students may share their completed organizers with the class.

Literature

- Students may enjoy reading other biographies. Pearson publishes a series of biographies entitled *Freedom Fighters.* Students may choose to read *Nelson Mandela, César Chávez,* or another biography.
- Students may use the Book Report reproducible found on page 333 of this *Teacher's Manual* to record their responses to the biographies.

12. MATTHEW HENSON, EXPLORER, PART 4

Henson got back to the U.S. in 1909. Right away, he found himself up against an old problem. He was African American. This had been no problem in the frozen north. Up there, people looked at a man for what he could do, not at his race.

But many people in the U.S. were not ready to see an African American as a hero. They asked Peary why he had taken an African American along on his trip. Why not a white man? they wanted to know. Without Henson, of course, Peary may never have made it to the North Pole. In some ways, it was Henson who took Peary along on that last trip. Most people know this now. But at the time, no one would believe such a thing.

Henson hardly even got to see his name in the paper. News stories talked only about Peary. They said little or nothing about Henson. They did not say much about the Inuit, either. It was as if Peary had gone to the North Pole by himself. Everyone called Peary **the first man to reach the North Pole**. Peary did little to set the story right.

In fact, Peary would not even talk to Henson for awhile. He was mad at Henson. At one point, a group asked Henson to go around the country, giving talks about his adventures. Henson was happy to do so. He asked Peary to let him use some of the pictures they had taken at the North Pole. But Peary would not give Henson any pictures. Peary said that only he should have the right to tell people about the trip.

Henson went out and gave his talks anyway. He was often attacked. Some people would not believe Peary had really gone to the North Pole. Henson stood up for his chief. Some screamed at Henson because he was African American. There was not much Henson could do about this. At last, he had to cut off his talks and go home.

Henson always said good things about Peary. Peary said very little about Henson—good or bad. In 1912, Henson put out a book about his adventures in the north. There, too, he gave first place to Peary. But he told about his own work, too. His book, however, did not sell very well. Henson could not even

64

Worktext page 64

get a good job. In the end, he got a job taking letters from room to room in a big building. Peary, on the other hand, moved up in the Navy. He made a lot of money. When he died in 1920, he was one of the most famous men on Earth.

Very late in life, Henson got some of the fame he had coming. The Navy did give him a medal at last, in 1945, and in 1954, Henson was asked to come to the White House. By then, he was known to many as a great explorer. But the late fame did Henson little good. He was 87 years old by that time. The next year, he died.

The Inuit of Greenland remember Henson to this day. He is the hero of many Inuit stories. These stories often paint a picture of a man who was bigger than life. What did Peary have to say about Henson in the end? "He was the best man I ever had."

In 1954, Henson points out the North Pole to President Eisenhower. Mrs. Henson is in the center of the group.

65

Worktext page 65

Making a Timeline

Now you have read the whole biography. See if you can make a timeline of Matthew Henson's life. In the box are some of the things that happened to him. Write each one on the timeline, next to the year when it happened.

Born	Gets a medal
First trip to Greenland	Goes to sea
Starts first trip to North Pole	Meets Peary
Gets to the North Pole	Dies
Asked to the White House	Writes a book

The Life of Matthew Henson

1866: ______

1879: ______

1887: ______

1891: ______

1898: ______

1908: ______

1912: ______

1945: ______

1954: ______

1955: ______

66

Worktext page 66

Level 6

FINAL NOVEL Under Fire

MATERIALS
Final Novel 6, *Under Fire*
Teacher's Manual, page 290
Assessment Manual, Final Assessment 6, pages 112–118

Summary *Will delivers food to The Sea House restaurant. He likes Ana, a girl who works there. When money is stolen from the restaurant, Will pays the money back because he thinks Ana took it. Once Will knows Ana didn't take the money, he sets out to find out who did. Will figures out that it was the cook.*

REVIEW AND ASSESSMENT

- Have students review their Memory Chips with partners or in small groups. Depending on your students' needs, review the following skills covered in Lessons 9–12: syllables; context clues; possessives; compound words; contractions; medial consonants; phonograms *en* and *ell*; and endings *s, ing, en, er, est, ment, ous,* and *ed.*

If you wish to assess students' progress at this point, use the *Assessment Manual,* pages 112–118. For students who need additional support, you may use the Reteach activities from previous lessons.

INTRODUCE THE NOVEL

Invite students to preview the book by reading the title, looking at the illustrations, and reading aloud the captions. Begin a discussion of story concepts by asking:

- **What do you say to someone you like but don't know very well?**
- **What would you do if you thought someone you liked stole something?**
- **Is it better to work for someone you like or someone who pays you well? Why do you think so?**

CHECK COMPREHENSION

Chapter 1 Why does Will like to make deliveries to The Sea House? (*Ana, a pretty girl he likes, works there.*)

Chapter 2 Why does Will's band call itself The Sick Dogs? (*They sound like sick dogs when they sing.*)

Chapter 3 Why is the Sea House an uncomfortable place for Ana to work? (*Matthew, the cook, bothers her and pesters her about going out with him.*)

Chapter 4 Why does Ana need $200? (*Her family needs the money because the rent went up.*)

Chapter 5 Who does Will think stole the $200 from The Sea House? Why does he think that? (*He thinks Ana stole it because she needed the money.*)

Chapter 6 Why do you think Ana is crying? (*Possible answers: She thinks Will stole the money, and she is upset about it. Or, she is upset because she stole the money.*)

Chapter 7 What does Lou tell Will to do about the money? (*He tells Will to tell the cops or Mr. Henson what happened; he also suggests Will ask Ana to go to the cops and turn herself in.*)

Chapter 8 How do Will and Ana end up in the freezer during the fire? (*The front door was locked, and the other exits were blocked. The freezer would protect them from the fire.*)

Chapter 9 What do Will and Ana figure out as they wait in the freezer? (*They find out that both of them thought the other stole the money, but actually neither of them did.*)

Chapter 10 Who took the $200 from the restaurant? (*Matthew*)

Chapter 11 How does the story end? (*Ana and Will both get new jobs and raises. Ana will sing with Will's band.*)

CONNECTION

Home/School Encourage students to bring home a copy of *Under Fire.* They might read the novel, or sections of the novel, to family members.

LEVEL 7

ORGANIZER

Level 7 of the *Caught Reading* program includes the following components:

Worktext 7

Worktext 7 includes 12 lessons, taking students from those words introduced in previous levels through a word list of 175 words (found on page 344 of this *Teacher's Manual*) by Lesson 12. The Practice Lessons provide students with opportunites to extend practice, and review the content of each lesson. The Response to Reading pages allow students to practice using their new vocabulary. Tear-out Memory Chips in the back of the student book reinforce new vocabulary and can be used both independently by students and in small groups.

Midway and Final Novels 7

These novels are designed to reinforce learned vocabulary and give students the opportunity to read for meaning. Their high-interest plots encourage successful reading experiences and an appreciation for literature.

- *Asking for Trouble* includes only vocabulary students have learned up to the midway point of this level.
- *Stepping Up* includes all vocabulary learned through Level 7.

Teacher's Manual

The *Teacher's Manual* provides detailed objectives and instruction for each skill taught in the Worktext, as well as additional teaching suggestions for meaningful practice and reinforcement. The *Teacher's Manual* provides choices for flexible instruction. Comprehension questions for the Midway and Final novels are included, as well as Answer Keys for the Worktext activities and the Practice Lessons.

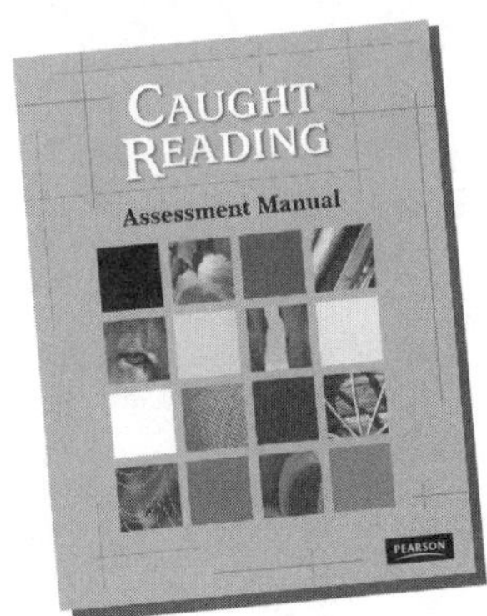

Assessment Manual

The *Assessment Manual* provides preassessment, ongoing assessment, and postassessment to administer to students throughout their work in *Caught Reading*. Within this Manual you will also find Midway and Final Assessments to determine the students' comprehension of the Midway and Final Novels.

OBJECTIVES

Vocabulary Development

- Read a base vocabulary, plus base vocabulary words with various endings; compound words; and contractions formed from base words.
- Use the word learning sequence to remember and spell words correctly.
- Review vocabulary independently, both in and out of context, using the Memory Chips.
- Learn vocabulary to read about survival skills, such as finding an apartment.

Phonics

- Recognize the letter groups *ore, ove, other, oice,* and *air.*
- Recognize the ending *tion* on base words.

Reading Comprehension

- Read and understand directions.
- Locate the parts of a newspaper.

Literary Analysis

- Determine the underlying theme or author's message in fiction.
- Identify the speaker or narrator in a selection.

Writing

- Fill out forms.
- Write several imaginary want ads.

Speaking and Listening

- Perform short interview plays for the whole class.
- Give precise directions and instructions.

INTRODUCTION & LESSON 7.1

OBJECTIVES

- Students will decode and blend words containing the *ore, ock,* and *ing* phonograms
- Students will use context clues to figure out unknown words
- Students will apply endings *es, s, ing,* and *ed* to base words to form new words
- Students will recognize and form compound words

PHONICS VOCABULARY

newspaper	brings	kinds	parts
news	interesting	events	politics
huts	breaks	pages	newspapers
jobs	gives	sports	teams
score	baskets	winning	articles
tonight	shows	movies	ads
going	businesses	however	clothes
cars	buys	store	listed
lines	houses	used	anything
looking	almost	articles	Dana
fill	forms	important	information
list	paragraphs	piece	signs
skills	sport	tool	basketball
shuts	teams	spaces	grouped
newspaper	shopping	bring	clock
interest	movie	yesterday	business

WORDS TO KNOW

basket	bench	bring	business
clock	clothes	event	fun
less	movie	score	state
yesterday	almost	article	Dana
fill	form	important	information
list	paragraph	piece	sign
skill	sport	tool	

MATERIALS

Worktext 7, pages 5–11
Teacher's Manual, pages 294–296
Practice Lesson 7.1, pages 66–67 of the Worktext

TEACH

- Before beginning the lesson, have students complete the exercises independently in the Introduction on Worktext pages 5–6.
- Using Worktext pages 8–9, introduce students to the vocabulary words. Give students an opportunity to practice writing the words.
- Students can organize their Memory Chips, found in the back of the Worktext. You may wish to say each word, having students repeat it after you. Students can take turns using each word in a sentence.

Worktext pages 8–9 can also be used to reinforce spelling. Use the five-step process detailed on page 71 of this *Teacher's Manual.*

Phonograms *ore, ock, ing*

Write this sentence on the board and read it aloud: **I hope the team can score before the game is over.** Ask students which two words rhyme. (*score, before*) Have a volunteer circle the letters *ore* in both words. Repeat for *ock* and *ing,* using these sentences: **I will buy the sock and the clock.** (*sock, clock*) **Please bring the ring.** (*bring, ring*)

Blending Write **score** on the board. Erase the *sc* and write **t**. Have students blend the sounds to make the new word. Repeat, making the words *sore* and *wore.* Then ask students to list rhyming words for *ring* and *clock.* (*sing, bring, fling, wing; sock, flock, rock*) List them on the board, and blend them as you read them aloud.

Context Clues

Remind students that when they see a word they do not know, they can read the words around it to help them guess how to read the word. Write these sentences on the board: **I needed to find out where I could buy a car. I looked in the newspaper to get the information.** Read the sentences, leaving out the word *information.* Ask students what they think the word is and what other words give them clues.

Endings *es, s, ing, ed*

Write **business** on the board, read it aloud, and tell students it is a base word. Then add *es,* and say the new word aloud: **businesses**. Remind students that when words end in *s, ss, x, ch,* or *sh,* the ending *es* and not *s* is added. In words like *space* or *team, s* is added instead. Then remind them that *ing* and *ed* can be added to base words.

Make New Words Write these base words and endings on index cards: **movie**, **break**, **business**, **page**, **group**, **interest**, **es**, **s**, **ing**, **ed**. Have students take turns putting two cards together to make a new word. (*movies; breaks, breaking; businesses; pages, paging, paged; groups, grouping, grouped; interests, interesting, interested*) They can write the words on the board and use each one in a sentence.

Compound Words

Remind students that words like *sometimes* and *into* are made up of two smaller words.

Make New Words Write these words on index cards, and have students put two of them together to make new words: **basket**, **ball**, **foot**, **news**, **paper**. (*basketball, football, newspaper*)

PRACTICE

- Let students practice the new words they have learned and formed by completing the activities found on pages 8–9 of the Worktext.
- If students are experiencing difficulty with the Words to Know section on pages 8–9, place the Memory Chips on the table. Pose a riddle and have students choose a word that answers it. For example: **This word tells what Ohio is.** (*state*) **I tick and tock. What am I?** (*clock*)

For further practice, have students complete Practice Lesson 7.1 on pages 66–67 of the Worktext. Answers can be found in the Answer Key on page 360 of this *Teacher's Manual.*

APPLY

- Have students talk about the story concept by discussing things they already know. Ask: **What can you find out when you read a newspaper?**
- Ask students to read the article on page 10 in the Worktext. Encourage students to decode the words, using the clues and patterns they have learned.
- After students have completed reading the article, have them complete the Comprehension Exercises (Finding Paragraphs and Finding Main Idea Sentences) on page 11 in their Worktext. Answers can be found in the Answer Key on page 359 of this *Teacher's Manual.*

INTRODUCTION: GET CAUGHT READING IN THE REAL WORLD

Letter Groups

tion The letter group **tion** is an ending that you can add to some words. You know how this letter group sounds in the word **direction.** You will find the same letter group as an ending in one of your new words: **information.** See if you can read this word by breaking it into four parts: **information = in + for + ma + tion.** Can you read the word? Write it in the sentence below.

I would like some ____________________ about dogs.

Words to Know

	Look	Say	Picture	Write
almost al-most	☐	☐	☐	____________
article ar-ti-cle	☐	☐	☐	____________
Dana Da-na	☐	☐	☐	____________
fill	☐	☐	☐	____________
form	☐	☐	☐	____________
important im-por-tant	☐	☐	☐	____________
information in-for-ma-tion	☐	☐	☐	____________
list	☐	☐	☐	____________
paragraph par-a-graph	☐	☐	☐	____________
piece	☐	☐	☐	____________
sign	☐	☐	☐	____________
skill	☐	☐	☐	____________
sport	☐	☐	☐	____________
tool	☐	☐	☐	____________

5

Worktext page 5

Word Attack

+s Add **s** to the words below to make the new words.

ad ____________ article ____________

form ____________ sign ____________

skill ____________ sport ____________

paragraph ____________

+ing You can add **ing** to **shop** to make a new word. But write one more **p** after **shop** before you add **ing**. Write the new word in this sentence.

You can't go ____________ if you have no money.

2=1 You know the words **news** and **paper**. Put them together to make one new word.

news + paper = ____________

6

Worktext page 6

GET CAUGHT READING IN THE REAL WORLD

You are about to start the last book—**Caught Reading Level 7**. In the first six books, you learned about 1,000 words. You learned skills to help you read science, social studies, and literature.

Reading, however, is not just a tool for doing well in school. It is an important tool for living in the real world. You need to read in order to drive a car, look for a job, go shopping, rent a place to live, or fill out a form. You need it to get information from ads, read signs, and vote. You have to read a newspaper to find out what is going on in sports, politics, and the news as a whole. You have to read to follow directions—how to run a DVD player, learn a skill or a sport, fix a car—the list goes on and on. In fact, reading comes into almost every part of life today.

This book describes some of the forms of writing you may come across in the real world. You will learn how sentences are put together to build one main idea in a paragraph. You will learn how paragraphs are used to build one or more main ideas in an article. Some of the pieces in this book are articles about forms of writing. Others tell the story of two young people, Dan and Dana, who are just starting life on their own. You will see how Dan and Dana use information from ads, newspaper articles, and other forms of writing as they make their way in the world.

Each time you see **MCR** it is time for a Memory Chip Review. Remember to practice first with side **A**, and then with side **B**. Check (√) the ones you read easily on side **B**. When a Memory Chip has three checks (√√√), put it in the **Words I Know** envelope.

7

Worktext page 7

Worktext Pages 8–11

1. THE PARTS OF A NEWSPAPER

Letter Groups You know the words **ring** and **lock**. Find each of these words in one of the new words below. Circle the word you know in each word. Read the new words. Then write the new words on the lines.

bring ____________ clock ____________

before Circle the letter group **ore** in each word below. You know the first two words. Read and write the new word.

before more score ____________

Base Word You already know the word **interested**. This is the base word **interest** with an **ed** ending. Write the base word in the sentence below. Then read the sentence.

Does science ____________ you at all?

Take a Guess Read the sentence below. See if you can guess the words in dark letters. Ask yourself, *What is a **star**? What would someone who is a star wear?*

The **movie** star is wearing fancy **clothes**.

Did you guess the words? Try another one: The shop was closed **yesterday**, but it's open for **business** today.

Write the four new words on the lines below.

____________ ____________

____________ ____________

Words to Know

	Look	Say	Picture	Write
basket bas-ket	☐	☐	☐	____________
bench	☐	☐	☐	____________
bring	☐	☐	☐	____________

8

Worktext page 8

1. THE PARTS OF A NEWSPAPER

A newspaper is not just a paper that brings you news. A newspaper brings you many other kinds of information as well. It is a tool you can use to help you live your life. To use this tool, you have to understand how it is put together. Every newspaper has different parts. Each part has a different kind of news or information.

The first part of a newspaper has what is called **hard news**. Hard news is any important or interesting event that has just happened. Many such events have to do with politics. But there are other kinds of hard news, too. A new President of the U.S.—that's hard news. A big storm that shuts down much of the city—that's hard news. A war that breaks out somewhere in the world—that's hard news, too. The most important news goes on the front page. Less important news goes on other pages inside.

A newspaper has different parts for different kinds of news. For example, all the news about your city and state may be in a part of its own. In most big-city newspapers, you will find all the news about money and jobs in one part. This news is of great interest to some people, but not to everyone.

Another part of the newspaper gives only sports news. Here, you can find out how all the teams did in every main sport. You can get the score for a basketball game yesterday. You can find out how many baskets each player had and who made the winning basket.

Still another part has articles about fun things to do and see around town. Do you want to know where to hear some music tonight? Do you want to know what big shows are coming to town? What movies are playing now? When and where to see a movie? You can find out from the newspaper.

Every newspaper has ads, too. A newspaper cannot keep going without ads. People and businesses pay to put ads in the newspaper. In fact, most of the money that a newspaper makes comes from ads.

There are, however, two kinds of ads in a newspaper. One kind is put in by businesses. These ads are found all through the newspaper. Some are big—they can take up a whole page. Some even take up two pages. Ads of this kind may have pictures and headings written in fancy letters. These ads try to make people stop and look. They give information that helps businesses sell things. This kind of ad may tell you of a clothes sale. It may tell you that the new cars for the year have come in. It may tell about some good buys down at the food store.

The other kind of ad is often known as a want ad. These are found in only one part of the paper. Want ads are very small. They are listed one after another in long lines. Some want ads tell of jobs that are open. Some tell of houses and apartments for sale or rent. Most want ads are taken out by people who have something for sale. If you want a used car or a used computer, the want ads are a good place to look. But anything else might turn up in the want ads, too. Are you looking for an old clock? Do you want to buy a used park bench? You may or may not find one in the want ads—but it's worth a look, anyway.

10

Worktext page 10

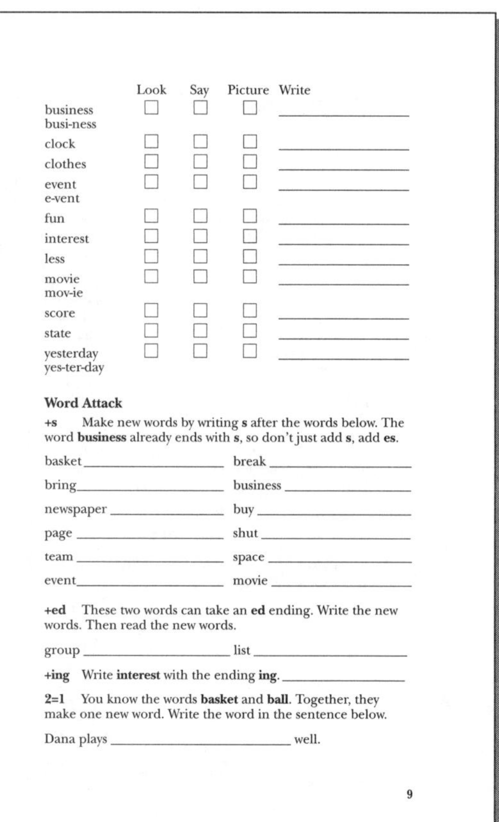

	Look	Say	Picture	Write
business busi-ness	☐	☐	☐	____________
clock	☐	☐	☐	____________
clothes	☐	☐	☐	____________
event e-vent	☐	☐	☐	____________
fun	☐	☐	☐	____________
interest	☐	☐	☐	____________
less	☐	☐	☐	____________
movie mov-ie	☐	☐	☐	____________
score	☐	☐	☐	____________
state	☐	☐	☐	____________
yesterday yes-ter-day	☐	☐	☐	____________

Word Attack

+s Make new words by writing **s** after the words below. The word **business** already ends with **s**, so don't just add **s**, add **es**.

basket ____________ break ____________

bring ____________ business ____________

newspaper ____________ buy ____________

page ____________ shut ____________

team ____________ space ____________

event ____________ movie ____________

+ed These two words can take an **ed** ending. Write the new words. Then read the new words.

group ____________ list ____________

+ing Write **interest** with the ending **ing**. ____________

2=1 You know the words **basket** and **ball**. Together, they make one new word. Write the word in the sentence below.

Dana plays ____________ well.

9

Worktext page 9

Finding Paragraphs

The sentences in a written work are grouped together. Each group is called a **paragraph**. A paragraph has only one main idea. All the sentences in the paragraph say something about this idea. You can tell where one paragraph ends and a new one starts just by looking at a page. Each new paragraph starts on a new line. It starts a few spaces in from the left side. Count the paragraphs in **Parts of a Newspaper**. How many do you find?

____

Finding Main Idea Sentences

Sometimes, one sentence in a paragraph tells the main idea. Look at the second paragraph in **Parts of a Newspaper**. The first sentence tells you the main idea. It is that the first part of a newspaper is for hard news. This is a main-idea sentence. All the other sentences give some detail about hard news.

Now look at the third, fourth, and fifth paragraphs. Look for the main-idea sentence in each of these paragraphs. Write the main-idea sentences on the lines below.

Paragraph 3 ____________

____

____

Paragraph 4 ____________

____

____

Paragraph 5 ____________

____

____

11

Worktext page 11

LESSON 7.2

OBJECTIVE
- Students will practice and apply skills to an extended passage

MATERIALS
Worktext 7, pages 12–15
Teacher's Manual, pages 297–298, 331, 333
Practice Lesson 7.2, pages 68–69 of the Worktext

SKILLS REVIEW

- Before reading, you may wish to review these words that apply phonics skills: *moved, outside, lived, years, finished, likes, willing, wants, things, runs, friends, takes, classes, rented, looking, someone, interested, bedroom, gets, living, neighborhood, moves, clothes, starts, hits, started, says, anywhere, getting, ads, changes, heads, remembers, bills, looks, coming, asks, seems, something, finds, gives.* Have students review the Memory Chips they have learned so far. Then ask: **What do you need to do to get an apartment of your own?**
- While reading, have students think about what kind of character Dana is.
- After reading, have students complete the Comprehension Exercises (Getting to Know Characters, Writting a Plot Summary, and Finding the Main Idea) on Worktext pages 14–15.

For further practice, have students complete Practice Lesson 7.2 on pages 68–69 of the Worktext. Answers can be found in the Answer Key on pages 359–360 of this *Teacher's Manual.*

RETEACH

If students need further review of phonics skills, you may wish to use the following activity:

Phonograms *ore, ing, ock*

Scavenger Hunt Divide students into small groups. Then give them this list, and have them look in the classroom for appropriate objects.

1. Bring something that you use before lunch.
2. Bring something that is more than 10.
3. Bring something that keeps score.
4. Bring a ball you use when you keep score.
5. Bring back something that is shaped like a clock.
6. Bring something you wore to school yesterday.
7. Bring something you wore before today.
8. Bring something you tore.
9. Bring something you wish you have more of.

CONNECTION

Response to Reading
- To reinforce students' understanding of the literary elements found in their reading material, have them complete the Character Cluster reproducible found on page 331.
- Students will demonstrate an understanding of characters by filling out the organizer.
- Students may share their completed organizers with the class.

Literature
- Students may enjoy reading or listening to other books about young women. *Jane Eyre* and *Little Women* are available in softcover texts and on audiocassette from Pearson's *Pacemaker™ Classics.*
- Students may use the Book Report reproducible found on page 333 of this *Teacher's Manual* to record their responses to the books they read.

2. DANA ON HER OWN

When Dana was young, her family moved to a place just outside the city. She has lived outside the city most of her life. Now she is 18 years old and has finished high school. She wants to move back to the city and start a life of her own. Her family likes the idea and is willing to help her any way they can. But Dana doesn't want a lot of help. That's just the point. She wants to do things on her own now.

One day, she runs into Jen. Dana and Jen were good friends in high school. Jen is a year older than Dana. She got out of school last year. She has a part-time job and takes college classes. Later, she and another woman rented an apartment in the city. But the other woman has just moved out. Jen can't

12

Worktext page 12

handle the rent by herself. She is looking for someone to move in with her.

"Say, how about you?" she says to Dana. "Would you be interested? The bedroom is big, and it gets a lot of sun. We have a big kitchen and living room, and the neighborhood is safe. Your part of the rent would come to $405. What do you think?"

"What do I think? I think it's a great idea," says Dana. That same week, Dana moves her things into the new place.

She doesn't have much—just her clothes. She will need a lot of things now that she is on her own. She starts to write down all the things she will need. Then it hits her that she can't buy any of these things—not yet. She will need some money first. To get some money, she will need a job. To get a job, she will have to go around town from business to business. To get around town, she will need a car. To get a car, she will need money. To get money—

"Wait," she says, "I'm back to where I started. First things first, they say—but what if there is no first thing? This is all one big circle."

"Look," says Jen, "you don't need a car at first. You can get around the city on a bus. Buy yourself a pass. With that, you can ride any bus, anytime, from anywhere to anywhere. You keep your mind on getting a job. You will need it to pay the rent! Go out and buy a newspaper. Look through the want ads. See what there is."

"Right away," says Dana. She changes to street clothes and heads off. On the way to the corner, she remembers that she will need some change. She looks through her bag. All she has are dollar bills. Will she have to go all the way back to the apartment? She turns. A guy is coming up behind her. He has to stop short so as not to crash into her. "Do you happen to have change for a dollar?" she asks.

He does not seem to even see her. He seems to be looking at something past her. Yet, he looks through his pocket and finds some change. He gives it to her and takes her dollar. Dana moves on.

13

Worktext page 13

Getting to Know Characters

So far you know two characters by name in this story. Write their names in the chart below. Write the name of the main character on the first line to the left. Write the name of the other character on the line below it.

Names of characters	*Facts about the characters*
________	________________
	________________
	________________
	________________
	________________
________	________________
	________________
	________________
	________________
	________________

Write three facts about each character in the chart. Use facts from the box below.

Is one year older	Just finished high school
Is living on her own	Wants to live on her own
Never lived in the city	Has a job

14

Worktext page 14

Writing a Plot Summary

The sentences below all tell things that have happened so far in this story. Use six of them to write a summary of what has happened so far. Remember that a summary tells only main events. So leave out sentences that give small details.

Dana runs into Jen, an old friend from high school.
Jen is taking classes at a college.
Jen asks Dana to move in with her.
She says the kitchen and living room of the apartment are big.
Dana is not sure where to start in setting up her new life.
Jen tells Dana to work on getting a job first of all.
Dana says, "Right away."
Dana goes out to buy a newspaper.
On the way, she takes change from a young man.

____
____
____
____
____
____

Finding the Main Idea

Each paragraph in a story has one main idea. But the story as a whole has one bigger main idea. Read these sentences about **Dana On Her Own**. Which one best tells the main idea of the whole story so far?

Dana moves into the city to start a life of her own.
Dana meets an old friend from high school.
Dana meets a boy on the way to the corner.

____
____

15

Worktext page 15

LESSON 7.3

OBJECTIVES

- Students will decode words containing the *ack, ock, ick,* and *eam* phonograms
- Students will use context clues to figure out unknown words
- Students will apply endings *ing, er, s,* and *ly* to base words to form new words
- Students will recognize and form possessives
- Students will recognize and form compound words

PHONICS VOCABULARY

blocks	ads	newspaper	grouped
jobs	apartments	heading	houses
kinds	things	cars	computers
headings	darker	bigger	inside
interested	sometimes	understand	words
letters	rooms	means	miles
asking	parts	gives	black
runs	look	stands	stormer
schools	block	dogs	dream
quick	playground	engine	loud
slows	letting	Bill's	neighborhood

WORDS TO KNOW

aunt	black	block	dream
engine	example	loud	model
number	power	quick	special
stormer	uncle		

MATERIALS

Worktext 7, pages 16–20
Teacher's Manual, pages 299–301
Practice Lesson 7.3, pages 70–71 of the Worktext

TEACH

- Using Worktext pages 16–17, introduce students to the vocabulary words. Give students an opportunity to practice writing the words.
- Students can organize their Memory Chips, found in the back of the Worktext. Students can divide them into groups of words they know and words they don't recognize. Then say each word, having students repeat it after you.

Worktext pages 16–17 can also be used to reinforce spelling. Use the five-step process detailed on page 71 of this *Teacher's Manual.*

Phonograms *ack, ock, ick, eam*

Write these words on the board, and ask students how they are alike: **black**, **sock**, **brick**. (*They all end in ck; all have short vowel sounds.*) Then say this sentence, and ask students which two words rhyme. **I dream of ice cream.** *(dream, cream)*

Blending Have students brainstorm words that rhyme with *black, sock, brick,* and *cream.* Write each word on the board, blending the sounds as you write. *(back, sack, tack, rack; tock, block, clock; sick, tick, click; dream, scream, team)*

Context Clues

Write this sentence on the board: **We opened the hood of the car and were surprised to find that the engine was missing!** Cover the word *engine* and tell students that when they see an unfamiliar word like this one, they can read the words around it and use what they know about letters and sounds to help them figure out the word. Read the sentence without *engine.* Uncover the word and have students look at the beginning syllable, *en.* Tell them that the *en* gives a clue as to how the word begins. Ask them what word they think goes in the sentence.

Endings *ing, er, s, ly*

Remind students that when *ing* and *er* are added to base words, the ending consonant is sometimes doubled.

Make New Words Write these words on the board, and invite students to add *ing, er, s,* and *ly* to the end of each: **let**, **quick**, **dark**, **block**. *(letting, lets; quicker, quickly; darker; blocking, blocker, blocks)* Students can use each new word they make in a sentence.

Possessives

Remind students that when they want to show ownership by a person or thing, they add an apostrophe and *s.*

Make New Words Have students add an apostrophe and *s* to these words and use them in sentences: *Bill, engine, boy.* (*Bill's, engine's, boy's*)

PRACTICE

- Let students practice the new words they have learned and formed by completing the activities found on pages 16–17 of the Worktext.
- If students are experiencing difficulty with the Words to Know section on pages 16–17, you may wish to scramble the letters of each word on the board. Then have partners look at the Memory Chips, unscramble the words, and read them aloud.

For further practice, have students complete Practice Lesson 7.3 on pages 70–71 of the Worktext. Answers can be found in the Answer Key on page 360 of this *Teacher's Manual.*

APPLY

- Have students talk about the story concept by sharing their experiences. Ask: **What kinds of things can you find advertised in want ads?** Tell students they are going to use the words they have learned to read an article about the want ads in a newspaper.
- Ask students to read the article on pages 18–19 in the Worktext. Offer assistance if necessary, but encourage students to decode the words independently, using the clues and patterns they have learned.
- After students have completed reading the article, have them complete the Comprehension Exercise (Reading for Facts) on page 20 in their Worktext. Answers can be found in the Answer Key on page 359 of this *Teacher's Manual.*

CONNECTION

Strategy for Reading After students finish reading the selection "Shopping the Want Ads" on Worktext pages 18–19, ask them to summarize it either aloud or in writing.

Speaking/Listening Student partners can read the selection aloud. The partners can alternate being speaker and listener.

Writing Students should be encouraged to keep a journal of their writings. They can use these journals to record responses to their reading, list new words they have learned, or record their thoughts about the reading selection.

Worktext Pages 16–17

3. SHOPPING THE WANT ADS

Letter Groups You know the first two words in each set of words below. The last word—the one in dark letters—is new. Circle the letter group that all three words in the set share. Then read the new word and write it on the line.

pack back **black** ______

lock rock **block** ______

team scream **dream** ______

pick stick **quick** ______

Take a Guess Read the sentence below. The words in dark letters are new. Try to guess these words. The words **car** and **hear** should help you.

The **engine** in that car is so **loud** that you can hear it for miles!

Did you guess the two new words? Now write them on the lines below.

______ ______

Words to Know

	Look	Say	Picture	Write
add	☐	☐	☐	______
aunt	☐	☐	☐	______
black	☐	☐	☐	______
block	☐	☐	☐	______
dream	☐	☐	☐	______
engine en-gine	☐	☐	☐	______
example ex-am-ple	☐	☐	☐	______

16

Worktext page 16

	Look	Say	Picture	Write
loud	☐	☐	☐	______
model mod-el	☐	☐	☐	______
number num-ber	☐	☐	☐	______
power pow-er	☐	☐	☐	______
quick	☐	☐	☐	______
special spe-cial	☐	☐	☐	______
uncle un-cle	☐	☐	☐	______

Word Attack

+s Write the words below with **s** at the end.

block ______ school ______

room ______ slow ______

ad ______

+er Add the ending **er** to **dark.** ______

Add the ending **er** to **storm.** ______

+ly Add the ending **ly** to **quick.** ______

+ing You can put the ending **ing** on **let.** You have to add one more **t** to **let.** Write the new word.

let (+t) + ing = ______

2=1 The word **playground** is made up of two words you know. Read this new word. Write the words that are in it.

playground = ______ + ______

+'s **Bill** can be a name. To show that **Bill** owns or has something, add **'s** at the end. Write the new word in the sentence below.

Hey, isn't this ______ house?

17

Worktext page 17

3. SHOPPING THE WANT ADS

Want ads in a newspaper are grouped together. All the ads for jobs will be in one place. All the apartments for rent will be under another heading. Houses for rent will make up another group. Houses for sale will show up under yet another heading. Then there are all the different kinds of things people want to buy and sell. Cars might make up one group. Computers make up another.

When you shop the want ads, look at the headings first. These are in darker, bigger letters. Each one may be inside a box. Use the headings to help you find the group of ads you are interested in. Then look through this group for the very thing you want.

Sometimes, want ads can be hard to understand. People have to pay for these ads by the word—or even by the letter. They don't want to use any more letters than they have to. At the same time, they want to pack in as much information as they can. So they leave out words not needed to get their idea across. Sometimes, they use just one or two letters to stand for a whole word. They may write **nu** for **new**—just to save a letter. They may write **rms** for **rooms** or **apt** for **apartment**. Because of this, you sometimes have to work a little to guess what a want ad means.

To help you guess, ask yourself what the ad is for. This will point you to the kind of information you should find. Just about any car ad will tell you what year the car was made. It will tell you the make and model of the car. The ad may tell you how many miles the car has on it. It is sure to tell how much money the owner is asking. It may tell what new parts, if any, the car has. Also, it gives a number to call if you are interested. Look at this ad.

**'97 Stormer, black.
Runs gd, looks great! 60K miles.
power+! $1400. Call 555-5555.**

18

Worktext page 18

In this ad, **'97** stands for the year 1997. **Stormer** is, of course, the make of the car. The letters **gd** stand for **good.** But what does **60K** mean? It means **60,000**. The letter **K** is often used to stand for **1,000. Power +** is a way of letting you know that the car has a strong engine.

An ad about an apartment for rent will give another whole set of information. It will tell you how big the place is, how much the rent is, and who to call. It may give other information, too. It may tell something about the neighborhood. It may tell you things you can or can't do there. Look at this ad.

**$575 5-room dream apt.
Close to schools. One block to playground;
two blocks to bus. No loud music. Dogs OK.
Call 555-5555 after 6. Ask for Mr. White.**

An ad for a job will tell what the job is, who you will work for, and what special skills you may need. Sometimes, it tells how much money you will get. More often you have to find out about the money when you go in to see about the job. Here is an ad for a job.

**COOK:
Uncle Bill's fast-food
restaurant needs full-time cook.
Great pay. Call 555-5555 between
2–10 PM.**

19

Worktext page 19

Reading for Facts

Sometimes, it is best to read every word and think about each sentence. But not always. If you are looking for just one detail or fact, you may want to read in a different way. You let your eye move over the page quickly. In this way, you read just enough of each line to see if it has the information you need. If not, you move on.

Try out this way of reading. Look through **Shopping the Want Ads**. Find an ad for a car. Then find the answer to each question below. Write each answer on the line.

What year is the car? ____________________

How much is the owner asking for it? ____________________

How many miles are there on the car? ____________________

What number should you call? ____________________

Now find the ad that tells about an apartment for rent. Answer these questions about the apartment.

How big is the apartment? ____________________

How much is the rent? ____________________

What is it close to? ____________________

Can you live there if you own a dog? ____________________

What number should you call? ____________________

Who should you ask for? ____________________

Now find the ad about a job. Answer the two questions.

What kind of work is it? ____________________

When should you call? ____________________

20

Worktext page 20

LESSON 7.4

OBJECTIVE

- Students will practice and apply skills to an extended passage

MATERIALS

Worktext 7, pages 21–24
Teacher's Manual, pages 302–303, 333
Practice Lesson 7.4, pages 72–73 of the Worktext

SKILLS REVIEW

- Before reading, you may wish to review these words that apply phonics skills: *miles, seems, feels, longer, Dan's, works, homes, houses, skills, helping, computers, bills, books, starting, worker, lives, moving, turns, looking, leaves, needs, living, wants, pushes, glasses, suddenly, stops, asks, takes, walks, uses, opens, buys, finds, ads, making, looks, happens, interesting, apartments, rooms.* Have students review the Memory Chips they have learned so far. Then ask: **What kind of job would be a dream job for you?**
- While reading, have students think about how Dan's and Dana's experiences are alike.
- After reading, have students complete the Comprehension Exercises (Finding the Main Idea and Alike and Different) on Worktext pages 23–24.

For further practice, have students complete Practice Lesson 7.4 on pages 72–73 of the Worktext. Answers can be found in the Answer Key on page 360 of this *Teacher's Manual.*

RETEACH

If students need further review of phonics skills, you may wish to use the following activity:

Phonograms *ack, ock, eam, ick*

Letter Scramble Relay Have students brainstorm words that rhyme with *pack, lock, team,* and *pick.* List the words on the board in a column under each word as they list them. If they suggest words like *seem,* put them in a different column. Then write these scrambled words on the board: **damer**, **ucikq**, **citks**, **kipc**, **recams**, **meta**, **cork**, **colk**, **cabk**, **cpak**, **clabk**. (*dream, quick, stick, pick, scream, team, rock, lock, back, pack, black*)

Divide the class into two teams. Have them have a relay race. Each team sends a member to unscramble a word. When they finish, they tag the next player until all the words are unscrambled. The first team to finish wins.

CONNECTION

Response to Reading

- Student partners can create two want ads—one selling an item and the second advertising a job opportunity.
- Students may use computers, if available, to give a professional look to their want ads.

Literature

- Students may enjoy reading or listening to another story that takes place in a city. *A Tale of Two Cities* is available in softcover text and on audiocassette from Pearson's *Pacemaker™ Classics.*
- Students may use the Book Report reproducible found on page 333 of this *Teacher's Manual* to record their responses to the book.

4. NEW IN THE CITY

Dan is new in the city. All through high school, he lived with his family in a small town about 75 miles north of the city. After high school, he didn't know what to do with his life. He could have gone back to a job he had the summer before—cooking at a fast-food place down by the freeway. But he doesn't want that job anymore. It doesn't pay enough, and it seems like a job for a kid. Dan feels he is no longer a kid. In his town, there are hardly any jobs for a young man. So Dan did a lot of nothing in his first summer out of high school. At first he liked it, but that way of life can get old fast.

One night, his uncle called from the city. Dan's uncle works for a business called Henson Homes. They build houses. Dan's uncle said that a job was about to open up at his place of work. It was not a great job. It did not call for any special skills. Most of the time, Dan would be helping out in the office.

21

Worktext page 21

"But," said his uncle, "the pay is OK. I'm sure it's better than anything you can get in your town, Dan. You can learn on this job. You can pick up some job skills. You like computers, don't you? Well, you would run a computer here. You'll make out bills. You can learn how to keep books for a business. What's more, Henson Homes is starting to grow. If you are a hard worker, you can move up as time goes on. Are you interested? I could put in a word for you."

Dan said he was very interested. The next week, his uncle called to say he had the job.

So Dan lives in the city now. Moving here was a big change, as it turns out. Maybe it was a little more change than he was looking for. He still feels lost here most of the time. But he is excited, too. Every day seems full of adventures. Every time he leaves the house, he feels as if anything could happen.

Today, he is going to the corner to buy a newspaper. He needs to look at the want ads. Dan is still living with his aunt and uncle, and that can't last. Their place is not big enough. Dan wants a place of his own.

On the way, a young woman pushes past him, going fast. She has a red hat and dark glasses. She is looking through her bag as she walks. Suddenly, she stops and turns. "Do you have change for a dollar?" she asks Dan.

"Sure." Dan gives her the change and takes the dollar bill from her hand. The girl walks on. When he gets to the newspaper box on the corner, he finds himself in line behind her. She uses the change she took from Dan to buy a paper. Then it's Dan's turn to buy a paper.

He opens the paper. He can't wait to look through the want ads. So he goes into a restaurant on the corner, buys a cool drink, and finds a place to sit. The girl with the dark glasses is in the same restaurant, sitting by herself.

Dan opens his paper to the want ads. He starts to look at apartments for rent. Most of them are too much money for Dan. One time, when he looks up, he sees that the girl has taken off her dark glasses. She, too, has her paper open to the want ads. *Now, what could she be looking for?* he asks himself. *Could she be new in town—like me?* he wants to ask her. She does not seem interested in making new friends. So he looks back at his own newspaper.

22

Worktext page 22

This time his eye happens to land on an interesting ad under **Apartments for Rent.** This is the ad:

> **$300: Big apartment. 3 rooms.**
> **New building. Quiet and sunny.**
> **All-electric kitchen. Call Mack, 555-5555.**

This looks great! Maybe this will be his new place. Dan wants to tell someone. He looks around for the girl with the red hat. But she is gone.

Finding the Main Idea

As you know, a paragraph is a group of sentences about the same main idea. Sometimes, the main idea is right there in one of the sentences. More often, the main idea is not in any one sentence. You can tell what the main idea is from looking at all the sentences that are there. You can see that all the sentences point toward one idea, or all the sentences together add up to one idea. Look at the first paragraph of **New in the City.** The main idea of this paragraph could be put as follows:

Dan couldn't find a good job in his hometown.

Every sentence in the paragraph adds some little piece to this main idea. Some tell when he couldn't find a good job (after high school). Some tell why he didn't want the job he could find (doesn't pay enough, and so on). Some tell why he can't find a good job (no jobs for a young man). Some tell where his hometown is (75 miles north of the city). All the sentences together add up to the main idea.

Now look at the second paragraph of the story. Which of the sentences below best gives the main idea of this whole paragraph? Circle the sentence.

Dan's uncle told him about a job in the city.

One night, a great thing happened.

Dan likes to talk to his uncle.

23

Worktext page 23

Try one more. Look at the third paragraph of the story. Now read the sentences below. Pick the one that best tells the main idea of the third paragraph. Circle it.

His uncle tells him about Henson Homes.

Dan finds out he can run a computer on this job.

His uncle tells him some good things about the job.

Alike and Different

You read about Dana in **Dana On Her Own.** Now you have read about Dan. In some ways, these two characters are **in the same boat.** In some ways, they face different problems. Look at each fact below. Write **Dan** if it tells only about Dan. Write **Dana** if it tells only about Dana. Write **Both** if it tells something about both characters.

__________ just finished high school

__________ wants to start a new life in the city

__________ is young

__________ needs a car

__________ was living just outside the city

__________ is moving away from home for the first time

__________ already has a place to live

__________ was living in a small town north of the city

__________ already has a job

__________ needs a place to live

__________ needs a job

24

Worktext page 24

LESSON 7.5

OBJECTIVES

- Students will decode and blend rhyming words containing the *ove, oke, ose, ark,* and *ore* phonograms
- Students will use context clues to figure out unknown words
- Students will apply endings *s, ing, er,* and *ed* to base words to form new words
- Students will recognize and form possessives
- Students will recognize and form contractions

PHONICS VOCABULARY

suppose	younger	brother	comes
pieces	directions	points	looking
don't	parts	things	tells
cooking	foods	there's	putting
tools	supposed	missing	pulling
it's	mark	won't	minutes
hours	store	kid's	hangs
listening	ones	uncle's	above
writing	you'll	means	smoke
once	steps	burned	boy's

WORDS TO KNOW

above	brother	easy	hour
mark	minute	once	second
step	store	suppose	table

MATERIALS

Worktext 7, pages 25–31
Teacher's Manual, pages 304–306
Practice Lesson 7.5, pages 74–75 of the Worktext

TEACH

- Using Worktext page 26, introduce students to the vocabulary words. Say each word, and have students repeat it after you.
- Students can organize their Memory Chips, found in the back of the Worktext. They can divide them into words that have one and two syllables.

Worktext page 26 can also be used to reinforce spelling. Use the five-step process detailed on page 71 of this *Teacher's Manual.*

Rhyming Words and Phonograms *ove, oke, ose, ark, ore*

Write these words on index cards, mix them up, and say them aloud as students repeat them after you: **move**, **prove**, **other**, **brother**, **joke**, **smoke**, **those**, **suppose**, **before**, **more**, **explore**, **mark**, **dark**, **park**.

Blending Mix up the cards, and have students find the words that rhyme. Have them say each word, blending the sounds. Then have them suggest other rhyming words. Write the words on index cards, and add them to the pile.

Context Clues

Write this sentence on the board: **I hope I can finish making the cake before the party.** Read the sentence aloud, leaving out *finish.* Frame *finish,* and have students figure out what the word means by reading the other words in the sentence. Then have them look at the beginning sound for other clues. Ask students to read the sentence aloud with you, pausing before you say *finish.*

Endings *s, ing, er, ed*

Remind students that they can add the endings *s, ing, er,* and *ed* to words. Remind them that if a word ends in *e,* they drop the *e,* and add *ed.*

Make New Words Write these words on the board, and have students take turns adding the endings *s, ing, er,* and *ed* to them to make new words: **young**, **burn**, **suppose**, **tool**. (*younger*; *burns, burning, burner, burned*; *supposes, supposing, supposed*; *tools*) Have them use each word in a sentence.

Possessives

Remind students that they can show ownership by adding an apostrophe and *s* to the end of a word.

Make New Words Have students add an apostrophe and *s* to these words: *uncle, Bill, brother.* (*uncle's, Bill's, brother's*)

Contractions

Remind students that they can sometimes make a shorter word out of two words. Write **there's** on the board, and ask students what two words it stands for. (*there is*)

Make New Words Write these word pairs on the board, and have volunteers take turns making contractions of each pair: **do not**, **is not**, **cannot**, **it is**. (*don't, isn't, can't, it's*)

PRACTICE

- Let students practice the new words they have learned and formed by completing the activities found on pages 25–27 of the Worktext.
- If students are experiencing difficulty with the Words to Know section on page 26, you may wish to have them write the troublesome words on laminated Tic-Tac-Toe cards. Have them play Tic-Tac-Toe with partners, saying each word before they make an O or X.

For further practice, have students complete Practice Lesson 7.5 on pages 74–75 of the Worktest. Answers can be found in the Answer Key on page 360 of this *Teacher's Manual.*

APPLY

- Have students predict what will happen next. Ask: **How can directions help you?**
- Ask students to read the article on pages 28–29 in the Worktext. Encourage students to decode the words independently, using the clues and patterns they have learned.
- After students have completed reading the article, have them complete the Comprehension Exercises (Following Directions and How to Follow Directions) on pages 30–31 in their Worktext. Answers can be found in the Answer Key on page 360 of this *Teacher's Manual.*

CONNECTION

Strategy for Reading Have students reread the selection "Reading Directions" on Worktext pages 28–29 to correct comprehension breakdowns. Students may achieve understanding by reprocessing the same text with greater attention focused on its meaning.

5. READING DIRECTIONS

Try This You know how the letter group **ove** sounds in **move** and **prove**. This letter group sounds differently in **love**. Try both ways in this new word: **above**. What is the word? Write it in this sentence.

Most of the building is ______________ the ground.

Letter Groups You know the word **other**. Put **br** before **other**, and you have the new word: **brother**. Can you read this word? Write it in the sentence.

This is my sister, and that is my ______________.

Read each set of words below. The word in dark letters is new. All the words in the same line share a letter group. Circle the letter group. Read the new word and then write it in the space.

joke **smoke** ____________

those **suppose** ____________

dark park **mark** ____________

before explore more **store** ____________

Take a Guess The word **once** is made from **one**. Look for this new word in the sentence below. See if you can guess what it means from the rest of the sentence. The words **not**, **but**, and **two** should help you.

Mu Lan went to California not **once** but two times.

Write the new word. ______________

25

Worktext page 25

Worktext Pages 25–27

Words to Know

	Look	Say	Picture	Write
above a-bove	☐	☐	☐	________
brother broth-er	☐	☐	☐	________
easy eas-y	☐	☐	☐	________
hour	☐	☐	☐	________
mark	☐	☐	☐	________
minute min-ute	☐	☐	☐	________
once	☐	☐	☐	________
second sec-ond	☐	☐	☐	________
step	☐	☐	☐	________
store	☐	☐	☐	________
suppose sup-pose	☐	☐	☐	________
table ta-ble	☐	☐	☐	________

Word Attack

+s Write each word below with an **s** ending.

tool ______________ food ______________

hour ______________ piece ______________

minute ______________ step ______________

hang ______________

+ing Add the ending **ing** to **miss**. ______________

Add the ending **ing** to **pull**. ______________

26

Worktext page 26

+ed You can add the **ed** ending to each of the words below. The word **suppose** already has an **e** at the end, so just add **d**.

burn ______________ suppose ______________

+er Write **young** with an **er** ending in the sentence below.

My brother is ______________ than I am.

+'s As you know, you can add the ending **'s** to show that someone owns or has something. Add **'s** to these words.

boy ______________ kid ______________

Now use the two new words in this sentence.

They found a __________ bike in that __________ house.

Write **uncle** with **'s** at the end. ______________

1+1 The words **there is** can be written as one new word: **there's**. Write the new word on the line below. Then circle the letters you left out of the two words to write the one word.

there is = ______________

27

Worktext page 27

5. READING DIRECTIONS

Suppose your younger brother comes to you with a problem. He has a new bike—but it is all in pieces. Can you put it together for him? "It's easy," you say. "Just follow the directions."

Well, maybe it is not so easy. Written directions are a fact of life—you come across them every day. But even well-written directions can be hard to follow. Many directions are not well written.

Here are some points that can help you follow any directions you come across. First, start by looking through the whole set of directions from start to finish one time. Don't try to follow them at this point. Just read for the big picture. Get an idea of how the whole job should go.

Most directions have two parts. One part tells what things you will need. Another part tells what you should do. After you read the whole set of directions once, read the first part again. When you finish this part, stop and see if you have everything you need.

28

Worktext page 28

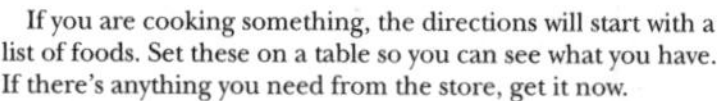

If you are cooking something, the directions will start with a list of foods. Set these on a table so you can see what you have. If there's anything you need from the store, get it now.

Suppose you are putting together a bike. The first part of the directions tell what tools you need and what parts are supposed to be in the box. It may even show a picture of the parts. After you finish reading the first part of the directions, stop. Get your tools together. Make sure you have all the parts shown. If something is missing, this is the time to go back to the store.

After you finish pulling your tools together, read the second part of the directions. Now it's time to follow the directions step by step. It's important to go one step at a time. Read each step, do that step, and then go on to the next one. Mark your place after you finish reading so that you can come back to the same place each time. That way you won't miss any steps. Above all, take your time. A job may take minutes if you are slow and hours if you are fast. Why? Because when you move too fast, you often do some things wrong.

Follow the steps in the order that they are written. Good directions will give you the steps in the right order. When you finish the last step, the kid's bike should be ready to ride. Or, if you were cooking, set the table—it's time to eat.

Some directions don't tell how to make something. They tell how to get from one place to another. Directions of this kind don't have a first part—the tools you will need. They only have part two—the steps you should take. Most of the time, you don't see these directions written out. You hear them—over the telephone more often than not. If you want to remember them, you have to write them down. Your main problem, then, is to write the directions in such a way that you can understand and follow them later.

You may not have time to take down every word as you are listening to the directions. Just be sure to get the most important ones. Suppose you want to go to your uncle's house. You call him up. He tells you, "Take the freeway north, get off at Main Street, and go two blocks—" Then he hangs up. You might write, *Freeway N, Main, 2.* As soon as you hang up the telephone, look at what you have written. Write the directions over again—right away while you still remember what was said. Remember that you will have to read your own writing later, so make sure that you'll know what every word means.

29

Worktext page 29

Following Directions

The article you have just read tells how to follow directions. Use the information in the article to fill in the directions below. First, find the best ending for each step. Next, circle the letter of the ending you have picked (**a**, **b**, or **c**). Then, write the missing words in the space that follows the step.

How to Follow Directions

1. For any kind of directions, start by

   a. doing what the first step tells you.
   b. reading the directions from start to finish once.
   c. going to the store.

   ____

   ____

2. If the directions are for making something,

   a. read the first part again and then stop.
   b. read through the whole set again.
   c. go right to the store and get what you need.

   ____

   ____

3. After reading the first part again,

   a. get together all the tools and other things you will need.
   b. go right on to part two.
   c. ask for help if you need it.

   ____

   ____

4. Next,

   a. read the rest of the directions to the end.
   b. follow part two of the directions, one step at a time.
   c. follow the directions two steps at a time.

   ____

   ____

30

Worktext page 30

5. If you are taking down directions for going somwhere,

   a. write down every other word.
   b. write down every word.
   c. write down every important word.

   ____

   ____

6. After you hang up the telephone,

   a. put the directions in your pocket till you need them.
   b. call the person back.
   c. look at the directions right away and write them over.

   ____

   ____

31

Worktext page 31

LESSON 7.6

OBJECTIVE
- Students will practice and apply skills to an extended passage

MATERIALS
Worktext 7, pages 32–34
Teacher's Manual, pages 307–308, 330–331, 333
Practice Lesson 7.6, pages 76–77 of the Worktext

SKILLS REVIEW

- Before reading, you may wish to review these words that apply phonics skills: *thinks, answers, says, calling, you're, sometimes, cuts, wants, coming, I'm, directions, talks, waiting, looks, words, letter, sees, woods, remembers, that's, gets, comes, sits, moves, keeps, going, laughs, stands, walks, waits, asks, driver, started, minutes, saved, suppose, other.* Have students review the Memory Chips they have learned so far. Then ask: **What makes directions easy to read? What makes them hard?**
- While reading, have students think about a time they went the wrong way on a bus.
- After reading, have students complete the Comprehension Exercises (Remembering Details and What Do You Think?) on Worktext page 34.

For further practice, have students complete Practice Lesson 7.6 on pages 76–77 of the Worktext. Answers can be found in the Answer Key on pages 360–361 of this *Teacher's Manual.*

RETEACH

If students need further review of phonics skills, you may wish to use the following activity:

Phonograms and Letter Groups *ove, oke, ose, ark, ore*

Finish the Ad Have students brainstorm words that rhyme with *move, love, joke, those, dark,* and *before.* (*prove, above, smoke, suppose, rose, park, mark, explore, more, store*) Write the words on the board in a list. Then write this ad on the board, and have students choose a word from the list to fill in each blank.

Do You Need to _______?

Look no _____! ____ you look any further, make a red _______ around this ad right now! Walk your dog in the beautiful green ______ across the street. Buy your groceries at the _____ next door. Three big rooms, and lots of light! Low, low rent. This is no _____! Call today! 555-1213.

(*Answers: move, more, Before, mark, park, store, joke*)

CONNECTION

Response to Reading
- To reinforce students' understanding of the literary elements found in their reading material, have them complete the Character Cluster reproducible found on page 331.
- Students will demonstrate an understanding of characters by filling out the organizer.
- Students may share their completed organizers with the class.

Literature
- Students may enjoy reading or listening to other adventures involving young male characters. *The Adventures of Tom Sawyer* and *Adventures of Huckleberry Finn* are available in softcover texts and on audiocassette from Pearson's *Pacemaker™ Classics.*
- Students may use the Book Report reproducible found on page 333 of this *Teacher's Manual* to record their responses to the books.

Independent Reading
- Encourage students to read for pleasure and information. Pearson's *Reading Explorations,* Levels C and D, cover social studies, science, math, and life-skills topics. For ESL students, vocabulary words are listed and defined before each reading. Comprehension and critical-thinking questions appear throughout the texts to encourage active reading. See page xvii of this *Teacher's Manual* for additional titles.
- After reading, students may form small groups and share what they learned.

6. DAN TAKES THE BUS

Dan thinks he has found an apartment that will be just right for him. He calls the number given in the ad. A man answers.

"Hi," says Dan. "I am calling about your ad in the paper."

"The dog has already been sold," the man says.

Before the man can hang up, Dan says, "No, wait! I was calling about an apartment. Is this the right number?"

"Oh—the apartment. Yes, this is the right number. But let me tell you, I am not going to rent it to just anyone. Have you got a job?"

"Yes," says Dan.

"All right," says the man. "How old are you?"

"Well—almost 19."

"You're 18," says the man. "I suppose you like loud music, do you?"

"Well," says Dan, "maybe sometimes. But could I—"

"OK, OK," the man cuts in, "you can look at the place. You're not the only one who wants it, you know. A lot of people are coming today. I'm not going to hold it for you or anyone. Get here fast, and have your money ready." He gives Dan directions for getting there on the bus. But he talks fast, and Dan has to write quickly.

Later, standing on Main Street waiting for the bus, he looks at the directions. Oh, no! What are all these words and letters he has written? What do they mean? Here is what he sees: **156N, Cruz, left 3, right 1, up, woods (not) 1453**

Then he remembers one thing. **156** is the bus line. Cruz? Yes, he remembers something about that, too. The man told him to get off at Cruz Street. Well, that's all he needs for now. He can call again when he gets to Cruz Street.

The bus comes, and Dan gets on. At this time of day, there are not many people on the bus. Dan sits by a window and reads street names as he moves along. The bus keeps going, and he never sees Cruz Street. At last, he calls to the bus driver. "What happened to Cruz Street? Is it coming up soon?"

32

Worktext page 32

"Cruz Street is back the other way, my friend—way back!" the driver laughs.

Dan looks at his directions again. He sees the letter **N** for the first time. Suddenly, he knows what the **N** stands for: north. He took the right bus, but going the wrong way. At the next stop, he gets off, walks across the street, and waits for the bus again.

This time he gets on the **156** going north. He asks the bus driver to let him know when they get close to Cruz Street. The bus goes right past the place where Dan started. That's when the driver calls out, "Cruz Street coming up!"

Dan was only two blocks south of Cruz when he started out! So it has taken him an hour to go two blocks by bus. He could have walked to the apartment in 10 minutes, and he would have saved a dollar!

33

Worktext page 33

Remembering Details

Dan has trouble finding his way to the apartment he wants to rent. Here are some sentences about Dan's bad day. One word is missing from each sentence. The missing words are in the box. Write the word that goes in each space. Look back at the story if you need to.

north Cruz south north Cruz Main south

1. Dan waits for the bus on _______________ Street.
2. He wants to take the bus to _______________ Street.
3. Dan starts out just _______________ of Cruz street.
4. He gets on a bus going _______________.
5. Dan gets off and waits for a bus going _______________.
6. He goes two blocks _______________ of where he started.
7. There, he finds _______________ Street at last!

What Do You Think?

One of the sentences above tells the thing that Dan did wrong. Circle the sentence. Now talk about the story with one or more friends who have read it. Why did Dan have this problem. What might he have done to make sure this wouldn't happen?

34

Worktext page 34

LESSON 7.7

OBJECTIVES

- Students will break words into syllables
- Students will decode and blend words containing the *ick* phonogram
- Students will use context clues to figure out unfamiliar words
- Students will apply endings *s, ing,* and *ly* to base words to form new words

PHONICS VOCABULARY

correctly	sick	years	days
filling	growing	questions	heading
carefully	comes	following	directions
closely	names	asks	asking
parents	brothers	wants	persons
numbers	papers	falls	stays

WORDS TO KNOW

ago	buzzer	company	correct
doctor	empty	month	parents
person	security	trick	

MATERIALS

Worktext 7, pages 35–39
Teacher's Manual, pages 309–311
Practice Lesson 7.7, pages 78–79 of the Worktext

TEACH

- Using Worktext pages 35–36, introduce students to the vocabulary words. Say each word, and have students repeat it after you.
- Students can organize their Memory Chips, found in the back of the Worktext. Students can divide them into words that have one, two, or more syllables. Then have students sort the words by beginning sounds.

Worktext pages 35–36 can also be used to reinforce spelling. Use the five-step process detailed on page 71 of this *Teacher's Manual.*

Syllables

Tell students that they can listen to how a word sounds to figure out the number of parts it has. Say **filling**, tapping its two syllables on your desk with a pencil eraser. Then have students beat the syllables with you, tapping their desks with their fingers. Repeat, using *security, company,* and *ago.* Say the following words, and have students tap on their desks each time they hear a syllable: **correctly**, **number**, **closely**, **paper**, **person**, **carefully**.

Phonogram *ick*

Write this sentence on the board, and read it aloud: **I was so sick I could not lick the ice cream.** Ask students what two words rhyme and how these two words are alike. (*sick, lick; they both end in* ick)

Blending Say *sick*, blending it for students: /*s*/ /*i*/ /*k*/. Repeat, using *lick.* Students can take turns suggesting words that rhyme with *sick* and writing them on the board, blending each sound as they go.

Context Clues

Write this sentence on the board: **I got to go to camp for four weeks, or about a month.** Read the sentence aloud, leaving out *month.* Frame *month,* and have students figure out what the word means by reading the other words in the sentence. Then have them look at the beginning sound for other clues. Finally, ask them to read the sentence with you, pausing before you say *month.*

Endings *s, ing, ly*

Remind students that *s, ing,* and *ly* can be added as word endings.

Make New Words Write these words on the board, and have students take turns adding the endings *s, ing,* and *ly* to them to make new words: **brother**, **careful**, **fill**, **correct**. (*brothers, brotherly; carefully; fills, filling; corrects, correcting, correctly*) Have students use each word in a sentence.

PRACTICE

- Let students practice the new words they have learned and formed by completing the activities found on pages 35–36 of the Worktext.
- If students are experiencing difficulty with the Words to Know section on pages 35–36, you may wish to have them write the troublesome words in random order on 16-grid Bingo cards. As you call out each word, students can cover the word in the square with a marker. When a student gets a row going across, down, or diagonally he or she yells "Bingo!"

For further practice, have students complete Practice Lesson 7.7 on pages 78–79 of the Worktext. Answers can be found in the Answer Key on page 361 of this *Teacher's Manual.*

APPLY

- Have students share their prior knowledge about filling out forms. Ask: **What forms have you filled out? What kind of information did the forms ask you to include?** Tell students they are going to use the words they have learned to find out more about filling out forms.

- Ask students to read the article on pages 37–38 in the Worktext. Offer assistance if necessary, but encourage students to decode the words independently, using the clues and patterns they have learned.
- After students have completed reading the article, have them complete the Comprehension Exercise (Fill Out a Form) on page 39 in their Worktext. Answers can be found in the Answer Key on page 360 of this *Teacher's Manual.*

CONNECTION

Strategy for Reading After students finish reading the selection "Filling Out Forms" on Worktext pages 37–38, ask them to summarize it aloud or in writing.

Speaking/Listening Have student partners read the selection aloud. The partners can alternate being speaker and listener.

Writing Ask students to write a few sentences on what they learned about filling out forms.

Worktext Pages 35–36

7. FILLING OUT FORMS

Break It Up You can find two words you know in the new word **ago**. The smaller words are **a** and **go**. They don't tell you what the bigger word means. But they can help you read the word. Try reading it now: **ago**. Write the new word in the sentence below, and read the sentence.

This place was different many years ________.

Letter Groups You know the first two words below. The last word is new. But all three words end with the same letter group. Circle that letter group. Read the new word which is in darker letters. Then write it on the line.

pick stick **trick** ________

Take a Guess Read the sentences below. See if you can guess the word in dark letters.

A **month** is four weeks long.

Did you guess the word? Write it. ________

Words to Know

	Look	Say	Picture	Write
ago a-go	☐	☐	☐	________
buzzer buzz-er	☐	☐	☐	________
company com-pa-ny	☐	☐	☐	________
correct cor-rect	☐	☐	☐	________
doctor doc-tor	☐	☐	☐	________
empty emp-ty	☐	☐	☐	________
month	☐	☐	☐	________

35

Worktext page 35

	Look	Say	Picture	Write
parents par-ents	☐	☐	☐	________
person per-son	☐	☐	☐	________
security se-cu-ri-ty	☐	☐	☐	________
trick	☐	☐	☐	________

Word Attack

+s Write these words with **s**. Read the new words.

brother ________ chance ________

number ________ paper ________

stay ________ person ________

+ly Add the ending **ly** to each of the words below.

careful ________ close ________

correct ________

+ing Write these words with an **ing** ending.

fill ________ grow ________

36

Worktext page 36

7. FILLING OUT FORMS

Do you want to take the driver's test? First, you will have to fill out a form. Do you want to try for a job at some big company? First, you will have to fill out a form. Do you feel sick? Do you need to see a doctor? Guess what? You have to fill out a form.

Many years ago, you could get through your whole life and never see a form, but those days are gone. Filling out forms is now a growing part of day-to-day life.

How can you be sure to fill out a form correctly? First, you need to know one thing. A form does not ask questions for the most part. It gives you headings. You are supposed to fill in the information that goes under each heading.

It is important to read a form carefully. Why? Because filling out a form really comes down to following directions. Almost every form asks for your full name. Now, in day-to-day life, you would write your first name first, your middle name next, and your last name last. But look closely at the form. Do you see some small headings just above, below, or next to the lines on which you are to write your name? Do they say **Last**, **First**, and **Middle**? These headings show the order in which you should write your name. The form may ask that you write your last name first, your first name second, and your middle name last. Whatever the form asks for, that's what you should do.

Here and there on a form, you may see special directions. Follow these, too. There may be a box with the words, **For office use only**. Leave a box like that empty. Or the directions may say, **Answer questions 1-13**. If that is what the form says, don't answer question 14. Make sure you understand each question, too. If the form has a name with a space after it, should you write your name? Look again. What if that part of the form is asking about your parents? If the form says brothers, don't write their names. Maybe the form just wants a number—it may be asking how many, not who. Just be careful. You're not in a race, and you don't have to beat a buzzer. Take your time.

37

Worktext page 37

Some questions turn up on many different forms. You almost always have to write down where you live, when you were born, and what your telephone number is. Often, you are asked to name someone who knows you well and to give a telephone number for this person (or persons). Another number you may have to write on a form is your social security number. You might write some of this information on a card and keep it with you. Then when you have to fill out a form, you will have the correct information at hand.

Also, there are some important numbers that you should not keep on yourself. Many people have money in the bank. They have a special number for their card for the bank machine. It's OK to write down this number, but keep the written number at home with other important papers. Don't take it with you when you go out. That way, even if your bank card falls into the wrong hands, your money stays in the bank.

38

Worktext page 38

Fill Out a Form

The form below asks for information about the article you have just read. Use the information in the article to fill out the form correctly.

Answer question 1 and questions 3-7.
DO NOT ANSWER QUESTION 2.

1. Name: ____________ ____________ ____________

2. Your telephone number: ____________________

3. Birth date: ________ ________ ________

4. Date when article was read: ______ ______ ______ (Day, Month, Year)

5. Name of article: ____________________

6. Number of paragraphs: ____________________

7. What article is about: (Circle the letter of your answer.)
   a. How to fill out forms
   b. How to follow directions
   c. How to keep your papers safe
   d. How to cook

Do not write in this space
Name
Number
Street
CRX ______ QTB ______ TT - YY - GG ______

39

Worktext page 39

LESSON 7.8

OBJECTIVE

- Students will practice and apply skills to an extended passage

MATERIALS

Worktext 7, pages 40–42
Teacher's Manual, pages 312–313, 333
Practice Lesson 7.8, pages 80–81 of the Worktext

SKILLS REVIEW

- Before reading, you may wish to review these words that apply phonics skills: *looks, directions, woods, words, plants, says, thinks, sees, building, answers, walks, sticks, follows, hears, having, throws, windows, rooms, points, getting, turns, hears, lets, stairs, shows, really, works, needs, finds, stands, remembers.* Have students review the Memory Chips they have learned so far. Then ask: **What kind of apartment would you like to have?**
- While reading, have students predict how they think the story will end.
- After reading, have students complete the Comprehension Exercises (Finding Details and Alike and Different) on Worktext page 42.

For further practice, have students complete Practice Lesson 7.8 on pages 80–81 of the Worktext. Answers can be found in the Answer Key on pages 360–361 of this *Teacher's Manual.*

RETEACH

If students need further review of phonics skills, you may wish to use the following activity:

Compound Words

Make a Match Write the two columns on the board, and have students take turns drawing lines to make compound words. They can write the compound word on the board and use it in a sentence.

a	self
a	ground
play	round
basket	live
news	head
a	paper
a	friend
him	go
boy	ball

(*Answers: around, alive, ahead, ago, playground, basketball, newspaper, himself, boyfriend*)

CONNECTION

Response to Reading

- Have students complete a chart with the headings "Apartment 1" and "Apartment 2."
- Students should show an understanding of the story "A Great Apartment" by noting the differences between the two apartments Dan sees.

Literature

- Students may enjoy reading or listening to another story about a young man coming into his own. *The Red Badge of Courage* is available in softcover text and on audiocassette from Pearson's *Pacemaker*™ *Classics.*
- Students may use the Book Report reproducible found on page 333 of this *Teacher's Manual* to record their responses to the book.

8. A GREAT APARTMENT

Dan has gone up one street and down another. He has turned left, and he has turned right. Now he looks again at his directions. He sees the words: **Woods (not)**.

He looks up and—well, well! Right next to the street is a little green space, about two feet by six feet. It has a few little plants. In front of it is a sign that says, **The Woods**.

Not, thinks Dan. *Good, I must be close.* Just then he sees the building up ahead. It is an old, green building. It looks like it is about to fall down.

No one answers Dan's ring. He tries the handle—the door is open. He walks in. "Hi!" he calls out. "Anyone here?"

A man sticks his head out of a door. "You called about the apartment?"

"I'm the one," says Dan.

"Follow me."

Dan follows the man down the hall. On the telephone, the man had said that many people were interested in the apartment. But they do not seem to be here now. Dan hears music from one apartment. He hears voices from another. Two people seem to be having a bad fight. This place is loud!

"Here we are," says the man, and he throws open a door.

Dan walks in and looks around. He sees just one room, and it is not very big. It has two small windows, but the room is pretty dark. "Didn't the ad say three rooms?" Dan asks.

"You got your kitchen over there," says the man, and he points to the corner.

"But that's not another room!" says Dan. "That's just a corner of this room. Anyway, the ad said, **all-electric kitchen**! What about that part?"

"There is electricity in that corner," says the man.

Dan is getting a bad feeling about this apartment. "Where is room three?" he wants to know. "Don't tell me. It's the other corner."

"Of course not. Look." The man opens a door that Dan did not happen to see till now. Behind it is a dark space with no windows at all. "You can sleep in there," says the man. "The last guy did. It's quiet."

40

Worktext page 40

"What?" cries Dan. "That's not a room!"

"If it's big enough to sleep in, it's a room. You interested? Sign here." The man sticks out a form. Dan looks through the form. Then he turns it over. On the back he sees some words in small letters. The words say that he must stay in the apartment for a year.

"Does the $300 pay for electricity and water?" he asks.

"No, that will run you $40 more. Then, of course, I have to ask for another $10 to keep the hall clean," says the man.

"Do you mean you want $350 in all? How can you ask that much for a place like this?" Dan can't believe what he hears.

"You get what you pay for," says the man.

"Not here, you don't," says Dan. "I'm not interested. Forget it."

"Hey!" The man follows him to the door. "By the time you change your mind, it will be too late. A lot of people want this apartment. It will be gone by tonight!"

But Dan just leaves. On the way to Main Street, he sees a sign in a window: **Room for rent**.

A woman lets him into this new building. "You have a room for rent?" Dan asks.

"Sure. It's up the stairs. Follow me." The woman shows Dan one big room with a really big window. A door on one wall opens into a small, clean kitchen.

"How much?" Dan asks.

"$300 a month," she says. "That takes care of everything—electricity, water, the works."

"This is great!" says Dan. "When can I move in?"

"Fill out the form," says the woman. "You look like a quiet young man. If you can prove you have a job, you can move into the room."

Dan has all the information the woman needs. He can—and does—fill out the form right then and there. He has the money, too. Soon, he finds himself alone in his own apartment! He stands by the big window in the empty room and looks down at the street. Suddenly, a woman steps out of the building across the way. Dan puts his head close to the glass to get a better look. She is wearing a red hat. It's the girl he saw on the way to buy a newspaper. Has he moved in across the street from her? Dan throws open the window and sticks his head out. He wants to call out to her. Then he remembers that he doesn't even know her name. So he doesn't call out after all.

41

Worktext page 41

Finding Details

In this story, Dan looks at two apartments. He has read about the first one in the want ads. Points from the ad are listed on the left. Next to each point, write what the apartment is really like.

Big	The apartment is ______________.
3 rooms	The apartment really has__________.
$300	The rent is really______________.
Quiet	The apartment is really __________.
Sunny	The apartment is really __________.
New building	The apartment is in ____________.
All-electric kitchen	The kitchen is ________________.

Alike and Different

Dan sees a sign for the second apartment on his way to Main Street. Each sentence below tells how the second apartment is different from the first one. Fill in the missing word. Pick one of the two words below each sentence.

The second apartment is ______________.
(bigger/smaller)

The second apartment gets ______________light.
(more/less)

The second apartment has a ___________kitchen.
(real/smaller)

The second apartment is ______________money.
(more/not as much)

42

Worktext page 42

MIDWAY NOVEL Asking for Trouble

MATERIALS

Midway Novel 7, *Asking for Trouble*
Teacher's Manual, page 314
Assessment Manual, Midway Assessment 7, pages 119–124

Summary *Ana moves to a new school. She and Jared both want to be the school's lead reporter. Ana breaks a big story involving drugs. Jared thinks she stole the story. He tricks Ana to get back at her. Then Ana is grabbed in an alley by the drug dealer. Jared shows up, they decide to work together from now on.*

REVIEW AND ASSESSMENT

- Have students review their Memory Chips with partners. Depending on your students' needs, review the following skills covered in Lessons 1–8: phonograms *ing, ock, ore, ack, eam, ick, oke, ose,* and *ark*; words that rhyme with *prove* and *other*; syllabication; compound words; contractions; context clues; singular possessives; and endings *s, ing, er, ly,* and *ed.*

If you wish to assess students' progress at this point, use *Assessment Manual*, pages 119–124. For students who need additional support, you may use the Reteach activities from previous lessons.

INTRODUCE THE NOVEL

Invite students to preview the book by reading the title, looking at the illustrations, and reading aloud the captions. Begin a discussion of story concepts by asking questions such as:

- **What do you think it would be like to write for a school newspaper?**
- **What do you think it takes to be a good reporter?**

CHECK COMPREHENSION

Chapter 1 Why is Robin showing Ana around? (*Ana is new to Henson High School.*)

Chapter 2 How do you predict Ana and Jared will get along at the newspaper? (*Possible answer: They won't get along because they both want to be head writers.*)

Chapter 3 What does Ana tell Jared about herself? (*She tells him that she will be the person who gets all the bylines in the newspaper from now on.*)

Chapter 4 What kind of column does Ana plan to write? (*She will write a column that gives questions and answers for students.*)

Chapter 5 What does Ana find in Locker 17? (*She finds a big bag of drugs.*)

Chapter 6 How did Ana get the story on the drugs? (*She took a call for Jared that gave her the information.*)

Chapter 7 What do you think Jared will do to get back at Ana for stealing his story? (*Likely answer: He will probably mess up the "Ask Ana" column in some way.*)

Chapter 8 Why is Ana so excited about Mike Fields's letter? (*She is excited because he is popular and plays on the basketball team; because he asked her to the ball, he probably likes her.*)

Chapter 9 What do you predict will happen next? (*Possible answer: Ana will be embarrassed when she finds out that Mike Fields did not write the letter; Jared will be happy that he fooled Ana.*)

Chapter 10 How does Ana react when she finds out that Jared tricked her with Mike's letter? (*She gets really mad and vows revenge.*)

Chapter 11 What does Mr. Shipman do to solve the problem between Ana and Jared? (*He assigns both of them to cover the Henson Sports Ball.*)

Chapter 12 Do you think Ana was right in taking Jared's story? Why or why not? (*Possible answers: Yes, because she was there when the call came, and Jared would not have worked on the story with her anyway; no, because the tip was for Jared, not her; they could have worked on the story together.*)

Chapter 13 What does Jared want Ana to do now that he thinks they are even? (*He wants her to stop writing for* The Explorer.)

Chapter 14 Why does the man attack Ana at the ball? (*He is upset because he lost money when she found the drugs and turned them in to the principal.*)

Chapter 15 How does Ana get away from the man? (*She sees a metal tool and hits him with it.*)

CONNECTION

Home/School Encourage students to bring home a copy of *Asking for Trouble.* They might read the novel, or sections of the novel, to family members.

LESSON 7.9

OBJECTIVES

- Students will decode and blend words with different sounds for vowels *oo*
- Students will decode and blend words with the *ap, ard, ow, air,* and *ot* phonograms
- Students will use context clues to figure out unfamiliar words
- Students will apply endings *s, ed,* and *ing* to base words to form new words
- Students will recognize and form compound words
- Students will recognize and form possessives
- Students will recognize and form contractions

PHONICS VOCABULARY

ads	facts	giving	selling
feelings	gives	hides	ideas
spiders	breaks	sunglasses	pairs
waiting	low	sells	rules
exciting	says	spider's	can't
shop	shops	words	wants
things	wearing	turns	faces
explorers	they're	makes	walks
everyone	works	excited	let's
guard	basketball	shoots	making
moves	jumps	seconds	gets
slams	scores	guarding	championship
shooting	points	champions	comes
passes	stars	clapping	he'll
eyes	you'll	weren't	shoot
clap	yours	streets	wears
pair	court	tricks	passed
understanding		themselves	

WORDS TO KNOW

clap	court	crowd	guard
jump	low	moment	pair
price	rule	shoot	shot
slam			

MATERIALS

Worktext 7, pages 43–50
Teacher's Manual, pages 315–318
Practice Lesson 7.9, pages 82–83 of the Worktext

TEACH

- Using Worktext pages 43–44, introduce students to the vocabulary words. Give students an opportunity to practice writing the words.
- Students can organize their Memory Chips, found in the back of the Worktext. Say each word, having students repeat it after you. Then have them sort the words according to words they know and those that are unfamiliar. Say each unfamiliar word together, and have students use it in a sentence.

Worktext pages 43–44 can also be used to reinforce spelling. Use the five-step process detailed on page 71 of this *Teacher's Manual.*

Vowel Sounds *oo*

Write these words on the board, and say them aloud: **poor, foot, shoot.** Point out the *oo* in each word, and tell students *oo* can have three different sounds.

Blending Write these words on cards and have students sort them by vowel sounds: **poor**, **door**, **soot**, **toot**, **foot**, **floor**, **moor**, **shoot**.

Phonograms *ap, ard, ow, air, ot*

Write these words on the board, and have students take turns suggesting rhyming words for each: **cap**, **hard**, **low**, **hair**, **got**.

Blending Have students make word ladders with *cap, hard, low, hair,* and *got.* They can work individually or with a partner.

cap	hard	low	hair	got
nap	guard	bow	fair	rot
tap	card	sow	chair	not

Context Clues

Write this sentence on the board: **My sneakers squeaked as I ran across the basketball court.** Cover *court,* and ask students how they would read this word if they did not know it. (*Read the sentence and use clues from the sentence along with decoding clues.*) Read the sentence, leaving out *court.* Ask students what they think the word might be and how they figured it out.

Endings *s, ed, ing*

Remind students that they can add the endings *s, ed,* and *ing* to base words. Remind them that:

- when a word ends in *ss,* the ending *es* instead of *s* is added
- when a word ends in *e,* the *e* is dropped and then the ending *ed* or *ing* is added
- if a word has a short vowel sound and ends in a consonant, the consonant is doubled and *ed* or *ing* is added.

Make New Words Write these words on the board, and invite students to add the endings *s, ed,* and *ing*: **pass, face, shoot, clap.** (*passes, passed, passing*; *faces, faced, facing*; *shoots, shooting*; *claps, clapped, clapping*) Students can use each word they make in a sentence.

Compound Words

Remind students that two words can be put together to make one longer word.

Make New Words Write these words on the board in random order and have students use them to make compound words: **sun**, **glasses**, **some**, **thing**, **flower**, **where**, **how**. (*sunglasses, sunflower, something, somewhere, somehow*)

Possessives

Remind students that they can add an apostrophe and *s* to a word to show ownership.

Make New Words Have students add an apostrophe and *s* to these words and use each word in a sentence: *spider, Jen, Bill.* (*spider's, Jen's, Bill's*)

Contractions

Remind students that sometimes two words can be written as one. An apostrophe is used to replace the missing letter(s) in the words.

Make New Words Have students write a contraction for each of these two words: **were not**, **he will**, **she will**, **you are**, **you have**. (*weren't, he'll, she'll, you're, you've*) Students can use each word in a sentence.

PRACTICE

- Let students practice the new words they have learned and formed by completing the activities found on pages 43–45 of the Worktext.
- If students are experiencing difficulty with the Words to Know section on pages 43–44, you can say sentences like the ones below, and have students choose the Memory Chip words they hear: **I see a <u>crowd</u> of people. The <u>guard</u> would not let us go into the museum.**

For further practice, have students complete Practice Lesson 7.9 on pages 82–83 of the Worktext. Answers can be found in the Answer Key on page 361 of this *Teacher's Manual.*

APPLY

- Have students talk about the story concept by sharing their prior knowledge. Ask: **What does an ad try to do? How does it do that?** Tell students they are going to use the words they have learned to read an article about ads.
- Ask students to read the article on pages 46–49 in the Worktext. Offer assistance if necessary, but encourage students to decode the words independently, using the clues and patterns they have learned.
- After students have completed reading the article, have them complete the Comprehension Exercises (Understanding Main Ideas and Understanding Ads) on page 50 in their Worktext. Answers can be found in the Answer Key on page 360 of this *Teacher's Manual.*

CONNECTION

Strategy for Reading After students finish reading the selection "Understanding Ads" on Worktext pages 46–49, ask them to summarize it either aloud or in writing.

Writing Give students an opportunity to write in their journals. Have students list their favorite ads and explain why they like these particular ads.

9. UNDERSTANDING ADS

Try This The vowel group **oo** can sound many different ways. It sounds one way in **foot**, another way in **floor**. Now look at the word: **shoot**. You know the sound of **sh** at the beginning and **t** at the end. Try three different sounds for **oo** till you get a word that would be right in the sentence below. Read the new word, **shoot**, and write it in the sentence.

Will likes to _______________ pictures of his family.

Letter Groups In each group of words below, you know the first two words. The word in dark letters is new. It ends with the same letter group as the first two. Circle the letter group you find in all the words. Read the new word and write it on the line.

map trap **clap** ____________________

card hard **guard** ____________________

slow below **low** ____________________

stairs fair **pair** ____________________

hot plot **shot** ____________________

Take a Guess Read the sentences below. See if you can guess the word in dark letters. The word **basketball** should help you. Think about where the game of basketball is played.

The basketball player steps onto the **court**.

Did you guess the word? Now write it. ____________________

43

Worktext page 43

Words to Know

	Look	Say	Picture	Write
clap	☐	☐	☐	____________
court	☐	☐	☐	____________
crowd	☐	☐	☐	____________
guard	☐	☐	☐	____________
jump	☐	☐	☐	____________
low	☐	☐	☐	____________
moment mo-ment	☐	☐	☐	____________
pair	☐	☐	☐	____________
price	☐	☐	☐	____________
rule	☐	☐	☐	____________
shoot	☐	☐	☐	____________
shot	☐	☐	☐	____________
slam	☐	☐	☐	____________

Word Attack

+s Write these words with an **s** ending. Add **e** to pass before you add **s**.

pass ____________________ rule ____________________

second ____________________ slam ____________________

trick ____________________ wear ____________________

your ____________________ jump ____________________

score ____________________ shoot ____________________

street ____________________ face ____________________

+ed Another ending you can add to **pass** is **ed**. Write this new word in the sentence below.

Tom ____________________ the ball to me.

44

Worktext page 44

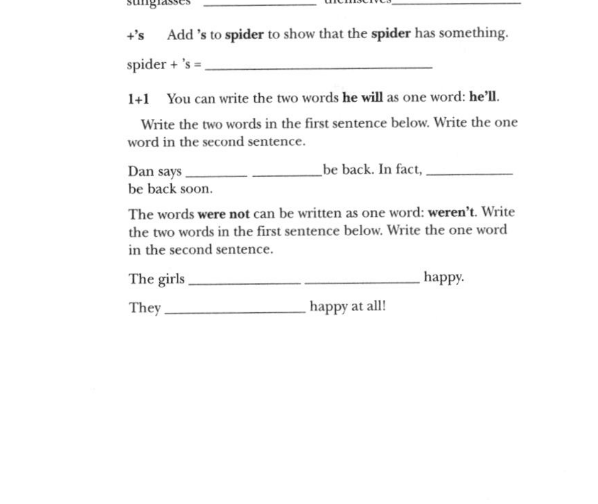

+ing Write the words below with the ending **ing**. Add one more **p** to **clap** before you add **ing**.

clap ____________________ guard ____________________

shoot ____________________ understand ____________________

2=1 Each of the words below is made up of two words. Circle the two words in each word. Then write each whole word on the line and read it out loud.

sunglasses ____________________ themselves ____________________

+'s Add **'s** to **spider** to show that the **spider** has something.

spider + 's = ____________________

1+1 You can write the two words **he will** as one word: **he'll**.

Write the two words in the first sentence below. Write the one word in the second sentence.

Dan says ________ ________ be back. In fact, ____________ be back soon.

The words **were not** can be written as one word: **weren't**. Write the two words in the first sentence below. Write the one word in the second sentence.

The girls ____________ ____________ happy.

They ____________________ happy at all!

45

Worktext page 45

9. UNDERSTANDING ADS

Some ads are full of facts—and the facts may be correct. But giving facts is not the point of most ads. The main point of most ads is to sell something. The ad tries to make you want the thing it is selling. So it tries to get to your feelings in some way. If it gives you facts, it hides some other ideas in with the facts. Take a look at this example.

TODAY ONLY!
SPIDER'S SUN SHOP BREAKS THE RULES!
EVERY PAIR of EXPLORER SUNGLASSES goes on sale. Yes, this is the sale you have been waiting for. Get new, NEW, NEW Explorer sunglasses for the low, LOW, LOW price of $39.95! Yes, that's right, yours for only $39.95. Or get two—yes, TWO—FOR ONLY $78.99! BRING A FRIEND!

46

Worktext page 46

This ad does have three facts in it. Here they are:

1. Spider's Sun Shop sells Explorer sunglasses.
2. One pair of these glasses goes for $39.95.
3. Two pairs go for $78.99.

That's it. All the other words in the ad are just there to get to your feelings. The ad says the shop is going to **break the rules** today. That sounds exciting. But what does it mean? Nothing, really. There is no rule against a shop having a sale. The ad says you have been waiting for this sale. But have you? How would Spider's Sun Shop know? Is $39.95 such a low, LOW, LOW price? Maybe yes, maybe no. You can't tell just from this ad. You have to ask how much they were before the sale, and how much they are in other shops. What if you can get them for $20 somewhere else? Then the price here is not so low, LOW, LOW.

To see the information in an ad, you have to see through the words. No one really wants to be left out or left behind. People want to be in the middle of things—part of the group. So an ad may say something like this: Hey, what are you waiting for? You want to be the last one in the world to get some really cool Explorer sunglasses? Get with it! Join the gang! Buy a pair of Explorers before life has passed you by.

On the other hand, most people like to think they are special. They like to think of themselves as one-of-a-kind. An ad may try to reach this side of people. Picture an ad for Explorer sunglasses on TV. You see a man on a mountain. He is all alone. Then you see him up close. He is wearing sunglasses. Suddenly, he turns and faces you. He says, "I've tried all those other sunglasses. They might work for other people—not for me. I make up my own mind. I go my own way. Explorers—they're the only sunglasses for me." He turns and walks away. A voice says, "Explorer sunglasses: they're not for everyone."

47

Worktext page 47

An ad like that will make some people want Explorer sunglasses. These are people who want to stand out in a crowd. Of course, if the ad really works, a crowd of people will soon be wearing the glasses. So the very thing that makes the ad work, soon makes it wrong. Right?

48

Worktext page 48

Let's say you turn on the TV and see the best point guard who ever lived. If you love basketball, you become excited. You want to clap. There he is on the court, making one of his great moves. He jumps! He shoots! He gets the ball back. He slams it through the basket. He scores again! You remember the time he won a championship at the last moment with a slam like that. His shot beat the buzzer by two seconds. Shooting 30 points a night is nothing for this guy. Guarding him is a bad dream. If only you could be more like him! Now as he comes down, he passes the ball off and turns. The great star gives you a cool smile. He puts on a pair of Explorer sunglasses. "I like these sunglasses," he says. Then the words show up on the TV: **EXPLORERS: the sunglasses that champions wear.**

An ad like this can really get to some people. Many people, after all, want to be like famous stars. They want to hear people clapping. They want to feel the eyes of the world on their every move. But wearing what some star wears won't bring about this change. If you buy Explorer sunglasses, all you'll get are glasses.

49

Worktext page 49

Understanding Main Ideas

Understanding Ads talks about some of the ways that ads try to trick people. Each way counts on different feelings that most people have. The three main feelings talked about in this article are listed below. Finish each sentence (**a**, **b**, and **c**) by writing one of the three endings given for it.

a. People want to be ____________________
   part of the group.
   better than the group.
   free from the group.

b. People want to feel that ____________________
   they are no one special.
   they are special.
   no one is special.

c. People want to be the same as ____________________
   their boss at work.
   their parents.
   famous stars.

Understanding Ads

The lines below come from different ads. Each ad tries to get to one of the feelings listed above. Next to each ad, write the letter of the feeling (**a**, **b**, or **c**).

_____ 1. "I just love a Gold Medal TV dinner after a long hard day on the set," says Jen Green, star of **Streets of Gold**.

_____ 2. Run, don't walk, to see **They Weren't So Bad After All**. It is the movie the whole country is talking about!

_____ 3. You're in a class by yourself. Step up to the car that is in a class by itself.

50

Worktext page 50

LESSON 7.10

OBJECTIVE

- Students will practice and apply skills to an extended passage

MATERIALS

Worktext 7, pages 51–53
Teacher's Manual, pages 319–320, 330–331
Practice Lesson 7.10, pages 84–85 of the Worktext

SKILLS REVIEW

- Before reading, you may wish to review these words that apply phonics skills: *good, wants, used, thinks, he'll, hears, guys, sounds, excited, we're, inside, low, don't, gets, freeway, faraway, signs, comes, puts, looks, news, lots, looking, too, door, walks, can't, takes, sunglasses, I'm, interested, turns, feels, he's, asks, listens, answers, looked, hood, saying, something, knows, living, someone, what's.* Have students review the Memory Chips they have learned so far. Then ask: **How do you go about buying a used car?**
- While reading, have students jot down tips for buying a used car.
- After reading, have students complete the Comprehension Exercise (Remembering Details) on Worktext page 53.

For further practice, have students complete Practice Lesson 7.10 on pages 84–85 of the Worktext. Answers can be found in the Answer Key on pages 360–361 of this *Teacher's Manual.*

RETEACH

If students need further review of phonics skills, you may wish to use the following activity:

Endings s, es

s or es? Remind students that when words end in *s, ss, x, ch, tch,* and *sh,* you add *es* as an ending instead of *s.* Give each student two cards, one with **s** and one with **es** written on it. Call out the words below, and have students hold up *s* or *es,* depending on which ending makes another word. Then have a volunteer write the word on the board.

pass	**rule**	**second**	**slam**
trick	**box**	**peach**	**wear**
patch	**your**	**jump**	**score**
shoot	**street**	**wish**	**face**
gas	**grass**	**eye**	**catch**
want	**sport**		

CONNECTION

Response to Reading

- To reinforce students' understanding of the literary elements found in their reading material, have them complete the Story Map and Character Cluster reproducibles found on pages 330–331.
- Students will demonstrate an understanding of setting, characters, and plot by filling out the organizers.
- Students may share their completed organizers with the class.

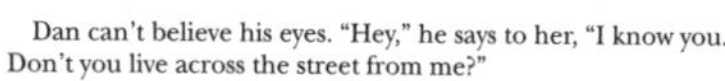

10. A GOOD USED CAR

Dan wants to buy a good used car. He thinks he'll have to save up for awhile. But one day, he hears an ad on the radio. It is for a used car place called the Car Guys. The man in the ad sounds so excited as he says, "Hey! Fast Jake here for the Car Guys. Come on over to the Car Guys! We're the guys who say YES! Yes, you can! YES, WE WILL! Yes, you do! YES! If you have a job, you can drive home a good used car tonight! YES, YOU CAN! Take a look at our Special of the Week. This is the Great One. Clean inside and out! LOW, LOW miles. Only one owner. What do you mean, you don't have money? You don't need MONEY to shop at the Car Guys. WE KNOW YOU! We LIKE you. We want to HELP you. We're the Car Guys! Put $100 down and take this monster machine home tonight!"

Dan thinks, *I have $100. Maybe I don't have to wait to buy a car. I could buy this Special of the Week right now.*

So he gets on a bus and goes over to the Car Guys. They have a big lot down by the freeway. It is full of used cars. All the cars look pretty good from far away. They all have signs that say things like **Special!** or **Great Buy!**

A man comes up and puts out his hand. "I'm Fast Jake. What can I do for you, my man?"

Dan says, "I heard your ad on the radio. I want to see that Special of the Week."

"Oh! Bad news! I just sold that one!" The man looks at his watch. "Oh, but hey! Good news! I have lots of other good buys. What kind of car are we looking for?"

"Well—just something I can count on," says Dan.

"I can get you into a very good little sports car for $5,500—"

"No, no—that's too much money," says Dan.

"How about a truck? I can sell you one for $3,000—"

"No, that's still too much," says Dan.

"OK, how about this little red two-door? It's a good city car. I drive one of these myself. I can let it go for $2,000." He walks Dan toward a red car. Just then, a young woman comes up to the car from the other side.

51

Worktext page 51

Dan can't believe his eyes. "Hey," he says to her, "I know you. Don't you live across the street from me?"

The woman takes off her sunglasses and gives Dan a close look. "What do you know! I do think I have seen you around. I'm Dana."

"I'm Dan. Were you interested in this car?"

"Yes, but you saw it first."

"No, no," says Dan, "you saw it first."

Fast Jake says, "Let me take the two of you out for a test drive. When you get back you can fight over the car."

So Dan and Dana take turns driving. The car feels good to Dan. He's ready to sign some papers. But Dana asks a lot of questions, and Dan listens to her. Fast Jake does not seem to know many answers. Back at the lot, Dana wants to look under the hood. After she has looked, she says, "Sorry, not for me. This car needs a ring job."

"A ring job!" Dan cries. "Isn't that like saying it needs a whole new engine?"

"Yes, something like that," says Dana.

"How do you know?"

Dana tells him all the signs she has seen. Fast Jake tries to cut in at first. But Dana knows what she is talking about. So after awhile, Fast Jake gives up.

Dan and Dana go home together on the bus that day. "How come you know so much about cars?" Dan asks.

Dana laughs. "I have been around cars all my life. Both my dad and my uncle fix cars for a living. They own a shop together."

"Oh, if only I had someone like you to help me buy a car," says Dan.

"Well," says Dana, "I could help you. I do have lots of time right now. I don't have a job."

"What's your number?" Dan asks.

52

Worktext page 52

Remembering Details

Write a detail from the story in each space below. Each detail can be one word or more than one word. Look back at the story if you need to.

Dan hears an ad on the ______________. The ad says that he can get a good used car from the ______________. The ad calls this good buy the ________________________.

When Dan goes to the used car place, he meets a man called ______________. This man says the special has been sold, but he has a __________________ for $5,500. Dan says that that's too much, so the man tells him about a truck for ______________. That is still too much money for Dan, so Fast Jake shows him a little ____________ two-door. Fast Jake says this is a good __________ car. Just then, a woman in sunglasses comes up to the same car. She says her name is ____________. After a test drive, she asks to look under the _________. Then she says the car needs a ______________ job. Later, on the bus, Dan asks how come she knows so much about ______________. She tells him that her dad and her uncle own a ______________ together. At the end, Dan asks for her ______________.

53

Worktext page 53

LESSON 7.11

OBJECTIVES

- Students will decode and blend words with different sounds for vowels *oo*
- Students will decode and blend words with the *oice* and *air* phonograms
- Students will use context clues to figure out unfamiliar words
- Students will apply endings *s*, *es*, and *ing* to base words to form new words
- Students will recognize and form contractions

PHONICS VOCABULARY

that's	choices	too	crowds
others	looking	questions	choice
getting	changes	keeping	forgets
sales	politics	kids	coming
problems	listening	jobs	helping
plants	building	taking	can't
working	things	hours	drivers
running	skills	school	wood
learning	doesn't	works	ads
ways	pages	businesses	friends
look	filling	clothes	hair
good	wearing	kinds	answers
knows	waiting	starts	listens
loses	loves	minds	haven't
foot	practice	tomorrow	catches
chances	hurts	interviews	

WORDS TO KNOW

breath	calm	catch	center
chance	choice	foot	forward
foster	hair	interview	practice
tomorrow			

MATERIALS

Worktext 7, pages 54–59
Teacher's Manual, pages 321–323
Practice Lesson 7.11, pages 86–87 of the Worktext

TEACH

- Using Worktext pages 54–55, introduce students to the vocabulary words. Give students an opportunity to practice writing the words.
- Students can organize their Memory Chips, found in the back of the Worktext. Say each word, having students repeat it after you. Then have students sort the words according to words they know and those that are unfamiliar. Say each unfamiliar word together and have students use it in a sentence.

SPELLING Worktext pages 54–55 can also be used to reinforce spelling. Use the five-step process detailed on page 71 of this *Teacher's Manual*.

Vowel Sounds for *oo*

Write these words on the board, and say them aloud: **look**, **cool**, **door**. Remind students that *oo* can have three different sounds. When they see *oo* in a word, students can try out these three sounds as they figure out what the word is.

Blending Write these words on cards, and have students sort them according to vowel sounds: **look**, **cook**, **wood**, **hood**, **door**, **floor**, **book**, **spook**, **cool**, **stool**, **food**, **pool**. (*look, cook, book, wood, hood*; *spook, stool, pool, cool, food*; *door, floor*)

Phonograms *oice*, *air*

Write these sentences on the board, and have students find the words *choice* and *hair*: **I had to make a choice between two colors. I had to decide if my hair would look better with a blue or green stripe.**

Blending Write **choice** on the board, saying the word and blending the sounds. Erase the *ch*, and replace the letters with *v*. Ask a volunteer to say the new word and use it in a sentence. Repeat, using *hair*, *pair*, and *stair*.

Context Clues

Write this sentence on the board: **I want to play basketball really well, so I practice every day for at least two hours.** Cover *practice*, and ask students how they would read this word if they did not know it. (*Read the sentence and use clues from the sentence along with decoding clues.*) Read the sentence, leaving out *practice*. Ask students what they think the word might be and how they figured it out.

Endings *s*, *es*, *ing*

Remind students that they can add *s*, *es*, and *ing* to the endings of words. Remind them that when a word ends in *ch*, the ending is *es*, instead of *s*.

Make New Words Write these words on the board, and invite students to add endings *s*, *es*, or *ing*: **catch**, **mind**, **lose**, **interview**, **crowd**. (*catches, catching*; *minds, minding*; *loses, losing*; *interviews, interviewing*; *crowds, crowding*) Students can use each word they make in a sentence.

Contractions

Remind students that sometimes two words can be written as one. Ask them what is used in place of the missing letters in the words. (*an apostrophe*)

Make New Words Have students write a contraction for each of these two words: *have not, could not.* (*haven't, couldn't*) Students can use each word in a sentence.

PRACTICE

- Let students practice the new words they have learned and formed by completing the activities found on pages 54–55 of the Worktext.
- If students are experiencing difficulty with the Words to Know section on pages 54–55, you can say sentences like these and have students fill in the blanks using the vocabulary words: **The day after today is ______.** (*tomorrow*) **I like to comb my ____.** (*hair*)

For further practice, have students complete Practice Lesson 7.11 on pages 86–87 of the Worktext. Answers can be found in the Answer Key on page 361 of this *Teacher's Manual.*

APPLY

- Have students talk about the story concept by sharing their prior knowledge. Ask: **How do you know what kind of job to look for? What are some things you should remember when interviewing for a job?** Tell them they are going to use the words they have learned to read an article about interviewing and getting jobs.
- Ask students to read the article on pages 56–58 in the Worktext. Offer assistance if necessary, but encourage students to decode the words independently, using the clues and patterns they have learned.
- After students have completed reading the article, have them complete the Comprehension Exercise (Finding Main Ideas and Details) on page 59 in their Worktext. Answers can be found in the Answer Key on page 360 of this *Teacher's Manual.*

CONNECTION

Strategy for Reading Have students reread the selection "Jobs" on Worktext pages 56–58 to correct comprehension breakdowns. Students may achieve understanding by reprocessing the same text with greater attention focused on its meaning.

Writing Students should be encouraged to keep a journal of their writings. They can use these journals to record responses to their reading, list new words they have learned, or record their thoughts and feelings about the reading selections.

Worktext Pages 54–55

11. JOBS

Try This The vowel pair **oo** can sound many different ways. It sounds one way in **look** and **book**, another way in **cool** and **food**, and another way in **door** and **floor**. Which way does it sound in this word: **foot**? Try all three sounds till you hit a word you know.

Write the word. ____________

Letter Groups You know the first word in each pair below. The word in dark letters is new. Circle the letters that are the same in each pair. Read the new word, and write it in the sentence.

voice **choice** You have made a good ____________.

pair **hair** Who cuts your ____________?

Take a Guess Read the sentences below. See if you can guess the words in dark letters.

The more you **practice**, the better you will be.
Forget about yesterday—get ready for **tomorrow**.

Write the new words. ____________ ____________

Words to Know

	Look	Say	Picture	Write
breath	☐	☐	☐	____________
calm	☐	☐	☐	____________
catch	☐	☐	☐	____________
center cen-ter	☐	☐	☐	____________
chance	☐	☐	☐	____________
choice	☐	☐	☐	____________
foot	☐	☐	☐	____________

54

Worktext page 54

	Look	Say	Picture	Write
forward for-ward	☐	☐	☐	____________
foster fos-ter	☐	☐	☐	____________
hair	☐	☐	☐	____________
interview in-ter-view	☐	☐	☐	____________
practice prac-tice	☐	☐	☐	____________
tomorrow to-mor-row	☐	☐	☐	____________

Word Attack

+s Add **s** to the words below to make new words. Add **e** to **catch** before you add **s**.

catch____________ chance ____________

choice ____________ crowd ____________

driver ____________ forget____________

hurt ____________ interview ____________

listen ____________ lose ____________

love____________ mind ____________

+ing Write the words **learn** and **listen** with the ending **ing**.

learn ____________listen ____________

1+1 You can put the words **have** and **not** together into one word. Here is the word: **haven't**. Write the two words on the lines to the left below. Write the one word on the right. Circle the letters in **have not** that are left out of **haven't**.

__________ __________ = ____________

55

Worktext page 55

11. JOBS

Money: we all need it, and that's a fact. To get money, most of us need a job. But what kind of job? That's where the choices begin.

Some people think one job is just like another. Every job is different—and people are different, too. Some people like crowds. Others like to be alone. A job that is right for some people may be wrong for others.

So the first step in looking for a job is to look at yourself. What are you like? What do you do for fun? Questions like these can help you make the right choice. After all, it's best to go for a job that will interest you. That's the kind of job you have the best chance of getting. Your chances of keeping such a job are better, too.

Do you like to talk? Do you like to meet new people? Are you someone who never forgets a face? Maybe you belong in sales or in politics. Do you get along best with young kids? Think about a job in day care. Are people always coming to you with their problems? Are you good at listening? Many jobs center around helping other people. You might run a home for kids who are in trouble, or you might work at a home for older people.

Do you get along better with plants than with people? Any big office building has many plants. Taking care of them is a big job. Maybe it can be your job. If you can't stand to be inside all day, you might like a job in a park. Someone has to take care of those plants, too.

Some people like working with things better than with people. Do you like cars? It would take hours to list all the jobs that might interest you. You could sell cars. You could fix them. You could drive them—yes, there are jobs for drivers of all kinds. You could work on cars to help keep them running. The list goes on and on.

After you know what kind of job you want, look at your skills. What can you do? How can you learn to do more? How can you get ready for the jobs that will be around tomorrow? School is one place to pick up special job skills. In some high school

56

Worktext page 56

classes, you can learn such office skills as running a computer. In some, you can learn to work with wood and metal or to fix cars. Some people pick up skills by learning on the job. But, of course, you have to get a job before you can pick up skills in this way. It will have to be a job that doesn't take a special skill. You might get a job helping someone who works with electricity. Then you can watch and learn from this person.

You already know one way to find a job in the real world: look in the want ads. But there are other ways, too. You might look through the yellow pages. What catches your eye? Call around to businesses that interest you. Ask if they need help. You might walk around and look for **Help Wanted** signs. Many people find jobs through family or friends. Is your uncle's company looking for someone? Do your friends who have jobs know of anything that might open up where they work? There is only one way to find out. Ask around.

Once you know of a job you want to go for, you have to put your best foot forward. Getting the job may well take more than filling out a form. You may have to go through some kind of interview. In an interview, you meet someone from the business and answer questions face to face. A good interview can get the job for you.

How can you do well in a job interview? Here are a few points to keep in mind.

1. Try to look right for the job. Your clothes and hair are important. If you have a chance, look around the place of work before your interview. See what other people are wearing. You should wear the same kinds of clothes.
2. Before the interview, think about the questions you may be asked. Practice your answers. You can't guess every question, of course. But some questions come up in most job interviews. Here are some of those questions.
   - Why do you want this job?
   - How far did you go in school?
   - What skills do you have?
   - Have you done work like this before? When?
   - Why did you leave your last job, if you had one?
   - Why will you be good at this job?
   - Who can we call that knows you and can tell us about your work?

57

Worktext page 57

3. Get to the interview on time. In fact, get there early. So what if you have to sit in the waiting room for awhile? You can use that time to calm down and catch your breath.
4. Once the interview starts, listen carefully to each question. Answer just what is asked. Look the other person in the eye as you talk.

58

Worktext page 58

Finding Main Ideas and Details

Jobs is all about how to get a job in the real world. It looks at four main ideas that have to do with getting a job. These main ideas are listed as headings below. Write a detail on each line under the four headings. Use the choices in the box.

Call around, walk around, and ask around. Take classes in school. Look in the want ads. Look right for the job. Be on time. Pick a job that goes with who you are and what you like. Learn on the job. Practice your answers. Be friendly.

1. How to pick the kind of work that would be best for you

   ____

2. How to get the skills you will need for the jobs of tomorrow

   ____

   ____

3. How to find out about jobs that may be open

   ____

   ____

4. How to do well in a job interview

   ____

   ____

   ____

   ____

59

Worktext page 59

Level 7

LESSON 7.12

OBJECTIVE

- Students practice and apply skills to an extended passage

MATERIALS

Worktext 7, pages 60–65
Teacher's Manual, pages 324–325
Practice Lesson 7.12, pages 88–89 of the Worktext

SKILLS REVIEW

- Before reading, you may wish to review these words that apply phonics skills: *looks, building, she's, needs, hopes, doors, finds, sitting, working, says, I'm, jumps, knows, aren't, forgets, gets, brings, good, look, book, don't, turns, minutes, comes, waiting, numbers, books, can't, moving, bills, running, machines, you're, didn't, houses, buildings, trucks, tools, things, that's, workers, listens, I'll, walks, meets, feeling, stands, looking, feels, taking.* Have students review the Memory Chips they have learned so far. Then ask: **Do you think there are some jobs that only men can do? Are there jobs that only women can do? Explain.**
- While reading, have students predict what they think will happen next in the story.
- After reading, have students complete the Comprehension Exercises (Writing a Summary, Getting to Know Characters, Who's Changed?, What Do You Think?, and Think About Tomorrow) on Worktext pages 63–65.

For further practice, have students complete Practice Lesson 7.12 on pages 88–89 of the Worktext. Answers can be found in the Answer Key on pages 360–361 of this *Teacher's Manual.*

RETEACH

If students need further review of phonics skills, you may wish to use the following activity:

Sounds of *oo*:

What's the New Word? Write the following letters on cards: **oo**, **f**, **l**, **b**, **c**, **d**, **r**, **t**, **sp**, **k**. Place the letters *oo* on the table. Call out the following words and have students choose the cards that make the word you say: **floor**, **door**, **fool**, **book**, **cook**, **food**, **look**, **flood**, **took**, **spool**. Then write all the words on index cards. Have students sort the words into groups of words that rhyme. (*floor, door; fool, spool; took, book, cook, look*)

Worktext Pages 60–61

12. DANA GETS A JOB

Dana looks at the number on the building. Yes, this is the place. She's scared, but she needs the job. She hopes she will do OK in this interview.

She goes through the front doors and finds herself in a big office. A young man is sitting there with his head down, working on something. "Hi," she says to him. "I called you yesterday about the ad in the paper—about the job. I was told to come in at 10:00 today. I hope I'm not late."

The young man looks up. Then he jumps to his feet. Dana says, "Oh!" She knows him. "Aren't you—" But she forgets his name. "You were at the used car place."

"Yes, I was. Good to see you again, Kate."

"Dana," she says.

His face gets all red. "Right, Dana. What brings you here?"

"As I said, I'm interested in the job."

"You are? I mean, you are! Right. Let me just look in the book. Oh, yes. Here you are. I don't know anything about it. Let me see if Mr. Henson is ready for you." The young man backs away, turns, and goes through a door. A few minutes later, he comes back out. "Go ahead," he says.

Dana goes into the office where Mr. Henson is waiting. He is a big man. He looks at her. "I'm Mr. Henson. Please sit down," he says. "Now, tell me about yourself. Do you know how to use a computer?"

"No. Is that important?"

"Important? I should say so. You are good with numbers, aren't you?"

"Not really," says Dana. "Numbers and I just don't get along—"

"Is that so? Well, did you ever keep books before?"

"No, I can't say that I did. But—"

"No? Young woman, you did not read our ad very carefully. This is a fast-moving business. A lot of bills come in and go out. A lot of money goes through this building. We must have

60

Worktext page 60

someone who already knows how to do this kind of work. We don't have time for someone who has to learn on the job. Now, Dan will show you to—"

"But Mr. Henson, the ad I saw said something about running machines."

"Oh, that job." A long moment goes by. At last, Mr. Henson says, "But you're a woman."

"Yes, but the ad didn't say the job was only for men."

"Well, no, but do you understand what the job is? We put up houses and other buildings. We have a lot of trucks and power tools and other machines. So we run our own shop to fix things that break. That's where we need someone. Why do you think you could do that kind of work?"

Just then, Dan's uncle comes into the room. He says, "May I talk to you for a moment, Henson?"

The two men go to a corner of the room and talk for awhile. Mr. Henson comes back. "I understand you know one of my workers. You helped him buy a car."

"No," says Dana, "I helped him **not** to buy a car. I let him know the car he was about to buy was no good."

"How could you tell?"

Dana tells Mr. Henson how she could tell the car had a bad engine. Then she tells him how she comes to know so much about machines.

Mr. Henson listens and looks interested. "Well," he says at last, "I'll tell you what. We have a truck with a bad engine in the shop right now. You come in tomorrow. Show me what you can do with it. If you can prove to me that you know your way around machines, you've got the job. It would be a first for us—a woman working in our machine shop. But if you can do the work—hey, why not, I guess."

Dana has a sunny face when she walks out of Mr. Henson's office. Dan meets her at the front door. "How did it go in there?" he asks.

"Not bad," she says. "I have a feeling you put in a good word for me. Am I right?"

"I just told my uncle what happened the other day at that used car place. He said he thought it would be of interest to Mr. Henson."

61

Worktext page 61

"You never called me," says Dana. "I guess you didn't need my help after all. Did you buy a car already?"

"No. In fact, I'm going out to look at one tonight. Would you like to go with me? It will put you to a lot of trouble, but I'll make it up to you. I'll buy you dinner."

"OK," says Dana. She walks out of the building then and stands there for awhile looking at the city. She feels as if her new life is really taking off at last. Inside the building, Dan is feeling just the same way.

62

Worktext page 62

Writing a Summary

The sentences below tell about events in **Dana Gets a Job**. Use seven of these sentences to write a summary of the story. Remember that a summary gives only the most important events. It leaves out details.

Dana comes to Henson Homes to interview for a job.
Dana looks at the number on the building.
Mr. Henson thinks she wants a job keeping books.
Dana tells him she wants the job in the machine shop.
Mr. Henson asks why she thinks she can do that job.
Dan's uncle talks to Mr. Henson about Dana.
Mr. Henson listens and looks interested.
Mr. Henson makes up his mind to let Dana try the job.
On her way out, Dana runs into Dan.
Dana finds out that Dan put in a good word for her.
Dan asks Dana out, and she says yes.

63

Worktext page 63

Getting to Know Characters

You know that characters are the people in a story. The way some characters look, talk, feel, and what they do changes over time. Other characters do not change.

You have read all about Dana and Dan. By the end of this book, are these characters the same or different from the way they were at the start? Use your own words to complete the sentences.

1. At first, Dana seems scared to be in the city. By the end of the story, she

2. At first, Dan does not do anything with his life. At the end of the story, he

3. At first, Mr. Henson does not want to give Dana a job. At the end of the story, he

64

Worktext page 64

Who's Changed?

Did all the characters change?

Who did not change? Write their names. ________________

Who did change? Write their names. ________________

What Do You Think?

Get together with one or more friends who have read this story. Talk about the new job Dana will be starting. Do you think this is a good job for her? Will she do well at it? Why or why not?

Think About Tomorrow

Where will you be in five years? Write a letter to yourself. Write down what kind of job you will have. Will you keep going to school? Where will you be living?

When you are done writing this letter to yourself, save it. You may want to open it in five years and see if your dreams came true.

Dear ________,

65

Worktext page 65

FINAL NOVEL Stepping Up

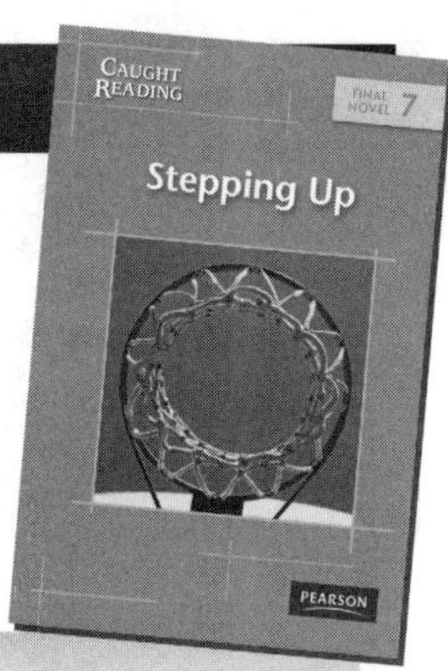

MATERIALS
Final Novel 7, *Stepping Up*
Teacher's Manual, page 326
Assessment Manual, Final Assessment 7, pages 125–129

Summary *Spider is a basketball star who meets a lost boy in the park. The boy can't remember who he is or how he got there. Spider is determined to help the little boy, even though it sometimes conflicts with basketball. In the end, Spider is able to reunite the little boy with his family.*

REVIEW AND ASSESSMENT

- Have students review their Memory Chips with partners or in small groups. Depending on your students' needs, review the following skills covered in Lessons 9–12: context clues; compound words; contractions; possessives; phonograms *ap, ard, ow, air, ot, oice,* and *air*; the sounds of *oo*; and endings *s, ing, es,* and *ed.*

If you wish to assess students' progress at this point, use *Assessment Manual*, pages 125–129. For students who need additional support, you may use the Reteach activities from previous lessons.

INTRODUCE THE NOVEL

Invite students to preview the book by reading the title, looking at the illustrations, and reading aloud the captions. Begin a discussion of story concepts by asking:

- **What do you think it would be like to sit on a bench game after game?**
- **What is it like to be a basketball star?**
- **What do you think is more important in high school, having a good job or playing a sport well? Why do you think so?**

CHECK COMPREHENSION

Chapter 1 What happens to change Spider's life? (*When Tyrone is injured, Spider is taken off the bench and put into a basketball game. Spider wins the game.*)

Chapter 2 Do you think Spider did the right thing when he got in the car with Venus and Red? (*Students should say no because they are not nice to Mark; they were not friends before Spider became a star. Spider should have stayed back to fix the car as he said he would.*)

Chapter 3 What choice do you think Spider made after his day with Venus? (*He is not as taken with Venus; he likes Dana; he is concerned with the boy more than being friends with Venus and Red.*)

Chapter 4 What does Spider do for the lost boy? (*He gets the boy to trust him, and he finds a social worker to help him.*)

Chapter 5 How is the coach deciding who will start, now that Tyrone is well? (*He will choose the one that is a team player, shows up on time, and sets an example for the other players.*)

Chapter 6 What does Spider say he will do for the lost boy? (*He says he will spend time with Bill and drive him around to see if he remembers anything about how he got lost.*)

Chapter 7 What does Spider's uncle want Spider to do? (*He wants Spider to give up playing basketball and concentrate on work.*)

Chapter 8 Why does Coach decide to start Spider? (*Tyrone said Spider was on drugs, and Coach thinks Tyrone is not a team player.*)

Chapter 9 What does Spider tell his uncle he has decided to do about playing basketball? (*He tells his uncle that he will cut back his hours at the shop and still be able to play.*)

Chapter 10 Who does Spider think the lost boy is? (*He thinks he is a boy everyone had thought died in a fire.*)

Chapter 11 What happens the day of the big game? (*The Cougars win the game because Tyrone plays well; the lost boy is reunited with his parents.*)

Chapter 12 What happened to Miles the day of the fire? (*He went outside the shop to play and climbed inside a car on a truck loaded with new cars. The truck took off. When it stopped, the truck driver ran Miles off the truck, and Miles went to the park.*)

CONNECTION

Home/School Encourage students to bring home a copy of *Stepping Up*. They might read the novel, or sections of the novel, to family members.

APPENDIX

STORY MAP

Caught Reading

Name: ______________________ Date: ______________

TITLE ______________________

AUTHOR ______________________

SETTING

CHARACTERS	PLACE	TIME

PROBLEM

EVENTS LEADING TO RESOLUTION

RESOLUTION

Caught Reading

CHARACTER CLUSTER

Name: ______________________ Date: ______________

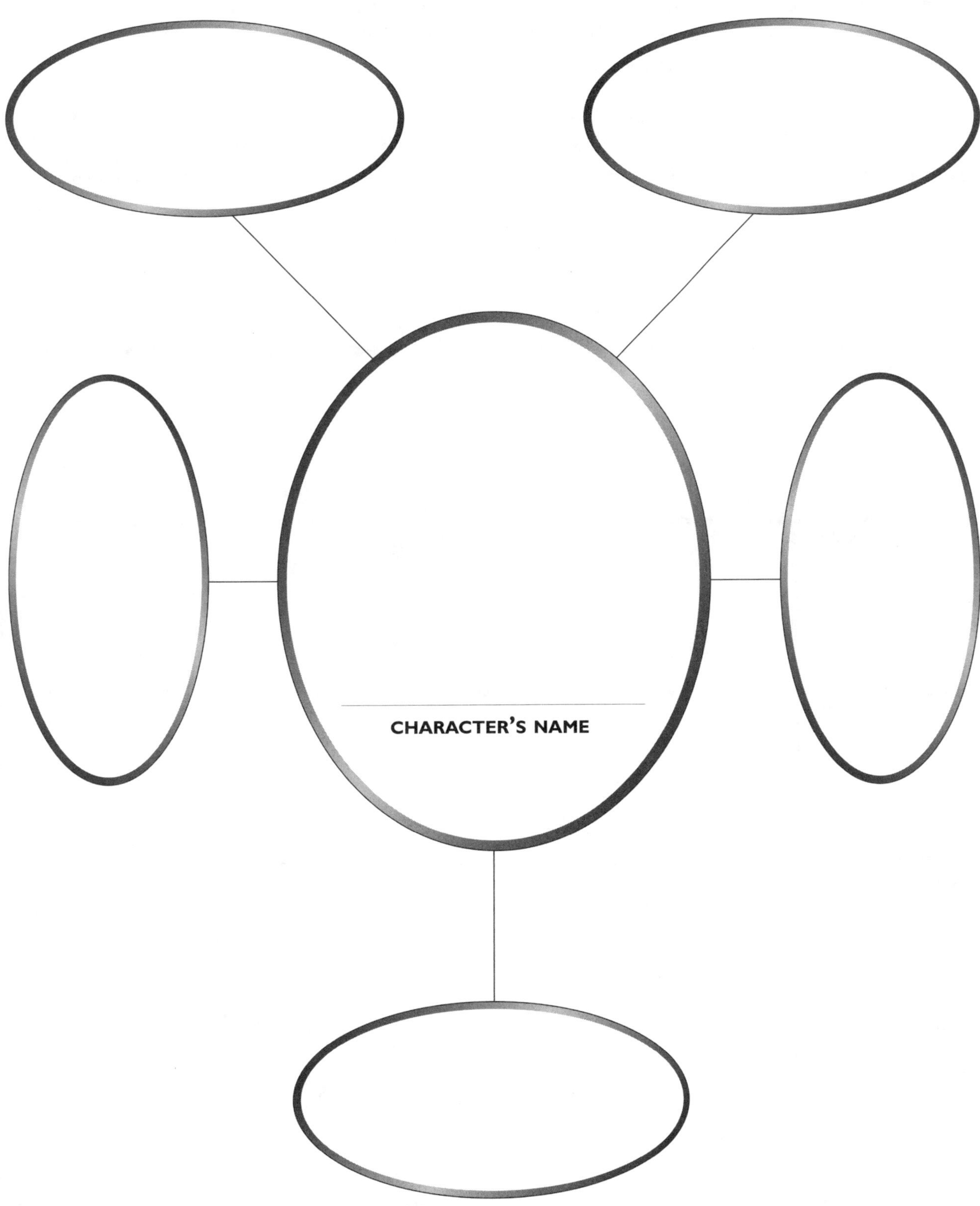

Caught Reading

Name: ______________________________ Date: ______________

Use the following chart to compare and contrast elements of the two novels you've just read. You may wish to review both novels before you fill out the chart. Write a sentence or phrase in each empty space.

	MIDWAY NOVEL	FINAL NOVEL
TITLE		
SETTING		
CHARACTER(S)		
PROBLEM		
TURNING POINT		
SOLUTION		

Caught Reading

BOOK REPORT

Name: ______________________ Date: ______________

Use the following form to write a book report on the novel you just read.

TITLE ______________________

AUTHOR ______________________

SETTING ______________________

____

MAIN CHARACTERS ______________________

____

WHAT THE BOOK IS ABOUT ______________________

____

____

____

____

____

____

WHAT I THINK ABOUT THE BOOK ______________________

____

____

____

____

____

____

Caught Reading

Name: ______________________________ Date: ____________________

DATE	TITLE	AUTHOR	HOW I FELT ABOUT IT

BOOKS I HAVE READ

Caught Reading

STUDENT PROGRESS REPORT

Name: ______________________ Date: ______________

Use the following form to track your students' progress. Place a check in the column that best describes your students' progress. For students that receive four or more "Partial Evidence" or "Little Evidence" checks, you may want to provide extra help.

READING BEHAVIORS	Little Evidence	Partial Evidence	Adequate Evidence	Substantial Evidence
BEFORE READING				
Previews titles and illustrations				
Uses prior knowledge				
Makes predictions				
Sets a purpose for reading				
DURING READING				
Reads independently				
Monitors comprehension				
Reads aloud fluently				
Recognizes and appreciates literary features				
AFTER READING				
Discusses selection				
Summarizes selection				
Writes about selection				
Evaluates and analyzes content				
Rereads to find information				

During this level, this student has shown progress by: ______________________

____

During this level, this student's most significant accomplishment is: ______________________

____

During the next level, this student needs to work on the following: ______________________

____

____

____

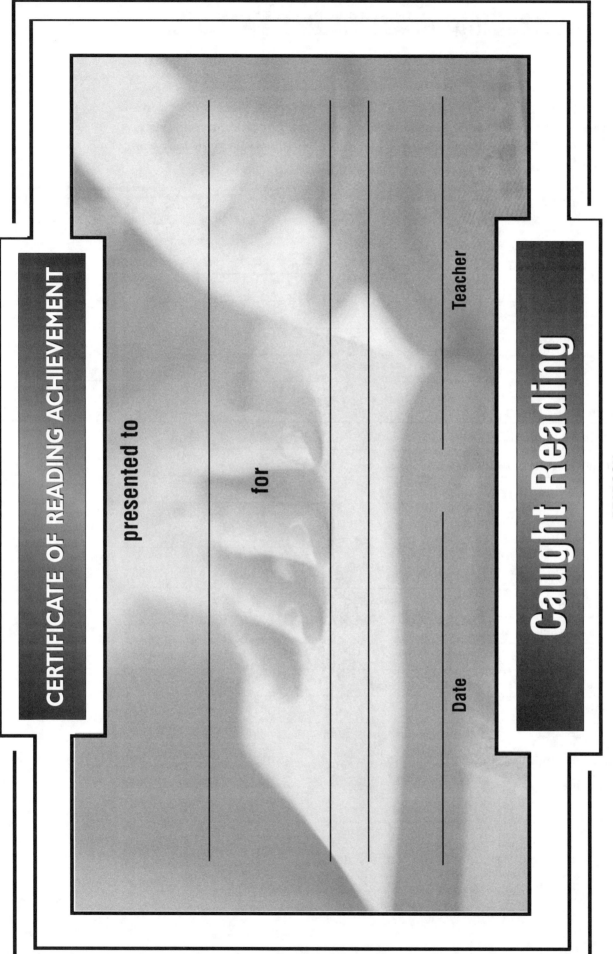

CERTIFICATE OF READING ACHIEVEMENT

presented to

____

for

____

____

______________________ ______________________

Date Teacher

Caught Reading

PEARSON

ADDITIONAL NONSENSE WORDS

Chapter 2

TIJ	MOZ	GAM	TUS	RAJ
KIJ	BOZ	GAD	TIS	REJ
LIJ	VOZ	GAV	TES	RUJ
MIJ	ROZ	GAF	TAS	RIJ
DIJ	TOZ	GAZ	TOS	ROJ
RIJ	VOZ	GAN		
PIJ	THOZ	GAJ		
VIJ		GAT		
SIJ		GAK		
WIJ		GAG		

Chapter 3

ZOOK	FAISH	MEEP	DOOP	LEEZ	SOOF	TOOT	TAISH	KOUF
ZOIK	FAIM	MAIP	DOOJ	LAIZ		TAIT	TOUSH	SHOUF
ZEEK	FAID	MOOP	DOOZ	LOOZ			TEESH	ROUF
ZIEK	FAIP	MAUP	DOOV	LOIZ			TOISH	DOUF
ZAIK	FAIZ	MOIP	DOOG	LOAZ			TOOSH	GOUF
		MOUP		LAWZ			TAUSH	LAIF
		MOAP		LOUZ				LAICH
		JOWP		TEEB				MAICH
		JOOP		IEEB				MAIZ
		JOAK		NEEB				MOIZ
				SEEB				
				CHEEB				
				SOUK				
				SOUF				

Chapter 4

ETS	SKOI	PROA	GLI	SNOU
EST	KOIS	ROAP	LIG	SOUN
TES	OISK	OARP	ILG	OUNS
STE	OIKS	POAR	GIL	NOUS

Chapter 5

STROI	ULFS	SPLEE	CHOUST
TROIS	LUFS	PLEES	SOUCHT
ROIST	SLUF	SPEEL	STOUCH
ROITS	SULT		CHOUTS

Chapter 6

SPROFT	SLOAKT	ROIMPT	TRAIKS
PROFTS	SKLOAT	PROIMT	STRAIK
PROFST	SKOALT	TROIMP	SKARAIT
SPROT	STOALK	TOIMP	SKAIRT
	SKOALT	TOIP	KAIRTS
		TOISP	KAIRST

LEVEL 1 WORD LIST

9th
10th
about
ad
am
are
at
back
bag
bags
be
big
bigger
bike
bikes
boss
boy
boyfriend
bus
but
by
call
calls
can
can't
cannot
car
careful
CD
CDs
class
classes
clean
cleaning
coach
college
come
comes
coming
cook
cooking
dad
Dan
Dan's
day
did
do
does
dog
dogs
doing
don't
Donna
drink
drinker
drive
drives
fast
faster
fastest
find
finds
fire
for
friend
friends
game
get
gets
girl
girls
going
grandma
hall
happy
have
he
hear
help
helped
helps
her
hide
his
hit
hitting
home
hot
house
I'm
if
is
it
Jake
Jake's
Jen
Jen's
job
Kate
keep
kid
kids
laugh
laughing
laughs
light
like
little
lost
lot
lots
make
makes
making
man
me
mom
money
more
MP3
MP3s
my
need
new
next
night
not
of
off
on
one
own
part
people
play
player
problem
problems
put
race
Saturday
say
saying
says
scared
school
scream
screams
see
sees
sell
selling
she
sick
sister
six
sleep
sleeping
sorry
stop
take
takes
talk
talking
talks
team
teamwork
that
the
then
think
thinking
this
three
time
to
Tom
Tom's
too
truck
trucks
try
trying
tryouts
us
waiting
walk
walks
want
wants
was
we
week
what
who
with
wood
woods
work
working
you
your

LEVEL 2 WORD LIST

after
alive
all
already
another
any
anymore
apartment
away
bad
band
bank
base
baseball
because
believe
biggest
boat
champion
championship
close
cold
cop
cops
cougar
cougars
Cruz
dark
days
didn't
dinner
doesn't
ever
family
feel
feels
field
fires
firetrucks
fish
fished
fishing
five
friendly
gave
getting
give
gives
graffiti
hard
has
having
him
hold
holds
homeless
I'll
idea
it's
Jared
just
Kay
kidding
know
knows
lighten
line
lines
long
longer
look
looking
looks
mad
may
maybe
meet
Mike
most
mountain
Mrs.
Mu Lan
needed
no
old
other
our
over
pack
packs
paint
painter
principal
raise
raised
raises
ring
run
running
screaming
sea
seen
shelter
ship
shop
should
smash
smashed
smashing
snow
snowball
snowing
sold
some
start
sun
taken
tell
tells
there
they
thinks
throw
throws
up
use
uses
vote
votes
walked
walking
wall
wanted
wave
waves
way
wear
wearing
when
where
will
window
woman
won
wooden
worked
worth

LEVEL 3 WORD LIST

again	gone	oh	somehow
always	good-looking	open	someone
anything	got	opens	something
anyway	group	or	somewhere
anywhere	guy	outside	sound
as	had	owns	sounds
asks	hand	paints	starts
attach	happen	place	stops
bases	happened	places	story
been	happens	players	than
before	he's	playing	that's
behind	hears	point	their
believes	here	points	them
below	himself	pretty	these
better	homework	pull	thing
box	houses	pulls	things
boxes	Inez	puts	through
buy	inside	read	till
called	into	reads	today
card	introduction	right	together
cards	keeps	room	told
Carmen	kitchen	runs	took
Carmen's	last	sad	tries
change	leave	safe	turn
circle	leaves	said	turns
could	let	sale	two
cries	let's	sales	under
dog's	lets	same	walls
done	letter	save	well
door	lights	saw	were
down	likes	self	what's
else	looked	sells	while
even	Luis	sentence	why
every	made	she's	without
everyone	mean	shops	word
everything	mind	show	words
everywhere	mouth	showing	works
face	move	shows	would
fame	much	side	write
far	must	sisters	wrong
feelings	myself	sit	yes
first	name	sits	you're
food	needs	smile	yourself
forget	news	smiles	
from	now	so	
games	off-base	someday	

LEVEL 4 WORD LIST

against
air
and
animal
animals
answers
ant
ants
arm
attacks
ball
balls
belongs
between
body
break
cage
cars
changed
changes
circles
clean
closes
closest
computer
computers
corner
count
course
crack
cracks
crash
creature
creatures
cut
darkest
die
different
direction
drug
each
Earth
eat
eats
eight
enough
eye
eyes
fall
falls
feelers
fight
fighting
fights
fix
fly
flytrap
front
gang
gas
given
glass
green
ground
grow
half
hands
harm
harmed
harmful
harmless
helping
helpless
hiding
hits
hole
hope
housework
in
insect
insects
interested
jobs
kind
kinds
known
land
legs
life
liquid
live
lives
living
lose
machine
machines
metal
monster
mountains
moves
names
never
oil
ones
outer
page
parts
pay
pictures
planet
planets
plant
plants
pointed
push
pushed
pushes
questions
radio
radios
red
remembers
robot
robot's
robots
rock
saved
scientist
scientists
seem
seems
shake
shakes
shark
sharks
sharks'
sickness
sitting
sky
small
solid
sometimes
space
spaceship
spider
spiders
stand
star
stars
steal
sticks
still
stories
studies
teeth
they're
those
times
toward
trap
trip
Tyrone
Tyrone's
used
using
Venus
voice
voices
wants
water
ways
weeks
win
year
years
yet
you'll

LEVEL 5 WORD LIST

accident
act
African
Americans
Arizona
asked
asking
badly
beat
become
becoming
believed
Beth
bill
blanket
born
build
building
buildings
burns
California
camp
camps
cares
César Chávez
Cherokee
Cherokees
chief
cleaned
closed
cloth
counts
crops
driver
dying
eating
else's
fair
families
Fannie Lou Hamer
farm
farmers
farming
farmworkers
fields
finding
finish
found
four
free
freeway
gold
good
grape
grapes
growers
growing
guys
Hamer's
handouts
hanged
harder
heads
high
highest
history
holding
homes
hood
hoped
hopes
hour
however
hurt
husband
jean
jeans
joke
kill
killed
lasted
late
law
laws
learn
Levi Strauss
listened
lived
married
meeting
mile
miles
mine
miners
Mississippi
named
nation
navy
neighbor
neighborhood
neighbors
office
Oklahoma
opened
others
outhouses
owned
pants
passed
paying
pick
pickers
pipe
pipeline
police
politics
poor
pulled
putting
reading
ready
register
registering
religious
rivet
rivets
ruin
sending
share
sharecropper's
sharecropping
showed
social
something
sometimes
south
started
starting
stay
stayed
stood
stopped
strike
strong
stronger
strongly
swim
talked
tent
tents
test
thief
town
tried
underwear
union
violence
voting
wagon
wagons
waited
went
white
whites
willing
Wilma Mankiller
wins
winter
worker
workers
writing
yellow

LEVEL 6 WORD LIST

across
adventures
alone
Ana
Ana's
anyone
apartments
arms
awhile
banks
beginning
bones
books
both
boys
breaking
breaks
burning
bursts
camping
César's
charts
coldest
cool
couldn't
country
dirt
dirty
dish
dishes
doors
driving
early
eaten
either
electric
electricity
excited
excitement
excites
explore
explorer
explorers
fallen
falling
fancy
fat
feeling
feet
fell
few
floor
follow
freeze
freezing
frozen
full
glasses
great
Greenland
guitar
gun
handle
hat
hearing
heat
helper
Henson
Henson's
hero
hey
hi
ice
Inuit
Inuits
isn't
knees
lands
letters
liked
liking
lock
longest
love
main
Matthew Henson
means
meat
medal
men
might
moved
moving
Mr.
music
musk ox
noise
north
nothing
older
outdoors
outlaw
packing
paper
park
placing
plays
poems
pole
prove
pushing
reach
rent
rest
restaurant
restaurants
rhymes
rich
ride
Robert Peary
rocks
secret
she'll
shut
since
sing
singing
sings
sled
slow
slowly
sometime
song
soon
stairs
standing
stolen
storm
street
such
sudden
suddenly
sure
telephone
telling
top
trips
trouble
turned
turning
very
war
wash
washing
wasn't
watch
we'll
we're
web
webs
whatever
whole
windows
won't
world
wouldn't
you've
young

LEVEL 7 WORD LIST

above	Dana	learning	score
ads	directions	less	scores
ago	doctor	list	second
almost	dream	listed	seconds
article	drivers	listening	security
articles	easy	loud	sells
aunt	empty	low	shoot
basket	engine	mark	shooting
basketball	event	minute	shoots
baskets	events	minutes	shot
bench	example	misses	sign
black	exciting	missing	skill
block	faces	model	skills
blocks	facts	moment	slam
breath	fill	month	slams
bring	filling	movie	special
brings	following	movies	spider's
brother	foods	newspaper	sport
brothers	foot	newspapers	sports
business	forgets	newsroom	stands
businesses	form	number	state
buys	forward	numbers	stays
buzzer	foster	once	step
calm	fun	pages	store
carefully	giving	pair	Stormer
catch	grouped	pairs	sunglasses
center	guard	papers	suppose
champions	guarding	paragraph	supposed
chance	hair	parents	table
choice	hangs	passes	taking
choices	heading	person	teams
clap	headings	persons	there's
clapping	hides	piece	tomorrow
clock	hours	pieces	tonight
closely	huts	playground	tool
clothes	ideas	power	tools
clothing	important	practice	trick
company	information	price	uncle
correct	interesting	pulling	uncle's
correctly	interview	quick	understand
court	jump	remembered	winning
crowd	jumps	rooms	yesterday
crowds	keeping	rule	younger
darker	kid's	rules	

Chapter 1

LESSON 1 a, e, i, o, and u should be circled; b, c, d, f, g, h, j, k, l, m, n, p, q, r, s, t, v, w, x, y, and z should have squares around them.

LESSON 2

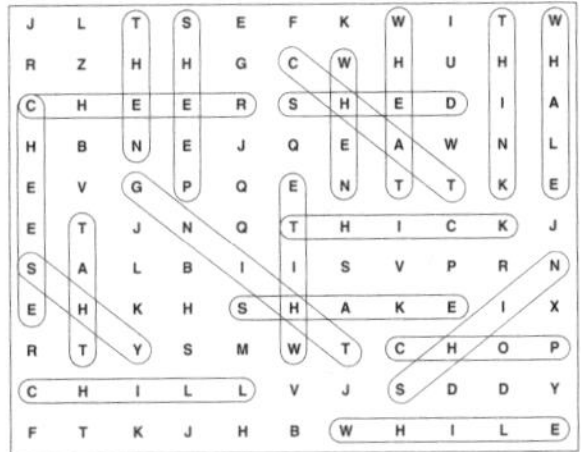

LESSON 3 1. game 2. need 3. bike 4. cove 5. tune 6. main 7. deep 8. tie 9. row 10. mule 11. day 12. meal 13. kite 14. boat 15. June 16. rain 17. each 18. pie 19. soap 20. cute

LESSON 4 A. *short a*: an, tap, at, am; *short e*: Ed, hen, get, beg; *short i*: it, if, in, sip; *short o*: mop, cot, on, log; *short u*: us, tub, bug, up; B. 1. pan, pen, pin, pun 2. tag, tog, tug 3. mat, met 4. bat, bet, bit, bot, but 5. fan, fin, fun 6. nod 7. ran, run 8. sap, sip, sop, sup 9. van 10. tab, tub

LESSON 5 A. *ou*: cloud, mouth, house; *ow*: bow, flower, crown; *oi*: coin, noise, oil; *oy*: boy, toy, joy; *au*: Paul, haul, pause; *aw*: crawl, yawn, paw; B. 1. coin 2. crawl 3. noise 4. mouth 5. flower 6. pause 7. cloud 8. crown 9. haul 10. yawn

Chapter 2

LESSON 1 B. *ll*: hill, fell, full, will, well; *ss*: pass, boss, miss, mess, less; *ff*: buff, stuff, cliff, puff, cuff; *ck*: back, pack, pick, kick, duck; C. 1. boss 2. chill 3. black 4. moss 5. less 6. fell 7. shack 8. pall, pass, pack 9. cuff 10. hill, hiss; D. Answers will vary.

LESSON 2 1. chat 2. cuff 3. tub or but 4. sit 5. met 6. chin 7. gab or bag 8. shop or posh 9. back 10. job 11. pick 12. lip 13. nap or pan 14. fog 15. chum or much 16. will 17. pet 18. hill 19. sad 20. duck

B. 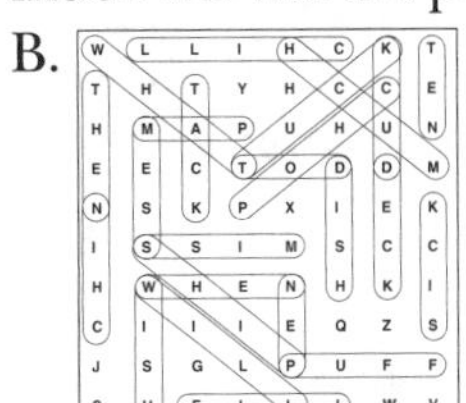

LESSON 3 B. *short a*: Pal, and, Pat, Pam; *short e*: Peg, pet, pen; *short i*: pickle, pig, pit, pigged, in, his, pickles; *short o*: pot, of, Pod, on; *short u*: put, Pug; Answers to the second part will vary. C. Answers will vary. E. 1. Red is washed. Red is fed. Red is petted. Red and his owner sit on the bed. 2. Red gets sick. Red and his owner go to the vet. Red licks the vet's chin. The vet gets all wet. 3. Red and his owner go to the shop. They buy a pot. They buy a pan. They buy a mop. 4. Red's owner puts the pot in her van. Red's owner puts the mop in the van. Red's owner puts the pan in the van. Red's owner puts Red in the van. 5. Red and his owner go home. Red sits in his owner's lap. Red is petted. Red and his owner take a nap.

Chapter 3

LESSON 1, PART 1 B. *a-consonant-e*: fate, cane, pane, tape, made; *i-consonant-e*: hide, kite, dime, ride, bite; *o-consonant-e*: note, mope, robe, cope, hope; *u-consonant-e*: cube, cure, tube, dude, cute; C. 1. cute 2. mope 3. tape 4. note 5. bite 6. dude 7. dime 8. kite 9. fate 10. ride; D. Answers will vary.

PART 2 B. *ee*: beet, peek, feet, cheep, meet; *ea*: peak, cheap, meat, feat, beat; *ai*: gain, nail, maid, paid; *ay*: way, may, day, hay, pay; *oa*: soap, coat, foam, boat, goal; C. 1. meet or meat 2. foam 3. feet or feat 4. peek or peak 5. day 6. coat 7. beat, beet, or boat 8. nail; D. (Order of the answers may vary.) 1. cheep and cheap 2. meet and meat 3. feat and feet 4. peek and peak

LESSON 2 B. Answers will vary.

LESSON 3 B. *a-consonant-e*: Kate, made, shape, race, Gabe, game, take, lake, save, date, Nate's, wake; *i-consonant-e*: time, hike, ride, bike, dive, while, mile, nine, miles, Mike; *o-consonant-e*: Hope, note; *ea*: Dear, team, seat; *ee*: need, week, sleep; *oa*: boat; C. (Answers must appear in this order, except for Gabe and Hope.) week, game, team, Gabe, Hope, need, take, beach, feed, wait, may; E. Answers will vary.

Chapter 4

LESSON 1, PART 1 B. /***s*** /: city, race, mice, dice, rice, face, ice; /***k*** / coal, cat, cake, coin, cut, cone, coat; C. 1. cat, mice 2. race 3. face 4. ice 5. coat 6. ice; cone

PART 2 B. /***g***/: game, goat, egg, gum, gift; /***j***/: sage, huge, gym, page, siege; C. 1. egg 2. game 3. gum 4. gift 5. page 6. gym

PART 3 B. /***i*** /: fly, my, sky, cry, by, try; /***e*** /: baby, funny, very, many, puppy, pretty; C. 1. underline puppy; circle shy, my 2. underline baby; circle cry 3. circle sky 4. underline funny 5. underline many, very, and funny; circle my 6. circle fly

LESSON 2

B.

C. 1. grew 2. arch or char 3. stay 4. clue 5. aunt 6. cat or act 7. seat or eats 8. true 9. free or reef 10. glue 11. plow 12. try 13. glow 14. stew 15. rat, tar or art 16. growl 17. math 18. three 19. oats 20. arm, ram, or mar

LESSON 3 B. 1. Cody, Jane, Ned, and Kate 2. organizing the food drive 3. Friday 4. Room 101 5. to help the homeless people in the city; D. 1. broke 2. arm 3. track 4. last 5. help 6. cast ; E. Answers will vary. F. Answers will vary.

Chapter 5

LESSON 1, PART 1 B. *kn*: knit, kneel, knob, know, knife; *wr*: wreck, wren, write, wrist, wrench; *gn*: design, sign, gnaw; *mb*: limb, comb, climb, lamb, thumb; Students should have circled the k's, w's, g's, and b's. C. wrist, thumb, knit, lamb, write.

PART 2 C. *ar*: car, march, large, hard; *er*: nerve, verb, serve, germ; *ir*: girl, first, thirst, skirt; *or*: corn, shore, sport, form, storm; *ur*: hurt, church, turn; C. 1. circle car and storm 2. circle First and shore 3. circle corn and large 4. circle skirt 5. circle turn 6. circle form 7. circle nerve 8. circle church

PART 3 B. *ch*: which, reach, march; *tch*: watch, pitch, catch; *ng*: wrong, long, sing; *nk*: pink, think, drink; C. 1. pitch 2. Which 3. catch 4. pink or long; D. 1. sing or sink 2. pitch 3. march 4. wrong 5. drink 6. which 7. think or thing 8. ring or rink

LESSON 2

A.

LESSON 3 C. circle front, school, form, next, curb, turn, front, left, Trail, train, tracks; D. Answers will vary. E. Answers will vary. G. Answers will vary.

Chapter 6

LESSON 1, PART 1 B. *No change*: pitched, cooking, loaded, jumping, walking, cleaned, talked, splashing, chirping; *doubled consonant*: running, grabbed, shopping, swimming, slipping, tripped, stopped; C. 1. stopped, swimming 2. talked 3. shopping, running, walking, or swimming 4. cleaned 5. tripped

PART 2 B. */p/*: puppy, supper, happy; */b/*: bubble, rubber; */r/*: carry, berry, borrow; */t/*: button, written, lettuce; */d/*: saddle, hidden, ladder; */l/*: balloon, follow; C. puppy, supper, carry, follow, happy

LESSON 2 A. 1. lamps 2. shrimp 3. desks 4. carrot 5. skunk 6. guppy 7. floats 8. stream 9. paddle 10. bottle 11. ground 12. street 13. claps 14. skipped 15. flippers; B. *three-sound words*: mill, theme, rule; *four-sound words*: gruff, found, check; *five-sound words*: spring, clasp, trick, wished, crisp; *six-sound words*: strict, streets, lunged, splint, plunk

C. 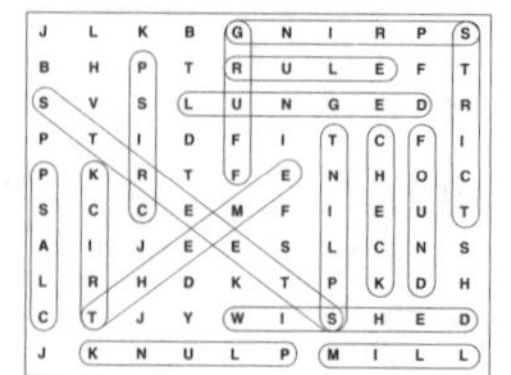

LESSON 3 B. Answers will vary. D. 1. last Saturday 2. Los Angeles 3. old rock tunes 4. four 5. guitar, keyboard, drums, and bass 6. they liked it and cheered 7. drummer 8. they are the best rock group that has ever played at Stone Park; E. Answers will vary.

Chapter 7

LESSON 1 B. 1. Welcome 2. lemon 3. invite 4. chicken 5. pencil 6. gallon 7. kitten or doctor, orchard 8. travel 9. quarter 10. visit; C. Sunday, invite, Steven, supper (twice), lemon, chicken, soda, After, into, apple (3 times), orchard, apples, filling, entire, barrel, inside, gallons, cider, and seven should be underlined.

LESSON 2 A. *sun*: sunflower, sunshine, Sunday, sunlight; *snow*: snowplow, snowball, snowsuit, snowflake; *rain*: raincoat, rainbow, raindrop; *-ball*: snowball, softball, fireball; *-port*: airport, carport, seaport; *-day*: Sunday, birthday, today; B. (Order of answers will vary.) 1. butterfly 2. goodbye 3. rattlesnake 4. understand; C. 1. underline snowsuit; raincoat 2. underline raindrop; sunflower 3. underline snowball; softball 4. underline carport; seaport

LESSON 3 B. 1. unfair 2. unhappy 3. reread 4. disagree 5. rebuild; C. 1. unhappy 2. unpack 3. express 4. return 5. reread

LESSON 4 B. 1. *ful*: careful, hopeful, thankful, harmful, thoughtful, painful, helpful, useful; *less*: helpless, harmless, painless, thankless, careless, hopeless, useless, thoughtless; *able*: honorable, sinkable, dependable, washable, reliable, breakable; C. 1. helpful or useful 2. breakable 3. thankful 4. thoughtful, thoughtless, dependable, or reliable 5. careful

LESSON 5 B. underline rain/coats, rain/drops, rain/bows, butter/cups, sun/flowers, summer/time, sea/shore, sea/shells, foot/ball, cheer/leaders, winter/time, snow/flakes, snow/balls, and snow/suits; C. Answers will vary. E. be/gin, un/beat/a/ble, un/a/fraid, de/scribe, in/act/ive, in/tol/er/ant, in/volved, in/ter/est/ed, a ble, re/li/a/ble, de/pend/a/ble, hon/or/a/ble, thank/ful, bash/ful, some/times, thought/ful, help/ful, al/ways, fool/ish, child/ish, ad/mi/ra/ble, qual/i/ties; F. Answers will vary. G. Answers will vary.

ANSWER KEY WORKTEXTS 1–7
PRACTICE LESSONS

Worktext 1

LESSON 1.1

Remembering Details: job or CD player, dog, money or $200, lost, money

LESSON 1.2

Remembering Details: lot, school, Saturday, sick
Finding the Main Idea: what to do on Saturday

LESSON 1.3

Remembering Details: sick, job, want, home
Finding the Main Idea: what makes Tom sick

LESSON 1.4

Remembering Details: money, trucks, house, happy
Putting Ideas in Order: My house is on fire! My mom gets the dog. I lost my money.

LESSON 1.5

Remembering Details: school, find, Mom, happy, say
Read It Again: c) money, a) need, b) think

LESSON 1.6

Remembering Details: talking, sick, girl, problem
Putting Ideas in Order: At home, I say I am sick. Then I see a big kid hit a little kid. The big kid backs off. Then I walk her home.

LESSON 1.7

Finding the Main Idea: My truck hits a dog.
Read It Again: b) finds, a) grandma, c) sick

LESSON 1.8

Remembering Details: house, friends, problem, sorry
Putting Ideas in Order: Dan, Tom, Jake, and I are friends. Jake says, "I don't need friends like Dan." Mom says, "People like to talk." But I just walk by.

LESSON 1.9

Finding the Main Idea: I want to do my own thinking.
Read It Again: c) sick, b) school, a) job

LESSON 1.10

Remembering Details: trying, fastest, team, helped, helped
Putting Ideas in Order: One day, she talks in class. The next day is bike team tryouts. I'm happy to have a new friend.

LESSON 1.11

Finding the Main Idea: What a sorry day!
Read It Again: a) sick, a) little kid, c) stop

LESSON 1.12

Remembering Details: back, keeping, sell, drives
Putting Ideas in Order: We work on the car for weeks and weeks. "I want the car," Dan says. "What about me?" I say. "It is your car and my car."

LESSON 1.13

Finding the Main Idea: I sell Dan's and my car.
Read It Again: b) home, a) house, a) dog

LESSON 1.14

Remembering Details: part, careful, talking, college
Putting Ideas in Order: "You are not working part-time," my dad says. The next week, Mom sells the car. My dad stops talking to her.

LESSON 1.15

Finding the Main Idea: Mom gets an "A", and we are happy.
Read It Again: c) in school, b) lost, a) do, c) happy

LESSON 1.16

Remembering Details: woods, thinking, scared, light, bigger, bigger
Putting Ideas in Order: We go out to the woods. Then we get in the sleeping bags. Kate screams.

LESSON 1.17

Finding the Main Idea: We get scared in the woods.
Read It Again: a) friends, c) problems, b) talk, c) sister

Practice Lessons 1

LESSON 1.1

A. day, Kay, play, pay, hay, may, ray, stay
B. 1. play 2. Kay 3. day 4. say 5. stay 6. may
C. Answers will vary.
D.

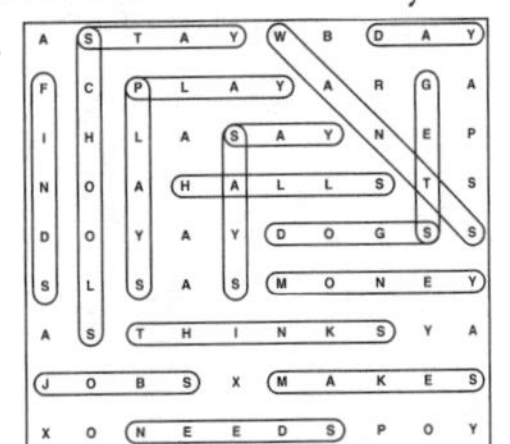

E. 1. player 2. money 3. find 4. school 5. job 6. money 7. hall 8. school
F. Answers will vary.

LESSON 1.2

A. 1. games, gaming 2. walks, walking 3. finds, finding 4. likes, liking 5. needs, needing 6. thinks, thinking 7. wants, wanting 8. gets, getting 9. plays, playing 10. schools, schooling
B. Answers will vary.
C. 1. e 2. f 3. b 4. a 5. d 6. c
D. 1. Grandma's 2. Jen's 3. coach's 4. Jen's 5. school's
E. 1. game 2. Saturday 3. walks 4. He 5. coach 6. says, wants 7. go, sick 8. coach, play 9. Get, off 10. going, Grandma's
F. Answers will vary.

LESSON 1.3

A. 1. goes 2. walking 3. likes 4. player 5. find 6. wants 7. coaching 8. sick, sicker
B. Answers will vary.

LESSON 1.4

A. dot, not, plot, pot, hot, got, rot
B. 1. hot 2. not 3. lot 4. got 5. not
C. 1. needs, needing. Answers will vary. 2. trucks, trucking. Answers will vary. 3. waits, waiting. Answers will vary. 4. finds, finding. Answers will vary. 5. thinks, thinking. Answers will vary. 6. says, saying. Answers will vary. 7. plays, playing. Answers will vary. 8. walks, walking. Answers will vary.
D. 1. sister 2. waiting 3. hide 4. fire trucks 5. not 6. school 7. car 8. back 9. wait 10. sister
E. Answers will vary.

LESSON 1.5

A. 1. hot 2. about 3. hides 4. go 5. walking 6. sister 7. truck 8. finds
B. Answers will vary.

LESSON 1.6

A. 1. bay, play, stay 2. walk, talk, chalk 3. day, say, play 4. balk, talk, walk
B. 1. sees, seeing, seer 2. kids, kidding, kidder 3. backs, backing, backer 4. halls 5. hits, hitting, hitter 6. walks, walking, walker 7. bigger 8. talks, talking, talker 9. thinks, thinking, thinker 10. says, saying 11. finds, finding, finder 12. stops, stopping, stopper
C. 1. player 2. thinker 3. talker 4. big 5. backs
D. 1. day 2. hit 3. are 4. says 5. cannot 6. talking 7. little 8. problem
E. Answers will vary.

LESSON 1.7

A. 1. cannot 2. new 3. problem 4. did 5. lost 6. hit 7. sorry 8. kids
B. Answers will vary.

LESSON 1.8

A. first ladder: tall, call, hall, fall, mall, stall; second ladder: van, Dan, pan, fan, tan, man
B. 1. tall, tan 2. hall 3. mall 4. call 5. Dan 6. can
C. 1. calls 2. Dan's 3. drinks 4. Jake's 5. wanting 6. talked 7. backed 8. fires 9. Grandma's 10. played 11. girls 12. coaching 13. backing 14. walked 15. friends 16. playing 17. sisters 18. called 19. waiting 20. Dad's
D. 1. calling 2. drinking 3. getting 4. friend's 5. Jen's 6. wanted
E. 1. by 2. big 3. want 4. sorry 5. own 6. can't 7. that 8. friend
F. Answers will vary.

LESSON 1.9

A. 1. drink 2. friends 3. own 4. big 5. wanted 6. sorry 7. by 8. I'm
B. Answers will vary.

MIDWAY ASSESSMENT

A. (Words must appear in this order.) game, waiting, with, am, problem, sister, sick, make, little, happy, thinking, people, house, players, friend
B. 1. Jake, fake, and cake should be circled, cake 2. dad, had, and mad should be circled, dad 3. an, Dan, and can should be circled, Dan 4. tall, hall, and call should be circled, tall 5. day and play should be circled, day 6. talk and chalk should be circled, talk 7. hot and got should be circled, hot
C. Answers will vary.
D. 1. dogs, dog's 2. bigger 3. talks, talked, talking, talker 4. halls, hall's 5. hits, hitting, hitter 6. Dan's 7. kids, kidded, kidding, kidder, kid's 8. stops, stopped, stopping, stopper 9. finds, finding, finder 10. trucks, trucked, trucking, trucker, truck's
E. 1. walked 2. Jen's 3. don't 4. problems 5. friend's 6. going 7. player 8. talker

LESSON 1.10

A. 1. Mike 2. like 3. bike 4. hike
B. 1. like 2. hike 3. Mike 4. bike
C. Answers will vary.
D. 1. fastest 2. fired 3. laughed 4. trying 5. laughing 6. 9th 7. 10th 8. helped 9. helping 10. friends 11. girls 12. comes 13. lots 14. calling 15. makes 16. helps 17. called 18. laughs 19. 5th 20. biggest
E. 1. biggest or fastest 2. fired 3. laughing 4. 5th, 9th, or 10th 5. laughing or helping 6. calling or helping 7. helped 8. trying
F. 1. fast 2. race 3. laugh 4. help 5. team 6. bike 7. try 8. come
G. Answers will vary.

LESSON 1.11

A. 1. fired 2. makes 3. team 4. comes 5. bikes 6. calls 7. one 8. faster 9. help 10. class
B. Answers will vary.

LESSON 1.12

A.

B. 1. can, man, fan 2. Jake, take, rake 3. Dad, sad, had 4. plan, man, Nan; answers will vary.
C. 1. drive 2. take 3. weeks 4. doing 5. keeping 6. man 7. sell 8. ad
D. Answers will vary.

LESSON 1.13

A. 1. thinks 2. drives 3. takes 4. plays 5. sell 6. take 7. keep 8. sell
B. Answers will vary.

LESSON 1.14

A. 1. classes 2. glasses 3. bosses 4. tosses 5. passes 6. crosses
B. 1. worked 2. cooked 3. cleaned 4. played 5. biked 6. fired 7. walked 8. needed
C. 1. making 2. taking 3. working 4. stopping 5. cleaning 6. biking
D. 1. got, pot, and hot should be circled 2. talk and chalk should be circled 3. sake, take, and wake should be circled 4. sad, had, and glad should be circled 5. like, hike, and spike should be circled 6. wall, tall, and fall should be circled 7. May, stay, and gray should be circled 8. Stan, pan, and tan should be circled.

E. 1. talk 2. bike 3. can 4. walk
F. Answers will vary.
G. 1. selling 2. be 3. cook 4. wait 5. time 6. clean 7. part, want 8. careful, the
H. Answers will vary.

LESSON 1.15

A. 1. cooking 2. sells 3. bus 4. college 5. with, clean 6. careful, night
B. Answers will vary.

LESSON 1.16

A. deep, sleep, beep, peep; light, bright, slight, fight; dream, scream, seam, beam
B.

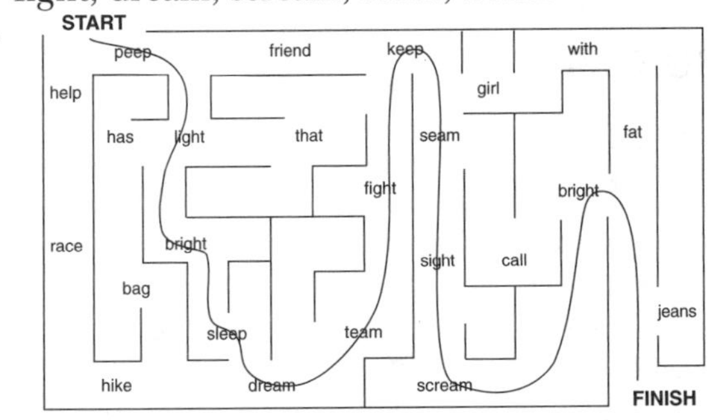

C. cannot, fire truck, teamwork, into, forget, without, boyfriend, driveway
D. Answers will vary.
E. 1. light 2. hot 3. sleep 4. making 5. scream 6. if 7. bag, home 8. boy, woods
F. Answers will vary.

LESSON 1.17

A. 1. calling 2. sleeping 3. coming 4. without 5. says, boyfriend
B. Answers will vary.

FINAL ASSESSMENT

A. (Words must appear in this order.) bus, teamwork, talk, game, sister, players, college, lost, man, problem, school, happy, does, hit, about
B. 1. making 2. scream 3. kid 4. friend, fire 5. boyfriend, bus 6. keeping, hall 7. days, work 8. class, not 9. problem, truck 10. scared, dogs
C. boyfriend, fire truck, without, driveway, into, forget
D. 1. boyfriend 2. forget 3. without 4. fire truck 5. into 6. driveway
E. 1. kids, kidded, kidding 2. plays, played, playing 3. stops, stopped, stopping 4. fires, fired, firing 5. calls, called, calling
F. 1. seam, dream, and scream should be circled, scream 2. bright, sight, and light should be circled, light 3. sleep and deep should be circled, sleep 4. ad, had, and glad should be circled, ad 5. like, spike, and hike should be circled, hike 6. sake, cake, and make should be circled, make 7. fall, stall, and call should be circled, call 8. talk and chalk should be circled, talk 9. stay, way, and pay should be circled, pay 10. spot, hot, and cot should be circled, hot

Worktext 2

LESSON 2.1

Remembering Details: principal, idea, friendly, graffiti
Putting Ideas in Order: I am getting scared. I want to scream, "What did I do?" The principal says, "Mrs. Selling says you are a painter." The principal says, "Wait, Jared."

LESSON 2.2

Remembering Details: painters, idea, problem, cleans
Finding the Main Idea: Jared paints walls at school to help stop graffiti.

LESSON 2.3

Making Predictions: There is no correct answer. Students may predict yes or no. However, students should be able to back up their prediction with good reasoning. Two sound responses would be to predict: 1) No. "The man gives me $500 for it." "No," my dad says. "It's sold." 2) Yes. "If we go fast, maybe we can get it back." Dad gives us the $500.

LESSON 2.4

Remembering Details: sold, boyfriend, grandma's, mom's, alive
Putting Ideas in Order: He drives after the man. The man stops and hears what I have to say. "Sorry. It's no longer your ring."

LESSON 2.5

Remembering Details: feels, cops, ring
Finding the Main Idea: She gets her mom's and grandma's ring back.

LESSON 2.6

Remembering Details: waiting, money, holdup, happy
Read It Again: b) the principal, c) graffiti, b) painting

LESSON 2.7

Making Predictions: There is no correct answer to this question. Students may predict yes or no. However, students should be able to back up their predictions with good reasoning. Two possible responses would be to predict: 1) No. The snow is coming down. Night is coming on fast. "I don't know the way back," Tom says. It just takes longer and longer to walk in the snow. 2) Yes. But Tom says he knows where he is going. Tom says he goes to the shelter all the time.

LESSON 2.8

Remembering Details: screaming, snow, shelter, dinner
Putting Ideas in Order: I think about making a shelter with snow. I make a big snowball. We eat the dinner without cooking it. We come out of the woods.

LESSON 2.9

Finding the Main Idea: The kids in the story find a family sleeping in the field.
Read It Again: a) money, c) hold-up, b) alive

LESSON 2.10

Remembering Details: family, playing, apartment
Putting Ideas in Order: "I'm going to tell the bank who did it." Jared says, "The family already talked to the bank people about it." "We will have to start over."

LESSON 2.11

Finding the Main Idea: The kids are going to vote to say where the money goes.
Read It Again: a) wooden shelter, b) snowballs, c) a hot dinner

LESSON 2.12

Remembering Details: cougar, baseball, believe, dinner
Putting Ideas in Order: Mu Lan and I are looking at the baseball game on TV. "I want to go find the cougar!" The man and the woman close up the back of the truck fast.

LESSON 2.13

Making Predictions: There is no correct answer to this question. Students may predict yes or no. However, students should be able to back up their predictions with good reasoning. Two possible responses would be to predict: 1) No. The sea looks dark. Waves smash up on the boat. Dad can't make the boat go the way he wants. 2) Yes. My dad, his dad, and **his** dad all fished. We are all champions.

LESSON 2.14

Finding the Main Idea: No championship is worth being thrown into the sea.
Read It Again: c) baseball, b) jobs, b) window, a) an apartment

LESSON 2.15

Remembering Details: married, smiles, marrying, Saturday
Putting Ideas in Order: "I'm getting married," she says. "You don't know this boy," I say. "What are you doing this for?" Then she starts to cry and runs out of the apartment.

LESSON 2.16

Finding the Main Idea: Robin makes up Mack because she doesn't want to think about school.

Practice Lessons 2

LESSON 2.1

A. 1. way, stay, pay, hay 2. wall, stall, tall, call 3. book, hook, look, took 4. well, fell, bell, sell
B.

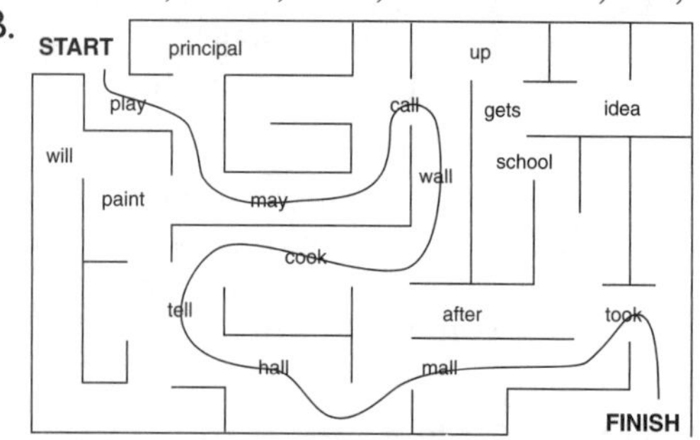

C. 1. painters 2. graffiti 3. principal 4. after 5. Mrs. 6. walls, paint 7. idea, clean 8. may, tell
D. Answers will vary.

LESSON 2.2

A. 1. puts 2. cleans 3. painting 4. putting 5. tells 6. keeps, paintings 7. painter, friendly 8. tells, principal 9. will, look 10. graffiti, wall
B. Answers will vary.

LESSON 2.3

A. Long e: see, scream, deep, seek, weed, keep, bean, sleep; Long a: wait, paint; Long o: goes, coach
B. 1. scream 2. seek 3. goes 4. coach 5. paint 6. see 7. sleep 8. bean
C. 1. bad 2. shop 3. No 4. sold 5. feel, at 6. about, truck 7. him, longer 8. just, give
D. Answers will vary.

LESSON 2.4

A. 1. Maybe 2. alive 3. drives 4. hears 5. gives 6. feel, ring 7. looking, just 8. give, long 9. sold, looks 10. longer, him
B. Answers will vary.

LESSON 2.5

A.

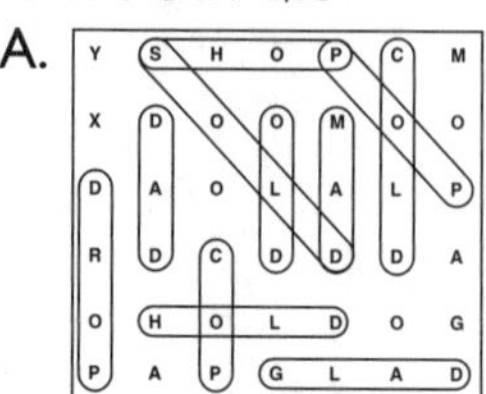

B. Answers will vary.
C. 1. I'll 2. didn't 3. hold 4. mad 5. teller, bank 6. screams, because 7. feeling, needed 8. talks, anymore
D. Answers will vary.

LESSON 2.6

A. 1. cop 2. gave 3. races 4. feels 5. mad 6. any, bank 7. bank, money 8. didn't, needed 9. tell, teller 10. hold, I'll
B. Answers will vary.

LESSON 2.7

A. 1. packing 2. woman's 3. lighten 4. knows 5. playing 6. cooking 7. shopping 8. frighten 9. snowing 10. mountains 11. snowballs 12. having 13. wears 14. screamed 15. where's 16. raced 17. snowed 18. packed 19. wooden 20. brighten
B. 1. snowballs 2. cooking 3. wooden 4. brighten 5. having
C. 1. sun 2. dinner 3. over 4. way 5. played, snow 6. know, painter 7. other, wooden 8. others, mountain
D. Answers will vary.

LESSON 2.8

A. 1. cars 2. ways 3. having 4. There 5. having 6. doesn't, others 7. snowing, there 8. walking, shelter 9. knows, snowball 10. where, dinner
B. Answers will vary.

MIDWAY ASSESSMENT

A. (Words must appear in this order.) others, up, principal, longer, painting, way, cold, where, finding, There, teller, over, about, made, bank
B. 1. pay, play, and may should be circled, may 2. wall, tall, and call should be circled, tall 3. took and book should be circled, took 4. sell, bell, and well should be circled, sell 5. Dad, bad, and mad should be circled, bad 6. shop, pop, and crop should be circled, shop 7. hold, cold, and fold should be

circled, hold 8. pack, rack, and tack should be circled, pack

C. 1. lights, lighted, lighting, lighten, lightly 2. woods, wooded, wooden 3. friends, friendly 4. cleans, cleaned, cleaning, cleanly 5. puts, putting

LESSON 2.9

A. first ladder: start, cart, dart, tart; second ladder: sun, bun, pun, nun, run, gun, stun

B.

						1 P		
					2 C	A	R	T
						R		
		3 S	T	A	4 R	T		
		U			U			
5 B	U	N			N			

C. 1. start 2. sleeping 3. should 4. already 5. family 6. field, window 7. smash, when 8. holds, jobs

D. Answers will vary.

LESSON 2.10

A. 1. telling 2. homeless 3. fires 4. start 5. holds 6. window, baseball 7. field, start 8. family, teller 9. should, apartment 10. sleeping, window

B. Answers will vary.

LESSON 2.11

A. 1. uses 2. raises 3. started 4. meeting 5. raised 6. raising 7. starting 8. votes 9. voting 10. cougars 11. runs 12. running 13. worked 14. bands 15. believed 16. believes

B. 1. raising 2. believes 3. running 4. voting 5. Cougars 6. starting 7. raised 8. worked

C. 1. cougars 2. raises 3. throw 4. close 5. band 6. worked, hard 7. started, used 8. use, meeting

D. Answers will vary.

LESSON 2.12

A. 1. meet 2. raise 3. band 4. runs 5. talk 6. started, worked 7. seen, hard 8. meeting, raising 9. used, close 10. This, uses

B. Answers will vary.

LESSON 2.13

A. first ladder: throw, crow, row, tow, grow; second ladder: pave, wave, Dave, save, grave

B. 1. gave 2. throw 3. wave 4. crow 5. save 6. pave 7. row 8. grow

C. 1. fish 2. champions 3. taken 4. line 5. throws 6. championship, three 7. waves, smashing 8. three, days

D. Answers will vary.

LESSON 2.14

A. 1. another 2. lighter 3. champion 4. worth 5. Our 6. thrown, lines 7. Three, fishing 8. ever, close 9. taken, championship 10. ship, days

B. Answers will vary.

LESSON 2.15

A. I am with I'm, you are with you're, does not with doesn't, what is with what's, do not with don't, cannot with can't, did not with didn't, I will with I'll

B. 1. You're 2. I'm 3. doesn't 4. can't 5. What's 6. didn't

C. 1. hardly 2. really 3. married 4. times 5. pass, classes 6. many, beach

D. Answers will vary.

LESSON 2.16

A. 1. cry 2. only 3. pass 4. What's 5. marries 6. really, good 7. How, marrying 8. hardly, smile 9. smile, what's 10. many, passing

B. Answers will vary.

FINAL ASSESSMENT

A. (Words must be in this order.) mountain, sleeping, bosses, shop, backpacks, idea, mad, working, call, talking, know, field, next, bags, paint

B. 1. bosses 2. backpacks 3. who 4. ballplayer 5. painting 6. happy 7. about 8. sometimes 9. closes 10. like

C. 1. married 2. waving 3. doesn't 4. classes 5. championship 6. biggest 7. faster 8. wooden 9. friends 10. homeless

D. 1. stop, hop, and cop should be circled, stop 2. pack, sack, and rack should be circled, rack 3. hold, gold, and fold should be circled, gold 4. band, sand, and grand should be circled, band

Worktext 3

LESSON 3.1

Putting Ideas in Order: A man with some boxes comes up. The man gives up and walks away. Tom runs after the man. The bus leaves without Tom. Tom gets on the bus with the box.
Remembering Details: bus, box, name, old

LESSON 3.2

Putting Ideas in Order: "It's my MP3 player," says Tom. Tom opens the box. Tom's sister looks into the box. "I call it—The Thing Without a Name," he says.
Finding the One Big Idea: The thing in the box is a thing no one wants.

LESSON 3.3

Remembering Details: The Thing Without a Name, Anything for a Laugh, kitchen
Describe It: long, dark **The Thing Without a Name:** sorry **The people on Carmen's show:** out of it **Anything for a Laugh:** so good **A boy on Anything for a Laugh:** good-looking

LESSON 3.4

Describe It: new, cold, good
Putting Ideas in Order: Inez says she will make a new drink. Inez looks at the drink but does not drink it. Carmen goes back to the TV. The dog has a drink.
Find the One Big Idea: Inez makes a drink that is good—but only for dogs.

LESSON 3.6

Read It Again: Sample responses: He was not at school that day. He was not feeling well. She wants to help him.
Describe It: Tom does not feel happy.

LESSON 3.7

Remembering Details: last Saturday, going by the school, writing on the wall.
What Comes Next?: Answers will vary.

LESSON 3.8

Putting Ideas in Order: Tom sees a boy writing on the wall. Carmen looks up and sees the ad. "Are you Luis?" she asks. "I know just the place," says Carmen. "Tom?" says Luis. "Who is Tom?"
Describe It: the letters are as big as people, his face lights up, the words come fast

LESSON 3.9

Putting Sentences in Order: Carmen takes Luis to the principal. The principal asks Luis about the graffiti. Luis says he was home from 4:00 to 6:00. The principal says that Luis did the graffiti.
Find the One Big Idea: he did the graffiti.

LESSON 3.10

Describe It: a big, open mouth; many, many people, laughing and talking; good
What Will Happen Next? Answers will vary.

LESSON 3.11

Describe It: Snow is coming down. The night is cold. It is dark.
Putting Ideas in Order: Tom shows up at 8:00 on Saturday. The truck starts to make a bad sound. His face comes closer and closer. He points the light into the back of the truck. Then the dark thing sits up.

LESSON 3.12

Putting Ideas in Order: Luis tells the man at the shop that he did the graffiti.
Describe It: pretty, little, walking hand in hand. Luis: my best work; Carmen: no-good; The man who owns the shop: good

LESSON 3.13

Putting Ideas in Order: Luis sees an ad for a bike sale. The line does not move much. Luis makes up a story about another sale. People start talking about the other sale. Luis thinks he will go to the other sale.
Remembering Details: bike, line, sale, Fire Mountain

LESSON 3.14

Remembering Details: the school, Hot Dog, Carmen, in a field by Luis's house
What Will Happen Next? Answers will vary.

LESSON 3.15

Remembering Details: Carmen, Luis, and Tom; Carmen; Tom; he fields
Finding the One Big Idea: he asks Carmen—not Luis—to play for the team.

LESSON 3.16

Describe It: How the card looks at first: pretty, clean. How the card looks that night: sad, words are gone
Putting Ideas in Order: Inez opens Carmen's letter. Inez tries to hide the card behind a painting. The card is gone. The card has gone through a sad change.

LESSON 3.17

Describe It: big apartment house, old cars, smashed-up car window, long dark hall, one light
Remembering Details: graffiti, at the far end, the card, it's pretty—or was, a card shop
Finding the One Big Idea: Inez meets Luis and likes him.

Practice Lessons 3

LESSON 3.1

A. first ladder: lit, hit, fit, sit; second ladder: lame, game, fame, same; third ladder: light, fight, sight, right; fourth ladder: gold, hold, fold, sold
B. 1. same 2. hit 3. game 4. hold 5. fit 6. sold 7. sit 8. gold 9. fight 10. light
C. 1. writer, reads 2. writing, sentence 3. Nothing, reading 4. read, sentences 5. words, alike 6. write, someone 7. open, box 8. group, word
D. Answers will vary.

LESSON 3.2

A. 1. has, story 2. introduction, sound 3. opens, letters 4. things, old 5. leave, sit 6. sits, right 7. or, here 8. Something, name 9. thing, these 10. leaves, boxes
B. Answers will vary.

LESSON 3.3

A. anyone, anything, anywhere, someone, something, somewhere, everyone, everything, everywhere, nothing, nowhere
B. 1. Carmen's 2. Inez's 3. Grandma's 4. Carmen, Inez's
C. 1. sisters, kitchen 2. Isn't, too 3. everything, better 4. had, everywhere 5. called, anything 6. made, groups
D. Answers will vary.

LESSON 3.4

A. 1. every, sisters 2. find, so 3. had, made 4. kitchen, everything 5. isn't, let 6. called, better 7. isn't, show 8. Every, too 9. last, everywhere 10. lets, anything
B. Answers will vary.

LESSON 3.5

A. 1. remembers, remembering 2. orders, ordering 3. ends, ending 4. pictures, picturing 5. details, detailing 6. shows, showing 7. opens, opening 8. answers, answering 9. leaves, leaving 10. votes, voting
B. 1. remembers 2. answering 3. describes 4. ends 5. ordering 6. vowels
C. 1. remember, details 2. will, answers 3. describe, again 4. guess, order 5. picture, detail 6. remembering, answer
D. Answers will vary.

LESSON 3.6

A. space, trace, grace; grind, kind, wind, bind; spell, well, sell, bell, cell, shell; would, should
B.

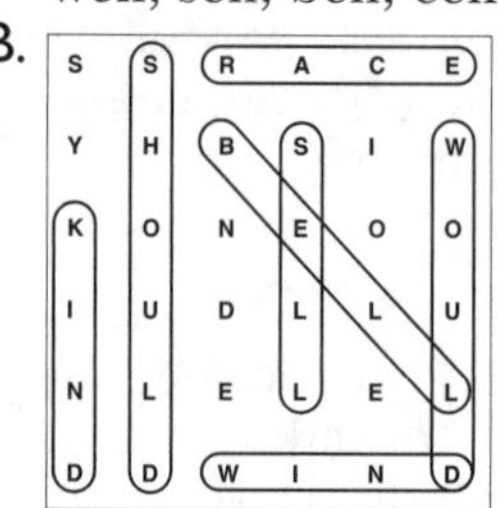

C. 1. guy, believes 2. Everyone, wrong 3. Today, goes 4. asked, face 5. he's, anyway 6. Why, cries
D. Answers will vary.

LESSON 3.7

A. 1. well, today 2. believes, somehow 3. saw, everyone 4. said, were 5. He's, asked 6. Why, than 7. Would, wrong 8. that's, mind 9. tries, cries 10. Let's, goes

B. Answers will vary.

LESSON 3.8

A. 1. someday 2. anyway 3. everyone 4. somehow

B. 1. Someday 2. anyway 3. Everyone 4. Somehow

C. 1. kitchen 2. point 3. always 4. graffiti

D. 1. Someday, move 2. always, himself 3. points, shops 4. lights, them 5. feelings, self 6. Yes, first

E. Answers will vary.

LESSON 3.9

A. 1. place, shops 2. places, them 3. himself, game 4. points, lights 5. Yes, first 6. Someday, apartment 7. shows, point 8. move, myself 9. Someday, feelings 10. always, shops

B. Answers will vary.

MIDWAY ASSESSMENT

A. (Words must appear in this order.) mind, down, another, family, job, know, almost, anything, time, herself, really, shop, ship, kitchen, doesn't

B. 1. fit, sit, and quit should be circled, quit 2. game, same, and shame should be circled, game 3. bright, sight, and night should be circled, sight 4. gold, cold, and told should be circled, told 5. grace, lace, and place should be circled, place 6. mind and wind should be circled, mind 7. could and would should be circled, would 8. letter, setter, and go-getter should be circled, letter

C. 1. boxes, boxed, boxer, boxing 2. passes, passed, passer, passing 3. places, placed, placing 4. faces, faced, facing 5. points, pointed, pointer, pointing

LESSON 3.10

A. guy; could, should; gave, cave, shave

B. 1. wave 2. homework 3. she's 4. guy 5. save 6. buy 7. Carmen's 8. truck

C. 1. happens, homework 2. happen, herself 3. She's, pull 4. door, mouth 5. buy, food 6. pulls, car

D. Answers will vary.

LESSON 3.11

A. 1. pull, somewhere 2. Hand, food 3. door, herself 4. eyes, smile 5. night, homework 6. Could, she's 7. moves, apartment 8. save, buy 9. happen, beach 10. pulls, window

B. Answers will vary.

LESSON 3.12

A. 1. sake 2. bake 3. lake 4. take 5. tape 6. cape 7. cope 8. hope 9. hole 10. pole

B. 1. bake 2. hole 3. hope 4. tape

C. 1. sales, change 2. pretty, mean 3. gone, himself 4. owns, far 5. came, sale 6. even, its

D. Answers will vary.

LESSON 3.13

A. 1. pretty, going 2. told, about 3. sale, its 4. owns, side 5. mean, far 6. paints, even 7. change, sales 8. came, himself 9. mean, much 10. owns, pretty

B. Answers will vary.

LESSON 3.14

A. game, fame, same, blame; got, forgot, not, rot; find, behind, wind, grind
Answers will vary for second part.

B. 1. behind 2. through 3. yourself 4. worked 5. fame 6. showing

C. 1. writes, players 2. bases, field 3. fame, news 4. behind, changes 5. got, works 6. Their, turn

D. Answers will vary.

LESSON 3.15

A. 1. got, fame 2. news, works 3. players, their 4. yourself, care 5. writes, done 6. bases, worked 7. behind, over 8. showing, changes 9. have, news 10. principal, done

B. Answers will vary.

LESSON 3.16

A. took with book, sad with mad, hard with card, just with must, smile with while
Answers will vary for second part.

B. 1. look 2. smile 3. while 4. just 5. cook 6. cards

C. 1. meets, outside 2. through, cards 3. Before, under 4. While, happened 5. Whoever, card 6. room, safe

D. Answers will vary.

LESSON 3.17

A. 1. took, cards 2. must, room 3. happened, card 4. through, before 5. dog's, under 6. Whoever, sad 7. safe, while 8. been, really 9. been, through 10. While, inside

B. Answers will vary.

FINAL ASSESSMENT

A. (Words must appear in this order.) homework, clean, sister, sale, forget, Where, points, cooking, Why, something, down, trying, outside, again, doesn't

B. 1. sale 2. sister 3. clean 4. dinner 5. herself 6. homework 7. dog 8. outside 9. get 10. bus

C.

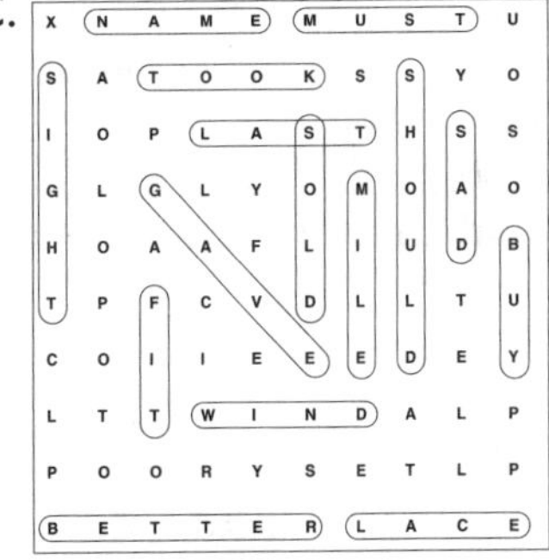

Worktext 4

LESSON 4.1

Remembering Details: Across: 3. people 4. scientist 6. science; Down: 1. food 2. glass 3. parts 5. fire

LESSON 4.2

Writing a Summary: In his sleep, Tyrone thinks he works for a mad scientist. Tyrone goes out to find fish parts for the scientist. He comes home and sees himself sleeping. Tyrone opens his eyes and sees a real scientist on TV.

LESSON 4.3

Make Headings into Questions: 1. What are sharks' teeth like? 2. How do sharks find food? 3. What things do sharks eat?
Now Find the Facts: What are sharks' teeth like? Facts: many lines; point to front when mouth opens, point back when mouth is closed; front ones fall out, next line moves to front, new teeth every one or two weeks.

LESSON 4.4

Write a Summary: Tom goes out in a boat by himself to fish. Then he pulls in a really big fish. A shark eats the fish on his way back. No one believes his story about the big fish.
Making a Chart: Tom, bigger than he is; Will, bigger than a bus; Mack, bigger than a house.
Reading a Chart: Mack

LESSON 4.5

Make a Heading into a Question: How do insects harm and help us?
Now Find the Facts: Harm: take sickness from place to place; eat our food; one kind eats wood and destroys houses. Help: help plants grow; are food for animals
Reading a Chart: spider, two, ant

LESSON 4.6

Remembering Details: Down: 1. science 2. hole 3. big; Across: 1. somewhere 3. balls 4. move 5. creature
What's in a Picture: B, down, E

LESSON 4.7

Remembering Details: plants, water, sticks, liquid, spider
Make Headings into Questions: 1. What does the Venus Flytrap look like? 2. How does the Venus Flytrap get its food? 3. What other plants eat animals?
Now Find the Facts: What does the Venus Flytrap look like? It has green leaves. Two of the leaves are bigger. They look like hands. These big leaves are green on the outside and light red on the inside. Close to the outside of the hands are some pointed parts.

LESSON 4.8

Putting Ideas in Order: Find two plants that look just the same. Put the plants in the same place in the house. Give one plant more water than the other. Look at the plants every week, and write what I see. After three weeks, see what the chart shows.
What's in a Chart: A, B, A, B, A, every day

LESSON 4.9

Use a Picture: land or crust, solid rock or mantle, solid or outer core, liquid or inner core
Remembering Details: Across: 3. hot 4. ring 5. shakes 7. solid; Down: 1. mountains 2. pushes 6. fire

LESSON 4.10

Read It Again: rock, metal, glass, metal, glass, rock
Putting Ideas in Order: Find the kind of rock that has metal in it. Get the rock really hot. Let the liquid metal run into something. Wait for the metal to get cold and turn solid. Make what you want out of the metal.

LESSON 4.11

Make Headings into Questions: 1. What is light like? 2. In what way is light like a thing? 3. What is another way that light changes directions? 4. How does light move?
Now Find the Facts: 1. like waves in the sea; like a thing 2. in a line; does not turn at a corner when it hits something; it goes off in another direction; changes direction when it goes from air to water or back; goes fast

LESSON 4.12

You Tell How the Box Works: Ask students to explain in their own words why the box works. Answers will vary but should follow the explanation given. For further practice in telling events in sequence, ask students to explain how to make a peanut butter and jelly sandwich or how to change the oil in a car. Students may wish to draw pictures to accompany their explanations. Encourage students to share their explanations with others.

LESSON 4.13

Make Headings into Questions: 1. Why is Venus called our sister planet? 2. What are some stories about life on Venus?
Now Find the Facts: Why is there no life on Venus? It has harmful gas; it is hot. Why is Venus so hot? The gas lets in light from the sun but it does not let it out.
What Are the Facts? Venus is closer to the sun than we are. We can see Venus from Earth. The gas around Venus is not like the air on Earth.

LESSON 4.14

Write a Summary: A light from a spaceship hits Donna. After that, everything she wants to happen does. She says, "I hope I run into my boyfriend." On her way to school, she does crash into her boyfriend. After the crash, she can't make things happen just by wanting them to happen.

LESSON 4.15

What Are the Facts? Not Fact: Computers may change life even more than cars did. Fact: Already, in some places robots are making cars. Not Fact: In some ways, life was better before the car came along. Not Fact: People should not be helping machines. Fact: The first computers could not do much more than count.

Practice Lessons 4

LESSON 4.1

A. 1. aren't, caught 2. bus, myself 3. ones, questions 4. study, scientist 5. question, front 6. living, glass 7. eyes, charts 8. eat, different
B. Answers will vary.
C. Answers will vary.

LESSON 4.2

A. 1. stories, summary 2. tried, science 3. kind, scientists 4. live, heading 5. life, different 6. memory, facts 7. scientist's, study 8. question, parts
B. Answers will vary.
C. Answers will vary.

LESSON 4.3

A. 1. monsters, attacked 2. creatures, darkest 3. small, closed 4. shark, attacks 5. water, cut 6. moving, die 7. monster, hiding 8. never, turn
B. Answers will vary.
C. Answers will vary.

LESSON 4.4

A. 1. fall, year 2. creatures, hiding 3. sharks', teeth 4. small, creatures 5. never, shark 6. moving, closed 7. shark, eats 8. using, run
B. Answers will vary.
C. Answers will vary.

LESSON 4.5

A. 1. ant, insect 2. hope, harmful 3. spider, legs 4. names, page 5. given, grow 6. ant, body 7. Those, feelers 8. They're, harm
B. Answers will vary.
C. Answers will vary.

LESSON 4.6

A. 1. insects, known 2. hope, sickness 3. falls, legs 4. grow, plants 5. insect, hole 6. those, ants 7. spider, feelers 8. kinds, harmful
B. Answers will vary.
C. Answers will vary.

LESSON 4.7

A. 1. trap, cage 2. spiders, harmless 3. one, sticks 4. green, pointed 5. drug, sickness 6. enough, fight 7. liquid, grows 8. changed, today
B. Answers will vary.
C. Answers will vary.

LESSON 4.8

A. 1. changed, course 2. drugs, harmless 3. liquid, drink 4. green, grows 5. closes, enough 6. trap, spiders 7. red, plant 8. pointed, game
B. Answers will vary.
C. Answers will vary.

MIDWAY ASSESSMENT

A. (Words must appear in this order.) name, pretty, monster, different, memory, good, pointing, raced, being, belongs, clean, someone, maybe, beach, problems
B. 1. sick 2. problems 3. happy 4. way 5. race 6. get it going 7. house 8. sorry for 9. right 10. mind
C. Answers will vary.

LESSON 4.9

A. 1. ball, crack 2. solid, ground 3. against, years 4. told, gotten 5. pushes, metal 6. rocks, shaking 7. push, running 8. running, rock
B. Answers will vary.
C. Answers will vary.

LESSON 4.10

A. 1. land, rock 2. shake, crash 3. rocks, solid 4. gotten, years 5. pushed, crack 6. ball, ground 7. pushes, against 8. shown, shaking
B. Answers will vary.
C. Answers will vary.

LESSON 4.11

A. 1. space, stars 2. corner, dark 3. ahead, direction 4. seem, itself 5. Sometimes, seems 6. stand, yet 7. understand, seems 8. outer, space
B. Answers will vary.
C. Answers will vary.

LESSON 4.12

A. 1. seem, ahead 2. Sometimes, dark 3. star, space 4. stand, yet 5. seems, understand 6. air, corner 7. itself, direction 8. toward, pass
B. Answers will vary.
C. Answers will vary.

LESSON 4.13

A. 1. steal, machine 2. stands, between 3. gang, fights 4. fighting, saved 5. lives, harmed 6. gas, drive 7. machines, break 8. cooked, means
B. Answers will vary.
C. Answers will vary.

LESSON 4.14

A. 1. lives, between 2. fighting, cooked 3. harmed, machine 4. planets, space 5. planet, sky 6. steal, saved 7. win, means 8. stands, fights
B. Answers will vary.
C. Answers will vary.

LESSON 4.15

A. 1. losing, oil 2. robot, help 3. spaceship, computer 4. You'll, orders 5. isn't, radio 6. count, pay 7. Today's, computers 8. We'll, robot's
B. Answers will vary.
C. Answers will vary.

FINAL ASSESSMENT

A. (Words must appear in this order.) problem, spaceship, own, trying, nothing, night, eyes, home, mind, computer, yourself, happens, other, interested, make
B 1. scared 2. each other 3. nothing 4. problems 5. Mu Lan 6. good at 7. being mad at everyone 8. good at many things 9. get along 10. pass the time
C. Answers will vary.

Worktext 5

LESSON 5.1

Describe It: She tried to register to vote. She was a sharecropper. She came from a big family. She would not give up.
What Will Happen Next?: Answers will vary. If students answer yes, good backup sentences are: Fannie Lou Hamer did not give up. She no longer had anything to lose. By law, African Americans had the right to vote. If students answer no, good backup sentences

are: African Americans will never vote in Mississippi. She will never have enough money. They will keep finding ways to stop her from voting.

LESSON 5.2

Remembering Details: African, vote, Rights
Who? What? Where? When? Why?: The answers to these questions will vary. The following are good possibilities. **Who:** Fanny Lou Hamer was a woman who worked for voting rights for African Americans. **What:** She tried over and over again to register to vote. She also talked to many people to make changes in laws and politics. **Where:** Mississippi **When:** She began her work in 1962. She worked until she died in 1977. **Why:** She believed all people had the right to vote.

LESSON 5.3

How Are People Alike and Different?: They are all 18 years old. They all live in the same neighborhood. They all can vote.
Putting Ideas in Order: Beth came to the door and stood next to me. "We can stop this," Jared said. "I am asking you to vote against Will Glass." "It can't hurt to vote," I said. "Why not try?"

LESSON 5.4

Write a Summary: Jared tried to get Mu Lan and Beth to vote. Will Glass won the race. They are taking down our neighborhood to put in a freeway.

LESSON 5.5

Who? What? Where? When? Why?: The answers to these questions will vary. The following are good possibilities. **Who:** Levi Strauss was a 17-year-old boy who wanted to earn a lot of money. **What:** He made the first jeans. **Where:** California
When: 1800s **Why:** He wanted to earn money. Or: He saw that miners wore their pants out quickly.

LESSON 5.6

What Will Happen Next?: Answers will vary. If students answer yes, good backup sentences are: The family wants to go there quickly. After they're over the mountains, they will be almost there. Robin, Mack, and Bill all seem strong. If students answer no, good backup sentences are: There is still a long trip ahead of them. They have no wagon. They have lost everything they own.
Describe It: hot and sunny, high mountains, lots of gold, miners live there

LESSON 5.7

Remembering Details: California, thief, wagon, highest

LESSON 5.8

Write a Summary: Robin, Mack, and Bill are going to the California gold fields. A rock pushes their wagon off the mountain. Bill dies. Mack and Robin make it to California and get jobs.
How Are People Alike and Different?: They went to California. They had ideas about making money in California. They do not want to mine for gold.

LESSON 5.9

Remembering Details: Cherokee, pipeline, accident, chief
What's the Main Idea?: After living through a bad car accident, Wilma Mankiller knew what she wanted to do with her life.

LESSON 5.10

Who? What? Where? When? Why?: The answers to these questions will vary. The following are good possibilities: **Who:** She is chief of the Cherokee Nation. **What:** She built a pipeline and became chief. **Where:** Oklahoma **When:** She became chief in 1987. **Why:** She wanted to give her people hope.
How Are People Alike and Different: did not think about being a chief, had problems getting her life together, didn't know what she wanted **After the Car Accident:** was ready to become chief of the Cherokees, believed people could find answers to their own problems, liked building houses and pipelines

LESSON 5.11

Who? What? Where? When? Why?: The answers to these questions will vary. The following are good possibilities. **Who:** A man who started a farmworkers' union. **What:** He got people to stop buying grapes until the grape growers gave in to the demands of the union. **Where:** He was born in Arizona. **When:** He lived from 1927 until 1993. This story tells about his work from 1962 until 1970. **Why:** He wanted to help farmworkers solve their work problems.
Making a Timeline: 1927: He was born. **1945:** He went off to the Navy and World War II. **1962:** He worked to start a farmworkers' union. **1964:** He had enough workers in the union to hold a meeting. **1965:** The union went on strike against the grape growers. **1970:** Twenty-three growers said they were ready to talk with Chávez and the union. **1993:** Chávez died.

LESSON 5.12

What Will Happen Next?: Answers will vary. If students answer yes, good backup sentences are: He was having problems in L.A. He didn't have his good friends anymore. Luis, who lives on the farm, is 16, like him. He will not have problems with the police on the farm. If students answer no, good backup sentences are: He is used to a big place like L.A. He will miss his mom. He will miss driving around with friends.

LESSON 5.13

Remembering Details: different, summer, lettuce, questions, pocket
What's the Main Idea?: I went to work on a farm for the summer, and I liked making money.

LESSON 5.14

Write a Summary: In the fall, Luis came back with me to L.A. At school, some of the guys gave him a hard time for asking so many questions in class. I gave up and started being friends with him.

Practice Lessons 5

LESSON 5.1

A. 1. taken, test 2. asked, cleaned 3. crops, farm 4. learning, bills 5. steal, law 6. police, kill 7. owned, yellow 8. went, beat

B. Answers will vary.

C. Answers will vary.

LESSON 5.2

A. 1. register, voter 2. husband, sharecropper 3. killed, laws 4. Americans, vote 5. rights, voting 6. learn, happily 7. African, voters 8. Americans, badly

B. Answers will vary.

C. Answers will vary.

LESSON 5.3

A. 1. moved, neighbors 2. office, building 3. hurt, poor 4. guys, hood 5. asking, joke 6. cares, builds 7. keep, ruin 8. stood, voted

B. Answers will vary.

C. Answers will vary.

LESSON 5.4

A. 1. cares, winning 2. poor, build 3. counts, free 4. office, neighbor 5. seen, guys 6. voted, wins 7. named, moved 8. joke, hurt

B. Answers will vary.

C. Answers will vary.

LESSON 5.5

A. 1. California, freeway 2. gold, miners 3. hopes, tent 4. heard, flying 5. become, stronger 6. jeans, mine 7. used, cloth 8. hope, rivets

B. Answers will vary.

C. Answers will vary.

LESSON 5.6

A. 1. strong, miners 2. California, gold 3. Mining, history 4. cloth, wagons 5. rivet, burns 6. pants, jeans 7. sunny, neighborhood 8. heard, headed

B. Answers will vary.

C. Answers will vary.

LESSON 5.7

A. 1. swim, camp 2. firewood, winter 3. thief, found 4. late, accident 5. families, miles 6. rooming, blanket 7. worker, else's 8. mile, heads

B. Answers will vary.

C. Answers will vary.

LESSON 5.8

A. 1. firewood, campers 2. families, camp 3. heads, highest 4. worker, cuts 5. miles, accident 6. high, got 7. thief, late 8. swim, mile

B. Answers will vary.

C. Answers will vary.

MIDWAY ASSESSMENT

A. (Words must appear in this order.) remembers, believed, bills, someday, weeks, blanket, wrong, anything, sound, count, family, answer, screamed, known, ahead

B. 1. mine 2. South America 3. gold 4. sounds 5. the woods 6. remembering 7. does not like 8. live

C. Answers will vary.

LESSON 5.9

A. 1. Cherokee, Oklahoma 2. born, town 3. chief, Cherokee 4. finished, killer 5. pipeline, homes 6. hoped, swimmer 7. stayed, two 8. died, believed

B. Answers will vary.

C. Answers will vary.

LESSON 5.10

A. 1. stay, finish 2. pipe, town 3. nation, people's 4. finished, ready 5. believed, thief 6. born, chief 7. killer, two 8. lived, Oklahoma

B. Answers will vary.

C. Answers will vary.

LESSON 5.11

A. 1. strike, union 2. girlfriend, religious 3. farm workers, grapes 4. pickers, violence 5. picked, hour 6. I'd, Navy 7. couldn't, eating 8. wasn't, showed

B. Answers will vary.

C. Answers will vary.

LESSON 5.12

A. 1. Arizona, picked 2. workers, showed 3. religious, violence 4. Navy, didn't 5. girlfriend, fair 6. I'd, farmer 7. holding, grapes 8. wasn't, pulled

B. Answers will vary.

C. Answers will vary.

LESSON 5.13

A. 1. thought, lettuce 2. left, pocket 3. dollar, miss 4. listen, answered 5. counted, send 6. listened, circled 7. hang, city 8. smiling, summer

B. Answers will vary.

C. Answers will vary.

LESSON 5.14

A. 1. missed, happening 2. hanging, thought 3. listened, miss 4. counted, pocket 5. lettuce, left 6. summer, listen 7. quiet, answered 8. hang, dollar

B. Answers will vary.

C. Answers will vary.

FINAL ASSESSMENT

A. (Words must appear in this order.) understands, news, someday, would, finish, homework, hall, meeting, last, talking, safe, already, People, even, school

B. 1. made her feel scared 2. a newswoman 3. cooks dinner 4. can't think 5. away in the Navy 6. Mrs. Well 7. there wasn't enough money to fix all the things that were wrong. 8. have to take a bus to another school 9. talked Mr. Singer into leaving the school open to finish the school year 10. had money problems for some time

C. Answers will vary.

Worktext 6

LESSON 6.1

Remembering Details: people, electric music, boy and girl, love
Writing the Rhymes: Street rhymes with beat. Night rhymes with light. Clean rhymes with seen.
Finding the Beat: Students should circle the italicized words: *Fancy* dog *has* meat to *eat*. *Mean* dog *is* a *street* dog. The beat is the same.

LESSON 6.2

Finding Rhymes: Poem: "Work Day." The word past rhymes with fast. Poem: "A Friend." The word hide rhymes with inside. The word too rhymes with you.
Hearing the Beat: "A Friend," "On a Day Like This," "Work Day"
Finding the Main Idea: a. everything you see and hear starts to run together.

LESSON 6.3

Meeting Characters: Mike: is 17 years old; is strong, fast, and full of life; thinks he can handle whatever comes up. César: is 16 years old; is careful; wants to be more like his friend.
Describing the Setting: Today, some American city. Answers will vary.

LESSON 6.4

What's the Problem?: César is scared to go into the old green building.
Looking Ahead: Answers will vary. Students may circle any of the sentences.

LESSON 6.5

Following the Plot: César hears voices somewhere. César finds a spider web in an open door. Mike falls through the floor. The room below is full of spider webs. César sees a big spider on Mike.
What Will Happen Next?: Answers will vary.

LESSON 6.6

Following the Plot: Mike, César, old green building, night, locked, a window, door, spider's web, Mike, spiders or webs, spider, secret, spiders, César, bag, Mike, laugh, careful

LESSON 6.7

Finding the Parts of a Play: Young woman, in those days bands played music!; Oh, Mom! Do I have to go?; Ana makes a face; Saturday, around 9 AM
What's the Problem?: Ana can't see the Burning Scream because she has to go to Green Woods.

LESSON 6.8

Following the Plot: Ana is made to go to Green Woods. Ana meets Bill Cage at Green Woods. Great Grandma Wilma tells a story about an old boyfriend. Bill says he will give Ana a ride back to the city. Ana finds out that Bill Cage is really Ice Machine.
Turning Point: Bill says he will give Ana a ride back to the city.

LESSON 6.9

What Is a Biography?: Matthew Henson
Read It Again: 1866, washing dishes, went all over the world working on ships, an older man, Henson was African American, 1887, back room of a hat shop, working

LESSON 6.10

Finding the Main Idea: c. explored Greenland with Robert Peary
Putting Facts in Time Order: Henson stayed with an Inuit family. Henson killed a musk ox. Peary and Henson had to eat their dogs. Peary and Henson took a big rock to the United States. Henson said he would go with Peary to the North Pole.

LESSON 6.11

Finding Facts to Back Up Ideas: Students may back up the statement that Henson was a great explorer with any of the following sentences. Henson was one of six men who made it to the North Pole. Henson took over at the end of the last trip. One man told Henson, "The rest is up to you." Henson fell into ice-cold water, but he wouldn't turn back. Henson got to the North Pole ahead of Peary.

LESSON 6.12

Making a Timeline: 1866, is born; 1879, goes to sea; 1887, meets Peary; 1891, makes the first trip to Greenland; 1898, starts first trip to North Pole; 1908, gets to the North Pole; 1912, writes a book; 1945, gets a medal; 1954, is asked to the White House; 1955, dies.

Practice Lessons 6

LESSON 6.1

A. 1. poems, rhyme 2. exciting, storyline 3. literature, often 4. bones, falling 5. electricity, dark 6. put, people 7. starting, noise 8. electric, that
B. Answers will vary.
C. 1. hatbox 2. streetcar 3. meatball 4. sometime 5. sidewalk
D. Answers will vary.

LESSON 6.2

A. 1. poem, love 2. world, heat 3. alone, longest 4. hat, street 5. meat, fat 6. dirt, care 7. hot, cooler 8. turns, music
B. Answers will vary.
C. 1. noise 2. dirty 3. bones 4. moving 5. electricity
D. Answers will vary.

LESSON 6.3

A. 1. liked, stick 2. watch, stolen 3. lock, doors 4. parked, locked 5. ride, shut 6. Both, camping 7. Tonight, describing 8. park, banks
B. Answers will vary.
C. 1. Rent 2. owner 3. stopped 4. windows 5. floor
D. Answers will vary.

LESSON 6.4

A. 1. parked, locked 2. closed, later 3. starting, apartments 4. Stick, handle 5. We're, restaurant 6. steal, might 7. owner, tonight 8. park, ride
B. Answers will vary.

C. 1. watch 2. shut 3. rich 4. Glasses 5. park
D. Answers will vary.

LESSON 6.5

A. 1. turned, paper 2. secret, wouldn't 3. main, slowly 4. suddenly, storm 5. standing, stairs 6. soon, follow 7. you've, web 8. pushing, very
B. Answers will vary.
C. 1. secret 2. Stairs 3. feet 4. soon 5. paper
D. Answers will vary.

LESSON 6.6

A. 1. sounded, breaking 2. Slow, following 3. sudden, top 4. wouldn't, hearing 5. standing, storm 6. stairs, feet 7. slowly, follows 8. webs, very
B. Answers will vary.
C. 1. you've 2. slow, 3. hasn't, 4. glasses, 5. wouldn't
D. Answers will vary.

LESSON 6.7

A. 1. washing, dishes 2. telephone, packing 3. young, miles 4. singer, bands, 5. She'll, directions 6. hi, wash 7. guitar, picks 8. describes, singing
B. Answers will vary.
C. 1. washed 2. turning 3. they'll 4. war 5. I've
D. Answers will vary.

LESSON 6.8

A. 1. I've, ice 2. Since, guitar 3. such, washed 4. telephone, early 5. turning, directions 6. played, song 7. singer, young 8. picks, wash
B. Answers will vary.
C. 1. telephone 2. packing 3. they've 4. hi 5. she'll
D. Answers will vary.

MIDWAY ASSESSMENT

A. (Words must appear in this order.) band, song, doesn't, stairs, something, starts, street, little, around, glass, joke
B. 1. song 2. good 3. problems 4. eat 5. followed
C. 1. there was just something about him 2. some got on the bus and some got in the car 3. Mike was driving 4. they wanted to miss running into other cars 5. wants to hurt them.
D. Answers will vary.
E. Answers will vary.

LESSON 6.9

A. 1. explorer, trips 2. musk ox, frozen 3. explore, lands 4. adventures, sled 5. helper, excitement 6. driving, sled 7. explorers, well-known 8. harder, prove
B. Answers will vary.
C. 1. frozen 2. adventures 3. helper 4. freeze 5. country
D. Answers will vary.

LESSON 6.10

A. 1. trips, Greenland 2. adventures, excitement 3. harder, well-known 4. freezing, sled 5. Driving, harder 6. musk ox, north 7. prove, explorer 8. helper, explorer
B. Answers will vary.
C. 1. hotdog 2. Greenland 3. newspaper 4. sunlight 5. countryside
D. Answers will vary.

LESSON 6.11

A. 1. men, across 2. rest, whole 3. sure, trouble 4. We've, either 5. oldest, fell 6. leaving, ended 7. eaten, few 8. older, excited
B. Answers will vary.
C. 1. few 2. arms 3. ended 4. reach 5. eaten
D. Answers will vary.

LESSON 6.12

A. 1. Henson's, fell 2. sure, leaving 3. trouble, oldest 4. few, reach 5. We've, either 6. excited, medal 7. rest, older 8. eaten, whole
B. Answers will vary.
C. 1. colder 2. We've 3. whole 4. leaving 5. trouble
D. Answers will vary.

FINAL ASSESSMENT

A. (Words must appear in this order.) door, follows, music, really, jobs, guitar, song, read, think, doesn't, something, Tonight, ready, name, guess, apart, pick, stolen, money, isn't
B. 1. are friends 2. for people they already know 3. aren't good enough to play for people they don't know 4. makes him think of Ana 5. he is playing well and is really into the music 6. ready to play for people they don't know 7. he thinks they sound like sick dogs when they sing 8. a new guitar because his old one has a crack in it 9. he needs to buy a car 10. believe they need Will with them to play at the Green Spider
C. Answers will vary.
D. Answers will vary.

Worktext 7

LESSON 7.1

Finding Paragraphs: 8
Finding Main Idea Sentences: Paragraph 3: A newspaper may have different parts for different kinds of news. Paragraph 4: Another part of the newspaper gives only sports news. Paragraph 5: Still another part has articles about fun things to do and see around town.

LESSON 7.2

Getting to Know Characters: Dana: just finished high school; wants to live on her own; never lived in the city. Jen: is one year older; is living on her own; has a job.
Writing a Plot Summary: Dana runs into Jen, an old friend from high school. Jen asks Dana to move in with her. Dana is not sure where to start in setting up her new life. Jen tells Dana to work on getting a job first of all. Dana goes out to buy a newspaper. On the way, she takes change from a young man.
Finding the Main Idea: Dana moves into the city to start a life of her own.

LESSON 7.3

Reading for Facts: 1997; $1,400; 60,000; 555-5555; 5 rooms; $575; schools, playground, bus; yes; 555-5555; Mr. White; cook; between 2–10 PM

LESSON 7.4

Finding the Main Idea: Dan's uncle told him about a job in the city. His uncle tells him some good things about the job.

Alike and Different: both, both, both, both, Dana, both, Dana, Dan, Dan, Dan, Dana

LESSON 7.5

Following Directions:

1. b. reading the directions from start to finish once
2. a. read the first part again and then stop
3. a. get together all the tools and other things you will need
4. b. follow part two of the directions, one step at a time
5. c. write down every important word
6. c. look at the directions right away and write them over

LESSON 7.6

Remembering Details: Main, Cruz, south, south, north, north, Cruz

What Do You Think? 4. He gets on a bus going south. Answers will vary. One possible response: He should have made a clean, clear copy of the directions as soon as possible after hearing them.

LESSON 7.7

Fill Out a Form: Answers to questions 1, 3, and 4 will vary. Question 2 should be left blank. 5. Filling Out Forms 6. 7. 7. a. Students not write anything in the last part of the form where it says, "Do not write in this space."

LESSON 7.8

Finding Details: little, one/two rooms, $350, loud, pretty dark, an old building, just a corner of the room

Alike and Different: bigger, more, real, not as much

LESSON 7.9

Understanding Main Ideas: a. part of the group b. they are special c. famous stars

Understanding Ads: 1. c 2. a 3. b

LESSON 7.10

Remembering Details: radio; Car Guys; Special of the Week; Fast Jake; sports car; $3,000; red; city; Dana; hood; ring; cars; shop; number

LESSON 7.11

Finding Main Ideas and Details: 1. Pick a job that goes with who you are and what you like. 2. Take classes in school. Learn on the job. 3. Call around, walk around, and ask around. Look in the want ads. 4. Look right for the job. Be on time. Practice your answers. Be friendly.

LESSON 7.12

Writing a Summary: Dana comes to Henson Homes to interview for a job. Mr. Henson thinks she wants a job keeping books. Dana tells him she wants the job in the machine shop. Dan's uncle talks to Mr. Henson about Dana. Mr. Henson makes up his mind to let Dana try the job. Dana finds out that Dan put in a good word for her. Dan asks Dana out, and she says yes.

Getting to Know Characters: 1. At first, Dana seems scared to be in the city. By the end of the story, she has her own apartment, the chance for a job, and has become friends with Dan. 2. At first, Dan does not do anything with his life. At the end of the story, he has rented an apartment, started a new job, and has become friends with Dana. 3. At first, Mr. Henson does not want to give Dana a job. At the end of the story, he gives Dana a chance to see what she can do on the job.

Who's Changed?: All the characters—Dan, Dana, and Mr. Henson changed.

What Do You Think?: Answers will vary. A possible answer is that Dana will do well at her new job because she is doing something she likes.

Think About Tomorrow: Answers will vary.

Practice Lessons 7

LESSON 7.1

A. 1. form, information 2. paragraphs, pages 3. listed, important 4. newspaper, movies 5. basketball, yesterday 6. baskets, score 7. fill, form 8. bench, basket

B. Answers will vary.

C. 1. fun 2. clothes 3. less 4. breaks 5. business

D. Answers will vary.

LESSON 7.2

A. 1. events, state 2. tool, businesses 3. bring, clothes 4. buys, sport 5. grouped, sports 6. shuts, sign 7. shopping, interesting 8. articles, interest

B. Answers will vary.

C. 1. skill 2. piece 3. list 4. sign 5. state

D. Answers will vary.

LESSON 7.3

A. 1. add, quickly 2. power, darker 3. aunt, uncle 4. special, playground 5. model, engine 6. black, blocks 7. dream, rooms 8. letting, block

B. Answers will vary.

C. 1. playground 2. darker 3. aunt 4. quickly 5. number

D. Answers will vary.

LESSON 7.4

A. 1. rooms, quick 2. aunt, schools 3. letting, black 4. block, blocks 5. model, number 6. dream, power 7. slows, playground 8. engine, quickly

B. Answers will vary.

C. 1. loud 2. dream 3. engine 4. slows 5. Blocks

D. Answers will vary.

LESSON 7.5

A. 1. hour, minutes 2. brother, burned 3. boy's, supposed 4. suppose, missing 5. steps, above 6. hangs, store 7. hours, minutes 8. uncle's, tools

B. Answers will vary.

C. 1. pulling 2. younger 3. pieces 4. once 5. second

D. Answers will vary.

LESSON 7.6

A. 1. missing, pieces 2. kid's, steps 3. supposed, minute 4. tools, steps 5. boy's, brother 6. Once, burned 7. younger, above 8. uncle's, hour
B. Answers will vary.
C. 1. minutes 2. table 3. brother 4. store 5. easy
D. Answers will vary.

LESSON 7.7

A. 1. doctor, closely 2. person, correctly 3. buzzer, company 4. carefully, correct 5. papers, numbers 6. empty, security 7. trick, filling 8. stays, growing
B. Answers will vary.
C. 1. persons 2. months 3. parents 4. ago 5. empty
D. Answers will vary.

LESSON 7.8

A. 1. filling, growing 2. month, company 3. correctly, parents 4. numbers, correct 5. brothers, buzzer 6. closely, trick 7. papers, ago 8. person, stays
B. Answers will vary.
C. 1. company 2. doctor 3. growing 4. correct 5. trick
D. Answers will vary.

MIDWAY ASSESSMENT

A. (Words must appear in this order.) across, around, middle, almost, enough, inside, map, news, move, sunny, north, flying, someone, window, winter, swimming, famous, newspaper, monster, shark
B. 1. they both know what it's like to be new 2. she has moved far north, and it's winter 3. Ana is used to living in Arizona where it's not cold 4. was on the swim team 5. her dad's work was up north, and Ana and her mom were trying to sell the house in Arizona 6. he knows about the school newspaper 7. the school newspaper and swimming 8. someone who Ana will need to watch carefully 9. like to make friends with others 10. Ana and Jared will have problems
C. Answers will vary.
D. Answers will vary.

LESSON 7.9

A. 1. He'll, guard 2. crowd, clapping 3. spider's, themselves 4. slams, scores 5. seconds, shoot 6. clap, court 7. faces, shoots 8. price, pair
B. Answers will vary.
C. 1. guarding 2. trick 3. passed 4. sunglasses 5. seconds
D. Answers will vary.

LESSON 7.10

A. 1. understanding, rules 2. tricks, guarding 3. streets, passes 4. slam, jump 5. He'll, court 6. passed, shooting 7. sunglasses, crowd 8. faces, clapping
B. Answers will vary.
C. 1. slam 2. price 3. moment 4. he'll 5. clap
D. Answers will vary.

LESSON 7.11

A. 1. interview, tomorrow 2. loves, crowds 3. Haven't, practice 4. catch, breath 5. catches, chance 6. minds, drivers 7. calm, forward 8. learning, foster
B. Answers will vary.
C. 1. hurts 2. hair 3. choice 4. haven't 5. tomorrow
D. Answers will vary.

LESSON 7.12

A. 1. listens, hurts 2. loses, hair 3. forgets, choice 4. interviews, listens 5. calm, mind 6. practice, tomorrow 7. chances, foster 8. chance, loves
B. Answers will vary.
C. 1. foot 2. breath 3. practice 4. forward 5. center
D. Answers will vary.

FINAL ASSESSMENT

A. (Words must appear in this order.) game, bench, friends, special, sometimes, couldn't, owned, money, always, Throw, enough, basket, city, famous, ads, never, feel, power, minutes, sick
B. 1. was quiet and not into sports 2. his parents died 3. learned the business and started to make more money 4. he was having trouble making his arms and legs do what he wanted them to do 5. by someone in the park 6. be in the basketball games in the park 7. he was still learning the game and needed more practice 8. he wasn't happy sitting on the bench all the time 9. Tyrone's backup is sick, and Tyrone will need a rest 10. works hard, studies the game, and wants to do his best
C. Answers will vary.
D. Answers will vary.